College Reading: The Science and Strategies of Expert Readers

Janet Nay Zadina, Ph.D.
Tulane University School of Medicine

Rita Smilkstein, Ph.D.
*North Seattle Community College,
emeritus Western Washington University*

Deborah B. Daiek, Ph.D.
Schoolcraft College

Nancy M. Anter
Schoolcraft College

Australia • Brazil • Canada • Mexico • Singapore • United Kingdom • United States

Cengage

College Reading: The Science and Strategies of Expert Readers
**Janet N. Zadina, Ph.D.,
Rita Smilkstein, Ph.D.,
Deborah B. Daiek, Ph.D., Nancy M. Anter**

Director: Annie Todd

Executive Editor: Shani Fisher

Senior Development Editor: Marita Sermolins

Editorial Assistant: Erin Nixon

Media Editor: Christian Biagetti

Brand Manager: Lydia LeStar

Senior Content Project Manager:
   Corinna Dibble

Art Director: Faith Brosnan

Manufacturing Planner: Betsy Donaghey

Rights Acquisition Specialist: Ann Hoffman

Production Service and Compositor:
   Integra Software Services

Cover Image: Sergio77/Shutterstock.com

Cover Designer: RHDG/Riezebos Holzbaur

Interior Designer: Anne Bell Carter

For product information and technology assistance, contact us at
**Cengage Customer & Sales Support, 1-800-354-9706
or support.cengage.com.**

For permission to use material from this text or product,
submit all requests online at **www.copyright.com.**

Library of Congress Control Number: 2012952820

Student Edition:
ISBN-13: 978-1-111-35001-7
ISBN-10: 1-111-35001-9

Cengage
200 Pier 4 Boulevard
Boston, MA 02210
USA

Cengage is a leading provider of customized learning solutions with employees residing in nearly 40 different countries and sales in more than 125 countries around the world. Find your local representative at: **www.cengage.com.**

To learn more about Cengage platforms and services, register or access your online learning solution, or purchase materials for your course, visit **www.cengage.com.**

For your course and learning solutions, visit **www.cengage.com**

Instructors: Please visit **login.cengage.com** and log in to access instructor-specific resources.

Printed in the United States of America
Print Number: 05   Print Year: 2022

Brief Contents

Contents

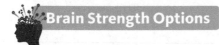

CHAPTER 2

Remembering What You Read   48

CHAPTER 3

Developing Your College Vocabulary 98

CHAPTER 4

Locating Stated Main Ideas   152

CHAPTER 5

Finding Supporting Details   198

CHAPTER 6

Using Inference to Identify Implied Main Ideas 244

CHAPTER 7

Recognizing Patterns of Organization 296

Practice with a Reading Passage   Neat People vs. Sloppy People 345

Post Test   We're Born to Learn 350

 **Brain Strength Options**   353

CHAPTER 8

Using Preview, Study-Read, and Review (PSR) 354

CHAPTER 9

Taking Control of Your Textbook: Marking and Note Taking 392

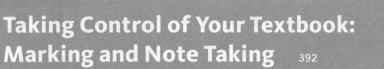

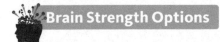

CHAPTER 11

Understanding and Creating Arguments 490

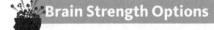

CHAPTER 12

Reading Arguments Critically   544

CHAPTER 13

Reading Beyond the Words   592

APPENDIX

Test-Taking Strategies 636

Preface

HOW DOES BRAIN-COMPATIBLE LEARNING HELP CREATE EXPERT READERS?

How does telling students to read and answer questions help them read? How does this actually make better readers? Teaching this way can help students with good decoding (reading fluency) skills think better and get more out of the reading, but does it help a struggling reader tackle difficult reading?

Much of what we teach when we teach reading skills are "thinking skills." But there is more to reading than just thinking. Many college developmental students are still struggling with reading skills involving basic decoding. They have problems with phonology and orthography—figuring out vocabulary and remembering sight words. They have underlying deficits in attention and working memory that appear as reading deficits.

College Reading: The Science and Strategies of Expert Readers bridges brain research and learning theory to offer reading strategies that are practical, interesting, and empirically grounded.

College Reading: The Science and Strategies of Expert Readers approaches reading not only from a thinking skills perspective but also from a knowledge of *how* one thinks, learns, and reads. The bridge from the scientific research to the classroom is built on expertise in both science and education. The translation from research to reading strategies that help struggling learners is clear, concise, and in layperson's terms. By explaining the brain science of reading, *Science and Strategies* teaches students how to read with the knowledge that they can change their brain into a more effective reading brain.

The benefits of teaching with an awareness of brain research are many. Research shows that when students learn that their brain is malleable—that it changes as a result of learning—their achievement rises. *Science and Strategies* is designed to increase student achievement by providing them with this important information immediately. And when students understand *why* something should be done, they are more willing to do it. Therefore, students learn about their brain and the *why* behind the activities and strategies, which is a unique feature of this book—the transparency of the learning process. Teachers and students learn about these new insights into learning together.

"The overall tone of the textbook is very accessible. The authors' voice is personal and informal, and students will find this approach refreshing and helpful. I can imagine my students commenting on how easy this textbook is to read and understand."

—MICHAEL BOYD, ILLINOIS CENTRAL COLLEGE

"This text bothers to explain the reasoning (the science) behind how students can become more effective readers while continually assuring students that they have the power to improve their reading based on that reasoning. Most other texts focus on why students should become more effective readers and basically issue prescriptions for improved reading without rationale."

—ROCHELLE WATSON, MONROE COMMUNITY COLLEGE

EXPERT AUTHORS TEACHING

College Reading: The Science and Strategies of Expert Readers brings together an expert group of authors to credibly incorporate widely proven brain research and learning theory into a user-friendly, dynamic reading textbook aimed at diverse learners. As international and national authorities on brain research and education and developmental educators with more than 30 years' experience who have conducted scientific research on reading, these authors are committed to helping your students become the expert readers they have the capabilities of being.

Janet N. Zadina, Ph.D., is an Adjunct Assistant Professor at Tulane University School of Medicine, Department of Neurology. She is a cognitive neuroscientist and former community college instructor of reading and English. She has conducted award-winning research on the neurobiology of dyslexia. She is an internationally known speaker on brain research and instruction and was invited to give a prestigious TED talk. She is also the author of several books and articles in the fields of science and education.

Her background as a teacher and reading specialist, along with her neuroimaging of dyslexia experience in the lab, serves her in her passionate devotion to developmental reading students. She sees reading instruction through the eyes of a teacher *and* a scientist. Because research shows that students who learn about their brain become higher achievers than those who don't, she is passionate about the importance of educating students as well as teachers about the brain.

She is the 2011 winner of the Society for Neuroscience Science Educator Award given to "an outstanding neuroscientist who has made a significant impact in informing the public about neuroscience." She is also a CLADEA Fellow of the Council of Learning Assistance and Developmental Education Associations, 2006, the highest honor in the field of Developmental Education, which recognized her lifetime achievement in helping college developmental students. She is a member of the Society for Neuroscience, Neurobiology of Language Society, National Association for Developmental Education, and College Reading and Learning Association.

Rita Smilkstein, Ph.D., has spoken nationally and internationally on brain-compatible education and the Natural Human Learning Process (NHLP). She has taught in middle school through graduate school, including 26 years in the Humanities Division at North Seattle Community College. Currently she is Professor Emerita, North Seattle Community College, and invited faculty in Secondary Education at Western Washington University's Woodring College of Education, Everett Campus. She has received many teaching awards, including the National Institute for Staff and Organizational Development's Excellence Award, 1991, 1995; the College Reading and Learning Association's highest honor, the Robert Griffin Award, 2005; and Induction as a Fellow of the Council of Learning Assistance and Developmental Education Associations (CLADEA), 2006, the highest honor in the field of Developmental Education. She is also a member of the Editorial Advisory Board of the *Journal of College Reading and Learning*.

Her B.A. was in English at the State University of Iowa, her M.A. in English was at Michigan State University, and her Ph.D. in Educational Psychology was at the University of Washington. Her book *We're*

STUDENTS TO BE EXPERT READERS

Born to Learn: Using the Brain's Natural Learning Process to Create Curriculum (Corwin Press, 2003; 2nd ed., 2011) won the Delta Kappa Gamma International Society's Educator's Award of the Year, 2004. A second edition of her book *Tools for Writing: Using the Natural Human Learning Process* was published by Many Kites Press in 2011.

She also frequently gives presentations at national conferences of educational organizations such as the College Reading and Learning Association and the National Association of Developmental Education.

Deborah B. Daiek, Ph.D., serves as the Associate Dean for Learning Support Services, Schoolcraft College, Livonia, Michigan. She oversees the College's Library, Collegiate Skills Reading Department, English as a Second Language courses, Education Transfer Program, and Learning Assistance Center (LAC), which houses tutoring, Peer Assisted Learning, Writing Fellows, Student-Athlete Support System, and University Bound. Under her direction, Schoolcraft's LAC was the recipient of the John Champaign Memorial Award for an Outstanding Developmental Education Program. She provides new faculty orientation workshops on ways to engage students in the learning process.

She holds a Bachelor of Arts degree cum laude as well as an M.A. in Adult Learning, both from Western Michigan University. Additionally, she holds a doctorate from Wayne State University in Instructional Technology, with an emphasis on cognition.

She is twice the Past President of MDEC, the Michigan Chapter of NADE, and remains actively involved. In 1998, she was given the Outstanding Developmental Educator Award. She is a member of NADE and CRLA as well. She co-chaired NADE's Brain Compatible Education SPIN and received NADE's Administrator for Outstanding Support of Developmental Education Award. She served as Treasurer and President for the North Central Reading Association (NCRA).

Nancy M. Anter is an educational consultant and freelance writer with more than 20 years of experience in the field of developmental education. She has taught reading and writing at the high school, community college, and university level and has offered national and local workshops and seminars on learning theory and composition.

She coordinated the learning center at Wayne State University. Her work involved instruction for student athletes, ESL students, and the general university population as well as individual students preparing for graduate-level exams. Because she witnessed student success at both ends of the academic spectrum, developmental level to graduate level, she understands the importance of starting instruction where students are comfortable and gradually leading them to higher levels.

She holds a B.A. in English from the University of Michigan and two M.A.s from Wayne State University—one in English education and the other in English, with an emphasis in composition theory. She currently serves as an adjunct faculty member at Schoolcraft College and is a member of MDEC, the Michigan chapter of NADE.

EXPERT READING STRATEGIES

Fire it until you wire it!

Repetition is important because the more a group of neurons fire together, the more likely they are to fire together again. Research shows that the more pathways by which information is encoded, the easier it is to learn and remember. We learn what is important to us, therefore students' brains need to be engaged to be in a state conducive to learning.

FIRE IT!

▶ *Making Connections* questions begin each chapter to activate students' existing network of knowledge about chapter topics to help them make connections to the new material introduced in that chapter. See p. 99 for example questions.

> **Tip** FROM THE
> **Brain Doctor**
> Did you know that intending to do something affects the brain? How can this help you? Research has shown that when students are given an assignment in class, if they write down when and where they intend to do it, they are more successful in completing it. Take advantage of this power. Every time you are given an assignment, write down when and where you intend to do it. Try it and see for yourself!

▶ *Tips from the Brain Doctor* introduce students to some of the research behind learning in a very user-friendly way while suggesting how students may use the latest scientific brain research to improve their learning and reading. Look for the tip boxes throughout the chapters.

"Tips from the Brain Doctor: This aspect is the most unique of this textbook. The author links science with the reading process in specific, easily understood ways."

—BARBARA COX, REDLANDS COMMUNITY COLLEGE

▶ *Activities* stimulate multiple pathways toward natural learning of reading and learning strategies, thus reaching a greater range of diverse learners. The design of many of the activities in *Science and Strategies* is implicitly compatible with the way the brain works. Students work together and are led through a process of constructing understanding through exploration. Students self-discover *before* being explicitly taught something. While most educators and textbooks address visual, auditory, and kinesthetic learners, this text includes other pathways involved in learning, such as attention, emotion, frontal lobe, social, and more. See Activity 6A (p. 249) and Activity 11A (p. 496) for examples of activities reaching diverse learners.

"I am thrilled that a college reading textbook finally has paired how to learn with the process of reading. It incorporates teaching the student about the brain and how it functions and then applies that to the process of reading. This is something I have tried to do for over twenty years. It's gratifying to find a text that does it so well."

—JONELLE BEATRICE, YOUNGSTOWN STATE UNIVERSITY

ACTIVITY 6A
Apply Prior Knowledge to Reading Comprehension
Read the following paragraph that illustrates the importance of prior knowledge, and try to figure out what it is about.

Schtolc Gnlhsaw

The procedure is actually quite simple. First, you arrange the items into different groups. Of course one pile may be sufficient depending on how much there is to do. If you have to go somewhere else due to lack of facilities that is the next step; otherwise, you are pretty well set. It is important not to overdo things. That is, it is better to do too few things at once than too many. In the short run this may not seem important but complications can easily arise. A mistake can be expensive as well. At first, the whole procedure will seem complicated. Soon, however, it will become just another facet of life. It is difficult to foresee any end to the necessity for this task in the immediate future; but then one never can tell. After the procedure is completed, one arranges the materials into different groups again. Then they can be put into their appropriate places. Eventually they will be used once more and the whole cycle will then have to be repeated. However, that is part of life.

Source: From Dooling, D. and Lautchman, R., "Effects of Comprehension on Retention of Prose," *Journal of Experimental Psychology* vol. 88 (pp. 216–222). Copyright © 1971 American Psychological Association. Reprinted with permission.

Continued on next page.

SUPPORTED BY SCIENTIFIC RESEARCH

WIRE IT!

▶ *Practice with a Reading Passage* allows students to solidify learning. Cumulative to that chapter, these practice readings allow students to build and strengthen their neural networks for reading skills over time. Repeated exposure via a variety of pathways helps learners "wire" the material, or learn it. Many students have never experienced reading as an enjoyable activity. And so, students are exposed to a variety of high-interest, multi-length, college-level readings in order to discover that they can love to read and learn. When students garner ideas and knowledge from reading, they are motivated to go on. See Chapter 5, Letting Justice Flow (p. 230) for a representative reading.

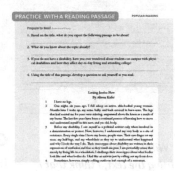

▶ *Post Tests* serve as a student learning outcome for each chapter, providing a cumulative critical reading activity for all the reading strategies presented. Post Tests encourage students to expect more from themselves and their reading course by testing their understanding of concepts in Part 1 and application of reading skills in Part 2. See Chapter 4 Post Test (p. 191) for an example.

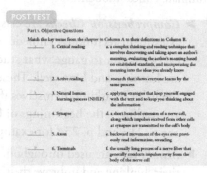

"*This text approaches reading organically, leading the student through the process, making connections between what the student already knows and what the student needs to learn. The pedagogy is not dry or boring (student's word). It is engaging and clear and, best of all, supportive. It addresses the student as someone who can join in on this great adventure and then shows the student how in a very personal and personable way.*"

—CHRISTINE TUTLEWSKI,
UNIVERSITY OF
WISCONSIN–PARKSIDE

▶ *Brain Strength Options* acknowledge that we are probably all wired differently. We know that every student has a different brain and learns differently. Neuroscience indicates that some students, those with dyslexia or severe reading difficulty, may use different brain pathways than typical readers. They need strategies to help them compensate. Designed for students to self-select according to their strengths, these chapter-culminating projects go beyond learning styles to address multiple pathways in learning, allowing students to effectively "wire" their reading skill knowledge. Some examples: Create a poster. Write song lyrics. Illustrate a graphic novel. Students will be empowered to show you how they have wired the chapter content. See p. 47 for an example.

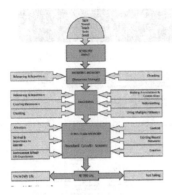

> ▶ *Chapter 2 is devoted to the encoding of memory from short-term to long-term*. Many times what appear to be reading comprehension problems are actually working memory problems. *Science and Strategies* may be the only book that shows students how to address the challenges of encoding memory. Recall of material read depends upon long-term memory, which must be actively encoded. Therefore, how it is encoded can make a big difference. Students also learn how to address working memory problems that can hinder their performance on tests or comprehension of what they read.

Good frontal lobes help you make good decisions.

If you engage in activities that stimulate the frontal lobes, you can actually improve them. The frontal lobes develop in response to experience, so if students need to be better critical thinkers, then they must be provided with opportunities that stimulate critical thought.

"Within a few weeks of using the text, I think that I would be able to convince my students that their developmental education could represent an 'overhaul' of their thinking processes, a radical change in how they approach intellectual tasks. In other words, I would use this text to engage them in a critical look at how their minds work and how to make their thinking more effective."

—MICHAEL BOYD, ILLINOIS CENTRAL COLLEGE

> ▶ *Comprehension Checks* are classroom assessment techniques embedded in every chapter to gauge what students are learning and how well. These prompts also get students into the habit of asking themselves if they are understanding what they are reading—the beginnings of being an expert critical reader. See p. 217 and p. 234 for examples.
>
> ▶ *Mind Maps* are used throughout the book to help students organize their thinking and improve their critical reading skills. Mind maps at the start of each chapter show students how the content can be organized visually. Using these maps as models, students can then organize other material they read. Maps prove especially useful when sorting out main ideas, details, and arguments.

Visual pathway is powerful!

The brain is very visual and learns best through pictures. When pictures are associated with information, a more powerful memory is created.

> ▶ Activities throughout the book encourage students to create images in order to improve memory.
>
> ▶ Chapter 10 is devoted to understanding visuals in textbooks. Students are taught how and why to create images as they study their other textbooks.

HELP CHANGE STUDENTS' BRAINS: DEVELOP LIFELONG LEARNING SKILLS

College Reading: The Science and Strategies of Expert Readers teaches students how to be better learners and readers by explaining the *science* of learning. Students will understand how what they do will change their reading skills and change their brain for the better for all their future coursework. Students make the connection that **reading is learning**. Not only will students **learn to read more efficiently**, but they will also **learn how to learn more efficiently**.

> "It's almost like being in on the secret of how to learn more effectively."
> —SHEILAH DOBYNS, FULLERTON COLLEGE

▶ *Natural Human Learning Process* is explained by the pioneer of the research, author Rita Smilkstein, an educational psychologist who over the years has collected empirical evidence to show that the process works. In Chapter 1 and revisited in Chapter 13, students are introduced to the basic process by which all humans learn, involving six stages:

  ▶ motivation (wanting to or having to learn something)

  ▶ practice (trying it)

  ▶ more practice (improving, gaining confidence)

  ▶ more practice (more understanding, some success)

  ▶ more skill (more success, becoming natural)

  ▶ mastery (able to teach it, able to build on it)

▶ *Brain Connections: Self-Assessments* give students an opportunity to visually connect their understanding of a topic to what they imagine their dendrites and neural networks might look like. Students assess their comprehension of chapter concepts as they progress through the chapter in relation to how the brain processes information and learns.

> "In my classes, I discuss building dendrites, but this book actually practices this theory in every chapter.... This book truly practices and reinforces brain theory. So many students do not have a clear understanding as to how they learn and how important it is to their reading and comprehension. This is truly innovative and relevant to present-day college students."
> —MARLYS CORDOBA, COLLEGE OF THE SISKIYOUS

Brain Connections: Self-Assessment

Draw on the brain cell how many dendrites you imagine you have for how much you know about how the memory works.

I don't understand too much about how memory works.	I have a pretty good understanding about how memory works.	I have a very good understanding about how memory works.

HELPING INSTRUCTORS TO BE EXPERT TEACHERS: INSTRUCTOR SUPPORT

Instructor's Manual and Test Bank

Designed for both instructors who are new to and familiar with implementing brain-compatible learning strategies in their courses, the Instructor's Manual includes an introduction on the benefits of brain-compatible learning and teaching strategies that foster brain-compatible learning. Author Spotlights highlight individual authors' experiences using strategies from the book and how instructors can successfully do the same. A detailed sample syllabus, classroom activities, course teaching tips, and handouts are among the many resources available. The Test Bank includes chapter quizzes that test students' comprehension and application of skills from the chapter. Pre Tests mirror the book's Post Tests and a mid-term and final exam of comprehension-based questions using a variety of readings to test cumulative skills are provided. For more information, contact your Cengage Learning sales representative.

ExamView®

Create, deliver, and customize tests and study guides (both print and online) in minutes with this easy-to-use assessment and tutorial system. ExamView offers both a Quick Test Wizard and an Online Test Wizard that guide you step by step through the process of creating tests, while its "what you see is what you get" interface allows you to see the test you are creating on the screen exactly as it will print or display online. For more information, contact your Cengage Learning sales representative.

Instructor Companion Site

The Instructor's Companion Site includes electronic versions of the Instructor's Manual and Test Bank and downloadable files to use with the ExamView® suite. Instructor PowerPoint presentations are available for download and cover chapter concepts and provide lecture ideas. A listing of additional web resources can also be found here. Log into the Instructor Companion Site at login.cengage.com.

HELPING STUDENTS TO BE EXPERT READERS: STUDENT SUPPORT

Aplia for Developmental Reading

Aplia for Developmental Reading is an online learning solution that improves comprehension and outcomes by increasing student effort and engagement. Students stay on top of coursework with regularly scheduled graded practice. The Grade It Now feature provides students with detailed, immediate explanations for every answer. Grades are automatically recorded in the instructor's Aplia grade book. Aplia assignments match the language, style, and structure of this text, allowing students to seamlessly apply chapter concepts. Find out more at www.aplia.com/developmentalenglish.

ACKNOWLEDGMENTS

Great appreciation and heartfelt thanks go to our team at Cengage Learning, whose support, insightfulness, and expertise from beginning to end was always given with kindness and understanding.

Marita Sermolins, Senior Development Editor: We are very grateful to Marita for sustaining our focus. It was not easy to keep herd on four different authors, but she did it amazingly. Her experience and expertise guided and shaped our book, making it better with every revision. We are indebted to her for her infinite patience, straightforward honesty, and talent.

Shani Fisher, Executive Editor: We thank Shani for her ongoing encouragement of our book and for her keen understanding of our vision. We are grateful for her support and steadfast optimism.

Annie Todd, Director of Developmental Studies: We thankfully acknowledge Annie's belief in our project and for working so hard to make it happen. Her energy and commitment to developmental education was the connection that got the ball rolling. We are grateful to her for championing our concept. She gave us strength and energy.

Corinna Dibble, Content Project Manager: We are thankful for Corinna's insight and invaluable suggestions for improving the text and activities.

Ann Courtney, Project Manager for Integra: We are deeply appreciative for the expertise that Ann brought to the project. She understood the importance of brain-compatible reading strategies and wonderfully handled all the details in making this book come alive.

Janet N. Zadina

I would also like to thank the many colleagues who supported the idea of this book, particularly all my colleagues who volunteered to review the book and are too numerous to mention. Thank you for your excitement and willingness to move the project forward. In addition, I would like to thank all of those who did submit reviews. It was heartwarming to see the attention to detail that you put into those reviews so that this book would be the best possible product.

Renee Casbergue, Deborah Christie, Denise DeFelice, Marina Morbiducci, Gayle Nolan, Charis Sawyer, and Lillian Tunceren for all the great conversations about teaching and learning! You are truly amazing friends and colleagues! Thank you to all who have kept me going through your expertise, support, and friendship: Monica Fiala, Lisa Irwin, Pat Kidder, Danny Meyer, Kerry Porter, McLaughlin, Victor Vazquez (RIP). You have all made my life and work better! For helping me unwind, thanks to the gang: Karen and Tom Blanchard, Jim and June Blount, Janie and Terry Clark, Percy Doiron and Marcia Warner, Ross and Claudine Foushee, Darlene and Dennis Ferrerio, and Margot and Bill King. I would like to thank my co-authors on this book for contributing their unique viewpoints. Because we don't agree on everything, the diversity of viewpoints has allowed us to create a book that can appeal to a diverse audience. While I did not always prevail, the discussions provided insight. In the end, we were able to create a book with multiple viewpoints and options.

A special thank you to my family: Larry and Joelan Nay, Jeff, Kathie, Alex, and Jason Nay, and my "adopted" family, Anne and Steve Capes! James E. Zadina, my husband and friend, thank you for supporting me in many ways, including never complaining when I travel the world to work with colleagues or to learn more and for putting up with me during the writing of this book!

Writing the book has been a journey, almost archetypal, and I have learned a great deal from both the vistas and the valleys. I am grateful to all of you who have been with me on this path.

Rita Smilkstein

There is no way I could have contributed to this book without the help of many wonderful people. First and foremost, my students over the 30 and more years I have been teaching, who taught me invaluable lessons about learning and teaching. Also thanks to my family and friends for their inspiration, support, and love, my daughters Jessica Dodge, Susanna Burney, Diana Phipps, and Georgia Franklin; grandkids Rome Davis, Laurel Dodge, Jesse and Isabella Franklin; friends Dale Chase, Dianne Hulscher, Edith Clarke, Dan Bockman (RIP), and especially Richard Blum, who was with me every step of the way.

I also want to acknowledge and express the deepest respect for—and thanks to—my excellent co-authors, Nancy Anter, Deborah Daiek, and Janet Nay Zadina, who were supportive, interactive, and helpful to the highest level of professionalism and friendship throughout our work together from beginning to end.

Deborah B. Daiek

I would like to thank my husband, Karl, my sons, David, Andy, and Ben, and my daughters-in-law, Erin and Lynde, for working around my intense schedule. Their love and patience is treasured. I want to thank my grandchildren, the future readers in our family: Ella, Logan, Luke, and Dillan for giving G-Ma fuel. I would like to express my gratitude to my MDEC, NADE, and Schoolcraft College colleagues for their encouragement and support. I would also like to thank all of the students who worked with me and made contributions to our book: Kalthoum Bayz, Mee Sook Choo, Matt Cornett, Brooke Frizzell, Brent Jacobsen, Suzanne Lenhardt, Tara Leach, Joseph Wafer, and Nathan Wagner; and to those who will contribute to the world of reading after reading our book. Special thanks in loving memory of my mother, Jacqueline R. Brooks, whose enthusiastic words, "How's the book coming?" helped sustain the journey.

Nancy M. Anter

I would like to thank the other authors on this project for their expertise and effort toward making this book happen. Thanks are also due to the students who shared their college stories with us, especially Erin Bishop, Preston Tindall, Niki Hudson, Serja Goram, Sowmya Rasa, Joselyn Evans, Elise Guido, and Alex Manion. Many others offered detailed feedback on the manuscript, practical advice, and abundant prayers, most notably Mary Pilat, Katherine Tombolesi, Clyde Manion, Thomas Manion, Mary O'Dowd, Laura Srinivasan, Suzy Stockmann, Helen Roarty, Lynette Mikula, and Gwyn Makara. To them I am deeply indebted. I am grateful for the support of my children, Thomas and Julia, who provided encouragement and humor when I needed it the most. I especially would like to thank my husband, Mark Anter, to whom this work is dedicated.

To our reviewers who enthusiastically supported us and provided valuable feedback that helped to shape this book into what you currently hold in your hands, a very grateful thank you:

Phillis Aaberg, University of Central Missouri

Nicole Aitken, Illinois Central College

James Andersen, Springfield Technical Community College

Bonnie Arnett, Washtenaw Community College

Kristi Barker, South Plains College

Melissa Barrett, Portland Community College

Jonelle Beatrice, Youngstown State University

Brenda Boshela, Cuyahoga Community College

Michael Boyd, Illinois Central College

Robyn Browder, Tidewater Community College

Carol Bustamante, Oakton Community College

Eileen Cain, Leeward Community College

David Chase, Raritan Valley Community College

Sandra Chumchal, Blinn College

Marlys Cordoba, College of the Siskiyous

Barbara Cox, Redlands Community College

Julie Damerell, Monroe Community College

Sherry Dilley, Minneapolis Community and Technical College

Luciana Diniz, Portland Community College

Sheilah Dobyns, Fullerton College

Kimberley Donnelly, College of Southern Maryland

Mary Dubbe, Thomas Nelson Community College

Juliet Dunphy, Concordia University

La Tonya Dyett, Community College of Baltimore County

Grant Eckstein, Brigham Young University

Teri Eckhoff, Hutchinson Community College

Marie Eckstrom, Rio Hondo College

Courtney Edwards, Red Rocks Community College

Janell Edwards, Brookhaven College

David Elias, Eastern Kentucky University

Priscilla Faucette, University of Hawaii at Manoa

Gail Fensom, University of New Hampshire at Manchester

Suzanne Franklin, Johnson County Community College

John French, Cape Cod Community College

Sally Gabb, Bristol Community College

Amy Garcia, Fullerton College

Janice Gardner, Peninsula College

Cathryn Jeffers-Goodwine, St. Clair County Community College

Geraldine Gough, Brevard Community College

Linda Gubbe, The University of Toledo

Sharon Hayes, Community College of Baltimore County

Beverly J. Hearn, University of Tennessee

Janice Hill, Moraine Valley Community College

Amye Howell, Copiah-Lincoln Community College

Judy Hubble, Austin Community College

Dianne Ida, Kapiolani Community College

Susie Johnston, Tyler Junior College

Sandra Jones, Community College of Baltimore County

Sally Keeton, Johnson County Community College

Sandra Kelley, Leeward Community College

Susan B. Larson, Portland Community College

Debra Lee, Nash Community College

Erlinda Legaspi, City College of San Francisco

Levia Loftus, College of Lake County

Naomi Ludman, Southwestern Michigan College

Gail Malone, South Plains College

Teresa Massey, Chemeketa Community College

Brook Mayo, Asheville-Buncombe Technical Community College

James McNamara, Alverno College

Elizabeth Patterson Melton, Mississippi Delta Community College

Dorothy Minor, Tulsa Community College

Betty Moffitt, Paris Junior College

Dan Moody, Southwestern College

Vicki Moulson, College of the Albemarle

Nancy Parker, Community College of Baltimore County

Rick Richards, St. Petersburg College

Stephen Rizzo, Bevill State Community College

Amelia Rodriguez (Wilson), Mesa Community College

Kathryn Ryder, Broome Community College

Dianna Sand, Delaware County Community College

Charis Sawyer, Johnson County Community College

Lynn Strong, Pulaski Technical College

Iris Strunc, Northwest Florida State College

Linda Talbert, Schoolcraft College

Bonny Tibbitts, American English Institute, University of Oregon

Christine Tutlewski, University of Wisconsin-Parkside

Shari Waldrop, Navarro College

Danhua Wang, Indiana University of Pennsylvania

Phyllis Watson, American River College

Rochelle Watson, Monroe Community College

Kimberly Whalen, Ozarks Technical Community College

Nicole Williams, Community College of Baltimore County

Victoria Williams, St. Cloud State University

Patricia Windon, St. Petersburg College

Barbara Wolfe, University of Hartford

Lynda Wolverton, Polk State College

Cynthia VanGieson, Baker College of Jackson

Chris Yockey, Mitchell Community College

Lynne Zimmer, North Central Michigan College

Making Brain Connections to Become an Expert Reader

TERRY CLARK

A tool and die skilled tradesman for an automotive company, a realtor, a real estate developer, an artist-mural painter, a remodeling designer and craftsman, and a poet

> *"The worth of a book is to be measured by what you can carry away from it."*
>
> —JAMES BRYCE

WHEN I WAS IN SCHOOL, it killed me to sit and read the books they make you read. I would do anything I could do to avoid reading the book. It was like taking a beating to read it. Then, at test time, I suffered. When you get out in life, you have to be more focused than in class. You can't just say, "I'm not good at this." You need to focus on something that attracts your interest. Once a person finds their focus in life, they are going to read about it.

Courtesy of Terry Clark

No one at a young age knows their strengths. Give yourself time to find your strengths. My advice is don't feel stupid. The "want to's" help you find your strengths. And remember, somewhere along the line, no matter what you do, you are going to have to read the directions.

Now I enjoy reading tax codes; they interest me because I have rental property. You must read well to understand the system or problem. Now I like to read about what is going on—meaningful, up-to-date information. If I am really interested, I could sit down and read for the better part of a day. Looking back, if I would have realized how much it would mean to me later in life, I would have taken more interest in reading.

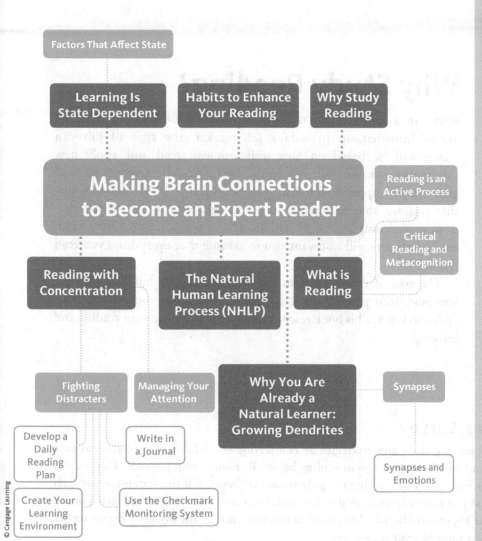

Factors That Affect State

Learning Is State Dependent

Habits to Enhance Your Reading

Why Study Reading

Making Brain Connections to Become an Expert Reader

Reading is an Active Process

Critical Reading and Metacognition

Reading with Concentration

The Natural Human Learning Process (NHLP)

What is Reading

Fighting Distracters

Managing Your Attention

Why You Are Already a Natural Learner: Growing Dendrites

Synapses

Develop a Daily Reading Plan

Write in a Journal

Synapses and Emotions

Create Your Learning Environment

Use the Checkmark Monitoring System

© Cengage Learning

Brain Connections: Self-Assessment

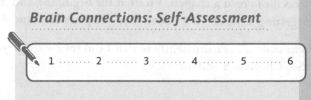

1 .... 2 .... 3 .... 4 .... 5 6

On the scale, with 1 meaning *nothing* and 6 meaning *a great deal*, circle the number for how much you understand right now about how the brain learns.

Why Study Reading?

NEVER HAVE READING AND THINKING BEEN SO IMPORTANT. This is the age of information. In today's job market, the type of job you secure will be based on how well you can read and apply new information—how well you learn. Being an effective reader will give you the upper hand. Your future employer will want to know that you are able to locate and access reliable sources of information, sort through a lot of details, and apply what you have read. And employers will not want you to assume that everything you read is true!

The goal of this book is to focus on reading by building on your strengths. Your greatest strengths are your brain and your natural-born ability to learn. This book teaches you how to optimize your reading and learning.

ACTIVITY 1A
Take a Reading Survey

Check your present reading skills and strategies by completing the following survey. Read each statement and respond based on your current reading habits. Be honest with yourself. This is a way to help you discover how well you are able to apply strategies. Write *Y* if the statement correctly describes you or what you currently do or *N* if it does not. Each statement will be addressed in this textbook. In Chapter 13, you will be asked to complete this same survey. Ideally, as an expert reader, you will have changed some of your responses.

_____ 1. I make every attempt to learn the words I don't understand while reading. (See Chapter 3.)

_____ 2. I create questions to ask myself before I begin to read a textbook chapter. (See Chapters 4 and 8.)

_____ 3. When I decide to read a chapter, I start at the beginning and read straight through, often forgetting most of what I read. (See Chapters 1, 4, and 8.)

_____ 4. I highlight main ideas consistently so that I can review the key points of a chapter easily. (See Chapters 8 and 9.)

_____ 5. Thinking at different levels has nothing to do with reading at different levels. (See Chapter 13.)

_____ 6. I don't make connections between what I know and new reading material. (See Chapter 1.)

_____ 7. When I detect an argument in my reading assignment, I locate and evaluate the reasons supporting it. (See Chapter 11.)

_____ 8. Detecting fallacies helps me understand authors' conclusions more effectively. (See Chapter 12.)

_____ 9. I am always able to identify the main ideas of textbooks. (See Chapters 4, 5, and 6.)

_____ 10. Sticking to a schedule seems too rigid for me. I'm too spontaneous to stick to a regular reading plan. (See Chapter 1.)

_____ 11. When I read, I try to locate organizational clue words. (See Chapter 7.)

_____ 12. Having a good attitude is related to how well I read. (See Chapters 1 and 2.)

_____ 13. It is important to actually say to myself that I intend to remember specific information in my textbook chapters. (See Chapter 2.)

_____ 14. Using authors' patterns of organization is not an important reading skill. It is more of a writing skill. (See Chapter 7.)

_____ 15. I create visuals for my most challenging textbook information. I use different visuals based on the type of information presented. (See Chapter 10.)

_____ 16. Tracking my concentration won't improve my ability to read. (See Chapter 1.)

_____ 17. I always look for clue words to help me gain deeper insight into the author's meaning. (See Chapters 7, 8, 9, and 13.)

_____ 18. I often try to create a metaphor to help me remember textbook information. Making comparisons makes recall easier. (See Chapters 2 and 6.)

_____ 19. I give up on trying to figure new information out. It is a waste of my time. (See Chapters 6 and 7.)

_____ 20. I use specific colors to identify main ideas and supporting details when marking my textbooks. (See Chapter 9.)

Continued on next page.

To calculate your score, your instructor will provide you with the answers of an expert reader. For every answer you have that matches that of an expert reader, give yourself 5 points.

Your Score: _____

100–95 Outstanding	Outstanding application of critical reading and thinking strategies.
90–85 Above Average	Above average application of critical reading strategies.
80–75 Average	Additional knowledge of skills and strategies will strengthen your ability to read and think more effectively.
70–65 Marginally Adequate	You may have difficulty getting the most out of your textbooks. Additional knowledge of skills and strategies will strengthen your ability to read and think more effectively.
60 and below Needs Work	You will benefit from learning and applying the strategies learned in this course. Not only will the strategies help you academically, but they will also benefit you in the world of work.

Knowledge is power. The more you read, the more you know. And the ability to use information in a meaningful way will always give you an advantage.

What Is Reading?

READING IS NOT NORMAL! Yes, you read that sentence correctly. Reading is a skill learned late in human history. It is not as old as music or drawing skills. There is no single area in the brain devoted to reading. Instead, parts of the brain designed for other tasks are used to read. Reading does not come naturally, though learning does. Reading requires skills that have to be learned, and college-level reading requires additional skills.

In school you are expected to read and understand what you read. But what does it mean to "read" a textbook? What exactly *is* reading? Have you ever thought about how you'd define reading? Probably not. It's just something you do. Take a few minutes to think about how you would define reading, and write down your definition here.

_____

_____

_____

You will probably be surprised to see that there is more than one way to define reading. Reading really involves a lot of activities. Reading is complicated, and if you don't know any reading strategies, such as vocabulary development, locating main ideas and details, identifying implied main ideas, and textbook marking, college reading will be especially challenging. If you have had difficulty with reading, you are not alone. Read your definition of reading and see if it includes any of the following.

Reading is:

- ▶ learning
- ▶ intentional (for a purpose)
- ▶ an active process (processes)
- ▶ a task that requires focus and concentration
- ▶ contextual (authors use clues to help readers understand information)
- ▶ a two-way communication between an author and the reader
- ▶ a two-way communication using written language or symbols
- ▶ a medium or a way for authors to share information
- ▶ understanding and interpreting
- ▶ thinking and reflecting
- ▶ making connections to previous experiences and learning

Did your definition include one or more of the items listed? All of the listed items are correct definitions of reading. It is a complicated process. Did you ever think about textbook reading as being a two-way communication between an author and the reader? Did you know that when you read well, you bring important information you have to the author's ideas? The author talks to you with words on the page and you add to this conversation with information you know on the subject.

It is equally important to know what reading is not. Just looking at words is not reading. Understanding is crucial. If you do not understand what you read, you will not learn or remember the information. Without understanding, you are just looking. For example, you can look at the words and characters in Russian, German, Greek, or Chinese books, but you will not be able to read those books unless you are familiar with and understand those languages. Read this sentence from a book about grammar: "Appositives are typically non-restrictive noun phrases that have the same references as the preceding noun phrases."* Do you understand what that means? If not, what would you have to do to be able to understand it? The same is true when reading college textbooks or any written information using the language of specific disciplines or subjects, like the language used by the grammarian in the quote and by other experts, such as mathematicians, biologists, historians, or engineers.

Critical Reading and Metacognition

critical reading a complex thinking technique that involves discovering and taking apart an author's meaning, evaluating the author's meaning based on established standards, and incorporating the meaning into the ideas you already know

CRITICAL READING is a complex thinking technique that involves discovering and taking apart an author's meaning, evaluating the author's meanings based on established standards, and incorporating the meaning into the ideas you already know. Critical reading, as required for textbooks and other college reading material, is more complicated than reading done for pleasure, which is why college reading is more difficult and takes more time than pleasure reading. Critical reading goes beyond basic understanding and requires more strategies, such as:

- ▶ understanding an author's ideas even if they are not stated directly
- ▶ recognizing patterns of organization in what you read
- ▶ using a questioning technique before, during, and after you read
- ▶ prioritizing an author's ideas
- ▶ translating an author's ideas into visuals
- ▶ identifying and evaluating an author's arguments
- ▶ creating new ideas using an author's ideas

All of these strategies can, and should, be used to get more out of your college reading. This textbook offers clear explanations and lots of practice with these essential critical reading strategies.

As you master the critical reading strategies presented in this book, apply them to the textbooks you are reading this semester. To purposely apply reading strategies that work involves metacognition. Metacognition is thinking about how you think. It is an awareness of your own knowledge and your ability to monitor and control your learning. Have you ever answered your cell phone in a crowded area with lots of noise? You most likely covered one ear with your hand while you listened to the call. You were aware that noise

metacognition thinking about how you think; an awareness of your own knowledge and an ability to monitor and control your learning

---

*Greenbaum. *The Oxford English Grammar*. Oxford: Oxford University Press, 1966, p. 205.

makes a phone call difficult to hear and you knew that blocking one ear helped cut down on the noise. You knew how to listen more effectively and created a strategy to help you. You actually used metacognition.

With the strategies presented in this book, you can take control over your learning by having a system for making sense of your textbook. Academic success is about perseverance—to keep going in spite of obstacles, discouragement, or difficulty—as well as actively engaging in your learning and maintaining a positive attitude. It is knowing what skills to apply and how and when to apply them.

ACTIVITY 1B
Determine Who Is Reading

Read the paragraph below, and then answer the following questions using complete sentences. Be specific in your answer.

> A volunteer community reader has been assigned to record a history chapter for a blind student. The volunteer pronounces all of the words correctly. He says that it is a challenging (monotonous) job, so he tries to keep his mind busy as he speaks into the recorder. He makes mental to-do lists or thinks about the next book that has to be recorded. When the blind student plays the recording of the history chapter, she stops it from time to time to summarize what she has heard. She identifies key points before continuing to play more of the recording, recording her own notes into a second tape recorder.
>
> Source: Adapted from Smith, Frank. *Reading Without Nonsense.* New York: Teacher's College Columbia University, 1985, pp. 48–49.

1. Is the volunteer reading? Explain your answer.

_____

_____

_____

2. Is the blind student reading? Explain your answer.

_____

_____

_____

Reading Is an Active Process

READING IS AN active process that depends on both an author's ability to communicate meaning using words and your ability to create meaning from those words. Successful reading requires you to constantly connect what you already know to what the author has written. So, if you don't understand the words the writer uses, it is unlikely that you will be able to remember much, if anything, that you read. The brain cannot remember what it does not understand.

Neuropsychologist Adele Diamond offers a good analogy for active reading. To read well, you need to be the "driver" of the process. She asks, "Who remembers a path to a destination better, the driver or the passengers?" The driver, of course. The driver is actively engaged in the activity and is acutely aware of what is going on around him. He remembers details like what streets to turn on and what the speed limits are, and he keeps in mind his main idea—the final destination. The passengers, on the other hand, could pay attention to the road, but they could also text their friends, listen to music, and even take a nap. The passengers are involved in the driving experience, but for the most part, they are along for the ride, passively seeing what is around them. The driver is actively involved, purposefully making choices about what to do, where to go, and what information to concentrate on.

To read well, you need to be active in your reading experience. Like a driver of a car, an active reader is purposefully engaged in the reading process. An active reader focuses attention on the words on the page just like the driver keeps eyes on the road. He reads carefully to understand the author, blocking out any distractions. An active reader slows his reading speed if an author's meaning is unclear. An active reader sometimes rereads passages and occasionally, looks up unfamiliar words. An active reader pauses to recall any information he already knows on the subject and tries to relate it to what he is reading. An active reader constantly monitors comprehension. If he becomes passive in his reading, he may read each word but not carefully monitor his understanding. Like the passenger of a car, he may shift his focus from one thing to another. He may daydream. He may even fall asleep. Active reading is always better than passive reading.

active reading applying strategies to stay engaged with text and to keep thinking about the information

Active reading requires that you purposely do something with the reading material to help you remember it. Several examples of active reading strategies that will be addressed in this book include:

▶ previewing all reading assignments so that you signal your brain what to look for

▶ developing questions so that you can answer them as you read

▶ connecting all new information to what you already know

▶ outlining/mapping/drawing your interpretation of the information to demonstrate your understanding

▶ using pictures, headings, subheadings, and titles to help you make sense of the new information and organize what you are learning

✓ **COMPREHENSION CHECK**

▶ What should you do to truly understand what you read?
▶ How is looking at words different from reading words?

ACTIVITY 1C
Identify Active and Passive Reading Strategies

Decide whether each of the following activities is passive or active by writing *P* next to the passive activities and *A* next to those you think are active.

_____ 1. Reading a textbook chapter from the beginning to end, straight through

_____ 2. Writing down everything your professor says during a lecture

_____ 3. Rewriting your lecture notes

_____ 4. Cramming for an exam the night before

_____ 5. Previewing each chapter and developing questions

_____ 6. Making a to-do list of weekend activities during a lecture

_____ 7. Summarizing what you have just read and then creating a mind map

_____ 8. Testing yourself on the information in your book

_____ 9. Giving a mini-lecture of the chapter information to an empty room

_____ 10. Skipping the pictures and charts in the textbook chapter because you don't have time

Now, truthfully answer the following questions. Honest answers will help you assess what kind of reader you are and what you need to do to become an expert reader.

11. How do you currently try to stay active during lectures and when you read a textbook chapter?

_____

_____

Continued on next page.

12. Do you believe that you are currently an active or passive reader?

_____

_____

13. Which subjects do you read more actively? Why?

_____

_____

14. Which subjects do you read more passively? Why?

_____

_____

15. For each item that you labeled as passive in the first set of questions, change the language in the statement so that it becomes an active reading strategy.

Why You Are Already a Natural Learner: Growing Dendrites

RECENTLY SCIENTISTS DISCOVERED SOMETHING NEW and amazing about the brain: it continues to change throughout your life as a result of what you do. The brain you have today is not the one you were born with. Even before you were born, your brain began shaping itself to your own environment. It started molding itself according to the early sounds you heard. After you were born, all of your experiences further shaped your brain. This ability of the brain to change as a result of experience is called plasticity because, like plastic, the brain can be molded or shaped. This textbook is going to show you how you can change your brain and become a better learner to learn faster and more effectively.

Think of a tree in winter with many bare branches and twigs (Figure 1.1). This is what our brain cells, called neurons, look like after we have learned something. Each brain cell has one trunk (like a tree trunk), called an axon. Also like trees, brain cells have many branches and twigs. Finally, like trees, our brain cells have many roots, called terminals on the axon.

Figure 1.2 is an artist's drawing of two large brain cells (neurons) with many other neurons behind them. As you can see, the neurons in this figure look a little like trees; the "roots" of the big neuron at the top are

neurons brain cells

axon the usually long process of a nerve fiber that generally conducts impulses away from the body of the nerve cell

terminals endings by which axons make synaptic contacts with other nerve cells

Figure 1.1 A Brain Cell (Neuron) Looks Like This Tree

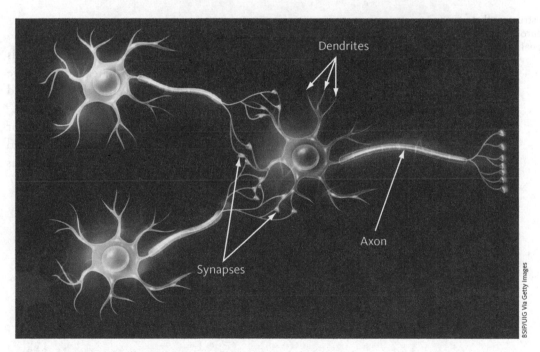

Figure 1.2 Brain Cells Connect to Form a Neural Network

touching, connecting to the "branches" or "twigs" of the big neuron next to it. Where neurons connect is called a synapse. Look at all the neurons in the background, and notice that they are also connecting to one another to form a network of neurons (a neural network). Scientists call the branches and twigs that grow from a neuron dendrites, which, in fact, means "tree-like."

As you work with, experience, explore, examine, think about, try to figure out, and practice a specific skill or concept, brain cells (neurons) in your brain grow new branches and twigs (dendrites) that connect that new knowledge, concept, or skill (Figure 1.3). The more we know, the more we grow. The more we grow, the more we know.

The neuron at the right in Figure 1.3 is an illustration to represent how dendrites might grow before and after learning. The more you think about, work with, and practice a specific new skill, concept, or area of knowledge, the more the dendrites can grow.

dendrites a short branched extension of a nerve cell, along which impulses received from other cells at synapses are transmitted to the cell body

Synapses

synapses a structure that permits a neuron to pass an electrical signal to another brain cell

SYNAPSES **CONNECT RELATED** neurons to create a neural network, which is what we have practiced, learned, and know about a skill or area of knowledge (Figure 1.4). Learning involves growing dendrites, connecting them at related synapses, and constructing stable neural networks.

The more we work on, think about, and practice a specific skill or area of knowledge, a larger, thicker neural network of specific connected neurons will grow. The neural network in Figure 1.4 shows four neurons

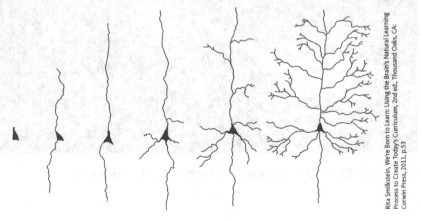

Rita Smilkstein, We're Born to Learn: Using the Brain's Natural Learning Process to Create Today's Curriculum, 2nd ed., Thousand Oaks, CA: Corwin Press, 2011, p.53

Figure 1.3 Growing Dendrites = Learning

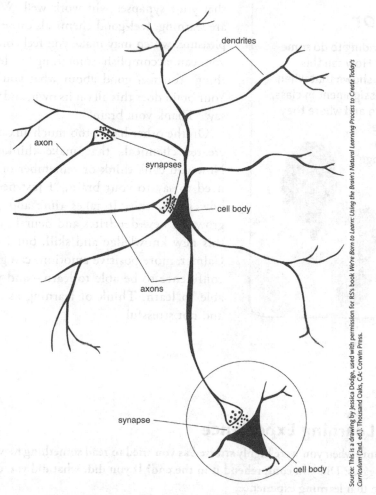

Source: This is a drawing by Jessica Dodge, used with permission for RS's book *We're Born to Learn: Using the Brain's Natural Learning Process to Create Today's Curriculum* (2nd. ed.), Thousand Oaks, CA: Corwin Press.

Figure 1.4 A Neural Network of Four Neurons

connecting at synapses. It is important to know how the synapses work because synapses are how our brain connects related neurons to create neural networks. The more we know and learn, the larger, fuller, and thicker that network will become.

Synapses and Emotions

When your synapses work well, your neurons are able to connect, which is what makes it possible for you to remember and use the knowledge and skill that you have learned. Synapses are affected by emotions, either helping

Tip FROM THE
Brain Doctor

Did you know that intending to do something affects the brain? How can this help you? Research has shown that when students are given an assignment in class, if they write down when and where they intend to do it, they are more successful in completing it. Take advantage of this power. Every time you are given an assignment, write down when and where you intend to do it. Try it and see for yourself!

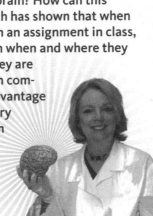

them work well or shutting them down, so you need to know how to control your emotions so that your synapses will work well. When brains are learning, feel-good chemicals cause you to feel pleasure, which may make you feel confident that you can accomplish something or learn something. You feel good about what you are doing. Your brain does this all on its own, and you should say, "Thank you, brain!"

On the other hand, too much anxiety or stress creates chemicals that make thinking harder. Now you can't think or remember or learn. You need to say to your brain, "I just need to learn how to do this. It takes time and practice to grow the new dendrites and neural networks for this new knowledge and skill, but I can do it." Calmer, more positive emotions can give you the confidence to be able to learn—and you will be able to learn. Think of learning as challenging and not stressful.

ACTIVITY 1D
Describe a Learning Experience

Think back to a time when you were highly stressed as you tried to read something new. What were your specific struggles? Did you comprehend it in the end? If you did, what did you do to understand it? Describe that learning experience.

✓ COMPREHENSION CHECK

▶ How can you "grow" new knowledge?
▶ How and why does the brain change when you are learning?

The Natural Human Learning Process (NHLP)

CAN YOU GUESS HOW MANY NEURONS you have in your brain? Brain scientists say that the human brain has one or two hundred billion nerve cells (neurons) and approximately 40 quadrillion connections (synapses) among them. They say this makes the human brain, which is a three-pound, soft, squishy organ, "the most complex object in the universe."*

The human brain, through human history, has created and made everything human beings have ever invented and produced. Fortunately, you do not need to know about all the vast complexities of the brain to learn well. You can learn some things about your brain that will help you be a more confident, successful learner and creator. Your brain was born to learn; therefore, you are a natural-born learner. It is important to know these major points about learning:

1. Your brain was born to learn, loves to learn, and knows how to learn.

2. You learn what you practice.
   - ▶ Practice is making mistakes, correcting mistakes, learning from them, and trying over, again and again.
   - ▶ Making and learning from mistakes are a natural and necessary part of learning.

3. You learn what you practice because, when you are practicing, your brain grows new fibers (dendrites) and connects them (at synapses) into neural networks.

4. Learning takes time because your brain needs time to grow and connect dendrites, synapses, and neural networks.

5. If you don't use what you learn, you can lose the new learning. Newly formed dendrites, synapses, and neural networks can begin to disappear if you don't use them—if you don't practice or use what you have learned. They just get absorbed into the brain tissue and are not stabilized.

6. Your emotions affect your brain's ability to learn, think, and remember.
   - ▶ Self-doubt, fear, and other negative emotions can prevent your brain from learning, thinking, and remembering.
   - ▶ Confidence and interest help your brain learn, think, and remember.

---

*Ratey, J. *A User's Guide to the Brain: Perception, Attention, and the Four Theaters of the Brain.* New York: Pantheon, 2001, p. 9.

ACTIVITY 1E
See the NHLP in Action

Think of something you learned to do well outside of school. It could be a sport, a hobby, an art, driving a car, something around the house, a people skill, maybe something you did when you were younger but don't do anymore. Think back to before you knew how to do it. Then think how you went from there to knowing how to do it. Write down some notes about how you got from not knowing how to do it to being good at it—maybe not the world's greatest expert, but pretty good.

1. If directed by your instructor, get together with a few others in your class, or complete the process by taking notes. Describe the thing you are good at. Then, if possible, share and compare in the group how everyone learned his or her thing.

2. Now share and compare with the whole class. What happened at the very beginning of learning your new thing? Your instructor will record your answers. This will be Stage 1.

3. Then what happened next? Share and compare; then your instructor will record your answers. This will be Stage 2.

4. Then what happened next? Share and compare; your instructor will record your answers. This will be Stage 3.

5. Keep answering what happened next until there are no more stages to report.

Did you all learn your different things pretty much this same way? Maybe not every word in this exact order—but pretty much in a similar way? More than 10,000 people have said they learned this same way. So just remember that learning takes time and practice.

Research with more than 10,000 students and teachers across subjects, ethnicities, genders, ages, and levels of education has found, thanks to our amazing brain, that there is a natural human sequence of stages of learning:

1. motivation (wanting to or having to learn something)
2. practice (trying it)
3. more practice (improving, gaining confidence)
4. more practice (more understanding, some success)
5. more skill (more success, becoming natural)
6. mastery (able to teach it, able to build on it)

natural human learning process (NHLP) research that shows everyone learns by the same process

This is the natural human learning process (NHLP). This research has found that every group, without exception, reports three to six stages. When fewer stages are reported, the middle stages usually have been reported as one or two stages of practice and/or the last stages have been reported as one stage of skillfulness, mastery, and teaching. Activity 1E proves to those who do it that they are successful, natural learners. In fact, after doing this activity, you have just proven that you know how to learn, that you have a brain that knows how to learn, and that you are a natural-born learner.

Table 1.1 shows the results of three NHLP research activities, following the steps you used in Activity 1E. Two were done with students in community college classes and the other with a group of college teachers. In each box is the list of the experiences and descriptions exactly as the individuals in the group reported their experiences. Notice the similar experiences the different groups reported even though some of the similar experiences are not at the same stage for each group.

Table 1.1 **Natural Human Learning Process Research Results**

Stage	Community College Students—Washington	Community College Students—North Carolina	College Teachers—Arizona
1. Motivation	failed, afraid and uncomfortable, frustrated, want to quit, filled with wonder, inspired	terrible at it, excited, scared of failing, mistakes, curiosity, nervous, carefree, hurt, practice a lot, watched it, had to trust someone, give it all you've got, picture it in your head, listen	observe, didn't have the aptitude, had motivation and a desire to learn, cried and got mad and got stubborn, made a lot of mistakes, it was very physically painful, there is anxiety, was excited
2. Practice	practice, had someone teach me, got more detailed, had encouragement from other people, it becomes more comfortable, made mistakes, really start to go through it	trial and error, action, learn it, practice, taking a class, asking questions, frustration, asking somebody who knows how to do it, anxious, got better, do it, encouragement	practice, asked for help, read about it, studied, learned from mistakes, took directions from others
3. More Practice	moved to more complex, practice, notice you're getting better, confidence, observation, appreciation, show someone else how to do it, really enjoy doing it, becomes natural	got good at it, practice, evaluate your progress, confident, persistence, refine, concentrate, input from peers	started having small successes, feeling satisfied, my confidence increased, tried again, motivation, received compliments, gaining self-confidence

Continued on next page.

Stage	Community College Students—Washington	Community College Students—North Carolina	College Teachers—Arizona
4. More Practice	keep evolving, there's always more to learn, other applications for it, becomes second nature	success, you succeed, independent, able to help others learn, make money, win, have fun, compete, pride, find your career	got more daring, started winning, more compliments, changed technique, got more creative, started teaching others, entered contests, rewards, started having fun, realized there was more to learn
5. More Skill	might move on to other activities, performing	continue, expand, teach, become an expert, help others, learn something new, higher level of difficulty	went back to stage 1 but at a different level, started selling my work
6. Mastery	mastery, teach somebody else	all the ones before, stop, start learning something else, parallel applications, celebrate, repeat all the stages again	teaching others

Brain Connections: Self-Assessment

Draw on the brain cell body provided here the amount and length of dendrites (tree-like branches and twigs) to represent how well you understand the section "The Natural Human Learning Process (NHLP)." If you don't understand it very well, draw only a few short dendrites. Then, read the section again and draw more dendrites to represent your learning progress. How many dendrites you draw represents how well you think you learned the material. You can use this method to keep track of your progress as you read this book.

I don't understand too much about the natural human learning process.	I have a pretty good understanding about the natural human learning process.	I have a very good understanding about the natural human learning process.

Reading with Concentration

TO READ WELL, YOU NEED TO READ WITH CONCENTRATION, which is focusing on what you are reading. Do you ever spend a couple of hours reading only to find that you cannot remember most of what you have read? If you are unable to concentrate, you won't remember much of what you read. Engaging with new material—discussing it, using it, or relating it to what you already know—is a very good strategy for concentrating. Research is clear that you must *concentrate* on doing something with the new information you are reading in order to learn, understand, and remember it. The more you can actively engage with new information, the more likely you will be able to remember it.

Managing Your Attention

IF YOU COULD set up a situation where your learning would be guaranteed, would you do it? If you knew the time you spent studying would result in real knowledge that would help you do better on exams, would you spend the time? Learning about attention and concentration cannot be over-emphasized. Many students who struggle with reading assignments do so because they have trouble staying focused. You can grow dendrites and create neural networks, which means that certain neural processes take over more "real estate" or space in the brain. For example, guitar players use their thumb a lot, so the part of the brain that is devoted to the thumb actually grows larger in guitar players' brains. And when you pay attention, there is even more change than what is created simply by usage alone.

Consider this research study scientists conducted with monkeys: Scientists had two kinds of sensory input going into the monkeys at the same time. One input was music, which goes to the auditory cortex in the brain, the part that enables you to hear. The second input was to make the monkeys' fingers move by hooking up wires so that pulling on the wires made the fingers move, much like a puppet. As you learned earlier, if you use a part of your body repeatedly, it makes a difference in the brain. So researchers

> ## Tip FROM THE
> ## Brain Doctor
>
> The scientific term for the type of concentration you need in school is *selective attention*. Managing your attention is managing your concentration and focus. This is a skill that you can get better at, and it is essential to being an effective reader and learner. If you cannot manage your attention, you will have difficulty in school and on the job.

expected two areas of the brain to get larger: the auditory part where the music was processed and the sensorimotor part where finger movements are registered in the brain. Now comes the important step: Using juice as a reward, scientists trained half of the monkeys to pay attention to the music and the other half to pay attention to their finger movements. Remember, both sound and movement are taking place for all the monkeys at the same time, but the monkeys are paying attention to either the sound or the movement. The results were shocking! It turns out that if the monkeys paid attention to the sound only, the auditory cortex got bigger but not the finger area even though using the fingers would normally affect the brain. However, if they paid attention to the finger movements and not the sound, the finger area got bigger but not the auditory area. In other words, whatever they focused on and paid attention to, those sections of their brains got bigger.

So what does that tell you? It may not be enough just to do something or go through the motions. You need to direct the brain's attention to the task. Both experience and attention cause the physical structure of the brain to change. Research indicates that just firing the brain, sending stimuli, even repeatedly, is necessary, but perhaps not sufficient. To wire the information in the brain seems to require attention. As Robert Leamnson, a learning expert, says, "There is a biological basis for the different effects of just reading, and reading with attention. If incoming stimuli are to have a lasting effect, they must be accompanied by *interest*." It turns out that paying attention with interest may be one of the most important keys to your success in school. This applies greatly to reading.

Tip FROM THE Brain Doctor

Studying halfheartedly, without focused attention, wastes your time. A shorter time of focused attention will probably pay bigger results. The tip? Turn off the TV, the iPhone, and the Internet, and pay attention. You want to create these positive brain changes, and now that you know more about how, you have the power to do so!

✔ COMPREHENSION CHECK

▶ Think of the monkey research study just described in terms of human behavior. Why is listening to your iPod while studying discouraged?

▶ What happens in the brain when you study while doing something else?

ACTIVITY 1F
Learn about Yourself

For each statement, score yourself as honestly as you can from 1 (if you strongly disagree) to 7 (if you strongly agree). A rating of 4 is neutral.

Strongly Disagree   Neutral   Strongly Agree

1 .... 2 .... 3 .... 4 .... 5 .... 6 7

_____ 1. *It is easy for me to concentrate on my activities.

_____ 2. Frequently when I am working I find myself worrying about other things.

_____ 3. Time always seems to be passing slowly.

_____ 4. I often find myself at "loose ends," not knowing what to do.

_____ 5. I am often trapped in situations where I have to do meaningless things.

_____ 6. Having to look at someone's home movies or travel slides bores me tremendously.

_____ 7. *I have projects in mind all the time, things to do.

_____ 8. *I find it easy to entertain myself.

_____ 9. Many things I have to do are repetitive and monotonous.

_____ 10. It takes more stimulation to get me going than most people.

_____ 11. *I get a kick out of most things I do.

_____ 12. I am seldom excited about my work.

_____ 13. *In any situation I can usually find something to do or see to keep me interested.

_____ 14. Much of the time I just sit around doing nothing.

_____ 15. *I am good at waiting patiently.

_____ 16. I often find myself with nothing to do, time on my hands.

_____ 17. In situations where I have to wait, such as in a line, I get very restless.

_____ 18. *I often wake up with a new idea.

_____ 19. It would be very hard for me to find a job that is exciting enough.

_____ 20. I would like more challenging things to do in life.

_____ 21. I feel that I am working below my abilities most of the time.

_____ 22. *Many people would say that I am a creative or imaginative person.

Continued on next page.

_____ 23. *I have so many interests, I don't have time to do everything.

_____ 24. *Among my friends, I am the one who keeps doing something the longest.

_____ 25. Unless I am doing something exciting, even dangerous, I feel half-dead and dull.

_____ 26. It takes a lot of change and variety to keep me really happy.

_____ 27. It seems that the same things are on television or in the movies all the time; it's getting old.

_____ 28. When I was young, I was often in monotonous and tiresome situations.

Source: From Farmer, R. & Sunberg, N.D., "Boredom Proneness—The Development and Correlates of a New Scale," *Journal of Personality Assessment.* 50:1. Copyright © 1986 Taylor & Francis. Reprinted with permission.

Do you ever say that you do not like a class or cannot pay attention because it is boring? Actually, boring is a state of your mind, not something inherent in or part of the person or material that you call boring. To add up your score for this activity, **score the statements with an asterisk (*) in front of it in the *reverse* direction.** In other words, for any statements with an asterisk, cross out your answer and use this scale:

Change 7 to 1	Change 3 to 5
Change 6 to 2	Change 2 to 6
Change 5 to 3	Change 1 to 7
Keep 4 the same	

Make this change only for those statements with an asterisk. Now add up your score and write the number here: _____

This is actually a test that scientists use to measure whether a person has a tendency toward being more bored than most people regardless of what a particular situation is. In other words, everyone is different in the level of stimulation that feels good. Some need more, some less. Those who need more stimulation often get bored easily. Therefore, situations that don't bore most people might bore them. And situations that bore everyone are even harder to take if you have a tendency toward boredom in general. Some people are more likely to get bored in school while others don't find it boring and find it very stimulating. Do you think you may have a tendency to get bored easily? If you scored higher than 117, then you are naturally more likely to get bored regardless of what is going on in the classroom.

Boredom leads to a lack of attention in the brain, and attention is critical to learning. If you get bored, you have to find a way to get mentally engaged. You will have to compensate and overcome a tendency to be bored by purposefully increasing your attention. Here are some ways to fight boredom when it occurs in school:

▶ **Take notes.** Even if you never look at them again (though you will learn better if you do), taking notes can help fight the boredom, thus increasing attention and improving your learning.

▶ **Doodle while you listen**. The brain can learn when it is relaxed, and doodling may help the processing, especially if you are listening and not thinking about what you are doodling.

▶ **Mentally outline what you are hearing**. Look for the major points. Hunting for main ideas will help keep you focused even if the material is not interesting to you.

▶ **Think about the goal.** Emotion drives attention, and attention drives learning. If you think about how good you will feel if you learn something or get a good grade, that may activate emotional systems that drive attention.

Remember, boredom is *your* problem because the bored feeling inside of you affects *your* learning and what is boring to you may not be boring to others. No one enjoys being bored, so use strategies to fight it and engage yourself in what you are learning.

Fighting Distracters

WHEN YOU ARE reading or studying, what distracts you? An important step in improving your concentration is knowing what prevents you from being able to read and study. Once you have identified your distracters, you can begin to correct them or, better yet, prevent them from occurring. There are two types of distracters:

▶ Internal distracters are those things that come from within you such as hunger, worry, daydreaming, boredom, money concerns, anger over a recent fight, price of gasoline, excitement about an upcoming event, or fear of failure.

▶ External distracters are those that come from the environment such as music, television, family conversations, fighting, phone calls, traffic, weather (good or bad), or visitors.

internal distracters things that come from within you, like feelings, emotions, or thoughts, that prevent you from being able to focus on your reading

external distracters things in your environment that prevent you from being able to focus on your reading

It is important for you to confirm what your distracters are so that you can begin to deal with them.

ACTIVITY 1G
Discover Your Distracters

Fold a lined sheet of writing paper in half vertically. Lay it open, and on one half, write down all your external distracters—the things that you find the most distracting from your environment. On the other half, write down all of the internal distracters you experience.

There are proven techniques designed to boost your attention that help you fight your distracters:

▶ Write in a journal
▶ Use the checkmark monitoring system
▶ Create your learning environment
▶ Develop a daily reading plan

Try them and see which ones work best for you.

Write in a Journal

journal a technique used to help you to think on paper about what you have just read and log what learning strategies do and do not work; a way to track and monitor concentration and progress

Using a journal helps you analyze your reading strategies and assess your learning. Journals help you think on paper about what you have read, and identify what you do (and do not) understand. Journals serve as a first step to explore how you think. Journaling is a metacognitive strategy—you are writing down what you think and how you think as you read. As you write, connect new material you have learned from your textbooks to information you already know about a subject. Journals also help you apply, monitor, and improve your critical reading strategies. Knowing which strategies work for you—and which do not—is essential for learning effectively. Some students are initially resistant to using journals; however, most experience the benefits immediately and continue to use them, even beyond this course. Why? Because journals work.

Journals usually use writing prompts to help you focus on what you have learned and read. Your responses to these prompts help you decide how well you have learned new information and what is unclear and requires follow-up. Journals are different from marking and note taking from your textbook (you will learn more about marking and note taking in Chapter 9) because the focus in your journal is your personal learning, not textbook content. You will actually be analyzing how you learn. You can use the Comprehension Checks in this textbook as journal prompts to think and write about what you are learning in each chapter. Another way to use journaling is when your instructor returns homework assignments to you. You can summarize the instructor's comments and use them to explore ways to improve your performance. An important key to learning is to know what works for you and what does not. If you do not do well on an assignment, analyze your mistakes so you do not repeat them. If you do well on an assignment, record the strategies you used so you *can* repeat them. Your journal is a great place for you to keep track of your progress and plan effective learning strategies.

It is ideal to have one journal for each of your classes, but you could use a spiral notebook with colored divider tabs, with each section as a journal for each different class. While there are no absolute rules for journal writing, here are some recommended guidelines:

▶ Date each entry on the top right side of the page.

▶ If your journal entry is in response to a reading assignment, write down the page numbers of your reading assignment with your journal entry in case you need to refer back to it.

▶ Highlight or otherwise mark any questions you have for your instructor. Highlighting helps you find your questions faster. When you learn the answers to your questions, write them in a different color pen, perhaps in the margin next to your questions, so that the right information stands out.

▶ Write a one- or two-word title for each entry to make locating the subjects of journal entries more efficient.

You can also use a journal to improve your ability to pay attention. This is a useful strategy if you are bothered by internal distracters such as anxiety or financial or personal problems. In your journal, write down your worries. Then mentally redirect yourself back to your studies, knowing that you have already addressed your internal concerns by writing them down in your journal. This journaling technique temporarily shelves a problem or worry.

Another use for your journal is to use it to write a letter to discuss your internal distracters. If there is something or someone that is really bothering you, don't walk away or give up on your studying. Take five minutes to write a letter in your journal. Address whatever may be bothering you (anger, excitement, worry). Write down exactly what you would like to say, at that moment, in a letter. Use all the language you would like to use regardless of how inappropriate it may seem. Then tear that page out of your journal, rip it up, and throw it away. This is a simple strategy that sounds ridiculous to many students, but it works. Somehow concerns are more noticeable right before a major exam or presentation. The act of writing down your concerns and then throwing them away helps you mentally (but temporarily) throw the problem away. Obviously it will not remove the problem forever, but it will allow you to concentrate on the task at hand. Try it once and see if it works for you.

ACTIVITY 1H
Use a Journal

1. Do you think that keeping a journal would be a good strategy for you? Why or why not?

_____

_____

2. What learning strategies do you already use well? Make a list. For each strategy on the list, explain why it works for you.

_____

_____

_____

Use the Checkmark Monitoring System

The checkmark monitoring system helps you keep track of the number of times you lose your concentration as you read. Once you become aware of when you lose concentration, you can begin to focus on why. Every time your mind wanders, you can make a conscious decision to refocus your attention, which will allow you to finish your homework. Tracking your attention helps reduce the number of times you get distracted. If you find yourself thinking about your date this weekend while reading, the checkmark monitoring system will help redirect your attention away from your daydreaming and back to your book. Here is how it works:

1. Start reading a textbook assignment. Every time you lose your attention, make a checkmark in your textbook.

2. After you have finished 50 minutes of reading, count how many checkmarks you made. This number will be your baseline.

3. As you practice the other attention techniques in this chapter, periodically use the checkmark monitoring system to assess how effective each technique is for you. As the number of checks decrease, you will know that your attention is improving.

It is important that you apply the checkmark monitoring system to reading from all of your courses so that you are able to see if there are differences in how well you concentrate in different subjects. You won't know this if you use just one textbook. You should notice a difference in how long it takes you to read different textbooks, as well as the number of times you get distracted.

ACTIVITY 1I
Use the Checkmark Monitoring System

Read from one of your current course reading assignments for 50 minutes, and apply the checkmark monitoring system.

1. How many checkmarks did you make?

_____

2. Why do you think you were as distracted as you were when reading?

_____

_____

3. Do you think you would make more or fewer checkmarks for a reading in another course? Explain your answer.

_____

_____

Create Your Learning Environment

If you find that you become distracted easily by external distracters, like cell phones ringing, the television, people talking, or traffic, it might be helpful for you to create your own personal study environment. Choose a space that is as private as possible, where you can organize your study materials so that they are easily accessible. Although the "perfect" environment varies from student to student, the following list offers general guidelines to follow:

▶ Turn off your cell phone when you study.

▶ Turn off the television. If you hear it at all, it will be too tempting to shift your attention from studying. You can reward yourself with a television show when you have finished studying.

▶ Stay away from the Internet. There are so many tempting and distracting things to do online. If you don't need it to do your studying, it is best to make it a reward after a study session.

▶ Have all of your study materials in one place before you begin to study: paper, pens, books, calculator, notebooks. Having to stop studying to hunt down another pencil or calculator could destroy your concentration, attention, and desire to study.

▶ Invest in a bright light. Dim light causes eyestrain and makes you tired faster.

▶ Sit in a firm, not-too-comfortable chair. You want to be alert and ready to work. A cushy chair may turn your study time into sleep time.

▶ Try not to do your homework in social areas in your home such as the living room or family room.

▶ Avoid reading college textbooks in bed. You will establish a habit of falling asleep every time you begin to read. You do not want to connect sleep with reading.

▶ Drink water. Before you study, make certain that you have taken care of your hunger and you have a bottle of water at hand. A dehydrated brain is sluggish and causes you to feel tired.

Remember that these are suggestions, so explore the types of environments that affect your individual needs. If you can't study while alone, how many people do you need to be around? Is working in the library a public but quiet enough space?

What if you have no place to study in your home? What if you share space and cannot find a good place to study? Always have a plan B. Put all of your essential study materials in a backpack: pencils, paper, appropriate books, and handouts. Go to your college or university library. Most academic libraries are collaborative and may seem noisy, but they all have quiet space. Many have study rooms that you can reserve. Having an environment to support your learning makes a difference in how well you learn.

Develop a Daily Reading Plan

Students usually intend to read all of the chapters assigned to them, but most have not developed a plan to ensure that they are able to follow through. Having a written plan—*I will read 16 pages of Chapter 4 at 6 p.m.*—is more of a commitment than thinking that you will read Chapter 4 sometime today or maybe tomorrow. The more specific you can make your plan, the more likely you will complete it on time and avoid any distracters. Making time and following a plan can be your greatest tools for success.

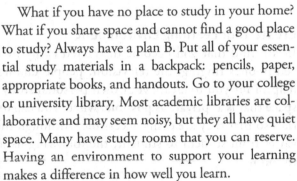

Tip FROM THE
Brain Doctor

Researcher Jill Shelton at Washington University in St. Louis, Missouri, found that students exposed to a cell phone ringing in class scored 25% worse on a test of material that was presented before the distraction. If she fumbled through her purse for the phone, creating more distraction, students performed even worse. Turn those cell phones off—in school or wherever you are studying!

ACTIVITY 1J
Create Your Daily Reading Plan

Using the calendar provided, create a daily reading plan for your current reading assignments for the coming week. Be specific in your plan, and schedule time for next week's reading assignments in your chart. Knowing how much time you have available makes it more likely that you will create an authentic plan, so add in other activities you know will take up your time, like sleeping, class, and work.

	Sunday	Monday	Tuesday	Wednesday	Thursday	Friday	Saturday
12 a.m.							
1 a.m.							
2 a.m.							
3 a.m.							
4 a.m.							
5 a.m.							
6 a.m.							
7 a.m.							
8 a.m.							
9 a.m.							
10 a.m.							

Continued on next page.

	Sunday	Monday	Tuesday	Wednesday	Thursday	Friday	Saturday
11 a.m.							
12 p.m.							
1 p.m.							
2 p.m.							
3 p.m.							
4 p.m.							
5 p.m.							
6 p.m.							
7 p.m.							
8 p.m.							
9 p.m.							
10 p.m.							
11 p.m.							

Learning Is State Dependent

IT IS COMMONLY UNDERSTOOD IN SCIENCE that learning is "state dependent." Put in terms of education, this means that it is easier to recall information if one is in the same state during testing as during learning. What is meant by "state"? "State" can mean anything that affects your senses or your brain. For example, if you are upset, you could say that you are in an emotional or agitated *state*. If you are in a noisy environment, then that is part of the *state* that you are in. The room you are in is part of your state.

Factors that Affect State

AS YOU READ the list of factors that can affect state, think of how you last studied. The following factors (effects) can influence state:

▶ **Environment effects:** If you take a test in the same physical environment (room, place) as where you studied, you will perform better. That is because the environment is encoded into the brain along with the learning. When you see the environment again, it tends to fire along with the network that contains the information that you studied. It is part of the neural network. Therefore, it is easier to remember.

▶ **Emotion effects:** Memory, as well as learning, is state dependent. If you are in a sad state, you are going to start remembering sad events because the sad state of mind triggers the sad memories. That can lead to a vicious downward spiral where the sadder you feel, the more you unconsciously retrieve sad memories, and, therefore, you feel even sadder. This plays out in the classroom so that if you are in the same focused, calm emotional state as when you studied, you are more likely to recall the information. You want to create and stay in a focused state of mind when you study and take a test. If you are joking around in the classroom, it will be harder to recall the information than if you have an attentive and focused attitude. That is not to say one can't laugh and enjoy the class. It simply means that

---

Tip FROM THE
Brain Doctor

It may be helpful to think of learning as *encoding* information in the brain. You encode through all your senses—what you see, hear, feel, taste, and smell. What are you encoding when you study? Look around you next time you study and see what you are putting into the neural network that you are forming with the information that you learn. What is your learning state? What should be removed or added to that state?

at those moments in class when you are trying to learn the material, it may be helpful to be in a calm, focused state.

▶ **Pathway effects:** You are going to learn more about the many pathways in the brain involved in learning in Chapter 2, but consider these two pathways: auditory (hearing) and visual (seeing). If you learn the material by the auditory pathway, it will be easier for you to recall it by remembering what you heard. However, if you learn it visually, it will be easier to recall it by remembering what you saw. If you study using *both* pathways, remembering both what you heard and what you saw, then you increase your chance of being able to remember the material.

Habits to Enhance Your Reading

THE FOLLOWING HABITS MAY HELP YOU when reading new and difficult information. They assist concentration and tend to improve reading effectiveness. However, just like anything taken to an extreme, they could be considered bad habits if they were practiced so severely that they hindered your ability to understand information. (For example, drinking water is considered healthy, unless you try to drink a gallon or two very quickly. Then water becomes toxic to your system [polydipsia] and dangerous.)

skimming reading only some of the words on a page

▶ **Skimming.** Reading only some of the words on a page is called skimming. Skimming is a great technique to use before you read a textbook assignment. Knowing what you are going to read about will help you mentally prepare for your reading, and skimming will give you an idea of the amount of time you will need to schedule. Skimming can also be helpful when you are researching and want to know if certain books and articles are going to be useful for your research. Skimming the headings and subheadings, dipping into introductory sentences, and viewing the visuals will let you know if the material is appropriate and can save you a lot of time.

regression backward movement of the eyes over previously read information; rereading

▶ **Rereading.** Sometimes when you have trouble understanding information, you will catch yourself rereading it. Rereading, also known as regression, can be a very helpful strategy. If you don't understand a word, rereading the sentence the word is in will help you figure out the meaning by using context clues (more about this in Chapter 3). Never skip over the difficult parts of a reading assignment. You may miss important and necessary points, context clues, or the full meaning of a chapter if you skip over pieces. Rereading gives you an opportunity to increase your comprehension.

▶ **Subvocalization.** Subvocalization is reading aloud. Years before there was research about learning and the brain, reading aloud was considered a bad reading habit. However, it is only a bad habit if it doesn't help you to understand what you are reading. When you are learning new information that is challenging, it sometimes helps to read the material aloud, especially if it is one of your strengths. Using both your eyes and voice to read helps you to fully pay attention to the material at hand. However, not everyone likes to read aloud. This will be a personal choice only you can make.

subvocalization reading aloud

▶ **Pacing.** Using your fingertips to read, or a bookmark placed horizontally under the line you are reading, is referred to as pacing. It allows you to follow each word or groups of words. This technique helps many students read. If you don't currently pace your reading with your finger or a bookmark, try it to see if it works for you. The sense of touch sometimes enhances learning. Because you are using more than your eyes to help you read, your attention is increased; you are more physically involved with the reading process. This habit can also help you keep your place if you are interrupted or if you are inclined to daydream.

pacing using your fingertips or a bookmark placed horizontally under the line you are reading

✔ COMPREHENSION CHECK

▶ Where in the chapter did you lose concentration or become confused?
▶ Of everything you learned in this chapter, what will you be sure to use in your other classes?
▶ If you could ask the authors a question about this chapter, what would you ask?

PRACTICE WITH A READING PASSAGE

Prepare to Read

1. Read the title and predict what you think the following passage will be about.

_____

2. Based on what you expect the passage to be about, what do you already know about the subject?

_____

3. Do you like the topic? Explain how liking the material affects your ability to read.

_____

4. What is your state of mind (mood, motivation, and/or energy level)?

_____

5. Read the following passage, and using the checkmark monitoring system, make a checkmark in the margin each time you lose your concentration.

Shanghai Girls
By Lisa See

pointedly
obviously
directed at
someone/
something

luminescent
light or beauty
coming from
something

permeate pass
into or through
every part

1   "Our daughter looks like a South China peasant with those cheeks," my father complains, pointedly ignoring the soup before him. "Can't you do something about them?"

2   Mama stares at Baba, but what can she say? My face is pretty enough—some might even say lovely—but not as luminescent as the pearl I'm named for. I tend to blush easily. Beyond that, my cheeks capture the sun. When I turned five, my mother began rubbing my face and arms with pearl creams, and mixing ground pearls into my morning _jook_, rice porridge—hoping the white essence would permeate my skin. It hasn't worked. Now my cheeks burn red—exactly what my father hates. I shrink down into my chair. I always slump when I'm near him, but I slump even more on those occasions when Baba takes his eyes off my sister to look at me. I'm taller than my father, which he loathes. We live in Shanghai, where the tallest car, the tallest wall,

or the tallest building sends a clear and unwavering message that the owner is a person of great importance. I am not a person of great importance.

3   "She thinks she's smart," Baba goes on. He wears a Western-style suit of good cut. His hair shows just a few strands of gray. He's been anxious lately, but tonight his mood is darker than usual. Perhaps his favorite horse didn't win or the dice refused to land his way. "But one thing she isn't is clever."

4   This is another of my father's standard criticisms and one he picked up from Confucius, who wrote, "An educated woman is a worthless woman." People call me bookish, which even in 1937 is not considered a good thing. But as smart as I am, I didn't know how to protect myself from my father's words.

5   Most families eat at a round dining table, so they will always be whole and connected, with no sharp edges. We have a square teakwood table, and we always sit in the exact same places: my father next to May on one side of the table, with my mother directly across from her so that my parents can share my sister equally. Every meal—day after day, year after year—is a reminder that I'm not the favorite and never will be.

STOP Reading

Try not to look back to the passage to answer these questions. This is a way for you to think about your reading and learn about what you find distracting.

6. Were you distracted? If yes, what distracted you?

_____

7. Was it easy for you to read?

_____

8. What is your state at this moment (focused, angry, happy, calm, positive)?

_____

9. Did you have to reread any of the sentences? If so, was it distracting or did it help understand the sentence or passage?

_____

10. Explain what you think the reading is about, up to this point.

_____

Continue reading the passage. However, this time, sit in front of a television or radio. Select something you really dislike, and purposely turn up the volume. Or if you are reading on campus, move to a busy, loud area. Now begin reading again, and continue to place checkmarks in the margin each time you lose your concentration.

Continued on next page.

6   As my father continues to pick on my faults, I shut him out and pretend an interest in our dining room. On the wall adjoining the kitchen, four scrolls depicting the four seasons usually hang. Tonight they've been removed, leaving shadow outlines on the wall. They aren't the only things missing. We used to have an overhead fan, but this past year Baba thought it would be more luxurious to have servants fan us while we ate. They aren't here tonight and the room is **sweltering**. Ordinarily an art deco chandelier and matching wall sconces of etched yellow-and-rose-tinted glass illuminate the room. These are missing as well. I don't give any of this much thought, assuming that the scrolls have been put away to prevent their silken edges from curling in the humidity, that Baba has given the servants a night off to celebrate a wedding or birthday with their own families, and that the lighting fixtures have been temporarily taken down for cleaning.

7   Cook—who has no wife and children of his own—removes our soup bowls and brings our dishes of shrimp with water chestnuts, pork stewed in soy sauce with dried vegetables and bamboo shoots, steamed eel, an eight-treasures vegetable dish, and rice, but the heat swallows my hunger. I would prefer a few sips of chilled sour plum juice, cold mint-flavored sweet green bean soup, or sweet almond broth.

8   When mama says, "The basket repairer charged too much today," I relax. If my father is predictable in his criticisms of me, then it's equally predictable that my mother will recite her daily woes. She looks elegant as always. Amber pins hold the bun at the back of her neck perfectly in place. Her gown, a *cheongsam*, made of midnight blue silk with midlength sleeves, has been expertly tailored to fit her age and status. A bracelet carved from a single piece of good jade hangs from her wrist. The *thump* of it when it hits the table edge is comforting and familiar.

Source: From *Shanghai Girls: A Novel* (pp. 3–4) by Lisa See. Copyright © 2009 by Lisa See. Used by permission of Random House, Inc and Bloomsbury Publishing.

sweltering
characterized by oppressive heat

Check Your Understanding

11. This time, were you more distracted? If yes, what distracted you?

_____

12. Was it easy to read with the additional noise and distractions?

_____

13. Explain what this second half of the passage is about.

_____

14. Did your state change? Were you anxious, irritated, or annoyed?

_____

15. Did you have to reread any of the sentences? How many times?

_____

16. Circle the statement that is a criticism that the father made.

   a. The dinner soup was sour.

   b. The mother spent too much.

   c. His daughter's cheeks weren't pale enough.

   d. The family painting was missing.

17. Even though you have not read the entire story, explain why you think the father made the criticism in question #15.

_____

_____

18. The family appears to be:

   a. Poor

   b. Wealthy

   c. Middle class

   d. Hard working

19. Why do you think the girl slouches when she is around her father?

_____

_____

20. What do you think may have happened to the wall sconces and art deco chandelier?

_____

_____

CHAPTER SUMMARY

Reading for college is different than other kinds of reading. College reading requires active participation on your part. Understanding how you learn (metacognition), and purposely using strategies that direct your attention as you learn, take you to a higher level of thinking called critical thinking. Learning to think critically is complicated, but necessary. Fortunately, your brain learns naturally. Current research suggests that people, no matter who they are, learn using the same process. The natural human learning process (NHLP) includes the following steps: motivation, practice, more practice, more practice, more skill, mastery. If you understand that you are a natural born learner, and you know some basic concepts of the how the brain learns, you can affect your own learning. You can help yourself learn better and faster. Your brain has neurons, brain cells that connect with one another and create neural networks. As you learn, your neurons ("trees") grow more dendrites ("branches"). The more you know, the more dendrites you grow, and the thicker your "trees" become. A dense neural network has a lot of information, knowledge, understanding, and/or skill. This process continues throughout your whole life.

This is helpful information to have as a college student because now you know you can shape your brain and create thick neural networks by using effective learning strategies such as:

▶ connecting newly learned information with information you already know

▶ controlling your emotions (good and bad)

▶ practicing which helps build neural networks

▶ managing your concentration and attention

▶ fighting distracters

▶ actively engaging with your reading material

▶ writing in a journal to analyze learning successes and failures

▶ using the checkmark monitoring system to track concentration

▶ controlling your learning environment because learning is "state" dependent

▶ developing a daily reading plan to make reading specific and intentional

Practice good habits to get the most out of what you read. Purposefully choose to learn, read, and study, and block everything else out. You already know what this feels like. Think of a time when you were completely absorbed in a video game or texting someone. Use that same level of paying attention every time you read. Know that multitasking does not work. Realize that although you may become bored when reading, you can still actively engage in your reading.

Brain Connections: Self-Assessment

Draw the amount of dendrites you imagine that you have now about the information in this chapter. Compare your drawing of dendrites now with those on page 20. If the amounts are different, explain why.

| I do not have a good understanding about information in this chapter. | I have a pretty good understanding about information in this chapter. | I have a very good understanding about information in this chapter. |

POST TEST

Part 1. Objective Questions

Match the key terms from the chapter in Column A to their definitions in Column B.

_____ 1. Critical reading   a. a complex thinking and reading technique that involves discovering and taking apart an author's meaning, evaluating the author's meaning based on established standards, and incorporating the meaning into the ideas you already know

_____ 2. Active reading   b. research that shows everyone learns by the same process

_____ 3. Natural human learning process (NHLP)   c. applying strategies that keep yourself engaged with the text and to keep you thinking about the information

_____ 4. Synapse   d. a short branched extension of a nerve cell, along which impulses received from other cells at synapses are transmitted to the cell's body

_____ 5. Axon   e. backward movement of the eyes over previously read information; rereading

_____ 6. Terminals   f. the usually long process of a nerve fiber that generally conducts impulses away from the body of the nerve cell

_____ 7. Dendrite   g. things that come from within you, like feelings, emotions, or thoughts, that prevent you from being able to focus on your reading

_____ 8. Metacognition   h. reading only some of the words on a page

_____ 9. Neuron   i. thinking about how you think; an awareness of your own knowledge and an ability to monitor and control your own learning

_____ 10. Journal   j. a structure that permits a neuron to pass an electrical signal to another brain cell

_____ 11. Skimming   k. a technique used to help you to think on paper about what you have just read and log what learning strategies do and do not work; a way to track and monitor concentration and progress

Continued on next page.

_____ 12. Regression	l. using your fingertips or a bookmark placed horizontally under the line of text you are reading
_____ 13. Subvocalization	m. things in your environment that prevent you from being able to focus on your reading
_____ 14. Pacing	n. brain cell
_____ 15. External distracters	o. reading aloud
_____ 16. Internal distracters	p. endings by which axons make synaptic contacts with other nerve cells

Indicate whether the following statements are true (T) or false (F).

_____ 17. Your brain continues to change throughout your life.

_____ 18. Hearing content increases your chances of remembering it.

_____ 19. The more you try to figure something out, the better chance you have to understand it.

_____ 20. Looking at words is reading.

_____ 21. Connecting new learning to something you already know is not necessary.

_____ 22. The checkmark monitoring system helps you increase your concentration.

Circle the best answer to the following multiple-choice questions.

23. Why are journals helpful?

   a. Journals give you a chance to vent your frustrations.

   b. Journals help you to analyze your learning behavior.

   c. Journals give you a chance to vent your frustrations and help you to analyze your learning.

   d. None of the responses is correct.

24. Which of the following is not an example of active reading?

   a. Reading the heading, subheadings, summary, and questions at the end of the chapter before reading the chapter thoroughly.

   b. Copying the chapter into a notebook.

   c. Analyzing your reading by making an entry in your journal.

   d. Drawing a picture of the content after reading the chapter.

25. See if you can remember: Draw the dendrites you would expect to see in the brain of someone who has very little background regarding the French language in the left box. Then draw the dendrites you would expect to see in the brain of someone who speaks French fluently in the right box. Explain why there is a difference.

_____

_____

_____

_____

Part 2. Reading Passage

POPULAR READING

Prepare to Read

1. Based on reading the first and last sentences of this passage, what do you expect the passage to be about?

_____

2. What do you already know about the subject?

_____

Continued on next page.

3. Create a question to ask yourself about the subject of this passage.

_____

4. Is your environment well lit? Is it clutter free? Do you have all of your reading materials so that you won't have to interrupt your reading?

_____

5. Read the following passage and use the checkmark monitoring system to make a checkmark in the margin each time you lose your concentration.

From *The Fattening of America*
By Eric A. Finkelstein and Laurie Zuckerman

1   The next time someone sneezes or coughs your way, you might not just want to worry about catching their runny nose, stuffy head, and fever—perhaps you should also worry about catching their obesity. This may sound surprising, but if you read the dense, nine-page spread in the *New York Times Magazine* last summer, you would have spent a few good hours reading about some new and little-known research being done in the area of *infectobesity* (the term that Dr. Nikhil V. Dhurandhar coined for contagious "fat"). The article covered the fascinating work of two scientists: Dhurandhar and Dr. Jeffrey Gordon.

2   There is now a growing interest in finding viral and bacterial agents that cause (and can potentially cure) obesity in humans. The goal? To either find a way to inoculate ourselves against them or cure ourselves if we've already caught the obesity bug.

3   Dhurandhar made a name for himself in obesity research when he noticed something strange about a plague that was killing chickens in India. Although the chickens were dying of infection, they weren't wasting away; they were actually gaining weight (and incidentally maintaining low cholesterol and triglyceride levels). Dhurandhar believes this weight gain is the result of a virus that is also contagious to humans. In fact, Dhurandhar found that the people he studied who carried antibodies for the chicken virus weighed an average of 33 pounds more than those who did not carry the antibody. The antibody-carrying individuals also exhibited the same low cholesterol and triglyceride levels as the infected chickens.

4   These findings brought him to the United States in search of a lab to conduct further research. When our government would not allow him to import the virus from India, Dhurandhar was able to find similar occurrences using several strains of adenoviruses—the "bugs" responsible for all sorts of nagging coughs, colds, and flus.

5   He has since extended his research to examine antibodies for these adenoviruses in humans. In one study, he looked at 502 volunteers from around the country, of which 360 were obese, and examined them for the presence of an antibody for

inoculate to inject something that can stimulate protection

triglyceride energy source containing much of the fat stored in the body

adenoviruses viruses that cause eye and respiratory diseases

the virus. Among obese subjects, 30 percent had them; among those who were not obese, only 11 percent had them. Another study with twins revealed similar findings. Out of 90 pairs of twins, those who had been infected with the virus were heavier (an average of 29.6 percent of body fat compared to 27.5 percent).

6   Based on his studies, several pharmaceutical companies are racing to produce a "fat vaccine." However, before you go out and get inoculated, we should point out that in his studies obesity was associated with low cholesterol and low triglyceride levels. For most obese individuals, their increasing weight results in higher values for both. Moreover, even in his studies, many obese individuals did not test positive for the antibodies; and some of those who had the antibodies were thin. Furthermore, even *if* the association proves accurate, it is not clear whether individuals get the virus and then gain weight as a result, or whether those who weigh more might be more susceptible to the virus. So far, I remain skeptical.

7   At the same time that Dr. Dhurandhar was looking to viruses to help explain the obesity crisis, Dr. Jeffrey Gordon had a gut instinct that took his obesity research in another direction.

8   In fact, he became captivated with the human gut or, more specifically, the wonderland of microorganisms our guts contain. Of the multi-trillion cells in each of our bodies, Gordon estimates that only 1 in 10 is human—the rest are microscopic organisms like fungi or bacteria. These organisms are everywhere, on every surface of our bodies; but the vast majority calls our guts home. We start off in the womb "germ" free, but right from our trek down the birth canal, we begin to adopt many of these microbes from our mother. "Microbes colonize our body surfaces from the moment of our birth," Gordon said in the *New York Times Magazine* article. "They are with us throughout our lives, and at the moment of our death they consume us."

microbes bacteria

9   Good thing, too. It may sound like science fiction; but in truth, without these microbes in our bodies, we would be unable to perform many of the tasks necessary for life (i.e., creating the capillaries that line our intestines or producing the enzymes that metabolize cholesterol). But it was the fact that these bacteria assist so much with digestion that caught Gordon's attention. Gut flora help extract calories from the food we eat and help store those calories in fat cells for later use. Gordon wondered why it was possible that two people could eat the exact same foods and engage in the exact same activities yet have two very different weights, and he began to speculate that these microorganisms might be the answer.

capillaries blood vessels

enzymes proteins

metabolize break down

Source: From Fineklsteing and Zuckerman, *The Fattening of America.* Copyright © 2008 John Wiley and Sons, Inc. Reprinted with permission.

Continued on next page.

Check Your Understanding

6. Did you lose concentration while reading this passage? If yes, what did you do to get back on track?

_____

_____

7. Has a cure for obesity been found? Why or why not?

_____

_____

8. What does *infectobesity* mean?

_____

_____

9. In your opinion, would we be better off without the microbes? Explain your answer and provide support.

_____

_____

10. Do you enjoy health-related articles? What kinds of articles do you enjoy reading more?

_____

_____

BRAIN STRENGTH OPTIONS

1. Make a poster that illustrates something that you are a natural learner of, such as skateboarding, knitting, or cooking. List the stages you went through and how they affected the outcome or quality of your skill at the time. Draw appropriate dendrites for each level or stage that you went through.

2. Use the Internet to learn more about how the brain learns. Individually or with no more than three other classmates, prepare a poster, PowerPoint presentation, Web page, or speech with a handout reviewing and elaborating on how the brain learns. Include information about neurons and synapses as well as explanatory information.

3. For one day, track your attention. Set your phone alarm or keep track of the time, and every 30 minutes stop and jot down what you are doing and the level of attention you are giving to the primary task. Use a scale of 1 to 5 with 5 representing the highest level of attention and 1 representing not even noticing. For example, if your primary task is driving, you may not even really be paying attention to the road. Notice it while you are driving and later write down any other tasks you may have been doing, such as listening to the radio or checking text messages. At the end of the day or the next morning, look over your list of tasks and attention levels and write a paragraph discussing how the tasks, multitasking, time of day, and any other factors affected your attention level. Summarize in a sentence or two your best attention levels and what was happening at those times. Conclude with a sentence describing what you learned from this experience.

4. Evaluate how you spend your time. First, write down how many hours a day you *think* you actually spend on the following: studying, sleeping, eating, watching television, gaming, using a computer or smartphone, and socializing with others. Estimate how much extra (or wasted) time you have per day. Next, create a timeline with half-hour increments throughout the day from 6 a.m. to midnight for seven days. During the week, write down what you are doing with that time—the primary, main, or most important activity only. Do not wait until the end of the day or you may not remember accurately what you did. Carry the list with you and add to it every time you are waiting or stopping or changing activities. Then add up how much time you spent on the items that you estimated. Add the totals for the week. Write a paragraph about what you learned about yourself and how you spent your time. What surprised you? What disappointed you? What changes do you want to make?

Remembering What You Read

STUDENT TO STUDENT

MONICA FIALA

A senior at University of South Florida majoring in psychology

"The true art of memory is the art of attention."
—SAMUEL JOHNSON

I'VE ALWAYS HAD TROUBLE retaining information for my exams so I need to work at it. A lot of times textbooks have information written in a way that is difficult to understand. I know that as students we need to learn how to read scholarly journals and things in professional lingo, but when you are learning a subject for the first time, it's sometimes hard to follow, in my opinion. I do read straight through at least once, but usually only as a refresher after I've listened to my professor's lecture. Before that I just skim through the necessary chapters highlighting and taking notes on the information that stands out to me. I never know what's important for sure until I listen to the professor's lecture. That's why I don't fully read the chapter until after the lecture. Then I look for important information in the chapter. Most of the time the key words and vocabulary are fairly important to pay attention to. I also try to pick out the general ideas in the chapter from what I already learned in the lectures. My system is the best I have been able to figure out. I think it works well for me because I am repeating the information in my head and I am able to remember it better.

Remembering What You Read

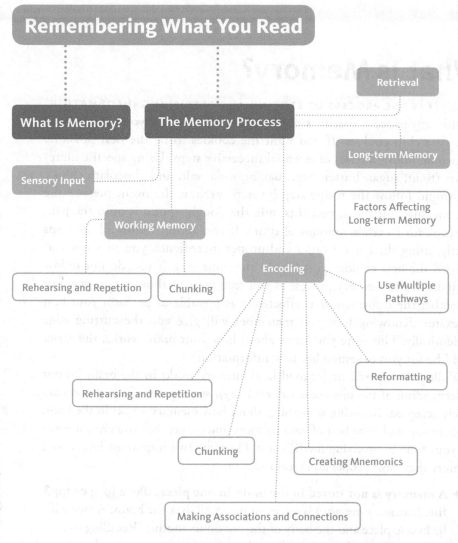

- **What Is Memory?**
- **The Memory Process**
- Retrieval
- Sensory Input
- Long-term Memory
- Working Memory
- Factors Affecting Long-term Memory
- Encoding
- Rehearsing and Repetition
- Chunking
- Use Multiple Pathways
- Reformatting
- Rehearsing and Repetition
- Chunking
- Creating Mnemonics
- Making Associations and Connections

© Cengage Learning

Making Connections

1. How good is your memory?
2. What strategies do you use in order to remember something?
3. How does memory affect your study habits? Test taking? Grades?
4. Can people improve their memory? Why or why not? If they could, how would they go about it?
5. Are some things easier to remember than others? Why? What would make the difference? Can you control that?
6. What interferes with your memory?
7. What does the phrase *garbage in, garbage out* mean?
8. How do you think the brain stores a memory?

Brain Connections: Self-Assessment

Draw on the brain cell how many dendrites you imagine you have for how much you know about how the memory works.

I don't understand too much about how memory works.	I have a pretty good understanding about how memory works.	I have a very good understanding about how memory works.
	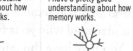	

What Is Memory?

memory the process of
storing and retrieving
information

MEMORY **IS THE PROCESS OF STORING AND RETRIEVING INFORMATION.**
Just like any process, specific steps are necessary. Suppose you want to bake
chocolate chip cookies. If you want the cookies to be the best possible,
you would follow a series of essential successive steps. Using specific ingredients (flour, sugar, butter, eggs, baking soda, salt, and chocolate chips),
you would follow the recipe step by step (preheat the oven, prepare the
pan, measure out the ingredients, mix the dough, spoon it onto the pan,
and cook for a certain amount of time). If you do not follow all the steps
exactly, using the correct order and proper ingredients, you may not end
up with the best cookies possible. In the same way, if you do not follow
the steps in the memory process as you read your textbooks, you may not
remember the information as effectively as possible or perform your best
on exams. Knowing how you remember will give you the cutting edge
academically. The more you know about how your brain works, the easier
it will be for you to remember new information.

While it is not well understood how memory works in the brain (as our
understanding of the process is still evolving), some parts of the process are
widely accepted. Knowing something about how memory works in the brain
can help you make the best of your memory and ensure that you are not wasting your time by studying inefficiently. There are two important facts about
memory that most people don't realize:

▶ **A memory is not stored in the brain in one piece, like a jpeg or mp3
file.** Instead, a memory is stored in pieces all over the brain. A face will
be in one place and the body of the person in another. Recalling the
person's voice will require pulling that piece from yet another location.
Meanwhile, non-human objects are stored in a different location. So
you don't actually retrieve or locate a memory; you reconstruct it.
This is why the police would rather have physical evidence than an
eyewitness account. Memories are not reliable; there are often pieces
missing. You have probably experienced something similar when you
and a friend discover that you recall an event differently. You may have
found it hard to understand why your friend doesn't remember it the
same way as you. You may have thought your friend was wrong and
you were right. Because you have to reassemble a memory, you might
leave something out in the process or even accidentally add something
that was not in the original memory (because it got associated with

something else during an earlier recall process). Because memory is distributed in the brain, you will learn later how to encode something multiple ways so that it will be easier to recall the entire memory accurately.

▶ **Most people do not realize that memory must be encoded, either unconsciously or consciously.** Encoding can be thought of as similar to filing hard copies of information. You make a decision that you need to keep something, and then you decide how you can store it so that you will be able to access it again. Unconscious encoding takes place when something happens that is so powerful or emotional that you can't forget it. For example, you see and meet someone you find attractive and because you are so interested in him or her, you remember that person's name immediately. Otherwise, most of the time you have to make a conscious effort to remember someone's name. A simple explanation of encoding memory is that a memory you decide you want to keep must be actively stored in the brain typically in a conscious way. The type of memory that you most often use when you study must be consciously and actively put into the brain. Activity 2A demonstrates this concept.

encoding doing something consciously with new information so that it can transfer from working memory to long-term memory

ACTIVITY 2A
See How You Organize Information

Set 1

Write in the requested items using the letters provided as the beginning of each word. The first one is modeled for you.

1. Name a bird beginning with the letter B   bluejay _____

2. Name an animal beginning with the letter C   _____

3. Name a fruit beginning with the letter P   _____

4. Name a metal beginning with the letter I   _____

5. Name a country beginning with the letter G   _____

6. Name a boy's name beginning with the letter M   _____

7. Name a girl's name beginning with the letter J   _____

8. Name a weapon beginning with the letter S   _____

9. Name a vegetable beginning with the letter P   _____

Continued on next page.

10. Name a classic fairytale beginning with the letter C _____

11. Name a flower beginning with the letter P _____

Set 2

Write in the requested items using the letter provided at the end of each word. The first one is modeled for you.

1. Name a bird ending with the letter W   _sparrow_____

2. Name an animal ending with the letter G   _____

3. Name a fruit ending with the letter H   _____

4. Name a metal ending with the letter R   _____

5. Name a country ending with the letter Y   _____

6. Name a boy's name ending with the letter N   _____

7. Name a girl's name ending with the letter E   _____

8. Name a weapon ending with the letter W   _____

9. Name a vegetable ending with the letter T   _____

10. Name a classic fairytale ending with the letter E   _____

11. Name a flower ending with the letter T   _____

Compare your answers for Set 1 with your answers in Set 2. Was Set 2 more challenging? In our culture, our brains are not used to organizing information right to left. We organize from left to right. If information is not organized in a way that makes sense to you, you will have trouble retrieving it.

In this chapter, you will learn how to consciously store information. Keep in mind that creating a memory is a process. Figure 2.1 on page 56 shows a diagram of the memory process. You will use Figure 2.1 throughout this chapter to make sense of the memory process.

The human brain is "arguably the most complex entity known to science."* However, knowing just a few facts about how the brain remembers will help you help yourself and your brain remember. To begin, remember or review the information about the brain in Chapter 1.

---

*Ratey, J. J. *A User's Guide to the Brain: Perception, Attention, and the Four Theaters of the Brain.* New York, NY: Pantheon, 2001, p. 358.

ACTIVITY 2B
Take a Memory Survey

Complete the following survey, which will help you identify the skills you are currently using and those you will learn and apply to coursework. Read each statement and respond to it based on your current reading habits. Write *yes* if the statement correctly describes you or *no* if it does not.

_____ 1. My use of concentration strategies affects how well I remember information.

_____ 2. I relate previously learned information to the information I am currently learning.

_____ 3. I have to understand information in order to remember it.

_____ 4. I do not wait to review my textbooks the night before an exam. Reviewing consistently and more frequently is necessary.

_____ 5. I do not have trouble understanding and remembering information that contains technical vocabulary because I always look up new vocabulary and create note cards.

_____ 6. I know why I sometimes forget what I read.

_____ 7. I use techniques to help me recall what I learned.

_____ 8. I use memory techniques but realize I need to do more with the textbook information.

_____ 9. When remembering new and difficult information, I read out loud.

_____ 10. I make a conscious effort to organize textbook information in my head, on paper, or with other students.

If you didn't answer *yes* for each response, you will want to focus on this chapter to help you address each item that does not currently describe you.

ACTIVITY 2C
Think about How You Read

Read the following passage regarding your memory. The point of this activity is to get you thinking about how you currently read textbook selections. Answer these questions first.

1. Read the title and predict what you think this passage will be about.

_____

2. What do you already know about the subject?

_____

3. What is your state of mind (mood, motivation, and/or energy level)?

_____

Continued on next page.

Beliefs about Memory Are Often Wrong
By Rick Nauert, Ph.D.

1   According to experts, people are poor at predicting or acknowledging what they have learned—a belief that leads to poor judgments.

2   "There's a disconnect among beliefs, judgments, and actual memory," according to Williams College psychologist Nate Kornell. Ask people to predict how or what they will learn and "in many situations, they do a breathtakingly bad job."

3   Why? A new study by Kornell and colleagues posits that we make predictions about memory based on how we feel while we're encountering the information to be learned—and that can lead us astray. Our beliefs about our memory are often wrong.

4   The researchers conducted three experiments, each with about 80 participants from teenagers to senior citizens.

5   To test the relationships between "metamemory"—or beliefs and judgments about memory—and performance, they looked at two factors: the ease of processing information and the promise of future study opportunities.

6   The participants were serially shown words in large or small fonts and asked to predict how well they'd remember each. In one iteration of the experiment, they knew they'd have either one more chance or none to study the words; in another, three more chances or none. Afterwards, they were tested on their memory of the words.

7   As expected, font size affected judgment but not memory. Because the larger fonts felt more fluently processed, participants thought they'd be easier to remember. But they weren't.

8   The number of study opportunities did affect memory—and the more repetitions, the better the performance. Participants predicted this would be so, but significantly underestimated the improvement additional study would yield. Belief affected judgment, but not much.

9   In a third experiment, participants were asked questions estimating the influence of font size and study on their learning. They still thought, incorrectly, that font size made a difference. But they were 10 times more sensitive to the number of study trials than in the earlier experiments.

10   This time, they based their answers on their beliefs, not their immediate experiences and judgments.

11   What fools us? First, "automatic processing": "If something is easy to process, you assume you will remember it well," says Kornell. Second, there's the "stability bias": "People act as though their memories will remain the same in the future as they are right now." Wrong again.

12   Actually, "effortful processing" leads to more stable learning. And "the way we encode information is not based on ease; it's based on meaning." In other words, we remember what is meaningful to us.

13   It's unlikely we'll start checking our judgments every time we make one, says Kornell, "That's too slow." So we'll just have to study more than we think we have to. And to preserve memories, we'd be wise to keep a journal.

4. Were you distracted? If yes, what distracted you?

_____

5. Did you need to use the dictionary? Was the passage easy to understand?

_____

6. In one or two sentences, using your own words, explain what you think the passage is about.

_____

7. What are some of the mistaken beliefs regarding our memory?

_____

8. Why do you think a reading book addresses memory?

_____

The Memory Process

THE FOLLOWING OUTLINE IS AN OVERVIEW of the memory process discussed in this chapter. Figure 2.1 will also help you understand the outline and the memory process as it is covered in this chapter. As you read this outline, look at Figure 2.1 to see where each item appears in it.

1. **Sensory Input:** First, information must come into your brain through your senses.

2. **Working Memory:** Information stays in your working memory very briefly and then disappears unless it is encoded. Sometimes you have to try to hold information a little longer in your working memory. For example, you try to remember a phone number or directions long enough to act on the information. Two common strategies people use to hold information in their working memory are:

   ▶ Rehearsing and repetition
   ▶ Chunking

3. **Encoding:** You must actively encode or store the information if you want it to stay longer than a very brief time and if you want it available in your long-term memory. Some common strategies for encoding information are:

   ▶ Rehearsing and repetition
   ▶ Chunking

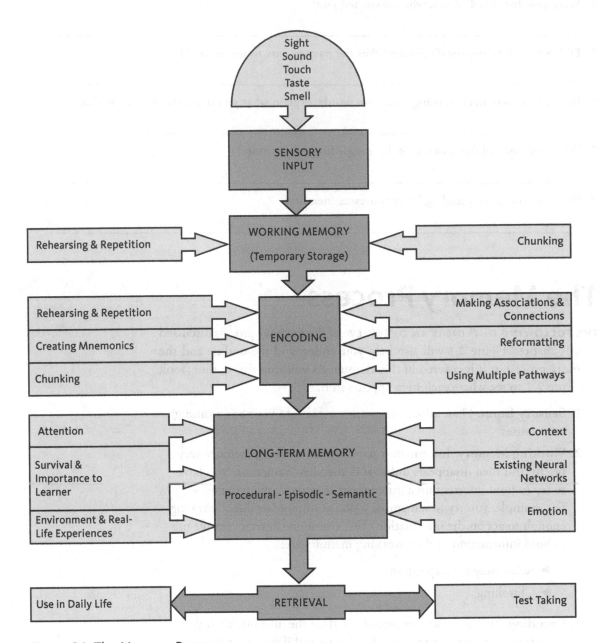

Figure 2.1 The Memory Process

Source: Used with permission. Copyright Janet N. Zadina, 2010.

▶ Creating mnemonics

▶ Reformatting

▶ Making associations and connections

▶ Using multiple pathways

4. **Long-term Memory**: Long-term memory is where memories are stored for future reference. There are several kinds of long-term memory; three are discussed in this chapter:

   ▶ Procedural: how you do something

   ▶ Episodic: what happens or happened to you

   ▶ Semantic: facts and information (the type usually used for school)

Some factors that affect how effectively something is stored in long-term memory are:

▶ Attention

▶ Environment and real-life experiences

▶ Survival and importance to learner

▶ Context

▶ Existing neural networks

▶ Emotion

5. **Retrieval**: Reassembling and recalling the memory (the information) so that you can do something with it such as recalling it for a test or using the information in daily life.

Tip FROM THE
Brain Doctor

Did you know that you can't have learning without memory? Attention drives memory, and memory drives learning. Without memory, there is no learning.

Sensory Input

SENSORY INPUT IS the first step in the memory process. New information enters your brain through your senses of taste, smell, sight, touch, and hearing, so it is called sensory input. However, at this stage the brain retains the information for only seconds or minutes. Sensory input usually has a limited capacity and can be easily lost unless you purposely decide to remember information and take action to encode it.

While you do not have as much control with this step as you do with the rest of the process, you do have some control. Sensory input can be affected by what you pay attention to. For example, sometimes you do not notice that

sensory input information coming to your brain through your sense of sight, hearing, touch, taste, or smell

a room is cold until someone points it out. Sensory input can also be affected by emotion. If you are powerfully affected by the beauty of something, the image may remain with you longer. When you are taking in information that you want to remember, keep in mind that focusing your attention and caring about the material can make a difference.

Working Memory

working memory the system in the brain where information is actively held temporarily while it is being worked with—previously called short-term memory

THE SECOND STAGE, working memory, is a temporary holding place for incoming information. Sometimes people call this short-term memory because it stays in your mind for only a very short period, such as seconds or minutes. Like sensory input, working memory is temporary and limited in what it can do; it is not designed for long-term storage. Working memory is designed to hold something so that you can "work" with it, such as entering a phone number, finding an address, or remembering what you went into a room to get. Information can be stored in your working memory for several minutes if you consciously do something with it to make it last longer than a moment. Two strategies are easy and helpful.

Rehearsing and Repetition

Something that you probably already do to keep information in working memory is repetition. You rehearse the information in your head and repeat it over and over. Think about memorizing a phone number: For example, you locate and enter a phone number because you want to order a pizza. Most people will think that they can remember 10 numbers (a typical phone number) until they get to the phone only to find that if they are distracted for a split second, the number is gone. So what do you do? You say the number over and over in your head until you enter it into the phone. This is called rehearsal.

rehearsal repeated practice of an activity

Chunking

chunking memory technique of taking small bits of information and putting them into larger groups

You also use the chunking method when you remember a phone number. Chunking works by condensing the amount of information you have to learn. Phone numbers are chunked into three sections: area code, first three digits, and last four digits. They are divided into these chunks visually when they are written because it is known that chunking into "bites" makes something easier to remember. According to current brain studies, the average person can hold onto between five and seven bits of information at a time, assuming that he or she has intended to remember it. For example, read the following set of numbers:

382205684

Now cover them up and continue reading. What are the numbers that you just read? Your difficulty remembering the numbers is partly due to the fact that there were more than seven items. But more importantly, the numbers did not come to you because you did nothing to keep them in your working memory. Try the activity again. This time, pretend the following numbers make up your Social Security number:

382-20-5684

Now, instead of trying to remember nine separate bits of information, try to remember the three groups of numbers. Repeat the numbers to yourself using this format, and then cover them up and see if you are able to remember them more effectively. The strategy you just used is an example of chunking.

Chunking increases the power of your working memory even though your working memory's capacity remains the same. Suppose you have a small bag that can hold only seven coins. If you put in seven pennies, the value is going to be only seven cents. But if you place seven quarters, seven silver dollars, or seven gold coins, its capacity will remain the same but its value will be significantly enhanced.

You can put chunking to use to help you comprehend what you read. Do you read a sentence and, by the time you get to the end, you can't remember the beginning? Do you finish a paragraph and feel that you did not get the main idea? Do you believe that you have a reading comprehension problem? Actually, sometimes this is not a reading problem but a working memory problem. Some sentences and most paragraphs are long and, therefore, hard to hold in working memory. This leads to comprehension problems, not because you do not understand what you read, but because it is hard to hold it in your working memory long enough to make the connection between the information at the beginning and at the end. Here is a key question to help you figure out if this is your problem: Do you read word by word or do you read in chunks? Expert readers read in phrases, not individual words. This is another way to chunk information. The important thing about this strategy is that you read in meaningful phrases. For example, read the following sentence:

> The heavy wool coat that the well-dressed handsome businessman wore was thoroughly soaked by the strong, windy, needle-like rain that was loudly pouring from the dark, cloudy skies after an earlier brief period of sunny skies had made everyone think it would be a lovely day.

That is a long sentence and almost impossible to hold in working memory. However, you can chunk it into short meaningful segments that you can visualize as you go along and, therefore, capture the entire meaning. Read it again here, pausing and visualizing where you see the backslash (/).

> The heavy wool coat/
> that the well-dressed handsome businessman wore/
> over his dark blue suit/
> was thoroughly soaked/
> by the strong, windy, needle-like rain/
> that was loudly pouring/
> from the dark, cloudy skies/
> after an earlier brief period of sunny skies/
> had made everyone think/
> that it would be a lovely day.

Was that easier? The key is to chunk the sentence into meaningful units that you can remember. You decide how the units are meaningful. An effective way to chunk the sentence is to chunk it after punctuation. Commas, semicolons, and dashes represent pauses when you read, so that is a natural place to break. Another way to make it easier to comprehend and recall the information in a long sentence is to rewrite it into several shorter sentences.

ACTIVITY 2D
Chunk a Sentence

Chunk the following sentence into four shorter sentences. You decide what small amount of information to put into each sentence.

The heavy wool coat that the well-dressed handsome businessman wore was thoroughly soaked by the strong, windy, needle-like rain that was loudly pouring from the dark, cloudy skies after an earlier brief period of sunny skies had made everyone think it would be a lovely day.

1. _____
2. _____
3. _____
4. _____

ACTIVITY 2E
Chunk a Passage

For the following passage, put a backslash (/) as needed to break the sentences into meaningful chunks. As you read, pause briefly at each slash. Reading aloud will help you find natural stopping points where you might pause.

Being Prey
By Val Plumwood

1   Escaping the crocodile was not the end of my struggle to survive. I was alone, severely injured, and many miles from help. During the attack, the pain from the injuries had not fully registered. As I took my first urgent steps, I knew something was wrong with my leg. I did not wait to inspect the damage but took off away from the crocodile toward the ranger station.

2   After putting more distance between me and the crocodile, I stopped and realized for the first time how serious my wounds were. I did not remove my clothing to see the damage to the groin area inflicted by the first hold. What I could see was bad enough. The left thigh hung open, with bits of fat, tendon, and muscle showing, and a sick, numb feeling suffused my entire body. I tore up some clothing to bind the wounds and made a tourniquet for my bleeding thigh, then staggered on, still elated by my escape. I went some distance before realizing with a sinking heart that I had crossed the swamp above the ranger station in a canoe and could not get back without it.

Source: Plumwood, Val. "Being Prey." *The Best American Science and Nature Writing*, ed. E. Wilson and B. Bilger, Houghton Mifflin Company, New York, p. 190.

Encoding

THE MOST IMPORTANT thing to know about working memory is that you must do something to retain information. Otherwise, this information will be lost in minutes or less. To remember information indefinitely, you must transfer it from your working memory to your long-term memory where information is permanently stored. This is called encoding.

Working memory is not sufficient enough for applying information to tests or using information in future situations. To learn, study, or remember over time requires moving information from working memory to long-term storage. This usually does not happen automatically, especially with textbook material. Instead, a person must actively store it, just like putting away groceries in sensible places rather than dumping them randomly into a pile and

encoding doing something with new information so that it can transfer from working memory to long-term memory.

hoping that you can find an item later. There are many strategies available to help you store information so that you can easily remember it for a test.

Have you ever taken an exam and *know* that you know the answer? It was "on the tip of your tongue." You reviewed the information, but the answer would not come. If you cannot access information easily, perhaps you did not store it properly. For example, imagine your instructor having more than 300 students enrolled in four classes during a semester. She creates a folder for each one to store each student's completed work. Say you decide to visit her office to review your folder; in order to access it, your instructor needs a system. She needs to store the files in an efficient and effective way for easy retrieval—a way that is meaningful for her. If she decides not to organize the files and, instead, piles them haphazardly on the floor, it will require a lot of time and effort to find your folder, which will waste your time and hers. If, however, your instructor stores her files in a file cabinet, in alphabetical order, she can access your folder immediately. She will have taken the information and reformatted it from a pile of papers into a folder system.

If information is not organized in a meaningful way for you, it will be difficult for you to remember it. During an exam, you do not have the luxury of unlimited time to retrieve the information you want. You need immediate access. The way to organize and study your information will determine how easily you retrieve it. The following six encoding strategies will enable you to effectively encode textbook material so that you can remember it better for future tests. The more of these strategies you use, the stronger the memory.

Rehearsing and Repetition

This is the same strategy that you use to keep something in working memory because it involves rehearsing or repeating the information. However, to encode for a longer period of time, the rehearsal and repetition must be more extensive. You learned in Chapter 1 that the brain learns by making a connection. The more times you activate a group of neurons (fire them), the more likely they are to activate again. This is learning. If you keep activating a group of neurons, you will get a strong network that is "wired" together, meaning that it will be easier to fire again in the future. This is why scientists say that "neurons that fire together wire together." In order to recall information, it is not enough just to "fire" the appropriate brain network when you study; you also need to "wire" it. This takes repetition. The following rehearsal and repetition strategies can help you repeat the material in a variety of ways:

> ▶ **Reviewing.** One of the best rehearsal and repetition memory strategies is tried-and-true reviewing. Read the chapter you are working on aloud and review it aloud. Reading aloud helps you attend to the new information

more effectively because you use more of your senses as you read and review. It also helps you block out external distracters such as internal and external noise. If you have been writing notes, review your notes aloud. If you are using a three-ring notebook, take your notes and spread them over a table. As you review, you may begin to see connections that you did not notice before. If your mind is giving you distracting thoughts (about dinner, about your friends or family), remind yourself that this is study time and promise yourself that you will pay attention to these thoughts and concerns after your study time is over.

When you review newly learned information, time of day is as important as the review process itself. If you attend a lecture today, review today. Most people will forget 50% of new textbook information within 24 hours if they do nothing with the information. It is actually easier for your brain to forget information than it is to learn (understand) and remember it. Schedule regular review sessions for yourself, perhaps even with a study partner or study group, shortly after you finish reading a chapter. A few minutes of consistent and same-day review are far more effective than having to relearn everything in a cram session three weeks later.

► **Teach it.** The highest level of learning is teaching. If you know the information well, you can teach it to others. Go into a private space of your house, dorm, or study room. Give a lecture to yourself about the chapter you are studying.

A variation of this activity is for you to connect with other students in a class. Be responsible for "owning" parts of a textbook chapter and teach them to the others; they will also be responsible for parts and teach them to you. Explaining something is an excellent way to find out how well you know and understand the information. You will know exactly where your weak spots are and can go back and relearn information. You will reinforce what you know, and you will also find out what you don't know.

► **Space it out.** Research shows that spaced intervals of repetition are more effective than a larger block of study time in which you repeat the information over and over. For example, if you have one hour to study, you are better off studying in two or three smaller segments than in one long segment. Compare it to eating an orange. Most people do not generally stuff the entire orange in their mouth for a reason. The body needs to be able to chew and process the food in smaller amounts. Or when you know that you are facing a busy day, you do not eat all your meals in the morning because you won't have time later. You know that your body can process the energy you are giving it only when spaced out over time. Just like the body performs more efficiently and uses its resources better under certain conditions, so does the brain, for several reasons.

▶ **Mental fatigue.** Just like your body, your brain gets tired after carrying a heavy cognitive (mental) load. Just like you might lift weights or do cardio in intervals where you work hard, rest briefly, and work hard again, the same plan works with learning. If you push too long at one sitting, the brain gets tired and begins to learn less and less as time goes on. This is called "diminishing returns."

▶ **Strengthening recall**. Cover material for 20 to 30 minutes and then give yourself a little time to get it out of working memory and start to forget a little. After 15 or 20 minutes, go back to that material again, but first try to recall it and then review it again. The process of trying to recall is like trying to lift a stronger weight—it builds muscle. In this case, it strengthens the neural network, the memory. When you go to recall it for the test, you will have practiced recalling it several times.

▶ **Primacy/recency effects**. Did you know that you are more likely to remember the first part of new information and the last part, but not so much of what is in between? That goes for when you are in class or when you are studying. The scientific reason for this is that the brain pays attention to beginnings and endings because they are when something new is happening. It is part of the survival pathway. When everything is just humming along status quo, the brain does not need to pay as much attention, so it conserves its resources and does not work as hard. Therefore, the more study sessions you have, the more beginnings and endings you have, the more you are likely to remember.

Spacing your sessions over time will save you time and improve performance. The most effective way to study is to review the information and take a brief break. For example, study 20 to 40 minutes; then take your morning shower. Study for another session and then throw in a load of laundry or fill the dishwasher. If you are somewhere else, take a quick walk or short break. Resist the urge to use technology as that activity uses the same resources that you need to study. Rest your brain. Be sure not to simply turn to another subject and study that. Research shows an interference effect where learning new material interferes with the material that was just learned, so don't study new material before studying for the test. Studying for a test should always be a review process. It is also quite appropriate to take a nap or sleep in between study sessions, as sleep gives the brain time to strengthen the memory network. When you wake up, you will know the material even better than before you slept, as the memory consolidates. After your break, review the information again and continue repeating the process.

However, repetition does not just mean going over the same information again and again in the same way. Use a different sense for the next repetition. For example, the first time read the material to yourself. The second time, read it aloud, explain it to someone, write it out, or draw it. Avoid cramming as information recall is only temporary and usually is not very useful. People cram because they have not started studying until the last minute. Some people think a Monday deadline means starting Sunday night. A deadline is not a signal to start working; it means the process should be almost finished before that date. If you reviewed material only 15 or 20 minutes a day, think how many times you could cover it before the test, getting faster and faster as time goes on. You do not have to continue spending a lot of time reviewing material that you have learned during the process. As they say, work smarter, not harder.

ACTIVITY 2F
Teach It

Go to a private area in your home or to a study room on your campus. Review Chapter 1 of this book for a few minutes, stand up, and teach it. Use the headings as an outline to help you recall information. Respond to the following questions about your experience.

1. Did you realize where in the chapter where you might need to learn information more effectively?

_____

2. Did teaching to an imaginary class let you know what you know?

_____

3. If you found that you had trouble teaching specific information, did you go back and try to understand it more thoroughly? If so, did you try a different strategy to help you understand and remember the information?

_____

Chunking

Chunking can be used to encode information, just as it can be used when transferring sensory input to your working memory. Before you were just chunking something to remember it for a moment. Now you are working with larger amounts of information and encoding for long-term memory. There are many ways to chunk information.

ACTIVITY 2G
Chunk to Encode

Study the following words for 60 seconds. Then cover them up and list as many as you can remember.

accounting	forest	government	painting
animals	executive	river	nature
art	mountain	king	politics
beauty	corporation	market	rules
business	currency	museum	song

Were you able to remember all the words from Activity 2G? Most people don't without a strategy. Go back and review the words. What could you do to help remember them? How can you chunk this information? Do you see any categories? Instead of trying to remember 20 separate words (or items), which overloads your short-term memory, you can chunk the information by placing the words into groups or categories. Try to determine how some of them are alike. When trying to organize, did you think of breaking the words into the following groups: alphabetical order, similar categories, or similarities/differences between items? Alphabetical order could be used. However, why would alphabetical order not be the most helpful with this group of words? There are 10 different beginning letters, which would make it difficult to group them according to the alphabet because 10 exceeds the five-to-seven rule. This is not to say you couldn't organize this way; it is just not the most effective way for this group of words.

Most students find that they can organize the group of words in Activity 2G into four similar categories. See if you can you figure out the four categories, which will serve as a trigger to help you remember all of the words. List the four categories that you discovered:

_____

✓ COMPREHENSION CHECK

▶ What is chunking?
▶ What are the benefits of chunking?
▶ Provide an example of chunking.

Creating Mnemonics

Mnemonics are tricks you can use to help you recall information once you understand and have learned it. The mnemonic you create serves as a trigger to help you remember information. For example, do you remember learning about Columbus by repeating the following rhyme? "*In 1492, Columbus sailed the ocean blue. He had three ships and left from Spain; He sailed through sunshine, wind, and rain.*" This is a type of mnemonic. By connecting your course information to a mnemonic, you create a memory tool for the topic you are studying. There are several common mnemonics:

> ▶ Acronyms are words created by using the first letter of each word or phrase that you intend to remember. One acronym is HOMES, which helps people remember the names of the Great Lakes: *H*uron, *O*ntario, *M*ichigan, *E*rie, and *S*uperior. Another acronym is FACE to remember the musical notes on sheet music in the spaces of the treble clef. Both HOMES and FACE are easy to remember because they are familiar words.

> ▶ Acrostics are created by using the first letter of each item you need to remember to make a phrase or sentence. For example, suppose you had to remember the order of classifications in the animal kingdom for a biology test: kingdom, phylum, class, order, family, genus, and species. Using the first letter of each word (K, P, C, O, F, G, S), you could create a variety of sentences using all seven letters in their correct order. For example, **K**ing **P**eter **C**alls **O**ften **F**or **G**reat **S**paghetti or **K**ing **P**eter **C**ries **O**ut **F**or **G**round **S**ausage. Another example is when people say **E**very **G**ood **B**ird **D**oes **F**ly to recall the notes that are on the lines in sheet music, *EGBDF*. The acrostic sentences you create are purely for your use. In cases in which the order of the keywords does not matter, you can rearrange the letters in any order. The funnier the phrase, the more memorable it is.

> ▶ Anagrams are created by rearranging the letters in a key word to create another word, phrase, or sentence. Consider the word *binary*, which is not a common word but one you may come across in a computer science class. To help yourself remember, try purposely associating the word *binary* with the word *brainy*. It contains the same letters, but in a different order. You could remember the word *mitochondria,* a word you would see in a biology class, by using the anagram sentence *A orchid I'm not.* Anagrams are especially helpful when committing individual words to memory, such as specialized or foreign language

mnemonics memory tricks

acronyms mnemonic where you create words by using the first letter of each word or phrase that you intend to remember

acrostics mnemonic where you use the first letter of each item to be remembered to make a phrase or sentence

anagrams mnemonic created by rearranging the letters in a key word to create another word, phrase, or sentence

vocabulary. The French word for grapefruit is *pamplemousse*. You may forget if the word has one "s" or two. This anagram for pamplemousse may help: *Measles Mop Up*.

▶ **Analogies** are comparisons between two different things in order to show a similarity. Analogies are a powerful way to make connections. Some examples are:

> ▶ Shells were the dollars and coins of trade during the ancient cultures.
>
> ▶ The snowflake fell to the earth like a tiny feather from heaven.
>
> ▶ The giant was like a gentle, frightened child, unaware of his strength and size.

Analogies can also be visual: If "This is your brain on drugs" were the caption to this photograph, how would you explain the connection? Is it positive or negative?

Today ago kids/Shutterstock.com

▶ **Key words** represent the topic or main ideas of the material you are reading. Instead of trying to remember an entire chapter word for word, you can use key words as memory cues by attaching related information to them. For example, if you were studying endangered species, key words could be *pollution* (attach related information on manufacturing, agricultural runoff, and sewage pollution), *commercialization* (attach information on the commercial use of turtle shells, elephant tusks, and rhinoceros horns), and *habitat* (attach information on the cutting of old growth forests and strip mining). Key words can also cue you to details if you chunk them using the same technique.

▶ **Rhymes** are an effective way to remember, especially if you prefer learning by listening. Do you remember "Thirty days have September, April, June, and November. All the rest have thirty-one, except February, which has twenty-eight and in Leap Year twenty-nine"?

▶ **Songs** are a great way to remember information and have been used to share key information throughout time, including songs about famous heroes, events, and relationships. Use key points from your notes to create new lyrics for your favorite song. It is easier for you to remember if you can relate the information to something you already know.

analogies comparison between two different things in order to show a similarity

key words words that represent the topic or main idea of the material you are reading

ACTIVITY 2H
Use a Song to Help Remember

Think of any song you know that tells a story based on a real event or thing. Write two or three sentences explaining the story or motive for the song. Here's an example using the song, The "Star-Spangled Banner."

> When the American flag was raised to celebrate America's victory in the War of 1812, the stripes and stars of the American flag were so inspiring to Francis Scott Key that he wrote a song about them that is now our national anthem. Each time we sing it, it is a reminder of the making of our country. It reminds us that we are a strong and great country and that many sacrifices were made for our freedom.

Now write your own song lyrics to help you remember important pieces of information from a textbook in one of your other courses. Be creative, and use your favorite song for the melody.

ACTIVITY 2I
Use Mnemonics

Read the following passage and then create a mnemonic to help you remember the information in the passage using one of the mnemonics you just learned about: acronyms, acrostics, anagrams, analogies, key words, rhymes, or songs.

> ### The Visual Record: Icons
>
> The word *icon* comes from the Greek *eikōn,* which means "image."...Icons portrayed saints, the Virgin Mary, and sometimes Jesus Christ. They were believed to be genuinely holy, to capture, in some mysterious way, the holiness of the person whom they represented. Icons may have arisen from funeral portraits, or they may have been miniature versions of much larger images on the walls of churches. One of the earlier examples of icons relates to Saint Symeon Stylites. Symeon was a recluse who lived for many years on top of a pillar in the Syrian desert. After his death, his reputation for holiness drew many people to worship at his tomb. Soon, people began to take away pictures of Symeon. We hear that in far-off Rome, shopkeepers affixed icons of Symeon to the doorposts outside their shops to ward off evil.
>
> Source: From NOBEL/STRAUSS/OSHEIM/NEUSCHEL. Western Civilization Beyond Boundaries 6e (p. 210). Copyright © 2011 Cengage Learning.

Your mnemonic:

_____

_____

Reformatting

reformatting strategy for making material easier to remember by putting into a format that is meaningful to you

Reformatting is a way of making material easier to remember by putting it into a format that is more visual or more familiar to you. You have probably done some of the following study strategies in the past without realizing that you were reformatting.

▶ **Put it in your own words.** An important part of reformatting is making sure you understand the vocabulary—reformatting the words into words that you understand. For example, you can reformat "exemplification" into "giving examples to show what you mean." You must understand the language of the discipline you are studying. Memorizing textbook information you do not understand is like memorizing nonsense. Just because you memorize something from a textbook does not mean you understand it and can apply it.

▶ **Make it more visual.** Sometimes translating paragraph information into a visual aid, like a table or diagram, is helpful. Using the Internet to search for images of the concept you are studying is another way to make something more visual and memorable.

▶ **Reorganize it**. Sometimes you can reorganize the material in a way that makes it more meaningful or clearer to you. You can often simplify it by reorganizing it, like when you create an outline. A lot of text is explanatory to help you understand the main points that you need to recall for later use. Reorganizing information into a briefer representation may make it easier to recall.

ACTIVITY 2J
Try to Understand What You Don't Know

Read the following paragraph and try to remember the information long enough to answer the questions that follow.

The Poxitation of Zraxquif

Each day, it has become more important that you bractoliote about Zraxquif. Zraxquif is a new griebe of zionter. It is poxitated each month in Arizantanna. The Arizantanninas gristerlate large frialtonda of fevon and then bracter it to quasel Zraxquif. Zraxquif is becoming one of our most precious snezlaus. Our zionter lescelidge and lack of current poxitated fevons. It could save millions of lives.

1. Why is it important to know about Zraxquif?

2. Where is Zraxquif poxitated?

3. How is Zraxquif quaseled?

4. What is Zraxquif?

Were you able to answer the questions? You probably were! By using context clues, you could answer the questions, but that doesn't mean you understand the content. What is zionter? What is griebe? What does *gristerlate* mean? If you were to be tested on this with the expectation that you understood the language and meaning, how well do you think you would do? Even though you may have been able to answer the questions, the words were all nonsense and you do not truly understand what any of them mean. There have probably been times when you experienced the same confusion reading passages from specialized textbooks.

Now read the following passage from a statistics textbook and try explaining it in your own words.

> To determine the $F_{critical}$, establish the level of α and calculate the degrees of freedom. The F-distribution has two degrees of freedom. The numerator degrees of freedom (df_N) is the degrees of freedom associated with the between-groups variance. The denominator degrees of freedom (df_D) is the degrees of freedom associated with the within-groups variance. For example, if $\alpha = .05$ and $df_N = 3$ and $df_D = 6$ $F_{critical} = 4.76$.
>
> Source: Runyon, Richard P., et al. *Fundamentals of Behavioral Statistics*, 9th Edition, McGraw-Hill, p. 523.

With this passage, real words are used. If the words were not familiar to you, you probably felt exactly the way you did when you read the nonsense paragraph: confused. And if you did not understand the paragraph, you were not able to explain it in your own words. You really cannot do anything (paraphrase, outline, draw, or create mnemonics) with information if you do not understand it. If, while reading any of your textbooks, you find that the content does not make sense, use the vocabulary strengthening strategies you will learn in Chapter 3. You might have known what a denominator and a numerator are, but did you know what $F_{critical}$ and degrees of freedom are? Do not skip unfamiliar vocabulary; it is crucial to comprehension.

Making Associations and Connections

The more you can relate new information to what you have already stored in your long-term memory, the easier it is to remember. Remembering one thing leads to remembering another. For example, if you are trying to remember where you put your keys, you may retrace your steps. You may recall that you came in through the garage and put some of the groceries on the stairs and went back for more. Then you put some groceries on the kitchen counter and went down and got the rest. When you think about the counter, you remember you tossed the keys on the table as you walked by. One memory triggers another. It is similar with facts that you try to remember. If you link a new fact to information that is relevant, then if you have trouble recalling the new information, you can recall the related information in the hopes that it will maintain the connection and trigger the recall of the new information.

There are three strategies to help you make strong associations and connections when learning new information:

► **Exemplification**. Exemplification is providing familiar examples to illustrate new information. An example from your biology class is that plants need light to bloom. Now think of an example of a plant you know that needs light to bloom. You know from your own experience that tulips need light to bloom. Now you have that new information in your long-term memory. Plants, like tulips, need light to bloom.

► **Comparison**. Be aware of the similarities between what you are studying and information you already know. If you are learning about the process of photosynthesis in biology, you can remember it by being aware of similarities regarding the digestive process in human beings. You can connect the details of the photosynthesis process (new information) to the human digestive process (familiar information)—plants need light to grow and humans need food to grow. When you need to recall for an exam how photosynthesis works, you may more easily locate the information in your memory with the similarity you identified regarding the digestive process. Here is an example of an explicit comparison from a communications textbook:

> In short, living without health insurance is as much of a risk as having uncontrolled diabetes or driving without a safety belt.

Source: Verderber & Verderber. *Communicate!* 12th Edition, Cengage Learning, 2008, p. 299.

What is the comparison being made? The level of danger involved in living with an untreated disease or driving without a safety belt is being compared to living without health insurance. All are dangerous. Sometimes, however, comparisons may not be directly stated.

> A calorie is a measure of energy expenditure. The calories referred to in diet and exercises are kilocalories (kcal). A pound of fat stores 3500 calories (kcal). To lose a pound of fat a week a person must eat approximately 50 fewer calories (kcal) per day than she expends.

Source: www.itansolariums.com/spaservices-fit-bodywraps.html

When comparisons aren't directly stated, you can create your own. A comparison you could make about this passage is: The calorie concept is like money in the bank. If you spend more than you put in the bank, you will lose. However, if you spend less (less exercise), your savings (fat) will grow.

▶ **Addition**. Consider adding new information to more familiar information. You can make even stronger connections between new information and prior knowledge by doing additional research on a topic. For example, plants need light (new information), but they also need soil and water (familiar information). If you are learning about human bones, for example, go to the library and check out additional information on the skeleton. Keep adding new information to familiar information, and you will be amazed how much easier it will be for you to remember. Seek out multiple explanations of a topic. The more you use additional materials, the deeper you process new information. The deeper you process new information, the easier it will be to access when you need it.

ACTIVITY 2K
Suggest Ways to Make Associations and Connections

Cheryl wants to be a history major. She reads history books in her spare time and is very good at answering history-related questions. However, in her first class on the American Civil War, she does poorly on essay tests. She cannot understand why her extensive factual knowledge is not enough to help her perform well on essay tests.

1. What are some possible reasons for Cheryl's poor performance on essay tests? Be prepared to share your answers with the class.

_____

_____

_____

Continued on next page.

2. Give some suggestions to help Cheryl make more effective associations and connections in order to remember details about the American Civil War.

_____

_____

_____

_____

ACTIVITY 2L
Establish Connections

Read the following passage. See how many connections you can make between what you learn in the passage and what you already know about Egyptian life, death, and religion. Use the chart following the passage to write down these connections.

Life and Afterlife

1   Egyptian life was full of religious practices, from daily rituals and seasonal festivals to ethical teachings and magic. Egyptian religion tended toward *syncretism*—that is, the blending of mutually opposed beliefs, principles, or practices. For example, Egyptian mythology taught variously that the sky was a cow, was held up by a god or by a post, or was a goddess stretched over the earth. No one was troubled by such inconsistencies, as a modern worshiper might be, because Egyptians believed that a fundamental unity underlay the varieties of nature.

2   Egypt's religion had many greater and lesser deities, including human, animal, and composite gods. Various animals, from cats and dogs to crocodiles and serpents, were thought to represent the divine. Important deities included Thorth, the moon-god and god of wisdom; Nut, goddess of the sky; Ptah, a creator-god; Osiris, who invented agriculture and became lord of the dead; Horus, son of Osiris, a sky-god imagined as a giant falcon; and Isis, wife of Osiris and mother of Horus, a mother-goddess. Temples were numerous and lavish.

3   Egyptian religion focused on the afterlife. Unlike the Mesopotamians, the Egyptians believed that death could be a pleasant continuation of life on earth. Hence, they actively sought immortality. The wealthy built tombs that were decorated with paintings and inscriptions and stocked with cherished possessions for use after death. The most cherished possession of all was the body, and the Egyptians provided its preservation through their mastery of the science of embalming—thus, the Egyptian mummies.

Source: From NOBEL/STRAUSS/OSHEIM/NEUSCHEL. Western Civilization Beyond Boundaries 6e (pp. 20–21). Copyright © 2011 Cengage Learning.

1. Brainstorm everything you believe you know or think you know about Egyptian life, mythology, customs, and death. The more you know, the easier it will be for you to remember the information in this passage.

2. Fill in the chart provided here. On the left side of the chart, list important information from this passage. On the right side, list what you know. This type of thinking takes practice but serves as a great study guide.

What You Learned from Passage	Related Information That You Already Know

ACTIVITY 2M
Connect by Making Comparisons

Read the following passages and write a comparison for each one. Remember that the act of making a comparison forces your brain to make a connection, which will become a trigger to help you remember key information. There is no one right answer. First, ask yourself what is being discussed. Then, ask yourself what you can compare it with that is very familiar to you.

> The acronym RAM stands for random access memory, which is the main memory the computer uses to write, store, and retrieve information while the computer is running.
>
> Source: www.ammas.com

1. RAM is like _____. Explain why.

> A very important type of interaction is competition among organisms for scarce resources. Organisms also exploit each other by consuming each other and by parasitism, a symbiotic relationship in which one organism benefits at the expense of another.
>
> From RUSSELL. Biology, Exploring the Diversity of Life, Volume 1, 1e (p. 61). Copyright © 2010 Cengage Learning.

2. Organisms are like _____. Explain why.

> Design is essentially the opposite of chance. In ordinary conversation, when we say "it happened by design" we mean something was planned—it did not occur just by accident.
>
> From LAUER/PENTAK. Design Basics 7e (p. 4). Copyright © 2008 Cengage Learning.

3. Design is like _____. Explain why.

> Many students have an unrealistic fear of math. Before they take a class, they are convinced that it will be a disaster and that they will fail. Their fear is often unfounded and based on their own imagination.

4. Math is like _____. Explain why.

The vice-presidential ritual demonstrates a phenomenon of political optics: few men or women look qualified before they get into office, either by winning it or taking the place of a fallen predecessor. Or, conversely, those who look abundantly qualified beforehand may prove to be disappointing. Presidential politics is inventive, bizarre, and addicted to surprise.

Source: Lowi, Ginsberg and Hearst. *American Government: Readings and Study Guide,* 2nd Edition. W.W. Norton and Company: New York, p. 147.

5. Vice-presidential ritual is like _____. Explain why.

Using Multiple Pathways

The final method for encoding or studying is putting the information into memory using as many pathways as possible. This means using your senses. You need to say it, hear it, see it, write it, and/or draw it. Attempt to work with whatever you are studying from your textbooks using as many pathways as possible. For example, when you preview your reading assignment, you might make an outline; therefore, you are seeing and writing. As you begin to read and look for main ideas, you might state the main idea aloud as you write it in your outline. Say the details as you write them.

If there is a visual aid in the textbook, see if you can redraw it in your notes. If there is not an illustration, you should draw one. Would it be helpful to have a diagram or illustration to make the information clearer? For example, suppose you are reading about the process of how neurons fire together to make a connection at the synapse. You could draw two neurons and connect them at the synapse as described in Chapter 1 on page 14. Now you have a strong visual to help you remember.

If you really want to boost your intensity of learning new information, record yourself reading your outline using your smartphone or computer recording device and play it back when you are walking, doing dishes, or folding laundry. Now you are using the auditory pathway. If you can visualize information as you listen, you are incorporating an additional pathway. Just as when you are working out in a gym and do two things at once, such as lifting hand weights while stepping up and down onto a step, you are increasing the intensity of the workout by engaging multiple pathways in the body. When you work with the new information in as many ways as possible at the same time, you are increasing the intensity of the learning process.

Long-term Memory

long-term memory the brain's system for storing, managing, and retrieving information for future use over the long term

Long-term memory is the next step in the process. Your goal is to get the information from sensory input and working memory and then, through encoding, into long-term memory. Long-term memory can be compared to putting your clothes in the closet rather than throwing them on the bed. You might throw your clothes on the bed, a chair, and other places around your home temporarily, but it is not effective for finding what you want when you want it. Sometimes you want to find something for a special event that you have not worn in a long time. You must get it out of storage—the closet. Long-term storage in the brain is where information is kept that you can later retrieve when needed.

Scientists have identified several types of memory and refer to the types by varying names, so it can get complicated. To keep it simple, here are three kinds of long-term memory using the most common names:

procedural memory the memory system for how we do things, particularly skills and procedure

▶ Procedural memory is what you use when you tie shoelaces, brush your teeth, or text message. The clue is in the name itself—it involves a procedure. Procedural memories are much easier to remember because they are heavily practiced when being encoded. For example, when you learned to drive a car, you had to repeat a procedure over and over until it became automatic. Once you encode a memory like that, the procedure seems to automatically take over when you engage the first step and you do not have to think about the rest of the procedure. For example, have you ever started driving on your day off and suddenly caught yourself automatically taking the route to work because you were lost in thought? Or you suddenly arrive somewhere and did not even think about the driving? While procedural memory is not usually involved in the type of material presented in textbooks, it can be in some courses. For example, if you are studying to be an emergency medical technician, your textbook may describe a procedure that you would use under a certain circumstance. However, the formation of procedural memory does not come as a result of reading about a procedure in a textbook; it comes from actually doing the procedure. It is sometimes referred to as kinesthetic memory, motor memory, or muscle memory. Your body carries some of the memory, as you do some things without even thinking about them.

► Episodic memory also contains a clue in the name. What is an episode? This is the type of memory that enables you to recall what you have done or experienced. This type of memory can be very easily recalled because it is a memory of your life and may have been emotionally encoded. On the other hand, we do not remember most of the events in our daily lives because they are not encoded into long-term memory. Events with more emotional impact are generally encoded because emotion is a powerful encoder; those episodes are more easily recalled. Other details, like what you ate two weeks ago Thursday, are not easily recalled. However, if you ate a special birthday dinner at your favorite restaurant, you may recall dozens of details about the memory. Episodic memory is what we use to remember our life and personal history.

episodic memory the memory system for remembering personal events and situations, memory of what happened

semantic memory memory of words, ideas, meanings, and concepts

► Semantic memory (sometimes called declarative memory because you can declare it on a test, for example) is the type of memory that you use in order to study. While procedural and episodic memory can occur naturally, semantic memory involves effort in the encoding process. This is the memory that you primarily use when taking tests. You can strengthen semantic memory by properly encoding for retrieval.

Factors Affecting Long-term Memory

Several things, some beyond your control, affect how easily and how well you store information in your long-term memory. See if you can find ways to make reading easier and to remember what you intend to remember.

► **Attention.** Attention is critical, as you learned in Chapter 1. For example, everyone can remember when they first heard about the terrorist attacks on September 11, 2001.

Tip FROM THE Brain Doctor

A new study reveals something important about when information is easily lost or more likely to be stored. Researchers discovered that if a person knew that he or she could easily find the information online by doing an Internet search, he or she was significantly less likely to recall the information later. However, if the person knew he or she would not have access to the information online, he or she was more likely to remember it. It is likely that you could find most of the information in your textbook on the Internet. However, if your instructor requires you to memorize the information from the text, then you have to make a special point of reminding your brain that this information will not be easily available to you and that you need to store it. Keep this in mind when you start the encoding process, and you will be more effective at remembering later.

(What type of memory is that?) You can remember where you were and what you were doing because you were really paying attention. The information was permanently stored in your memory because some of the other factors you will read about here were also involved.

▶ **Emotion**. When information has an emotional connection to you, it is more easily remembered. If it is powerfully emotional, you do not have to work at encoding it. In fact, you might not even be able to stop it from encoding. If the brain believes that something is important, it is more likely to remember it. Sometimes feelings in the body, such as goose bumps or feelings of excitement, tell the brain to pay attention and remember. However, you can sabotage yourself by worrying and feeling insecure or afraid. These emotions make it harder to think and learn. So remind yourself, if you studied and reviewed periodically, you have created the conditions for good recall.

▶ **Survival and/or importance to learner**. This factor is huge when it comes to information being stored in long-term memory. Think again of the 9/11 terrorist attacks. They were instantly stored in long-term memory because of your relationship to survival and the fact that the event was very important to you. The best you can do with this factor is to try to think of the material you are studying as important, even if only for the test.

▶ **Environment and real-life experience**. This has a huge impact on long-term memory. Remember when you learned how to use a new smartphone, software, or social networking tool? If you think the information has real-life relevance, you will be more likely to recall it. If it relates to something important in your environment, it may be stronger in your long-term memory. How can you activate this factor? Try thinking of how the information might apply in real life.

▶ **Context**. The context (the environment) in which you learn something can become part of the memory itself. You do not learn in isolation. You are in your environment—all of the sights and sounds and objects and activities around you. That environment creates a *context* in which the learning is embedded. Perhaps you recall the expression on the teacher's face and that the classroom was really hot and everyone was in a bad mood that day. That context was built into the memory. Sometimes context strengthens a memory. You might even be able to activate this by consciously thinking about the context in which you learned something or the context in which the information would be useful. It is easier to recall information, for example, when you take a test in the same room in which you studied for the test.

▶ **Existing neural networks**. The more you already know about a subject, the easier it may be to add new information to your network. You can actively affect this factor by deliberately connecting the information to what you already know.

Sometimes more than one factor will be used when encoding to long-term memory. For example, remember when you learned to use social media. How did the factors affect you? Were you excited and confident or did you have fear of the new technology that made it hard for you to think? Was it real life and meaningful or something that you were pressured into by your family or friends? Did the context affect your attention? If a relative was just showing a program to you as she or he used it, you might not pay as much attention as if someone was showing it to you so that you could stay in touch with your family. Did your existing neural networks (typing skills, video gaming skills, or other skills) affect your ability to learn to use the technology? How important was it to you? Was your social "survival" affected?

✓ **COMPREHENSION CHECK**

▶ Explain the difference between procedural memory and semantic memory.
▶ What, up to this point in the chapter, is unclear?

ACTIVITY 2N
Examine Your Factors

Using the following examples, examine how the factors affected your learning.

1. Think about your memory of how to use a new cell phone. That memory is called _____ memory. Circle the factors that contributed to your ability to remember that skill over a long period of time.

Attention	Environment and Real-Life Experience
Emotion	Context
Survival and/or Importance to Learner	Existing Neural Networks

2. Think about the last time you studied for a test. Circle the factors that contributed to your ability to store that information well.

Attention	Environment and Real-Life Experience
Emotion	Context
Survival and/or Importance to Learner	Existing Neural Networks

3. Think about a time that you felt you were in danger. Circle the factors that contributed to your ability to store the memory of that event.

Attention	Environment and Real-Life Experience
Emotion	Context
Survival and/or Importance to Learner	Existing Neural Networks

Retrieval

retrieval recall and reassemble information from your memory

THE FINAL STAGE of memory is being able to retrieve the information when you need it. Retrieval means that you can recall and reassemble the information as needed. But you have probably experienced times when that step failed and you could not remember something. Maybe you had the "tip of my tongue" experience where you know it is in there but you just cannot find it. That is normal. You do not want to panic when you cannot recall something for the test, as that will make it even harder to remember. There are better ways to get that information back into active working memory.

First, think back to the context in which you studied the information. Put yourself mentally back there. Does that trigger the information? If not, mentally think through the encoding process. Did you make a mnemonic? Use the mnemonic to retrieve the information. Did you associate it with something? If you did, then thinking about the associated information should bring it back. Continue mentally listing the encoding steps until you can recall which one(s) you used and try to find the information.

If you still cannot retrieve the bit of information, again, do not panic. If you encoded it, you can probably find it. Move ahead to another question. Information involved in subsequent questions may trigger associations or context encoded with the missing information and bring it back into working memory. Remember that no one's memory is perfect; memory itself is not a perfect process. That is why it takes so much time and effort during the encoding process. You may have had a great deal of information to cover, making it harder to recall every last bit of information. On the other hand, be sure to question yourself and think about your encoding process. Did you "fire it until you wired it"? Did you engage in enough retrieval practice? In order to improve your overall memory skills and your study and test-taking performance, it is important to evaluate your procedures and look for ways to improve.

Tip FROM THE Brain Doctor

What does the phrase *garbage in, garbage out* mean? You cannot get information out in a meaningful way if you did not put it there in a meaningful way. Context makes information more meaningful.

✔ COMPREHENSION CHECK

▶ Of everything you learned in this chapter, what will you be sure to use in your other classes?
▶ If you could ask the authors a question about this chapter, what would you ask?

PRACTICE WITH A READING PASSAGE

This Practice with a Reading Passage is intentionally different from others in this textbook to give you an opportunity to thoroughly apply all of the stages of memory. As you read, you will work through activities to test your ability to apply what you have learned about the memory process.

STAGE ONE: SENSORY INPUT

This is the stage where you take in information through your senses—in this case by reading.

Activity A

Read the following passage.

The New Rules of Social Networking
By Ferris Jabr

He Stands Alone

1   Males are far less likely than females to mention significant others in the "About Me" sections of their MySpace profiles, perhaps because they're inherently less inclined to define themselves through their relationships.

Teacher's Pet

2   "OMG, r u kidding me? My prof just friended me on FB!" One-third of surveyed students believe faculty should not be permitted access to Facebook, citing concerns of identity management and privacy. Males are more than twice as likely to be OK with faculty presence on Facebook.

Last Night Rocked

3   "Things got pretty crazy at your party last night and your caring friends have already started uploading incriminating photos and anecdotes." Studies show that comments indicating misbehavior increase males' perceived physical attractiveness, but the same kind of comments have the opposite effect on females.

Be My Friend?

4   According to one study, having too few or too many Facebook friends greatly decreases your social attractiveness: 300 was judged the optimal number. Any more and you start looking desperate.

Your God Here

5   Many Facebook users mute aspects of their lives that might be very meaningful to them for the sake of creating acceptable online personas. For example, only 13 percent make explicit claims of religious identity (versus 85 percent in the U.S. census).

Leveling the Field

6   Despite students' reluctance to integrate teachers and professors into online social networks, instructors who disclose information about their social lives on their Facebook profiles increase student motivation and create a more comfortable classroom climate.

Source: From Ferris Jabr, "The New Rules of Social Networking," *Psychologytoday.com* (November 2008). Copyright © 2008 Psychology Today. Reprinted with permission.

STAGE TWO: WORKING MEMORY

This stage occurs as you read, enabling you to comprehend long sentences and paragraphs and make sense of the material. In this stage, you must first understand the vocabulary and concepts in order to *comprehend* what you read and put it into working memory.

Activity B

Using what you know, see if you can figure out these words from the passage using the context (words and sentences) around them. Think carefully about the meaning of the sentence and what the word *might* mean. Reformat that sentence by writing a synonym (a word that has a similar meaning), then read the sentence again, inserting your synonym, and see if it makes sense. If not, change the synonym. You may have to consult a thesaurus or dictionary.

1. inherently (paragraph 1)   _____

2. inclined (paragraph 1)   _____

3. citing (paragraph 2)   _____

4. presence (paragraph 2)   _____

5. incriminating (paragraph 3)   _____

6. optimal (paragraph 4)   _____

7. personas (paragraph 5)   _____

8. explicit (paragraph 5)   _____

9. integrate (paragraph 6)   _____

STAGE THREE: ENCODING

Now start working with the encoding process. You will not always be able to use every strategy for every stage, but the more you use, the better.

▶ **Rehearsing and Repetition:** If you were studying for a test, you might review all the main ideas repeatedly over a series of days. You will not practice this strategy in this activity.

Continued on next page.

▶ **Chunking:** Recall that chunking is breaking something into meaningful units so that there are not so many pieces to remember all at once. In this case, to remember six facts about social networking, you want manageable chunks.

Activity C

In each paragraph of the reading, circle a keyword that will remind you of the information. For example, "alone" could be the keyword for the first paragraph.

▶ **Creating Mnemonics:** Creating a mnemonic can help you recall information for a test.

Activity D

Create an acrostic.

1. Write the first letter of each keyword in the headings of the passage.

   _____

2. Then choose words that start with each letter to make a sentence that you can remember.

   _____

3. Now using the first letter from the key words, write the original word from which you took the key word. Write it in your own words if you like.

   _____

4. Using the key words, write the original headings as they appeared or in your own words:

   _____

▶ **Making Associations and Connections:** The next strategy in encoding is to make associations and connections between the new material and what you already know.

Activity E

Answer the following questions to activate what you already know that relates to the information in this passage.

1. Have you experienced any of what is described in the reading on social networks?

   _____

   _____

2. Do you think males and females behave differently online? If so, how?

   _____

   _____

3. How do you feel about your professors visiting your social networks? Do you visit theirs?

_____

_____

4. Do you hide things online? What sort of things do you find it best not to reveal?

_____

_____

▶ **Reformatting:** Paragraph format makes things harder to remember. You can often reformat paragraphs into an outline or, even better, into a list. Each of the six paragraphs in the passage has a heading, so there are six items in the numbered list to remember. You still need to do more reformatting to help you remember the information in that list of rules. Notice that the headings or titles may be there to get your interest, but they are not necessarily specific enough to help you recall the six rules. Therefore, reformat the headings to include the main ideas.

Activity F: Part One

Write the headings of each paragraph of the passage.

1. _____

2. _____

3. _____

4. _____

5. _____

6. _____

You can see that these rules are actually statements about how people behave. To reformat this information, rewrite it in your own words. For example, "He Stands Alone" could be rewritten as "Males, much more than females, don't give information about their relationships online maybe because they don't think of themselves in terms of their relationships."

Activity F: Part Two

Rewrite the headings of the passage in your own words. Include information that makes the main point of the paragraph clear.

1. _____

2. _____

3. _____

Continued on next page.

4. _____

5. _____

6. _____

▶ **Using Multiple Pathways:** Another method of storing information in your memory is to see how many different ways you can encode the information you want to remember. In this passage, the information to remember is the list of rules.

Activity G
Draw a picture that symbolizes each rule. For example, to remind you of the information about how people may not reveal religion, you could draw a religious symbol. Say the rules aloud as you write them out. That gives you triple coding: visual, motor, and auditory.

STAGE FOUR: LONG-TERM MEMORY
You have now completed the encoding process, so the information should be in long-term memory. In this chapter, you learned six factors that affect how easily the material will be encoded and how likely it will be stored in long-term memory. See how these factors affected your encoding of the information you learned about social networking

Activity H
Write a sentence for each factor explaining how that factor influenced or increased your ability to recall this information in the future.

1. Attention

   _____

2. Environment and real-life experiences

   _____

3. Survival and importance to learner

   _____

4. Context

   _____

5. Emotion

   _____

6. Existing neural networks

   _____

Do you think you have enough factors to hold the information long term (until the test or until you need it in real life)?

STAGE FIVE: RETRIEVAL

The final stage of the memory process is the one that is most important to you—getting the information out when you need it!

Activity I

Write a paragraph summarizing the passage without looking at it or your notes. Hint: Using your acrostic may help. See how well you can remember the information, and add as much detail as you can recall.

CHAPTER SUMMARY

Without memory, learning cannot occur. Memory is the active process of storing and retrieving information. To learn well in your classes and to get information stored in your brain (and keep it there), you have to actively do something with new information.

Memories are stored in places and parts all over your brain. To ensure that memories or any new information get stored well and are retrievable, they must be encoded. For factual information, which involves semantic memory, encoding means actively storing information in a conscious way.

The stages of the memory process are sensory input, working memory, encoding, long-term memory, and retrieval. Sensory input is that which comes to you through your senses. Working memory is where information stays briefly, unless you actively begin to engage with it. Some of the ways to engage with information that is in your working memory are through rehearsing, repetition, and chunking. Information can then be encoded. Ways to encode information include rehearsing and repetition, chunking, creating mnemonics, reformatting, making associations and connections, and using multiple pathways. Encoding information leads to long-term storage.

There are many factors that can affect long-term memory storage, both positively and negatively, including attention, environment, survival/importance to the learner, context, emotion, and existing neural networks. Once information makes it to long-term storage, it can be retrieved, which means the information is pulled together from different parts of your brain when you need to use it.

Brain Connections: Self-Assessment

Draw the amount of dendrites you imagine that you have now about how the memory works. Compare your drawing of dendrites now with what you drew at the beginning of this chapter. If the amounts are different, explain why.

| I don't understand too much about how memory works. | I have a pretty good understanding about how memory works. | I have a very good understanding about how memory works. |

POST TEST

Part 1: Objective Questions

Match the key terms from the chapter in Column A to their definitions in Column B.

_____	1. Memory	a. mnemonic where you use the first letter of each item to be remembered to make a phrase or sentence
_____	2. Sensory input	b. doing something with new information so that it can transfer from working memory to long-term memory
_____	3. Working memory	c. repeated practice of an activity
_____	4. Rehearsal	d. memory of words, ideas, meanings, and concepts
_____	5. Chunking	e. strategy for making material easier to remember by putting into a format that is meaningful to you
_____	6. Encoding	f. the system in the brain where information is actively held temporarily while it is being worked with—previously called short-term memory
_____	7. Mnemonics	g. the process of storing and retrieving information
_____	8. Acronyms	h. the memory system for how we do things, particularly skills and procedure
_____	9. Acrostics	i. words that represent the topic or main idea of the material you are reading
_____	10. Anagrams	j. memory tricks
_____	11. Analogies	k. information coming to your brain through your sense of sight, hearing, touch, taste, or smell
_____	12. Key words	l. memory technique of taking small bits of information and putting them into larger groups
_____	13. Reformatting	m. mnemonic where you create words by using the first letter of each word or phrase that you intend to remember
_____	14. Long-term memory	n. mnemonic created by rearranging the letters in a key word to create another word, phrase, or sentence
_____	15. Procedural memory	o. comparison between two different things in order to show a similarity
_____	16. Episodic memory	p. the brain's system for storing, managing, and retrieving information for future use over the long term
_____	17. Semantic memory	q. the memory system for remembering personal events and situations, memory of what happened

18. The five steps in the memory process are

   ▶ _____   ▶ _____
   ▶ _____   ▶ _____
   ▶ _____

19. List the six strategies you can use to help you encode new information.

   ▶ _____   ▶ _____
   ▶ _____   ▶ _____
   ▶ _____   ▶ _____

20. Imagine you are in a biology class. Using the five steps of the memory process and Figure 2.2, explain how you could memorize the parts of a plant cell. (Note: You don't have to actually memorize them; just explain how you would.)

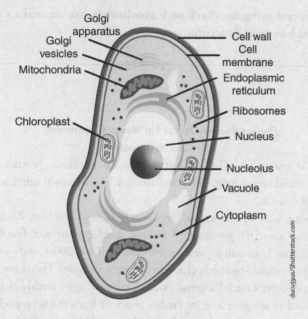

Figure 2.2 Plant Cell Structure

_____

_____

_____

Continued on next page.

Part 2: Reading Passage   POPULAR READING

Prepare to Read

1. Based on the title, what do you expect this passage to be about?

   _____

2. What do you already know about the topic of this passage?

   _____

3. What is your state of mind (mood, motivation, and/or energy level)?

   _____

4. Read the following passage, and using the checkmark monitoring system, make a checkmark in the margin each time you lose your concentration.

   _____

Project Runway Spices Up Sleepy Classrooms
By Katy Steinmetz

vapid flat, lacking life

voyeuristic finding joy in watching others

1   Reality TV wears a lot of hats: entertainment, talent search, portrait of culture at its most vapid and voyeuristic. But it has another, lesser-known function: spicing up bland college courses.

2   In the spring issue of *Journal on Excellence in College Teaching*, Brad van Eeden-Moorefield, an associate professor of human development and family studies at Central Michigan University, presents the results of his 2006 study on the effects of modeling a research-methods class after *Project Runway*. The show makes budding fashion designers vie for a grand prize by competing in weekly challenges. And though it's hard to imagine a realm farther removed from the sexy world of fashion than a small-town campus in sleepy Mount Pleasant, Mich., van Eeden-Moorefield's Project M (the *M* is for *Methodology*) proved successful. By the end of the semester, 100% of the students said they thought the curriculum should be used in future classes. They reported being more invested and also retaining more material. And perhaps most important, they said they actually had fun in a class in which students are trained to write theses, academic papers and similarly mind-numbing (but necessary) stuff.

3   So what is it about *Project Runway*, a show that each week has German supermodel Heidi Klum dismissing a contestant with a cool "Auf Wiedersehen," that made the Michigan students dive into developing data-collection strategies

and writing abstracts? The answer is, of course, the age-old spirit of competition. Although the most disappointing students weren't voted off the class roster at regular intervals, faculty and student judges ranked teams almost weekly in 11 challenges based on how the students applied research skills, whether in writing a literature review or understanding ethics. "It's human nature. People want to win. People want to excel," says Christine Walsh, who was a senior in the class when van Eeden-Moorefield first tried the method in 2006. "You can shove a bad test grade in your folder. When you're presenting in front of peers and professors, you want to be on your best game." (The prize and grand finale for Project M involved a grade bump, mentorship and presentation at a college-wide exhibition.)

4   There is also the element of reaching young people through a pop-culture platform, which turned a class that elicits soporific images of spreadsheets and bibliographies into something relatable. "Research methods is an important skill, even for people who [will never] inject lab rats with anything," says van Eeden-Moorefield, explaining that Project M made students less apprehensive about—and less bored by—the topic. He has continued to use the format since its 2006 debut and has achieved good if not better results by honing the method and incorporating suggestions from students, like giving second- and third-place winners a little prize action too.

5   In a 2004 study examining why people like reality TV, Steven Reiss, a professor emeritus of psychology at Ohio State University, found that reality shows allowed people to repeatedly and vicariously experience some of their basic desires, specifically their yearning for status and vengeance, the latter being closely tied to human enjoyment of competition. "The message of reality television—that millions of people are interested in watching real-life experiences of ordinary people—implies that ordinary people are important," Reiss wrote. And injecting some student exhibitionism into a class often governed by teacher-centric lectures and handouts "helps break down some of that power hierarchy," van Eeden-Moorefield says.

6   But there are also factors particular to *Project Runway* and similar shows that came into play, one of the biggest being its interactive form of critique, which often comes from the show's resident mentor, Tim Gunn. University of Tennessee law professor Michael Higdon has been giving lectures for years on why teachers should be more like Gunn, a silver-haired, bespectacled fashionisto (and former academic) who guides contestants before they present their creations to the judges. Higdon believes there is an essential overlap between teaching and talent-competition reality shows like *Project Runway*—at their basic levels, individuals are given a particular task and critiqued on their different approaches to completing that task, and giving meaningful criticism that is specific and informed, delicate yet honest, is integral to improvement. "Tim Gunn is the master of critique," Higdon says. "His slogan is 'Make it work.' There are some teachers who will just dictate to their students, and that just doesn't work."

Continued on next page.

abstracts summaries of academic work

soporific something that makes you sleepy

emeritus retired

vicariously enjoyed through imaginary participation

7   Van Eeden-Moorefield says he took on Gunn's role and let others do the judging. In presenting their work to a panel of judges, students, like the competing designers on TV, are exposed to a variety of critical perspectives, something van Eeden-Moorefield says is important in getting them to assess their approaches without getting defensive. In one challenge, students were asked to summarize previous research regarding their particular topic but to do so in the form of comic-book storyboards, a quirky assignment that could elicit very different reactions from peers compared with professors'. "You're getting feedback, you're getting challenged," Walsh says. "Part of it isn't awesome, but that's the reality of life."

8   Although van Eeden-Moorefield's study merely presents a promising method, Jane Cha, executive producer and co-creator of *Project Runway*, says she can see how the show's formulaic approach would be appealing to teachers. "[The contestants] hit on the same beats every time, but they can still be creative," says Cha, who understands all too well the burden teachers face in returning to the same basic material year after year. "The designers know what to expect," she says. "So the onus is on us to make [the challenges] more interesting every single time."

onus responsibility

Source: From Katy Steinmetz, "Project Runway Spices Up Sleepy Classrooms," *TIME Magazine* (Aug. 02, 2010). Copyright © 2010 Time Inc. Reprinted with permission.

Check Your Understanding

Circle the best answer to the following multiple-choice questions.

5. What were the results of the 2006 study mentioned in the reading?

    a. All of the students endorsed the study.

    b. All of the students reported being more invested in the class.

    c. All of the students reported that they retained more.

    d. All of the given answers.

6. What is Project M?

    a. an experimental teaching method that has student teams compete with one another

    b. an experimental teaching method that has student teams help each other

    c. an experimental teaching method that has student teams design fashions

    d. an experimental teaching method that has students on a reality TV show

7. According to Christine Walsh, a student in van Eeden-Moorefield's class, why did Project M work?

    a. People like reality TV.

    b. People did not want to be voted out of the class.

    c. People like to perform.

    d. People like to win.

8. According to Professor Steven Reiss, why do people like reality TV?

    a. It is real and not fiction.

    b. It allows people to enjoy being watched and judged by their peers in a fair competition.

    c. It allows people to enjoy something over and over, by their imaginary participation in something.

    d. It is a form of learning.

9. What are soporific images?

    a. graphic pictures

    b. images that cause people to sleep

    c. images of sophomores in college

    d. images of students sleeping

Answer the following short-answer questions.

10. What class are you currently taking that you think Project M might work for? Why?

    _____

    _____

    _____

11. How could the success of this experiment be credited in part to the idea of survival, one of the factors affecting long-term memory?

    _____

    _____

    _____

Continued on next page.

12. How can the students' emotional response to this teaching experiment affect their learning in a positive way? How can it affect learning in a negative way?

_____

_____

_____

13. Why might the idea of "dictating to students" not work well as a teaching method? Explain your answer using what you learned in this chapter.

_____

_____

_____

14. How do student presentations enhance learning for other students?

_____

_____

_____

15. Do you think Project M is a good idea for a college class? Why or why not?

_____

_____

_____

BRAIN STRENGTH OPTIONS

Select one of the following. You will present this to the class or instructor in the format associated with the project. The product should contain enough information to provide a thorough review of the material.

1. Diagram the memory process in a poster using circles, boxes, and lines to show relationships.

2. Outline the material in the memory process in a handout. Use headings and subheadings as needed.

3. Illustrate the memory process using pictures and captions, as in a comic strip.

4. Create a PowerPoint presentation about the memory process.

5. Working with four classmates, divide up the stages of the memory process. Each one of you will teach your part to the classroom. You will be the "expert" on that part of the process, so know it well and explain it clearly. All steps in the memory process must be covered by your group.

Developing Your College Vocabulary

ERIN BISHOP

A junior at University of Phoenix majoring in psychology and minoring in biology with plans to continue on to medical school

> *"One forgets words as one forgets names. One's vocabulary needs constant fertilizing or it will die."*
>
> —EVELYN WAUGH

Courtesy of Erin Bishop

I HAVE ALWAYS been a word geek. Even as a little girl I had to know the meaning of a new word. When my mom was working on her master's degree, I would talk to her as she did her homework, and when a new and fascinating word came up, I would go and get the dictionary. I remember when I learned the word *psychotic* I walked around for a week telling people that their behavior was psychotic. The best trick that I know for memorizing vocabulary is to try to find a way to use the word in a sentence every day.

In my classes, technical vocabulary is very important because most of the diagnoses in psychology and the terms in biology are not commonplace. So you have to know the proper name and meaning, and the proper use of the word until you know it by heart. I just make flash cards with the words and meanings on them. When I have a test coming up, I cover my refrigerator with flashcards of terms and key phrases so every time I open the refrigerator, I see the word. This helps me remember things a lot easier because, well ... I open the refrigerator a lot!

Develop a Strong Vocabulary

Types of Context Clues

Context Clues

Prefixes

Developing Your College Vocabulary

Word Part Analysis

Suffixes

Roots

Methods to Help You Learn and Remember Vocabulary

Word Maps

Sounding It Out

Specialized Vocabulary

The Card Review System (CRS)

Exam Terminology

© Cengage Learning

Brain Connections: Self-Assessment

Draw on the brain cell how many dendrites you imagine you have for how much you know about vocabulary.

Develop a Strong Vocabulary

DEVELOPING A STRONG VOCABULARY HAS MANY BENEFITS. Increasing your vocabulary increases your ability to think critically about new information. Knowing more words means you not only increase your reading comprehension, you also develop your listening comprehension. When you know more vocabulary, college lectures will begin to make more sense. You may not have made the connection to the words in your reading with those used in your professor's lectures because words are sometimes spelled differently from how they sound. Also, many college courses build upon each other, so learning the language of entry-level courses will better prepare you for the next level.

Owning your own dictionary and thesaurus or being able to access them online will be worth the investment. There are also smartphone applications for dictionaries and thesauri; just search the words for which you need definitions. Your reading comprehension is at stake, and using a dictionary and thesaurus will help you to begin developing good reading habits. The more words you learn, the easier it will be for you to understand, remember, and learn what you are reading. You cannot learn a concept if you do not understand the key words in it. Understanding a word's meaning is very different from just recognizing or knowing how to pronounce the word; meaning is the key to understanding. Most students' reading difficulty stems from their weak vocabulary, and many do not take the time to look up new words. Begin using the new words in your conversations. The more you use them, the easier it will be for you to remember the words and their meanings.

There are two important ways you can try to figure out the meaning of unfamiliar words without having to immediately consult a dictionary:

context clues using the words around a word to determine meaning

1. **Pay attention to context clues.** Context clues are the words around a word. These clues will help you figure out the meaning of a word without having to stop and look it up. This is how most people learn new vocabulary.

2. **Know and understand word parts.** Knowing word parts allows you to make an educated guess regarding the meaning of the word. This strategy is known as word-part analysis. There are three primary word parts:

   ▶ **prefixes**
   ▶ **suffixes**
   ▶ **roots**

Context Clues

Read this sentence:

> I could charge the expense of the dinner on my credit card and you could pay me the cash. Conversely, you could charge it on your credit card and I could give you the cash.

► What does *conversely* mean? _____

► How did you figure it out? _____

► Write a sentence using *conversely.* _____

If you figured out the meaning of *conversely*, you used context clues. If you were not able to figure it out, you may not be familiar with context clues. Read the following sentence:

> Although Karl is usually quite <u>polemical</u> during study sessions, today he didn't argue at any time during the session.

See if you can locate two clues to the meaning of the word *polemical*. The first clue tells you that Karl is *usually* polemical during study sessions. The second clue helps define the meaning of the word—today he didn't *argue* at any point. After reading the two clues, you can work out that *polemical* means "argumentative."

Even if you think you can figure out the meaning of a new word using context clues, you never want to assume you know the meaning. Read this next example to see why just thinking you understand the context clues is not always enough.

> Nancy looked everywhere for pencils, pens, and paper. In the storage room, she found, to her surprise, a <u>dearth</u> of supplies.

What do you think *dearth* means? It seems like it should mean "a lot" or "surplus," but it actually means "shortage," "lack," or "absence." If you assumed it meant a lot, your understanding would be completely wrong. Depending on what you are reading, it may not be practical to look up every new word. If, however, you are reading a textbook, you should take the

Tip FROM THE
Brain Doctor

The brain does not like memorizing vocabulary out of context because it is not meaningful. Remember, learning means making connections! It is best to learn a new word in context—in the sentence in which it is used. When you are reading online, you may notice that some words are in color or underlined to stand out. Often, these links take you to a definition of the word.
This is an easy way to learn vocabulary because you are storing it right along with the information that you are reading—in other words, in context—which will make it easier to remember.

time to look up and learn the meaning of unknown words, with or without context clues. If you are reading for pleasure, it may not be necessary. Ask yourself, "Can I keep reading, not knowing a troublesome word?" If not, then look it up.

ACTIVITY 3A
Begin to Use Context Clues

Read the following sentence, and think about what the underlined word means.

The little boy was thin and dirty. He hadn't eaten anything in days and was <u>famished</u>. When the boy's mother came into the room and gave him a slice of dry bread, the little boy stuffed it quickly into his mouth.

1. What does *famished* mean?

_____

2. Explain how you figured out the meaning of *famished*.

_____

Tip FROM THE
Brain Doctor

Using context clues is very natural for the brain because it is always searching for meaning and making connections. Reflecting on a word and looking at the words around the unknown word for a context clue can take advantage of the brain's natural desire to make sense of things.

Types of Context Clues

Authors use different types of context clues in their writing to help you define an unfamiliar word.

▶ **Punctuation.** Authors use punctuation to set words off from the rest of a sentence through the use of commas, dashes, brackets, or parentheses. For example, when commas surround a word or words, they set them off from the rest of the sentence; when dashes set a word or words off, they emphasize their importance; and when parentheses or brackets set them off, they indicate the words are less important. An author may also restate material in between punctuation in order to make the meaning more clear, as in these examples. Note how the word to be restated is followed by a comma.

Karla's father, Mr. Jones, is a nice guy.

The tiny Pomeranian, a breed of dog, stole the show.

▶ **Synonyms**. Authors use synonyms, words that mean the same or similar to an unfamiliar word, as clues.

The little girl was famished; in other words, she was starving.

The hockey player was angry, or ireful, when he skated off the ice.

The following words are often used to introduce synonyms:

▶ *or*

▶ *also known as*

▶ *in other words*

▶ *the same as*

▶ **Antonyms**. Authors also use antonyms, words that mean the opposite of unfamiliar words, as clues.

The new movie by Joe Daida was unimaginative, unlike his first, which was so creative.

Our new contract was immaterial; however, it was meant to be important.

Tip FROM THE
Brain Doctor

We have many more words in our receptive vocabulary (words that we understand when we see or hear them) than we do in our expressive vocabulary (words that we actually speak). Receptive and expressive pathways are different brain pathways. In order to remember a new vocabulary word you are reading, it is best to speak it aloud. That way you are incorporating both the receptive and expressive pathways and making the memory stronger. In order to "fire and wire" the expressive pathway, you need to actually speak aloud. Many times you will hear a word in your head just fine, but find that when it comes to saying it, you cannot pronounce it. This is because you have not formed the pathway by actually speaking it aloud. Say new words aloud and you will remember them better and be more likely to add them to your expressive, speaking vocabulary.

The following words are often used to introduce antonyms:

▶ *on the other hand*

▶ *however*

▶ *although*

▶ *unlike*

▶ **Definitions**. Authors provide a brief explanation of what a word means.

Photosynthesis is the process plants use to convert sunlight into energy.

Maria used the fine grater, also known as a microplane, to shred cheese on top of the pasta.

When authors use definitions as context clues, the following words are often used:

▶ *is*

▶ *is known as*

► *also known as*
► *is the same as*
► *is called*
► *means the same as*
► *i.e.* (a Latin abbreviation meaning "that is")

► **Examples**. Authors use examples to illustrate what a word means.

> Sensory input involves new information coming into the brain from a person's senses, such as hearing a news report on the radio.

Examples are often introduced by words like:
► *for example*
► *such as*
► *for instance*
► *e.g.* (a Latin abbreviation meaning "for example")

► **Personal experiences, opinions, and knowledge**. Authors often provide their readers with personal or additional information to enhance the point they are making and help define difficult words and concepts.

> Having known Sheila all of her life, she came forward of her own volition; no one can talk her into doing anything she doesn't want to do.

ACTIVITY 3B
Identify Different Context Clues

See if you can figure out the meaning of the words in boldfaced type by using context clues in the following sentences. Then determine the type of clue the author uses. Highlight or underline the clues. The first one is done as an example for you.

Example: My mother's **brooch**, a silver pin, was her treasure. It was the only piece of jewelry her
husband ever gave to her.

► What is the definition of *brooch*?

pin
_____

► What type of clue did the author give you?

punctuation
_____

1. In other words, the **precocious** little girl was unusually bright for her age.

   ▶ What is the definition of *precocious*?

   _____

   ▶ What type of clue did the author give you?

   _____

2. A **mala,** a string of prayer beads, is worn by Hindu monks.

   ▶ What is the definition of *mala*?

   _____

   ▶ What type of clue did the author give you?

   _____

3. The **nefarious** little child hid her true self from everyone around her. Only I knew. When no one else was looking, she stuck out her evil tongue as she kicked the dog.

   ▶ What is the definition of *nefarious*?

   _____

   ▶ What type of clue did the author give you?

   _____

4. Although writing songs is not always a **lucrative** profession, I know that I would not want to do anything else. Singing with others and making music are far more important than money.

   ▶ What is the definition of *lucrative*?

   _____

   ▶ What type of clue did the author give you?

   _____

5. Jed is a very **morose** young boy, unlike his sister who is always happy.

   ▶ What is the definition of *morose*?

   _____

   ▶ What type of clue did the author give you?

   _____

ACTIVITY 3C
Practice with Context Clues

Select the definition of the boldfaced word by using context clues to determine the word's meaning.

1. The cookies were a simple way to **assuage** the angry students for having to wait so long to see a counselor. Their angry frowns were quickly replaced by smiles.

   a. increase
   b. criticize
   c. soothe
   d. hide

2. Even with his busy schedule, Brad Pitt keeps up a **voluminous** correspondence with his fans in America and abroad. He writes to millions.

   a. sizeable or numerous
   b. see clearly
   c. loud
   d. fake

3. The politician took a **pedagogic** approach with his speech, hoping that those attending would learn something meaningful from it.

   a. incomplete
   b. something that opens the door
   c. brightens
   d. instructional

4. The adoring fan stared at his hand, touched by Lady Gaga. When asked how he felt about being touched, he smiled and took a long time to respond. He then said it was **ineffable.**

   a. hateful
   b. boring
   c. incapable of being expressed in words
   d. critical

5. Some people flip a coin to make all of their decisions. It is a very **capricious** way to live.

   a. certain
   b. unpredictable
   c. green
   d. expected

List the six types of contexts clues authors use and provide an example for each type.

1. _____

2. _____

3. _____

4. _____

5. _____

6. _____

ACTIVITY 3D
Use Context Clues in a Passage

Read the following passage about code cracking during World War II, and determine the meaning of the boldfaced words. Remember to make connections to what you already know as you read.

1. What do you know about this topic?

_____

2. Why do you think it might be difficult to translate the Navajo language?

_____

The Language Barrier
By Simon Singh

1   One war **correspondent** described the difficulties of communication during the heat of jungle battle: "When the fighting became confined to a small area, everything had to move on a split-second schedule. There was not time for **enciphering** and **deciphering**. At such times, the King's English became a last resort—the **profaner** the better." Unfortunately for the Americans, many Japanese soldiers had attended American colleges and were fluent in English, including the profanities. Valuable information about American strategy and tactics was falling into the hands of the enemy.

2   One of the first to react to this problem was Philip Johnston, an engineer based in Los Angeles, who was too old to fight but still wanted to contribute to the war effort. At the beginning of 1942 he began to **formulate** an encryption system inspired by his childhood experiences. The son of a Protestant missionary, Johnston had grown up on the Navajo reservations of Arizona, and as a result he had become fully **immersed** in Navajo culture. He was one of the few people outside the tribe who could speak their language fluently, which allowed him to act as an interpreter for discussions between the Navajo and government agents. His work in this capacity **culminated** in a visit to the White House, when, as a nine-year-old, Johnston translated for two Navajos who were appealing to President Theodore Roosevelt for fairer treatment for their community. Fully aware of how **impenetrable** the language was for those outside the tribe, Johnston was struck by the notion that Navajo, or any other Native American language, could act as a **virtually** unbreakable code. If each battalion in the Pacific employed a pair of Native Americans as radio operators, secure communication could be guaranteed.

3   He took his idea to Lieutenant Colonel James E. Jones, the area signal officer at Camp Elliott, just outside San Diego. Merely by throwing a few Navajo phrases at the bewildered officer, Johnston was able to persuade him that the idea was worthy of serious consideration. A fortnight later he returned with two Navajos, ready to conduct a test demonstration in front of senior marine officers. The Navajos were isolated from each other; and one was given six typical messages in English, which he translated into Navajo and transmitted to his colleague

Continued on next page.

via a radio. The Navajo receiver translated the messages back into English, wrote them down, and handed them over to the officers, who compared them with the originals. The game of Navajo whispers proved to be flawless, and the marine officers authorized a pilot project and ordered recruitment to begin immediately. . . .

4   At the time of America's entry into the Second World War, the Navajo were living in harsh conditions and being treated as inferior people. Yet their tribal council supported the war effort and declared their loyalty: "There exists no purer concentration of Americanism than among the First Americans." The Navajos were so eager to fight that some of them lied about their age or gorged themselves on bunches of bananas and swallowed great quantities of water in order to reach the minimum weight requirement of 55 kg. Similarly, there was no difficulty in finding suitable candidates to serve as Navajo code talkers, as they were to become known. Within four months of the bombing of Pearl Harbor, 29 Navajos, some as young as fifteen, began an eight-week communications course with the Marine Corps.

5   Before training could begin, the Marine Corps had to overcome a problem that had **plagued** the only other code to have been based on a Native American language. In Northern France during the First World War, Captain E. W. Homer of Company D, 141st Infantry, ordered that eight men from the Choctaw tribe be employed as radio operators. Obviously none of the enemy understood their language, so the Choctaw provided secure communications. However, this encryption system was fundamentally flawed because the Choctaw language had no equivalent for modern military **jargon**. A specific technical term in a message might therefore have to be translated into a vague Choctaw expression, with the risk that this could be misinterpreted by the receiver.

6   The same problem would have arisen with the Navajo language, but the Marine Corps planned to construct a **lexicon** of Navajo terms to replace otherwise untranslatable English words, thus removing any **ambiguities**. The trainees helped to compile the lexicon, tending to choose words describing the natural world to indicate specific military terms. Thus, the names of birds were used for planes, and fish for ships (Table 3.1). Commanding officers

Table 3.1 Navajo Code Words for Planes and Ships

Planes and Ships	Code Word	Navajo
Fighter plane	Hummingbird	Da-he-tih-hi
Observation plane	Owl	Ne-as-jah
Torpedo plane	Swallow	Tas-chizzie
Bomber	Buzzard	Jay-sho
Dive-bomber	Chicken hawk	Gini
Bombs	Eggs	A-ye-shi
Amphibious vehicle	Frog	Chat
Battleship	Whale	Lo-tso
Destroyer	Shark	Ca-10
Submarine	Iron fish	Besh-lo

became "war chiefs," platoons were "mud-clans," fortifications turned into "cave dwellings" and mortars were known as "guns that squat."

7   Even though the complete lexicon contained 274 words, there was still the problem of translating less predictable words and the names of people and places. The solution was to devise an encoded phonetic alphabet for spelling out difficult words. For example, the word "Pacific" would be spelled out as "pig, ant, cat, ice, fox, ice, cat," which would then be translated into Navajo as bi-sodih, wol-la-chee, moasi, tkin, ma-e, tkin, moasi. The complete Navajo alphabet is given in Table 3.2. Within eight weeks, the trainee code talkers had learned the entire lexicon and alphabet, thus **obviating** the need for codebooks which might fall into enemy hands. For the Navajos, committing everything to memory was trivial because traditionally their language had no written script, so they were used to memorizing their folk stories and family histories. As William McCabe, one of the trainees, said, "In Navajo everything is in the memory—songs, prayers, everything. That's the way we were raised."

8   At the end of their training, the Navajos were put to the test. Senders translated a series of messages from English into Navajo, transmitted them, and then receivers translated the messages back into English, using the memorized lexicon and alphabet when necessary. The results were word-perfect. To check the strength of the system, a recording of the transmissions was given to Navy Intelligence, the unit that had cracked Purple, the toughest Japanese cipher. After three weeks of intense **cryptanalysis**, the Naval codebreakers were still baffled by the messages. They called the Navajo language a "weird succession of guttural, nasal, tongue-twisting sounds … we couldn't even **transcribe** it, much less crack it." The Navajo code was judged a success. Two Navajo soldiers, John Benally and Johnny Manuelito, were asked to stay and train the next batch of recruits while the other 27 Navajo code talkers were assigned to four regiments and sent to the Pacific …

Table 3.2 The Navajo Alphabet Code

A	Ant	Wol-la-chee	N	Nut	Nesh-chee
B	Bear	Shush	O	Owl	Ne-ahs-jsh
C	Cat	Moasi	P	Pig	Bi-sodih
D	Deer	Be	Q	Quiver	Ca-yeilth
E	Elk	Dzeh	R	Rabbit	Gah
F	Fox	Ma-e	S	Sheep	Dibeh
G	Goat	Klizzie	T	Turkey	Than-zie
H	Horse	Lin	U	Ute	No-da-ih
I	Ice	Tkin	V	Victor	A-keh-di-gJini
J	Jackass	Tkele-cho-gi	W	Weasel	Gloe-ih
K	Kid	Klizzie-yazzi	X	Cross	Al-an-as-dzoh
L	Lamb	Dibeh-yazzi	Y	Yucca	Tsah-as-zih
M	Mouse	Na-as-tso-si	Z	Zinc	Besh-do-gliz

Continued on next page.

9   The reputation of the code talkers soon spread, and by the end of 1942 there was a request for 83 more men. The Navajo were to serve in all six Marine Corps divisions and were sometimes borrowed by other American forces. Their war of words soon turned the Navajos into heroes. Other soldiers would offer to carry their radios and rifles; and they were even given personal bodyguards, partly to protect them from their own comrades. On at least three occasions code talkers were mistaken for Japanese soldiers and captured by fellow Americans. They were released only when colleagues from their own battalion **vouched** for them. ...

10   Altogether, there were 420 Navajo code talkers. Although their bravery as fighting men was acknowledged, their special role in securing communications was classified information. The government **forbade** them to talk about their work, and their unique contribution was not made public. Just like Turing and the cryptanalysts at Bletchley Park, the Navajo were ignored for decades. Eventually, in 1968, the Navajo code was declassified; and the following year the code talkers held their first reunion. Then, in 1982, they were honored when the U.S. Government named August 14 "National Navajo Code Talkers Day." However, the greatest tribute to the work of the Navajo is the simple fact that their code is one of very few throughout history that was never broken.

Source: From *The Code Book: The Evolution of Secrecy from Mary Queen of Scots to Quantum Cryptography* (pp.195–196) by Simon Singh. Copyright © 1999 by Simon Singh. Used by permission of Doubleday, a division of Random House, Inc. and Fourth Estate, a division of Harper Collins (UK).

Using context clues, provide definitions for the following words from the passage.

3. correspondent (paragraph 1)

_____

4. enciphering (paragraph 1)

_____

5. deciphering (paragraph 1)

_____

6. profaner (paragraph 1)

_____

7. formulate (paragraph 2)

_____

8. immersed (paragraph 2)

_____

9. culminated (paragraph 2)

_____

10. impenetrable (paragraph 2)

_____

11. virtually (paragraph 2)

_____

12. plagued (paragraph 5)

_____

13. jargon (paragraph 5)

_____

14. lexicon (paragraph 6)

_____

15. ambiguities (paragraph 6)

_____

16. obviating (paragraph 7)

_____

17. cryptanalysis (paragraph 8)

_____

18. transcribe (paragraph 8)

_____

19. vouched (paragraph 9)

_____

20. forbade (paragraph 10)

_____

ACTIVITY 3E
Use Context Clues in Textbooks

Read the following passages adapted from college textbooks. Using the authors' context clues, define each boldfaced word. Then, from the options provided, circle the answer closest in meaning to your definition.

1.   **Coleoptera** means "sheath wings," a reference to the armored forewings on a beetle.

Source: Adapted from Imes, R. *The Practical Entomologist.* New York: Simon and Schuster, 1992, p. 94.

What do you think *coleoptera* means?

_____

Which answer is closest in meaning to your definition?

    a. hairy legs

    b. armored forewings on a beetle

    c. fur

2.   Alcoholism **exacts** a horrible toll on the drinker and the drinker's family, but the damage doesn't stop there. Drunk driving, workplace losses, and overburdened health care systems are only some of the larger-scale loss issues related to alcohol abuse.

Source: Halonen, J. and Santrock, J. *Psychology: Contexts and Applications.* New York: McGraw Hill, 1999.

What do you think *exacts* means?

_____

Which answer is closest in meaning to your definition?

    a. diminishes

    b. demands

    c. feels

3.   The assassination created an emotionally charged atmosphere that the new president, Lyndon Baines Johnson, **adroitly** exploited. Seizing the moment, Johnson cleverly added new provisions to the legislation.

Source: Adapted from Judd D. and Swanstrom, T. *City Politics: The Political Economy of Urban America,* 7th Edition, New York: Longman, 2010, p. 191.

What do you think *adroitly* means?

_____

Which answer is closest in meaning to your definition?
   a. skillfully
   b. civilly
   c. frantically

4.   Just when an appliance seems sold out and least available, it becomes most desirable. Many customers do agree to purchase at this time. Thus, when the salesperson **invariably** returns with the news that an additional supply of the appliance has been found, it is also with a pen and a sales contract in hand.

Source: Adapted from Cialdini, R. *Influence: Science and Practice,* 5th ed. Boston: Pearson, 2009, p. 202.

What do you think *invariably* means?

_____

Which answer is closest in meaning to your definition?
   a. never
   b. sometimes
   c. always

5.   Given ideal conditions, populations of many organisms can grow **exponentially;** that is, they can expand at a constant rate per unit of time. This can produce an enormous population.

Source: Adapted from Cunningham, Cunningham and Easton. *Environmental Science: A Global Concern,* 10th ed. Boston: McGraw Hill, 2008, p. 128.

What do you think *exponentially* means?

_____

Which answer is closest in meaning to your definition?
   a. grow slowly
   b. grow tremendously
   c. grow openly

▶ In your own words, write your definition of what context clues in textbooks are.

▶ What does it mean to understand a word in its context?

Word Part Analysis

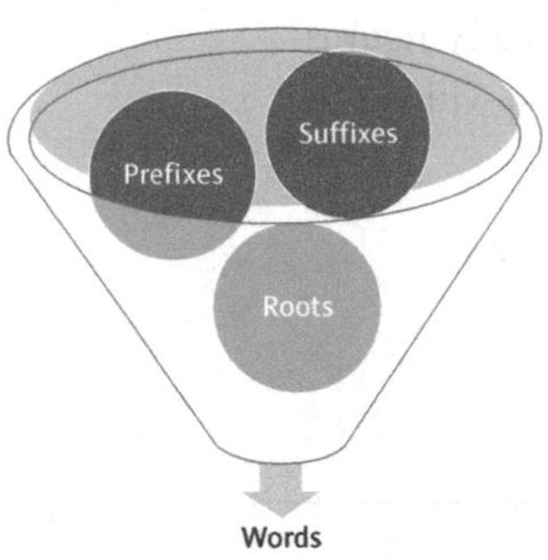

Figure 3.1 **Word Parts**

IN ADDITION TO CONTEXT CLUES, you can use word parts as clues to determine the meaning of unfamiliar words. There are three primary word parts:

▶ **prefixes**

▶ **suffixes**

▶ **roots**

More than 50% of English vocabulary comes from ancient Greek and Latin, so when you learn some words parts that come from the original Greek and Latin words, you can figure out many English words. Table 3.3 shows examples of English words based on Latin word parts.

Table 3.3 English Words from the Latin Root *duc* Using Prefixes and Suffixes

duc = a Latin root as in the Latin word *ducere* = to lead	
*ab*duct (prefix *ab-* = away, leads away)	*in*duce (prefix *in-* = leads in)
*con*duct (prefix *con-* = with, leads together with)	*intro*duce (prefix *intro-* = leads into)
conduc*tor* (suffix *-or* = the one who does it)	introduc*tion* (suffix *-tion* = an action)
*de*duct (prefix *de-* = away, leads away from)	*pro*duce (prefix *pro-* = forward, leads forward)
*e*ducate (prefix *e-* = out, leads it out)	*re*duce (prefix *re-* = back, leads backward)
educa*tor* (suffix *-or* = the one who does it)	reduc*ing* (suffix *-ing* = an action happening)

The following sentences use words from Table 3.3 that are based on Latin word parts.

A good **educator** will introduce students to how to **produce** good writing without having to **reduce** their creativity.

A criminal might **abduct** a child in order to **induce** the parents to pay ransom.

We try to **conduct** peaceful interrelationships by **reducing** everyone's stress.

You may **deduct** your business expenses from your income tax.

See how many word parts you already know. Read this sentence:

My computer got some *malware* on it.

▶ What word associated with computer ends in *-ware*?

_____

▶ What are words that mean "bad cancer" or "bad nutrition" (just two of many possible examples) that begin with *mal-*?

_____

▶ Therefore, *malware* means:

_____

▶ Describe the strategy that you just used to figure out the word.

_____

▶ Write a sentence using the word *malware*.

_____

Prefixes

PREFIXES **ARE WORD** parts or syllables placed at the beginning of words. They can change the meaning of a word. For example, consider the prefixes *a-, bi-, homo-*, and *hetero-* when each one is attached to the root word *sexual*, which means "intimately involving" or "having sex."

prefixes word part, syllable, or syllables placed at the beginning of words

asexual	not intimate; not having or involving sex
bisexual	intimate with both (two) sexes
homosexual	intimate with the same sex
heterosexual	intimate with the opposite (different) sex

The word *sexual* is common to all of the words. Each prefix changes the word's meaning. Knowing a prefix can help you figure out the word's meaning.

ACTIVITY 3F
Learn Common Prefixes

Using a sheet of paper, cover up the prefix definition column for the following list of prefixes. Next to each prefix, write down what you think the definition of that prefix is. You may be familiar with the words using the prefixes, which will help you to determine what the definition of the prefix is. Check your responses by uncovering the prefix definition column.

Table 3.4 Common Prefixes

Prefix	Word(s) Using the Prefix	Prefix Definition
a-	aside, atheist	not, away from
ab-	abhor	away from
ac-	accede	to, toward
ad-	adhere, advance	to, toward
ambi-	ambidextrous	both
amphi-	amphitheatre	around, on both sides
annu-, anni-	annual	year
ante-	antecedent	before
anti-	antibiotic	against, opposed to
audi-, aur-	audio	hear
auto-	autograph	self
bene-	beneficial	well, good
bi-	biped, bilingual	two
bio-	biography	life
carn-	carnivore	flesh
circum-	circumvent	around
co-	cohesive	with, together
com-	company	with, together
con-	convenient	with, together
corp-	corporation	body
cred-	credible	believe
de-	detach	away, from
dem-	democracy	people
dis-	disengage, distrust	apart, no longer, not
e-	emit	out, out of

Prefix	Word(s) Using the Prefix	Prefix Definition
ef-	effaced	out of, from
em-	empower	make, or cause to be
ex-	exit	out of, from
extra-	extraordinary	beyond
hetero-	heterogeneous	different, other
homo-	homogenized	same
hyper-	hyperactive	more than usual
hypo-	hypodermic	below, under
il-	illegal	not
im-	imposter	not, into
in-	instill	not, into, toward
ir-	irrational	not, into
kilo-	kilometers	thousand
mal-	malicious, malfunction	wrong, bad
meta-	metabolic	after, change
mis-	misconduct	wrong
mono-	monologue	one, single
multi-	multidimensional	many, much
neo-	neophyte	new
non-	nonsense	not
ob-	object	against
omni-	omnipotent	all
op-	opposed	against
over-	overwork	above, too much, beyond
pan-	panacea	all, every
para-	paranormal	beside, near
ped-	pedestrian	foot
per-	persecute	through
poly-	polygon	many, several
port-	portable	carry
post-	postpone	after, behind, later
pre-	precede	before, in front of
pro-	propel	advancing forward
proto-	prototype	first

Continued on next page.

Prefix	Word(s) Using the Prefix	Prefix Definition
quad-	quadruple	four
re-	readmit	again, back, against
retro-	retrospect	backward, behind
se-	secede	apart, away from
semi-	semiannual	half, partly
sub-	submarine	under, below
super-	superimpose, superlative	above, beyond
sym-	sympathy	with, together
syn-	synchronous	with, together
techn-	technician	skill, art
trans-	transform	across, over, change
tri-	triangle	three
ultra-	ultramodern	very, beyond
un-	unbelievable	not
under-	undermine	beneath, lower
uni-	uniform	one

ACTIVITY 3G
Use Prefixes

Use the following prefixes to create two words for each.

1. ab- _____   _____

2. con- _____   _____

3. corp- _____   _____

4. derm- _____   _____

5. hypo- _____   _____

6. proto- _____   _____

7. sub- _____   _____

8. super- _____   _____

9. trans- _____   _____

10. uni- _____   _____

ACTIVITY 3H
Identify Prefixes and Build Words

Identify the appropriate prefix being defined, and then provide two words using each prefix. The first one is modeled for you.

1. A prefix that means "out of, from": ___ex_____

   a. ___exit_____   b. ___exclaim_____

2. A prefix that means "half": _____

   a. _____   b. _____

3. A prefix that means "together, with": _____

   a. _____   b. _____

4. A prefix that means "under": _____

   a. _____   b. _____

5. A prefix that means "one": _____

   a. _____   b. _____

6. A prefix that means "thousand": _____

   a. _____   b. _____

7. A prefix that means "forward": _____

   a. _____   b. _____

8. A prefix that means "carry": _____

   a. _____   b. _____

9. A prefix that means "against": _____

   a. _____   b. _____

10. A prefix that means "three": _____

   a. _____   b. _____

Suffixes

A SUFFIX IS a word part attached to the end of a word. Suffixes usually do not change the meaning of a word as much as prefixes do, though they can change verbs to the present, past, or future tense. Did you know that different verb

suffix word part attached to the end of a word

tenses use suffixes (*-ed* and *-ing*)? For example, the verb *stay* can be *stayed* yesterday or *will be staying* tomorrow. A suffix can also change the way words are used. For example, the verb *laugh* can be changed to an adjective by adding the suffix *-able*, which means "able to be":

laugh + -able = laughable   means "able to be laughed at"

Usually when you add a suffix to a root word, the spelling of both stays the same such as with *laughable*. But there are times when the spelling of a root word changes when you add a suffix:

educate + -tion → education (*e* drops)

Following are several rules that serve as a general spelling guideline, but if you are unsure, it is always a good idea to use a dictionary to check the spelling.

1. For most words that are short, have one syllable, and end in a single consonant, double the last letter in the word when you add a suffix:

hum + -ing → humming

2. For most longer words with more than one syllable that end in *l*, double the last consonant when adding a suffix:

control + -ed → controlled

3. For longer words with stress on the last syllable that end in a single consonant, double the last letter:

begin + -er → beginner

prefer + -ing → preferring

4. When a word ends in a consonant and a suffix starts with a consonant, you do not need to double the last letter of the word:

commit + -ment → commitment

ACTIVITY 31
Learn Common Suffixes

Using a sheet of paper, cover up the suffix definition column for the following list of suffixes. Next to each suffix, write down what you think the definition of that suffix is. You may be familiar with the words using the suffixes, which will help you to determine what the definition of the suffix is. Check your responses by uncovering the suffix definition column.

Table 3.5 Common Suffixes

Suffix	Word(s) Using the Suffix	Suffix Definition
-able, -ible	legible	able to be
-al, -ic	angelic, comical	like, pertaining to
-an, -or, -er	musician, worker	person who
-ance	resistance	state of, action
-ant	participant	causing, being
-ation	information	state, condition
-ful	harmful, beautiful	full of
-fy	simplify, magnify	to make
-hood	brotherhood	condition
-ible	divisible	capable
-ion	vision	state of being
-ious	suspicious	characterized by
-ism	symbolism	system
-ist	scientist	agent, doer, specialist
-ity	community	condition, degree
-ive	active	tending toward
-ize	legalize	to make
-less	heartless	without
-ly	slowly	like
-ment	movement	state of being
-ness	happiness	state, quality
-or	actor	performer of action
-ous	frivolous	characterized by
-ship	friendship	condition, state
-some	awesome	tending to
-tion	election	act, process
-ty	frailty	state, condition
-ward	homeward	direction
-y	cloudy	full of

ACTIVITY 3J
Create Words with Suffixes

Write a word using a suffix that fits each definition provided. The first one is done for you.

1. able to bend   bendable
2. like a father   _____
3. full of hurt   _____
4. one who provides instruction   _____
5. without a home   _____
6. one who specializes in biology   _____
7. to make alphabetical   _____
8. without money   _____
9. state of censoring   _____
10. characterized by harmony   _____

Roots

root a word's most basic part

A WORD'S ROOT is its most basic part. As word parts, roots can be found anywhere in a word, whereas prefixes typically appear at the beginning and a suffix typically at the end. It provides the reader with the core meaning of a word. For example, suppose you read in your local newspaper that an amateur aquarist has added two rare fish to his collection. Looking at the first part of the word, *aqua*, which means "water," you could safely guess that the *aqua*rist (-*ist* means "one who specializes in it") has something to do with water. Because the fish live in water, he would have to keep them in an *aqua*rium, so it would be reasonable to conclude that the *aqua*rist is someone who keeps or maintains *aqua*riums.

ACTIVITY 3K
Learn Common Roots

Using a sheet of paper, cover up the definition column for the following list of roots. Next to each root, write down what you think the definition of that root is. You may be familiar with the words using the roots, which will help you to determine what the definition of the root is. Check your responses by uncovering the root definition column.

Table 3.6 Common Roots

Root	Word(s) Using the Root	Root Definition
anthrop	anthropology	man
aqua	aquarium	water
audio	audition	hear
bibl	bibliography	book
bio	biography	life
cap	capture	take
capit	capital	head
cede	precede	to go
chron(o)	chronological	time
cred	credible	believe
cur	current	run
dict	dictate	tell, say
dog	dogma	thought, idea
duc	conduct	lead
equ	equal	equal
fact	factory	make
fid	fidelity	trust
geo	geography	earth
graph	autograph	write
gyn	gynecologist	woman
hemi	hemisphere	half
ject	trajectory	throw
lith	monolith	stone
log, logo, logy	biology	study, thought
man	manual	hand
mit, mis	transmit	send
mort	mortal	death
path	empathy	feeling
peri	periscope	all around
philo	philosophic	love
phobia	xenophobia	fear

Continued on next page.

Root	Word(s) Using the Root	Root Definition
poli	metropolitan	city
rupt	disrupt	break
scop	telescope	see
scrib, sript	prescription	write
sect	section	cut
sen, sent	sentiment	eel
spec, spick, specit	spectacle	look
tract	detract	drag, draw
vac	vacuum, vacant	empty
ver	verify	true
verb	verbose	word
vert	convertible	turn
vis	visible	see
viv	vivid	live

ACTIVITY 3L
Use Roots

Create two words for each of the following roots.

1. spec _____   _____

2. scribe _____   _____

3. sect _____   _____

4. graph _____   _____

5. hemi _____   _____

6. bio _____   _____

7. phobia _____   _____

8. mort _____   _____

9. cede _____   _____

10. aqua _____   _____

ACTIVITY 3M
Identify Roots

Each of the following words contains one or more prefixes or suffixes. Identify the root of each word. Do not include any prefixes or suffixes in the root word you write. The first one is modeled for you.

1. mindfulness   mind _____

2. sinfulness _____

3. absent _____

4. predict _____

5. motorcycle _____

6. ectoderm _____

7. theist _____

8. misanthropist _____

9. biography _____

10. subtract _____

ACTIVITY 3N
Define Words Using Word Parts

Underline the root in each of the following words; then review the list of prefixes and suffixes to write a definition of the word.

1. remit

_____

2. circumscribe

_____

3. credible

_____

4. reject

_____

5. predict

_____

Provide a definition for each of the following words using your knowledge of word parts. You can refer back to all the prefixes, suffixes, and roots that you have learned in this chapter. Try not to use a dictionary. The first one is modeled for you.

Continued on next page.

Example: infidelity
     unfaithful
_____

6. confidential

_____

7. autonomous

_____

8. bibliography

_____

9. posthumous

_____

10. misogynist

_____

11. chronological

_____

_____

12. emit

_____

_____

Specialized Vocabulary

All course subjects have their own unique vocabulary. In order to do your best in your courses, it is important for you to learn the language of your discipline or field of study. Your instructors will use specific words from the discipline and will expect you to understand and use the same vocabulary. Before you move to the next level in your major, you should begin to master the discipline's specialized vocabulary. Your lectures will make more sense, and you will remember more.

    Knowing a discipline's specialized vocabulary will also help you to answer essay questions. For example, read the following paragraph taken from a textbook for a film course. It would be critical for you to know the language of this

specialized vocabulary
words common to specific
disciplines

course in order for you to really understand and remember the information. Circle all of the words that you think would be considered specialized.

> The opening scene of *L'eclisse* demonstrates the extraordinary complexity and power of Antonioni's compositions. The first shot of the film is a close up of a lamp and books with a white object resting on top of the books. Significantly, this composition lacks any apparent human presence. After a few seconds, though, the camera pans right to reveal Ricardo sitting at his desk. The white object on top of the books turns out to be his elbow. His body is bisected by a pyramid sculpture and bordered by a second lamp on the right of the frame.

Source: Prince, Stephen. *Movies and Meaning: An Introduction to Film.* Allyn and Bacon: Boston, 1997, p. 283.

ACTIVITY 3O
Identify Your Courses' Specialized Vocabulary

Identify 10 course-specific words from one or more of your current courses. These should be words that you have been hearing in lectures and seeing in your textbooks for those courses. Also provide their definitions.

1. _____   6. _____
2. _____   7. _____
3. _____   8. _____
4. _____   9. _____
5. _____   10. _____

ACTIVITY 3P
Use Context Clues to Define Specialized Vocabulary

Identify the prefixes, roots, and suffixes of the words in boldfaced type in the following passage from a marketing textbook. Then use the context clues surrounding those words to see if you are able to define them.

> After marketers select a **target market,** they direct company activities toward profitably satisfying that **segment**. Although they must manipulate thousands of **variables** to reach this goal, marketing decision making can be divided into four **strategies**: product, pricing, **distribution,**

Continued on next page.

and **promotion** strategies. The total package forms the **marketing mix**—the blending of the four strategy elements to fit the needs and preferences of a specific target market. Each strategy is a variable in the mix.

Source: Boone and Kurtz. *Contemporary Marketing Wired,* 9th ed. The Dryden Press: Fort Worth, Texas, 1998, p. 24.

1. target market

_____

2. segment

_____

3. variables

_____

4. strategies

_____

5. distribution

_____

6. promotion

_____

7. marketing mix

_____

Exam Terminology

APART FROM KNOWING specialized vocabulary, it is equally important that you understand exam terminology, which includes some unfamiliar terms. You may know all of the content, but if you do not understand what is being asked of you in an exam question, your answer may be wrong. For more assistance with test-taking terminology and skills, refer to the Appendix on page A1 on test-taking strategies.

ACTIVITY 3Q
Learn Exam Terminology

Match the key word on the left with the correct definition on the right to see how much you understand exam terminology. The first one is modeled for you.

____d____   1. illustrate   a. state the meaning of a word or concept

_____   2. outline   b. list and explain each point

_____   3. justify   c. acknowledge the points of similarity

_____   4. compare   d. use a chart, word picture, diagram, or concrete example
                                       of something

_____   5. criticize   e. acknowledge the points of difference

_____   6. contrast   f. make a judgment based on specific criteria

_____   7. summarize   g. look at individual parts and examine each critically

_____   8. define   h. summarize by using a series of headings

_____   9. enumerate   i. tell how to do, or make clear by giving an example

_____   10. explain   j. tell about, give an account of or characteristics of
                                       something

_____   11. describe   k. state your opinion—you can either support or not support
                                       an issue, but support your opinion using examples

_____   12. prove   l. show good reasons for, give evidence to support your
                                       position

_____   13. analyze   m. provide a brief overview of the main points in
                                       paragraph form

_____   14. evaluate   n. establish the truth by providing factual evidence or
                                       logical reasons

Methods to Help You Learn and Remember Vocabulary

THERE ARE METHODS YOU CAN USE TO HELP YOU make connections with unfamiliar words. You can create word maps, use a card review system, and sound it out. Remember that making strong connections will allow you to create pathways for easy access to the meaning of new words. It is also important to understand new words beyond their definitions, like knowing what part of speech a word is, for example, whether it is a noun or a verb. This will help you see how words are used in sentences so that you can to use them correctly. The more connections you make, the more likely you will remember new vocabulary.

Word Maps

word map a visual way to represent a word

A WORD MAP is a visual way to represent a word. When you create a word map using the steps explained here, you should understand its meaning and how to use it. The goal is to begin using your new vocabulary in your everyday life. Suppose you wanted to learn the word *precede;* Figure 3.2 is an example of a word map you could create.

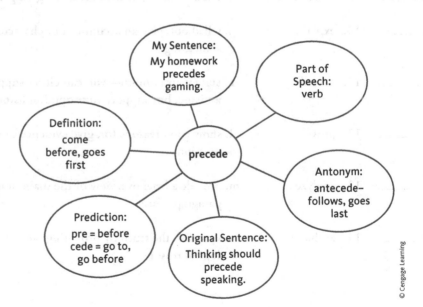

Figure 3.2 Word Map for *Precede*

© Cengage Learning

There are seven steps to creating your own word map:

1. **Circle 1—Vocabulary Word.** Draw a circle in the center of a page or index card, and write the new vocabulary word in the center.

2. **Circle 2—Original Sentence.** Draw another circle anywhere around the center circle, label this *Original Sentence,* and write in it the sentence in which you found the vocabulary word (including the page number, if the word is from a textbook). Connect this circle by a line to the center circle.

3. **Circle 3—Prediction.** Draw another circle, and write in it your prediction of what you think the word means, using context clues and word part analysis. Label this *Prediction,* and connect the circle by a line to the center circle.

4. **Circle 4—Dictionary Definition.** Draw another circle, and write in it the actual definition from a dictionary. Label this *Definition,* and connect the circle by a line to the center circle.

5. **Circle 5—Your Own Sentence.** Draw another circle anywhere, and write in it your own sentence using the vocabulary word. Label this *My Sentence,* and connect the circle by a line to the center circle.

6. **Circle 6—Part of Speech.** Draw another circle, and write in it what part of speech the word is—adjective, noun, verb, or adverb. Label this *Part of Speech,* and connect the circle by a line to the center circle.

7. **Circle 7—Antonym.** Draw one last circle, and write in it an antonym (a word that has the opposite meaning) of the vocabulary word. Label this *Antonym,* and connect the circle by a line to the center circle.

Some students like to use different colors for each component of their word map. Just like road maps, word maps help guide you to understand and remember new vocabulary words.

ACTIVITY 3R
Create Word Maps

Create word maps for the following words after reading each paragraph.

1. Undaunted

Continued on next page.

Andrew had never played hockey. His friend David asked him to go to the local ice arena to play a game. He borrowed equipment, pulled on his old skates, and hit the ice, literally. He fell hard, hurting his hip. **Undaunted,** he picked himself up and headed to the net to score his first goal.

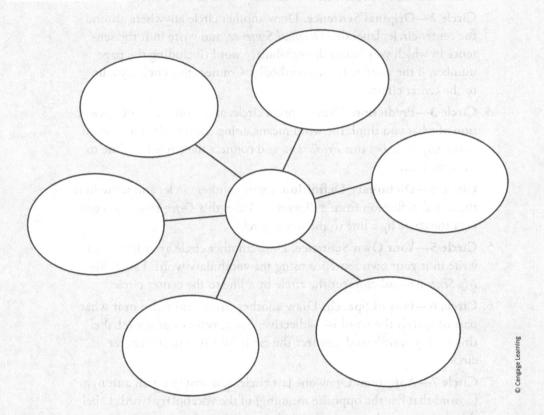

2. Concocted

It was the first time he had spoken publicly since early November, when stories first filtered out that his father and would-be marketer had **concocted** a pay-for-play scheme to sell Cam's services to Mississippi State. This much is fact: Cecil Newton told NCAA investigators it happened, and the NCAA deemed that, according to the information it currently has, Cam Newton knew nothing about the scheme.

Source: Hayes, Matt. "Cam...a lot." *Sporting News.* Week of December 20, 2010, p. 34.

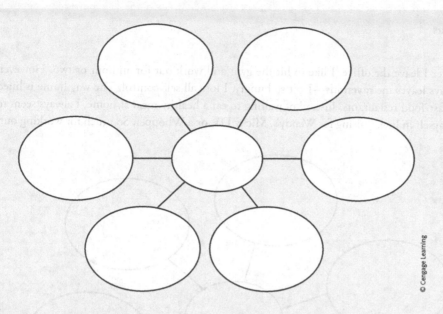

3. Flak

> Her folks, Carole and Michael Middleton, really have the high-pressure job: introducing themselves to the Queen on the big day. They joined a shooting party at Balmoral at Will's invitation, but she wasn't on hand. Carole has already taken **flak**, for apparently chewing gum at William's 2006 graduation from Sandhurst Military Academy (a source contends it was a lozenge).
>
> Source: Westfall, Zuckerman, and Corcoran. "Doing It Her Way." *People,* March 7, 2011, p. 62.

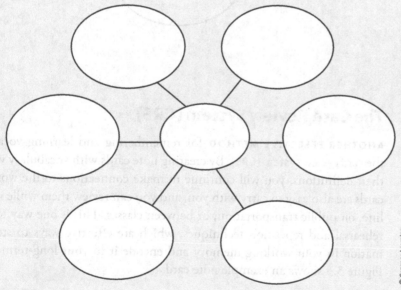

Continued on next page.

4. Ravenous

After I leave the office, I like to hit the gym and work out for an hour or two. However, it always leaves me **ravenous**—I get so hungry, I lose all self-control. The way home is lined with fast-food restaurants. Instead of waiting to eat a healthy meal at home, I always seem to find myself in line, waiting for Wendy's, Micky D's, or a Whopper. So much for working out.

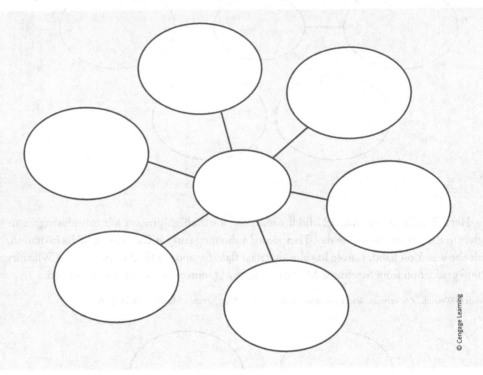

The Card Review System (CRS)

card review system (CRS) a vocabulary-building activity where words and their definitions are written on note cards for easy and frequent review

ANOTHER EFFECTIVE METHOD for remembering and learning vocabulary is the card review system (CRS). By creating note cards with vocabulary words and their definitions, you will continue to make connections to the words. Note cards are also easy to carry with you, and you can review them while waiting in line, on public transportation, or between classes. This is one way to practice rehearsal and repetition techniques, which are effective ways to store information in your working memory and encode it to your long-term memory. Figure 3.3 shows an example note card.

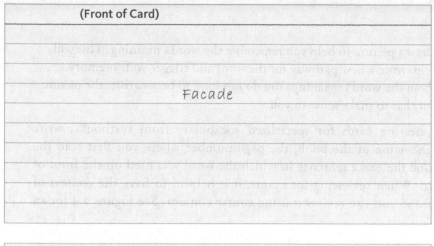

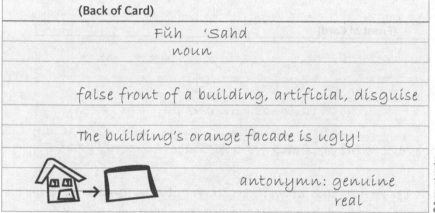

Figure 3.3 Example Note Card for *Facade*

To create a card for the CRS, follow these steps:

1. Write down the vocabulary word on the front of a 3 × 5 index card.

2. Look up the word in a dictionary. On the back of the card, write how the word should be pronounced and identify what part of speech it is (noun, verb, adjective, adverb).

3. Write down the word's definition.

4. Then write a sentence using the word.

5. Write down an antonym of the word (a word that is opposite in meaning).

6. Draw a picture to help you remember the word's meaning. This will help create a new pathway for the word and trigger your memory about the word's meaning. You do not have to be an artist; the picture only has to make sense to you.

When creating cards for specialized vocabulary from textbooks, write down the name of the book, the page number where you first read the word, and the exact sentence in which the word was used on the front of the card. When reviewing for exams, it is helpful to have the context of the word so you can review it using course content. See Figure 3.4 for an example.

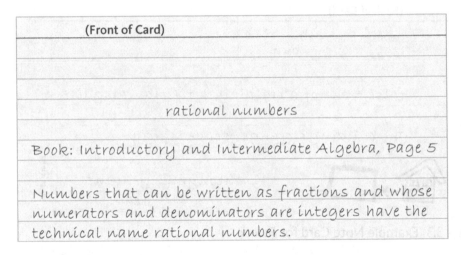

(Front of Card)

rational numbers

Book: Introductory and Intermediate Algebra, Page 5

Numbers that can be written as fractions and whose numerators and denominators are integers have the technical name rational numbers.

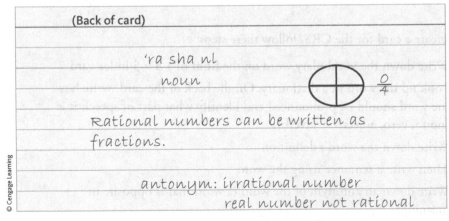

(Back of card)

'ra sha nl

noun

$\frac{0}{4}$

Rational numbers can be written as fractions.

antonym: irrational number

real number not rational

© Cengage Learning

Figure 3.4 Example of a Specialized Vocabulary Note Card for *Rational Numbers*

As you create more and more cards with vocabulary words that you encounter in your reading, organize the words in chronological order (in the order you found them in your textbooks) to help you remember the source and context of each word (if you are organizing your cards by course). Or you can organize your cards alphabetically if that makes more sense for you. Some students find it convenient to punch a hole in the top left-hand corner and place the cards on a ring to keep the cards together and organized.

Remember to carry the cards with you so that you can review them when you have a few free minutes each day, like when you are waiting for a class to begin. Reviewing your cards whenever you have time will help you to quickly learn the words and is a painless and effective way to learn any type of vocabulary. When you can, review the words by saying them out loud. Recording new words and playing them back can be especially useful because you are using several senses (speaking and hearing) to learn them.

ACTIVITY 3S
Use the Card Review System (CRS)

Read the following passage, identify all of the words you are not familiar with, and practice using the CRS by creating a card for each unfamiliar word.

> The same Indians who gave the world quinine also gave it coca, which Indian farmers cultivated in approximately the same area at the foot of the Andes. One of the traditional uses of coca was a ritual antiseptic applied to the body of the patient by a healer. More commonly, the leaves of the coca bush are masticated or made into tea that appeases the body and alleviates pain as well as the discomfort of thirst, hunger, itching, and fatigue.
>
> Source: Weatherford. J. *Indian Givers: How the Indians of the Americas Transformed the World.* New York: Crown Publishers, p. 190.

Sounding It Out

IMPROVING YOUR VOCABULARY includes knowing a word's meaning as well as its pronunciation. A third technique for remembering and learning new words is to sound them out. Sometimes saying a word out loud triggers a memory of having heard the word before. For example, you may see the word *calamari*. If you sound it out, you recall hearing it in a restaurant and eating it and make the connection that it is octopus. Pronouncing a word will help you remember it and will give you the confidence to use the word. Sounding out a word creates a learning pathway in the brain from something unfamiliar (the new word) to something familiar in your brain (words you already know that have similar sounds and related meanings).

If you are unsure about how to pronounce a new word, look it up in a dictionary. Dictionaries usually include pronunciation guides in the front to help you understand what the marks mean. Consider the word *eclectic*. One dictionary has this guide: *e'klek tik*. The mark before *klek* shows that this syllable is emphasized. Sound it out. Some dictionaries also include a pronunciation guide at the bottom of every page. Online dictionaries usually provide an audio pronunciation that can help you confirm exactly how the word is pronounced. For example, if you had never seen and did not know the word *knee*, how would you sound it out? And what about the word *pneumonia*? Or *psychology*?

ACTIVITY 3T
Use Pronunciation Keys

Using the pronunciation key here, sound out the following phonetically spelled words and then write them in the spaces provided, using the correct English spelling. The first one is modeled for you.

ă	pat	k	kick, cat, pique	zh	vision, pleasure, garage
ā	pay	l	lid, needle	ə	about, item, edible, gallop, circus
â	care	m	mum		
ä	father	n	no, sudden	ōō	boot
b	bib	ng	thing	ou	out
ch	church	ŏ	pot	p	pop
d	deed, milled	ō	toe	r	roar
ĕ	pet	ô	caught, paw, for, horrid, hoarse	s	sauce
ē	bee			sh	ship, dish
f	fife, phase, rough	oi	noise	t	tight, stopped
g	gag	ōō	took	th	thin
h	hat	û	urge, term, firm, word, heard	*th*	this
hw	which			ŭ	cut
ĭ	pit	v	valve	ər	butter
ī	pie, by	w	with		
î	pier	y	yes		
j	judge	z	zebra, xylem		

1. tə-mā-tō   tomato _____

2. sī-n-ti-fik _____

3. tō-nāl _____

4. kän-trə-dikt _____

5. nīt kləb _____

6. ter-ə-bəl _____

7. äk-tə-pəs _____

8. mir-i-kəl _____

9. kä-lij _____

10. hi-pə-pä-tə-məs _____

Compare your answers for this activity with other students in your class. Did any of you have different words? Try sounding the words out together again to see if you can agree on the correct word.

✓ COMPREHENSION CHECK

▶ What strategies presented in this chapter create pathways in your brain for learning new vocabulary?

▶ Why is creating many pathways better than creating only one?

PRACTICE WITH A READING PASSAGE

POPULAR READING

Prepare to Read

1. Based on the title, what do you expect the passage to be about?

_____

2. What do you already know about the subject?

_____

Physics Major Has a Name for a Really Big Number

By Steve Chawkins

hitherto up to this time

exuberance enthusiasm

Austin Sendek, a 20-year-old UC Davis student, is trying to get scientists from Boise to Beijing to use the term "hella" to denote the unimaginably huge, seldom-cited quantity of 10 to the 27th power.

immortalize give everlasting fame to

1   When Austin Sendek was growing up in Northern California, he was never allowed to use the regional slang term "hella." Now the 20-year-old physics major at UC Davis uses "hella" often—and he's trying to get scientists from Boise to Beijing to do the same. Sendek, who was forced to use "hecka" as a child, has petitioned an international scientific body to make "hella" the name for the hitherto nameless, unimaginably huge, seldom-cited quantity of 10 to the 27th power—or 1 followed by 27 zeros.

2   It started as a joke, but Sendek's Facebook petition to the Consultative Committee on Units, a subdivision of the Bureau International des Poids et Mesures, has drawn more than 60,000 supporters. Its chances for formal adoption by the global weights-and-measures community are hella dim, but Google was so taken with Sendek's modest proposal that it incorporated "hella" in its online calculator.

3   "As Google goes," Sendek says hopefully, "so goes the world."

4   "Hella," a term many Southern Californians find as irritating as teary-eyed renditions of "I Left My Heart in San Francisco," is used mainly to make adjectives more intense, as in: "This lentil pizza is hella healthful!" It also can convey simple exuberance: "That party at Sunshine's house? Hella!"

5   "Hella" probably derived from "helluva" and, for reasons unknown, morphed into "hella" in the Bay Area before taking wing in the 1990s. In 2001, Gwen Stefani and her band No Doubt—out of Orange County—took it national with their mega-hit "Hella Good."

6   "A lot of people around the U.S. know it comes from Northern California, where there have been so many contributions to science at Davis, Berkeley, Stanford and Lawrence Livermore," Sendek says of "hella." "It would be a really good way to immortalize this part of the state."

© Nathan Morgan Photography

7   As for slang in scientific terminology, at least one linguist says right on. "Anything that takes vernacular speech and treats it well—gives it its props—is fine with me," said Carmen Fought, a professor at Pitzer College in Claremont. In a Facebook posting, a friend of Fought related the regional pride he felt on overhearing a Berkeley teenager use "hella": "I nodded and smiled and thought to myself, 'Keep the torch lit, my young friend.'"

8   For Sendek, the idea sprang from a physics class. "I asked my lab partner how many volts were in this electric field and she said, offhandedly, 'Oh, man—there's hella volts,'" he recalled. "It kind of clicked."

9   At Google, software engineers, who are accustomed to planting "Easter eggs"—hidden delights—in their programs, got wind of "hella" through one of Sendek's friends and installed it in the service's calculator. Now users can find out, with a little finagling, that our $13-trillion national debt, when expressed in hella-dollars, is a pleasingly tiny 1.3 times 10 to the minus 14th. Of course, Google also planted pig Latin and Klingon in its translator function, so its embrace of "hella" may not reflect a rigorous intellectual assessment of the term.

10   For that, the world's scientists turn to the Consultative Committee on Units, an advisory body of the International System of Units—which in French, the language of weights and measures, is more stylishly known as the Systeme Internationale, or SI. Hella's chances at the committee's next meeting, in September, are remote. In an e-mail to colleagues, Ian Mills, the British chemist who serves as the CCU's president, wrote that "it will be received with smiles—but I doubt that it will go further!"

11   The SI is not known for whimsy. It generally chooses prefixes suggested by Greek or Latin. In 1991, the last time prefixes were added to the world's quantitative lexicon, the choices were "zepta" for 10 to the 21st and "zetto" for its tiny cousin in the realm of negative numbers, and "yotta" and "yocto" for 10 to the 24th and 10 to the minus 24th. (Above 1,000, prefixes are selected at every third power: "mega" for 10 to the sixth, "giga" for 10 to the ninth, etc.).

12   "The biggest question is whether the scientific community needs a prefix for 10 to the 27th," said Ben Stein, a spokesman for the National Institute of Standards and Technology. "Zepta" and "yotta" haven't exactly caught fire, he said, and the science is delving ever deeper into the unimaginably small—a realm Sendek's proposal does not address.

13   Sendek, who skis for UC Davis when he's not pounding the drum for large quantities, insists that the term would simplify scientific descriptions. The theoretical diameter of the universe, he points out, is 1.4 hellameters.

14   Still, he acknowledges that getting an official blessing for a term that means a million billion trillion is a long shot, despite headlines around the U.S. and a surge of pro-hella sentiment on his home turf.

15   "There's not a huge chance of it happening," he says, "but maybe if they're having a great day."

Continued on next page.

---

vernacular language particular to a group

pig Latin a humorous form of English where the first consonant or consonant cluster of each word is moved to the end of the word and the "a" sound is added to the end, for example *say* = aysa

Klingon language spoken by characters in the television series *Star Trek*

rigorous harsh, severe

whimsy playfulness

quantitative pertaining to quantity, something you can count

lexicon vocabulary of a particular language, profession, or field of study

delving probe, explore

Check Your Understanding

3. What did college student Austin Sendek petition to do with the term *hella*?

   a. He petitioned for the right to use the term in his classes, even though he was forbidden to use the term as a child.

   b. He petitioned an international scientific body to have the term officially stand for the numerical amount of 10 to the 27th power.

   c. He petitioned an international scientific body to have the term officially stand for the numerical amount of 27,000.

   d. He petitioned an international scientific body to have the term officially used on Facebook.

4. According to the passage, the word *hella*'s chances for formal adoption by the global weights-and-measures community are:

   a. great

   b. possible

   c. likely

   d. not likely

5. What did Google do with the word *hella*?

   a. Google added it to its online calculator.

   b. Google added it to its home page.

   c. Google added it to its translator function.

   d. Google added Klingon to its translator function.

6. What other prefix is added to the world's quantitative lexicon?

   a. mini

   b. hella

   c. mega

   d. gimongous

7. Sendek points out that the theoretical diameter of the universe is:

   a. .14 hellameters

   b. 14 hellameters

   c. 140 hellameters

   d. 1.4 hellameters

8. If adopted, the term *hella* would be a:

    a. suffix

    b. prefix

    c. root

    d. context

9. What slang terms can you think of that have become part of the larger culture and seen in print or heard on television?

_____

10. What slang words can you think of that are still known only to an exclusive group?

_____

11. Can you think of a slang word that would be good to describe a really big number?

_____

12. Do you think the word *hella* will be adopted by the scientific community? Why or why not?

_____

CHAPTER SUMMARY

College students are expected to grow their vocabularies throughout their college careers. To increase your vocabulary, actively use context clues, words around an unfamiliar word, to help you discover a word's meaning. Authors will use different types of context of clues—like punctuation, synonyms, antonyms, definitions, examples, and personal experiences, opinions, and knowledge—to help readers uncover the meaning of unfamiliar words and to make their meaning more clear. Analyze the parts of a word—prefixes, roots, suffixes—so you can see how the parts fit together to create meaning. If context clues and word part analysis do not help you to understand the meaning of a word, consult a dictionary. Every academic discipline has specialized vocabulary, and textbooks will include a rich variety of new words that you will probably be unfamiliar with. Challenge yourself to look up unfamiliar words as you encounter them in your reading material. If you are a biology student, you shouldn't just memorize words such as *endothermic* for a test; you will need that word for a lifetime. Knowledge builds as you progress in your field.

Brain Connections: Self-Assessment

Draw the amount of dendrites you imagine that you have now about vocabulary. Compare your drawing of dendrites now with what you drew at the beginning of this chapter. If the amounts are different, explain why.

Make a firm vocabulary foundation for yourself by committing new vocabulary words to memory by drawing word maps, using the card review system (CRS), and sounding words out. Purposefully create pathways in your brain. Hearing the word and seeing the word creates different pathways in your brain. Remember that the greater number of pathways activated, the better the learning.

✓ COMPREHENSION CHECK

▶ Where in the chapter did you lose concentration or become confused?

▶ If you could ask the authors a question about this chapter, what would you ask?

POST TEST

Part 1: Objective Questions

Match the key terms from the chapter in Column A to their definitions in Column B.

_____   1. context clues

a. a vocabulary-building activity where words and their definitions are written on note cards for easy and frequent review

_____   2. prefix

b. word part attached to the end of a word

_____   3. suffix

c. a visual way to represent a word

_____   4. root

d. using the words around a word to determine meaning

_____   5. specialized vocabulary

e. word part, syllable, or syllables placed at the beginning of a word

_____   6. word map

f. a word's most basic part

_____   7. card review system (CRS)

g. words common to specific disciplines

Match the prefixes, suffixes, and roots from the chapter in Column A to their definitions in Column B.

_____   8. a   a. around

_____   9. terr   b. life

_____   10. circum   c. not, away from

_____   11. hypo   d. people

_____   12. ver   e. true

_____   13. rupt   f. believe

_____   14. post   g. against, opposed to

_____   15. bio   h. land

_____   16. ism   i. after, behind, later

_____   17. mis   j. wrong

_____   18. dem   k. break

_____   19. cred   l. below, under

_____   20. anti   m. system

_____   21. ist   n. state, quality

_____   22. ness   o. one who does, doer, studies, agent

Continued on next page.

23. Which of the following is not a type of context clue?

    a. definition   b. punctuation

    c. duplication   d. example

24. When using the CRS, which of the following should be written on the front of your note card?

    a. part of speech   b. word

    c. definition   d. pronunciation

25. Using a dictionary, create a word map for the word *homonym*.

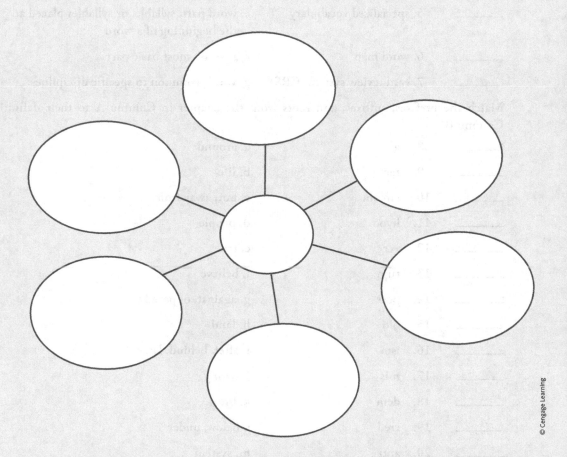

Using the context clues you have learned in this chapter, define the following boldfaced words and identify the type of context clue used.

26. I never met a more **apathetic** group of participants; they were completely indifferent and unresponsive to the needs of those around them.

▶ Define *apathetic*: _____

▶ Type of context clue: _____

27. A **homestead** is the home and adjoining land occupied by a family.

▶ Define *homestead*: _____

▶ Type of context clue: _____

28. I don't think he can be believed; in other words, a witness can lose all **credibility** after being caught in a lie.

▶ Define *credibility*: _____

▶ Type of context clue: _____

29. His argument was **specious** and false, and it will send him home.

▶ Define *specious*: _____

▶ Type of context clue: _____

Match the selected testing terminology in Column A with its definition in Column B.

_____ 30. justify   a. bring out the points of similarity

_____ 31. compare   b. bring out the points of difference

_____ 32. contrast   c. look at individual parts and examine each critically

_____ 33. summarize   d. make clear, make plain, tell how to do, make clear by giving an example

_____ 34. explain   e. show good reasons for, give evidence to support your position

_____ 35. analyze   f. provide a brief overview of the main points

Part 2: Reading Passage   **POPULAR READING**

Prepare to Read

1. Based on the title and heading, what do you expect this passage to be about?

_____

2. What do you already know about the topic?

_____

Continued on next page.

Learn Something New—Your Brain Will Thank You
By Gary Marcus

1   The idea that learning a new skill—say juggling, cooking, or playing guitar—can be like an addiction is no joke.

2   I should know. As a college professor/scientist, who has written about the dynamics of narcotics and self-control, I have spent the last 3 1/2 years all but addicted to learning to play guitar. Despite lacking anything that might remotely resemble musical talent, I find no day is complete without at least a little bit of time on the guitar.

3   Even listening to music can be a little like a drug. A brain imaging study that came out last year proved what many scientists long suspected: Listening to music can lead the brain to release the neurotransmitter dopamine. Dopamine is the brain's universal signal for pleasure, an internal system that tells the brain (sometimes rightly, sometimes wrongly) that it is doing the right thing.

4   Drugs elicit dopamine artificially by fooling the brain, while activities like sex and eating elicit dopamine naturally. Listening to music taps into the dopamine system in part because hearing something new is a signal that the brain is learning something, and we have evolved to enjoy acquiring new information.

5   Shortcuts like drugs, however are fleeting. Although narcotics can elicit dopamine fairly directly, over time it takes a bigger and bigger dose to get the same rush, and can lead people to destroy families, risk their health and even lose their lives.

6   Learning new things is a lot safer, and ultimately a lot more satisfying.

7   There is a myth that children (and for that matter adults) don't really enjoy learning new things, but as every video game maker has realized, the truth is just the opposite. From "Space Invaders" to "Halo," "Grand Theft Auto" and "Zelda," practically every video game is in part about mastering new skills.

8   As video game designers realized long ago, if you can keep a player poised on the knife's edge of conquering new challenges, neither too easy and too hard but square in what the cognitive psychologist Vygotsky called the Zone of Proximal Development, you can keep gamers engaged for hours. As long as we constantly feel challenged but never overwhelmed, we keep coming back for more and constantly sharpen new skills.

9   The trouble, though, with most video games lies in what they teach, which often stays with the game when the game is complete. A game that makes you good at shooting aliens may have little application in the real world.

10   Learning a more lasting new skill—be it playing guitar or learning to speak a foreign language—can equally harness the brain's joy of learning new things, but leave you with something of permanent value, in a way that neither drugs nor video games ever could. It leaves you with a sense of fulfillment, which goes back to what pioneering psychologist Abraham Maslow called "self-actualization."

11   As Aristotle realized, there is a difference between the pleasures of the moment (hedonia), and the satisfaction that comes from constantly developing and living one's life to the fullest (eudaimonia). In recent years, scientists have finally begun to study eudaimonia. Research suggests that the greater sense of purpose and personal growth associated with eudaimonia correlates with lower cortisol levels, better immune function and more efficient sleep.

12   From the strict "Selfish Gene" perspective—in which all that we do is driven by the self-perpetuating interests of our individual genes—hobbies like playing music rarely make sense, especially for mere amateurs. But maybe the art of reinvention and acquiring new skills, even as adults, can give us a sense of a life well-lived.

13   According to a 2009 Gallup Poll, 85% of Americans who don't play a musical instrument wish that they could. Why not start today? As it happens, this week is National Wanna Play Music Week, a perfect time to pick up a new skill that will bring satisfaction throughout life.

14   What stops many people from learning something new is the thought that they are too old, not good enough or just plain busy. If my own experience is any guide, none of these matter much. Taking up an instrument (starting at age 38) has been one of the most challenging but rewarding things I've ever done.

15   So long as your goal is growth rather than stardom, learning something new may just turn out to be one of the most rewarding things you ever do. Your brain will thank you for it.

Source: From "Learn something new - your brain will thank you" by Gary Marcus. Copyright © 2012 by Gary Marcus. Reprinted by permission. http://thechart.blogs.cnn.com/2012/05/10/learn-something-new-your-brain-will-thank-you/

Check Your Understanding

1. Using context clues, define dopamine as it is used in paragraph 3. Then list two activities that produce dopamine.

_____

_____

_____

2. Provide your own definition for the *Zone of Proximal Development*, based on what you read about it in reference to "gamers."

_____

_____

_____

3. Use an Internet search to see what else you can learn about the two Greek words *hedonia* and *eudaimonia*. How are the two words similar and different? How does doing extra investigating on difficult words help your understanding of the reading?

_____

_____

_____

4. Analyze the word parts and provide a definition of the following words:

   ▶ remotely (paragraph 2): _____

   _____

   ▶ universal (paragraph 3): _____

   _____

5. Using context clues, define the word *imaging* in paragraph 3.

   _____

   _____

6. Create a word map on a separate piece of paper for a word unknown to you from the reading passage.

7. Create a CRS card for a word unknown to you from the reading passage.

8. Define *self-actualization*. Then explain how you could use a journal to help you understand what the author means by self-actualization.

   _____

   _____

   _____

BRAIN STRENGTH OPTIONS

From the list below, select one individual activity and one group activity.

1. Find something in a magazine, advertisement, or article that provides a context clue. You may use articles from the Internet. Hint: The clue may be a picture. Remember, it must be a clue to the meaning of a *word* not an explanation of a product in an advertisement. This is an individual activity.

2. Find an example of each type of context clue using sentences from a textbook or making up your own sentences. Make a poster or presentation with the sentences, and label each example accordingly. The poster or presentation will be used in class to enhance other students' learning about context clues. This is a group activity of no more than three people.

3. Write a song using new vocabulary with context clues in the lyrics. Use at least five new-to-you words in the song. Sing the song to the class, and provide written lyrics either on handouts or projected on a screen. The lyrics must be turned in before your performance for your instructor's approval. This is a group activity of no more than three people.

4. Create a graphic novel or cartoon that includes at least five vocabulary words in which the picture or story line contains context clues to the meaning of the words. You may use any type of context clues. This is an individual option.

5. Photocopy five context clues from another textbook, label them with the type of context clue, and submit them to your instructor. No students should have the same excerpts even if they use the same textbook in other courses. This is an individual option.

CHAPTER 4

Locating Stated Main Ideas

"Once you learn to read you will be forever free."

—FREDERICK DOUGLASS

Courtesy of Preston Tindall

WHEN I READ, I go from beginning to end and take notes. I figure out the topic from the headings and subheadings and I fill in the rest as I go along. I typically don't read the summary at the end because it gives it all away. It tells you everything. I like to figure it out as I go.

I usually don't have trouble as I read because I have a lot of background knowledge in the subject matter. If I do have a problem, though, I reread and sometimes ask someone else who knows more about the topic than I do. Vocabulary is possibly the hardest part of reading in my discipline. Sometimes I come across a word in print that I don't understand initially, but then usually when I sound it out, I hear it and then recognize it. I guess I know more words by ear than I do by sight, but that's probably normal.

My current knowledge base helps me as I approach new material. I have a couple of apps on my phone to help me such as *Word of the Day*, *Business Weekly*, and *Wall Street Journal*.

Main Ideas Help You Understand Your Reading

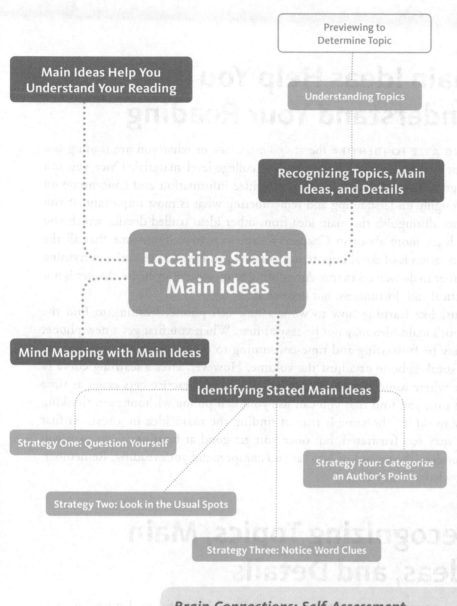

Previewing to Determine Topic

Main Ideas Help You Understand Your Reading

Understanding Topics

Recognizing Topics, Main Ideas, and Details

Locating Stated Main Ideas

Mind Mapping with Main Ideas

Identifying Stated Main Ideas

Strategy One: Question Yourself

Strategy Two: Look in the Usual Spots

Strategy Three: Notice Word Clues

Strategy Four: Categorize an Author's Points

Making Connections

1. What is a theme park? Why is the word *theme* used? Could you use the term *main idea* to describe the park instead of the word *theme*? Explain.

2. Have you ever heard the phrase *main idea*? Describe the context in which you have heard it used.

3. How would you define the term *main idea*?

4. If you had a suggestion for how to improve the packing and shipping procedures in an office where you worked and you were asked to write a memo explaining your suggestion, what would be the main idea of your memo? How would you get your idea across?

5. How do you think an author helps the reader see his or her main idea?

Brain Connections: Self-Assessment

Draw on the brain cell how many dendrites you imagine you have for how much you know about stated main ideas.

Main Ideas Help You Understand Your Reading

stated main idea major points the author makes about the topic directly stated in a sentence

BEING ABLE TO IDENTIFY the stated main idea of what you are reading is a major first step toward understanding college-level material. Once you can recognize the main idea, you can prioritize information and concentrate on thoroughly understanding and remembering what is most important. If you cannot distinguish the main idea from other ideas (called details, which you will learn more about in Chapter 5), you can wrongly assume that all the information is of equal importance and feel you have to memorize everything in order to do well on exams. Attempting to memorize an entire chapter is not practical and, fortunately, not necessary.

Just like learning how to work a new cell phone, learning to find the author's main idea may not be easy at first. When you first get a new phone, it may be frustrating and time-consuming to do simple functions, like use the speakerphone or adjust the volume. However, after a learning curve (a time where something starts out hard and with practice gets easier as time goes on), you find that you can use your cell phone without even thinking how to do it. The same is true of finding the main idea in a text. At first you may feel frustrated, but once you get good at figuring it out, you will experience the reward of "aha" as you comprehend your reading. Remember: Knowledge is power.

Recognizing Topics, Main Ideas, and Details

topic a word or phrase that is the subject of a reading

TO UNDERSTAND WHAT MAIN IDEAS ARE, it is helpful to distinguish them from topics and supporting details. A topic is what a reading is about, the subject of a reading. It can be stated in a word or a phrase. Usually, the title of an article or chapter will offer a hint about what the topic is. For example, the title of this chapter, "Locating Stated Main Ideas," is also its topic, what this chapter is about.

A main idea is the major point the author makes about the topic. A topic and main idea are not the same thing. The main idea is a complete thought, usually in the form of a sentence, and gives more detailed information about the topic. The topic is just a word or phrase.

Topic   Older college students
Main Idea   Students over the age of 40 are entering college in record numbers.

Each main idea is supported by evidence or details called supporting details. Details, which will be discussed in Chapter 5, are more specific than a main idea. They prove, clarify, justify, or support a main idea.

supporting details ideas that prove, clarify, justify, or otherwise support the main idea

All college reading contains topics, main ideas, and details. Topics are the most general ideas, and details are the most specific. To demonstrate the general-to-specific relationship between topics, main ideas, and details, examine the mind map in Figure 4.1. Mind maps are line drawings that show the relationship between ideas. They begin with the most general idea at the top, or in the center, and then visually separate out the topic, main ideas, and supporting details. The mind maps that are at the beginning of each chapter of this textbook demonstrate this as well.

mind maps line drawings that show the relationship between ideas

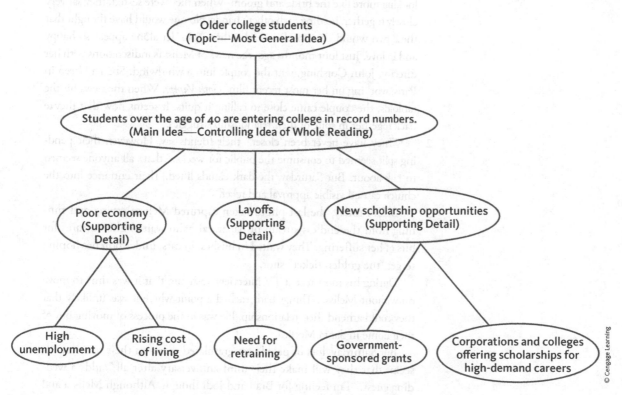

Figure 4.1 Example of a Mind Map for Topic *Older College Students*

Table 4.1 Topics of Textbook Chapters

Textbook	Chapter Topic
earth science	climate change
psychology	addiction
history	Gulf War

Understanding Topics

TOPICS ARE THE general ideas of what you are reading. A chapter title can tell you what the topic is. See Table 4.1 for examples of possible topics of textbook chapters.

However, it is important to remember that a topic is not the main idea. For example, the Gulf War might be the topic in your textbook. *What about* the Gulf War? That is a pretty big topic. The main idea might be reasons for the Gulf War, a comparison of the Gulf War with the war in Vietnam, or the people involved in the Gulf War.

Consider the following passage. It is like something you might find thumbing through a magazine while standing in line at the grocery store:

Melissa and Josh – Together!

1   Last Saturday, almost three years to the date of their own wedding, Melissa and Josh found themselves walking down the aisle again, this time as wedding guests of their dear friends Brad and Jodi. Both of them were beaming, looking more like the bride and groom. When they were seated, they sat very closely together, holding each other's hands. No one would have thought that these two would ever speak to each other again, let alone appear so happy and in love. Just four months ago, the news of Melissa's indiscretions with her director, John Gorshing, sent the couple into a whirlwind. She had been in Paris, working on her most recent film, *Goth Vamps*. When the news hit the tabloids, the couple came close to calling it quits. It seems now that they're back together in spite of their relationship struggles.

2   "They have never been closer," their friends say. However, their pending split seemed to consume the public for weeks…that's all anyone seemed to talk about. But Saturday, the dark clouds lifted. Their entrance into the church caused visible approval and relief.

3   Before today, the last photo taken captured Melissa crying and running from the endless stream of paparazzi, who waited like vultures for bits of her suffering. They waited in bushes, in cars, under porches hoping to get "the golden ticket" shot.

4   During his most recent TV interview, Josh said that it was time to move on without Melissa. Things had reached a point where it was unlikely that they could amend their relationship. He was in the process of moving out of their home in Santa Monica.

5   But Saturday, lots of people congratulated them on their reunion. "It seems that they will make their third anniversary after all," adds a wedding guest. "I'm feeling for Brad and Jodi though. Although Melissa and Josh tried to keep a low profile during the ceremony, all eyes were on

them anyway. But the twosome didn't stay long. They never intended to take attention away from the bride and groom." Not wanting to cause additional commotion they left immediately following the ceremony.

6   Their romantic plans? Some say they were headed to their honeymoon hut on a private island in the Pacific.

This short article is one you could easily read without much effort, and quickly identify the topic. What do you think it is? If you thought the topic is *Melissa and Josh being together,* you would be correct. The title, "Melissa and Josh – Together!," focuses your attention on that topic right away. Many phrases in the passage continue on that topic: "Both of them were beaming, looking more like the bride and groom," and "When they were seated, they sat very closely together, holding each other's hands." What do you think the main idea is? What is the passage focused on? What point is made about their being together? The last sentence in the first paragraph tells you: "It seems now that they're back together in spite of their relationship struggles." Sentences throughout the article explain why their relationship was at risk ("Just four months ago, the news of Melissa's indiscretions with her director, John Gorshing, sent the couple into a whirlwind.") and what the status of their relationship is now ("But Saturday, lots of people congratulated them on their reunion").

Magazines usually have shorter articles with familiar information, and you might be wondering how discussing this type of leisure reading helps with college reading. The reading skills you use to quickly determine the topic from a magazine article can also be used to determine topics of college reading assignments. For both leisure and academic reading, you look at the title and glance at, or skim, the reading to get an idea of content.

> **skim** to scan or look over something quickly

ACTIVITY 4A
Identify the General Topic

When determining topics, it is helpful to compare ideas and decide which ones are general and which are more specific. The more general ideas are likely to be topics. Read the words in each group, and circle the word that is likely to be the topic in each set. The first one is modeled for you.

1. apple	2. dogs	3. Lady Gaga
peach	rottweiler	pop stars
(fruit)	golden lab	Britney Spears
lemon	poodle	Katy Perry

Continued on next page.

4. Bachelor of Arts
   Ph.D.
   college degrees
   Master's

5. Michigan
   states
   Illinois
   Colorado

6. humerus
   phalanges
   sternum
   bones

7. Saab
   Audi
   Mustang
   car

8. Buddhism
   Catholicism
   Sikhism
   religions

9. keyboard
   computer system
   monitor
   hard drive

10. egg salad
    sandwiches
    ham and cheese
    BLT

Think about this activity for a moment. Did you struggle a bit to come up with any of the answers, specifically #6? Did unfamiliar words make it difficult? If you do not know what *phalanges* are, you could have had difficulty identifying the topic of the words in that list. Look up unfamiliar words as you read to help your comprehension.

ACTIVITY 4B
Decide the Topic

For each list, think about what the separate items have in common and decide what the general topic is. The first one is modeled for you.

1. Topic: ____women's shoes____

   flats

   heels

   boots

   clogs

2. Topic: _____

   cancer

   Parkinson's

   HIV/AIDS

   muscular dystrophy

3. Topic: _____

   Golden Gate

   Brooklyn

   Ambassador

   London/Tower

4. Topic: _____

   Facebook

   Google +

   YouTube

   Twitter

5. Topic: _____

  lacrosse

  hockey

  baseball

  soccer

ACTIVITY 4C
Identify Topics in Paragraphs

Read the following passages, and determine what the topic is for each.

1. From a magazine article titled "Grouchily Ever After: It's the Good-Natured Grumbling that Keeps Our Marriage from Crumbling"

  Shared humor is a litmus test of love, a key predictor in whether a couple will stay together. A recently completed study backs me up. In it, University of California, Berkeley, psychologists Patrick Whalen and Robert Levenson looked at stress among long-married couples measured in terms of blood pressure, heart rate, and sweating, and they found that affectionate humor (but not teasing and sarcasm) makes us calmer and more responsive to our partners during anxious times. The upshot: We like them more because they make us feel better. So of course, we'll hang out with them longer. We already intuitively knew this, but it's nice to have science on our side.

Source: Newman, Judith. "Grouchily Ever After: It's the good-natured grumbling that keeps our marriage from crumbling," *Reader's Digest* September, 2010. p. 111.

Topic: _____

2. From a newspaper article titled "Sensible Option"

1 With gasoline prices on the rise, it's important to make sure your vehicle's engine is running effectively and efficiently. April is National Car Care Month and an ideal time to talk with a professional automotive technician to see if repowering your vehicle with a remanufactured/rebuilt engine is the right choice for you.

Continued on next page.

2   A rebuilt engine gets better gas mileage and emits fewer pollutants than worn out engine. If your car or truck is experiencing major engine damage, but is in relatively good shape otherwise, repowering it with a remanufactured/rebuilt engine is sensible financial option that is much more cost effective than purchasing a new or used car.

Source: Carter, Ken. Livonia Observer and Eccentric. *Sensible Option*. Thursday, 2012, April 26, p. A-12.

Topic: _____

3. From a journal article titled "About Faces, in Art and in the Brain"

Almost all creatures, from dogs to canaries, gorillas to penguins, salamanders to crocodiles, kangaroos to spiders, and certainly members of our human family, manifest the same formula for facial composition: a forehead, two eyes, a nose, a mouth, and a chin that are in the same relative positions. Why was nature so consistent in composing faces? Essentially, the arrangement optimizes survival: the eyes located high for a commanding view of the world, the nose turned down to avoid rain, and the mouth situated to ingest food that has been perused by the nose and eyes above it.

perused read, examined in detail

Source: Solso, Robert, L. "About Faces, in Art and in the Brain". *Cerebrum: The Dana Forum on Brain Science,* 6(3), 2004, 8.

Topic: _____

4. From a book titled *Rethinking Homework: Best Practices That Support Diverse Needs*

Homework is a long-standing education tradition that, until recently, has seldom been questioned. The concept of homework has become so ingrained in the U.S. culture that the word *homework* is part of the common vernacular, as exemplified by statements such as these: "Do your homework before taking a trip," "It's obvious they didn't do their homework before they presented their proposal," or "The marriage counselor gave us homework to do." Homework began generations ago when schooling consisted primarily of reading, writing, and arithmetic, and rote learning dominated. Simple tasks of memorization and practice were easy for children to do at home, and the belief was that such mental exercise disciplined the mind. Homework has generally been viewed as a positive practice and accepted without question as part of the student routine. But over the years, homework in U.S. schools has evolved from the once simple tasks of memorizing math facts or writing spelling words to complex projects.

vernacular plain, ordinary language

Source: Vatterott. *Rethinking Homework: Best Practices That Support Diverse Needs*. ASCD, 2009, p. 1.

Topic: _____

5. From a book titled *The Learning Paradigm College*

> Academic success or learning for its own sake in a classroom setting does not offer most students any significant personal rewards. If we separate learning and cognitive development in the classroom from the external rewards tied to it—grades, graduation, college admission—we discover that most high school students find learning in the classroom setting neither motivating nor rewarding and find failure to learn neither unpleasant nor threatening. Most of those students who thrive academically in high school do so through an exercise of will, managing to devote a high level of attention to matters they find intrinsically unrewarding.

Source: Tagg, J. *The Learning Paradigm College.* Anker Publishing Company, Inc., 2003, p. 46.

Topic: _____

Previewing to Determine Topic

Previewing is a strategy that helps you mentally prepare for reading new material. It is skimming with a goal. To preview, you skim the reading assignment, reading the title, introduction, headings, subheadings, visuals, and, if there is one, chapter summary. Once you have done this, you should be able to predict the topic. Based on your more thorough reading of the assignment, you can then determine whether your topic prediction is accurate or needs revising. Previewing will be addressed in more detail in Chapter 9.

Previewing a reading is similar to the process you go through when finding out about a movie. If you were looking for a good matinee, you might check the Web site of your local theater to see the list of movies offered. The title *Taken 2* might not mean anything to you initially, but then you remember statistics about it from television, how it was a box office hit, holding the number one spot for weeks. Intrigued, you investigate further by viewing a movie trailer and reading reviews. From this, you figure out that the topic of *Taken 2* is a action movie about a kidnapping, a sequel to the 2008 hit movie *Taken*. You think you would be interested, so you decide to see it.

As you approach a reading assignment, use the same approach. Anticipating what you are about to get from a movie or a reading helps you ready your brain to receive it. As you take in the movie or reading, your brain actively works toward making meaning and begins to form networks. Previewing and identifying the topic help you connect the new information to what you already know and to see connections within the new information.

previewing looking over your reading material before you thoroughly read it, looking for specific things to mentally prepare yourself to read

Identifying Stated Main Ideas

THE MAIN IDEA OF A READING, paragraph, journal article, or whole textbook chapter is the principal point that an author makes about a topic. It is what the author believes and emphasizes as the central point of his or her writing. Main ideas often are stated directly, or explicitly, in the text. In textbook chapters, you usually find the main idea in a sentence or two in the opening paragraphs. In other types of readings, the stated main idea can generally be found in the first one-third of the reading, though there are no rules of where the main idea can go. The main idea can be found anywhere within a reading. There are various strategies to help you identify stated main ideas in a reading.

Strategy One: Question Yourself

THE FIRST STEP toward understanding an author's main point is to have in mind the question "What is this all about?" before you start reading. Then preview your reading assignment to get an idea of the topic. Remember to look at the title, any headings, visuals, and the chapter summary to get an idea about the content of the reading. Then read the first couple of paragraphs and develop questions based on what you think the reading is about—the topic. Continue reading the reading all the way through, asking yourself questions about what you are reading, like "What is the most obvious, most important, or most repeated point the author makes about the topic?" The answer to this question most likely will be the main idea, and it is useful to highlight it in green (or another "main idea" color that you choose) and then write down the main idea in your own words.

The following short passage shows the questioning strategy put into practice. After reading the title but before reading the passage, ask yourself, "What is this all about? What is the topic?" After reading the passage, ask, "What is the author telling me specifically about the topic? What point is the author making?"

Try answering these questions in your head as you read.

The Development of the Brain Sciences

What is the passage about? What is the topic of the passage? If you said *brain science* or the *study of the brain*, you would be correct. The title tells you right away what the topic is.

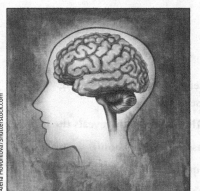

The brain is biology's greatest challenge. Perhaps in a sense it is the greatest challenge for science as a whole, beyond moon landing, the ultimate particles of the physicist and the depths of astronomical space. The engineering of a space shot or of a giant particle accelerator or radio telescope, the mathematics to analyze the results, the vision to design or to ask the questions in the first instance, are all the products of human society—a society itself made possible only when humans had evolved to *be* human—to possess that key feature that distinguishes them from animals, the human brain....The task of this book is to attempt an explanation of the functioning of the brain, in terms which relate its unique properties...to the ground rules that are known to operate in the rest of biology.

Source: Rose, S. *The Conscious Brain*. NY: Vintage Books, 1976, p. 21.

particle accelerator
machine used to propel charged particles at high speed in a beam

1. What important information is presented about the topic?

   Brain science is a tremendous challenge

   Ability to analyze separates humans from other animal

   Task of the book the author discusses is to explain functions of brain as it relates to biology

2. What is the main idea of the passage? Highlight it using a green highlighter.

Tip FROM THE Brain Doctor

One way the brain learns is by making associations. You can use highlighters to make associations and to make the main idea stand out. Use certain highlighter colors for specific purposes, so that each color becomes associated with the purpose, which can make it easier to analyze and organize information. Here is how it works: You could use the green highlighter for all main ideas. From now on, as you are reading your textbooks, you could always highlight every main idea with green, which will not only remind you to look for the main idea, so that you are organizing the information logically in your memory, but will also help you to go back and refer to it. This is a thinking and memory strategy.

✓ COMPREHENSION CHECK

▶ What is the difference between a topic and a main idea? Restate the most important points of what you have read up to this point.

▶ What does not make sense to you up to this point in the chapter?

ACTIVITY 4D
Question Yourself

Before reading the first passage, ready your mind to receive the passage by asking yourself the question "What is this all about?" Then follow these steps:

▶ **Read the title and quickly preview each passage. (This task usually reveals the topic.)**

▶ **Develop questions based on what you think the passage will be about.**

▶ **Read the passage, looking for the answers to your questions.**

▶ **After reading the passage, ask yourself the more specific questions, "What is the most important point the author makes about the topic? What idea is supported by all of the sentences in the passage?" Highlight in green the sentence in the passage that best answers these questions.**

The first two reading passages are from nonfiction essays, the type of reading you might encounter in an English or humanities class. The final two are passages from textbooks. The questioning technique works for any reading.

1. From a book titled *Stealing Buddha's Dinner*

1   So I began stealing food.

2   I would bring a book with me, pretending to be on my way to the basement to do some reading. If Rosa was in the living room she couldn't see the kitchen but could hear everything, so I had to move silently. More often than not she would be working at the dining table, in full view of the kitchen. I would wait for her to go to the bathroom or become otherwise distracted, then hoist myself up onto the counter, open the cupboard, reach for the cookies—I knew exactly where they were, of course—and take away a handful, hiding them behind my book. All done in a matter of seconds. In the summer, I tucked popsicles into the waistband of my shorts, shielding the evidence with another book. I honed my method over the years so that I could slide in and out of the kitchen with nearly entire meals carried between my shorts and T-shirt. I brought my spoils up to my bunk bed, where they could be hidden under the sheets if necessary. If Crissy and Anh were there in a

hoist lift, raise

tattletale mood, I would retreat to Noi's closet. I sat there often, peaceful among her *ao dais*, hand-knitted sweaters, and sensible shoes, reading, writing notes to myself, and eating my contraband.

Source: Nguyen, Bich Minh. *Stealing Buddha's Dinner*. NY: Penguin Books, 2007, p. 41.

2. From an article titled "Take Advantage of the Short-Word Economy of English"

1   When I was a kid, I read everything, including the backs and sides of cereal boxes. I still try to read everything, even on airplanes, killing time not just with novels and newspapers but also product catalogs and the text on airsickness bags. Since I can read a little Spanish, I also enjoy studying the bilingual safety-information cards.

© Eye-Stock/Alamy

2   Now the Spanish equivalent of the phrase "safety information" is "information de seguridad." It takes three Spanish words to translate two English words, twenty-two letters to translate seventeen. That discovery led me to hypothesize that, in general, it takes more language (more letters, more words) to express oneself in Spanish than in English, and that, in some respects, English is the "shorter" or "tighter" language.

hypothesize state a scientific argument or belief

3   My suspicion was reinforced when Barack Obama's supporters chanted one of his campaign catch phrases: "Yes we can." There's a lot of meaning squeezed in those three words and eight letters. Or how about this for economy: "To be or not to be …."

Source: Clark, Roy Peter. "Take advantage of the short-word economy of English," *The Glamour of Grammar: A Guide to the Magic and Mystery of Practical English*. NY: Little, Brown and Co., 2010, p. 49.

3. From an anthropology textbook

Cultural Anthropology and Sociology

1   Cultural anthropology and sociology share an interest in social relations, organization, and behavior. However, important differences between these disciplines arose from the kinds of societies each traditionally studied. Initially sociologists focused on the industrial West; anthropologists, on nonindustrial societies. Different methods of data collection and analysis emerged to deal with those different kinds of societies. To study large-scale, complex nations, sociologists came to rely on questionnaires and other means of gathering masses of

Continued on next page.

quantifiable able to be measured

ethnographers those who study cultures

quantifiable data. For many years, sampling and statistical techniques have been basic to sociology, whereas statistical training has been less common in anthropology (although this is changing as anthropologists increasingly work in modern nations).

2   Traditional ethnographers studied small and nonliterate (without writing) populations and relied on methods appropriate to that context. "Ethnography is a research process in which the anthropologist closely observes, records, and engages in the daily life of another culture—an experience labeled as the fieldwork method—and then writes accounts of this culture, emphasizing descriptive detail" (Marcus and Fischer 1986, p. 18). One key method described in this quote is participant observation—taking part in the events one is observing, describing, and analyzing.

3   In many areas and topics, anthropology and sociology now are converging. As the modern world system grows, sociologists now do research in developing countries and in other places that were once mainly within the anthropological orbit. As industrialization spreads, many anthropologists now work in industrial nations, where they study diverse topics, including rural decline, inner-city life, and the role of the mass media in creating national cultural patterns.

Source: Kottak, Conrad. *Anthropology: Appreciating Human Diversity,* 14th Edition. NY: McGraw-Hill, 2011, p.14.

4. From a political science textbook

The Two Revolutions Compared

utopian ideal, perfect

1   If the American Revolution was a revolution of sober goals, the French Revolution was one of infinite expectations. In the beginning, the French revolutionaries believed everything was possible for the pure of heart. The extremists' goals were utopian, and to realize them they were forced to use extreme means, including terror. Incredibly, America's best-known radical, Thomas Paine, found himself in a French prison during the revolution because his politics were not sufficiently extreme. In the thirteen colonies, most of the revolutionaries were political moderates. In France, moderates were executed or imprisoned.

moderates those avoiding extreme behavior

eradicate eliminate

2   The American Revolution, with its more modest aims, managed to produce the first great example of republican government in the modern age. France had no such luck. Yet the many revolutionary movements of the twentieth century were influenced far more by the French than the American example. It is understandable why the French Revolution—with its desire to eradicate poverty and its compassion for the oppressed—has fired the imagination of revolutionaries everywhere. But if concrete and lasting results are to be achieved, political ends must be realistic; otherwise, impossible dreams can turn into inescapable nightmares.

Source: From MAGSTADT. *Understanding Politics: Ideas, Institutions, and Issues* 9e (p. 451). Copyright © 2011 Cengage Learning.

Strategy Two: Look in the Usual Spots

WHEN AUTHORS WRITE an essay or chapter in a book, they usually use one main idea that is central to the whole work. This kind of main idea is called a thesis. Within the essay or chapter, though, other sections or even single paragraphs can have their own central points. These central points are main ideas for the smaller parts (sections and paragraphs) of a larger work. One way to think of the difference between these types of main ideas is to think of a football game. The main idea of the entire game is *Win the game*. The plays within the game have smaller objectives or main ideas. One play might have the main idea of *Get the first down*. Another play might be *Run out the clock so the other team can't score*. All of the plays in a football game support or help the larger main idea. The same is true in reading; main ideas of sections or single paragraphs help the larger main idea (thesis).

thesis a main idea of an entire work of writing

Authors want to make their ideas clear. To achieve this goal, they usually put stated main ideas in predictable places. The main idea of a paragraph, also called the topic sentence, can be placed at the beginning, middle, or end of a paragraph. The following paragraph from a sociology textbook begins with a topic sentence:

topic sentence the main idea of a paragraph

> On some level culture is a blueprint that guides and, in some cases, even determines behavior. Think about it; for the most part, people do not question the origin of the objects around them, the beliefs they hold, or the words they use to communicate and think about the world " any more than a baby analyzes the atmosphere before it begins to breathe it" (Sumner 1907, p. 76). Much of the time people think and behave as they do simply because it seems natural and they know of no other way.

Source: From FERRANTE. *Seeing Sociology: An Introduction* 1e (pp. 52–53). Copyright © 2011 Cengage Learning.

In this next paragraph, excerpted from the same sociology textbook, the main idea is in the middle of the paragraph:

Passing on Culture

The process by which people create and pass on culture suggests that it is more than a blueprint. Babies enter the world and virtually everything the child experiences—being born, being bathed, being toilet trained, learning to talk, playing, and so on—involves people. The people present in a child's life at any one time—father, mother, grandparents, brothers, sisters, playmates, caregivers, and others—expose the child to their "versions" of culture. In this sense people are carriers and transmitters of culture with a capacity to accept, modify, and reject cultural experiences to which they have been exposed and to selectively pass on those cultural experiences to those in subsequent generations. As a case in point, consider that Christmas is celebrated in the United States as if everyone in the country participates in the festivities. Businesses close on Christmas Eve and Day; public schools give children the week of Christmas off; stores, houses, and streets are decorated as early as October; and television commercials and shows run Christmas themes for a month or more. Yet despite this exposure many people in the United States reject this cultural option, as this reflection from one of my students illustrates: "I grew up in a religion that did not celebrate Christmas or Easter even though we called ourselves Christian. … While growing up I never challenged these practices. I just did what I was told." Yet this same student as an adult decided to celebrate Christmas and other holidays that her family rejected in her youth. "Now that I am older and have a child. … This year was the first year I put up a Christmas tree. I didn't know how to decorate it and I didn't know any Christmas carols but I learned. I decided that I don't want my children growing up the way I did."

Source: From FERRANTE. *Seeing Sociology: An Introduction* 1e (p. 50). Copyright © 2011 Cengage Learning.

In this last paragraph from a communications textbook, the main idea is the last sentence in the paragraph:

hegemony influence or authority over others

I first learned about **hegemony** sitting in my undergraduate introduction to communication course when my instructor, a smart, interesting, and attractive TA named Brent, said the word in passing. My classmate Cindy asked Brent to explain the term. I had never heard the term before, so I was glad when she asked for clarification. Brent asked whether it was easier for him to get students to do an assignment by helping them want to do it or by threatening to beat up the class. While the class was still thinking about where he was headed with this, Brent added: "If we want to do it, then the teacher doesn't have to force us. The teacher doesn't have to do much at all." He then explained that wielding power is easiest when those without power (students, in this case) want those with power (the teachers) to be in control. Teachers give assignments and, because students want to get good grades and to please their teachers, the students do them. Even knowing, as students do, that not all students can get As or succeed in the same way, even knowing that they are able to change the balance of power in the classroom, students will continue to strive to please the teacher. Participating in an imbalanced system that guarantees that not everyone will succeed—that is, students don't want everyone to get As or our As wouldn't mean as much—might seem a little strange; yet, we do the work because we see it as "good for us." This is hegemony; this is domination by consent.

Source: Warren, John T. and Fassett, Deanna L. *Communication: A Critical/Cultural Introduction*. Thousand Oaks, CA: Sage Publications, Inc. 2011, p. 46.

In journal articles, editorials, or short essays consisting of more than one paragraph, an author is likely to put the main idea of the whole piece (thesis) at the beginning, somewhere in the introductory paragraphs or the first third of the writing. Authors also frequently restate the main idea at the end of a reading in the concluding paragraph.

In textbooks, authors normally state the main idea of a chapter in the beginning, during the introduction to the chapter, and usually in very direct language: *In this chapter, we will focus on the two most treatable causes of obesity.* It is also common for textbook authors to restate the main idea of a chapter in their conclusion and again in the chapter summary. However, sometimes main ideas in a chapter or a longer reading are not stated directly. They are called implied main ideas and will be discussed in Chapter 7.

Strategy Three: Notice Word Clues

AUTHORS FREQUENTLY use word clues, words and phrases that signal what logical path the author's ideas are taking. Just as GPS navigation systems in cars guide drivers along unfamiliar roads, word clues provide readers with directions for understanding the main idea and details. They indicate changes in the course of an author's thinking, and by using them, you can follow an author's thought path, no matter how winding it is. For the purpose of understanding the concept of a main idea, word clues are introduced in Activity 4E to help you to recognize that all details support the main idea, either directly or indirectly. More instruction on the concept of word clues and details can be found in Chapter 5.

> word clues words and phrases that signal what logical path the author's ideas are taking

ACTIVITY 4E
Figure Out Word Clues

Three types of word clues are especially helpful when looking for main ideas. Read these three passages and determine what these types of word clues are.

Example 1

Read the following passage. What type of words are being used repeatedly throughout the passage to help you focus on specific ideas? Highlight the main idea in green. Then, circle the words you think draw your attention to certain ideas.

Continued on next page.

Most importantly, reading is a critical life skill. Learning to develop your ability to read will help you to prepare for the world of work. Develop a solid vocabulary and especially your ability to organize large amounts of information. Above all, learn how to effectively locate the main points of all reading materials. In summary, take the time to develop and strengthen your reading skills; reading well has benefits beyond college.

emphasis word clues words and phrases used to signal what is most important in a reading

Word clues that are used to get your attention and indicate which ideas are especially important to remember are referred to as emphasis word clues. **You would be correct if you noticed that the word clues in Example 1 all emphasize an idea. Table 4.2 provides some examples of emphasis word clues. When you see these words, slow down and pay attention; they may signal the main idea.**

Table 4.2 Emphasis Word Clues

most importantly	thus	to reiterate	in summary
therefore	hence	above all	especially

Example 2
Read the following passage. What types of words are being used repeatedly throughout the passage to help you focus on key details? First highlight the main idea in green. Then circle the words you think help support the main idea.

1   I need to sell you on the reasons why avoiding failure is counterproductive. First, let's make a list of people who have made a career out of starting (and thus often failing): Harlan Ellison, Steve Carrell, Oprah Winfrey, Richard Wright, Dr. Oz, George Orwell, Gloria Steinem and the list goes on and on. I didn't have to do any research at all to come up with this list; I just wrote down the names of a bunch of famous and respected successful people.

2   For instance, Oprah has had failed shows, failed projects, failed predictions. She starts something everyday, sometimes a few times a day, and there's a long list of things that haven't worked out. No one keeps track of that list, though, because the market (and our society) has such respect for the work she's done that *has* succeeded. Dr. Oz has lost patients. Mark Cuban has backed failed businesses. The more you do, the more you fail.

3   Second, let's think about the sort of failure we're talking about. Not the failure of disrespect, of the shortcut that shouldn't have been taken or the shoddy work of someone who doesn't care. No, we're talking about the failure of people with good intent, people seeking connection and joy and the ability to make a difference.

4   No one is suggesting that you wing it in your job at the nuclear power plant, or erratically jump from task to task instead of studying. Hard work is going to be here no matter what. For instance, the kind of initiative I'm talking about is difficult because it's important and frightening and new. Finally, if you sign up for the initiative path and continue on it when others fret about "quality" and "predictability," you will ultimately succeed.

Source: Adapted from Godin, Seth. *Poke the Box. Do You Zoom: Amazon*, 2011, pp. 16–17.

erratically with no fixed course

Did you notice clues that support the details by providing examples and key points? Authors also use support word clues to let you know when they are presenting details that support their main idea or argument. Table 4.3 contains a partial list of words and phrases that authors often use to do this. When you come across these clues, or similar ones, pause and ask yourself what larger point the details being discussed support. The larger point is most likely the main idea. Supporting details will be explained further in Chapter 5.

support word clues words and phrases used to signal that what is being presented in the text supports the main idea

Table 4.3 Support Word Clues

for example	one of the reasons	to illustrate the point	first of all	therefore
for instance	a case in point	also	second of all	finally

See that the author used the word *counterproductive* in this sentence:

I need to sell you on the reasons why avoiding failure is counterproductive.

You can use context clues and word part analysis to figure out what this word means. The context clue is that the word has something to do with avoiding failure. The word part analysis will gives us the answer. The prefix *counter-* means "against, opposite to"; the prefix *pro-* means "in favor of or for something"; the root *duct* means "to lead or bring forward"; the suffix *-ive* means "the quality or state of what is before it in the word." *Counterproductive* describes something that is against or opposite to what others are in favor of or want to bring forward.

Using context clues and word part analysis, define the word *predictions*, as used in this sentence from the passage:

Oprah has had failed shows, failed projects, failed predictions.

_____

_____

_____

Continued on next page.

Example 3

Read the following passage. What type of words are being used repeatedly throughout the passage to help you see a contrast in ideas? First highlight the main idea in green. Then, circle the words you think signal a contrast.

Even though both candidates are from the same party, their views are strikingly different in many ways. For example, each one's view regarding taxing is rather diverse. Candidate A believes that tax increases is the only way to cut our nation's deficits and will serve to strengthen the economy, long-term. On the other hand, Candidate B believes that reducing taxes is the only solution to growing the economy. It allows families to spend more and creates more job opportunities. Another difference is their views regarding health care reform. Candidate A challenges the law to provide coverage to all citizens, whereas Candidate B believes that health care is best left up to the decision of individual states. Candidate A believes that education reform begins with teaching our educators and reducing the number of charter schools. Too many schools are not graduating students when most future jobs will require a college education. However, Candidate B enforces standardized testing as the solution and supports the concept of charter schools.

Source: From MAGSTADT. *Understanding Politics: Ideas, Institutions, and Issues* 9e (p. 451). Copyright © 2011 Cengage Learning.

Although authors use many different word clues to help you see a main point more clearly or to understand how details support a main idea, some words and phrases serve both purposes. The words in Table 4.4 are examples of commonly used contrast word clues. Contrast word clues tell you that an author has stopped discussing one point and is moving on to discuss another point. Whenever you encounter these contrast word clues, pay careful attention to the new direction the author is taking; authors often place main ideas or important details right next to these phrases.

contrast word clues words and phrases used to signal when an author has stopped discussing one point and is moving on to a different point

Table 4.4 Contrast Word Clues

however	but	on the other hand	to the contrary
in contrast	conversely	on the contrary	whereas

ACTIVITY 4F
Find the Main Idea

Read the following passage from a political science textbook. Prepare yourself by asking "What is this all about?" As you read, notice the word clues that are purposely written in italics to guide you in this activity. At the end of reading this passage, ask yourself (1) "What is the topic?" and (2) "What is the most important point the author makes about the topic?" Then highlight in green the sentence that best answers the second question— the main idea.

Is the Party Over?

1   Many in the United States say neither major party any longer reflects the realities of U.S. life and society. Others see the parties as evidence of a failed political system. The very idea of party politics or partisanship has sometimes come into conflict with the ideal of democracy. At the same time, *however*, participatory democracy is here to stay. State primary elections, once the exception, have become the rule. States now compete to hold the earliest primaries. (The elections themselves have become a bonanza for some states, attracting revenue and wide media attention.) *Other* states hold party caucuses, where rank-and-file party members choose delegates who later attend state conventions that, in turn, select delegates pledged to support particular candidates at the party's national convention.

2   Such reforms make the average citizen at least feel a part of the party's nominating process and diminish the power of both state party and national party regulars. *But* there is a downside: U.S. presidential campaigns are costly and prolonged; the nomination and election process can last well over a year. (British parliamentary elections often last less than a month and cost a tiny fraction of what U.S. elections cost.) Fund-raising is a full-time endeavor, not only for presidential hopefuls but also for serious candidates in Senate and House races, prompting cynics to remark that U.S. elections have become nonstop events.

3   No other liberal democracy in the world spends so much time and treasure choosing its chief executive. Parties play a role in elections, *but* money plays a far bigger role. Where do candidates turn for financial backing? Next we look at the role of interest groups in contemporary U.S. politics.

Source: From MAGSTADT. *Understanding Politics: Ideas, Institutions, and Issues 9e* (p. 451). Copyright © 2011 Cengage Learning.

Continued on next page.

As you read the title and begin to read the passage, you can quickly tell that the topic is *political parties*. What about them? As you read and look for the answer to your question, you are stopped by the contrast word clue *however*, and then you see your answer: *participatory democracy (use of political systems) is here to stay*, which is the main idea of the passage. The other major points in the passage—primary elections, early primaries, party caucuses, cost, length of elections—are supporting details that show how the whole political process depends on political parties; they support the main idea, *participatory democracy is here to stay*.

1. What additional word clues can you locate in this passage?

   _____

2. What kind of word clues were they?

   _____

3. Did recognizing the word clues help you to understand the passage? If so, how?

   _____

4. Brainstorm what you know about political parties in the United States. How can this help you remember what you just read in the reading passage about political parties?

   _____

   _____

Use the vocabulary strategies you learned in Chapter 3 to help you unlock the meaning of the following words and phrases from the passage. If you cannot figure out the definitions, look the words up in a dictionary. Breezing over these words without fully understanding them can cause you to miss the meaning of this passage. You need to understand these definitions, not just recognize that the words look familiar, in order to see how deeply political parties are integrated into our political systems.

5. partisanship (paragraph 1):

   _____

6. party caucuses (paragraph 1):

   _____

7. delegates (paragraph 1):

   _____

8. national convention (paragraph 1):

   _____

Strategy Four: Categorize an Author's Points

AS YOU USE the strategies of asking questions, looking in the usual spots, and noticing word clues, you will begin to see that not all ideas are created equal—some are more important than others. You can use a fourth strategy, categorization, to help you decide which ideas are the main ideas. You do this by deciding how specific an idea is and looking at how it functions in a reading. General sentences are most likely to be main ideas, while very specific ones are usually the details that support them.

categorization arrange something into categories or classes

ACTIVITY 4G
Identify the General and Specific Sentences

Read each of the following pairs of sentences, and circle the more general statement. The first one is modeled for you.

Example (a.) Poisonous snakes can be found all over the world.
　　　　　 b.   Asian cobras kill more people than any other snake in the world.

1. a.   Self-improvement begins with self-examination.

   b.   Many negative beliefs about body image can contribute to low self-esteem.

2. a.   Dyslexia is a learning disorder that affects reading ability and sometimes math ability.

   b.   People with learning disabilities usually have above-average or at least average intelligence.

3. a.   Food additives enhance the appearance or flavor of foods.

   b.   Yellow food coloring is added to banana ice cream.

4. a.   Moore's law states that the number of transistors that can be placed inexpensively on an integrated circuit doubles every two years.

   b.   Computers will be faster and cheaper as years go by.

5. a.   Most people have brown hair.

   b.   Red heads make up 2% of the U.S. population.

✔ COMPREHENSION CHECK

▶ Describe the four strategies for identifying the main idea. Include as much detail as possible. Repeat them to yourself several times so that you feel comfortable using them in your other courses. Create a mnemonic to help you remember the four strategies.

▶ What strategies do you use to determine the main ideas in your readings? Have you used any of the strategies discussed in this chapter? If so, how effective are they? What works for you?

Tip FROM THE
Brain Doctor

Remember that when you get better at something, you are creating a pathway in the brain, such as the one that you use when you drive a car or ride a bike. Then you can do the activity without having to devote much attention to *how* you do it. Your goal in learning to search for main ideas and details is to create an efficient reading pathway. By the time you finish this course, you will not have to devote the effort to reading in this new fashion that you now have to. You will have a *reading superhighway*. However, building the highway takes time, practice, and effort until it becomes automatic, just like learning another skill or a sport.

Remember that identifying main ideas is not like completing a math problem. In math, 4 times 6 is always 24. In reading, the main idea is not always exact. It is what the author emphasizes as central to his or her point.

The four main idea strategies presented in this chapter make you examine your reading material closely, which is why they work. With practice, you will find yourself reading an article or textbook chapter and automatically understanding the main ideas without purposely applying each strategy as a separate step. It may be like the first time you drove a car with a manual transmission. Your first efforts at trying to use the clutch, stick shift, and accelerator simultaneously would probably have been clumsy. But as you practiced, your movements became more fluid, and eventually you drove without consciously thinking about each step in the process.

ACTIVITY 4H
Practice More with Main Ideas

Read the following passages, and use the four strategies presented in this chapter to highlight the main idea in green. Circle any word clues you find. The first one is modeled for you.

1.   When a tiny word gives you a big headache, it's probably a pronoun. Pronouns are usually small (I, me, he, she, it), but they're among the biggest troublemakers in the language. If you've ever been picked on by the pronoun police, don't despair. You're in good company. Hundreds of years after the first Ophelia cried, "Woe is me," only a pedant would argue that Shakespeare should have written, "Woe is I" or "Woe is unto me." (Never mind that the rules of English grammar weren't

even formalized in Shakespeare's day). The point is that no one is exempt from having his pronouns second-guessed.

Source: O'Conner, Patrick T. *Woe Is I: The Grammarphobe's Guide to Better English in Plain English*. New York: Penguin Books, 2009, p. 1.

You might have thought the first sentence should have been identified as the main idea instead of the second sentence. Either choice is correct as they both say essentially the same thing. After noticing the circled word clue *the point is*, you might ask yourself, "What is the point?" The answer to that question leads you to the main idea, which is that pronouns can be a problem.

2. 1   Pablo Picasso, one of the richest artists in history, liked to talk about his days as a poor man. He especially enjoyed telling the sausage story.

    2   As a struggling artist in Paris in 1902, Picasso shared an attic room with a friend, poet Max Jacob. Their flat was unheated and only had one bed. Jacob worked at a department store by day and claimed the bed at night. Picasso created artwork at night and slept during the day. At times, the two had to burn Picasso's drawings and watercolors to stay warm.

    3   One day when Jacob and Picasso were especially destitute, they bought a sausage from a street stall. Bringing it home with great anticipation, they warmed it and it grew bigger, and bigger and bigger, and then it exploded into nothingness, leaving only a stinky smell.

Source: Jacob, M. and Jacob, M. *What the Great Ate*. Three Rivers Press: New York, 2010, p. 87.

The Ethical Challenges Marketing Faces

3. 1   Marketing does not simply surround us, but envelops us, permeating our lives. Television, radio, newspapers, magazines, billboards, clothes with labels, packaging, the internet, posters, the movies, sky writing—virtually wherever anyone turns there is evidence that it has been touched by some marketer intent on promoting, informing, persuading, and/or selling us something. Marketing is how we get our food, clothes, and the items we use every day. It influences and reflects how we think about the world, though surely marketing is not the sole influence to which we are subjected. In turn, marketing is influenced by what people themselves want and are willing to do. The influences run back and forth. As such, marketing plays a large role in people's lives. It is, in part, how a society defines itself and its treatment of its members.

    2   A person might think that such a pervasive and important activity on which so much time and money are spent would be the object of relatively wide-spread moral agreement. How else has it achieved such significance in people's lives? Why else do people wear clothes with brand names,

Continued on next page.

seek out brand products, watch commercials, and envision a better life in terms of acquiring more (and larger) products?

ambivalent having mixed feelings

3   However, we are very ambivalent when it comes to marketing. It may satisfy us in many ways, but it infuriates us in others. We rely on it, but there are parts of it we dislike intensely. Marketing speaks to a larger drama in our lives of the conflicts between different sets of values and norms – between those related to the role of competition, identity, desire, greed, and fear in our society, but also those involving certainty, dependable quality, consumer-friendly service, trust, and inexpensive products and services. In short, to talk about marketing is to address an ongoing ethical conflict.

Source: From George Brenkert, *Marketing Ethics*. Copyright © 2008 John Wiley and Sons, Inc. Reprinted with permission.

Reading Mathematics

4.   1   Alan Natapoff says that our math learning is not "oral" or "aural" enough, and attempts to compensate for this in his remedial classes by having people speak out loud what they are being told. Another criticism of conventional math teaching is that we are not taught to read mathematics so that we can learn it on our own. Those of us who do not go on in math, it is true, never really learn to study mathematics the way we study other subjects. Studying math as we do it in the lower grades consists of review and drill. Studying on our own involves learning to understand new material without the help of a teacher. To do this effectively, we have to learn to read math, and that is what many of us do not know how to do.

2   One way to begin to read mathematics is to recognize how we read other subjects. Most texts in the humanities and even in the social sciences state important ideas and facts more than once. Therefore, those of us who enjoy reading this kind of material learn to read quickly, even to skim, to get the gist of what is intended, and we do not worry too much about missing something. Chances are, if a fact or an interpretive statement is important, it will be repeated or paraphrased. Topic sentences, paragraphs, the structure of a well-written essay are all signposts to tell the rapid reader where to slow down and even to stop. But reading mathematics is reading for immediate mastery. Things are stated only once and must be well understood before we move on. The process is so different from ordinary, even serious reading that the word "reading" might itself be misapplied.

3   Mathematicians tell me they would not think of tackling a math book without pencil and paper. They try to sketch, if possible, what is being said. They stop and imagine examples that would illustrate the problem at hand. They ask themselves questions and try to answer them. Above all, they move slowly, very slowly, over each part of each statement.

Source: Tobias, Sheila. *Overcoming Math Anxiety*. NY: W.W. Norton & Co., 1993, p. 249.

✓ COMPREHENSION CHECK

▶ Up to this point in the chapter, what is unclear?
▶ What is the difference between a topic and a main idea?

Mind Mapping with Main Ideas

Remember from earlier in this chapter what you learned about mind maps—they are line drawings that show the relationship between ideas, typically beginning with the most general idea at the top or in the center and then visually separating out the topic, main ideas, and supporting details. Read the following passage, and look at the mind map that follows it. When you are trying to sort out ideas, especially in a complicated reading, it helps to draw a mind map to clarify the difference between the topic, main idea, and supporting details. Mind maps let you visualize the relationships between ideas. (Chapter 10 offers more information about mind maps.)

Tip FROM THE Brain Doctor

A mind map is kind of like a neural network in the brain. You are making the pattern of connections visible. When you make mind maps, you are working in a way similar to the way the brain works (making connections between ideas), making it easier for you to learn and remember. Be sure to give this strategy enough effort and attempts so that you can see how helpful it can be to you. Once you are good at it, it will save you time and effort.

1   For some unimaginable reason a handful of my teachers didn't give up on me as a hopeless moron. Mr. Robicheaud, my history teacher, never doubted that I had a brain that was actually functional. He always made me want to rise to any challenge. Same with Ms. Samara, my homeroom teacher. And my English teacher, Mrs. Hawkes, urged me to take her creative writing class. I figured, "What the hell, sounds easy!" But it wasn't—at first, anyway. One day, after class, she took me aside and said, "You know, I always hear you telling funny stories and we can make that your homework assignment." Hey, it sounded better than poetry!

2   So I gave it a try and—amazingly—it turned out to be the first time I ever did homework where I wasn't waiting for Ricky Nelson to come on TV. I actually enjoyed it. I'd spend hours writing a story (usually about something stupid that happened at school), reading it to myself, crossing out things that weren't funny. I'd do four or five drafts, then hand it in. Suddenly, it was fun to go to class and stand up to read my funny story—and, best of all, to get some laughs. I was always grateful to Mrs. Hawkes for that.

3   Another teacher who made a huge impression was Mr. Walsh. For whatever reason, he was always assigned to oversee detention duty in the library. And since I was always in detention, we'd sit together almost every day. Mr. Walsh was one of those guys who would laugh at anything. Tell him the simplest joke and he'd break up. Everything was hilarious to this man. So I'd have new stories for him all the time. One day he said to me, "Why don't you think about going into show business?"

revelation the act of revealing/disclosure

4   This was a revelation. The idea never even occurred to me. I didn't know anybody in show business. The closest thing was an eighth-grade teacher named Mr. Duncan, who did magic tricks at student assemblies. And that was unbelievable! Someone we knew who could actually entertain people! When you grow up in a small town like Andover, show business is the furthest thing from being a career option.

Source: Leno, Jay. *Leading with My Chin*. New York: HarperCollins, 1996, pp. 55–56.

Figure 4.2 shows how the ideas in this passage are related to each other: The topic (a phrase) is at the top, the main idea (a complete sentence) is immediately below it, and the details that support the main idea branch off it. The further an idea is from the topic and main idea, the less important it is to the overall meaning of the passage. These details far away from the topic and main idea are minor.

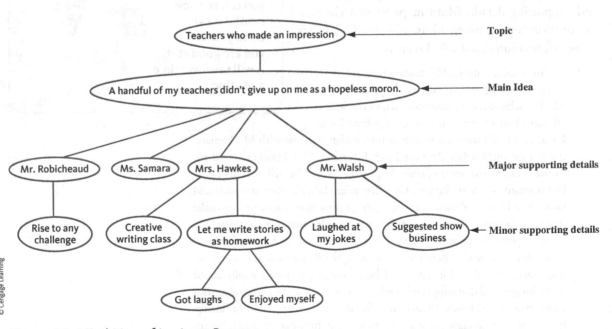

Figure 4.2 Mind Map of Jay Leno Passage

ACTIVITY 41
Create Your Own Mind Maps

Read the following passages and create a mind map for each. State the topic in a word or phrase at the top of your map. Draw a vertical line down from the topic and write the main idea in a sentence. Then draw lines extending away from the main idea statement and add details at the end of each line. Apply the main idea strategies you have been using in this chapter: 1) Question yourself, 2) Look in the usual spots, 3) Notice word clues, and 4) Categorize.

A common mistake is slicing sandwich meats thick instead of thin. A few thick slices of meat stacked on a sandwich will have far less volume and therefore look like less than an equal amount of thinly sliced meat. See Figure 4.3. Also, thicker cut meats tend to be chewier, especially when cold. Thinly sliced sandwich meats make the sandwich portion appear larger, are more tender, and are generally easier to eat.

Figure 4.3 Meat Fillings
Thinly sliced meat gives sandwich more volume than thick slices of meat.

Source: McCreal, Michael. *Culinary Art Principles and Applications.* American Technical Publishers, Inc., 2012, p. 393.

Continued on next page.

Don't Catch Me If You Can

1   Might we have better luck avoiding colds in the first place? My friend Cathy carries those little bottles of Purell everywhere she goes. She has them in her purse and her computer bag, in her desk drawers and her car. She uses them after she shakes hands with anyone or goes into a store, particularly a pharmacy. She never opens a door with her bare hands but uses her sweater or a shirt. She flushes toilets with her foot, presses elevator buttons with her elbow. If she is seated in a plane next to someone with a cough she says that "It totally freaks me out. I do everything I can to move. Even if it means creating a story like, I have cancer and can't be near a sick person. Yes, I did use that one," she admits. "If I absolutely have to stay there, I try not to talk and keep my face averted. Afterwards, I take vitamin C."

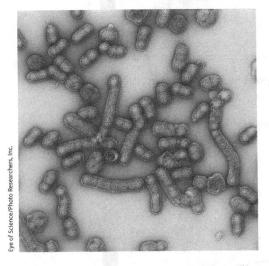

Eye of Science/Photo Researchers, Inc.

2   Cathy's pediatrician father put the fear of germs in her. At parties, he instructed his children which guests to avoid kissing and which to stay away from altogether. Her mother's constant refrain was "Keep your fingers away from your face. Don't put your fingers in your mouth!" "As a result, I pretty much see the world with an overlay of little floating germs," she says, "and my goal is to avoid them in every way possible." In the past 12 years, Cathy hasn't had a single cold. Germ prevention is possible, but at what cost? "Before I go on vacation, I won't go anywhere or see anyone except my fiancé," she says. "And I definitely won't go to a movie theater or any other place where there are lots of people or, God forbid, kids. I love kids, but they make me really nervous on the germ front. My cousins have gotten used to my asking if they are sick before I commit to coming over to their house; they completely understand now when I back out."

barbaric wild, primitive

aversion desire to avoid something

3   Cathy is in famously good company. Marcel Proust, Marlene Dietrich, and Howard Hughes were germaphobes. Jessica Alba of *Fantastic Four* fame reportedly carries a UV light to zap germs in her hotel rooms. Donald Trump considers shaking hands "barbaric"—an aversion that got him in hot water with the unwashed masses during the 2000 presidential campaign. "People always come up to me wanting to shake hands and I never know where that hand has been," he writes in his blog. "I say let's copy the wonderful Japanese custom of bowing. It's respectful and it's sanitary." Trump's campaign reportedly handed out half-ounce bottles of hand sanitizer to his constituents (tagged with his website address). The comedian Howie Mandel, who once wowed his audiences by blowing up a surgical glove using only his nose, fist-bumps acquaintances instead of shaking hands to avoid germs. The jacket of his new book, *Don't Touch Me*, shows Mandel inside a man-size plastic bubble; his website sells blue wristbands reading "Skip the Shake." Word has it that he even built a special guesthouse that he could retreat to when his kids got sick.

4   Our society as a whole is far more germ conscious than it was, say 10 or 15 years ago, says Harley Rotbart. "This is in part because we're inundated with news stories about health and infection. The types of stories that a decade ago might not have made the newspaper are now breaking news on all of the cable channels. When there are five cases of peanut butter associated with salmonella or two cases of *E. coli* linked with spinach, it becomes a huge national story and people wonder whether they should be eating spinach or peanut butter," says Rotbart. "But," he adds, "there's also clearly a sales job going on here." The enterprising germ-fighting industry exploits our fears, flooding the market with antimicrobial lotions, soaps, shampoos, toothpaste, perfume, air fresheners. You can buy hundreds of products infused with the antimicrobial chemical triclosan (the antibiotic present in most antibacterial soaps), including pencils and protractors for children. This is a complete scam, says Rotbart. "How can anyone believe that an antibiotic embedded in plastic can kill a bug that lands on the surface of an object? I understand the economics of it but not the biology. A plain protractor costs $0.35 and one impregnated with antibiotic costs $1.50. But how does an antimicrobial in a protractor or a hairbrush or a toilet seat find the bacteria it's supposed to destroy? This is the sort of nonsense that preys on the paranoia of people prone to paranoia."

5   The kind of hypervigilance that has come to characterize our culture may have some subtle psychological effects. Rotbart doesn't worry too much about its impact on children—he believes they're resilient and won't succumb to obsession over cleanliness. But at least one study suggests that even educated adults are affected by the germ hype in unexpected ways, making us overreact to something as simple as a sneeze. The study, led by Spike Wing Sing Lee of the University of Michigan, suggests that awareness of the danger of infectious disease heightens our perception of risks posed by other, unrelated hazards. Last May, just when swine flu was beginning to emerge as a serious threat, Lee and his colleagues positioned an actor in a busy building on the Michigan campus. As students passed, the actor occasionally sneezed loudly. Then the psychologists waylaid the students and interviewed them. Those who had witnessed the sneeze perceived a greater risk not only of getting sick but also of risk utterly unrelated to germs—such as having a heart attack before age 50 or dying in an accident or as a result of a violent crime. When asked about their views on this country's health-care system (was it a disaster or working pretty much okay?), the sneeze perceivers tended to pan the current system and express the view that resources should be shifted from the creation of green jobs to vaccine development.

6   In other words, in an atmosphere of hypervigilance, a simple sneeze can trigger sweeping fears and even color people's views on something as abstract as government allocation of resources.

7   It's hard not to be conscious of germs when there's a hand sanitizer dispenser outside every classroom and in every public bathroom," says Rotbart. "We're a Purell-inundated society." In Rotbart's view, this is not necessarily a bad thing. For starters, it means that people who are sick are generally more aware that they may be contagious and thus take more precautions. "More often these days, you hear people with a cold saying, 'Hey, you

Continued on next page.

---

conscious aware, noticing

enterprising readiness to act upon, assertive, ambitious

protractor an instrument for drawing angles

paranoia tendency toward irrational suspiciousness, distrustfulness

hypervigilance heightened awareness

resilient having a tendency to recover from or adjust to easily

perceivers those who are aware or who observe

allocation distribution

precautions care taken in advance

don't want to shake my hand; let's do an elbow bump instead.' It's not necessarily that the potential recipients of a bug are more paranoid, it's that the 'donors' have become more conscientious."

conscientious
careful

Source: From AH-CHOO! by *Jennifer Ackerman*. Copyright © 2010 by Jennifer Ackerman. Reprinted by permission of Grand Central Publishing. All rights reserved.

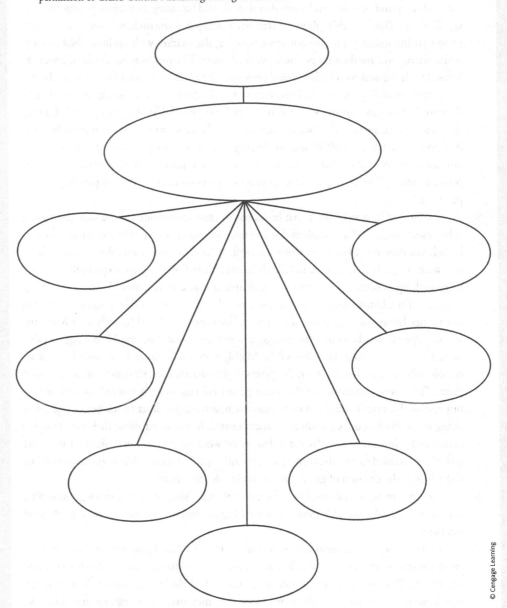

PRACTICE WITH A READING PASSAGE

Prepare to Read

1. Based on the title, what do you expect the following passage to be about?

_____

2. What do you know about the topic already? Are you comfortable with spiders and wasps?

_____

3. Develop a question, using the title of this passage, to ask yourself before you read.

_____

4. As you read the passage, circle any word clues and highlight the main idea in green.

From "The Spider and the Wasp"
By Alexander Petrunkevitch

1   In the adult stage the [pepsis] wasp lives only a few months. The female produces but a few eggs, one at a time at intervals of two or three days. For each egg the mother must provide one adult tarantula, alive but paralyzed. The mother wasp attaches the egg to the paralyzed spider's abdomen. Upon hatching from the egg, the larva is many hundreds of times smaller than its living but helpless victim. It eats no other food and drinks no water. By the time it has finished its single gargantuan meal and become ready for wasphood, nothing remains of the tarantula but its indigestible chitinous skeleton.

chitinous
hard, protective

2   The mother wasp goes tarantula hunting when the egg in her ovary is almost ready to be laid. Flying low over the ground late on a sunny afternoon, the wasp looks for its victim or for the mouth of a tarantula burrow, a round hole edged by a bit of silk. The sex of the spider makes no difference, but the mother is highly discriminating as to species. Each species of pepsis requires a certain species of tarantula, and the wasp will not attack the wrong species. In a cage with a tarantula, which is not its normal prey, the wasp avoids the spider and is usually killed by it at night.

MARK MOFFETT/MINDEN PICTURES/National Geographic Stock

Continued on next page.

3   Yet when a wasp finds the correct species, it is the other way about. To identify the species the wasp apparently must explore the spider with her antennae. The tarantula shows an amazing tolerance to this exploration. The wasp crawls under it and walks over it without evoking any hostile response. The molestation is so great and persistent that the tarantula often rises on all eight legs, as if it were on stilts. It may stand this way for several minutes. Meanwhile the wasp, having satisfied itself that the victim is of the right species, moves off a few inches to dig the spider's grave. Working vigorously with legs and jaws, it excavates—like a machine—a hole 8 to 10 inches deep with a diameter slightly larger than the spider's girth. Now and again the wasp pops out of the hole to make sure that the spider is still there.

4   When the grave is finished, the wasp returns to the tarantula to complete her ghastly enterprise. First she feels it all over once more with her antennae. Then her behavior becomes more aggressive. She bends her abdomen, protruding her sting, and searches for the soft membrane at the point where the spider's legs join its body—the only spot where she can penetrate the horny skeleton. From time to time, as the exasperated spider slowly shifts ground, the wasp turns on her back and slides along with the aid of her wings, trying to get under the tarantula for a shot at the vital spot. During all this maneuvering, which can last for several minutes, the tarantula makes no move to save itself. Finally the wasp corners it against some obstruction and grasps one of its legs in her powerful jaws. Now at last the harassed spider tries a desperate but vain defense. The two contestants roll over and over on the ground. It is a terrifying sight and the outcome is always the same. The wasp finally manages to thrust her sting into the soft spot and holds it there for a few seconds while she pumps in the poison. Almost immediately the tarantula falls paralyzed on its back. Its legs stop twitching; its heart stops beating. Yet it is not dead, as is shown by the fact that if taken from the wasp it can be restored to some sensitivity by being kept in a moist chamber for several months.

5   After paralyzing the tarantula, the wasp cleans herself by dragging her body around the ground and rubbing her feet, sucks the drop of blood oozing from the wound in the spider's abdomen, then grabs a leg of the flabby, helpless animal in her jaws and drags it down to the bottom of the grave. She stays there for many minutes, sometimes several hours, and what she does all that time in the dark we do not know. Eventually she lays her egg and attaches it to the side of the spider's abdomen with a sticky secretion. Then she emerges, fills the grave with soil carried bit by bit in her jaws, and finally tramples the ground all around to hide any trace of the grave from prowlers. Then she flies away, leaving her descendant safely started in life.

6   In all this the behavior of the wasp evidently is qualitatively different from that of the spider. The wasp acts like an intelligent animal. This is not to say that instinct plays no part or that she reasons as man does. But her actions are to the point; they are not automatic and can be modified to fit the situation. We do not

know for certain how she identifies the tarantula—probably it is by some olfactory or chemo-tactile sense—but she does it purposefully and does not blindly tackle a wrong species.

7　　On the other hand, the tarantula's behavior shows only confusion. Evidently the wasp's pawing gives it no pleasure, for it tries to move away. That the wasp is not stimulating sexual stimulation is certain because male and female tarantulas react in the same way to its advances. That the spider is not anesthetized by some odorless secretion is easily shown by blowing lightly at the tarantula and making it jump suddenly. What, then, makes the tarantula behave as stupidly as it does?

8　　No clear, simple answer is available. Possibly the stimulation by the wasp's antennae is masked by a heavier pressure on the spider's body so that it reacts when prodded by a pencil. But the explanation may be much more complex. Initiative in attack is not the nature of tarantulas; most species fight only when cornered so that escape is impossible. Their inherited patterns of behavior apparently prompt them to avoid problems rather than attack them. For example, spiders always weave their webs in three dimensions, and when a spider finds that there is insufficient space to attach certain threads in the third dimension, it leaves the place and seeks another, instead of finishing the web in a single plane. This urge to escape seems to arise under all circumstances, in all phases of life, and to take the place of reasoning. For a spider to change the pattern of its web is as impossible as for an inexperienced man to build a bridge across a chasm obstructing his way.

chasm a deep, wide gap

9　　In a way the instinctive urge to escape is not only easier but often more efficient than reasoning. The tarantula does exactly what is most efficient in all cases except in an encounter with a ruthless and determined attacker dependent for the existence of her own species on killing as many tarantulas as she can lay eggs. Perhaps in this case the spider follows its usual pattern of trying to escape, instead of seizing and killing the wasp, because it is not aware of its danger. In any case, the survival of the tarantula species as a whole is protected by the fact that the spider is much more fertile than the wasp.

Continued on next page.

Check Your Understanding

5. Use context clues and word part analysis to define the following words from the passage.

- discriminating (paragraph 2): _____

- molestation (paragraph 3): _____

- encounter (paragraph 9): _____

6. Were you able to answer the question you created in question #3? Provide the answer to your question.

_____

7. What is the topic?

_____

8. What is the main idea being supported by all of the sentences in the reading?

_____

9. If you could rewrite the title of the passage, what would your title be?

_____

10. What does the tarantula do when the wasp explores it?

_____

11. How does the wasp attack the tarantula?

_____

12. Why doesn't the wasp kill the tarantula completely?

_____

13. What answer does the author give for the tarantula's unusually compliant behavior?

_____

14. Did you enjoy the reading? Why or why not?

_____

15. What strategies did you use to help you concentrate on the reading?

_____

Circle the best answer to the following multiple-choice questions.

16. The wasp has to provide her egg with:

    a. a fresh, three-dimensional web.

    b. a live tarantula.

    c. a male tarantula.

    d. an egg from the tarantula's nest.

17. Which of the following statements is true?

    a. The wasp seeks a male tarantula to attach its egg to.

    b. Each species of pepsis requires a certain species of tarantula, and the wasp will not attack the wrong species.

    c. Male and female tarantulas react differently to the female wasp.

    d. Only male tarantulas are suitable for the female wasps' eggs.

18. What happens after the wasp digs a grave?

    a. The wasp grasps one of the spider's legs in her jaws.

    b. The spider fights the wasp.

    c. The tarantula becomes paralyzed.

    d. The wasp feels all over the spider once more with her antennae.

19. What happens after the wasp drops the spider into the grave?

    a. She stays in the grave for a while.

    b. She leaves to lay her egg.

    c. She kills the spider.

    d. She buries the spider.

20. How does the tarantula species survive?

    a. The wasps usually cannot find the right species very easily.

    b. The tarantula can run faster than the wasp can fly.

    c. The wasps have more babies than the tarantulas.

    d. The tarantulas have more babies than the wasps.

Chapter Summary

Main ideas are the author's important points, so figuring them out can lead to good comprehension and easier studying. The first step to understanding main ideas is realizing that main ideas and topics are not the same thing. Topics are subjects that can usually be described in one or two words. Main ideas are the points authors make about topics. Previewing helps you recognize the topic and begin to predict a pattern. Then ask yourself some questions. As you read, look for the answers to your questions by looking in the usual spots and by recognizing word clues when you see them. Also, categorize the author's points as you read them. Some are more general, which could be the main idea, and others are more specific, which are probably details. Mind mapping, line drawings that show the relationship between ideas, help you to visualize the general-to-specific relationships between topic, main idea, and details an author can use in a passage.

Brain Connections: Self-Assessment

Draw the amount of dendrites you imagine that you have now about stated main ideas. Compare your drawing of dendrites now with what you drew at the beginning of this chapter. If the amounts are different, explain why.

✔ COMPREHENSION CHECK

▶ Where in the chapter did you lose concentration or become confused?

▶ If you could ask the authors a question about this chapter, what would you ask?

POST TEST

Part 1: Objective Questions

Match the key terms from the chapter in Column A to their definitions in Column B.

_____   1. topic   a. to scan or look over something quickly

_____   2. stated main idea   b. words and phrases used to signal when an author has stopped discussing one point and is moving on to a different point

_____   3. thesis   c. looking over your reading material before you thoroughly read it, looking for specific things to mentally prepare yourself to read

_____   4. word clues   d. a word or phrase that is the subject of a reading

_____   5. topic sentence   e. line drawings that show the relationship between ideas

_____   6. contrast word clues   f. major points the author makes about the topic directly stated in a sentence

_____   7. emphasis word clues   g. ideas that prove, clarify, justify, or otherwise support the main idea

_____   8. support word clues   h. arrange something in categories or classes

_____   9. supporting details   i. the main idea of a paragraph

_____   10. mind maps   j. words and phrases that signal what logical path the author's ideas are taking

_____   11. skim   k. words and phrases used to signal that what is being presented in the text supports the main idea

_____   12. previewing   l. words and phrases used to signal what is most important in a reading

_____   13. categorization   m. a main idea of an entire work of writing

Indicate whether the following statements are true (T) or false (F).

_____   14. If several people read a textbook chapter, they should all identify the same main idea.

_____   15. To identify the main idea of a reading, all you have to do it look for word clues.

Continued on next page.

Part 2. Reading Passage

Prepare to Read

1. Based on the title, what do you expect the following passage to be about?

_____

2. What do you already know about the subject?

_____

3. Develop a question from the title. As you read the passage, try to answer that question.

_____

The "Thrill" of Theft
By Jerry Adler with Julie Scelfo, Gretel C. Kovach,
Karen Springen, and Tara Weingarten

1   If all you've ever done is pay for stuff, you'd never know how it felt. It was thrilling, she says, a heart-pounding rush of greed and fear as she stuffed the bathing suits into her bag, two identical sets of tops and bottoms, because she was going to a concert the next night with a friend and they wanted to wear the same thing. She was in eighth grade then, and she'd been stealing for a year, partly for the fun of getting away with something, but also partly because no way was she going to spend $70 on one of those suits. "I think, 'I could be spending my money on this, but I'm getting it for free'," she told *Newsweek.* "Then I get to spend my money on things my parents don't know I'm buying—like beer, drugs and cigarettes." But there's always danger. "Your heart starts to race, and all you can think about is getting out of the store. It's like, 'I've taken what I need to take, let's get out of here.' But I get really excited because I'm thinking, 'I already got a bunch of stuff in my bag and I can get a whole lot more'." She moved on to the rack of Mudd jeans. For some people, shoplifting is a thrill.

2   Some 800,000 times a day, this tableau of temptation, fear and exhilaration plays out in the humdrum aisles of department stores and supermarkets, frequently over such unlikely objects of avarice as batteries and souvenir knickknacks. It's a window into our desires: retailers like Brandy Samson, who manages a jewelry and accessories store in the Sherman Oaks (Calif.) Fashion Square, uses shoplifting as a guide to taste. "We know what's hot among teens by seeing what they steal," she says. It can be a cry for help on the part of troubled celebrities like Bess Myerson, Hedy Lamarr and maybe Winona Ryder, who was arrested in December on felony charges of taking $4,760 in clothes from the Beverly Hills branch of Saks Fifth

avarice greed

Avenue. She pleaded not guilty and was freed on bail, although her fans continue to protest the injustice of the arrest with free winona T shirts. And it's an economic **bellweather** thrills and temptation won out over fear in 2000 to the tune of some $13 billion, according to Checkpoint, a top retail-security company (which notes that employees steal the most by far). And in the current recession, the company is predicting a $1 billion jump in shoplifting losses, with more people out of a job, and fewer salesclerks to watch them as they nervously sidle down the aisles heaped with DVDs, lingerie and balsamic vinegar.

bellweather indicator

3   Shoplifting was the first distinctly modern crime, a product of late-19th-century mass merchandising. "Consumer culture manipulates the senses of the shoppers, seduces them, weakening their ability to resist temptation," says Lisa Tiersten, a cultural historian at Barnard College in New York. Department stores, bursting with fans and muffs and bustles stocked conveniently out of sight of the distant shop clerks, proved an irresistible lure to otherwise respectable housewives. The spectacle of middle-class women stuffing their corsets with swag was so unnerving to the Victorian sensibility that in 1890 a new mental disorder was **postulated** to explain it, "kleptomania." Shrinks no longer believe, as they once did, that it originates in the uterus, but kleptomania is still a recognized condition, although rarely diagnosed these days. By far the largest category of habitual shoplifters, experts say, are suffering from nothing more exotic than addictive-compulsive disorder; the rest include professional criminals, drug addicts supporting their habits—and thrill seekers, who are often high-school kids. By some estimates, a quarter of all shoplifters are teenagers.

postulated offered as a theory, claimed

4   She made only one mistake that day, but it was a costly one: she began her spree by taking an empty shopping bag from another store, to hold the items she planned to steal. A clerk at the first store watched her go and alerted the manager of the boutique where she was headed. As she left with the bathing suits, the jeans, and a couple of beaded T shirts stashed in her bag, she was stopped by a clerk. "They arrested me and walked me through the mall, they took me to the juvenile center and called my parents. I got grounded for probably like a month and a half, but it was the first month of summer vacation so it was really bad." She was not prosecuted, although she had to write a 25-page report on how shoplifting affects the economy.

5   A few decades after the invention of kleptomania, a 6-year-old named Gretchen Grimm began what may be one of the longest criminal careers in history, swiping a lipstick for her mother at a Woolworth's. The only daughter in a family with seven older sons, Grimm felt overlooked and began stealing, she believes, to win her mother's attention and affection. It ended last year when Grimm, at the age of 83, finally kicked the habit with the help of psychotherapy and the anti-anxiety drug Paxil. Over the intervening years, while she raised five children and worked as a nurse at the University of Iowa, she stole, by her own account, "clothes, jewelry, toilet paper, towels, pencils, pieces of stone—everything." At the moment of theft,

Continued on next page.

she says, "you feel wonderful, elated, slick and cool and cunning." But immediately afterward, guilt would set in, and often she would actually sneak her loot back into the stores.

condoned pardoned

6   Grimm's story illustrates two important truths about shoplifting. The first is the powerful ego boost it can provide, especially to insecure young people. In that context, experts say, while stealing can never be condoned, a single episode—especially as part of a group—is not necessarily a cause for parents to panic. "As an isolated thing, most 12-year-old girls with a peppery personality do it once," says child psychiatrist Elizabeth Berger, author of *Raising Children With Character*. "It shows you're a real badass."

7   The other lesson is that a crime that can be perpetrated with equal ease by first graders and old ladies is pretty hard to stop. Grimm had only one serious arrest, and hid her habit from her family for almost her entire life. She started getting caught more often in her 80s, and would call her psychiatrist, Dr. Donald Black. "She usually gets off because she's old," Black says. Technology has provided merchants with a new generation of sensor tags sewn inside clothes or hidden in packaging. Cameras now are ubiquitous in large retail stores, hidden in clocks, smoke alarms, even the pushbars on fire-exit doors. But most stores, as every shoplifter knows, are reluctant to pursue criminal cases against amateur crooks, reasoning that the cost in publicity—and possible liability for false arrest—isn't worth the gain.

ubiquitous everywhere, ever present

8   She's 17 now, and she's learned her lesson, which is to be more careful and steal stuff only when she really needs it—like last week, when because her car insurance payment was due she was out of cash for a Valentine's Day present for her boyfriend. So she picked up a nice candle for him, and, while she was at it, a Bob Marley T shirt for herself. "Anything free is cooler," she says. "And I still get a rush from it."

Source: Adapted from "The Thrill of Theft," by Jerry Adler from *Newsweek* (Feb. 25, 2002). Copyright © 2002 The Newsweek/Daily Beast Company LLC. Reprinted with permission.www.newsweek.com.

Check Your Understanding

Circle the best answer to the following multiple-choice questions.

4. According to the passage, which of the following statements is *not* true?

   a. One store used shoplifting as a guide to know what items are desirable among teenagers.

   b. Shoplifters usually steal things that they really need but cannot afford.

   c. Winona Ryder was arrested on felony charges for taking $4,760 in clothes from a Saks Fifth Avenue store.

   d. Shoplifting was the first distinctly modern crime.

5. Which is the largest category of habitual shoplifters?

  a. drug addicts supporting their habits

  b. professional criminals

  c. those suffering from addictive-compulsive disorder

  d. thrill seekers

6. What are the two important truths about shoplifting that are mentioned in the passage?

  a. Shoplifting provides a powerful ego boost and is hard to prevent.

  b. Shoplifting provides a powerful ego boost and is usually committed by men.

  c. Shoplifters usually are not arrested and they are good at avoiding security cameras.

  d. Shoplifters usually steal batteries and they usually strike during the day, when stores are the busiest.

7. According to the passage, what is one measure retailers are taking to prevent shoplifting?

  a. They are installing cameras in their stores.

  b. They are profiling certain people and following them around stores.

  c. They are watching their employees more carefully as they are the biggest offenders in shoplifting.

  d. They are hiring more security guards.

8. Why did Gretchen Grimm believe she started to steal things?

  a. She started shoplifting because she suffered no guilt from it.

  b. She started shoplifting because she knew that even if she were caught, she would never be prosecuted.

  c. She started shoplifting because she refused the anti-anxiety drug Paxil, even though she needed it.

  d. She started shoplifting because she felt overlooked and wanted to win her mother's attention and affection.

Short-Answer Questions

9. Use context clues and word part analysis to define the following words from the passage.

  • exhilaration (paragraph 2): _____

  • recession (paragraph 2): _____

  • intervening (paragraph 5): _____

Continued on next page.

10. Were you able to answer the question you created in question #3? Provide your answer to that question.

_____

11. What is the topic? What is the main idea being supported by all of the sentences in the reading?

_____

_____

12. Were you able to maintain your concentration throughout the entire passage? If you were, what factors do you think contributed to your ability to stay focused? If you were not able to maintain your concentration well, where in the passage did you become distracted and why?

_____

_____

13. In your opinion, does the author approve of shoplifting? Explain your answer.

_____

_____

14. List two word clues from the passage, and explain what they signal.

_____

_____

15. Why do you think the author included stories of shoplifters' experiences?

_____

_____

BRAIN STRENGTH OPTIONS

Working individually or in groups of no more than three people, complete one of the following options.

1. Create a PowerPoint presentation explaining the concepts of topic and main idea. You will present to the class (or the instructor may have you post your presentation online for other students to use to review the chapter).

   ▶ Be sure to define both terms and make the difference between them clear.

   ▶ Provide four examples. These examples will be a brief paragraph with the main idea indicated by highlighting or other formatting.

   ▶ Explain how you determined the topic and main idea.

2. Create a poster. Apply the same guidelines as in Option #1.

3. Find a popular song. Print out the lyrics for each class member or present them on a screen, and have the class identify the main idea. Then tell the class what you identified as the main idea. Realize that this means that you must find a song that has a clear message!

4. Take one article from a magazine or the Internet, and highlight the main idea and label the topic. Because you are highlighting what is actually printed, you will have to select material that has directly stated (explicit) main ideas and details, not implied (implicit) main ideas.

Finding Supporting Details

NIKI HUDSON

Recently graduated from Baker College with a degree in diagnostic medical stenography and is currently studying to take her board exams

"I've always wanted to be somebody, but I see now I should have been more specific."

—LILY TOMLIN

I LIKE THE GARBAGE! I'm not going to lie. *People, Us, OK.* Love those magazines. I have a crazy interest in that kind of stuff. I guess they're easy to read. I have a hard time comprehending things I'm not interested in, especially physics. I had to read it over and over just to understand. I have to admit, I struggle.

Courtesy of Niki Hudson

For all of my classes, I read the chapter once through to figure out what I'm reading. Then I reread the chapter to process what I read the first time. While I'm reading the chapter the second time, I pull out important parts, which are anything in bold or italics, anything that is underlined, any boxes on the side of the page that have the heading *Note*. I not only "note" these things, I highlight them and make flash cards to study from. I use this strategy for all my classes, and it usually works, except for physics. It only kind of works for that. I get the main idea of the chapters in physics because they're pretty clearly stated. It's the details: the math, the formulas. Some things are inversely proportional, directly proportional. Density affects speeds in some materials. There's a lot. It's not just memorization. If physics were song lyrics, I could breeze through.

Making Connections

1. Would you describe yourself as a "detail person"? Why or why not?

2. What is the purpose of details in a paragraph?

3. How do you remember large amounts of detail?

4. Which details do you choose to remember from your textbooks? How do you make that choice?

Using Your Entire Brain: Big Picture and Detail

Looking for the Big Picture in Longer Readings

What Are Supporting Details?

Finding Supporting Details

Identifying Minor Supporting Details

Identifying Major Supporting Details

Strategy One: Ask Questions

Strategy Two: Look for Support Word Clues

Strategy Three: Look for Implied Word Clues

Brain Connections: Self-Assessment

Draw on the brain cell how many dendrites you imagine you have for how much you know about supporting details.

Using Your Entire Brain: Big Picture and Detail

HAVE YOU HEARD PEOPLE TALK ABOUT "being in the right brain" or "being in the left brain" or saying that someone is "left-brained" or "right-brained"? This is actually not an accurate description of how the brain works. The misconception comes from the fact that the brain has two halves (called hemispheres), kind of like a walnut split down the middle; these halves are called right brain and left brain. The two halves have different primary functions, though they are highly interactive and share many functions. They always work together because they are connected by a large white-matter structure called the corpus callosum, a thick band of nerve fibers. This structure sends information back and forth between the two halves so they can work together. One example of this is how you can process both the "big picture" and details at the same time. For example, if you are walking and come upon a forest, you can understand that you are looking at both a forest (the big picture) and trees (the details).

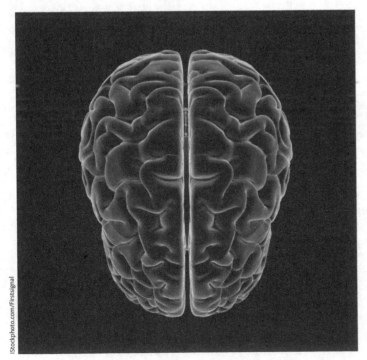

iStockphoto.com/Firstsignal

However, if someone has had surgery to cut the corpus callosum, the two halves cannot communicate, and the left side does not know what the right side is doing. Doctors and scientists working with someone who has had this surgery can present information to only one side of the brain because the two halves can no longer communicate. When a picture of a wooded area is presented to only the left side (sees details), the patient can see only *trees* but cannot see the *forest*—the patient is unable to understand the idea of a forest. However, if the doctor sets up the situation so that material is presented to only the right hemisphere (sees the big picture), the patient can see the *forest* but does not understand the *trees*. It takes both parts of your brain to see the big picture and the details. Both are important in order to have a complete understanding of the world. The same reasoning applies to reading.

What Are Supporting Details?

IN ORDER TO GET A COMPLETE UNDERSTANDING of your textbook material, you need to understand how all the textbook information is connected. Authors use supporting details to illustrate and explain their main ideas. Unlike topics or main ideas, which are more general in nature, details consist of facts, examples, definitions, and other more specific information. There are two types of details: major supporting details and minor supporting details. Major supporting details are the ideas and arguments an author uses to validate his or her main point or points. Major supporting details can be arguments, examples, illustrations, facts, opinions, and definitions. Minor supporting details are used to clarify and enhance major details. Minor supporting details are even more detailed than major supporting details. They exemplify, illustrate, or offer other related information about the major supporting details. They enhance the major details but are not absolutely necessary for basic comprehension of the reading. Keep in mind that supporting details, both major and minor, can be as small as single words in a sentence or as big as an entire sentence. Details are major or minor based on how and what they support, not their size.

supporting details
additional information an author provides to add meaning to the main idea

major supporting details
details that directly support the main idea

minor supporting details
details that directly support the major details

Identifying Major Supporting Details

MAJOR SUPPORTING DETAILS ARE TO A READING PASSAGE what engine parts are to a car; they make it work. The minor supporting details of a reading passage are extras, like the car's paint color, heated seats, and stereo system. They do not make it work, but they make it look nice and sound better. Once you recognize details and can distinguish major ones from minor ones, you will be able to follow an author's line of reasoning and see how the ideas in a reading text are related to each other.

In Chapter 4, you learned about main ideas. Many times finding the main idea leads easily to finding the supporting details because the supporting details are clearly examples of the main idea.

Tip FROM THE Brain Doctor

Remember that learning involves making connections in the brain. You will remember the details better if you connect them to the main ideas. Therefore, it is important that you identify the main idea first and then focus on the details and how they connect to the main idea.

ACTIVITY 5A
Identify Major Supporting Details

Read the following passage, and answer the questions that follow.

Waging War

One of the gravest charges against the human race is that only humans make war. The German writer Hans Magnus Enzensberger began his recent book on European civil war by saying, "Animals fight, but they do not wage war." We are supposed to be shamed by the fact that animals do not make war. Yet some animals do. Ant wars are the best known, but insects are sufficiently dissimilar to us that people seldom take that to heart. In recent years it has become clear that animals as closely related to us as chimpanzees can go to war. The famous chimps of Gombe attack other bands with no provocation and with deadly intent, not only patrolling their borders but making raids. They may kill and eat one another.

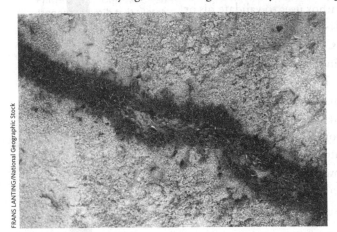

FRANS LANTING/National Geographic Stock

Source: Masson, J. M. & McCarthy, S. *When Elephants Weep: The Emotional Lives of Animals*. Delta Books, New York, 1995, p. 135.

1. The title gives you a clue to the main idea. Highlight the main idea of the passage in green.

2. The author clearly does not believe that only humans wage war. Find two examples to support his claim.

   a. _____

   b. _____

These two examples are major supporting details.

Now read the following passage. As you read, ask yourself, "What is the author's point?" Then ask yourself what sentences directly support the main idea (these are the major supporting details).

Thanks for the Topsoil

1   Earthworms, the "intestines of the earth," as Aristotle called them, dramatically alter soil structure, water movement, nutrient dynamics, and plant growth, according to the U.S. Department of Agriculture. These segmented vertebrates have been around for half a billion years, but they have

no eyes, ears, or lungs. They digest organic material (such as dead leaves), soil, and even tiny stones which are excreted as castings that enrich and aerate the soil.

2   Worms are pretty much responsible for all the rich soil on the planet. There can be as many as a million worms per acre in temperate regions. Some species are able to regenerate themselves: if one is cut in half, it can grow a new tail (but the pieces don't become two whole new worms.)

Source: Malesky, Kee. *All Facts Considered: The Essential Library of Inessential Knowledge*. John Wiley and Sons, Inc.: New Jersey, 2010, p. 121.

3. The title gives you a clue to the main idea. Highlight the main idea of the passage in green.

4. What are the major supporting details?

  a. _____

  b. _____

  c. _____

5. Explain why you selected each major supporting detail.

  a. _____

  b. _____

  c. _____

6. Why are worms referred to as the intestines of the soil? Why is this significant?

  _____

  _____

  _____

ACTIVITY 5B
Identify More Major Supporting Details

Read the following passage about families in China. Highlight the main idea in green and the major supporting details in yellow. Then answer the questions that follow.

Continued on next page.

1   It might seem an innocuous move to outsiders but in China it was a game-changer. Authorities in Shanghai began encouraging newly married couples in the city to have two children.

2   The rationale: Under China's vaunted one-child policy—a cornerstone of economic and social planning for decades—the population has been aging too rapidly. Indeed, Shanghai, which has always had a relatively youthful populace, now has the same proportion of retirees as an average city in the United States or Europe.

3   The move last summer by the city of Shanghai marked the first time since 1979 that officials have exhorted couples to have more offspring. More important, it symbolizes a sharpening debate in the world's most populous country over one of Beijing's most fundamental totems.

4   A growing chorus of critics is warning that unless the government changes course, the nation's one-child policy will drive the Asian powerhouse into a demographic dead end. They see China growing old before it grows rich.

5   Officials are beginning to take note. Spooked by the prospect of only 1.7 active workers for every pensioner by 2050, they are quietly chipping away at Beijing's signature population edict.

6   They have another reason to worry, too—forecasts are that within 30 years, 15 percent of marriage-aged men will be unable to find brides. The combination of the one-child policy and the Chinese preference for male offspring has proved deadly for female fetuses: 120 boys are born for every 100 girls—the highest ratio in the world.

Source: Ford, Peter. "China's crib conundrum," *The Christian Science Monitor*, Volume 102/Issues 5 & 6, Dec 2009 – Jan 2010, p. 23.

ACTIVITY 5C
Fill in the Missing Details

Suppose you are a college reporter and are asked to cover a story on graduation. Provide your own main idea and details for the topic *Ben's Graduation Day*. Complete the provided mind map based on your current understanding of major and minor supporting details. Explain what happened by providing readers with three major details. For each major detail, provide two minor supporting details. For example, one of the major supporting details could be:

Ben went to the graduation ceremony with two friends.

Two of the minor supporting details could be:

One of the girls was named Lucy.
The other girl was named Laura.

Be creative; it is your story. This activity is intended to introduce you to how details reinforce and support the main idea and how the details provide meaning and substance to what you are reading. Without the details, there is no story!

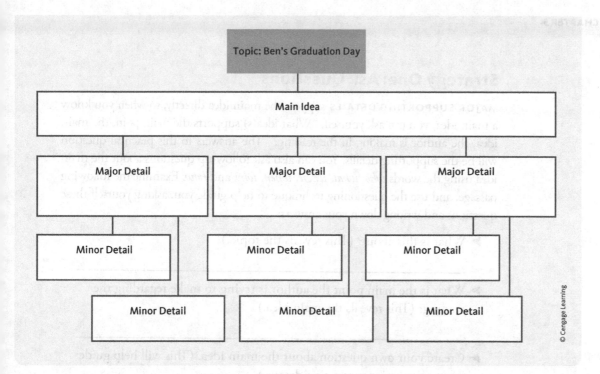

© Cengage Learning

ACTIVITY 5D
Remember the Day's Details: Part 1

On a sheet of paper, write the words "I made it to class." Below that sentence, write down every detail you can think of that describes anything you encountered from the time you closed the door of your house to the time you sat down in class today. (For example, if you were to list some details of what you did between waking up until an hour later, you might list: woke up, took a shower, read news on the Internet, stubbed my toe, had coffee.) It might be easier to think of the details between leaving your house and sitting down in class if you think in chronological order, but you do not have to. Your goal is to come up with as many details as you can. Try to fill a whole page if possible. Later in this chapter, you will return to this activity and work on it further.

There are three specific strategies you can use to identify major supporting details:

► Ask questions.
► Look for support word clues.
► Look for implied word clues.

Strategy One: Ask Questions

MAJOR SUPPORTING DETAILS support the main idea directly, so when you know a main idea, you can ask yourself, "What idea(s) supports the main poin, the main idea, the author is making in the reading?" The answers to this practical question will be the supporting details. You can also ask follow-up questions about the main idea using the words *who, what, where, when, why,* and *how*. Examine the following passage, and use the questioning technique to help guide you, asking yourself these questions and writing down your answers:

▶ What is this about? (This reveals the topic.)

_____

▶ What is the main point the author is trying to make regarding the reading? (This reveals the main idea.)

_____

▶ Create your own question about the main idea. (This will help guide you to the major supporting details.)

_____

▶ What in the passage supports the main idea directly? (This reveals the major supporting details.)

_____

> One of the many signs by which joy in animals can be recognized is vocalization. Pet cats are admired for purring, a sound that usually indicates contentment, though it may also be used to appease another animal. Big cats purr too. Cheetahs purr loudly when they lick each other, and cubs purr when they rest with their mother. Lions purr, though not as often as house cats, and only while exhaling. Both young and adult lions also have a soft hum they utter in similar circumstances—when playing gently, rubbing their cheeks together, licking each other, or resting.
>
> Source: Masson, J. M. & McCarthy, S. *When Elephants Weep: The Emotional Lives of Animals.* Delta Books, New York, 1995, p. 112.

Now read the following answers to the questions and compare them with yours.

▶ The passage is about signs of joy in animals.
▶ The main idea of the passage is that one of the signs animals make to show their joy is vocalization. You know that the main idea is vocalization because all of the sentences give examples of how animals vocalize when they are content, resting, and happy.

▶ A question about the main idea: How do animals vocalize joy?

▶ Cats were used to provide support (major supporting details) in this paragraph.

   ▶ Pet cats purr.

   ▶ Big cats purr, too.

   ▶ Lions hum.

ACTIVITY 5E
Ask Questions to Find Major Supporting Details

Read the following passages. For each passage, identify the topic, highlight the main idea in green, and then write a *who? what? where? when? why?* or *how?* question about the main idea. The answer to your question will reveal the major supporting details.

The adult brain, like the young child's, thrives on experience. If we are able to make the fullest use of its innate potential and continue to grow in mental abilities throughout life, it is essential we give our brains as rich, as varied, and as stimulating an environment as possible. One of the principal reasons that mental faculties appear to drop off after about the age of twenty is that formal education ceases around this age and we do not provide the brain with so many challenges and exercise. After leaving school, or college, many people stop using their brains as much, and with this comes an apparent decline of the brain's potential. Like any other organ, the brain atrophies if not in constant use.

Source: Russell, Peter. *The Brain Book*. New York, NY: Hawthorn Books, Inc., 1979, p. 74.

1. What is the topic?

   _____

2. Highlight the main idea in green.

3. Create a question about the main idea.

   _____

   _____

4. Answer your question to find major supporting details.

   _____

   _____

Continued on next page.

1   Multiplication is one of the basic math concepts that will enable you to calculate more quickly. It is a shortcut for repeated addition. One of the uses of multiplication is determining the total amount owed when you purchase more than one item costing the same amount, such as 6 CDs at $9.95 each. You can add $9.95 six times, but it is quicker to multiply $9.95 by 6. Through the use of multiplication, you will be able to determine if your paycheck has been computed correctly and if the charges on your monthly bills are correct.

2   Multiplication is the mathematical procedure for finding the product of two numbers. The number to be multiplied is called the multiplicand, and the number that indicates how many times to multiply is the multiplier. The result, or the answer, is known as the product. Sometimes the multiplicand and multiplier are referred to as factors.

Source: From BURTON/SHELDON. *Practical Math Applications 3e.* Copyright © 2011 Cengage Learning.

5. What is the topic?

_____

6. Highlight the main idea in green.

7. Create a question about the main idea.

_____

_____

8. Answer your question to find major supporting details.

_____

_____

_____

Covenant

1   Covenant is the crucial concept for setting out the relationship between God and the Hebrew people. The covenant can be summed up in the simple biblical phrase "I will be your God; you will be my people." In Hebrew history, the Bible insists, God has always been faithful to that covenant that was made with the people of Israel while the people must learn and relearn how to be faithful to it. Scholars have pointed out that the biblical covenant may be based on the language of ancient marriage covenants (for example, "I will be your husband; you will be my wife"); if that is true, it gives us an even deeper understanding of the term: the relationship of God and Israel is as close as the relationship of husband and wife.

2   This strong portrait of a single, deeply involved God who is beyond image or portrayal has had a profound impact on the shape of the Judeo-Christian worldview. The notion of covenant religion not only gave form to Hebrew religion, the idea of a renewed covenant became the central claim of Christianity. (Remember that another word for covenant is testament; hence the popular Old/

New Testament split Christianity insists upon.) The idea has even spilled over from synagogues and churches into our national civil religion, where we affirm a belief in "One nation under God" and "In God we trust"—both sentiments rooted in the idea of a covenant.

Source: From CUNNINGHAM/REICH. *Culture and Values, Volume I: A Survey of the Humanities with Readings* *7e* (p. 136). Copyright © 2010 Cengage Learning.

9. **What is the topic?**

_____

10. **Highlight the main idea in green.**

11. **Create a question about the main idea.**

_____

_____

12. **Answer your question to find major supporting details.**

_____

_____

_____

The Power of Effective Public Speaking for Free People

1   Just as the democratic civilizations throughout history have understood the importance of public speaking education, so do we know that being able to effectively present your ideas in a speech empowers you in several ways.

2   First, public speaking skills empower you to participate in democratic processes. Free speech is a hallmark of democracy. The strategies and policies our government adopts are a direct result of the debate that occurs across the nation: in living rooms; over pizza at the local hangout; on blogs and social networking sites; in the media; as well as in our executive, legislative, and judicial branches of government. When equipped with effective public speaking skills, you have the confidence to speak out and voice your ideas on important public issues.

3   Second, public speaking skills empower you to communicate complex ideas and information in ways that all audience members can understand. Most of us have had an unfortunate experience with a teacher who "talked over our heads." The teacher understood the material but was unable to

Continued on next page.

express it clearly to us. When we can express our ideas clearly, we are more likely to share them. When others understand our ideas, they learn from us. This confidence equips us to share our knowledge to the benefit of others.

4   Third, public speaking skills empower you to achieve your career goals and be self-sufficient. Research shows that, for almost any job, one of the most highly sought-after skills in new hires is oral communication skills.

5   So, whether you aspire to a career in business, industry, government, the arts, or education, good communication skills are a prerequisite to your success. Although you might be hired on the basis of your technical competence, your success will depend on your ability to communicate what you know to others, including your manager, your clients, and your colleagues.

Source: From VERDERBER/SELLNOW/VERDERBER. *The Challenge of Effective Speaking,* 15e (pp. 6–7). Copyright © 2012 Cengage Learning.

13. **What is the topic?**

_____

14. **Highlight the main idea in green.**

15. **Create a question about the main idea.**

_____

_____

16. **Answer your question to find major supporting details.**

_____

_____

_____

The Trust Economy

1   In the August 2007 issue of *Scientific American Mind* there was an article by Christoph Uhlhaas entitled "Is Greed Good?" The story describes how eBay should simply not work. After all, if you send money to a complete stranger, why would he send you anything in return? According to the article, "This is a borderline miracle, because it contradicts the concept of Homo economicus (economic man) as a rational, selfish person who single-mindedly strives for maximum profit. According to this notion, sellers should pocket buyers' payments and send nothing in return. For their part, buyers should not trust sellers—and the market should collapse."

2   So why does the online auction eBay work? Why do most people buy from someone they do not know, based on a bunch of positive peer reviews and ratings from people they do not

know? At first strike, this doesn't make any sense, but this type of behavior is commonplace online. We have an inherent trust in those who have taken the time to publish their personal feedback.

3   There is a "Wisdom of Crowds" at play here (to quote bestselling author James Surowiecki) and an overriding faith in groups of individuals who have never met. The online trust economy is a powerful force that favors the crowd over companies. Look no farther than Amazon. com. When reviewing book selections, the traffic and attention given to these peer reviews is so powerful that the online merchant's description of the book from the publisher and subsequent mass media reviews pale in comparison to the conversion rate to sale that they get from the consumer-generated reviews. Ultimately, you'll trust Sally from Carefree, Arizona, over the *New York Times Book Review*.

4   In fact, it works so well that Amazon.com also has a feature called "Customers Who Bought This Item Also Bought," which is one of the best tools to get consumers to buy more books. After all, if you like the book you're about to purchase and other people who bought this book also found value in some other titles, they might be worth checking out as well.

5   Those who are part of the *participatory culture* (and give abundantly) tend to build powerful and respected personal brands. They are connected through intricate networks based on information and content as the currency, and their ability to provide value translates into their status in the disjointed hierarchy online. Among all communities, individuals hope to achieve some level of status and reputation. The pecking order online is simply bigger, and it has no face.

6   This unique trust economy is counter to everything you ever thought about how a business grows. A great salesperson knows that the ultimate customer is one who has given you his or her trust. Trust is earned by an overall great experience with a foundation of authenticity, open communication, knowledge, and value from that customer's perspective.

17. **What is the topic?**

_____

18. **Highlight the main idea in green.**

19. **Create a question about the main idea.**

_____

_____

20. **Answer your question to find major supporting details.**

_____

_____

_____

Strategy Two: Look for Support Word Clues

support word clues words and phrases used to signal that what is being presented in the text supports the main idea

IN CHAPTER 4, you were introduced to support word clues as you were learning to distinguish main ideas from details. As you ask the question "What directly supports the main idea?" use support word clues to guide you to the answer—the major supporting details. Table 5.1 gives you some examples of support word clues. Can you think of others?

Table 5.1 Examples of Support Word Clues

for example	one of the reasons	to illustrate the point	first of all
for instance	a case in point	also	second of all
this is to say	for example	in addition	in other words

Look at the following passage from a communications textbook regarding hegemony.

1   Social theorist Antonio Gramsci (1971) referred to hegemony as domination by consent. In other words, hegemony is a process of granting some group with more power and privilege the ability to shape our worldviews, attitudes, beliefs, expectations, and actions. Perhaps one of the most common examples of hegemony concerns women's clothing in general and shoes in particular. Feminist scholars have argued that women have, to the extent that they embrace high-heeled, pointy-toed shoes and plunging necklines, assumed, perhaps unreflectively, the male gaze; this is to say, they have internalized (and thus embraced and made a part of their "style") a perspective and a look that functions to objectify them, making them seem more like objects for others' consumption than complex, thinking, and feeling individuals. This is especially complicated by the fact that wearing high heels can cause permanent damage to women's calf muscles. The concept of hegemony attempts to reveal how people or groups who are oppressed, or who have less power, participate in that process, even when it's harmful to them; however, this process of participation is complex.

2   For example, Deanna owns a pair of black Kenneth Cole mary janes with three-inch stacked wood heels. They are a smooth black matte leather, and they are lined, unexpectedly, with a vivid

Tip FROM THE Brain Doctor

If you set your intention, as in telling your brain, to actively look for something, you are more likely to find it. Study word clues, and then remind yourself to actively look for them when you read. This will make your reading more active, rather than passive, as well.

purple leather. She not only loves the way they look but also the way they sound when she walks, sort of a resonant "clock, clock, clock." They are a little bit uncomfortable; though they are roomy in the toe box, the height of the heel pitches her forward onto the balls of her feet, which, after about an hour or so, begin to feel bruisey, and causes her lower back to ache and complain. But she gets a lot of compliments when she wears them—about their style, about her legs, about the look—and, quite simply, it feels good to be recognized in this way. So, we could argue that this is as simple as "The shoes hurt, so toss them!" but so much in our culture—our friends, television and movies, historical and cultural trends in fashion—reinforces a vision of femininity that renders women available to the straight, male vision of beauty, one that comes at a cost for both women and men (in the form of unrealistic expectations of body image and disordered eating, sexism and violence against women, and so forth). That Deanna knows all this, and yet, the next time she is invited to a swanky dinner party, she's still likely to wear these shoes because of how attractive she feels when she wears them (even though they make her feel terrible at the same time) raises an interesting question in terms of Gramsci's definition: Has she consented to domination? Or, is being critical of all the different influences and contradictions in this experience resistance?

Source: From John T. Warren and Deanna L. Fassett, *Communication: A Critical/Cultural Introduction* (pp. 46–47). Copyright © 2011 Sage Publications, Inc. Reprinted with permission.

The first sentence is the main idea. Some might say that the second sentence looks like the main idea because the second sentence restates the first. Both sentences define hegemony, so either would be correct.

Ask yourself, "What directly supports the main idea?" Ask follow-up questions such as "*What* is hegemony?," "*Why* would someone consent to domination?," and "*What* does it look like to consent to domination?" What support word clues help point out the answers to these questions?

► First Support Word Clue: *in other words* emphasizes the main idea by restating it. It answers the question "What is hegemony?" by defining it and leading us into the passage regarding how powerful it is.

► Second Support Word Clue: *this is to say* reinforces the idea that a man's gaze regarding what they wear would have more power over women's thinking and actions than the consequences of their fashion choices. This answers the question "Why would someone consent to domination?"

▶ Third Support Word Clue: The second paragraph begins with the word clue *for example*. It answers the questions "What is hegemony?" and "What does it look like to consent to domination?" An example of hegemony is presented: granting some group with more power and privilege the ability to shape our worldviews, attitudes, beliefs, expectations, and actions.

ACTIVITY 5F
Locate Support Word Clues

1. Preview the following passage, and develop a question to answer.

_____

_____

Now read the passage.

1   Throughout the ages, poets have been waxing poetic about the beauties of white teeth. In the Old Testament's Song of Solomon, the beloved's teeth are compared to a flock of sheep, fresh-washed, evenly shorn, all twins.

2   But how do you get white healthy teeth? It's a pursuit that dates back to the pharaohs and beyond. Egyptians used to rub their teeth with a chew stick coated with a paste made from granulated pumice stone and wine vinegar. In Europe in the Middle Ages and Renaissance, barber-surgeons filed the surface of the teeth and slathered on aqua fortis, a corrosive nitric acid. A dazzling smile would be followed in middle age by tooth decay because the filing and acid took all the protective enamel off the teeth.

3   Another early popular approach was human urine. In ancient Rome, women gargled and brushed with urine to help keep their teeth sparkling, and most prized was Portuguese urine, reputed to be the strongest. (Actually, the long delivery time might make that claim true.)

Source: Richard Zacks, *An Underground Education*, New York: Doubleday, 1997, p. 203.

2. After reading the passage, what do you think is the topic?

_____

3. What is the most important point the author makes about the topic?

_____

4. Highlight the main idea in green.

5. What are the major supporting details? What points directly support the main idea?

_____

_____

_____

_____

6. Highlight in yellow any support word clues.

7. Use word part analysis to define what *reputed* means in this sentence: *In ancient Rome, women gargled and brushed with urine to help keep their teeth sparkling, and most prized was Portuguese urine,* reputed *to be the strongest.*

_____

_____

Strategy Three: Look for Implied Word Clues

SOMETIMES THE AUTHOR gives other clues to the major supporting details. The author may give examples without using specific word clues. The details may be in a pattern or have some similarity among them. Recognizing that similarity helps you find the details.

ACTIVITY 5G
Find Implied Word Clues

Read the following passage, looking for something similar that is repeated.

I have no doubt that Einstein, and other great scientists, have also been motivated by aesthetics in their search for new laws of nature. The Nobel physicist Steven Weinberg, who proposed the successful unified theory of the electromagnetic and weak nuclear forces far ahead of experimental evidence, uses words like *beautiful* and *ugly* to describe theories he likes and doesn't like. Dirac, whose equation for the electron has widely been described as

Continued on next page.

© GL Archive/Alamy

one of the most "elegant" and "beautiful" in all of physics, used to say "Find the mathematics first, and think what it means afterwards." The Nobel chemist Roald Hoffmann tells his students that it is the awareness and appreciation of the "aesthetic aspects of science," rather than mere quantitative analysis, that leads to discovery. And Einstein himself, in his *Autobiographical Notes,* says that the selection of physical theories has always been guided by considerations of "naturalness" and "logical simplicity" and "inner perfection." Perhaps aesthetic criteria are part of Einstein's "free inventions" of the mind.

Source: Lightman, Allen. *A Sense of the Mysterious.* Pantheon Books, New York, 2005, p. 76.

1. List the scientists mentioned in the passage. Next to each name, write the viewpoint of that scientist.

▶ _____

_____

▶ _____

_____

▶ _____

_____

▶ _____

_____

2. Underline the main idea in green.

Do you see how the major supporting details are the viewpoints of scientists regarding the main idea?

ACTIVITY 5H
Remember the Day's Details: Part 2

In Activity 5D, you were asked to recall the details of your day. Read over what you wrote. Consider the title your main idea, and highlight it in green. Now highlight in yellow the major details only—the ones that show *how* you got to class. The rest of the details on your page are minor supporting details.

Identifying Minor Supporting Details

MINOR SUPPORTING DETAILS CLARIFY or enhance the major supporting details and are usually not considered as important as major supporting details or main ideas. However, some of them are significant and useful to remember because they help make sense of the major details. They also help you visualize or picture what you read. Here are two strategies you can use to decide which minor details are worth remembering:

1. **Remember the minor details that make the major supporting details easier to remember.** For example, if you had to remember Stalin, the Soviet leader, his role during World War II, and the controversy he brought to his own country, you might picture Stalin in your mind, committing to memory this minor detail: Stalin had small pox as a child, which left permanent scars on his face; his schoolmates mercilessly called him "Pocky." Picture the face of Stalin with lots of scars. As you learn material about him, visualize him. The visual may make it easier to reconstruct the memory. All of the major details related to Stalin can be pictured in your mind, attached to this minor detail.

2. **Remember any minor details that are emphasized in lecture or in classroom discussions.** Many professors will stress points in lecture that they want you to know. Even if these points were minor supporting details from your textbook, you should remember them.

When you find minor supporting details in your reading you feel will help you remember the major details, you should mark them by underlining or circling them.

✓ COMPREHENSION CHECK

▶ Using your own words, differentiate between major supporting details and minor supporting details.
▶ Up to this point in the chapter, what is unclear?

ACTIVITY 51
Use Minor Supporting Details to Remember

Read the following passages, and highlight the main idea in green and major supporting details in yellow. From each passage, pick one minor detail that you think is worth noting, circle it, and explain why you think it is important in the space provided. The first one is modeled for you.

A Spherical Planet

1   We all have heard that some people believed Earth to be flat. Yet Earth's sphericity, or round-ness, is not as modern a concept as many think. For instance, more than two millennia ago, the Greek mathematician and philosopher Pythagoras (CA. 580–500 B.C.) determined through observation that Earth is spherical. We do not know what observations led Pythagoras to this conclusion. Can you guess what he saw to deduce Earth's roundness?

2   He might have noticed ships sailing beyond the horizon and apparently sinking below the water's surface, only to arrive back at port with dry decks. Perhaps he noticed Earth's curved shadow cast on the lunar surface during an eclipse of the Moon. He might have deduced that the Sun and Moon are not just the flat disks they appear to be in the sky, but are spherical, and that Earth must be a sphere as well. Earth's sphericity was generally accepted by the educated populace as early as the first century A.D. Christopher Columbus, for example, knew he was sailing around a sphere in 1492; that is one reason why he thought he had arrived in the East Indies.

Source: Christopherson, Robert. *Geosystems: An Introduction to Physical Geography.* NJ: Pearson, 2009, p. 15.

Why do you think the minor detail is worth noting? It is a clear visual, it is easy to remember, and it illustrates Pythagoras's possible observation.

We take our technological world, and our memories within it, very much for granted. We leave messages on answering machines or computers for absent friends; we consult our diaries as to free dates and write notes to colleagues arranging dinner, a theater or a meeting; we check the fridge and write ourselves a shopping list. Each of these is an act of individual memory—but an act in which we have manipulated technologies external to ourselves in order to aid or supplement or replace our internal brain memory system. It was not always thus: individual our memories may be, but they are structured, their very brain mechanism affected, by the collective, social nature of the way we as humans live. For each of us as individuals and for all of us as a society, technologies, some as old as the act of writing, some as modern as the electronic personal organizer, transfer the way we conceive of and the way we use memory. To understand memory we need also understand the nature and dynamics of this process of transformation.

Source: Rose, Steven. *The Making of Memory.* Anchor Books, New York, NY: 1992, p. 60.

Why do you think the minor detail is worth noting?

_____

_____

_____

1   Indian religion, later called the Hindu religion (derived from an Arabic word meaning "those who live in the Indus Valley"), combined, then, a highly ritualized worship of the gods of the pantheon (many believe these gods are merely faces or names for the ultimate reality) with a strong speculative tradition that tries to grasp the ultimate meaning of the cosmos and those who live in it. Indian religion, in short, is both a religion of the priest and the temple as well as the religion of solitary meditation and study. Most Indian homes to this day have a small altar for a god or goddess in order for the family to show respect and worship (called puja) in the home. The fundamental aim of Indian religion, however, is to find the path that leads one to the correct knowledge of ultimate reality, which, when known, leads one to be liberated from the illusory world of empirical reality and be absorbed into the one true reality, Brahman.

Malgorzata Kistryn/Shutterstock.com

2   Broadly speaking, three paths have been proposed for attaining such knowledge:

1. The path or discipline (that is, yoga) of asceticism (fasting, nonpossession, bodily discipline, and so on) by which one lives so that the material world becomes accidental and the person becomes enlightened. This is the hardest path of all, which, if at all undertaken, usually comes after one has had a normal life as a householder.

2. The path or discipline of karma, in which one does one's duty according to one's caste obligations (for example, priests should sacrifice; warriors fight) and not out of greed or ambition—motives that cloud the mind.

3. The path of devotion, in which all people refer all of their deeds as an act of devotion (bhakti) to the gods or to the one god to whom a person has a special devotion. By doing everything out of devotion, one does not fall into the trap of greed or self-centeredness.

Source: From CUNNINGHAM/REICH. *Culture and Values, Volume I: A Survey of the Humanities with Readings 7e* (p. 117) Copyright © 2010 Cengage Learning.

Continued on next page.

Why do you think the minor detail is worth noting?

_____

_____

_____

1   Culture shock is the disorientation that people feel when they encounter cultures radically different from their own and believe they cannot depend on their own taken-for-granted assumptions about life. When people travel to another society, they may not know how to respond to that setting. For example, Napoleon Chagnon (1992) described his initial shock at seeing the Yanomamö (pronounced yah-noh-MAH-mah) tribe of South America on his first trip in 1964.

2   The Yanomamö (also referred to as the "Yano-mami") are a tribe of about 20,000 South American Indians who live in the rain forest. Although Chagnon traveled in a small aluminum motorboat for three days to reach these people, he was not prepared for the sight that met his eyes when he arrived:

> I looked up and gasped to see a dozen burly, naked, sweaty, hideous men staring at us down the shafts of their drawn arrows. Immense wads of green tobacco were stuck between their lower teeth and lips, making them look even more hideous, and strands of dark-green slime dripped from their nostrils—strands so long that they reached down to their pectoral muscles or drizzled down their chins and stuck to their chests and bellies. We arrived as the men were blowing ebene, a hallucinogenic drug, up their noses. ... I was horrified. What kind of welcome was this for someone who had come to live with these people and learn their way of life—to become friends with them? But when they recognized Barker [a guide], they put their weapons down and returned to their chanting, while keeping a nervous eye on the village entrances. (Chagnon, 1992: 12–14)

3   The Yanomamö have no written language, system of numbers, or calendar. They lead a nomadic life-style, carrying everything they own on their backs. They wear no clothes and paint their bodies; the women insert slender sticks through holes in the lower lip and through the pierced nasal septum. In other words, the Yanomamö—like the members of thousands of other cultures around the world—live in a culture very different from that of the United States.

Source: From KENDALL. *Sociology in Our Times: The Essentials* 8e (pp. 60–61). Copyright © 2012 Cengage Learning.

3. **Why do you think the minor detail is worth noting?**

_____

_____

_____

ACTIVITY 5J
Differentiate Major from Minor Supporting Details

The following passage, *Thanks for the Topsoil*, should be familiar; you read it when practicing with major supporting details in Activity 5A. Read it again, but this time, after you read it, ask yourself, "What are the minor supporting details?" As you try to differentiate between major and minor supporting details, ask yourself what each detail supports. If it directly supports the main idea, it is a major supporting detail—and you will have already identified it. If the detail supports the major detail, it is a minor supporting detail. Think of it this way: If the detail could be left out without the passage losing its main idea, it is probably a minor detail.

1   Earthworms, the "intestines of the earth," as Aristotle called them, dramatically alter soil structure, water movement, nutrient dynamics, and plant growth, according to the U.S. Department of Agriculture. These segmented vertebrates have been around for half a billion years, but they have no eyes, ears, or lungs. They digest organic material (such as dead leaves), soil, and even tiny stones which are excreted as castings that enrich and aerate the soil.

2   Worms are pretty much responsible for all the rich soil on the planet. There can be as many as a million worms per acre in temperate regions. Some species are able to regenerate themselves: if one is cut in half, it can grow a new tail (but the pieces don't become two whole new worms.)

Source: Malesky, Kee. *All Facts Considered: The Essential Library of Inessential Knowledge.* John Wiley and Sons, Inc.: New Jersey, 2010, p. 121.

List all the minor supporting details, and explain why they are not major supporting details.

_____

_____

_____

_____

_____

ACTIVITY 5K
Unscramble the Paragraph

The paragraph on the next page is scrambled. Decide what the correct order of the paragraph should be by renumbering the sentences in the order they should appear. Identify the main idea and major and minor supporting details. When you finish, read the sentences aloud to check for accuracy.

Continued on next page.

_____   1. For example, suppose a student thinks, "I'm never going to pass this test."

_____   2. Keep track of your own negative self-talk.

_____   3. Your journal is a great place to write it down.

_____   4. Learn to substitute neutral statements.

_____   5. Listen to the words you use.

_____   6. Negative self-talk consists of irrational statements that must be recognized and changed.

_____   7. "I failed the last one, and I know the same thing will happen again."

_____   8. Write it down.

_____   9. Examine what you say to yourself.

_____   10. Negative self-talk can have a negative effect on a student's test performance.

Source: Adapted from Sembera and Hovis. *at: A Four Letter Word!* Whimberley, Texas: Wimberly Press, 1993, p. 23.

Was this process easy or difficult for you? Explain your answer.

_____

_____

Looking for the Big Picture in Longer Readings

When reading long reading assignments, especially entire textbook chapters, it is important to create in your mind a big picture of how all of the ideas relate to one another. You do not want to read facts and examples in isolation. When you see them as related and that they fill in the puzzle pieces (facts, examples, or arguments) of your mental picture as you read, you will be able to prioritize ideas. Although all ideas in a reading are related, they are not all equally important. The mental picture you create as you read will help you see this. You might even consider trying to draw your mental picture.

Textbook chapters usually have more than one main idea, so it is useful to break chapters down into smaller parts or sections and then seek the main idea and supporting details for each part. A section of a chapter can be a paragraph or group of paragraphs that make a single, important point about an overall topic. Textbook chapters are often separated into these sections by headings, which you can use as guides. Look for the main idea for each section, labeled by a heading, and then determine which ideas are the major supporting details. Once you can see the main point of each part and how the supporting details relate, you are on your way to understanding the whole chapter.

When you read textbook chapters, instead of looking for one topic with only one main idea, supported by several major and minor details, you should look at the bigger picture: one topic with a number of main ideas, each supported by a variety of major and minor supporting details.

Look at the mind map in Figure 5.1, which is based on a chapter from a sociology textbook. This chapter was divided into six sections, each with its own heading.

> ## Tip FROM THE
> # Brain Doctor
>
> Seeing the big picture and seeing details are two brain processes that work together. Most people will see both naturally. But sometimes you want to focus on one or the other. Because the brain learns by making connections, you want to focus on the big picture on the first reading and then reread the material focusing on the details. In this way, the information you focus on during the second reading will be able to connect to the big picture. When reading material in order to learn it, it is advisable to do two complete read-throughs.

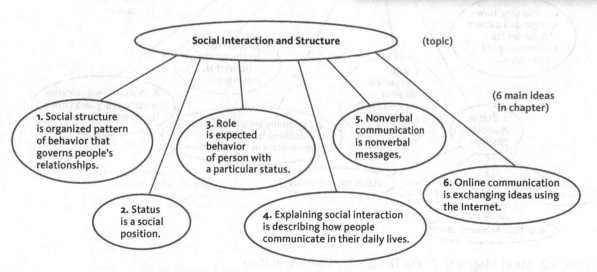

Figure 5.1 Mind Map with Main Ideas
Source: Based on Nijole V. Benokraitis, *SOC.* Belmont, CA: Wadsworth, 2010, pp. 80–97.

Tip FROM THE Brain Doctor

The brain is very visual. If you make the relationship between the main idea and the details visual, it will be easier to recall. There are many ways to do this, as you will learn in Chapter 10. But for now, a simple mind map will help, with the main idea in the center circle and lines to outside circles with the details.

The mind map in Figure 5.1 shows the topic, taken from the chapter's title, "Social Interaction and Social Structure," and six main ideas, which were suggested by the six headings within the chapter. The major supporting details you would need to remember could be found by asking a *who? what? why? where? when?* or *how?* question about each main idea. In the textbook chapter, however, there are subheadings under each heading, which are the major supporting details. Consider the following four subheadings (the major supporting details) under the main idea of: *Status is a social position.*

> *Status Set*
> *Ascribed and Achieved Status*
> *Master Status*
> *Status Inconsistency*

With these added major supporting details, your new mind map would look like Figure 5.2.

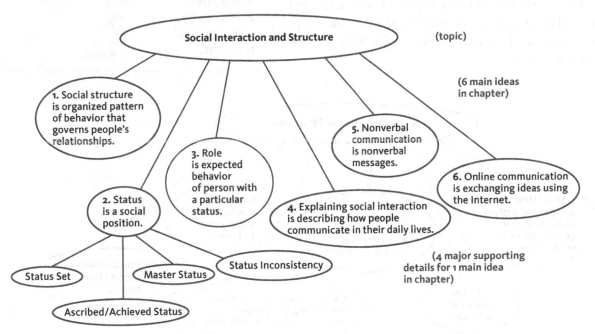

Figure 5.2 Mind Map with Major Details for One Main Idea

Source: Based on Nijole V. Benokraitis, *SOC.* Belmont, CA: Wadsworth, 2010, pp. 80–97.

Figure 5.2 shows that the ideas are all related but that there is a hierarchy. Learn the ideas with the hierarchy in mind. When you think about a main idea, such as *Status is a social position*, think about it in terms of its major supporting ideas. Try to see the main idea and its major supporting details completely so you can visualize a full picture. According to the textbook chapter, *status set* is the group of societal places one occupies at a given time. For example, you may be a college student, a registered voter, a brother, and a health club member. *Ascribed and achieved statuses* are those positions we are born into and are ascribed to us (sex, age, ethnicity) and those we choose or achieve (employee, graduate, spouse). *Master status* is a position that determines a person's identity. They are visible things or things people assess very quickly, such as ethnicity, occupation, and income level. *Status inconsistency* is conflict in statuses. A chemical engineer might be working at the local movie theater because of recent job shortages. His educational status is inconsistent with his occupational status.

Your instructors want you to understand what you read in a complete and deep way. This means understanding the main ideas clearly and linking them with necessary supporting details. This might seem like a lot to memorize at first, but if you visualize ideas so you can memorize them in groups of main ideas with their supporting details, you will have an easier time.

ACTIVITY 5L
Connect What You Know

Add to the mind map provided on the next page with information that describes your statuses. Here are some definitions to help you:

Status Set: group of societal places one occupies at a given time (student, voter, child)

Ascribed Status: those positions we are born into (sex, age, ethnicity)

Achieved Status: those positions we choose (employee, graduate, spouse)

Master Status: a position that determines a person's identity

Status Inconsistency: inconsistency in statuses

Continued on next page.

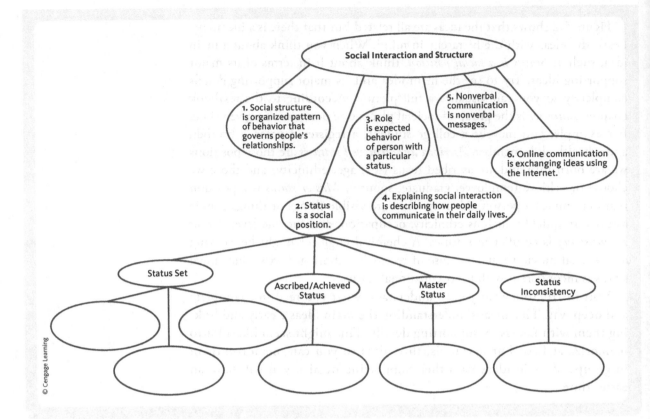

ACTIVITY 5M
Create a Mind Map Using Main Idea and Supporting Details

Read the following passage from a business textbook. Look for the main idea, major supporting details, and minor supporting details.

Ethical Criticisms

1   The criticisms of marketing are both well known and widespread. They are raised not simply in North America or Europe, but appear in most countries around the world. Advertising is, of course, a favorite target of moral criticism. Its use of sex and fear to increase sales, not to mention its deceptive practices, are condemned by many. Retailers are often charged with privacy invasion. For example, when customers use their credit cards at retail stores the data from their use not only informs the company of which goods to restock but also is mined as part of a data profile which data processors can develop on individuals and various market segments. The amount and detail of the information

moral pertaining to the principles of right and wrong

can be impressive. Similarly, telemarketers are criticized for intruding on people at home with their telephone calls. When laws are passed regulating this activity, they seek ways around those laws, while insisting on their right to call potential customers.

2   Marketers are also faulted for how they treat their business customers when, for example, salespeople offer money, bribes, or other "special considerations" to suppliers or retailers to obtain special favors. Large retailers are attacked for exercising their considerable economic power over smaller retailers and suppliers. Some of these methods inhibit open competition by requiring smaller retailers only to stock the products of one marketer rather than those of others. For example, Coca-Cola insists that those who handle its products not handle Pepsi Cola. If they do, then Coke will withdraw its product, as well as other favorable financing arrangements they provide to the handlers. Microsoft has been repeatedly taken to court for the pressure that it has placed on other businesses to use its products. And Wal-Mart is frequently attacked for driving local enterprises out of business while destroying the central business districts of small towns. These criticisms resonate around the world.

3   If this were not enough, marketing has been criticized more generally as simply being wasteful, expending billions of dollars to persuade people to buy products they don't need. It is accused of bringing about the commercialization of society and human relations. It is reproached for promoting both materialism and consumerism. Marketers are said to foster conditions under which people take their identities from the brands they buy and wear, as opposed to developing their own, non-commercial identities. The current problem of obesity is attributed, at least in part, to the marketing practices of fast-food producers and advertisers.

4   Finally, an important part of anti-globalization protests relates to marketing. International marketers have been charged with imposing the values of their home countries on the countries in which they do business, destroying local businesses, and manipulating people to want things they cannot afford.

Source: From George Brenkert, *Marketing Ethics*. Copyright © 2008 John Wiley and Sons, Inc. Reprinted with permission.

---

inhibit to hold back, restrain

resonate evoke feelings of shared beliefs

reproached expression of disapproval

Using the title, what is the topic?

_____

What is the main idea?

_____

_____

Complete the following mind maps, one for each paragraph, identifying the major and minor details as well as support word clues. The stars represent support word clues.

Continued on next page.

Paragraph 1

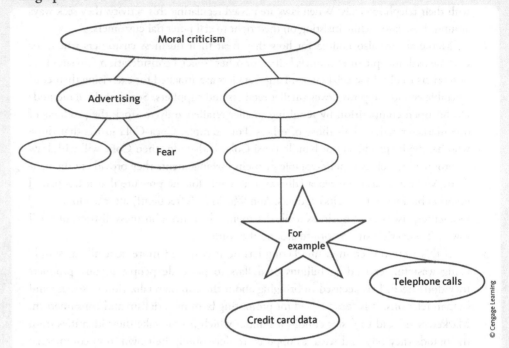

© Cengage Learning

Paragraph 2

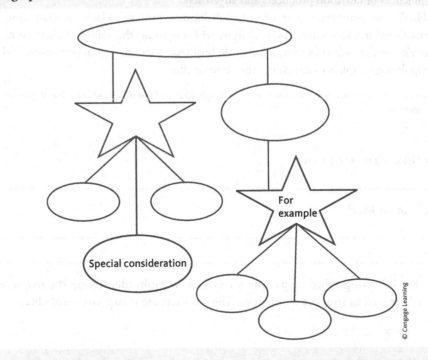

© Cengage Learning

Paragraph 3

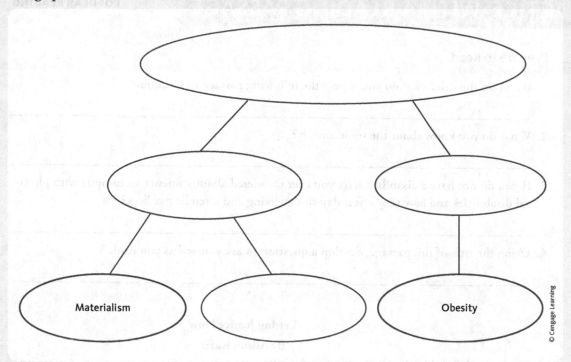

Paragraph 4

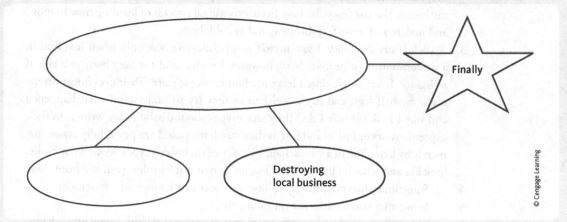

PRACTICE WITH A READING PASSAGE

Prepare to Read

1. Based on the title, what do you expect the following passage to be about?

_____

2. What do you know about the topic already?

_____

3. If you do not have a disability, have you ever wondered about students on campus with physical disabilities and how they affect day-to-day living and attending college?

_____

4. Using the title of this passage, develop a question to ask yourself as you read.

_____

Letting Justice Flow

By Alison Kafer

1   I have no legs.

2   One night, six years ago, I fell asleep an active, able-bodied young woman. Months later I woke up, my arms, belly, and back covered in burn scars. The legs that had carried me for years were missing, amputated above the knees as a result of my burns. The last few years have been a continual process of learning how to move and understand myself in this new, and yet old, body.

3   Before my disability, I saw myself as a political activist only when involved in a demonstration or protest. Now, however, I understand my very body as a site of resistance. Every single time I leave my house, people stare. Their eyes linger on my scars, my half-legs, and my wheelchair as they try to understand what happened and why I look the way I do. Their stereotypes about disability are written in their expressions of confusion and fear as they watch me pass. I am powerfully aware that merely by living life in a wheelchair, I challenge their stereotypes about what bodies look like and what bodies do. I feel like an activist just by rolling out my front door.

4   Sometimes, however, simply rolling outdoors isn't enough of a statement.

5   Sometimes you have to pee outdoors, too.

6   Three years ago, during my first semester of graduate school, I took an exchange class at a local seminary. A month into the course, I was assigned to give a presentation on the week's readings. Halfway through class we took a break, after which I was to give my talk. I desperately had to pee, and I rolled over to the library, sure I'd

seminary a special school providing instruction in theology find accessible toilets there. I was met only with a wall of narrow stalls—too narrow to slide my wheels into.

7   I dashed about campus, rolling from one building to another, hoping to find a wide stall door, muttering to myself, "There *has* to be an accessible can somewhere on this damn campus." After checking every bathroom in every building, I realized I was wrong.

8   What the hell was I going to do?

9   Going home wasn't possible because I would never make it back to school in time to give my presentation. "Holding it" also wasn't possible because … well, when a girl's gotta go, a girl's gotta go. I exercised my only remaining option: I went outside, searched for a dark and secluded part of campus, hiked up my skirt, leaned my body over the edge of my wheelchair, and pissed on the grass.

10   It just so happened that the dark, secluded place I'd found was the Bible meditation garden.

11   I went back to class angry. With mild embarrassment, I told the professor what had happened. I felt validated when she stopped the class to tell everyone the seminary president's name so they could write letters demanding an accessible bathroom at the school.

12   The next day, I, too, wrote a letter to the president informing him of both my accessibility problem and my solution. "Odds are," I wrote, "I will need a bathroom again. And I am doubtful that my 'christening' of the Bible garden is a practice you would like me to continue." In closing, I mentioned the Bible verse I'd found emblazoned on the garden wall (the one I'd practically peed on), and hoped its irony would not escape him. "Let justice roll down like waters," the words proclaimed, "and righteousness like an everlasting stream." Never before had the Bible seemed so relevant to me!

13   Within forty-eight hours, I had an appointment with the school president. He ushered me into his office and sat down across from me. "Before we discuss possible construction," he said, "I just want to give you a moment to share your pain."

14   I paused, thinking his comment a rather condescending way to begin a meeting. "I'm not in any pain," I said curtly, "I just want a place to go to the bathroom."

15   Our conversation could only go downhill from there.

16   The president informed me that although he wanted to provide me with an accessible bathroom, the school could not currently afford such construction. When I suggested that removing a forty-year-old stinky couch from one of the woman's rooms would free up space for an accessible stall, he responded with a sentiment as old as the couch: "Well, I'm reluctant to remove the sofa because some of the lady students like to rest there *during their time*."

17   Right. I'd forgotten how much we lady students, brains overtaxed by academia, liked to rest, bleeding, on musty couches in dank bathrooms. What a traitor to my sisters I must have been to suggest that my need to pee was more important than a couch that hadn't seen human contact since 1973.

Continued on next page.

christening baptism

emblazoned prominently displayed

irony situation where the actual meaning is the opposite of the literal meaning

relevant applicable, pertinent

18   Not surprisingly, that meeting did not result in an accessible toilet. So, as threatened, I continued to piss in the garden and complain in the halls. What had started out as a necessity became an interesting combination of necessity *and* protest—a pee protest. Word got around, and to my delight most students supported me. Petitions were signed in a number of classes. One student even proposed a documentary on *The Bathroom Debates* to her film class, showing them a short teaser clip she'd made. I became a bit of a celebrity, known in the halls as "the bathroom girl."

19   About a month after the first incident, I fired off another letter to the president informing him of my continued use of the Bible meditation site. This time I meant business. I told him I was ready to expose his total disregard of the needs of disabled Americans by going to the press with my story. Bingo. Construction began on the most beautiful accessible bathroom you ever did see.

20   Justice and righteousness were rolling down at last. They had just needed a little boost from a girl, her wheelchair, and a full bladder.

Alison Kafer is a graduate student in Women's Studies and Religion. In between battles with university administrators about inaccessible buildings, she kayaks, camps, and hikes. A relentless optimist, Alison insists that most people stare at her not because of her disability, but because of her Southern charm and dazzling physical grace.

Source: From THAT TAKES OVARIES: BOLD FEMALES AND THEIR BRAZEN ACTS by Alison Kafer (pp. 127–130) edited by Rivka Solomon. Copyright © 2002 by Rivka Solomon. Used by permission of Three Rivers Press, a division of Random House, Inc. and Alison Kafer.

Check Your Understanding

5. Use context clues and word part analysis to define the following words from the passage.

   • accessible (paragraph 6): _____

   • validated (paragraph 11): _____

   • condescending (paragraph 14) _____

Circle the best answer to the following multiple-choice questions.

6. What was the author's problem in the essay?

   a. She had a difficult time with her wheelchair.

   b. She found her graduate-level classes difficult.

   c. There were no wheelchair-accessible bathrooms.

   d. There were no clean bathrooms.

7. How did she finally solve her problem?

   a. She waited until she went home.

   b. She went to the library to find a bathroom.

   c. She went to the student union.

   d. She relieved herself outside in the meditation garden.

8. What did her professor do when she told her about her problem and described how she solved it?

   a. She told the students the school president's name so they could write letters.

   b. She ignored her problem and continued teaching class.

   c. The professor wrote a letter of protest.

   d. She gave the students a few minutes to talk so they could share her pain.

9. What did the president of the school say when the author had a meeting with him to discuss the problem?

   a. He suggested removing an old couch from one of the women's bathrooms to free up space for an accessible stall.

   b. He said that building construction was not up to him and that she should contact the ombudsman of the school.

   c. He said the school was already constructing a new bathroom in another wing of the building.

   d. He said the school could not currently afford to build an accessible bathroom stall.

10. What made the university president finally agree to build an accessible bathroom?

    a. The author threatened to continue to relieve herself outside.

    b. The author threatened to expose the problem to the press.

    c. Other students protested on the author's behalf.

    d. He felt it would be expensive but worth it.

Short-Answer Questions

11. Did you enjoy reading the passage? Why or why not?

_____

_____

Continued on next page.

12. The main idea is not stated explicitly but implied, a subject that will be discussed in the next chapter. The main idea is: Sometimes you have to do something radical to achieve justice. Knowing this, identify at least three major supporting details.

_____

_____

13. What details does the author use to make you, the reader, understand her frustration at not being able to find an accessible bathroom?

_____

_____

14. What details does the author use to show how other students supported her request for an accessible bathroom?

_____

_____

15. Do you agree or disagree with how the author handled her situation? Would you have acted differently to get the college to provide accessibility?

_____

_____

✔ COMPREHENSION CHECK

▶ Create three questions about this chapter you would ask students if you were the instructor.
▶ Of everything you have read in this chapter, what will you be sure to use in other classes?
▶ If you could ask the authors a question about this chapter, what would you ask?

CHAPTER SUMMARY

Major supporting details add strength and clarity to the main idea by providing more specific information, explanation, and examples. Minor supporting details flesh out the major supporting details with more explanation and examples. Ideas go from general (topic) to very specific (minor detail), depending on what function they serve in the reading. Question yourself about the main idea in order to locate the major supporting details. Ask "what backs this up?" and *who? what? where? when? why?* or *how?* questions about the main idea, and then find the answers in the supporting details. Use support word clues and implied word clues to help you determine where the supporting details are.

Most textbook chapters have more than one main idea and a lot of details. Make it a practice to always look for the big picture in what you read. From there, fill in the blanks of the framework with main ideas of sections and details within those sections that you know are important. Decide what is important by taking cues from your instructor during lecture or class discussion. Include minor details, too, if they help you remember the more major details or the main ideas. It can be helpful to visualize or draw a mind map to identify the main idea and details of your readings. Visualizing what you read helps your brain remember better.

Brain Connections: Self-Assessment

Draw the amount of dendrites you imagine that you have now about supporting details. Compare your drawing of dendrites now with what you drew at the beginning of this chapter. If the amounts are different, explain why.

POST TEST

Part 1: Objective Questions

Match the key terms from the chapter in Column A to their definitions in Column B.

_____ 1. supporting details   a. words and phrases used to signal that what is being presented in the text supports the main idea

_____ 2. major supporting details   b. additional information an author provides to add to the meaning to the main idea

_____ 3. minor supporting details   c. details that directly support the main idea

_____ 4. support word clues   d. details that directly support the major details

Circle the best answer to the following multiple-choice questions.

5. Which of the following is *not* a strategy for locating main ideas?

a. Question yourself.

b. Discover your concentration blocks.

c. Notice word clues.

d. Look in the usual spots.

6. Minor supporting details:

a. are always very important.

b. are not at all important.

c. usually support major supporting details.

d. are located at the beginning or end of a paragraph, but never in the middle.

7. Textbook chapters:

a. sometimes have no main idea.

b. usually have more than one main idea.

c. usually have only one main idea.

d. do not include minor supporting details.

8. To help organize textbook information, you can:

a. create mind maps.

b. read your textbook aloud.

c. avoid looking up unfamiliar words so as not to lose concentration when you read.

d. avoid questioning yourself as you read in order to save time.

9. Mind maps are effective because:

a. they test your spelling skills.

b. they are difficult to complete.

c. they show others that you have memorized the information.

d. they show relationships between ideas.

Part 2. Reading Passage

ACADEMIC READING

Prepare to Read

1. Based on the title, what do you already know about this topic?

_____

2. Using the title, develop a question to ask yourself as you read.

_____

3. What memory technique would you use to help you recall information in this passage?

_____

4. Highlight the main idea in green and the major supporting details in yellow. Circle or Underline minor details if they help you understand what you have read.

McDonald's
By Conrad Kottak

1   Each day, on the average, a new McDonald's restaurant opens somewhere in the world. The number of McDonald's outlets today far surpasses the total number of all fast-food restaurants in the United States in 1945. McDonald's has grown from a single hamburger stand in San Bernardino, California, into today's international web

Continued on next page.

propaganda
information
deliberately spread
to influence others

liturgical formal,
public worship

transcends
to rise above or
go beyond

invariance
no variation,
sameness

doctrine
something that
is taught

sanctuary a sacred
place

of thousands of outlets. Have factors less obvious to American natives than relatively low cost, fast service, and taste contributed to McDonald's success? Could it be that natives—in consuming the products and propaganda of McDonald's—are not just eating but experiencing something comparable in certain respects to participation in religious rituals? To answer this question, we must briefly review the nature of ritual.

2   Rituals, we know from the chapter on religion, are formal—stylized, repetitive, and stereotyped. They are performed in special places at set times. Rituals include liturgical orders—set sequences of words and actions laid down by someone other than the current performers. Rituals also convey information about participants and their cultural traditions. Performed year after year, generation after generation, rituals translate messages, values, and sentiments into action. Rituals are social acts. Inevitably, some participants are more strongly committed than others are to beliefs on which the rituals are founded. However, just by taking part in a joint public act, people signal that they accept an order that transcends their status as mere individuals.

3   For many years, like millions of other Americans, I have occasionally eaten at McDonald's. Eventually I began to notice certain ritual-like aspects of Americans' behavior at these fast-food restaurants. Tell your fellow Americans that going to McDonald's is similar in some ways to going to church and their bias as natives will reveal itself in laughter, denial, or questions about your sanity. Just as football is a game and *Star Trek* is "entertainment," McDonald's, for natives, is just a place to eat. However, an analysis of what natives do at McDonald's will reveal a very high degree of formal, uniform behavior by staff members and customers alike. It is particularly interesting that this invariance in word and deed has developed without any theological doctrine. McDonald's ritual aspect is founded on 20th-century technology, particularly automobiles, television, work away from home, and the short lunch break. It is striking, nevertheless, that one commercial organization should be so much more successful than other businesses, the schools, the military, and even many religions in producing behavioral invariance. Factors other than low cost, fast service, and the taste of the food—all of which are approximated by other chains—have contributed to our acceptance of McDonald's and adherence to its rules.

4   Remarkably, when Americans travel abroad, even in countries noted for their food, many visit the local McDonald's outlet. The same factors that lead us to frequent McDonald's at home are responsible. Because Americans are thoroughly familiar with how to eat and more or less what they will pay at McDonald's in its outlets overseas, they have a home away from home. In Paris, whose people aren't known for making tourists, particularly Americans, feel at home, McDonald's offers sanctuary (along with relatively clean, free restrooms). It is, after all, an originally American institution, where natives, programmed by years of prior experience, can feel completely at home. Given its international spread, McDonald's is

no longer merely an American institution—a fact that McDonald's advertising has not ignored. A TV commercial linked to the 1996 Olympics (of which McDonald's was an "official sponsor") portrayed an Asian athlete finding sanctuary from an alien American culture at a McDonald's restaurant in Atlanta. For her, the ad proclaimed, McDonald's was home-culture turf.

5   This devotion to McDonald's rests in part on uniformities associated with its outlets: food, setting, architecture, ambience, acts, and utterances. The McDonald's symbol, the golden arches, is an almost universal landmark, as familiar to Americans as Mickey Mouse, Mr. Rogers, and the flag. A McDonald's (now closed) near my university was a brick structure whose stained-glass windows had golden arches as their central theme. Sunlight flooded in through a skylight that was like the clerestory of a church.

6   Americans enter a McDonald's restaurant for an ordinary, secular act—eating. However, the surroundings tell us that we are somehow apart from the variability of the world outside. We know what we are going to see, what we are going to say, and what will be said to us. We know what we will eat, how it will taste, and how much it will cost. Behind the counter in every McDonald's, agents wear similar attire. Permissible utterances by customer and worker are written above the counter. Throughout the United States, with only minor variation, the menu is in the same place, contains the same items, and has the same prices. The food, again with only minor regional variation, is prepared according to plan and varies little in taste. Obviously, customers are limited to what they can choose. Less obviously, they are limited in what they can say. Each item has its appropriate designation: "large fry," "quarter pounder with cheese." The novice who innocently asks, "What kind of hamburgers do you have?" or "What's a Big Mac?" is out of place.

7   Other ritual phrases are uttered by the person behind the counter. After the customer has completed an order, if no potatoes are requested, the agent ritually asks, "Any fries?" Once food is presented and picked up, the agent conventionally says, "Have a nice day." (McDonald's has surely played a strong role in the diffusion of this cliché into every corner of contemporary American life.) Nonverbal behavior also is programmed. As customers request food, agents look back to see if the desired sandwich item is available. If not, they tell you, "That'll be a few minutes," and prepare your drink. After this, a proper agent will take the order of the next customer in line. McDonald's lore and customs are even taught at a "seminary" called Hamburger University in Illinois. Managers who attend the program pass on what they learn to the people who work in their restaurants.

8   It isn't simply the formality and regularity of behavior at McDonald's but its total ambience that invites comparison with ritual settings. McDonald's image makers stress "clean living" and refer to a set of values that transcends McDonald's itself. Employees submit to dress codes. Kitchens, grills, and counters should sparkle. Understandably, as the world's number one fast-food chain, McDonald's also has evoked hostility. In 1975, the Ann Arbor campus McDonald's was the scene

clerestory a high point of a structure that has windows in it to let light in

secular non-religious

variability changes

ambience atmosphere, surroundings

evoked called up

Continued on next page.

of a ritual rebellion—desecration by the Radical Vegetarian League, which held a "puke-in." Standing on the second-story balcony just below the clerestory, a dozen vegetarians gorged themselves on mustard and water and vomited down on the customer waiting area. McDonald's, defiled, lost many customers that day.

demarcated defined, marked off

analogies similarities between two things

9   The formality and invariance of behavior in a **demarcated** setting suggests **analogies** between McDonald's and religious rituals. Furthermore, as in a ritual, participation in McDonald's occurs at specific times. In American culture, our daily food consumption is supposed to occur as three meals: breakfast, lunch, and dinner. Americans who have traveled abroad are aware that cultures differ in which meal they emphasize. In many countries, the midday meal is primary. Americans are away from home at lunchtime because of their jobs and usually take less than an hour for lunch. They view dinner as the main meal. Lunch is a lighter meal symbolized by the sandwich. McDonald's provides relatively hot and fresh sandwiches and a variety of **subsidiary fare** that many American **palates** can tolerate.

subsidiary secondary

fare food

palates sense of taste

10   The ritual of eating at McDonald's is confined to ordinary, everyday life. Eating at McDonald's and religious feasts are in complementary distribution in American life. That is, when one occurs, the other doesn't. Most Americans would consider it inappropriate to eat at a fast-food restaurant on Christmas, Thanksgiving, Easter, or Passover. Our culture regards these as family days, occasions when relatives and close friends get together. However, although Americans neglect McDonald's on holidays, television reminds us that McDonald's still endures, that it will welcome us back once our holiday is over. The television presence of McDonald's is particularly evident on such occasions–whether through a float in the Macy's Thanksgiving Day parade or through sponsorship of special programs, particularly "family entertainment."

11   Although Burger King, Wendy's and Arby's compete with McDonald's for the fast-food business, none has equaled McDonald's success. The explanation may lie in the particularly skillful ways in which McDonald's advertising plays up the features just discussed. For decades, its commercials have been varied to appeal to different audiences. On Saturday morning television, with its steady stream of cartoons, McDonald's has been a **ubiquitous** sponsor. The McDonald's commercials for children's shows usually differ from the ones adults see in the evening and on sports programs. Children are reminded of McDonald's through fantasy characters, headed by clown Ronald McDonald. Children can meet "McDonaldland" characters again at outlets. Their pictures appear on cookie boxes and plastic cups. Children also have a chance to meet Ronald McDonald as actors scatter visits throughout the country. One can even rent a Ronald for a birthday party.

ubiquitous existing everywhere

12   Adult advertising has different but equally effective themes. Breakfast at McDonald's has been promoted by a fresh-faced, sincere, happy, clean-cut young woman. Actors gambol on ski slopes or in mountain pastures. The single theme, however, that for years has run through the commercials is personalism. McDonald's, the commercials drone on, is something other than a fast-food restaurant. It's a warm, friendly place where you are graciously welcomed and feel at

home, where your children won't get into trouble. McDonald's commercials tell you that you aren't simply an anonymous face in an **amorphous** crowd. You find **respite** from a hectic and impersonal society, the break you deserve. Your individuality and dignity are respected at McDonald's.

> **amorphous** formless
>
> **respite** a break, a rest

13   McDonald's advertising tries to de-emphasize the fact that the chain is a commercial organization. One jingle proclaimed, "You, you're the one; we're fixin' breakfast for ya"—not "We're making millions off ya." Commercials make McDonald's seem like a charitable organization by stressing its program of community good works. "Family" television entertainment is often "brought to you by McDonald's." McDonald's commercials regularly tell us that it supports and works to maintain the values of American family life.

14   I am not at all arguing here that McDonald's has become a religion. I am merely suggesting that specific ways in which Americans participate in McDonald's bear analogies to religious systems involving myth, symbol, and ritual. Just as in rituals, participation in McDonald's requires temporary **subordination** of individual differences in a social and cultural collectivity. In a land of ethnic, social, economic, and religious diversity, we demonstrate that we share something with millions of others. Furthermore, as in rituals, participation in McDonald's is linked to a cultural system that transcends the chain itself. By eating there, we say something about ourselves as Americans, about our acceptance of certain collective values, customs, and ways of living.

> **subordination** placing below

Source: From Conrad Kottak, *Cultural Anthropology 9e* (pp. 466–468). Copyright © 2002 McGraw-Hill. Reprinted with permission.

Check Your Understanding

5. Use context clues and word part analysis to define the following words from the passage.

- designation (paragraph 6): _____
- lore (paragraph 7): _____
- inappropriate (paragraph 10): _____

Circle the best answer to the following multiple-choice questions.

6. According to the author, why do people eat at McDonald's?

a. The French fries are only $.99.

b. Americans are not really concerned with their health.

c. They are familiar with how to eat and what they will pay at McDonald's.

d. Americans do not like to pay a lot for lunch because it is not considered the main meal of the day.

Continued on next page.

7. The author argues that people are devoted to McDonald's because:

    a. they believe that Wendy's has greasy hamburgers.

    b. they like the uniformities associated with McDonald's outlets.

    c. each McDonald's is different.

    d. McDonald's was an "official sponsor" of the 1996 Olympics.

8. According to the author, what nonverbal behavior is customary for McDonald's employees?

    a. As customers request food, employees look back to see if the desired sandwich item is available.

    b. If no potatoes are ordered with a meal, employees routinely ask, "Any fries?"

    c. If a food item is not available, employees will say, "That'll be a few minutes."

    d. Employees frequently stare off into space and yell, "Next in line!"

9. What hostility occurred in a McDonald's in Ann Arbor, Michigan?

    a. University of Michigan undergraduates critiqued the grammar on the menu over the loudspeaker.

    b. Michigan State football fans attempted to rally at the restaurant but couldn't remember their school's fight song.

    c. Vegetarians picketed outside.

    d. The Radical Vegetarian League held a "puke-in."

10. According to the author, in what way has McDonald's promoted the idea of personal attention in their advertisements?

    a. They have a catch phrase in their commercials: "Have it your way."

    b. The commercials tell you that you aren't simply an anonymous face in an amorphous crowd.

    c. They include a guy name "Dave" in all of their commercials.

    d. They advertise McNuggets for McYou.

Short-Answer Questions

11. What is the main idea of the passage?

    _____

    _____

12. What rituals are performed at McDonald's?

    _____

    _____

13. According to the author, what do we say about ourselves when we eat at McDonald's?

_____

_____

14. Do you agree with the author when he states that Americans have created religious-like rituals regarding McDonald's? Explain.

_____

_____

15. Create your own title for this reading.

_____

_____

BRAIN STRENGTH OPTIONS

This project will combine what you learned in Chapter 4 and in this chapter. Working individually or in groups of no more than three people, complete one of the following options.

1. Create a PowerPoint presentation explaining the concepts of topic, main idea, and supporting details. You will present what you create to the class (or the instructor may have you post your presentation online for other students to use to review the chapter).

   ▶ Be sure to define *topic, main idea,* and *supporting details.*

   ▶ Provide examples of all of these from two readings. Each main idea should have at least two details.

   ▶ Explain how you determined that reading's topic, main idea, and details.

2. Create a poster, applying the same guidelines as in Option 1.

3. Find an article from a magazine or the Internet that is at least two pages long. Highlight the topic, main ideas, and supporting details. Because you are highlighting what is actually printed, you will have to select material that has directly stated main ideas and details.

Using Inference to Identify Implied Main Ideas

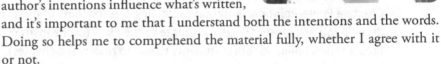

STUDENT TO STUDENT

SERJA GORAM

A graduate student at Ashland University studying pastoral counseling

"More than anything else, being an educated person means being able to see connections that allow one to make sense of the world and act within it in creative ways."

—GEORGE KUH

I WANT TO UNDERSTAND where an author is coming from when I read because I don't always agree with their views. I give them a chance, though. I try to see what an author is saying from their point of view. Are they just being informative or persuasive? Are there opposing views on the subject? An author's intentions influence what's written, and it's important to me that I understand both the intentions and the words. Doing so helps me to comprehend the material fully, whether I agree with it or not.

Reading always comes easier to me when I have some background information on the subject. I usually take a number of different approaches to get acquainted with a subject before I dive into the reading. This includes skimming the assigned chapter (sometimes even the previous chapter) to see what is familiar to me. I frequently use the Internet to access information on the subject area or terms that I am unfamiliar with.

I integrate what I already know on the subject with what I am reading, but I don't want to extend my understanding beyond the author's intent. One way I gauge whether my inferences are accurate is by comparing the professor's lecture with the class readings. They should complement one another. If they don't, something is amiss. With the current popularity of student postings online being required in many courses, I am also able to measure my understanding of the text in comparison to my fellow students. This gives me an idea whether I have a "middle-ground understanding" or if my comprehension of the material is off.

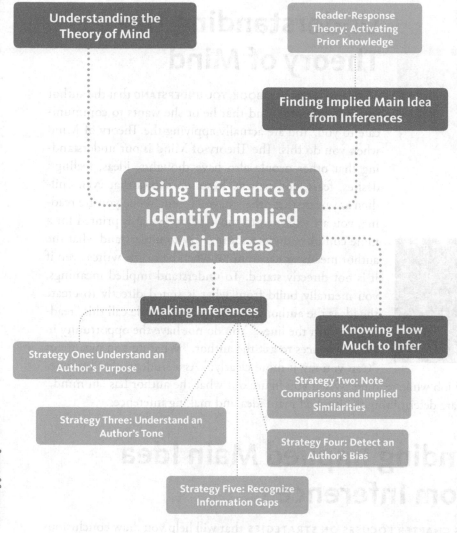

Understanding the Theory of Mind

Reader-Response Theory: Activating Prior Knowledge

Finding Implied Main Idea from Inferences

Using Inference to Identify Implied Main Ideas

Making Inferences

Knowing How Much to Infer

Strategy One: Understand an Author's Purpose

Strategy Two: Note Comparisons and Implied Similarities

Strategy Three: Understand an Author's Tone

Strategy Four: Detect an Author's Bias

Strategy Five: Recognize Information Gaps

© Cengage Learning

Understanding the Theory of Mind

Pakhnyushcha/Shutterstock.com

WHEN YOU READ A TEXTBOOK, YOU UNDERSTAND that the author has something in mind that he or she wants to communicate to you. You are actually applying the Theory of Mind when you do this. The Theory of Mind is our understanding that other people also have thoughts, ideas, feelings, desires, fears, and beliefs. Research shows that even children are aware that others have a mind. When you are reading, you are expected to move *beyond* what is printed for a more complete understanding. Try to understand what the author means or has in mind when he or she writes even if it is not directly stated. To understand implied meanings, you mentally build from what is stated directly to create the ideas the author intended. Some people call this "reading between the lines." You do not have the opportunity in most instances to ask the author, "What do you mean?" or "Can you say it more clearly?" As a student, that becomes your job while reading. When you figure out what the author has "in mind," you are determining the implied main idea and making inferences.

Finding Implied Main Idea from Inferences

THIS CHAPTER FOCUSES ON STRATEGIES that will help you draw conclusions from your reading assignments by noting both what is said and what is not said by an author. Combine this information with what you already know to determine implied main ideas.

Sometimes when you are reading a textbook, the main idea is directly stated in a sentence. In Chapter 4, you learned different strategies for locating a stated main idea:

1. Question yourself.
2. Look in the usual spots.
3. Notice word clues.
4. Categorize an author's points.

However, sometimes authors use implied main ideas, which are the main points in a paragraph, section, or chapter that are *not* stated directly. The implied main idea should be what you think the author intends you to find. You cannot just look in the usual spots to find the main idea, and you may not find word clues that help you. You have to do more. You have to work with the text to *figure out* the main idea and ask yourself what idea the sentences support. Working with the text means taking what you read, adding to it what you already know, and making inferences that lead you to a reasonable main idea.

Inference is the process of drawing conclusions about information when an author's opinions or ideas are not directly stated. Remember that when you read, you participate in a two-way conversation with an author. Some books present literal information or facts, like these stated main ideas from a math textbook:

> An angle is the union of two rays that have the same end point.
>
> The Pythagorean Theorem involves the relationship of the sides of a triangle.

However, some textbooks only offer clues that hint at or imply the main idea. Your job in this conversation is to take the hint and infer meaning.

Consider this story. You will be surprised when you realize you know more about inference than you think you do. See if you can figure it out.

> Juan dropped the letters, packages, and advertisements through the slot, ignored the barking, and moved away. He breathed a sigh of relief that he was finished for the day, just as it started to get dark.

Use your ability to infer by answering the following questions.

1. Who is Juan? _____
2. Where is Juan? _____
3. What time of day is it? _____
4. What kind of animal did Juan come across? _____
5. What is Juan wearing? _____
6. What was he doing? _____
7. Why did he put those objects in the slot? _____
8. How did he feel? _____
9. What happens as a result of what Juan did? _____

implied main ideas main point in a paragraph, section, or chapter that is not stated directly

inference the process of drawing conclusions about information when an author's opinions or ideas are not directly stated

Look at how much information you inferred from a few short sentences. You made inferences and understood the implied meaning when you answered the questions about Juan. You were able to "read between the lines" and fill out the story. You infer information in a similar way all the time, every day. The inference questions you just answered are similar to the types of questions you should ask yourself when you read textbooks. You learn information directly from printed words, but often you are expected to move *beyond* what is printed for a more complete understanding.

Reader-Response Theory: Activating Prior Knowledge

READER-RESPONSE THEORY says that in order for you, the reader, to understand what you are reading, you need to have knowledge about what you are reading so that you can connect it with what you already know. If you have knowledge about the writer's topic, your prior knowledge, also called your schema, will be activated. As a result, you will be able to understand and respond to what the writer tells you. Your neural network will be activated, and you will connect what you already know to what you are reading. You will be able to respond by agreeing or disagreeing with the writer or by knowing that you need to do more research to be sure you understand what you are reading.

prior knowledge
everything you have learned or experienced about a topic previously

For example, if you took Biology 101 last term and are now taking Biology 102, you will probably have enough of a basic schema or neural network to be activated for the neurons to connect. When this happens, you can understand and catch on relatively easily and quickly to the material in the next, higher-level course. On the other hand, if you took an algebra course when you were a sophomore in high school and did not take any more math classes until your calculus course in college, you will probably not have the necessary knowledge to make it possible for you to easily understand this higher level course.

The same is true about anything you are reading. If what you are reading is above and beyond what you know, you need time to develop and increase

Tip FROM THE Brain Doctor

Remember that prior knowledge creates neural networks that new information can activate. In order to make inferences as you read, connect what you are reading to what you already know. If you do not have the prior knowledge or think you do not, the sentences are difficult, if not impossible, to understand. The more frustrated and upset you get about not understanding what you are reading, the more difficult it is for you to learn. Once you make a connection, suddenly the information will seem to fall into place and make sense.

your prior knowledge and grow and connect a new neural network about the new or more advanced topic. In other words, if you do not have prior knowledge about the topic, you will not easily be able to understand and respond to what you are reading.

Without knowledge and experiences similar to the writer's, you may find it difficult to make correct inferences about what you are reading and to understand what the writer is saying. You need to remember to look up new words as you are reading to connect what you already know and understand the points the author makes.

✓ COMPREHENSION CHECK

▶ Imagine you are reading a magazine article about the stock market and what people need to do to prevent bankruptcy. However, you do not know anything about the stock market. What will you need to do to be able to read and respond with understanding to this article?

ACTIVITY 6A
Apply Prior Knowledge to Reading Comprehension

Read the following paragraph that illustrates the importance of prior knowledge, and try to figure out what it is about.

Sehtolc Gnihsaw

The procedure is actually quite simple. First, you arrange the items into different groups. Of course one pile may be sufficient depending on how much there is to do. If you have to go somewhere else due to lack of facilities that is the next step; otherwise, you are pretty well set. It is important not to overdo things. That is, it is better to do too few things at once than too many. In the short run this may not seem important but complications can easily arise. A mistake can be expensive as well. At first, the whole procedure will seem complicated. Soon, however, it will become just another facet of life. It is difficult to foresee any end to the necessity for this task in the immediate future; but then one never can tell. After the procedure is completed, one arranges the materials into different groups again. Then they can be put into their appropriate places. Eventually they will be used once more and the whole cycle will then have to be repeated. However, that is part of life.

Source: From Dooling, D. and Lauchman, R., "Effects of Comprehension on Retention of Prose," *Journal of Experimental Psychology* vol. 88 (pp. 216–222). Copyright © 1971 American Psychological Association. Reprinted with permission.

Continued on next page.

1. What do you think the Sehtolc Gnihsaw procedure is about?

   _____

2. What do you infer from the paragraph?

   _____

3. If you had trouble understanding this paragraph, what made it difficult for you to understand?

   _____

4. Now read the title backward. What does it say?

   _____

5. Now that you know what the topic of the paragraph is, does it change your understanding of its meaning? How did your understanding about the reading change once you knew the title?

   _____

Making Inferences

MAKING AN INFERENCE OR CONCLUSION about what you read involves many factors—your assumptions, the author's words, other facts. As you make inferences while reading, check these factors. Ask useful questions to help you judge the accuracy of your inferences. What is the author's purpose for writing? What are the facts? What assumptions are you making? What might the author want you to get from his writing?

Very often when you are trying to infer what an author is saying, you make personal assumptions that lead you to that inference. Assumptions are beliefs and ideas that you have collected over your lifetime from your experiences. These assumptions may or may not be factual and many times include information you might not have ever questioned. For example, the sun sets each day and you assume it will rise again the next day. You accept this as true. We are greatly influenced by our own assumptions and use them, sometimes unknowingly, as we read.

For example, imagine walking into a person's house and seeing a framed picture on a table. You look at the picture and take in the facts. How many people are in it? Are they close together in the picture? Are they smiling? Is the picture in color, black-and-white, sepia? Was the picture taken outside

assumptions
beliefs and ideas collected over a lifetime from experiences

or inside? What is everyone wearing? Then you think about what you know of the person whose house you are in. Does this person have brothers or sisters? Where did this person grow up? Then you add your own assumptions. *Displaying family pictures is common, desirable. Having pictures of people in your house shows that you have a close relationship with them.* After all of this thinking, which may take only seconds, you may infer (or conclude) that the picture is of the person's family members.

ACTIVITY 6B
Make Assumptions and Inferences

Complete the unfinished sentences with the words you think should be there.

1. It is raining very hard outside. When Jane goes out, she will need to take a(n) _____ to keep her dry.

2. Joe is going to the beach. Remind him to pack his _____ so he can go swimming.

3. Michael always loved flying. When he had to select between being an airline pilot or a businessman, of course he chose being a(n) _____.

4. We can infer from the woman's sighing, red eyes, and smudged eye makeup that she has been _____.

5. We can infer from the sounding of the weather alert alarm that _____.

None of your responses may be 100% correct, but, based on the words on the page, what you know to be true, and your past experiences, your responses are most likely good conclusions or inferences.

Now read the following passage from *The Great Gatsby*. Write a short paragraph about what you think you know (infer) about the person being discussed. Provide at least three pieces of evidence from the paragraph to support what you think.

There was music from my neighbor's house through the summer nights. In his blue gardens men and girls came and went like moths among the whisperings and the champagne and the stars. At high tide in the afternoon I watched his guests driving from the tower of his raft, or taking the sun on the hot sand of his beach while his two motor-boats slit the waters of the Sound, drawing aquaplanes over cataracts of foam. On week-ends his Rolls-Royce became an omnibus, bearing parties to and from the city, between nine

© Corbis

Continued on next page.

in the morning and long past midnight, while his station wagon scampered like a brisk yellow bug to meet all trains.

Source: Fitzgerald, F. Scott. *The Great Gatsby.* Simon and Schuster: New York, 1925, 1925, p. 43.

1. Your inference:

_____

2. Evidence 1:

_____

3. Evidence 2:

_____

4. Evidence 3:

_____

5. Using your knowledge of word parts and context clues, what do you think the word *omnibus* means as used in this passage?

_____

_____

ACTIVITY 6C
Infer from Proverbs

Practice making inferences by explaining what the following proverbs mean.

Example: A closed mouth catches no flies.

Possible response: If you are quiet, you are less likely to say something you will regret.

1. A penny saved is a penny earned.

_____

2. A leopard cannot change its spots.

_____

3. She who marries for money will earn it.

_____

4. A drowning man will clutch at a straw.

_____

5. A golden key can open any door.

_____

The following strategies will help you infer meaning when an author does not directly state it. Using these will help you put the pieces together so that you can understand the author's main idea:

▶ Understand an author's purpose.

▶ Note comparisons and implied similarities.

▶ Understand an author's tone.

▶ Detect an author's bias.

▶ Recognize information gaps.

ACTIVITY 6D
You Already Use Inference Strategies

Before reading about inference strategies, see if you can figure out inferences by reading the poem here. Answer the following questions. You may be surprised by how many inference strategies you used. This poem is one of several poems that make up a play written in the mid-1970s. Since then, the play has been performed off-Broadway and has been adapted into a 2010 film titled _For Colored Girls_. The main idea is timeless, which is why it is still relevant after 40 years. The language is written like texting language is today, but long before texting became popular.

"no assistance"

1   without any assistance or guidance from you
      i have loved you assiduously for 8 months 2 wks & a day
      i have been stood up four times
      i've left 7 packages on yr doorstep
5   forty poems 2 plants & 3 handmade notecards i left
      town so i cd send to you

Continued on next page.

you have been no help to me
on my job
you call at 3:00 in the mornin on weekdays
10   so i cd drive 27 1/2 miles cross the bay before i go to work
charmin charmin
but you are of no assistance

i want you to know
this waz an experiment
15   to see how selfish i cd be
if i wd really carry on to snare a possible lover
if i waz capable of debasin my self for the love of another
if i cd stand not being wanted
when i wanted to be wanted
20   & i cannot
so
with no further assistance & no guidance from you
i am endin this affair

this note is attached to a plant
25   i've been watering since the day i met you
you may water it
yr damn self

1. The main idea is implied. What is it?

_____

_____

2. The author says, "i have loved you assiduously for 8 months 2 wks & a day." Using context clues, define *assiduously*. Why would the author use that word in this poem when the other words are easy, more familiar words?

_____

_____

3. Why does the author give the exact amount of time—"8 months 2 wks & a day"? What does that tell you about her?

_____

_____

4. The author provides a lot of specific detail. Why do you think she does this? What is her purpose?

_____

_____

5. She is not really carrying out an experiment in stanza 3 (lines 13–23). Why does she tell him she is?

_____

_____

6. What is her point about the plant? What assistance did she need that she did not get?

_____

_____

Strategy One: Understand an Author's Purpose

AN author's purpose is his or her reason for writing. A textbook author wants to inform you about a specific subject such as psychology, biology, history, or business. Authors also, at times, write to persuade you or to explain ideas. For example, an author of a biology text might want to persuade you of the importance of addressing climate change. A sociology textbook author might explain how one's culture affects one's decisions in life. Authors of other types of college reading material, such as essays, journal articles, and stories, write for other purposes, perhaps to stimulate your imagination as you read about possible technological advances or entertain you with stories.

author's purpose reason for writing

An author's purpose is frequently implied. To understand an author's purpose, begin by asking yourself, "What is the author's reason for writing this?" In the poem from Activity 6D, the author's purpose for writing was to express her anger and disappointment.

Read the following passage and ask yourself, "What is the author's purpose?"

> The ACT, like the SAT, is designed to test what a student has learned and to demonstrate the application of ideas. It uses both multiple-choice and essay questions. The ACT is the most common college admission test in Michigan, and test administrators make slight adjustments to maintain the same degree of difficulty each year.
>
> Source: Jodi Upton, *The Detroit News*, August 25, 2002.

There is no attempt at humor in this paragraph, no persuasion. The author's purpose is simply to inform. The author offers facts about the ACT. The following passage from a political science textbook has a different purpose. Can you figure it out?

> The most basic service that most governments are expected to offer their people is education. This is a prerequisite of economic development for the country as a whole, and it greatly expands the world of the individuals who are educated. Many nations of the Third World, whose populations were largely illiterate at the time independence was acquired, have had an uphill fight in bringing education to their peoples, but this story over the last fifty years is in the main one of success.
>
> Source: Shively W. Phillips. *Power & Choice: An Introduction to Political Science, 12th Edition*. NY: McGraw-Hill, 2011, p. 85.

When you ask yourself, "What is the author's purpose in writing this?" you can decide right away that it is not to entertain. There is actually not a lot of information in the passage or much detailed explanation. The author seeks to persuade you to see the value education has to an entire nation. Here is another passage from a sociology textbook. What do you think the author's purpose is here?

> 1   Cultures change because people are continually finding new ways of doing things. Invention, the process of creating new things, brought about products such as toothpaste (invented in 3000 BC), eyeglasses (262 AD), flushable toilets (the sixteenth century), can openers (1813), fax machines (1843— that's right, invented in 1843!), credit cards (1920s), sliced bread (1928), computer mouses (1964), Post-It notes (1980), and DVDs (1995).
>
> 2   Innovation—turning inventions into mass-market products—also sparks cultural changes. An innovator is someone determined to market an invention, even if it's someone else's good idea. For example, Henry Ford invented nothing new but "assembled into a car the discoveries of other men behind whom were centuries of work," an innovation that changed people's lives.
>
> Source: From BENOKRAITIS. *SOC* 1e (p. 55). Copyright © 2010 Cengage Learning.

There is a lot of detailed explanation in this passage. The author's purpose is to explain. The following passage is a little different. It is not from a textbook. What is the author's purpose?

> 1   I asked my mother, "What was Daddy like?"
> 2   "Crunchy, a bit salty, rich in fiber."
> 3   "Before you ate him, I mean."
> 4   "He was a little guy, insecure, anxious, neurotic ... pretty much like all you baby boys."
> 5   I felt closer than ever to the parent I had never known, who'd been dissolved in Mom's stomach just as I was being conceived. From whom I had

gotten not nurturing but nourishment. I thought, thank you, Dad. I know what it means for a [praying] mantis to sacrifice himself for the family.

Source: Boffa, Alesandro. "You're Losing Your Head, Viskovitz," in *You're an Animal, Viskovitz!* New York: Alfred A. Kopf, 2002, p. 27.

As you read the passage, you may have realized that praying mantises are talking to one another. It seems more like fantasy than just straight information. The author's purpose is to entertain.

ACTIVITY 6E
Identify an Author's Purpose

Read the following passages, and decide what the author's purpose is for each passage.

1.   Some of the latest research suggests that your taste in food can be formed even before you're born. The fluid in a mother's womb may carry the flavors of whatever she's been eating, and that fluid is often swallowed by the fetus growing in there. Julia Mennella conducted an experiment on how tastes are formed, studying mothers who drank carrot juice while they were pregnant or breastfeeding. She compared babies whose mothers drank carrot juice with those whose mothers didn't. All of the babies were given cereal mixed with water and then cereal mixed with carrot juice. The babies who had learned the taste of carrot juice from their mothers—either from breast milk or from amniotic fluid—liked the carrot juice/cereal combination much more than the other babies did. You probably have to be fed carrot juice at an early age (before you're old enough to say no) in order to want it on your cereal.

Source: Schlosser & Wilson, *Chew on This*, New York: Houghton Mifflin Company, pp. 108–109.

The author's purpose is:

a. to entertain   b. to inform   c. to illustrate   d. to praise

2.   In the midst of a pleasant dream I opened my eyes as the dawn was silently pushing the darkness from my bedroom window. Wavy streamers of pink and gold peeked out from behind the shrouded clouds. The freshly brewed breeze of the young day filled my room. I could hear the full-throated birds chanting their morning psalms of praise. Joyful peacefulness had come to visit me, and I was grateful. Sounds of gladness floated through the open window of the room, through my mind. The mistakes of yesterday took flight, and new and

Continued on next page.

better possibilities were present. As the horizon was lifting the great orange ball, I heard a distant echo of ancient words: "Let there be light."

Source: McKams, Fr. James. *In Living Faith*, Fenton, MO: Creative Communications for the Parish, 2012, Volume 27, Number 4.

The author's purpose is:

a. to persuade   b. to support   c. to disprove   d. to inspire

3.   1   Under the palm of one hand the child became aware of the scab of an old cut on his knee-cap. He bent forward to examine it closely. A scab was always a fascinating thing; it presented a special challenge he was never able to resist.

     2   Yes, he thought, I will pick it off, even if it isn't ready, even if the middle of it sticks, even if it hurts like anything.

     3   With a fingernail he began to explore cautiously around the edges of the scab. He got a nail underneath it, and when he raised it, but ever so slightly, it suddenly came off, the whole hard brown scab came off beautifully, leaving an interesting little circle of smooth red skin.

Source: Roald Dahl, *Skin and Other Stories*, Penguin Books, 2000, p. 90.

The author's purpose is:

a. to persuade   b. to encourage   c. to describe   d. to insult

4.   1   Adolf Hitler launched a war against cigarette smoking and sought to confiscate all guns. In *Hitler, Great Lives Observed*, it says that if Hitler's "people had found that he intended after the war to prohibit smoking and make the world of the future vegetarian it is probable that even the SS would have rebelled."

     2   We quite properly call Hitler's regime totalitarian. But Americans accept government invasion in other areas of private conduct—cigarette smoking—as an example of enlightened big government intervention. In one Northern California city, laws bar people from smoking in public parks! What's next? Americans' intake of meat and sugar? Don't laugh. Yale University professor Dr. Kelly Brownell believes that government should tax fatty, unhealthy foods to discourage their consumption. Said Brownell, "To me, there is no difference between Ronald McDonald and Joe Camel." He thinks the government should subsidize fruits and vegetables, to make them dirt cheap, but tax foods containing too many calories or grams of fat, so that people will think twice about their food purchases, knowing a Twinkie will hurt your wallet once you reach the cash register.

Source: Elder, Larry. *The Ten Things You Can't Say in America*, St. Martin Press, 2000, pp. 219–220.

The author's purpose is:

a. to persuade   b. to encourage   c. to entertain   d. to insult

5.   People vary in the extent to which they know and use a large variety of words. If you have made a conscious effort to expand your vocabulary, are an avid reader, or have spent time conversing with others who use a large and varied selection of words, then you probably have a large vocabulary. As a speaker, the larger your vocabulary, the more choices you have from which to select the words you want. Having a larger vocabulary, however, can present challenges when communicating with people whose vocabulary is more limited. As a speaker, you must try to adapt your vocabulary to the level of your listener so that your words will be understood. One strategy for assessing another's vocabulary level is to listen to the types and complexity of words the other person uses and to take your signal from your communication partner. When you have determined that your vocabulary exceeds that of your partner, you can use simpler synonyms for your words or use word phrases composed of more familiar terms. Adjusting your vocabulary to others does not mean talking down to them. It is merely polite behavior and effective communication to try to select words that others understand.

Source: From VERDERBER/VERDERBER. *Communicate!* 12e (p. 68). Copyright © 2008 Cengage Learning.

The author's purpose is:

a. to inform   b. to illustrate   c. to entertain   d. to object

Strategy Two: Note Comparisons and Implied Similarities

IN TEXTBOOKS, AUTHORS sometimes use comparisons to illustrate their points. For example, the author of a history text might use a familiar situation, such as that of parent and child, to illustrate and explain an unfamiliar situation, like the relationship between Britain and the colonies before the American Revolution. A biology text author might liken the human circulatory system (unfamiliar) to a road map (familiar).

comparisons
characteristics that are common to two or more things

Consider this example of a comparison and implied similarity. What two things are being compared?

> Learn to do the drudgery of scientific work. Although a bird's wing is perfect, the bird could never soar if it did not lean upon air. Facts are the air on which the scientist leans.

Source: Hergenhahn, B.R. *An Introduction to Theories of Learning.* Englewood Cliffs, NJ: Prentice Hall, 1982.

It seems from this statement that a bird needs air to fly just as a scientist needs hard work to arrive at factual information. Being implied here is that both the bird and the scientist are dependent on something. Even though the author does not directly state this dependence, he implies it with his comparison.

similes comparisons using the words *like* or *as*

Sometimes writers signal that they are making a comparison by using words such as *like* or *as*. Such comparisons are called similes. You have probably heard the expressions "worked like a dog," "cold as ice," or "light as a feather." Those are all similes.

With similes, authors add emotion, emphasis, and clarity to their words. Look at the photograph here taken from a photography book. At first glance, you may think it is a boy just looking at the light coming into the room. It is actually much more.

© Charles Harbutt

The boy is blind. He is in The Lighthouse, an institute in New York. He is not looking at the light. He is feeling the heat from the light, which is how he recognizes it. Read the following poem written in response to this picture, and take note of the simile in bold.

The Photograph

Shutter release button squeezed
like a thin hollow egg pushed beneath water,
and this blind boy
will always be
5 a blind boy
on his knees,
hands flat on the wall
like lips on a kiss.
His fingertips reach
10 for the familiar rope of heat,
he grabs for an instant,
and pulls himself into unexpected light;
it washes the dark dream from his eyes

until he is again, nothing
15 more than a photograph
in a closed book.

Source: D.A. Brooks. Used with permission.

In the poem, the author compares the blind boy's happiness of finding his rope of light everyday at noon to a tender kiss on the lips. His hands on the wall, lovingly touching the light, are being compared to lips kissing. A kiss is loving and soft. When we think of kissing someone, it usually means that we trust, embrace, and count on that someone. Described in this poem is a time of day when the boy feels connected to the world, which is otherwise a dark space for him. The rope of light becomes his "someone" or "everything." Notice that the word *like* in the sentence signals the comparison.

Sometimes, authors present two apparently dissimilar pieces of information next to one another *without* using any comparison words and expect you to infer what they mean. These kinds of comparisons are called metaphors. Consider these words by William Carlos Williams:

> **metaphors** strong comparison where one idea is described as another

Let the snake wait under
his weed
and the writing
be of words, slow and quick, sharp
to strike, quiet to wait,
sleepless.

Source: By William Carlos Williams, from THE COLLECTED POEMS: VOLUME II, 1939–1962, copyright ©1944 by William Carlos Williams. Reprinted by permission of New Directions Publishing Corp. and Carcanet Press Limited.

What do you think this is about? Writing and the creative process are being compared with nature. The snake makes the comparison more dramatic. Snakes are unpredictable, striking when one least expects it. The poet waits for the right words (waits for the snake to strike). The process cannot be forced, but the creative juices never rest—they are just waiting for the right moment. A metaphor is a comparison, like a simile, but stronger.

In the poem from Activity 6D, the author uses a plant as a metaphor for the relationship. She implies that a plant, like a relationship, needs attention and care. She says she watered it every day, implying that she did all the work in the relationship. In the end, she gives him the plant. He now has to do the work to keep it (the plant/their relationship) alive.

Have you ever sweat bullets while taking an exam, cried your eyes out, worked your butt off, or felt like a million bucks? If you are a native English speaker, you probably use metaphors and similes like these as well as other types of comparisons all the time. Begin looking for them in writing and purposefully thinking about what is being compared and why.

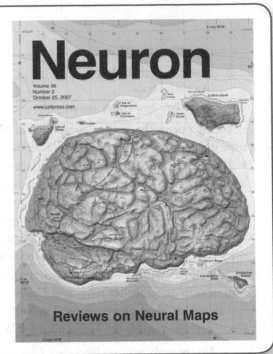

Tip FROM THE Brain Doctor

The brain loves metaphors because they are so visual and are connected to a large network of experience. If you can make comparisons when you think about information, it may be easier to remember, especially if you visualize what you are comparing the information to. Examine the cover of this scientific journal. What is the visual metaphor? What is being compared? How is the illustrator helping you see the comparison?

Neuron

Volume 56
Number 2
October 25, 2007
www.cellpress.com

Reviews on Neural Maps

ACTIVITY 6F
Identify Comparisons

Read the following passages. Identify what two items are being compared, and explain the implied similarity.

1.   Mentally, Tiger simply loved the competition, "I like the feeling of trying my hardest under pressure," he said. "But it's so intense, it's hard to describe. It feels like a lion is tearing at my heart." Physically, Tiger had developed golf muscles that would allow him to drive the ball over 300 yards.

Source: Rosaforte, Tim. *Tiger Woods: The Making of a Champion*. New York: St. Martin Press. 1997, pp. 27–28.

Comparison between:

_____

Implied similarity:

_____

2.   On a molecular scale, liquids resemble the people in the stadium aisles, who move more freely than when sitting in their seats. A liquid is an example of a fluid, which is any substance that flows. Flowing occurs when molecules are free to slide past one another and continually change their relative positions. The molecules are in constant motion. They are free to flow under, over, and around their neighboring molecules.

Source: *Heath Chemistry* (New York: D.C. Heath and Company. 1987).

Comparison between:

_____

Implied similarity:

_____

_____

3.   A social movement is a large and organized activity to promote or resist some particular social change. Examples of social movements include groups that focus on civil rights, the rights of the disabled, crime victims, gun control, and drunk driving to name just a few. Social movements are as American as apple pie, notes sociologist Lynda Ann Ewen.

Source: Nijole V. Benokraitis. *SOC*. Belmont, CA: Cengage Learning, 2012, p. 321.

Comparison between:

_____

Implied similarity:

_____

_____

4.   Viewing data as weapons and programs as their delivery system, the [computer] hacker considers himself a privateer of the modern era. He likens his computer to a vessel, a battleship for him to cruise the world's computer networks, assailing the weak and subverting the unsuspecting.

Source: Ritter, Jonathan. "The World View of a Computer Hacker," in M. Connelly, *The Sundance Reader*, 2nd ed. New York: Harcourt Brace College Publishers, 2000, p. 187.

Continued on next page.

Comparison between:

_____

Implied similarity:

_____

_____

5.   Culture is the principal tool we use to feed ourselves. That is, human beings, in groups, develop forms of knowledge and technologies that enable them to get the necessary energy from the environment to make life more secure.

Source: From NANDA/WARMS. *Cultural Anthropology* 9e (p. 103). Copyright © 2007 Cengage Learning.

Comparison between:

_____

Implied similarity:

_____

_____

Strategy Three: Understand an Author's Tone

TONE IN WRITING is like facial expressions in speaking. If you are good at reading facial expressions, you may be good at Theory of Mind, or figuring out what others are thinking. This skill should also help you when you read to figure out tone and the author's implied meaning.

A famous scientist named Paul Ekman determined that there are some universal facial expressions. In every culture around the world that he studied, he found that these expressions conveyed the same basic emotions regardless of where people lived. See if you can infer the emotions from the following facial expressions and, thus, discover these basic emotions according to Ekman.

Read the following passage, and think about the ways authors use their writing to express emotions, similar to facial expressions.

The Universality of Facial Expressions

Human facial expressions are also designed to arouse reactions from others. The early work of Darwin (who took full advantage of the British Empire's broad geography) indicated that people all over the world both express and perceive facial expression in similar ways. These early observations were confirmed recently by Paul Ekman, Ph.D., of the University of California Medical School at San Francisco, who enlarged Darwin's observations, using more sophisticated methods. Traveling to exotic locations such as Papua New Guinea where the residents had little contact with outsiders, Ekman showed the natives photographs of people expressing anger, happiness, disgust, surprise, sadness, and fear and asked them to say what emotion was being expressed. He found

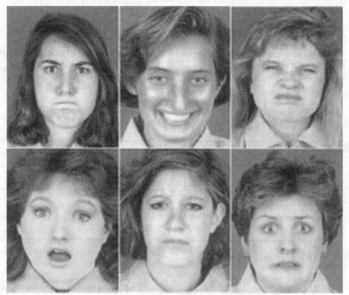

Source: Solso, RL. "The cognitive neuroscience of art: A preliminary fMRI observation." *Journal of Consciousness Studies* 2000, 7: 75–85. Permission courtesy Imprint Academic. All Rights Reserved. Photo by Anne Solso.

wide general agreement in the emotions identified, which he interpreted as meaning "our evolution gives us universal expressions, which tell others some important information about us." In these universal signals we are able to read another's emotions, attitudes, and truthfulness. Of course, exceptions abound, such as the everyday deceptions put forward for our benefit by, for example, actors on stage and salespeople who have learned to mimic genuine facial expressions. Although culture shapes the nuances of facial expressions, nature seems to endow us with a limited number of basic emotions and ways to convey them, much like a language, which is basically the same everywhere it is used but is subject to local dialects.

Source: From Robert L. Solso "About Faces, in Art and in the Brain," *Cerebrum* (July 01, 2004). Copyright © 2004 The Dana Foundation. Reprinted with permission.

ACTIVITY 6G
Detect Emotions

Describe a time when you knew someone was angry or upset with you, even though he or she did not say a word. How did you know? What did he or she do that convinced you? And, when he or she did speak, what made you know that this person was not happy?

_____

_____

_____

_____

ACTIVITY 6H
Design Emoticons

How do you show emotion or tone in an email? Draw an emoticon that you would use in an e-mail to represent the following emotions. It can be letters that stand for something or a drawing of symbols.

1. amused

_____

2. laughing

_____

3. sad

_____

4. offhand remark

_____

List as many emoticons as you can, and write the emotion or tone they are intended to convey. Review a reading in this chapter, and draw appropriate emoticons in the margin.

author's tone the emotion or feeling that an author's words give

The tone authors use to discuss their subject matter can reveal their attitude toward it. You can assess an author's tone by examining the words used and by taking the time to picture the images created with figurative language. Tone is a subtle aspect of an author's writing. An author's tone also emphasizes the author's purpose for writing. If the purpose is to entertain, the tone may be humorous; if the purpose is to persuade, the tone may be authoritative or even sarcastic; if the purpose is to inform, the tone may be formal and emotionless.

An author's diction or word choice is a good place to start when you are trying to determine the author's tone. In the poem from Activity 6D, the author chooses specific words to express her anger: *i've been stood up, you have been no help to me, water it yr damn self.*

Read the following sentences, and decide which one is positive and which one is negative.

Example 1:   Pushy children hawking overpriced cookies to unsuspecting grocery store shoppers for class-trip money is an American tradition.

Example 2:   Hard-working students who raise money from supportive community members are keeping up an American tradition.

Did you notice a difference? What is the author talking about in each example? Complete the following chart by listing words used in each example.

Topic of examples: _____

Example 1: Negative Language	Example 2: Positive Language

Even though the topic is the same, what is the implied main idea for each example?

_____

_____

_____

_____

Consider the following example from a history textbook.

> Although the development of gas masks significantly reduced the impact of this (menacing) new chemical warfare, the (threat) of poison gas added another (nightmarish) element to the experience of those who fought the war.
>
> Source: From NOBEL/STRAUSS/OSHEIM/NEUSCHEL. _Western Civilization Beyond Boundaries_ 6e (p. 699). Copyright © 2011 Cengage Learning.

The words _menacing_, _threat_, and _nightmarish_ help you infer the hardship of war. There are other aspects to war such as bravery, pride, and heroism, but this writer wants readers to focus on the difficulties, and he directs them with his choice of words. Contrast that passage with this one about Thomas Aquinas from the same textbook.

> Thomas Aquinas (1225–1274) was the (greatest) of the Scholastics, the most (sensitive) to Greek and Arab thought, and the most (prolific) medieval philosopher.
>
> Source: From NOBEL/STRAUSS/OSHEIM/NEUSCHEL. _Western Civilization Beyond Boundaries_ 6e (p. 275). Copyright © 2011 Cengage Learning.

Notice the words _greatest_, _sensitive_, and _prolific_. These words imply a positive meaning.

Emotive language are words authors use that are intended to persuade you and guide your thinking. They are words that let you know if there is additional or implied meaning to the text. For example, suppose an author talks about a

emotive language words that, when read, bring about certain feelings and emotions

politician he does not like. He may refer to the politician as *shady* or *slippery*. However, if the same author refers to a politician he likes, he may use terms such as *honest* or *innovative*. Or suppose an author wants to refer to a heavy-set person. She may use the word *husky* or *obese*. In our culture, it is acceptable for a young man to be husky, so if the author chooses that word, she presents a positive spin on the person. *Obese* would imply a more negative meaning. Words are powerful. They plant seeds of images in the minds of readers.

ACTIVITY 61
Work with Emotive Language

For each word, provide a word that means the same that is positive and one that means the same that is negative.

Word	Positive Word	Negative Word
Example: heavy-set	husky	obese
little		
unfriendly		
loud		
quiet		
new		
old		
hungry		
thirsty		
unattractive		
inexpensive		

ACTIVITY 6J
Set the Tone

Read the following passages, and choose the word that best matches the author's tone. As you read, circle words that help you identify the tone. The first one is modeled for you.

Example:

> The body of Richard Milhous Nixon was (scarcely) in the ground when the (struggle) for (control) of his legacy had begun. That day on the plane, the (dark forces) that (haunted) Nixon in life seemed to (reach beyond) the grave. Somewhere between the two coasts, Ed Cox, Tricia's New York attorney husband, brought up a plan to ensure the Nixon library would be (tightly controlled) by the family rather than by hired hands.
>
> Source: Adapted from "Nixon Daughters Spar over Library," *The Detroit News*, April 28, 2002, p. 8a.

The tone of this passage can best be described as:

a. joyful.   b. sarcastic.   (c.) troubled.   d. inspirational.

Explain why you selected your response.

<u>Emotive words such as *dark forces* and *haunted* give the passage a troubled tone.</u>

1.   The Complete Rules of Good Writing

Do not use, unnecessary, commas.

Do not use a foreign word when there is an adequate English quid pro quo.

Do not use hyperbole; not even one in a million can do it effectively.

Don't repeat yourself and avoid being repetitive.

Don't use no double negatives. The double negative is a no-no.

Don't be redundant; don't use more words than necessary it's highly superfluous.

Don't indulge in sesquipedalian lexicological constructions.

Don't overuse exclamation marks!!!

Don't repeat yourself, or say again what you have said before.

"Don't use unattributed quotations."

Source: Antal. Parody. *Eats, Shoots, & Leaves: Crap English and How to Use It*. Michael O'Mara Books Limited. Great Britain. 2004.

The tone of this passage can best be described as:

a. humorous.   b. sarcastic.   c. troubled.   d. inspirational.

Explain why you selected your response.

_____

_____

Continued on next page.

2.   To sum up, in philosophy, as in so many other endeavors, the Archaic Greeks were great borrowers and even greater innovators who left a profound mark on later ages. Lyric poetry and Archaic sculpture display a ground-breaking interest in individual feelings and the human body. By the late sixth century B.C., Archaic Greece was poised on the brink of a revolution that would give birth to the Classical period of Greek civilization.

Source: From NOBEL/STRAUSS/OSHEIM/NEUSCHEL. *Western Civilization Beyond Boundaries* 6e (p. 66). Copyright © 2011 Cengage Learning.

The tone of this passage can best be described as:

a. joyful.   b. sarcastic.   c. religious.   d. inspirational.

Explain why you selected your response.

_____

_____

3.   As humans expand and continue to devour land, water and natural resources, it is critical to remember that we are only one part of a vastly complex, organic mosaic composed of myriad life forms—all of which are dependent on the earth for survival.

 By appropriating more and more of this planet with our growing numbers and our technology, humans are effectively condemning other life on earth to an increasingly diminished existence.

Source: Ettingoff, S. "How Population Growth Effects the Planet" *New York Times,* The Opinion Page. October 27, 2011.

The tone of this passage can best be described as:

a. humorous.   b. sentimental.   c. warning.   d. sarcastic.

Explain why you selected your response.

_____

_____

4.   The United States established the Internet, a global media network that uses mainly English and is heavily saturated with American advertising and popular culture (Louw 2001). Iran's government has recently denounced Batman, Spider- Man, and Harry Potter toys as a form of "cultural invasion" that challenges the country's conservative and religious values. The curvaceous and often scantily clad Barbie dolls with peroxide-blond hair have been especially singled out as "destructive culturally and a social danger." However, many of the girls who watch foreign television and (illegal) satellite want the dolls.

Source: From NOBEL/STRAUSS/OSHEIM/NEUSCHEL. *Western Civilization Beyond Boundaries* 6e (p. 66). Copyright © 2011 Cengage Learning.

The tone of this passage can best be described as:

a. angry.   b. condescending.   c. serious.   d. humorous.

Explain why you selected your response.

_____

_____

5.   I learned on that day that it was fruitless to expect Jaclyn to apologize for any of her bad behavior as I expected my other children to do. Jaclyn would have sat in the time-out chair for days before she proffered an apology. I was angered by her stubborn refusal to offer this simple act of contrition. I joined a group of moms who had adopted older children from China; it was a support group that I desperately needed. One of the things I discovered through my conversation with others in the group was that Jaclyn's behavior reflected a cultural norm: to "lose face" was much worse than to accept punishment. Her past, still a puzzle to me, had made her who she was, and I knew that I needed to understand that better to really know how to parent her.

Source: Champnella, Cindy. (2003). *The Waiting Child.* St. Martin's Griffin: New York. p. 43.

The tone of this passage can best be described as:

a. sentimental.   b. angry.   c. mocking.   d. frustrated.

Explain why you selected your response.

_____

_____

Strategy Four: Detect an Author's Bias

TO DETECT AN author's bias, picture the author. Remember the Theory of Mind, that all people have personal feelings, beliefs, and opinions? These feelings, beliefs, and opinions color what authors write. The fact that authors write based on their own feelings, beliefs, and opinions does not necessarily make what they write wrong, though it can. It makes what they write a result of what they think and who they are. The words on a page are not always completely neutral.

author's bias a tendency toward a specific view, a prejudice

Most writing has some bias, even textbooks. When you read, ask yourself, "Is the author biased? How does the bias affect what the author says?"

Tip FROM THE Brain Doctor

Did you know that brain scans show that when someone reads emotional material, the emotional area of the brain lights up, as if the reader is actually experiencing the emotion? If you read material containing words with strong negative associations, such as *violent, bloody, fearful, angry, dying,* and so forth, your brain reacts to those negative emotions and experiences them. Do you like to fire up angry, negative emotions in yourself, do you like to experience fear through reading scary stories, or do you prefer to conjure up positive emotions? What you read can make a difference in how you feel afterward.

An author's bias can result in an imbalanced picture of an issue, either because authors omit information that contradicts their own points of view or they downplay or cancel out other viewpoints. An author's bias also can emphasize a point or direct the reader down a certain path of thinking. It is important to be able to detect bias so you can make an informed decision about whether to accept or challenge what an author says.

One way to detect an author's bias is to notice the use of emotive language—just as you did with noting the author's tone. When a writer uses words that convey emotion, he or she usually asserts an opinion. Opinions may or may not be founded on facts, but basing textbook material on opinions can promote bias. In the following passage from a biology textbook, the emotive words are circled.

> Endangered species are also collected or killed for profit. It is a (sad) commentary on human nature that the rarer a species becomes, the higher the price it (fetches) on the black market.
>
> Source: From STARR. Biology: *The Unity and Diversity of Life* 12e (p. 895). Copyright © 2009 Cengage Learning.

What types of feelings do the words *sad* and *fetches* evoke? The word *sad* evokes unhappy emotions and the word *fetches* means "to bring" but implies casualness, an action done without much thought or concern. The author's choice of words implies that she has sympathy for endangered animals and disdain for those who sacrifice them for money.

✓ COMPREHENSION CHECK

▶ What is bias?
▶ Name one bias that you have. (Biases can be positive, too.)
▶ Name a negative bias that people have.

ACTIVITY 6K
Detect Bias

Read the following passages, and answer the questions that follow. The emotive words have been circled.

1.   These (false) underlying assumptions about racism have led the general public, scholars, and activists all over the world to (misread) and (misunderstand) contemporary racism. The most notable of these well intended (misreadings) in the United States is Wilson's (mistitled) book, *The Declining Significance of Race* (1978).

   Source: Browser, Benjamin. *Racism and Anti-Racism in World Perspective* (Sage Publications,1995).

   What is the author's bias?

   _____

   _____

2.   To put all of this another way: think of this book as your own, private apprenticeship (alongside me,) the (Cake Boss) himself. I am going to teach you everything I learned at (my family's bakery,) in the same order I learned to do it. We're going to start by making his cookies, then work our way up through the Carlo's "curriculum" of pastries, pies, basic cakes, and theme cakes.

   Source: Valastro, Buddy. (2011). U.S. Airways, *Must Read.* US Airways - Pace Communications, Inc., p. 116.

   What is the author's bias?

   _____

   _____

3.   But it is (our) children—the children of farm workers and Hispanics and other minorities— who are seeking a better life. (It is for them, for their future—and for the future of California)— that we must say "no" to suspending Proposition 98. We must say "no" to cutting (essential services for the needy) instead of tax (loopholes for the wealthy.) We must say "no" to making (our) children and (their) teachers (scapegoats) for the budget crisis.

   Source: Chavez, Cesar. (1991). Statement From Cesar Chavez President, United Farm Workers, Sacramento, April 3, 1991.

Continued on next page.

What is the author's bias?

_____

_____

4.   Walter Hagen won 11 major championships from 1914–1929, and was one of the most charismatic players the game has ever known. He once said, "I never wanted to be a million-aire, I just wanted to live like one." Although he wasn't the straightest hitter, The Haig had amazing powers of recovery. His swing had a lot of lateral movement, but this classic position at the top shows a beautiful turn. It's worth copying: Left arm relaxed, hands soft, ready to make a full release on the downswing.

Source: Leadbetter, David. (2011). Golf Digest, _Learn for the Legends._ November, 2011, p. 25.

What is the author's bias?

_____

_____

5.   The emergence of powerful technologies that make it easier to track people's movements and their activities online has raised difficult questions about where to draw the line when it comes to protecting individual privacy. The issue discussed before the U.S. Supreme Court, however, does not fall in the difficult category. It involved a GPS tracking device that FBI agents put on the vehicle of a suspected drug dealer without a search warrant. An appellate court held this was a violation of the 4th Amendment guarantee against unreasonable searches. Both conservative and liberal justices were uncomfortable with the FBI practice. We're troubled, too. We doubt the signers of the Constitution—so concerned about individual rights—envisioned a federal government with unlimited power to conduct surveillance on its citizens.

Source: From _The San Diego Union Tribune_ (November 10, 2011, B-6). Copyright © 2011. Reprinted with permission.

What is the author's bias?

_____

_____

Strategy Five: Recognize Information Gaps

IT IS PARTICULARLY difficult to draw inferences from reading material when limited information is presented or when information appears to be missing, which are known as information gaps. Sometimes as you read, you may find that an author leaps from one idea to the next, seemingly skipping the information that should be in the middle. When writers do this, they assume that you have a certain amount of background knowledge and can fill in the gaps that are left on the page. Read the following example.

information gaps places in readings where information appears to be missing or where an author intends for the reader to infer meaning

China Pulls Off Tricky Satellite Maneuver

Experts say China pulled off a tricky and uncommon feat in space by maneuvering a satellite to within about 300 yards of another while they were orbiting Earth. Analysts say the August encounter could have been a test of China's ability to inspect its own satellites or to spy on others. It also could have been practice for docking orbiting vehicles, a skill required to build the space station China is expected to begin work on next year. The analysts, whom the Associated Press did not name, said the exercise probably wasn't meant solely to practice an attack on another country's satellite by ramming it. U.S. military officials confirm that the exercise occurred but have released few details. Chinese space officials didn't respond to questions.

Source: From "China shows space skills with satellite," *Detroit Free Press* (November 14, 2010 p. 26-A) Copyright © 2010 The Associated Press. Reprinted with permission.

The author does not tell you why there is concern nor confirms what actually took place. Instead, the author intentionally plants seeds of doubt, which could be alarming if taken out of context. How does the author do this? What is implied in this short article? Circle the words that are used to help plant doubt in the reader's mind.

▶ The author says that it "could have been" a test to inspect its own satellites."

▶ Or, "it could have been a test to spy on others." (Spy on whom? And why? This is a big leap in thinking.)

▶ The author then says, "It could have been practice for docking orbiting vehicles."

▶ But then in the next sentence he says, "It probably wasn't meant solely to practice an attack on another country's satellite by ramming it." What a leap the author makes! Note the use of words—"It probably wasn't meant to solely" ... meaning that it will probably do this. It will attack another country's satellite by ramming it. It may be used for other purposes, but it will be used to attack.

This is a very strong article that at first does not appear to say much. Nothing is proven. But, by leaving information gaps, the author leads the reader to believe that China is up to no good. The author never directly says that China is doing something negative but implies it. What did you think when you read this article?

The following steps can help you recognize information gaps in your textbooks and other reading materials.

1. In order to decide whether information is missing, read the entire reading and consider all the information presented.

2. Note the author's use of key words and phrases that represent the topic and main ideas of what you are reading.

3. Look for information gaps or leaps from one idea to the next following key words. Pause to mentally fill in any information gaps.

To help clarify how you would use these steps, read this passage from a political science textbook.

1   The original version of the Electoral College worked as the Framers intended only for as long as George Washington was willing to seek and hold the presidency. That is, in 1789 and again in 1792, each elector cast one of his two ballots for the great Virginian.

2   Flaws began to appear in the system in 1796, however. By then, political parties had begun to form. John Adams, the Federalist candidate, was elected to the presidency. Thomas Jefferson, an arch-rival and Democratic-Republican, who lost to Adams by just three votes in the electoral balloting, became his Vice-President.

Source: W. McClenaghan. *Magruder's American Government* (New York: Prentice Hall, 1994).

Reread the first sentence in the second paragraph. What word does the author use to let you know how he feels regarding the Electoral College? What is the word that lets you know the author's bias? What alternative word could be used that would change the meaning?

The author says flaws began to appear in the system. The next sentence leaps to the idea that political parties had already begun to form. There is an information gap here, signaled by the key words *flaws* and *political parties,* which are close to each other and suggest that the reader should pause to draw an inference. The inference is that in governmental evolution, political party formation revealed a flaw in the system—that candidates from the opposing parties could be placed in office together as president and vice president.

ACTIVITY 6L
Look for Information Gaps

Read the following textbook passages, and look for information gaps. Answer the inference questions that follow. Key words and phrases are circled.

1. For thousands of years, human beings have fashioned natural materials into useful products. Modern chemistry certainly has its roots in this endeavor. After the discovery of fire, people began to notice changes in certain rocks and minerals exposed to high temperatures. From these observations came the development of ceramics, glass, and metals, which today are among our most useful materials. Dyes and medicines were other early products obtained from natural substances. For example, the ancient Phoenicians extracted a bright purple dye, known as Tyrian purple, from a species of sea snail. One ounce of Tyrian purple required over 200,000 snails. Because of its brilliant hue and scarcity, the dye became the choice of royalty.

    Source: Ebbing, Darrell. *General Chemistry.* New York: Houghton Mifflin Company, 1943, p. 4.

    Although it is not directly stated, why would something with a "brilliant hue" that is "scarce" be suitable for royalty? What can you infer the author means when he mentions the brilliant hue and scarcity?

    _____

    _____

2. The Sophists took this idea to its extreme and asserted that it makes no sense to ask "What is something like really?" The only "answer" is that it "really" is the way it appears to me, the way it appears to you, and the way it appears to everyone else when they observe it. If there are no absolutes and if everything is relative, then opposite conclusions can both be supported. The way something seems to me is the way it is. In a sense, the Sophists turned the distinction between appearances and reality on its head.

    Source: Mitchell, Helen. *Roots of Wisdom.* Belmont, CA: Wadsworth. 2008. p. 27.

    Although the author does not directly say how she feels about the Sophists' point of view, what can you infer?

    _____

    _____

3. When European settlers first arrived in North America, they found 3 billion to 5 billion passenger pigeons. In the 1800s, commercial hunting caused a steep decline in the bird's numbers.

    Continued on next page.

The last time anyone saw a wild passenger pigeon was in 1900—and he shot it. The last captive bird died in 1914.

Source: From STARR. *Biology: The Unity and Diversity of Life* 12e (p. 894). Copyright © 2009 Cengage Learning.

Although the author never directly states his feelings, how do you think he feels about the destruction of passenger pigeons?

_____

_____

4.   A door just opened on a street—
        I, lost, was passing by—
        An instant's width of warmth disclosed
        And wealth, and company.

5   The door as sudden shut, and I,
        I, lost, was passing by,—
        Lost doubly, but by contrast most,
        Enlightening misery.

        —Emily Dickinson

Emily Dickinson does not state directly how she feels, but what can you infer when she says "enlightening misery?" What does she see that causes her to feel "lost doubly"?

_____

_____

5.   Ring around the rosy
        A pocketful of posies
        "Ashes, Ashes"
        We all fall down!

What would be a good title for this common children's poem? What meaning do you infer from this poem?

_____

_____

The concept of information gaps is brilliantly illustrated in cartoons and sarcastic photographs. The information that is not specifically stated in words is what makes them so funny. Your mind infers the punch line. Look at the cartoon here regarding progress and the explanation that follows. These are types of questions you should ask yourself when reading a cartoon or looking at a photograph.

"In return for an increase in my allowance, I can offer you free unlimited in-home computer tech support."

▶ **What do you think is the implied main idea, or punch line, of this cartoon?** Children are better with technology than adults. The older generation relies on their expertise to help, instead of teaching them. Roles have changed.

▶ **What are some of the details the cartoonist uses to make his point(s)?** The child is very confident and has business savvy. The blank look on the father's face means he is taking the child seriously. The father seems professional working on the computer, which makes the comic a little more ironic. Do you see anything else?

ACTIVITY 6M
Identify Information Gaps in a Cartoon

Read the cartoon, and answer the questions that follow.

Continued on next page.

1. What is the implied main idea, or punch line, that the cartoonist is making?

_____

_____

2. What are some of the details the author uses to make his point?

_____

_____

3. Based on how the cows are positioned, what is the implied meaning?

_____

_____

4. Do the position of the cows and the implied meaning (see question #3) strengthen the cartoon? Why or why not?

_____

_____

5. Provide your own title for this cartoon based on your understanding of it.

_____

_____

✓ **COMPREHENSION CHECK**

▶ What are the five strategies for making inferences introduced in this chapter?

Knowing How Much to Infer

ONE PROBLEM THAT CAN OCCUR when making inferences to establish the implied main idea is inferring too much. You can sometimes quickly jump to a conclusion when you read without establishing sound reasons for that conclusion. Remember that reading is a two-way conversation. You cannot ignore the other person speaking—the author. Here are some strategies to ensure that your inferences are accurate.

▶ **Recognize an author's perspective.** When you read, attend carefully to what an author says and try to see things from his or her perspective. For example, suppose the author of a cultural anthropology textbook writes, "Many similarities between man and his closest primate relations, the great apes, have been described." You should not conclude from the words *man, closest relations,* and *apes* that the author implies that humans and apes are as closely related as human siblings. The words do not support that conclusion. The inference that humans and apes are as closely related as siblings is an assumption that is not based on the actual content of the sentence. The author is a cultural anthropologist who defines the term *closest primate relations* in the context of thousands of years of history and the separate development of humans and ape. When he uses the term *closest,* he is not talking in terms of the two to three years that commonly separate siblings.

▶ **Use the text to support your conclusion.** When you infer something, you need to test your conclusion against the rest of the material in the text. Is there any information in the text that challenges your inference? If so, perhaps you are inferring too much. Are there details in the text that support your inference? If there are, your inference is probably accurate.

ACTIVITY 6N
Practice How Much to Infer

Read the following questions before you read the sociology textbook passage. You will answer them *after* you read the passage, but think about them as you read.

1. What is the author's perspective?

2. Why does she include the commentary from the homeless man? What is his bias? What in the text supports your answer?

3. What purpose does the quiz serve? Why do you think the author includes it?

4. What is the tone of the commentary? What is the tone of the passage? What in the text supports your answer?

5. Do you think the author has a bias? What in the text supports your answer?

Continued on next page.

The passage begins with commentary from a homeless man who is now an author. After the commentary, there is a question that serves as the passage's heading. After the heading, the sociology chapter begins. Then there is a sociology quiz at the end. Read all the parts of the passage, take the quiz, and then answer the questions that follow the passage.

1   I began dumpster diving [scavenging in a large garbage bin] about a year before I became homeless. ... The area I frequent is inhabited by many affluent college students. I am not here by chance; the Dumpsters in this area are very rich. Students throw out many good things, including food. In particular they tend to throw everything out when they move at the end of a semester, before and after breaks, and around midterm, when many of them despair of college. So I find it advantageous to keep an eye on the academic calendar. I learned to scavenge gradually, on my own. Since then I have initiated several companions into the trade. I have learned that there is a predictable series of stages a person goes through in learning to scavenge.

2   At first the new scavenger is filled with disgust and self-loathing. He is ashamed of being seen and may lurk around, trying to duck behind things, or he may dive at night. (In fact, most people instinctively look away from a scavenger. By skulking around, the novice calls attention to himself and arouses suspicion. Diving at night is ineffective and needlessly messy.) ... That stage passes with experience. The scavenger finds a pair of running shoes that fit and look and smell brand-new. ... He begins to understand: People throw away perfectly good stuff, a lot of perfectly good stuff.

3   At this stage, Dumpster shyness begins to dissipate. The diver, after all, has the last laugh. He is finding all manner of good things that are his for the taking. Those who disparage his profession are the fools, not he.

—Author Lars Eighner recalls his experiences as a Dumpster diver while living under a shower curtain in a stand of bamboo in a public park. Eighner became homeless when he was evicted from his "shack" after being unemployed for about a year. (Eighner, 1993: 111–119).

How is Homelessness Related to the Social Structure of a Society?

4   Eighner's "diving" activities reflect a specific pattern of social behavior. All activities in life—including scavenging in garbage bins and living "on the streets"—are social in nature. Homeless persons and domiciled persons (those with homes) live in social worlds that have predictable patterns of social interaction. **Social interaction is the process by which people act toward or respond to other people and is the foundation for all relationships and groups in society.** In this chapter, we look at the relationship between social structure and social interaction. In the process, homelessness is used as an example of how social problems occur and how they may be perpetuated within social structures and patterns of interaction.

5   **Social structure** is the complex framework of societal institutions (such as the economy, politics, and religion) and the social practices (such as rules and social roles) that make up a society and that organize and establish limits on people's behavior.

This structure is essential for the survival of society and for the well-being of individuals because it provides a social web of familial support and social relationships that connects each of us to the larger society. Many homeless people have lost this vital linkage. As a result, they often experience a loss of personal dignity and a sense of moral worth because of their " homeless" condition (Snow and Anderson, 1993).

6   Homeless persons such as Eighner come from all walks of life. They include full-time and part-time workers, parolees, runaway youths and children, veterans, and the elderly. They live in cities, suburbs, and rural areas. Contrary to popular myths, most of the homeless are not on the streets by choice or because they are mentally ill. Before reading on, learn more about homeless persons and the pressing national problem of homelessness by taking the quiz in the Sociology and Everyday Life box.

Source: From KENDALL. *Sociology in Our Times: The Essentials* 8e (pp. 104–5). Copyright © 2012 Cengage Learning.

How Much Do You Know about Homeless Persons?

True	False	
T	F	1. A significant increase in family homelessness has occurred in the United States in recent years.
T	F	2. Alcoholism and domestic violence are the primary factors that bring about family homelessness.
T	F	3. Many homeless people have full-time employment.
T	F	4. Many homeless people are mentally ill.
T	F	5. Homeless people typically panhandle (beg for money) so that they can buy alcohol or drugs.
T	F	6. Shelters for the homeless consistently have clients who sleep on overflow cots, in chairs, in hallways, and other nonstandard sleeping arrangements.
T	F	7. There have always been homeless persons throughout the history of the United States.
T	F	8. In large urban areas such as Los Angeles, many homeless people live in tent cities or other large on encampments.

Answers to the Sociology Quiz on Homelessness and Homeless Persons

1. True   Recently, a significant increase has occurred in the number of homeless families while there has been a decrease or leveling in the number of homeless single adults, partly due to policies aimed at ending chronic homelessness among single adults with disabilities.

2. False   Primary causes of family homelessness are as follows: job loss, foreclosures on homes brought about by the recession, and a lack of affordable housing in many cities.

Continued on next page.

3. True   Many homeless people do have full-time employment, but they are among the working poor. The minimum-wage jobs they hold do not pay enough for them to support their families and pay the high rents that are typical in many cities.

4. False   Most homeless people are not mentally ill; estimates suggest that about one-fourth of the homeless are emotionally disturbed.

5. False   Many homeless persons panhandle to pay for food, a bed at a shelter, or other survival needs.

6. True   Overcrowded shelters throughout the nation often attempt to accommodate as many homeless people as possible on a given night, particularly when the weather is bad. As a result, any available spaces—including offices, closets, and hallways—are used as sleeping areas until the individuals can find another location or weather conditions improve.

7. True   Scholars have found that homelessness has always existed in the United States. However, the number of homeless persons has increased or decreased with fluctuations in the national economy.

8. False   Although media reports frequently show homeless individuals and families living in tent cities or other large homeless encampments in major U.S. cities, official studies by the U.S. Conference of Mayors (2009) have found that only ten large U.S. cities have tent cities and that these cities hold only very small percentage of people who are homeless.

Source: U.S. Conference of Mayors, 2009.

Source: From KENDALL. *Sociology in Our Times: The Essentials* 8e (pp. 107–8). Copyright © 2012 Cengage Learning.

1. What is the author's perspective?

_____

_____

_____

2. Why does she include the commentary from the homeless man? What is his bias? What in the text supports your answer?

_____

_____

_____

3. What purpose does the quiz serve? Why do you think the author includes it?

_____

_____

_____

4. What is the tone of the commentary? What is the tone of the passage? What in the text supports your answers?

_____

_____

_____

5. Do you think the author has a bias? What in the text supports your answer?

_____

_____

_____

PRACTICE WITH A READING PASSAGE

Prepare to Read

1. Based on the title, what do you expect the following passage to be about?

_____

2. What do you know about the topic?

_____

From *The Hunger Games*
By Suzanne Collins

1   Effie Trinket crosses back to the podium, smoothes the slip of paper, and reads out the name in a clear voice. And it's not me. It's Primrose Everdeen.

blind space hidden from view

2   One time, when I was in a blind in a tree, waiting motionless for game to wander by, I dozed off and fell ten feet to the ground, landing on my back. It was as if the impact had knocked every wisp of air from my lungs, and I lay there struggling to inhale, to exhale, to do anything.

3   That's how I feel now, trying to remember how to breathe, unable to speak, totally stunned as the name bounces around the inside of my skull. Someone is gripping my arm, a boy from the Seam, and I think maybe I started to fall and he caught me.

Seam the poorest part of the fictional District 12, where the narrator lives

tesserae small square tile used in ancient times as a ticket or identification

4   There must have been a mistake. This can't be happening. Prim was one slip of paper in thousands! Her chances of being chosen so remote that I'd not even bothered to worry about her. Hadn't I done everything? Taken the tesserae, refused to let her do the same? One slip. One slip in thousands. The odds had been entirely in her favor. But it hadn't mattered.

5   Somewhere far away, I can hear the crowd murmuring unhappily as they always do when a twelve-year-old gets chosen because no one thinks this is fair. And then I see her, the blood drained from her face, hands clenched in fists at her sides, walking with stiff, small steps up toward the stage, passing me, and I see the back of her blouse has become untucked and hangs out over her skirt. It's this detail, the untucked blouse forming a ducktail, that brings me back to myself.

tribute residents of the 12 districts of a future (fictional) civilization who are forced to participate in the Hunger Games

6   "Prim!" The strangled cry comes out of my throat, and my muscles begin to move again. "Prim!" I don't need to shove through the crowd. The other kids make way immediately allowing me a straight path to the stage. I reach her just as she is about to mount the steps. With one sweep of my arm, I push her behind me.

7   "I volunteer!" I gasp. "I volunteer as tribute!"

8   There's some confusion on the stage. District 12 hasn't had a volunteer in decades and the protocol has become rusty. The rule is that once a tribute's name has been pulled from the ball, another eligible boy, if a boy's name has been read, or girl, if a girl's name has been read, can step forward to take his or her place. In some districts, in which winning the reaping is such a great honor, people are eager to risk their lives, the volunteering is complicated. But in District 12, where the word *tribute* is pretty much synonymous with the word *corpse*, volunteers are all but extinct.

> **reaping** annual (fictional) event where tributes are chosen to participate in the Hunger Games

9   "Lovely!" says Effie Trinket. "But I believe there's a small matter of introducing the reaping winner and then asking for volunteers, and if one does come forth then we, um …" she trails off, unsure of herself.

10   "What does it matter?" says the mayor. He's looking at me with a pained expression on his face. He doesn't know me really, but there is a faint recognition there. I am the girl who brings the strawberries. The girl his daughter might have spoken of on occasion. The girl who five years ago stood huddled with her mother and sister, as he presented her, the oldest child, with a medal of valor. A medal for her father, vaporized in the mines. Does he remember that? "What does it matter?" he repeats gruffly. "Let her come forward."

11   Prim is screaming hysterically behind me. She's wrapped her skinny arms around me like a vice. "No, Katniss! No! You can't go!"

> **vice** tool used to clamp items in place

12   "Prim, let go," I say harshly, because this is upsetting me and I don't want to cry. When they televise the replay of the reapings tonight, everyone will make note of my tears, and I'll be marked as an easy target. A weakling. I will give no one that satisfaction. "Let go!"

13   I can feel someone pulling her from my back. I turn and see Gale has lifted Prim off the ground and she's thrashing in his arms. "Up you go, Catnip," he says, in a voice he's fighting to keep steady, and then he carries Prim off toward my mother. I steel myself and climb the stairs.

14   "Well, bravo!" gushes Effie Trinket. "That's the spirit of the Games!" She's pleased to finally have a district with a little action going on in it. "What's your name?"

15   I swallow hard. "Katniss Everdeen," I say.

16   "I bet my buttons that was your sister. Don't want her to steal all the glory, do we? Come on, everybody! Let's give a big round of applause to our newest tribute!" trills Effie Trinket.

17   To the everlasting credit of the people of District 12, not one person claps. Not even the ones holding betting slips, the ones who are usually beyond caring. Possibly because they know me from the Hob, or knew my father, or have encountered Prim, who no one can help loving. So instead of acknowledging applause, I stand there unmoving while they take part in the boldest form of dissent they can manage. Silence. Which says we do not agree. We do not condone. All of this is wrong.

> **dissent** a disagreement with the opinion or decision of the majority

Source: From THE HUNGER GAMES by Suzanne Collins. Scholastic Inc./Scholastic Press. Copyright © 2008 by Suzanne Collins. Used by permission.

Continued on next page.

Check Your Understanding

3. Use context clues and word part analysis to define the following words from the passage.
   - protocol (paragraph 8): _____
   - valor (paragraph 10): _____

4. What comparison is made between paragraphs 2 and 3? Why do you think the comparison is made? In your opinion, does it add to the passage?

   _____

   _____

   _____

5. How can you tell Prim is unhappy about being selected? Use text from the passage to support your answer.

   _____

   _____

   _____

6. Why do you think the image of Prim's untucked blouse makes Katniss realize that she must do something to help her (paragraph 5)?

   _____

   _____

   _____

7. What can you infer about the mayor? How does he feel about Katniss volunteering? Use text from the passage to support your answer.

   _____

   _____

   _____

8. What do the people of District 12 do when asked to applaud for Katniss? What does their behavior signal to you?

   _____

   _____

   _____

9. In what other situations in life could silence be a form of dissent?

_____

_____

_____

10. What is the implied main idea?

_____

_____

_____

CHAPTER SUMMARY

College instructors require you not only to read and understand what is explicitly stated on the page, but also to detect ideas that are implied, or indirectly stated. Just as the Theory of Mind acknowledges our understanding that other people also have thoughts, ideas, feelings, desires, fears, and beliefs, you should realize that an author's have something to tell you. Sometimes, to fully comprehend an author's main idea, you have to read between the lines. Begin by questioning yourself about the topic of the reading. Recall what you already know on the subject (using Reader–Response Theory), and then draw reasonable conclusions.

To draw reasonable conclusions about an author's implied main idea, you need to practice making inferences. While making inferences is something you do every day, inferring meaning from textbooks and other college reading material requires you to use specific strategies such as understanding an author's purpose, noting comparisons and similarities, understanding an author's tone, detecting an author's bias, and recognizing information gaps. It is important that you double-check your inferences by recognizing an author's perspective and making sure there is something in the text that supports your inference. Without this step, you could infer too much and assume something that the author did not intend.

Brain Connections: Self-Assessment

Draw the amount of dendrites you imagine that you have now about making inferences. Compare your drawing of dendrites now with what you drew at the beginning of this chapter. If the amounts are different, explain why.

✔ COMPREHENSION CHECK

▶ What is the most valuable point you learned in this chapter?
▶ If you could ask the authors a question about this chapter, what would you ask?

POST TEST

Part 1. Objective Questions

Match the key terms from the chapter in Column A to their definitions in Column B.

	Column A	Column B
_____	1. inference	a. the emotion or feeling that an author's words give
_____	2. prior knowledge	b. main point in a paragraph, section, or chapter that is not stated directly
_____	3. assumptions	c. a tendency toward a specific view, a prejudice
_____	4. author's purpose	d. the process of drawing conclusions about information when an author's opinions or ideas are not directly stated
_____	5. author's tone	e. reason for writing
_____	6. author's bias	f. place in reading where information appears to be missing or where an author intends for the reader to infer meaning
_____	7. information gap	g. beliefs and ideas collected over a lifetime from experiences
_____	8. implied main idea	h. everything you have learned or experienced about a topic previously
_____	9. comparison	i. characteristics that are common to two or more things
_____	10. emotive language	j. words that, when read, bring about certain feelings and emotions
_____	11. simile	k. strong comparison where one idea is described as another
_____	12. metaphor	l. comparisons using the words *like* or *as*

Circle the best answer to the following multiple-choice question.

13. Which of the following statements does not contain emotive language?

   a. The adorable child waited quietly and patiently for his mother.

   b. The child waited for his mother.

   c. The mischievous child trampled through the delicate grass and plucked flowers while waiting for his mother.

   d. The dim-witted child ate a cup of dirt while waiting for his mother.

Short-Answer Questions

14. How do you make sure you are not inferring too much or incorrectly?

_____

_____

15. When inferring a main idea from a reading assignment, is it necessary that all the students in your class agree on what the implied main idea is? Explain your answer.

_____

_____

Part 2. Reading Passage

Prepare to Read

1. Read the title of the following passage, and skim over the paragraphs, including the information about the author. What do you expect the passage to be about?

_____

2. What do you already know about the topic?

_____

3. Using the title, develop a question to ask yourself as you read.

_____

The Cat Lady
By Chris Rose

1   Ellen Montgomery's house near Audubon Park was already almost invisible from the street before Hurricane Katrina shattered the massive cedar tree in her front yard and left a tangled, camouflaged mess that now obliterates the view of just about everything.

2   If anything, that helped her hide from the National Guard during the tense days—now ancient weeks ago—when word came that they were forcing those who had remained in New Orleans to leave.

3   "If I was out walking in the neighborhood and I heard the Hummers coming, I would duck down behind a porch or some broken shutters," she said. "I felt like a Confederate spy in enemy territory."

4   Montgomery was a holdout. A straggler. The resistance.

5   She stayed behind without power or running water or even a generator. The simple reason: "My babies," she says. Thirty-four cats. (It was thirty-three for several weeks, until one that had gone missing returned home last Saturday night "to say hello," Montgomery says.)

Continued on next page.

6   She knows what you're thinking. It used to bug her but not anymore.

7   "Years ago, I said to my vet: 'But I don't *want* to be a cat lady!'" Montgomery recalls. "And he says to me: 'But you *are* a cat lady.' So there you are."

8   And so, for thirty days, what has she done?

9   "Well," she pauses. "I sleep late. Let's see… and then I feed the cats. I read *The Journal of Beatrix Potter*. It's a lovely book. And then I have my cup of coffee. And that usually lasts a couple of hours. And then I paint and—I don't know. The days just fly by. I'm in another world here. I don't feel the heat. I don't feel anything. I am very able to exist on my own. I just paint, and that's what keeps me from going bonkers. That's my therapy."

10   Montgomery has been painting since 1977, when she read the book of Vincent Van Gogh's correspondence, *Letters to Theo*.

11   "I read it and I said, 'I want to do that,'" she says. "So I got down and did that and have been doing it ever since."

12   Indeed. She sits on the floor in the front room of her house—it would be a stretch to call it a "studio"—and she fills canvas after canvas, board after board, paper after paper. If you stood still in front of her for a long enough, she'd probably paint you.

13   Her home is filled with thousands of paintings she has made over the past three decades. She admittedly has sold few works, so mostly they line her walls, floor-to-ceiling in every room, and then they fill stacks and piles randomly assigned through her cluttered 1890s cottage.

14   And, having recently run out of canvases to work on, she is now working a medium that only a hurricane could provide. She has gathered scores of slate roofing tiles that were scattered off the roofs of her neighbors' homes into the street, and now she paints them.

15   "They're so beautiful," she says. "I couldn't bear the thought of the National Guardsmen or some contractors trampling over them, so I collected them. I won't have enough time in my life to paint them all."

16   Over the years, she has painted various abstracts and florals and faces and landscapes, but now her work is fairly dark and muddied and swirly, work clearly influenced by the monstrous forces that have visited upon her life this past month.

17   Funny thing is, in the beginning, she didn't really know what had happened.

18   Montgomery has been living the consummate, isolated cat lady existence for years and she was only vaguely aware that a storm was even coming.

19   The shattered cedar tree and the loss of power, water, and phone—and the disappearance of all her neighbors—told her it was something big.

20   "I went to church that Sunday morning before the storm and a sign on the door said, 'Services canceled,' so I bought a paper and that was the last news I heard," she says.

21   "There were four or five days where I had absolutely no idea what had happened. But I was safe, the cats were safe, so I thought: why be scared? I firmly believe in God and prayer. I knew I would just ride it out. I am probably more prepared than anyone else in the world to spend time alone."

22   It wasn't until several days later, when a neighbor returning to retrieve some items loaned her a radio—and stocked her with food and water before leaving again—that the magnitude of the event settled upon her.

23   "I try to listen to the news a couple of hours a day and it's unimaginable, really," she says. But she has seen no images of it at all; has not seen that more than half of the city was underwater and has not seen the human misery that filled the Superdome and Convention Center, sights that are now burned into the American consciousness.

24   "At first, actually, it was kind of nice around here," she says. "The birds came back and the squirrels would come deliver me the news. It's all been so peaceful, really. But it's nice to have the thought of people coming back. I suppose there'll be lots of chainsaws and hammers and all that, so I might miss the silence. But the truth is, I'm just about out of candles."

Chris Rose is a writer who gained popularity for his writings on the personal and public struggles of Louisiana after Hurricane Katrina.

Check Your Understanding

Circle the best answer to the following multiple-choice questions.

4. What is a typical "cat lady" in American culture? If you are not sure, look at the passage again, and use the details of the cat lady, Ellen Montgomery, to infer what "cat ladies" are like.

    a. a lady who has a cat and lives alone

    b. a lady who likes cats but doesn't have any

    c. a lady who thinks cats are better than dogs

    d. a lady who has many cats and lives alone

5. What are some characteristics of typical cats?

    a. They are independent and tend to be alone.

    b. They constantly seek the approval of their owners.

    c. They listen well to commands.

    d. They are dependent on other animals.

6. How was the cat lady able to live during the aftermath of the storm?

    a. She worked for a company that handled emergency relief.

    b. She was generally self-sufficient and used to being alone.

    c. She was generally dependent on others.

    d. She was generally a good painter.

Continued on next page.

7. What was the purpose of this passage?

   a. to inspire   b. to inform   c. to persuade   d. to explain

8. The author's tone was:

   a. sarcastic.   b. humorous.   c. negative.   d. understanding.

Short-Answer Questions

9. What biases might the author have?

_____

_____

10. What did Montgomery mean when she said, "I felt like a Confederate spy in enemy territory"?

_____

_____

11. What are some implied similarities between Ellen Montgomery and cats? Fill in the gaps the author left.

_____

_____

12. What does the author imply when he says that Montgomery "has seen no images of it [the aftermath of hurricane Katrina]"?

_____

_____

13. What does *consummate* mean in this sentence: "Montgomery has been living the consummate, isolated cat lady existence for years and she was only vaguely aware that a storm was even coming."

14. In the last line of the passage, the author quotes Montgomery as saying, "'But the truth is, I'm just about out of candles.'" What could the author be implying here? How do you think Montgomery feels about everyone returning back to the neighborhood?

_____

_____

15. In the passage, the author uses the cat lady to imply a point about people in general. What point can you infer about people from this passage? In other words, what is true about the cat lady that is also true about people in general?

_____

_____

BRAIN STRENGTH OPTIONS

Working individually or in groups of no more than three people, complete one of the following options.

1. Prepare a poster that illustrates these strategies for finding implied main ideas:
   ▶ author's purpose
   ▶ comparison
   ▶ tone
   ▶ author's bias
   ▶ information gaps

   Find and use selections from any text of your choice: textbook, magazine article, Internet article, song lyrics, or anything else you find that demonstrates the strategies for finding implied main ideas. Use as much text as necessary to illustrate each strategy, which should be named and highlighted in some manner (in bold, color, underlined). For example, if the sentence shows bias, you would highlight the parts that indicate bias and title it "Example of Bias."

2. Create a PowerPoint presentation that you will either present aloud or otherwise distribute to the class, as determined by your instructor. Follow the same guidelines as Option 1.

3. Lead the class in using the strategies listed in Option 1. Read a text aloud, and tell your classmates what they are looking for. For example, you might say, "In the following reading, determine the author's purpose" and then read your selection and guide them through the process. Do this for each strategy in Option 1. If the class has trouble finding the correct answer, perhaps you did not select appropriate examples; to avoid this, make sure to select clear examples of each strategy.

4. Can you draw? Create a short graphic novel illustrating each strategy. On the bottom of each frame, list the strategy and indicate the clues. Follow the same guidelines as Option 1.

5. Create an online lesson that teaches the strategies for finding implied main idea. Follow the same guidelines as Option 1.

6. Propose your own project in writing to your instructor. Indicate what you will do and how it will be considered successful. What will be the criteria?

Recognizing Patterns of Organization

SOWMYA RASA

A third-year medical student at St. George's University in Granada, West Indies

Courtesy of Sowmya Rasa

"Order is the sanity of the mind, the health of the body, the peace of the city, the security of the state. Like beams in a house or bones to a body, so is order to all things."

—ROBERT SOUTHEY

THROUGH MY EXPERIENCES with exams and essays, I learned to hone my study skills to fit my personality in order to help me become an efficient reader. It is an ongoing process and changes with the type of subject matter and field you are exposed to. It takes some time, but once you figure out what works for you, you start to learn more easily as well as enjoy what you are reading.

One thing I learned about reading textbooks is that it is important to understand the sequence of events. A lot of times, chapters went off on a tangent and started talking about history and other facts that were somewhat relevant but would not help me to understand medicine in a way that a doctor needs to. Therefore, it helped me to take parts of the chapter and rewrite them in sequential order. I used arrows to show the sequence. For example, to understand a biochemical process, like gluconeogenesis, I rewrote the different reactions in a sequence that would help me understand the topic better. In addition, it helped to make a table of all the enzymes in gluconeogenesis, making it easier to group them together because there are several processes in biochemistry and a lot of the enzyme names sound very similar. In the table I would write the name of the enzyme in one column and then the purpose of it in the next. On top I would write the heading to describe the category under which the enzymes belonged. I did this for a lot of different processes, grouping and reviewing. It made the reading clear and easier to remember. Once I remembered the different names, I could make comparisons between the tables and take relevant notes. This also helped me understand the lectures more easily, making the whole learning process worthwhile.

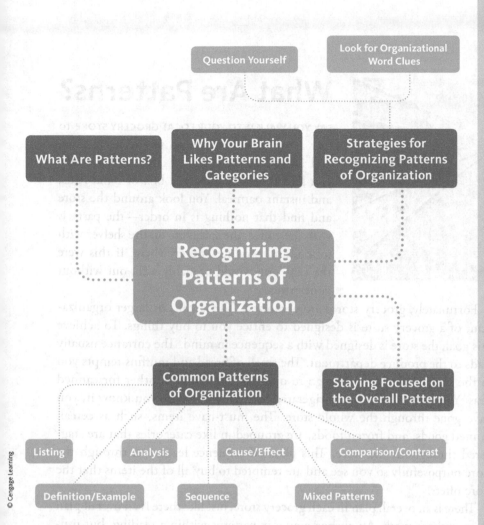

Question Yourself

Look for Organizational Word Clues

What Are Patterns?

Why Your Brain Likes Patterns and Categories

Strategies for Recognizing Patterns of Organization

Recognizing Patterns of Organization

Common Patterns of Organization

Staying Focused on the Overall Pattern

Listing

Analysis

Cause/Effect

Comparison/Contrast

Definition/Example

Sequence

Mixed Patterns

Making Connections

1. What kind of puzzles do you like?

2. Why do you like doing puzzles? How do they make you feel when you finish? What do you do when they become difficult? Why don't people just choose easy puzzles so they can do them quickly?

3. How is a puzzle like a pattern?

4. Name three things that have a pattern.

5. How could something you read have a pattern?

6. If you saw these words in something you were reading, what kind of a pattern would you guess the reading would have?

  then

  afterward

  later

  next

  finally

Brain Connections: Self-Assessment

Draw on the brain cell how many dendrites you imagine you have for how much you know about recognizing patterns of organization.

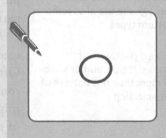

Katrina Wittkamp/Digital Vision/JupiterImages

What Are Patterns?

SAY YOU WALK INTO YOUR LOCAL GROCERY STORE to buy a bag of Fritos. You go to the snack aisle, and instead of the expected chips and pretzels, you find three cucumbers, a box of Band-Aids, and instant oatmeal. You look around the store and find that nothing is in order—the pasta is with the coffee, the spices are on the shelves with lotion, and produce is everywhere. If this were the case, you would probably walk out without your Fritos.

Fortunately, grocery stores are organized. The layout, or larger organization, of a grocery store is designed to entice you to buy things. To achieve this goal, the store is designed with a sequence in mind. The entrance usually leads to the produce department. The smell of bread and muffins tempts you to the back of the store. You go to one aisle for cereal, another for canned peas. You grab milk in the refrigerated section, and before you know it, you have gone through the whole store. The must-have items, such as cereal, canned goods, and frozen foods, are grouped in like categories that are staggered throughout the store. This planned sequence leads you through the store purposefully so you see and are tempted to buy all of the items that the store offers.

There is an overall plan in each grocery store, just like there is an overall plan in an author's work. An author may mix patterns within a reading, but usually there is one big pattern or logical structure to the entire reading. Actively looking for that larger pattern helps you understand how an author's ideas are related. Every time you start a new reading, think of it as exploring a new grocery store. Look for clues to the pattern so you can find all the information you need in the reading. A pattern of organization is the way that an author purposefully chooses to present his or her ideas through the use of specific pattern types.

pattern of organization a way to organize ideas through the use of specific pattern types

mixed patterns of organization author's use of more than one pattern of organization

At times, an author will use more than one pattern of organization within a reading. The use of multiple patterns is known as mixed patterns of organization. Often, one pattern does not describe the overall organization. For example, some stores might sell vegetables and nursery stock. The outside of the store might have pine trees, rose bushes, and annual plants and flowers. The inside of the store might have produce. The store has two goals—to sell plants and to sell produce. Likewise, an author might define democracy, giving a detailed example, and also providing an analysis of effective political systems. Both organizational patterns, definition/example and analysis, might be equally prominent in an author's order of ideas. The overall organizational pattern would be mixed.

In a grocery store, you can see a similar embedded organization. One aisle might have snack foods. Within that aisle, though, the products might be organized in groups—popcorn and peanuts at one end, pretzels of different brands in the middle, chips on the other end. In the next aisle, you might find cereals, hot and cold, and breakfast bars. There is, as they say, a method to the madness. Each aisle has its own organization—snacks in one aisle, cereal in the next. Different areas of the store have bigger organizational structures. The refrigerated area not only is bigger than an aisle but also includes a broader categories of items—milk, cheese, yogurt, eggs, cottage cheese, sour cream, and meats.

Authors use patterns of organization in their writing in order to achieve their goal: to get you, the reader, to understand and accept what they write. Like the grocery store owner, the author wants you to "buy" something. In order to critically examine what an author is "selling," you must first understand it. An author writing a book on climate change might organize a chapter by comparing and contrasting temperature and precipitation changes over the past 100 years. When you read this information, you note that the author's comparison/contrast organization helps him showcase his points. An author writing about cell division might explain her ideas in a sequence organization. The sequence moves you through the process from beginning to end. A researcher studying voting habits might write using a cause/effect pattern, illustrating his belief that something causes people to vote (or not).

Authors have a purpose behind the order in which they present ideas. Ideas in a textbook chapter are related to one another. If you do not see the relationship, you might have difficulty identifying the main idea and critically thinking about it. You also might have trouble remembering the details from the chapter because, like a disorganized grocery store, stuff can be everywhere. The details from the chapter might not be "shelved" anywhere that seems obviously

Tip FROM THE
Brain Doctor

The brain is a natural pattern seeker! It naturally notices patterns without even trying. Why? Because seeing patterns is essential to survival. Actually, it is *deviation* from patterns—a difference in a pattern—that the brain notices. Humans would not survive long if they did not notice these things. For example, a difference in the pattern in water indicates that fish might be feeding there, enabling fisherman to catch fish more easily. A difference in the branch of a tree might signal a snake is coiled there ready to spring. Take advantage of this natural skill, and use it to enhance learning.

logical. However, knowing an author's overall pattern of organization helps you mentally shelve ideas in their proper place in your brain.

ACTIVITY 7A
Create a Pattern

Imagine a grocery store that has all of the regular items a grocery store carries but whose goal is to urge customers to buy only healthy items. How would this store be laid out? Draw a picture of a possible layout and include the following items: canned goods, meat, frozen items, snacks, produce, deli items, pet food, paper items, cereals, spices, and candy. Add a paragraph to your drawing describing how the items would be displayed on the shelves.

Why Your Brain Likes Patterns and Categories

Look at the inkblots in this picture.

What do you see? Inkblots? Fallen leaves? Something else? Sometimes people think they see a dog in the pattern. If the text asked you to see inkblots and yet you saw a dog, what was your brain trying to do?

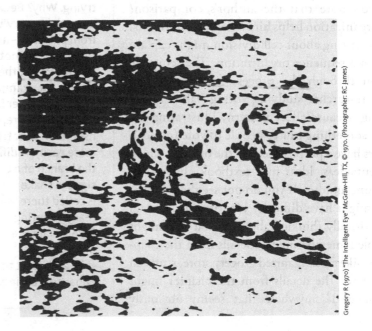

Gregory R (1970) "The Intelligent Eye" McGraw-Hill, TX, © 1970. (Photographer: RC James)

If you said something like "make sense of it," you are absolutely correct. The brain likes to make sense of things, and one of the most powerful ways it does so is by seeing patterns. It is a survival mechanism. Throughout time, if humans were to survive, they needed to see patterns. In fact, the human brain rewards the seeing of a pattern with a burst of a positive, good feeling. That is why people persist in figuring out a Sudoku, crossword or jigsaw puzzle—or even how to put a car engine back together. The brain loves to see patterns and to figure things out!

Categories are a type of pattern. Putting things into categories before you study them helps the brain make sense of the material. It helps you think better and more easily recall information. The first step is to figure out what the categories are. As you are reading, try to determine the pattern of organization the author uses—your brain will reward you with pleasure and a feeling of satisfaction just like completing a puzzle.

Tip FROM THE Brain Doctor

Looking for patterns helps you learn because it is a way of connecting information in your neural networks. It also helps you remember what you have read because you are not memorizing facts in isolation but are relating the facts to each other to form patterns. These patterns hold and organize the facts in your memory.

✔ **COMPREHENSION CHECK**

▶ Explain why patterns of organization are important.

Strategies for Recognizing Patterns of Organization

TO RECOGNIZE AN AUTHOR'S OVERALL PATTERN OF ORGANIZATION, make sure you question yourself and look for organizational word clues. You will notice that these strategies are similar to the ones you learned in Chapter 4 for finding stated main ideas. Reading strategies presented in this book are meant to be used together. It is not recommended, for example, to simply distinguish general ideas from specific ones to understand a stated main idea,

Tip FROM THE Brain Doctor

The brain has two pathways for visual information: the *what* and the *where*. You will learn about the *where* pathway later, but think about the *what* pathway now. The *what* pathway creates categories. There is a category for faces, for example, where all the faces you know are stored. Because the brain "likes" categories, creating categories as a study skill will make your learning easier and more effective.

or to only look for information gaps in reading to find an implied main idea. Use as many strategies as it takes in order to accomplish your reading goal.

Question Yourself

WITH ANYTHING YOU read, you should question yourself. (Refer to Chapter 4 for a review of this reading strategy, if necessary.) Read the title or heading and make a question from it. Look for the answer to that question as you read. That answer can lead you to the main idea and can help you identify the author's overall pattern of organization.

You can also question yourself about the details. Details that support a main idea are usually organized in identifiable patterns. For example, if you recognize a list of ideas as you read, you might ask yourself, "What is this a list of?" If you can tell that events are being described in chronological order, you can ask, "What is this sequence about?"

Look at the following example from a history textbook.

The Philosophy of Colonialism

reminiscent similar

pseudoscientific false, fake

To justify their conquests, the colonial powers appealed, in part, to the time-honored maxim of "might makes right." In a manner reminiscent of the Western attitude toward the oil reserves in the Persian Gulf today, the European powers viewed industrial resources as vital to national survival and security and felt that no moral justification was needed for any action to protect access to them. By the end of the nineteenth century, that attitude received pseudoscientific validity from the concept of social Darwinism, which maintained that only societies that moved aggressively to adapt to changing circumstances would survive and prosper in a world governed by the Darwinist law of "survival of the fittest."

Source: From DUIKER. *Contemporary World History 5e* (p. 29). Copyright © 2010 Cengage Learning.

What question could you create from the title of this passage?

What is the philosophy of colonialism?

The answer you look for might be an explanation or definition of colonialism. This answer leads you closer to the main idea and suggests a possible overall pattern of organization—definition/example. You will not know for sure using just the strategy of questioning yourself, but other strategies will help support your answer.

Look for Organizational Word Clues

AFTER YOU QUESTION yourself, look for clues that signal a pattern of organization. In Chapter 4, you learned that word clues alert you to the twists and turns in the path of an author's thinking. Organizational word clues are similar to the word clues that you learned about in Chapter 4, but instead of just showing how single ideas are connected, organizational word clues signal a reading's overall organization.

organizational word clues words or phrases that signal a pattern of organization an author uses for a reading

Sometimes these organizational word clues are obvious and present in the text. Other times, authors omit them but still expect you to infer the larger organization. Table 7.1 shows you some of the common organizational word clues associated with the patterns.

Organizational word clues can also help you determine the level of importance of an author's ideas. Those like *most importantly* tell you that what you are about to read is really important. Others such as *for example* let you know that a point is going to be illustrated. (An example is usually not the main idea.) When an author uses *on the other hand*, he or she shows another viewpoint (which could be the main idea). When an author uses *first, second,* and *third,* a process or sequence is introduced; what follows are often major supporting details. Being aware of these clues helps you make sense of what you are reading; knowing the pattern helps you to organize the information.

Common Patterns of Organization

KNOWING THE DIFFERENT PATTERNS OF ORGANIZATION helps you make sense of what you are reading and will also help you remember the content more accurately. Table 7.1 shows common patterns of organization along with their definitions and commonly used organizational word clues.

Table 7.1 Common Patterns of Organization

Pattern	Definition	Organizational Word Clues	
Listing	One thing after another in a list Example I have several items on my shopping list: ▶ first is milk, ▶ second—eggs ▶ third—chicken ▶ fourth—spinach, and ▶ finally, whole wheat bread.	▶ and ▶ first…second…third ▶ first of all ▶ secondly…finally ▶ the four levels of ▶ one way…another way…a third way ▶ further, furthermore ▶ additionally, last	
Analysis	Shows the parts of something Example Textbooks include several features that help readers navigate the text, including a title page, a table of contents, chapters, and an index.	▶ features ▶ properties ▶ characteristics ▶ one sense or one part ▶ aspects ▶ one way, another way ▶ is made up of ▶ includes ▶ categories ▶ classified as ▶ traits	▶ involves ▶ elements ▶ components ▶ functions ▶ attributes ▶ levels ▶ findings ▶ analysis ▶ in this case ▶ types
Cause/Effect	Tells the cause of something happening and the effect caused by it Example When there is a big storm, schools are closed due to past experiences. There are many reasons, but the primary one is safety.	▶ since ▶ thus ▶ because, because of ▶ consequently ▶ as a result of ▶ cause(s) ▶ effect(s) ▶ reason(s) ▶ indicates ▶ result(s) ▶ for this reason, for these reasons	▶ if…then ▶ is due to, may be due to ▶ creates ▶ occurred ▶ consequence(s) ▶ finding(s) ▶ leads to ▶ then, therefore ▶ affect ▶ it is evident
Comparison/ Contrast	Explains how things are compared. Author will show likenesses and differences.	▶ however ▶ compared with ▶ on the other hand ▶ but ▶ different from	▶ although ▶ on the contrary ▶ in opposition ▶ unlike ▶ although

Pattern	Definition	Organizational Word Clues	
	Example These two stories are similar because they are both about families. They also have obvious differences. The first story is rich with humor, unlike the second story, which seems to be one tragedy after another.	▸ whereas ▸ as compared with ▸ like ▸ contrasted with ▸ yet ▸ in the same way ▸ similar to	▸ in other words ▸ along ▸ similarly ▸ too ▸ as with ▸ opposed to
Definition/ Example	Defines something and/or uses an example to help readers' understanding Example A dessert is something sweet, which might be a piece of cake, a slice of pie, ice cream, or chocolate candy.	▸ for example ▸ as defined as ▸ means the same as ▸ translated as ▸ is called ▸ synonymous with ▸ another meaning	▸ also refers to ▸ as ▸ to illustrate ▸ interpreted as ▸ such as ▸ states that ▸ is
Sequence/ Time or Process	The order in which things appear or occur or outline of a process or procedure Examples Sequence/Time Several events caused the war. First, none of the countries would sign the nuclear weapons ban. Second, the invasion into France forced smaller countries to come together. Process The first step in baking cookies is to have a recipe. Next, you need the ingredients listed. Then, everything needs to be measured and mixed. The final step is to spoon the dough onto the cookie sheet and bake the cookies.	▸ first…second…third ▸ first of all…secondly…finally ▸ one way…another way ▸ after that… ▸ then… ▸ following… ▸ next ▸ before ▸ after ▸ subsequently ▸ yesterday/today/tomorrow ▸ eventually ▸ step, steps ▸ procedure, process	

ACTIVITY 7B
Figure Out the Pattern

Using Table 7.1, figure out which pattern the author uses in the following passage. The organizational word clues that signal the pattern are circled. You will be asked to identify those on your own in future activities. Don't forget to think about the author's purpose; it can be the best clue.

Despite Warnings, False Memories Occur

1   Some people who undergo hypnosis may be influenced to develop false memories, even when they are warned in advance about the possibility of creating fictional past events. In a study at Ohio State University's Lima campus, 28% of subjects who underwent hypnosis were induced by a researcher to develop false memories about recent incidents in their lives. This (occurred) even though they were warned that "hypnotized participants may confuse what they imagine with what really occurred." Moreover, 44% of participants who were not warned about possible pseudomemories (were induced) to develop a false memory.

2   The (results suggest) that many people have unrealistic and distorted views of the power of hypnosis, (indicates) professor of psychology Joseph Green. "There's a cultural expectation that hypnosis will lead to more accurate and earlier memories, (but) that's not true. Hypnosis can be helpful for some people, (but) it is subject to the same restrictions and pitfalls of any other memory-retrieval method."

3   The issue of false memories has grown in recent years as more clinicians have used hypnosis to help patients recover lost memories of early traumatic events. There has been controversy about whether these recovered memories always are real.

Source: From Jeff Grabmeier, "Despite Warning, People May Form False Memories During Hypnosis." Reprinted by permission of the author.

cause of false memory

cause

effect of hypnosis and false memories

effect

1. What pattern is used in this passage? (Keep in mind that you have not yet fully learned about patterns of organization. You are basing your answer on what you currently know about patterns.)

_____

Listing

USING WHAT YOU know about asking questions and organizational word clues, read the following passage from a communications textbook and see if a pattern becomes apparent to you. Using Table 7.1 as a guide, circle any organizational word clues you notice.

1　Think about the last time you experienced a conflict. How did you react? Did you avoid it? Give in? Force the other person to accept your will? Did you compromise? Or did the two of you use a problem-solving approach? When faced with a conflict, you can withdraw, accommodate, force, compromise, or collaborate (Lulofs & Cahn, 2000, pp. 101–102).

2　One of the most common and easiest ways to deal with conflict is withdrawing or avoiding the conflict. **Withdrawing** involves physically or psychologically removing yourself from the conflict. You withdraw physically by leaving the site. For instance, imagine Eduardo and Justina get into an argument about their financial situation. Eduardo may withdraw physically by saying, I don't want to talk about this and walk out the door. Psychological withdrawal occurs when you simply ignore what the other person is saying. So, when Justina begins to talk about their financial situation, Eduardo may ignore her and act as though she has not spoken. When you repeatedly use withdrawing, you risk damaging your relationship. First, in terms of the dialectical tension in the relationship, withdrawing signals closedness rather than openness and autonomy rather than connection. Further, withdrawing doesn't eliminate the source of the conflict and it often increases the tension. In many cases, not confronting the problem when it occurs only makes it more difficult to deal with in the long run. Nevertheless, as a temporary strategy, withdrawing allows tempers to cool and may be appropriate when neither an issue nor a relationship is important.

3　A second style of managing conflict is **accommodating**, which means satisfying others needs or accepting others' ideas while neglecting your own. So people who adopt the accommodating style of conflict will use passive behavior. For instance, during a discussion of their upcoming vacation, Mariana and Juan disagree in their thinking about whether to invite friends to join them. Juan uses accommodation when Mariana says, "I think it would be fun to go with another couple, don't you?" and he replies, "OK, whatever you want."

4　Accommodating can result in poor communication because important facts, arguments, and positions are not voiced. There are situations, of course, in which it is appropriate and effective to accommodate. When the issue is not important to you, but the relationship is, accommodating is the preferred style. Hal and Yvonne are trying to decide where to go for dinner. Hal says, I really have a craving for some Thai food tonight. Yvonne, who prefers pizza, says, OK, that will be fine. Yvonne's interest in pizza was not very strong, and because Hal really seemed excited by Thai food, Yvonne accommodated.

5　A third style of dealing with conflict is **forcing** or competing. Forcing means satisfying your own needs or advancing your own ideas with no

dialectical method of argument to get to the truth

autonomy independence

coercion to make one do something against one's will through threats

concern for the needs or ideas of the other and no concern for the harm done to the relationship. Forcing may use aggressive behavior such as physical threats, verbal attacks, coercion, or manipulation. If you use forcing in a conflict and your partner avoids or accommodates, the conflict seems to subside. If, however, your partner answers your forcing style with a forcing style, the conflict escalates.

6   Although forcing may result in a person getting her or his own way, it usually hurts a relationship, at least in the short term. There are times, however, when forcing is an effective means to resolve conflict. In emergencies, when quick and decisive action must be taken to ensure safety or minimize harm, forcing is useful. When an issue is critical to your own or the others' welfare and you know you are right, you may find forcing necessary. Finally, if you are interacting with someone who will take advantage of you if you do not force the issue, this style is appropriate. For example, David knows that, statistically speaking, the likelihood of death or serious injury increases dramatically if one does not wear a helmet when riding a motorcycle. So he insists that his sister wear one when she rides with him, even though she complains bitterly about wearing one.

7   A fourth way to manage conflict is through **compromising**, which involves giving up part of what each wants, to provide at least some satisfaction for both parties. Under this approach, both people have to give up part of what they really want or believe, or they have to trade one thing they want to get something else. For example, if Heather and Paul are working together on a class project and need to meet outside of class but both have busy schedules, they may compromise on a time to meet.

8   Although compromising is a popular and effective style, there are drawbacks associated with it. One drawback is that the quality of a decision is affected if one of the parties trades away a better solution to find a compromise. Compromising is appropriate when the issue is moderately important, when there are time constraints, and when attempts at forcing or collaborating have not been successful.

9   A fifth style of dealing with conflict is through problem-solving discussion, or **collaboration**. When you collaborate, you both try to fully address the needs and issues of each of you and arrive at a solution that is mutually satisfying. In this approach, both of you view the disagreement as a problem to be solved, so you discuss the issues, describe your feelings, and identify the characteristics of an effective solution. With collaboration, both people's needs are met and both sides feel that they have been heard. For example, if Juan and Mariana decide to collaborate on their conflict about asking friends to join them on vacation, Mariana may explain to Juan how she thinks that, by vacationing with friends, they can share expenses and lower their costs. Juan may describe his desire to have alone time with Mariana. As they explore what each wants from the vacation, they may arrive at a plan that meets both of

their needs. So, they may end up vacationing alone, but spending several nights camping to lower their expenses.

Source: From VERDERBER/VERDERBER. *Communicate!* 12e (pp. 188–9). Copyright © 2008 Cengage Learning.

What did you notice? Some questions you can ask about the passage are:

> *What choices are there when faced with a conflict?*
> *What are the ways someone can deal with conflict?*

As you read and questioned yourself, you may have noticed a pattern right away. At the end of the first paragraph, the authors write: *When faced with a conflict, you can withdraw, accommodate, force, compromise, or collaborate.* This paragraph gives a list of choices: withdraw, accommodate, force, compromise, collaborate. Then, the paragraphs that follow describe each item on the list. Most of the paragraphs begin with organizational word clues: Paragraph 2 begins "*One of the ways.* . . ." Paragraph 3, "A *second* style. . . ." Paragraph 5, "A *third* style. . . ." Paragraph 7, "A *fourth* way. . . ." Paragraph 9, "A *fifth* style. . . ." These organizational word clues signal the overall pattern of organization is listing.

Authors use listing to enumerate events, ideas, or other concepts. Lists can be organized in a variety of ways: alphabetically, numerically, by order of importance, or by category. For example, an author of a political science text might list the Amendments to the Constitution, an author of a chemistry textbook might list the elements in order of their atomic number, and a history textbook might list articles of clothing worn for battle in the Middle Ages. Listing is sometimes also known as addition. Table 7.2 provides examples of organizational word clues that signal an author's use of listing.

listing pattern that lists ideas, events, or concepts

Table 7.2 Organizational Word Clues for Listing Pattern

first . . . second . . . third	first of all	. . . secondly	. . . finally
the four levels of. . . .	one way	. . . another way	. . . a third way
further	furthermore	additionally	last

After you identify an author's pattern of organization as listing, you can visually represent the information in your notes. Figure 7.1 is an example of how to visually show the passage's listing relationship.

Here's an important test-taking tip: Want to know how to guess what will be on the test?

Choices When Faced with Conflict

1. withdraw
2. accommodate
3. force
4. compromise
5. collaborate

Figure 7.1 Visual for Listing Pattern

Questions that you ask yourself about a reading passage and jot down in your notes or in your textbook are very likely to be questions an instructor might ask on an exam. Here is an example of a question you could ask yourself about the previous passage in order to prepare for a test:

What choices does one have when faced with a conflict?

ACTIVITY 7C
Practice Identifying a Listing Pattern

Read this passage from a criminal law textbook. The author uses listing as an overall pattern of organization, but there aren't many organizational word clues. How do you know the pattern is listing?

Crime on City Streets

1　City governments, understandably enough, wish to minimize the amount of street crimes that occur. The use of criminal laws directed at conduct or persons believed to be related to criminal acts is common, but they must be tailored to avoid infringing on individual rights. Some such laws include:

infringing overstepping or going somewhere it doesn't belong

▶ Anti-cruising laws: Fines for prohibited cruising—driving cars on designated routes on certain streets during late night hours—can be as high as $1,000 in some places and may also include short jail sentences. The *Milwaukee Journal Sentinel* reported on April 24, 2007, that the city's new anti-cruising laws resulted in the issuance of 658 tickets and 86 arrests in one weekend. Four shootings occurred in that same weekend.

truancy one who should but doesn't go to school

detentions holding or keeping from moving freely

▶ Truancy arrests or detentions: State laws vary on the treatment of truancy, but in many states authorities are authorized to detain a school-age child not attending school and in some cases obtain criminal convictions of the child's parents. Enforcement of truancy laws has been shown to cut down on crimes such as burglary, criminal damage to property, theft, and criminal graffiti.

▶ Juvenile curfew laws: Daytime curfew laws are aimed at keeping children in school, while nighttime curfews seek to minimize teen drinking, drug use, fighting, vandalism, and gang activities. Such curfews have generally been upheld, if they are not overbroad, that is, written to prohibit conduct that is permitted, like attending school or church events in the evening.

Source: From GARDNER/ANDERSON. *Criminal Law* 11e (p. 239). Copyright © 2012 Cengage Learning.

1. What organizational word clues did you find in the passage?

_____

_____

2. What else helped you determine that the overall organizational pattern is listing?

_____

_____

3. What is the main idea of the passage?

_____

_____

✔ COMPREHENSION CHECK

▶ What do you understand about what you have read so far?

▶ Using your own words, explain patterns of organization and organizational word clues.

Analysis

USING WHAT YOU know about asking questions and organizational word clues, read the following passage and see if a pattern becomes apparent to you. Using Table 7.1 as a guide, circle any organizational word clues you notice.

Aspects of Business

1   Business is a broad domain. Within it, there are many different kinds of jobs, from human resources management to sales to finance to accounting. So you might wonder whether our genes influence our preference for functional areas of business as well. "Yes" is the answer. Let's take a look at what some of the studies show.

2   One aspect of work in the business world is managing other people. Like the character Michael Scott on the hit TV show "The Office," supervising others is what many business people do on a day-to-day basis. You might be surprised to learn that your interest in this kind of work is more heavily influenced by your genetic endowment than by how your mom and dad raised you. About 25 percent of the variation in interest in managing people is attributed to genes, while only 8 percent is accounted for by family environment. (Note to the producers of "The Office": You might consider an episode that explores the genetic origins of Michael Scott's and Dwight Schrute's desire to manage others.)

3   Another kind of work in the business world involves managing the ongoing operations of companies, what researchers have called "the day-to-day functioning of business and commercial organizations." After all, companies don't order raw materials, manage their own inventory, or run

their own assembly lines. Someone has to do that for them. Like managing other people, this aspect of business attracts some people more than others. And, as with managing other people, the appeal of this work is affected by your genes. Studies show that genetic factors account for the approximately 59 percent of the variation in people's interest in "the day-to-day functioning of business and commercial organizations."

Source: *Born Entrepreneurs, Born Leaders: How Your Genes Affect Your Work Life*, NY: Oxford University Press, 2010, pp. 53-54.

What about the heading of this passage gives you a clue to how the passage is organized? What question could you ask?

What are the different aspects of business?

The different aspects or parts of business might be listed, defined, and discussed. The first sentence helps you picture in your mind how the author sees business—as a domain (a range, area, or realm). Then the author identifies that the domain of business has many related parts or aspects. These clues suggest that the passage is organized with analysis.

analysis pattern that breaks a concept down into its specific characteristics, properties, or basic elements

With analysis, authors break a concept down into its specific characteristics, properties, or basic elements. The authors' purpose might be to show the different parts or details of a complex issue in order to make it easier to understand. For example, a medical writer discussing diabetes could give readers information about its cause, symptoms, and treatment options. Analysis is also sometimes known as classification.

In a way, the analysis pattern of organization is like listing because it lists parts. The difference is that a list can be organized randomly, such as a list of favorite activities: swimming, shopping, and reading. Analysis is more than listing because it shows the parts with respect to and in relation to the whole. Think about the skills needed to excel in swimming: you need the skills of agility, coordination, speed, strength, and quick mental processing. All of these skills are related to the whole (swimming). If swimmers had agility but no coordination, they would not be very good. This would be considered an analysis of the skills needed for a good swimmer.

ACTIVITY 7D
Analyze What You Know

Choose your favorite sport or activity, and create a list that includes the parts, elements, or aspects that make it your favorite. Then write a paragraph explaining how each part you identified relates to the activity you chose. Circle the words that you used to show the specific parts—these are the organization word clues you used.

Table 7.3 Organizational Word Clues for Analysis Pattern

features	properties	characteristics	one sense
aspects	one way	another way	is made up of
categories	classified as	traits	includes
involves	elements	components	functions
attributes	levels	findings	analysis
in this case	types	one part	

Table 7.3 provides examples of organizational word clues that signal an author's use of analysis.

To help you identify analysis as an author's pattern of organization, you can visually represent the information in your notes. Seeing the relationship visually might help you distinguish between a random listing and a discussion of parts of a whole. Figure 7.2 is an example of how to visually show the analysis relationship in the previous passage.

Knowing that an author has purposefully used the analysis pattern of organization helps you predict possible test questions. Here is an example of an analysis question an instructor might ask about the earlier passage.

What are some aspects of the business world?

Now examine the following world history passage. In it, the author describes an ancient Japanese art form that includes realistic and highly detailed representations of people. Keep in mind what the analysis pattern of organization does—it breaks something down into parts. Circle any organizational word clues that signal that analysis is being used.

Tip FROM THE Brain Doctor

Earlier in this chapter, the second visual pathway in the brain was mentioned—the *where* pathway—which organizes information about where you are, as the name implies. However, it also appears to be involved in organizing the understanding of relationships. The brain makes sense of material by understanding and organizing relationships. To use your brain well when you read, analyze the relationships between ideas.

Aspects of Business

Managing other people	Managing the ongoing operations of companies
5% of variation due to genes	59% of variation due to genes

Figure 7.2 Visual for Analysis Pattern

© BeBa/Iberfoto/The Image Works

During the Kamakura period (1185–1333) the hand scroll with its physical realism and action-packed paintings of the new warrior class achieved great popularity. Reflecting these chaotic times, the art of portraiture flourished, and a scroll would include a full gallery of warriors and holy men in starkly realistic detail, including such unflattering features as stubble, worry lines on a forehead, and crooked teeth. Japanese sculptors also produced naturalistic wooden statues of generals, nobles, and saints. By far the most distinctive, however, were the fierce heavenly "guardian kings," who still intimidate the viewer today.

Source: From DUIKER/SPIELVOGEL. *World History* 4e (p. 303). Copyright © 2004 Cengage Learning.

One way to know that the overall pattern of organization is analysis is to ask yourself good questions. Your answers help you infer what pattern is used.

▶ **What are the authors talking about (topic)?** Ancient Japanese art

▶ **How do the authors explain the art?** They offer lots of detail, but the detail is not just a list of things. The authors describe the subject of the art (people) and aspects (analysis organizational word clue) of those subjects (warriors, holy men, saints, kings—action-packed scenes—worry lines, stubble, crooked teeth).

▶ **In the last sentence, the authors say, "By far the most distinctive...."** **The most distinctive what?** The most distinctive feature (analysis organizational word clue) of this type of art.

Another way to infer an author's pattern of organization is by ruling out patterns that do not fit the reading. The Japanese art passage presents more than a list. Also, it does not compare or contrast anything. The authors say this kind of art gained popularity but do not say why. What caused this art to be popular? The reader does not know. A process of elimination like this can help you make a reasonable inference about what pattern an author uses.

ACTIVITY 7E
Use Inference with an Analysis Pattern

1. Based on the distinctive features described in the Japanese art passage on page 313, what can you infer about the value the Japanese placed on realism? In other words, what was the point of providing the features of the art?

_____

_____

2. What did the analysis of the art teach you about the art?

_____

_____

Cause/Effect

USING WHAT YOU know about asking questions and organizational word clues, read the following passage and see if a pattern becomes apparent to you. Using Table 7.1 as a guide, circle any organizational word clues you notice.

1   For my job I spent 300 days traveling the world last year. I met a lot of happy people. Who they are and where they live will surprise you.

2   The other day, as I took a taxi ride across Manhattan, the driver was pondering the state of the world. "I can't believe all these disasters happening everywhere," he said. "If it's not a flood, it's a tsunami. There are fires and hurricanes and earthquakes...then there are riots and bombs and wars and shootings." He kept shaking his head as he muttered, "What is this world coming to?"

pondering to think about

3   On the one hand, it's difficult not to agree with him. We need look no further, after all, than the latest headlines to see the world has turned into a pretty horrifying place. But then again: Is this really the case?

4   Let me explain. My job as a brand guy has a few advantages. One of them is that I get to see a lot of different places—I spent 300 days away from home last year—and my research takes me into a lot of private homes. And the upshot? I've begun seeing people in a new light. I've begun to question the reasons why some people find happiness wherever they may be, and others don't. Last week I visited one of the poorest districts in Medellin, Colombia. The town's very first escalator had recently been installed. The technology was so unfamiliar, it required strategically located spotters with the sole purpose of instructing people how to ride it. I was thoroughly absorbed watching the looks on the faces of the kids who were transfixed by the site of moving stairs. When I asked them about happiness, they waved their hands in the air and laughed. They dismissed happiness as a Western thing, and suggested we stop talking about it and just get on with the business of living.

transfixed to hold motionless

5   I had a similar encounter in a remote region of Thailand, where even though electricity was scarce, there was a general sense of well-being in the village. Therefore, I found that the kids happily played in the streets, a sight one rarely encounters these days in Western suburbs. A kindly older woman told me that happiness is because the family is together. Given the fairly intact nature of the rural village, people looked pretty content with their lot.

intact untouched by things that can harm

© Thomas Cockrem/Alamy

6   Another journey took me way into the Australian bush to a place where a toilet capable of flushing would be a novelty. Kids were busy kicking around a football on the street, but almost all took time out to speak to me, curious about who I was and what I was doing there. A young man told me that he felt happy because he helped others. He tried to perform one act of kindness a day. Consequently, this young man had only seen television twice in his life.

7   But it was when I got the chance to visit some of the 60 million newly built homes in China that all this really hit, well, home. Each new home was wired for the 21st century. Every room had television screens hooked up to high-speed Internet and each home came equipped with the latest in electronic gadgetry. In fact, the entire block was connected to a community intranet designed to help the neighbors stay in touch. As a result, I couldn't help noticing that there was an important element missing: smiles. I didn't see one of them.

8   I pursued my questions of happiness with a young Chinese family who had only been living in the city for two years. Their responses were measured. They said, "We're doing fine, but there is still so much to achieve before we will become truly happy." It seems the family **aspired** to all the things they were seeing being won on the daily online video shows. "I've seen what you can get, and we still don't have many of the things. So, for this reason we need to work harder. Then, I'm sure, one day we will get there."

aspired to seek to attain or accomplish

9   The city was orderly. There were no children playing outside. I'd been instructed to wear a mask, wrap my shoes in plastic, and sit on a cover on the chair. Everything was to stay clean and uncontaminated. Almost all the homes I visited around Beijing and Shanghai shared the same idea that sanitary living meant living a longer life.

10   An old boss of mine once instructed me never to reveal my salary to anyone. He maintained that it was a necessary secret because, if people knew what others earned, the results would only lead to unhappiness. He was right. I came to realize that the more informed we are, the less happy we become because of our tendency to get caught up in constant comparisons. Working on this principle, it seems that the more limited the access to electronic media, the more time people spend together as friends and family and the higher the happiness quotient seemed to be. (Of course, this is

just one man's observation: There is no shortage of studies and best-selling books on the subject.) Meanwhile, my Chinese family, who had the chance to compare their life with others, seemed unhappier than ever. Using a bar set by the mass media, they felt they'd failed to achieve their full potential.

11   Now I know what I should have told my despairing taxi driver. The reality is that the additional effects of our contemporary techno-media wonderland means that whenever a disaster occurs, almost anywhere in the world, we know about it within hours. Only recently, we heard about a cruise ship sinking off the coast of Italy, a shooting incident in Belgium, and a bushfire in Western Australia. Our brains are not really wired to accommodate such a proliferation of bad news, regardless of it happening thousands of miles away. As a result of one disaster after another compounds, and increases feelings of helplessness.

12   Does that mean that on some level we've lost our way? Absolutely not. But what it does mean is that we need to realize that with the ever-increasing media outlets, we must be vigilant in maintaining our own personal view of happiness. No matter how high you set your goals, you may never actually get there. So, what is my definition of happiness? A good friend once said to me, "Happiness is not measured by the number of days you live but, rather, by the number of days you remember."

13   I'll buy that. One thing is for sure, I won't be forgetting my time with all those happy people.

Source: Reprinted by permission of Martin Lindstrom. More information on Martin Lindstrom can be found at martinlindstrom.com.

despairing giving in to pessimism

proliferation buildup, increase

vigilant alert, watchful of danger

As you read this passage, you may have noticed a pattern. Although the author compares reasons for happiness and unhappiness, the overall pattern of organization is cause and effect. The author focuses on people's happiness and why others do not find happiness. The author states the main idea in paragraph 4: "I've begun to question the reasons why some people find happiness wherever they may be, and others don't." The unhappiness he experiences around him is the original cause for his study. Some questions you can ask about the passage are:

> *What organizational word clues does the author use?*
> *What is the main idea of this reading?*
> *What is the cause for some people's happiness?*
> *What are the effects of their happiness?*
> *How does technology seem to affect happiness?*

When authors use cause/effect, they show why something happened, the effects of something that occurred, or the outcome of an event. When you locate the main idea, the author states or implies a question asking why something happens and what the effects are. In the previous passage, the author looks at the effects of people's happiness. The author clearly uses cause/effect organizational word clues: *reasons, therefore, is because, consequently, as a result, results, effects.* The author

cause/effect pattern that shows why something happened, the effects of something that occurred, or the outcome of an event

explains to the reader what causes happiness and unhappiness and how that affects people. It seems that the less people know and have directly relates to states of happiness. The author also describes the places where these happier people live as having a "general sense of well being." Where technology was more advanced, the people seem less happy. The gadgetry connects them to the world around them, exposing them to more sadness. They can see how much others have and feel driven to try to achieve more. Technology allows people to lose their own personal view of happiness and begin comparing what they have to what others have.

Table 7.4 provides examples of organizational word clues that signal an author's use of the cause/effect pattern.

Table 7.4 Organizational Word Clues for Cause/Effect Pattern

since	because	consequently	as a result of	account for
reasons	results	effect	for these reasons	leads to
if…then	causes	for this reason	may be due to	explains why
creates	because of	the consequences	findings	thus
analysis	in this case	types	therefore	through this

To help you understand the cause/effect relationship between ideas in a passage, you can visually represent the information in your notes by using arrows. Figure 7.3 is an example of how to visually show the cause/effect relationship from the earlier passage.

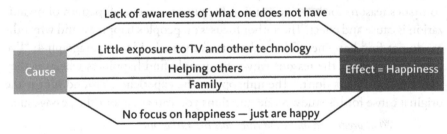

Figure 7.3 Visual for Cause/Effect Pattern

Now that you understand cause/effect and the organizational word clues for this pattern, you can predict the types of exam questions your professor may ask, such as:

What was the cause of some people's happiness?
What were the happiness states of the Chinese families who owned advanced technology?
What are some of the reasons for unhappiness?

ACTIVITY 7F
Practice Identifying a Cause/Effect Pattern

Read the following passage from a sociology textbook, and circle the cause/effect organizational word clues.

1   The number of Americans in their 20s and early 30s living with their parents has increased rapidly in recent decades. One reason for this phenomenon is economic. In the first few decades after World War II, housing and education costs were low, and the number of years one had to spend in school to get a steady, well-paying job was modest. Today, housing and education costs are high, and young people must typically spend more years in school before starting their careers (Furstenberg et al., 2004). As a result, many young people continue to live in their parents' home into their 20s and 30s as a matter of economic necessity.

2   For upper-middle-class families, a change in child-rearing practices also seems to account in part for the reluctance of some young adults to grow up. Many well-educated and well-to-do parents seem to be raising children who are simply too dependent. They are reluctant to insist that their children get part-time jobs when they are in their mid-teens, and they neglect to teach them the importance of saving money by always giving them as much money as they want. They provide too much assistance with schoolwork (either by themselves or by hiring tutors), and they organize too many extracurricular activities for their children, thus not giving them enough space to figure out their interests for themselves.

Source: From BRYM/LIE. *Sociology: Your Compass to a New World Brief Edition* 2e (p. 68). Copyright © 2010 Cengage Learning.

1. What reasons does the author give for adult children living with their parents?

_____

_____

Comparison/Contrast

USING WHAT YOU know about asking questions and organizational word clues, read the following passage and see if a pattern becomes apparent to you. Using Table 7.1 as a guide, circle any organizational word clues you notice.

1   There is no universal definition of family because contemporary household arrangements are complex. Family structures vary across cultures and have changed over time. In some societies, a family

includes uncles, aunts, and other relatives. In other societies, only parents and their children are viewed as a family.

How Families are Similar

2   The institution of the family exists in some form in all societies. Worldwide, families are similar in fulfilling some functions, encouraging marriage, and trying to ensure that people select appropriate mates.

Family Functions

3   Families vary considerably in the United States and globally but must fulfill at least five important functions to ensure a society's survival (Parsons and Bales 1955):

- ▶ Sexual regulation. Every society has norms regarding who may engage in sexual relations, with whom, and under what circumstances. In the United States, having sexual intercourse with someone younger than 18 (or 16 in some states) is a crime, but some societies permit marriage with girls as young as 8. One of the oldest rules that regulate sexual behavior is the incest taboo, a set of cultural norms and laws that forbid sexual intercourse between close blood relatives, such as brother and sister, father and daughter, or uncle and niece.

- ▶ Reproduction and socialization. Reproduction replenishes a country's population. Through socialization, children acquire language; absorb the accumulated knowledge, attitudes, beliefs, and values of their culture; and learn the social and interpersonal skills needed to function effectively in society.

- ▶ Economic security. Families provide food, shelter, clothing, and other material resources for their members. Increasingly in the United States, as you'll see shortly, both parents must work to purchase life's basic necessities such as housing and food.

- ▶ Emotional support. Families supply the nurturance, love, and emotional sustenance that people need to be happy, healthy, and secure. Our friends may come and go, but our family is usually our emotional anchor.

- ▶ Social placement. We inherit a social position based on our parents' social class. Family resources affect children's ability to pursue opportunities such as higher education, but we can move up or down the social hierarchy in adulthood. Many contemporary sociologists now include recreation as a basic U.S. family function. It's not critical for survival but since the 1950s, many parents have focused on having fun with their children and spending much more time with them on leisure activities, such as visiting amusements parks and playing video games together (see Coontz 2005).

Marriage

4   Marriage, a socially approved mating relationship that people expect to be stable and enduring, is also universal. Countries vary in their specific norms and laws dictating who can marry whom and at what age, but marriage everywhere is an important rite of passage that marks adulthood and its related responsibilities, especially providing for a family.

Endogamy and Exogamy

5   All societies have rules, formal or informal, defining an acceptable marriage partner. Endogamy (sometimes called homogamy) is the practice of selecting mates from within one's group. The partners are similar in religion, race, ethnicity, social class, and/or age. Across the Arab world and in some African nations, about half of married couples consist of first or second cousins because such unions reinforce kinship ties and increase a family's resources (Aizenman 2005; Bobroff-Hajal 2006). Exogamy (sometimes called heterogamy) is the practice of selecting mates from outside one's group. In the United States, for example, 24 states prohibit marriage between first cousins, even though violations are rarely prosecuted. In some parts of India, where most people still follow strict caste rules, the government is encouraging exogamy by offering a $1,250 cash award to any-one who marries someone from a lower caste. This is a hefty sum in areas where the annual income is less than half that amount (Chu 2007).

How Families Differ

6   There are also considerable worldwide variations in many family characteristics. Some variations affect the structure of the family, whereas others regulate household composition, as well as other behaviors.

Nuclear and Extended Families

7   In Western societies, the typical family form is a nuclear family that is made up of married parents and their biological or adopted children. In much of the world, however, the most common family form is the extended family, which consists of parents and children, as well as other kin, such as uncles and aunts, nieces and nephews, cousins, and grandparents. As the number of single-parent families increases in industrialized countries, extended families are becoming more common. By helping out with household tasks and child care, adult members of extended families make it easier for a single parent to work outside the home. Because the rates of unmarried people who are living together are high, nuclear families now comprise only

23 percent of all U.S. families, down from 40 percent in 1970 (U.S. Census Bureau 2010). Residence and Authority Families also differ in their living arrangements, how they trace their descent, and who has the most power. In a patrilocal residence pattern, newly married couples live with the husband's family; in a matrilocal residence pattern, they live with the wife's family; and in a neolocal residence pattern, the newly married couple sets up its own residence.

8   Around the world, the most common residence pattern is patrilocal. In industrialized societies, married couples are typically neolocal. Since the early 1990s, however, the tendency for young married adults to live with the parents of either the wife or the husband—or sometimes with the grandparents of one of the partners—has increased. At least half of all young American couples can't afford a medium-priced house; others have low-income jobs, are supporting children after a divorce, or just enjoy the comforts of a parental nest.

9   As a result, a recent phenomenon is the boomerang generation, young adults (and twice as many are men compared with women) who move back into their parents' home after living independently for a while or who never leave home in the first place. Parents try to launch their children into the adult world but, like boomerangs, some keep coming back. Some U.S. journalists call this group adultolescents because they're still "mooching off their parents" instead of living on their own.

10   Residence patterns often reflect who has authority within the family. In a matriarchal family system, the oldest women (usually grandmothers and mothers) control cultural, political, and economic resources, and consequently, have power over males. Some American Indian tribes were matriarchal, and in some African countries, the eldest women have considerable authority and influence. For the most part, however, matriarchal societies are rare.

11   A more widespread system is a patriarchal family system, in which the oldest men control cultural, political, and economic resources, and consequently, have power over females. In some patriarchal societies, women have few rights within the family and none outside the family, such as not being permitted to vote, drive, work outside the home, or attend college. In other patriarchal societies, women may have considerable decision-making power in the home, but few legal or political rights, such as the right to obtain a divorce or to run for a political office.

12   In an egalitarian family system, both partners share power and authority fairly equally. Many Americans think they have egalitarian families, but patriarchal families are more common. For example, employed

women shoulder twice as much child care as men. As you'll see shortly, women are considerably more likely than men to experience intimate partner violence (IPV) and economic hardship after a divorce. Also, employed women are twice as likely as their male counterparts to provide caregiving to aging family members (Houser 2007).

Source: From BENOKRAITIS. *SOC* 2e (pp. 233–6). Copyright © 2012 Cengage Learning.

What about the headings of this passage gives you a clue about how the passage might be organized? What questions could you ask? When looking for the overall pattern of organization of a reading, look to the major headings to begin looking for clues.

How are families similar?
How are families different?

The first paragraph introduces the topic of the reading—families. After skimming the headings, notice that the major ones have the words *similar* and *differ.* What similarities do families have? What differences do they have? Paragraph 2 includes this sentence, which establishes similarities: "The institution of the family exists in some form in all societies." Paragraph 3 lists the functions of families, but it appears a listing organization is limited to only that paragraph. In paragraph 6, the author uses the phrase *worldwide variations,* which suggests that differences will be discussed. Paragraphs 6–9 explore the differences between patrilocal, matrilocal, and neolocal residence patterns. Paragraphs 10 and 11 bring out *differences* in patriarchal families. The reading is set up in an overall comparison/contrast pattern of organization.

When authors use comparison/contrast, they examine the similarities and/ or differences between two or more ideas, people, objects, and events. For example, a political science author might explore the similarities and differences between a monarchy and a democracy. An author of a biology textbook could detail the similarities among animal cells. A textbook on criminal justice might include differences in prison systems in different countries.

Tip FROM THE
Brain Doctor

The brain loves metaphors because a metaphor compares two things. By bringing in another idea to compare to a new idea, the brain activates a larger network with more information. It is especially helpful when someone compares something you do not know much about to something for which you have a good network of information. In that way, you can use what you do know to help understand what you do not know. Looking at ways things are similar (comparison) and ways they are different (contrast) brings a larger network of information to the thought process while making information easier to remember. When you study, ask yourself, "How is this like something I already understand?" The metaphor's image will stay in your mind more easily and help you recall the new information.

comparison/contrast
pattern that examines the similarities or differences between two or more ideas, people, objects, or events

ACTIVITY 7G
Describe Similarities and Differences

Describe the similarities and differences between reading for pleasure and reading required assignments for classes. Complete the chart provided here.

Similarities		Differences	
Reading for Pleasure	Required Reading Assignments	Reading for Pleasure	Required Reading Assignments

Table 7.5 provides examples of organizational word clues that signal an author's use of the comparison/contrast pattern.

To help you identify the comparison/contrast pattern of organization, you can visually represent the information in your notes. Using charts or tables can help you organize the similarities and differences you find in a passage.

Table 7.5 Organizational Word Clues for Comparison/Contrast Pattern

however	on the other hand	but	different	variation
although	on the contrary	as	compared with	some…others
like	contrasted with	yet	in the same way	although
similar to	in other words	in opposition	unlike	too
whereas	as compared with	along	similar	similarly

Figure 7.4 is an example of how to visually show the previous passage's comparison/contrast relationship.

Families

	Similarities	Differences
1	Five important functions of a family	Family forms (nuclear, extended)
2	Marriage is important	Different residence patterns (patrilocal, matrilocal, neolocal)
3	Rules defining marriage partners	Differences among patriarchal family systems

Figure 7.4 Visual for Comparison/Contrast Pattern

Here are some examples of the types of comparison/contrast questions an instructor might ask on a test about the earlier passage and, therefore, the kind you should ask yourself before a test:

What similarities does the idea of marriage have among cultures?
How are patrilocal and neolocal residence patterns different?

ACTIVITY 7H
Practice Identifying a Comparison/Contrast Pattern

Read the following passage, and circle the comparison/contrast organizational word clues.

One of the greatest things about being a professor of English is that you get to keep meeting old friends. For beginning readers, though, every story may seem new, and the resulting experience of reading is highly disjointed. Think of reading on one level, as one of those papers from elementary school where you connect the dots. I could

disjointed not well connected

Continued on next page.

predisposition
to make more
likely

never see the picture in a connect-the-dot drawing until I'd put in virtually every line. Other kids could look at a full page of dots and say, 'Oh, that's an elephant,' 'That's a locomotive.' Me, I saw dots. I think it's partly predisposition—some people handle two-dimensional visualization better than others—but largely a matter of practice: the more connect-the-dot drawings you do, the more likely you are to recognize the design early on. Same with literature. Part of pattern recognition is talent, but a whole lot of it is practice: if you read enough and give what you read enough thought, you begin to see patterns, archetypes, recurrences. And as with those pictures among the dots, it's a matter of learning to look.

Source: Foster, Thomas, C. *How to Read Literature Like a Professor*. NY: HarperCollins, 2003, pp. 28–29.

1. **List two organizational word clues that do not signal comparison/contrast in this passage.**

   _____

   _____

2. **What two things does the author compare?**

   _____

   _____

Definition/Example

USING WHAT YOU know about asking questions and organizational word clues, read the following passage and see if a pattern becomes apparent to you. Using Table 7.1 as a guide, circle any organizational word clues you notice.

Contracts

1   Both oral and written communication with your company's customers must meet the requirements of several laws. Among the most important forms of communication is the **contract**, a legally binding agreement between two or more parties. A proposal or offer by one party and acceptance by the other party or parties creates a contract. The contract may involve completing a particular action, providing a particular item or service, or refraining from doing a certain action.

2   An enforceable contract may result from an exchange of letters—one that makes a clear and definite offer and another that accepts the offer

without making conditions on the acceptance—or a series of letters that makes clear the parties have reached agreement about material elements of the contract. A contract does not have to be written in a letter or on a particular form if it includes essential elements of the agreement and has the necessary signatures. Oral agreements are sometimes valid contracts. A valid contract must have the following elements:

1. Offer and acceptance
2. Competency of parties
3. Legality of subject matter
4. Consideration (money, motive, or promise exchanged)

Businesses generally use the services of a lawyer or forms reviewed by a lawyer for all but the simplest contracts. Examples of contracts are agreements for the sale of goods or services, transfer of property or interests in property, and contracts of employment.

Source: From KRIZAN. *Business Communication* 7e (p. 79). Copyright © 2008 Cengage Learning.

Use the title of the passage to create a question: "What are contracts?" or "What about contracts?" The answer can be found in the passage, where contracts are clearly defined and examples are given. The organizational word clue *is* is a subtle example because *is* is such a common word. However, in this passage, the word *is* signals a definition. The title of the passage tells you that the subject is contracts. What else is in the passage? More information about what a contract is (definition) and examples of a contract.

Authors use definition/example to clarify the meaning of key concepts. Definition/example is not always obvious at first. Boldface type can sometimes signal a definition of a key term. When you suspect a definition/example pattern, look for other clues to confirm your hunch. Headings and organizational word clues can lead you to decide whether the entire reading is organized in a definition/example pattern.

definition/example pattern that clarifies the meaning of key concepts by defining them or providing examples

Table 7.6 provides examples of organizational word clues that signal an author's use of the definition/example pattern.

Table 7.6 Organizational Word Clues for Definition/Example Pattern

for example	as defined as	means the same as	translated as
synonymous with	another meaning	also referred to as	interpreted as
such as	states that	which means	seen as

After reading this passage and identifying the author's pattern of organization as definition/example, you can visually represent the information as shown in Figure 7.5.

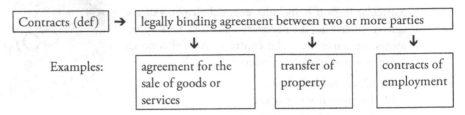

Figure 7.5 Visual for Definition/Example Pattern

Here are some examples of the types of definition questions an instructor might ask on an exam based on the passage and, therefore, the kind you should ask yourself:

What are contracts?
Give an example of a contract.

ACTIVITY 71
Practice Identifying a Definition/Example Pattern

The following passage from a biology textbook uses a definition/example pattern of organization. Circle the organizational word clues; you might notice that there are not many in this passage.

1   You could test your hypothesis by performing an **experiment**. An experiment is a procedure designed to test some idea. In this case, all you would need to do would be to try the light switch in the kitchen. If the lights in the kitchen worked, you would reject your original hypothesis and form a new one. Perhaps, you hypothesize, the circuit breaker to your study had been tripped. To test this idea, you would "perform" another experiment, locating the circuit breaker to see if it was turned off. If the circuit breaker was off, you would conclude that your second hypothesis was correct. To substantiate your conclusion, you would throw the switch and see if your computer worked.

2   This process involving observations, hypothesis, and experimentation forms the foundation of the scientific method. Although scientific experimentation may be much more complicated than discovering the reason for a computer failure, the process itself is the same.

3   Proper experimentation in biology usually requires two groups: experimental and control. The experimental group is the one that is tested or manipulated in some way. The control group is not tested or manipulated. Valid conclusions come from such comparisons because, in a properly run

experiment, both groups are treated identically except in one way. The difference in treatment is known as the experimental variable. Consider an example to illustrate this point. In order to test the effect of a new drug on laboratory mice, a good scientist would start with a group of mice of the same age, sex, weight, genetic composition, and so on. These animals would be divided into two groups, the experimental and control groups. Both groups would be treated the same throughout the experiment, receiving the same diet and being housed in the same type of cage at the same temperature. The only difference between the two should be the drug given to the experimental group. Consequently, any observed differences between the groups could be attributed to the treatment (the experimental variable).

Source: Chiras, Daniel D. *Human Biology*. Jones & Bartlett Learning, 2012, pp. 10–11.

1. What is the definition of experiment?

_____

2. What example of an experiment is given?

_____

Sequence

USING WHAT YOU know about asking questions and organizational word clues, read the following passage and see if a pattern becomes apparent to you. Using Table 7.1 as a guide, circle any organizational word clues you notice.

Journals

1   Professors assign weekly or monthly journals to illustrate more vividly the importance of journal writing for the study of history. In the computer and telephone age, people rarely write diaries or journals. For centuries, however, this was a common means by which people organized their thoughts and described their lives.

2   Journals written by historical figures such as Abigail Adams, Marco Polo, or Christopher Columbus will appear in class syllabi. Reading them provides you with an invaluable insight into their thoughts and their activities at pivotal moments in world history. But writing your own journal will give you added insight into the experiences and motivations of these men and women. You will discover that it is more difficult to articulate your opinions on paper than in your own

pivotal vitally important, critical

articulate express

mind. As you write your own journal, going through the same process as these other journal writers, you will be better equipped to analyze their words and deeds. You will recognize, for example, how opinions change as external circumstances change. Did Marco Polo's views of non-Europeans change during the course of his travels? If so, why did they change? What were the circumstances surrounding his change of opinion?

3   The first step in journal writing is to do the assignment required by the professor. Even if she collects the journals only once or twice during the semester, you have to keep up with the work. If the professor requires you to write in your journal once a week, write in it once a week. Don't wait until the deadline to write out three or four quick entries. The professor wants to see the progression of your views, which may change dramatically as new information comes to light in the classroom and the class readings.

4   The second step is to think of the journal in the same way you think of any other written assignment. In other words, you should follow all grammar and spelling rules. Finally, make sure you follow the professor's instructions. Some journal assignments require that you give personal insights about your own life; some ask you to analyze the different readings and topics in class. If you do not understand the assignment, ask the professor to clarify what he wants.

Source: From BERKIN/ANDERSON. *The History Handbook* (pp. 48–9). Copyright © 2012 Cengage Learning.

When you see the title of this passage, you might decide that the author will define journals. As you read the first paragraph, you realize, instead, that he assumes you know what journals are and spends his time trying to persuade you that they are worthwhile. The author continues with the benefits of journal writing in paragraph 2 and then mentions the word *process*. Paragraphs 3 and 4 actually begin with sequence/process organizational word clues: *the first step*, *the second step*. The author uses a sequence pattern of organization.

sequence pattern that shows the steps in a process or the chronological order of certain events

When authors use sequence, they show the steps in a process or the chronological order of certain events. The sequence pattern is also sometimes known as process. Most writing organized in a sequential pattern is fairly easy to recognize. However, sequence is not to be confused with listing because in sequence the order in which the steps or events occurred is important. A list is just a list. When you begin your semester, you get lists of books you need to purchase for your classes. It will not matter if you buy your biology textbook before your history book, as long you buy both before classes start. On the other hand, if you write down directions to a different campus where your friend attends college, the order of the directions matter because they must be followed in sequence.

Table 7.7 provides examples of organizational word clues that signal an author's use of sequence.

Table 7.7 Organizational Word Clues for Sequence Pattern

first...second...third	next	order of events	stages
the following phases	processes	cycles	sequence
steps	procedures	first of all	finally
another way	presented as a series of events in a particular order		

To help you understand the sequence of steps or events in a passage, you can visually represent the information in your notes. Timelines or flowcharts are especially useful for representing sequence. Figure 7.6 is an example of how to visually show the sequence relationship from the earlier passage.

Journals

1. Do the assignment required by the professor. (Do not wait until the last minute.)

2. Think of the journal like any other written assignment. (Observe grammar and spelling rules.)

3. Follow professor's instructions.

Figure 7.6 Visual for Sequence Pattern

Here are some examples of the types of exam questions an instructor might ask based on the passage and, therefore, the kind you should ask yourself before a test:

Why is the first step in journal writing important?
What is the second step in journal writing?

ACTIVITY 7J
Practice Identifying a Sequence Pattern

Read the following passage from a history textbook. Circle any organizational word clues that help you identify a sequence pattern, and notice how the dates help you follow the sequence.

COMBAT OF THE INFANTRY.

iStockphoto.com/Duncan Walker

siege military action in which forces surround an area

anarchy a condition without governmental control or military

resurgent rise that happens after a time of no movement

1   The Ottoman army, led by Sultan Suleyman the Magnificent, arrived at Mohcs, on the plains of Hungary, on an August morning in 1526. The Turkish force numbered about 100,000 men, and in its baggage were three hundred new long- range cannons. Facing them was a somewhat larger European force, clothed in heavy armor but armed with only one hundred older cannons.

2   The battle began at noon and was over in two hours. The flower of Hungarian cavalry had been destroyed, and twenty thousand foot soldiers had drowned in a nearby swamp. The Ottomans had lost fewer than two hundred men. Two weeks later, they seized the Hungarian capital at Budapest and prepared to lay siege to the nearby Austrian city of Vienna. Europe was in a panic. It was to be the high point of Turkish expansion in Europe.

3   In launching their Age of Exploration, European rulers had hoped that by controlling global markets, they could cripple the power of Islam and reduce its threat to the security of Europe. But the dream of Christian nations to expand their influence around the globe at the expense of their great Muslim rival had not been achieved. On the contrary, the Muslim world, which seemed to have entered a period of decline with the collapse of the Abbasid caliphate during the era of the Mongols, managed to revive in the shadow of Europe's Age of Exploration, a period that witnessed the rise of three great Muslim empires. These powerful Muslim states of the Ottomans, the Safavids, and the Mughals dominated the Middle East and the South Asian subcontinent and brought stability to a region that had been in turmoil for centuries.

4   This stability lasted for about two hundred years. By the end of the eighteenth century, much of India and the Middle East had come under severe European pressure and had returned to a state of anarchy, and the Ottoman Empire had entered a period of gradual decline. But that decline was due more to internal factors than to the challenge posed by a resurgent Europe.

Source: From DUIKER/SPIELVOGEL. *World History* 6e (pp. 419–420). Copyright © 2011 Cengage Learning.

1. What can you tell from the sequence of events about the Muslim empires?

_____

_____

2. Create a visual that depicts the sequence pattern of this passage.

3. What is the main idea of the passage?

_____

_____

ACTIVITY 7K
Identify Patterns of Organization

Based on what you have learned about patterns of organization, try to determine what pattern is used in each of the following passages. Circle any organizational word clues that signal the overall pattern of organization.

1.   If for some reason you left college without developing the basic skills in the ten know-how groups, graduate school can accomplish what your college education did not. First of all, most of your peers, if you go to a halfway program, will have those skills. Just associating

Continued on next page.

and competing with them will raise your level. In addition, they will have other more advanced skills than you might have, which they will help you learn. Second, graduate programs tend to be more skill oriented. They will have some courses that provide the opportunity to develop basic and advanced skills. Third, most good graduate programs will have significant internship or fieldwork requirements.

Source: Coplin, Bill. (2003. *10 Things Employers Want You to Learn in College*. Ten Speed Press: Berkeley, California. p. 196.

What is the overall pattern of organization? _____

2.   If you were arrested for a crime in France, the very fact that you were arrested would place the responsibility on your shoulders to prove that you were innocent. On the other hand, if you are arrested for a crime in the United States, the responsibility is on the state (processing attorney) to prove that you are guilty. In France there is a presumption of guilt when you are accused of a crime. But, in this country there is always a presumption that the person accused of a crime is innocent until he is proven guilty. This is a great protection to the individual. It prevents many innocent people from being sent to a prison for crimes they didn't commit. On the other hand, it is not uncommon for the accused in France to spend three months or more in prison; accused, but never convicted.

Source: Crabtree, Arthur. (1964). *The Law and You*. Holt, Rinehart and Winston: New York.

What is the overall method of organization? _____

3.   Poverty is staying up all night on cold nights to watch the fire, knowing one spark on the newspaper covering the walls means your sleeping children die in flames. In summer, poverty is watching gnats and flies devour your baby's tears when he cries. The screens are torn and you pay so little rent you know they will never be fixed. Poverty means insects in your food, in your nose, in your eyes, and crawling over you when you sleep. Poverty is hoping it never rains because diapers won't dry when it rains and soon you are using newspapers. Poverty is seeing your children forever with runny noses. Paper handkerchiefs cost money and all your rags you need for other things. Even more costly are antihistamines. Poverty is cooking without food and cleaning without soap.

Source: Goodwin Parker, Jo. *What is Poverty? America's Other Children: Public Schools Outside Suburbia by George Henderson*. University of Oklahoma Press, 1971.

What is the overall pattern of organization? _____

4.   The Thirty Years' War ruined the economy and decimated the population in many parts of the empire and had long-term political consequences for the empire as a whole. One reason for the war's devastation was a novel application of firepower to warfare that increased both the size of armies and their deadly force in battle. This was the use of volley fire, the arrangement of foot soldier in parallel lines so that one line of men could fire while another reloaded. This tactic, pioneered in the Netherlands around the turn of the century, was refined by Gustav Adolf of Sweden. He amassed large numbers of troops and increased the rate of fire so that virtually continuous barrage was maintained. He also used maneuverable field artillery to protect the massed infantry from cavalry charges.

Source: From NOBEL/STRAUSS/OSHEIM/NEUSCHEL. *Western Civilization Beyond Boundaries* 6e. Copyright © 2011 Cengage Learning.

What is the overall pattern of organization? _____

5.   1   Biologists look at all aspects of life, past and present. Their focus takes them all the way down to atoms, and all the way up to global relationships among organisms and the environment. Through their work, we glimpse a great pattern of organization in nature.

        2   The pattern starts at the level of atoms. Atoms are fundamental building blocks of all substances, living and nonliving.

        3   At the next level of organization, atoms join with other atoms, forming molecules. Among the molecules are complex carbohydrates and lipids, proteins, and nucleic acids. Today, only living cells make these "molecules of life" in nature.

        4   The pattern crosses the threshold to life when many molecules are organized as cells. A cell is the smallest unit of life that can survive and reproduce on its own, given information in DNA, energy inputs, raw materials, and suitable environmental conditions.

        5   An organism is an individual that consists of one or more cells. In larger multicelled organisms, trillions of cells organize into tissues, organs, and organ systems, all interacting in tasks that keep the whole body alive.

        Source: From STARR. Biology: *The Unity and Diversity of Life* 12e (pp. 4–5). Copyright © 2009 Cengage Learning.

What is the overall pattern of organization? _____

6.   Blood returning to the heart from the body tissues is low in oxygen and high in carbon dioxide. This blood first enters the right atrium and flows into the right ventricle. Next, the right ventricle pumps it through the pulmonary arteries to the lungs. The pulmonary arteries are the only arteries that carry oxygen-poor blood. All other arteries carry

Continued on next page.

oxygen-rich blood. As the blood travels through the capillaries in the lungs, it gains oxygen and gets rid of carbon dioxide.

Source: Cebco. *Biology: The Study of Life*. Allyn and Bacon: Newton, MA. p. 155.

What is the overall pattern of organization? _____

7.   1   Suppose you had been born in 1940. Your childhood and adolescence would have been very different from today: no Internet, computers, IPods, cell phones, air conditioners, automatic dishwashers, or appliances for washing and drying clothes. You would have listened to radio instead of watching television. Long-distance telephone calls were a luxury. Few women or minorities went to college, and those few had limited job opportunities afterward. If you had lived then, how would you have been different?

2   People of different generations differ in many ways, which psychologists call cohort effects. A **cohort** group of people born at a particular time, or a group of people who enter an organization at a particular time is a group of people born at a particular time or a group of people who enter an organization at a particular time.

era a time period with general characteristics

reigned ruled the country

3   The era in which you grew up is a powerful influence on your personality, social behavior, and attitudes. For example, people whose youth spanned the Great Depression and World War II learned to save money and to sacrifice their own pleasures for the needs of the country. Even after the war was over and prosperity reigned, most remained thrifty and cautious (Rogler, 2002). In contrast, young people of today have had much more leisure time (Larson, 2001). Jean Twenge (2006) has compared cohort effects to the differences among cultures. Indeed, the technology you have grown up with may seem unfamiliar and alien to your grandparents, who in some ways are like "immigrants" to modern culture. Many aspects of intellect and personality differ between generations, as we shall examine in later chapters.

Source: From KALAT. *Introduction to Psychology* 9e (pp. 160–1). Copyright © 2011 Cengage Learning.

What is the overall pattern of organization? _____

8.   1   Sports were foreign to me until I gave birth to three sons. Sports can be defined as *a particular activity, as in athletic game*. But I learned it was more…Webster didn't play sports! Each one of my sons introduced me to this leisure obsession simply as a result of his being born. It's as if the sports were born right along with them, through them; in a sense I guess they were. For example, each one had a golf club, custom made, before he learned how to walk. Each one had been gifted hockey, baseball, and soccer jerseys, in sizes birth to Toddler 2 before taking his first breath of air. Each one had at least one or three of every sport's balls manufactured at the time of his birth. And, I'm sure I remember that their first spoken words were "Red Wings, Tigers and Lions….oh my."

2   Ah, yes, to illustrate my point: the lessons. The lessons began the moment each one could balance himself. Each was put into the middle of the ice with a small chair and encouraged for 30 minutes to skate forward, thrown into a pool to see if he could float, lined up against a wall to learn how to hold and swing a bat, put into a sand-trap to punch a little white ball out with that miniature club, or to run and kick the "big ball." Even eating dinner became a sport.

3   In addition to hockey, swimming, and soccer there was T-Ball, track, and softball along with college golf and lacrosse. My sons were rewarded with souvenirs for their efforts. Their efforts are synonymous with rooms filled with team photos, posters, plaques, team books, medallions, sticks, and certificates.

What is the overall pattern of organization? _____

9.   These facts have serious implications. They tell us a great deal about the impact geography and especially climate have on the people of an area and their economy. Much of Eurasia is subject to great ranges of temperature. Russia and the former Soviet Union have occupied a very extensive landmass with no large bodies of water to modify temperature extremes. Thus, much of Siberia can be blisteringly hot in the summer and frigidly cold in the winter.

Source: Richards and Vaillant. *From Russia to USSR and Beyond,* 2nd Ed. White Plains, NY: Longman. pp. 4–5.

What is the overall pattern of organization? _____

10.   1   Every living thing on earth is made up of primarily water. A tomato is about 95% H_2O. Human beings are approximately 65% water (a character on *Star Trek: The Next Generation* referred to us as "ugly bags of mostly water"), and men are sloshier than women. We can live without food for about thirty days, but without water we would last only a week. Americans use more than 175 gallons of water a day per person.

2   The traits of water are interesting. Water is the only substance to be found in solid, liquid, and gaseous states in normal earth conditions. "Because of nature's water cycle," the *World Book Encyclopedia* tells us an important finding, "there is as much water on the earth today as there ever was—or ever will be. Water changes only from one form to another, and moves from one place to another. The water you bathed in last night might have flowed in Russia's Volga River last year. Or perhaps Alexander the Great drank it more than 2,000 years ago."

Source: Adapted from Malesky, Kee. *All Facts Considered.* John Wiley & Sons: Hoboken, New Jersey, 2010, pp. 125–126.

What is the overall pattern of organization? _____

Mixed Patterns

SOME LONGER READINGS use more than one pattern of organization within sentences, different patterns between paragraphs, and an altogether different overall pattern. Other readings have a mix of dominant overall patterns, not just one. No matter what the reading, begin by questioning yourself as you read so you can figure out an author's point and the path he or she takes to get to that point.

To do this, ask questions of headings and subheadings if there are any. If there are no headings, question yourself from the topic. The answers to all these questions will lead you close to the main idea. As you look for it, search also for the pattern the main idea fits into, the pattern of organization that the author purposefully picked in order to make his point. When you recognize any organizational word clues, look at what is around them and decide if they tell you something about the sentence, paragraph, or whole reading.

Consider the following passage from novelist Stephen King about writing. Notice that the organizational word clues are circled. Read the passage carefully, and ask yourself questions to figure out the main idea and overall pattern of organization.

1   In my view, stories and novels consist of three parts: narration, which moves the story from point A to point B and finally to point Z; description, which creates a sensory reality for the reader; and dialogue, which brings characters to life through their speech.

2   You may wonder where plot is in all this. The answer—my answer, anyway—is nowhere. I won't try to convince you that I've never plotted any more than I'd try to convince you that I never told a lie, but I do both as infrequently as possible. I distrust plots for two reasons: first, because our *lives* are largely plotless, even when you add in all our reasonable precautions and careful planning; and second, because I believe plotting and the spontaneity of real creation aren't compatible. It's best that I be as clear about this as I can—I want you to understand that my basic belief about the making of stories is that they pretty much make themselves. The job of the writer is to give them a place to grow (and transcribe them, of course). If you can see things this way (or at least try to), we can work together comfortably. If, on the other hand, you decide I'm crazy, that's fine. You won't be the first.

3   When, during the course of an interview for *The New Yorker*, I told the interviewer (Mark Singer) that I believed stories are found things, like fossils in the ground, he said that he didn't believe me. I replied that that was fine, as long as he believed that *I* believed it. And I do. Stories aren't souvenir tee-shirts or GameBoys. Stories are relics, part of

an undiscovered pre-existing world. The writer's job is to use the tools in his or her toolbox to get as much of each one out of the ground intact as possible. Sometimes the (fossil) you uncover (is) small; a seashell. Sometimes it's enormous, a *Tyrannosaurus Rex* with all those gigantic ribs and grinning teeth. Either way, short story or thousand-page whopper of a novel, the techniques of excavation remain basically the same.

is a metaphor here for story

4   No matter how good you are, no matter how much experience you have, it's probably impossible to get the entire fossil out of the ground without a few breaks and losses. To get even *most* of it, the shovel must give way to more delicate tools: airhose, palm-pick, perhaps even a toothbrush. Plot is a far bigger tool, the writer's jackhammer. You can liberate a fossil from hard ground with a jackhammer, no argument there, but you know as well as I do that the jackhammer is going to break almost as much stuff as it liberates. It's clumsy, mechanical, anti-creative. Plot is, I think, the good writer's last resort and the dullard's first choice. The story which results from it is apt to feel artificial and labored.

5   I lean more heavily on intuition, and have been able to do that because my books tend to be based on situation rather than story. Some of the ideas which have produced those books are more complex than others, (but) the majority (start out) with the stark simplicity of a department store window display or a waxwork tableau. I want to put a group of characters (perhaps a pair; perhaps even just one) in some sort of predicament and then watch them try to work themselves free. My job isn't to help them work their way free, or manipulate them to safety—those are jobs which require the noisy jackhammer of plot—(but) to watch what happens and then write it down.

6   The situation comes (first.) The characters—always flat and unfeatured, to begin with—come next. Once these things are fixed in my mind, I (begin) to narrate. I often have an idea of what the outcome may be, but I have never demanded of a set of characters that they do things my way. (On the contrary,) I want them to do things *their* way. In some instances, the outcome is what I visualized. In most, (however,) it's something I never expected. For a suspense novelist, this is a great thing. I am, after all, not just the novel's creator but its first reader. And if *I'm* not able to guess with any accuracy how the damned thing is going to turn out, even with my inside knowledge of coming events, I can be pretty sure of keeping the reader in a state of page-turning anxiety. Any why worry about the ending anyway? Why be such a control freak? (Sooner or later) every story comes out *somewhere*.

This passage has no headings or subheadings, so you have to begin reading and ask yourself, "What is the author saying about writing?" Look for that answer as you read, and note organizational word clues as you go along. Paragraph 1 talks about parts of a story. Could this be analysis? Paragraph 2 deals with why the author does not like planned plots in books. Could this be cause/effect? In the same paragraph, the author draws our attention to one point: "It's best that I be as clear about this as I can—I want you to understand that my basic belief about the making of stories is that they pretty much make themselves." He gets our attention by using phrases of emphasis. At the end of paragraph 2, you find the organizational word clue, *on the other hand*. What is being contrasted? Opinions about Stephen King—is he crazy or not? The reading is about stories, not King, so *on the other hand* just organizes those two ideas (is he crazy or not) and not the larger reading.

Paragraph 3 goes in depth about what stories are. Is this analysis? King even creates a metaphor of excavating a fossil to illustrate his point that stories are there to be uncovered. Paragraph 4 continues with the analysis. Paragraph 5 contains a sequence word clue and two comparison/contrast word clues. What is the author's purpose in paragraph 5? To describe the process of creating a story. Paragraph 6 continues with this process.

Now put it all together: The topic is writing stories. What is the main idea? What does the author say about stories? What is emphasized as a central point? How does the author frame his support for this main idea? He used a lot of word clues but some showed relationships among sentences and other relationships among ideas in paragraphs. What is the overall pattern? Ask yourself a question about the main idea. How do stories make themselves? To answer this question, the author takes a lot of time to make sure you understand what a story is, how it is a fossil waiting to be unearthed. He uses analysis to do this. Then he explains the process he takes in writing a story. He uses sequence to do this. The overall pattern is mixed: analysis and sequence.

Remember that the main idea and the overall pattern of organization should complement one another. The main idea fits into the pattern. Good questioning helps you uncover both.

ACTIVITY 7L
Identify Mixed Patterns

The following passage has a mixed pattern of organization. The main idea is highlighted for you. Organizational clue words are circled, but not all of them relate to the overall pattern. Read through the passage carefully, and question yourself using what you have learned.

1   Attending a political rally has a profound (effect) on a young adult, less (effect) on a pre-teen, and none on an infant. Playing with a pile of blocks is a more stimulating experience of a young child than for anyone older. The (effect) of any experience depends on someone's maturity. The theorist who made this point most influentially was Jean Piaget (pee-ah-ZHAY) (1896–1980).

2   Early in his career, while administering IQ tests to French-speaking children in Switzerland, Piaget was fascinated that so many children of a given age gave the same incorrect answer to a given question. He concluded that children have qualitatively different thought processes from adults. Piaget made extensive longitudinal studies of children, especially his own. According to Piaget, intellectual development is not merely an accumulation of experience. Rather, the child constructs new mental processes as he or she interacts with the environment.

qualitatively
having to do with opinions, feelings, or judgments

3   In Piaget's terminology, behavior is based on schemata (the plural of schema). A schema is an organized way of interacting with objects. (For instance,) infants have a grasping schema and a sucking schema. Older infants gradually add new schemata to their repertoire and adapt their old ones. The adaptation takes place through the processes of assimilation and accommodation.

4   Assimilation means applying an old schema to new objects or problems. (For example,) a child who observes that animals move on their own may believe that the sun and moon, which seem to move, must be alive also. (Many ancient adults believed the same thing.) Accommodation means modifying an old schema to fit a new object or problem. (For example,) a child may learn that "only living things move on their own" is a rule with exceptions and that the sun and moon are not alive.

5   Infants shift back and forth between assimilation and accommodation. Equilibration is the establishment of harmony or balance between the two, and according to Piaget, equilibration is the key to intellectual growth. A discrepancy occurs between the child's current understanding and some evidence to the contrary. The child accommodates to that discrepancy and achieves an equilibration at a higher level.

equilibration
sense of balance

6   The (same processes) occur in adults. When you see a new mathematical problem, you try several methods until you hit upon one that works. In other words, you assimilate the new problem to your old schema. However, if the new problem is different from previous problems, you modify (accommodate) your schema to find a solution. (Through) processes like these, said Piaget, intellectual growth occurs.

Source: From KALAT. *Introduction to Psychology* 9e (p. 161). Copyright © 2011 Cengage Learning.

Continued on next page.

1. What is the organization of paragraph 1?

   _____

2. In paragraph 2, what is the word clue *concluded* a clue to? Is it an organizational word clue or a clue to something else?

   _____

3. How are paragraphs 3 and 4 organized?

   _____

4. What is compared in paragraphs 5 and 6?

   _____

5. What is the author's purpose in paragraphs 5 and 6? What causes intellectual growth?

   _____

6. What two patterns dominate the organization of the passage?

   _____

Staying Focused on the Overall Pattern

IT IS EASY TO GET DISTRACTED by the individual paragraphs and miss the overall pattern of organization of the larger reading. One way you can stay focused on the overall pattern within a longer reading is using the note card technique.

This technique is simple and effective. Using index cards or half sheets of paper, write the main idea and pattern of organization of each paragraph. Then spread the cards or sheets out and determine which primary pattern of organization was used by the author. This technique makes it easier to see the larger, overall pattern no matter what is going on with each individual paragraph.

ACTIVITY 7M
Practice the Note Card Technique

Use the note card technique to help you recognize which patterns are being used in the following passage from a sociology textbook. Read the passage, and complete the following tasks to help you determine the overall pattern of organization:

1. Circle organizational word clues, and identify which pattern of organization is being used in each paragraph.

2. Write each paragraph's pattern of organization on a separate note card. On the same note card, write the paragraph's main idea.

3. Put cards in piles according to their pattern of organization.

4. Decide the overall pattern of organization of the passage by seeing which pile has the most cards. **Note:** If a paragraph does not have obvious word clues, you can still determine its organization. For example, an author may elaborate on examples, a cause, or a reason without using organizational word clues.

Resocialization and Total Institutions

1   In concluding our discussion of socialization agents, we must underline the importance of resocialization in contributing to the lifelong process of social learning. Resocialization takes place when powerful socializing agents deliberately cause rapid change in people's values, roles, and self-conceptions, sometimes against their will.

2   You can see resocialization at work in the ceremonies that are staged when someone joins a fraternity, a sorority, the U.S. Marines, or a religious order. Such a ceremony, or initiation rite, for example, signifies the transition of the individual from one group to another and ensures his or her loyalty to the new group. Initiation rites require new recruits to abandon old self-perceptions and assume new identities. To illustrate this point, when initiation rites take place during resocialization, they typically involve a three-stage ceremony: (1) separation from one's old status and identity (ritual rejection); (2) degradation, disorientation, and stress (ritual death); and (3) acceptance of the new group culture and status (ritual rebirth).

3   Much resocialization takes place in what sociologist Erving Goffman (1961) called total institutions. Total institutions are settings where people are isolated from the larger society and under the strict control and constant supervision of a specialized staff. Asylums and prisons are examples of total institutions. Because of the "pressure cooker" atmosphere in such institutions, resocialization in total institutions is often rapid and thorough, even in the absence of initiation rites.

4   A famous failed experiment illustrates the immense resocializing capacity of total institutions (Haney, Banks, and Zimbardo, 1973; Zimbardo, 1972). In the early

resocialization
process of learning new attitudes and norms required for a new social role

degradation
lower in the opinion of others or in self respect

Continued on next page.

1970s, researchers at Stanford University created their own mock prison. They paid two dozen male volunteers to act as guards and inmates. The volunteers were mature, emotionally stable, intelligent college students from middle-class homes. By the flip of a coin, half the volunteers were designated prisoners, the other half guards. At the mock prison, each prisoner was stripped, deloused, put into prison-issue clothes, given a number, and placed in a cell with two other inmates. The guards made up their own rules for maintaining law and order.

5   To understand better what it means to be a prisoner or a prison guard, the researchers wanted to observe and record social interaction in the mock prison for 2 weeks. However, they were forced to end the experiment abruptly after only 6 days because what they witnessed frightened them. In less than a week, the prisoners and prison guards could no longer tell the difference between the roles they were playing and their "real" selves. Much of the socialization that these young men had undergone over a period of about 20 years was quickly suspended.

despicable
shamefully bad

6   About a third of the guards began to treat the prisoners like despicable animals, taking pleasure in cruelty. Even the guards who were regarded by the prisoners as tough but fair stopped short of interfering in the tyrannical and arbitrary use of power by the most sadistic guards. All of the prisoners became servile and dehumanized, thinking only about survival, escape, and their growing hatred of the guards. If they were thinking as college students, they could have walked out of the experiment at any time. Some of the prisoners did in fact beg for parole. However, by the fifth day of the experiment they were so programmed to think of themselves as prisoners that they returned docilely to their cells when their request for parole was denied.

sadistic
deriving pleasure
from hurting
others

docilely in an
easy-to-manage
way

7   The Stanford experiment suggests that your sense of self and the roles you play are not as fixed as you may think. Radically alter your social setting, and like the college students in the experiment, your self-conception and patterned behavior are likely to change too. Such change is most evident among people undergoing resocialization in total institutions. However, the sociological eye is able to observe the flexibility of the self in all social settings, including those that routinely greet the individual in adult life.

Adapted Source: From BRYM/LIE. *Sociology: Your Compass to a New World Brief Edition* 2e (pp. 75–6). Copyright © 2010 Cengage Learning.

5. What is the overall pattern of organization of this passage?

_____

PRACTICE WITH A READING PASSAGE

Prepare to Read

1. Based on the title, what do you expect the following passage to be about?

_____

2. Before you read, predict what you think the author is going to say about neat and sloppy people.

_____

3. As you read, circle all the organizational word clues that signal the overall pattern of organization.

Neat People vs. Sloppy People
By Suzanne Britt

1   I've finally figured out the difference between neat people and sloppy people. The distinction is, as always, moral. Neat people are lazier and meaner than sloppy people.

2   Sloppy people, you see, are not really sloppy. Their sloppiness is merely the unfortunate consequence of their extreme moral rectitude. Sloppy people carry in their mind's eye a heavenly vision, a precise plan that is so stupendous, so perfect, it can't be achieved in this world or the next.

3   Sloppy people live in Never-Never Land. Someday is their métier. Someday they are planning to alphabetize all their books and set up home catalogs. Someday they will go through their wardrobes and mark certain items for tentative mending and certain items for passing on to relatives of similar shape and size. Someday sloppy people will make family scrapbooks into which they will put newspaper clippings, postcards, locks of hair, and the dried corsage from their senior prom. Someday they will file everything on the surface of their desks, including the cash receipts from coffee purchases at the snack shop. Someday they will sit down and read all the back issues of _The New Yorker_.

4   For all these noble reasons and more, sloppy people never get neat. They aim too high and wide. They save everything, planning someday to file, order, and straighten out the world. But while these ambitious plans take clearer and clearer shape in their heads, the books spill from the shelves onto the floor, the clothes pile up in the hamper and closet, the family mementos accumulate in every drawer, the surface of the desk is buried under mounds of paper, and the unread magazines threaten to reach the ceiling.

5   Sloppy people can't bear to part with anything. They give loving attention to every detail. When sloppy people say they're going to tackle the surface of a desk, they really mean it. Not a paper will go unturned; not a rubber band will go unboxed. Four

rectitude
correctness of
procedure

métier area
in which one is
considered an
expert

Continued on next page.

excavation area
dug out

meticulously
extremely careful
in attending to
details

hours or two weeks into the excavation, the desk looks exactly the same, primarily because the sloppy person is meticulously creating new piles of papers with new headings and scrupulously stopping to read all the old book catalogs before he throws them away. On the other hand, a neat person would just bulldoze the desk.

6   Neat people are bums and clods at heart. They have cavalier attitudes toward possessions, including family heirlooms. Everything is just another dust-catcher to them. If anything collects dust, it's got to go and that's that. Neat people will toy with the idea of throwing the children out of the house just to cut down on the clutter.

7   Neat people don't care about process. They like results. What they want to do is get the whole thing over with so they can sit down and watch the rasslin' on TV. Neat people operate on two unvarying principles: Never handle any item twice, and throw everything away.

8   Unlike the messy person, the only thing messy in a neat person's house is the trash can. The minute something comes to a neat person's hand, he will look at it, try to decide if it has immediate use and, finding none, throw it in the trash.

9   Neat people are especially vicious with mail. They never go through their mail unless they are standing directly over a trash can. If the trash can is beside the mailbox, even better. All ads, catalogs, pleas for charitable contributions, church bulletins, and money-saving coupons go straight into the trash can without being opened. All letters from home, postcards from Europe, bills and paychecks are opened, immediately responded to, and then dropped in the trash can. Neat people keep their receipts only for tax purposes. That's it. No sentimental salvaging of birthday cards or the last letter a dying relative ever wrote. Into the trash it goes.

10   Neat people place neatness above everything else, even economics. They are incredibly wasteful. Neat people throw away several toys every time they walk through the den. I knew a neat person once who threw away a perfectly good dish drainer because it had mold on it. The drainer was too much trouble to wash. And neat people sell their furniture when they move. They will sell a La-Z-Boy recliner while you are reclining in it.

11   Neat people are no good to borrow from. Neat people buy everything in expensive little single portions. They get their flour and sugar in two-pound bags. They wouldn't consider clipping a coupon, saving a leftover, reusing plastic nondairy whipped cream containers, or rinsing off tin foil and draping it over the unmoldy dish drainer. You can never borrow a neat person's newspaper to see what's playing at the movies. Neat people have the paper all wadded up and in the trash by 7:05 A.M.

swath a path

12   Neat people cut a clean swath through the organic as well as the inorganic world. People, animals, and things are all one to them. They are so insensitive. After they've finished with the pantry, the medicine cabinet, and the attic, they will throw out the red geranium (too many leaves), sell the dog (too many fleas), and send the children off to boarding school (too many scuff-marks on the hardwood floors).

Check Your Understanding

4. Use context clues and word part analysis to define the following words from this passage.

   • tentative (paragraph 3): _____

   • accumulate (paragraph 4): _____

   • scrupulously (paragraph 5): _____

5. Highlight the main idea of this passage in green.

6. Identify the overall pattern of organization of this passage, and explain how you determined it.

   _____

7. Create a visual representation of this passage on a separate piece of paper that covers at least four of its paragraphs.

8. What is the author's purpose for writing this essay?

   _____

9. List the major supporting details of this passage.

   _____

   _____

   _____

   _____

   _____

   _____

   _____

   _____

   _____

10. Decide if you think the author is a neat or sloppy person, and provide at least two reasons for your decision.

   _____

   _____

   _____

CHAPTER SUMMARY

Patterns are everywhere. You have recognized them and used them your whole life, from understanding the organization of a grocery store to figuring out a Sudoku puzzle. Your brain naturally seeks order in things, which is why it is satisfying when you can figure out things around you. Maximize this tendency in your brain to make order of things by looking for patterns in your college reading. Authors write in organized ways with the hope that you understand what they are saying. As you read, look for these patterns of organization. They will help you understand what authors are thinking.

Effective strategies for recognizing patterns of organization are to question yourself and look for organizational word clues. You should question yourself not only about the title or heading, if there is one, but also about each paragraph you are reading. The answers to your questions can lead you to the main idea and can help you navigate an author's pattern of organization. Common patterns of organization are: listing, analysis, cause/effect, comparison/contrast, definition/example, and sequence. These patterns can be found in individual paragraphs but can also be the larger organization of an entire reading. Sometimes authors will use more than one pattern of organization as the dominant pattern, called mixed patterns. The note card technique can help you stay focused on the overall pattern of organization of what you read.

Brain Connections: Self-Assessment

Draw the amount of dendrites you imagine that you have now about recognizing patterns of organization. Compare your drawing of dendrites with what you drew at the beginning of the chapter. If the amounts are different, explain why.

✓ COMPREHENSION CHECK

▶ What is the most valuable point you learned in this chapter?

▶ If you could ask the authors a question about this chapter, what would you ask?

POST TEST

Part 1. Objective Questions

Match the key terms from the chapter in Column A to their definitions in Column B.

	Column A		Column B
_____	1. pattern of organization	a.	pattern that shows why something happened, the effects of something that occurred, or the outcome of an event
_____	2. organizational word clues	b.	pattern that clarifies the meaning of key concepts by defining them or providing examples
_____	3. listing	c.	words or phrases that signal a pattern of organization an author uses for a reading
_____	4. analysis	d.	pattern that examines the similarities or differences between two or more ideas, people, objects, or events
_____	5. cause/effect	e.	pattern that lists ideas, events, or concepts
_____	6. comparison/contrast	f.	pattern that breaks a concept down into its specific characteristics, properties, or basic elements
_____	7. definition/example	g.	pattern that shows the steps in a process or the chronological order of certain events
_____	8. sequence	h.	a way to organize ideas through the use of specific pattern types
_____	9. mixed patterns of organization	i.	author's use of more than one pattern of organization

Circle the best answer to the following true/false questions.

10. The brain does not like patterns.

   True   False

11. Authors use comparison/contrast to show why events occur.

   True   False

12. Authors tend to use only one pattern per reading.

   True   False

Provide three organizational word clues for the following patterns of organization.

13. listing

_____

Continued on next page.

14. analysis

_____

15. cause/effect

_____

16. comparison/contrast

_____

17. definition/example

_____

18. sequence

_____

Part 2. Reading Passage

Prepare to Read

1. Based on the title, what do you expect the following passage to be about?

   _____

2. Develop two questions that you think the passage will answer.

   _____

4. Write down any words that may have prevented you from completely understanding the passage as you read.

   _____

5.   Circle any organizational word clues that signal a pattern as you read.

We're Born to Learn
By Rita Smilkstein

1   Recently I was working with a sixth-grade class. First, we did the natural human learning process (NHLP) activity. Then I showed them pictures of the brain, and we talked about how the brain learns. I said to them, "Your brains are no different from the brains of adults in the way you learn. You are just as capable of learning as adults are. The only difference is that adults have lived a longer time and, because of that, have had more opportunities to learn from more experiences. This means they have grown and connected more dendrites and synapses so they know more. That's the only difference. Your brains want to learn, know how to learn, and are, in fact, learning all the time, just like adult brains."

2   A strange thing happened as I spoke to them. I began seeing them as I had just described, as small beings with adultlike brains eager and ready to learn, but not yet having had the time and opportunity to grow and connect as many dendrites, synapses, and neural networks as adults. So of course, they knew less.

3   They seem transfixed by what they had been hearing about how the brain learns; they were intensely attentive and alert. When some of them came up afterward to ask more questions, I looked down at their faces and saw their intelligence and intellectual excitement. I had theorized before that the child's brain is similar to the adult's brain in its nature and capabilities, but now I really knew it. The brain of a child must grow trillions of dendrites on, and synapses between, billions of neurons to learn about the world, what is going on in it, how it works. This includes learning about life, self, other, language, communication (verbal and nonverbal), cause and effect, things, quantity, emotions, social interaction, ad infinitum. Everything. The child does this from personal experience.

4   The child's brain, apparently operating with the same power as an adult brain, grows dendrites, new ones constructed on prerequisite ones. Over time this learning produces a brain filled with networks that are completely interrelated.

5   We are seeing a work in progress when we watch a child negotiate the world, trying to see how to be empowered in it, feeling, acting, reacting, interacting, communicating, playing, trying to figure something out, or solving a puzzle at the level of network growth the child has thus far achieved.

6   If these learning drives and capabilities seem to disappear when children get older, it is only because the children are somehow prevented from enjoying them. If they seem to disappear in school, while the students, young or old, are learning with interest and motivation outside school, perhaps there is a lack of opportunity in the classroom to use their innate resources and some of the brain's rules for learning, to think, explore, experiment—in short, to be the natural and naturally motivated learners they were born to be.

Source: From Rita Smilkstein, *We're Born to Learn: Using The Brain's Natural Learning Process To Create Today's Curriculum.* Copyright © 2011 Sage Publications Inc. Reprinted with permission.

Check Your Understanding

6. Using context clues and word part analysis, define each of the following words from the passage:

   • transfixed (paragraph 3): _____

   • theorized (paragraph 3): _____

   • ad infinitum (paragraph 3): _____

   • prerequisite (paragraph 4): _____

   • innate (paragraph 6): _____

Continued on next page.

7. What is the purpose of the passage?

_____

_____

8. What is the main idea?

_____

_____

9. List the pattern of organization and main idea for each paragraph.

Paragraph 1

　　Pattern of organization:

_____

　　Main idea:

_____

_____

Paragraph 2

　　Pattern of organization:

_____

　　Main idea:

_____

_____

Paragraph 3

　　Pattern of organization:

_____

　　Main idea:

_____

_____

Paragraph 4

　　Pattern of organization:

_____

　　Main idea:

_____

_____

_____

Paragraph 5

Pattern of organization:

_____

Main idea:

_____

_____

Paragraph 6

Pattern of organization:

_____

Main idea:

_____

_____

10. What is the overall pattern of organization of the passage?

_____

BRAIN STRENGTH OPTIONS

Your project for this chapter consists of a presentation of each type of pattern of organization. Refer to Table 7.1 on page 304 to make sure you include each pattern. The presentation must include at a minimum the name of each pattern of organization with some kind of example or illustration of that pattern that you either find using your textbooks, Internet sources, magazines, or books you are reading or create by writing or drawing. You may work by yourself or in a group of no more than four students. You will be graded on the following:

▶ Completeness of the list
▶ Accuracy of the examples: Does your example _really_ show that pattern?
▶ Effectiveness of the examples: Does your example convey to others the nature of that pattern?

You can select your presentation format from the following or propose an alternative to the instructor:

▶ PowerPoint with examples typed or scanned in
▶ Poster with examples pasted on
▶ Written report with examples embedded by scanning or typing

Using Preview, Study-Read, and Review (PSR)

STUDENT TO STUDENT

DEMIS DROGANICI

Currently attends Keiser University and works at The Westin Diplomat Resort and Spa in Hollywood, Florida

"Reading without reflecting is like eating without digestion."

—EDMUND BURKE

THE FIRST TIME I attended college was about 12 years ago. Now I am back in school with the hopes of finishing what I started then. Even though I find my classes to be extremely difficult after a 12-year layoff, to my surprise, I find that maturity and life experiences lead me to achieve better grades. Back in my first college, I earned a D in English Composition, but now I've managed to achieve an A for the same class. I think the difference from then to now is the fact that I am a little bit older and more realistic to the realities of life. It is well established that "a mind is a terrible thing to waste," and I believe that with dedication and focus people can achieve their goals. I have a career goal now that I am excited about and I know that the classes and textbooks will help me get to my goal. Now I approach my textbooks with the attitude that I want to learn, not just do. I really study the book and don't just do the assignments. I follow the steps the teachers suggest, even though it seemed at first like they would take more time. By looking over the chapter first, then studying it, and taking time to review, I get the most out of my study time. I found out I learned the material better. If only I knew then what I know now, things would've been a lot different.

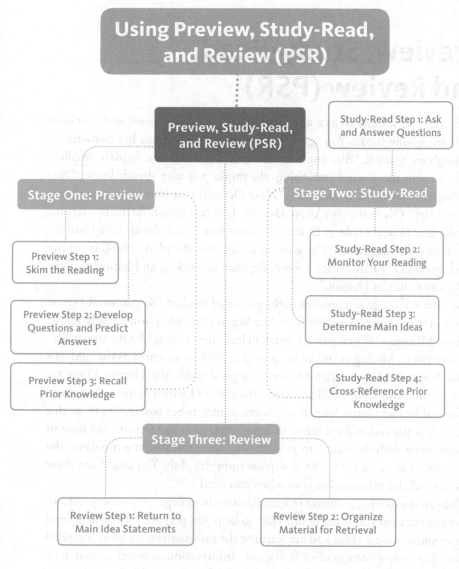

Using Preview, Study-Read, and Review (PSR)

Preview, Study-Read, and Review (PSR)

Stage One: Preview

Preview Step 1: Skim the Reading

Preview Step 2: Develop Questions and Predict Answers

Preview Step 3: Recall Prior Knowledge

Stage Two: Study-Read

Study-Read Step 1: Ask and Answer Questions

Study-Read Step 2: Monitor Your Reading

Study-Read Step 3: Determine Main Ideas

Study-Read Step 4: Cross-Reference Prior Knowledge

Stage Three: Review

Review Step 1: Return to Main Idea Statements

Review Step 2: Organize Material for Retrieval

© Cengage Learning

Making Connections

1. Describe your method for tackling a chapter or reading assignment. How do you begin? Do you have a process or steps that you take?
2. When you finish reading a chapter, what is your next step?
3. Where in your daily life do you come across previews?
4. What is the value to you of a preview?
5. Where in school have you come across a preview?
6. How is a preview like the framing of a house?

Brain Connections: Self-Assessment

Draw on the brain cell how many dendrites you imagine you have for how much you know about previewing, study-reading, and reviewing.

Preview, Study-Read, and Review (PSR)

IMAGINE THAT A CLASSMATE ASKS YOU to visit her hometown with her during Thanksgiving break. You agree, not knowing much about her hometown, Birmingham. You ask, "Birmingham, Alabama?" She begins to explain by offering facts about the general area, things she thinks you may already know. "No, Birmingham, Michigan," she says. "Near Detroit, you know, Motown? The Motor City?" Oh yeah, you know Detroit. Is Birmingham far from Detroit, you wonder? Hey, it's cold in Detroit in November! "Yes," she says, "it's usually cold during Thanksgiving." She goes on to describe the plan. "We'll go to the Thanksgiving Day Parade, see a football game, eat turkey, and Saturday night we'll go to a club in Detroit."

Your friend just gave a preview of the proposed weekend so you would know what you were getting yourself into. She began with what you already knew: Detroit, Michigan. When you go, you will learn new things like the unpredictable weather in Michigan (it can be as cold as 30°F or as warm as the mid-70s in late November), your friend's mom is a good cook, the Detroit Lions are Detroit's professional football team, and the club in Detroit features live music performed by local musicians. If you want to remember particulars from this trip, such as the recipe for a moist turkey or that club in Detroit, you have to do something with the new information you learn. You might write down the turkey recipe or keep the cocktail napkin from the club. You could use these cues to recall the information later when you need it.

You can approach a textbook in a similar way. In college, you are expected to know the material you learn in one class to help you prepare for the next-level course; and in many cases, you are learning the information for your intended career. The course information is aligned. Information covered in exit tests and finals in one course (100 level) is often the foundational information you are expected to know for the next level (200 level). In order to optimize your learning, you need to use a reading method that will help you read, learn, and remember effectively. You have learned that repetition is a key to learning. If you use a study system that builds in repetition using the least amount of time and the most efficient method, you can make the best use of your study time. One such method is called PSR—preview, study-read, review. Using this method, you get multiple repetitions of the most important material. Preview the chapter, calling to mind information you already know on the subject. Study-read the chapter, taking care to notice important points and details. Review the chapter so you can retrieve important information later for an exam.

preview preparing to read by skimming, asking questions, predicting answers, and recalling prior knowledge about the topic

study-read critically reading by asking and answering questions, monitoring your reading, and determining the main idea(s)

review last stage of reading by returning to main idea statements and reorganizing information for retrieval

The key to previewing, study-reading, and reviewing is purposeful, direct questioning before, during, and after reading. Creating effective questions about your reading material, and then answering them, helps you confirm that you have correctly identified main ideas and details. What you should ask yourself depends on when in the reading process you are asking the questions. There are several benefits to questioning yourself during all the stages of your reading:

▶ You establish a purpose for reading, which gets your brain ready to learn.

▶ You create a mental framework that holds new information in an organized way.

▶ You give yourself the opportunity to react to what you read and not just accept what an author says.

▶ You read more closely because you are looking for answers to your questions.

Stage One: Preview

BEFORE GPS IN cars, people who found themselves lost frequently stopped to ask directions at a nearby gas station or convenience store. The store clerk or gas station attendant usually began with a phrase like, "Keep going on the street you were on, Mack Avenue. Go down to …." The clerk or attendant started with what the driver knew, the street she was just on, and acquainted her with what else to expect—construction, a stop sign, a bank on the corner—in a logical way until he led her to her destination. She then knew her path before she got back into her car.

Open your textbooks with the same plan. First, ask yourself what your purpose is for reading. What are you expected to learn? Why did the instructor assign this reading? What type of information do you expect the reading to provide? How does this information connect with the course lectures or discussions? What do you intend to get out of the reading? Remember what you have learned in every chapter so far about making connections. It is critical for you to continually ask yourself what you predict you will be learning and connect it with what you already know.

Tip FROM THE
Brain Doctor

Remember that in order to "wire" your new learning, you must make a connection to your existing neural network—the information you already know. The preview step in reading is critical because it starts that process. Now that you know more about how you learn, you know that taking that step is a time-saver in the long run. It gives you the first "firing" so you can begin to "wire" the information.

Previewing is like looking at a map to see where you are and where you are going. To preview, skim what you are about to read, think of good questions to ask yourself, predict what you will be reading about, and recall information you already know about the topic. In other words, get yourself mentally ready to interact with what the author is about to say.

When you preview, you develop a framework of ideas that you fill in as you read. Previewing also lets you gauge how difficult or long a chapter is so you can plan the appropriate amount of study time. It also encourages you to read actively. When you develop questions (beginning with the reading's title), you naturally begin to seek out answers. Remember that your brain is a natural problem solver and loves to figure things out.

ACTIVITY 8A
Try Previewing

Look at the picture for exactly one minute. As you look, try to remember as many details as you can.

After one minute, turn to page 379 and answer the questions and then come back to this page.

Did you have a difficult time answering the questions? There is no reason for you to know what the answers are. It is an overcluttered picture intended to be difficult for you to recall so the following point could be made: If you knew what questions you were going to be asked about the picture, you would have been more focused on finding the answers.

You probably had a difficult time answering the questions in Activity 8A. This activity shows that if you know what you are looking for before you read, you will be better able to answer questions about your readings. If you know the questions before you read, finding the answers will be easier. Previewing requires that you develop questions *before* you read, which prompts you to actively search for answers as you read. You improve your focus and create your purpose for reading.

When you first looked at the photo in Activity 8A, you may have noticed that it has a lot of detail. Without focus and purpose, your mind may have taken in the detail but not retained much of it, which made answering the questions difficult. The same is true about reading textbooks. Reading a textbook chapter without first creating questions or reading the questions provided at the end of the chapter can be a lot like looking at a picture with lots of detail: overwhelming. After reading, you may find yourself asking, "What did I just read?" You will find that consistently developing questions or reading end-of-chapter questions results in understanding and remembering more of what you read.

There are three steps to the previewing stage:

► Preview Step 1: Skim the reading.
► Preview Step 2: Develop questions and predict answers.
► Preview Step 3: Recall prior knowledge.

Preview Step 1: Skim the Reading

Skim the amount of reading you plan to accomplish in one study session. Skimming means reading through quickly, skipping details, and focusing on the title of the chapter and, when available, the introduction, main headings, subheadings, and summary. If a book doesn't have these resources, skim the first sentence of every paragraph to help you get an overview of the content. Also, read any questions included at the end of the chapter. Skimming provides the framework or mental outline you need before you begin to study-read.

skimming reading only some of the words on a page

Tip FROM THE
Brain Doctor

Suppose you are going to read an article about the BP oil spill in the Gulf of Mexico. The headline is "Oil Slick Endangers Sea Birds." You may know about the oil leak but do not really know what an "oil slick" is. If you can't visualize "oil slick" it may be hard for you to get the full understanding of the article. Searching the Internet yields many images of oil slicks, such as the one shown here. Images like this one can really help you picture the situation before you read the article. Talk about an effective preview!

Source: http://ic1.ecolocalizer.com/files/2007/12/oiled-bird-south-korea.jpg

Look at the following passage from a sociology textbook, and take note of the highlighted text. If you were skimming this passage, you would read only what is highlighted.

Popular Culture and the Media

1   Because of iPods, iPhones, texting, YouTube, and social networking sites such as Facebook, young people are rarely out of the reach of the electronic media. How does such technology affect socialization?

Electronic Media

2   The American Academy of Pediatrics (2001: 424) advises parents to avoid television entirely for children younger than 2 and to limit the viewing time of elementary school children to no more than 2 hours a day, to encourage more interactive activities "that will promote proper brain development, such as talking, playing, singing, and reading together." Still, 68 percent of children under age 2 view 2 to 3 hours of television daily, and 20 percent have a television in their bedroom, as do one-third of 3- to 6-year-olds (Garrison and Christakis 2005; Vandewater et al. 2007).

3   The average young American now spends practically every waking minute—except for the time in school—using a smartphone, computer, television, or other electronic device. In 2009, those ages 8 to 18 spent 7.5 hours a day engaged with some type of electronic media, up from 6.5 hours in 2004. The 53 hours in 2009 were greater than the amount of time most adults spend at a full-time job. Generally, youths who spend more time with media have lower grades and lower levels of personal contentment (see Table 4.4). These findings are similar across all ages, for girls and boys, race/ethnicity, parents' social class, and single- and two-parent households (Rideout et al. 2010).

4   High media usage can decrease academic success, but two-thirds of parents are especially concerned that the media contributes to young people's violent or sexual behaviors (Borzekowski and Robinson 2005; Rideout 2007). Are such concerns justified? Many researchers agree that there are negative aspects of electronic media, such as obesity (because frequent sitting replaces playing outside and encourages eating foods advertised on children's programs that are high in fat and sugar). They contend, however, that there is still no evidence that television viewing causes violence. For example, violent crimes in society have decreased despite the increased depiction of

contend to state formally as true

violence on television and other electronic media (Powell et al. 2007; Sternheimer 2007).

5   A recent study found that middle-school-aged children, both girls and boys, who almost exclusively played rated M (for mature) games more than 15 hours a week were more likely than their counterparts to be bullies in school, get into fights, destroy property, and argue with their teachers. The researchers point out that it may be that more aggressive children are drawn to more violent games, and not that the games themselves are to blame (Kutner and Olson 2008). There is growing consensus, however, that violent video games make violence seem normal. Playing violent video games such as Grand Theft Auto: Chinatown Wars and God of War 3 can increase a person's aggressive thoughts, feelings, and behavior both in laboratory settings and in real life. Violent video games also encourage male-to-female aggression because much of the violence is directed at women (Anderson et al. 2003; Carnagey and Anderson 2005).

consensus agreement reached among members in a group

6   Still, it's not clear why violent video games affect people differently. Many young males enjoy playing such video games, for example, but aren't any more aggressive, vicious, or destructive than those who aren't video-game enthusiasts (Williams and Skoric 2005; Kutner and Olson 2008).

Advertising

7   Increasingly, advertisers are targeting children as early as possible. A new form of advertising called adver-gaming combines free online games with advertising. Advergaming is growing rapidly. Sites such as those operated by Nestlé (http://www. wonka.com), Mattel (Barbie.com), and M&Ms (http://mms.com/us/fun-games) attract millions of young children and provide marketers with an inexpensive way to "draw attention to their brand in a playful way, and for an extended period of time" (Moore 2006: 5).

8   In the print media, young people see 45 percent more beer ads and 27 percent more ads for hard liquor in teen magazines than adults do in their magazines (Strasburger et al. 2006). It's been estimated that girls ages 11 to 14 are subjected to about 500 advertisements a day on

Tip FROM THE
Brain Doctor

Sometimes when you see a reading title, nothing will fire in your mind. You just cannot imagine what the reading could be about! For example, a highly entertaining book is called *The Man Who Mistook His Wife for a Hat*. What in the world does that title mean? You cannot connect it to what you already know, but it does arouse your curiosity, doesn't it? Curiosity is also powerful for the brain. Reading the book, you would find out that, amazingly, there is a brain disease wherein people cannot recognize faces. The book talks about that amazing and unusual medical case, as well as others.

the Internet, billboards, and magazines, but that "the majority of [the models are] nipped, tucked, and airbrushed to perfection" (Bennett 2009: 43).

9   What effect do such ads have on girls' and women's self-image? About 43 percent of 6- to 9-year-old American girls use lipstick or lip gloss, 38 percent use hairstyling products, and 12 percent use other cosmetics. Eight- to 12-year-old girls spend more than $40 million a month on beauty products (Bennett 2009). Many women, especially white women, are unhappy with their bodies. In an analysis of 77 recent studies of media images of women, the researchers concluded that there is a strong association between exposure to media depicting ultra-thin actresses and models, and many women's dissatisfaction with their bodies and their likelihood of engaging in unhealthy eating behaviors, such as excessive dieting (Grabe et al. 2008).

Source: From BENOKRAITIS. *SOC* 2e (pp. 73–5). Copyright © 2012 Cengage Learning.

Notice that only the main heading, introduction, and two subheadings are highlighted? This content is all you would read while skimming. If you were previewing a larger reading assignment, such as an entire chapter, you would also read over the chapter summary and questions at the end of the chapter, if provided.

Preview Step 2: Develop Questions and Predict Answers

Reread the title, headings, and, whenever available, the subheadings and chapter summary, and develop questions about them using these six words: *who, what, when, where, why,* and *how.* (If you happen to be working with a textbook that does not have some of these features, you can still preview by looking at the first sentence of each paragraph to get an idea of what the reading is about.) Although many of the questions you create during this step may be basic, they will help you pay closer attention as you read. As questioning becomes more of a habit for you, you will probably be able to ask the questions in your head, but while you are learning this technique, write your questions in the margin

Tip FROM THE Brain Doctor

Make the most of your brain by giving it a purpose. Set questions before you read, and let your brain seek out the answers. You are not wasting time when you take the time to mentally create questions—you are actually working with your brain more efficiently. You will save time and have better results in the long run. You know what they say: "Work smarter, not harder."

of the reading or on a separate piece of paper. Then predict the answers to your questions.

One preview question you could ask about the passage from the sociology textbook on page 360 is:

How is popular culture affected by the media?

A prediction of an answer to this question might be:

Our culture is exposed to so much violence in video games and on television that people have become desensitized to violence.

ACTIVITY 8B
Ask Preview Questions and Predict Answers

1. What other questions could you ask about the passage from the sociology textbook on page 360? Remember to use information from skimming along with these question words: *who, what, when, where, how,* and *why.*

   _____

   _____

2. Now predict answers to the questions you developed in #1.

   _____

   _____

3. What pattern of organization does it look the like author may be using?

   _____

Preview Step 3: Recall Prior Knowledge

Now that you have a framework for what you think the reading will be about, consider what else you know about the topic. Search your memory for every experience and every piece of information or knowledge you have stored there about that topic. New information is best remembered when purposefully connected to information you already know about a subject. While you are learning this technique, you may want to write out what you already know to help you focus. Then you—and your brain—will be prepared to study-read successfully.

ACTIVITY 8C
Recall Prior Knowledge

1. What prior knowledge do you have about the topic of the sociology passage on page 360?

_____

_____

✓ COMPREHENSION CHECK

▶ Explain the previewing stage of reading.
▶ What do you think is meant by "giving your brain a purpose" when reading?

ACTIVITY 8D
Practice Previewing

Practice previewing using the following passage from a political science textbook. Even though the passage is an excerpt from a larger chapter, use the same previewing steps you would with a longer reading such as an entire chapter. Practice here and then try the steps with your own textbooks. Remember that you do not need to read the passage in its entirety. Complete the following previewing tasks to prepare yourself to read:

▶ Step 1: Skim the passage.
▶ Step 2: Develop questions from the title, heading, subheadings, summary, and/or end-of-chapter questions.
▶ Step 3: Predict content and recall your own knowledge on the subject (making connections).

Chapter 10 Political Socialization: The Making of a Good Citizen

1   The year is 1932. The Soviet Union is suffering a severe shortage of food, and millions go hungry. Joseph Stalin, leader of the Communist Party and head of the Soviet government, has undertaken a vast reordering of Soviet agriculture that eliminates a whole class of landholders (the kulaks) and collectivizes all farmland. Henceforth, every farm and all farm products belong to the state. To deter theft of what is now considered state property, the Soviet government enacts a law prohibiting individual farmers from appropriating any grain for their own private use. Acting under this law, a young boy reports his father to the authorities for concealing grain. The father is shot for stealing state property. Soon after, the boy is killed by a group of peasants, led by his uncle, who are outraged that he would betray

vast large, immense

collectivizes groups together

deter stop or prevent

appropriating taking by force of law

his own father. The government, taking a radically different view of the affair, extols the boy as a patriotic martyr. Stalin considered the little boy in this story a model citizen, a hero. How citizenship is defined says a lot about a government and the philosophy or ideology that underpins it.

The Good Citizen

2   Stalin's celebration of a child's act of betrayal as heroic points to a distinction Aristotle originally made: The good citizen is defined by laws, regimes, and rulers, but the moral fiber (and universal characteristics) of a good person is fixed, and it transcends the expectations of any particular political regime.

3   Good citizenship includes behaving in accordance with the rules, norms, and expectations of our own state and society. Thus the actual requirements vary widely. A good citizen in Soviet Russia of the 1930s was a person whose first loyalty was to the Communist Party. The test of good citizenship in a totalitarian state is this: Are you willing to subordinate all personal convictions and even family loyalties to the dictates of political authority, and to follow the dictator's whims no matter where they may lead? In marked contrast are the standards of citizenship in constitutional democracies, which prize and protect freedom of conscience and speech.

4   Where the requirements of the abstract good citizen—always defined by the state— come into conflict with the moral compass of actual citizens, and where the state seeks to obscure or obliterate the difference between the two, a serious problem arises in both theory and practice. At what point do people cease to be real citizens and become mere cogs in a machine—unthinking and unfeeling subjects or even slaves? Do we obey the state, or the dictates of our own conscience?

5   This question gained renewed relevance in the United States when captured "illegal combatants" were subjected to " enhanced interrogation techniques"—an Orwellian euphemism for torture—during the Bush administration's war on terror from 2002 to 2008. One prisoner was waterboarded 183 times (strapped to a board with towels wrapped around his head while water was poured slowly onto the towels until he smothered). Other harsh interrogation methods were also used.

6   Torture is outlawed by the Third Geneva Convention (1949), to which the United States is a party, as well as by the U.S. Code (Title 18, Chapter 113C). In addition, torture is a gross violation of the moral code we are taught to observe in our everyday lives from earliest childhood. As a presidential candidate, Barack Obama denounced torture and the use of "extraordinary" methods and procedures in the war on terror. As president, he ordered the closing of the Guantanamo Bay detention camp (Gitmo) and an end to waterboarding and other extremely harsh interrogation techniques practiced there and elsewhere.

7   Question Number One: Can anyone in any position of authority who orders the use of torture be justified in so doing? Question Number Two: Can anyone who carries out such an order be a good citizen? Question Number Three: Is it ever right to obey orders that are wrong—that is, illegal and (or) immoral? Keep these questions in mind as you read on.

Continued on next page.

---

extols praises

subordinate make not as important, secondary

obscure hide

obliterate destroy, remove all signs of

euphemism mild word or description used to replace a strong, offensive or hurtful one

Defining Citizenship

8   Throughout history, people of diverse moral character have claimed to be models of good citizenship. The relationship between the moral character of citizens and different forms of government underscores Aristotle's observation that the true measure of a political system is the kind of citizen it produces. According to this view, a good state is one whose model citizen is also a good person; a bad state is one whose model citizen obeys orders without regard for questions of good or evil. Simple though this formulation may sound, it offers striking insights into the relationship between governments and citizens, including, for example, the fact that we cannot divorce civic virtue or public morality from our personal integrity or private morality.

9   It is little wonder that different political systems embrace different definitions of citizenship. In many authoritarian states, people can be classified as citizens only in the narrowest sense of the word—that is, they reside within the territory of a certain state and are subject to its laws. The relationship between state and citizen is a one-way street. Ordinary citizens have no voice in deciding who rules or how, or even whether they have a vote. In general, the government leaves them alone as long as they acquiesce in the system.

10   By contrast, in totalitarian states, where the government seeks to transform society and create a new kind of citizen, people are compelled to participate in the political system. From the standpoint of citizenship, however, their participation is meaningless because it is not voluntary and stresses duties without corresponding rights. Loyalty and zealotry form the core of good citizenship, and citizens may be forced to carry out orders they find morally repugnant.

repugnant disgusting, unpleasant

11   In democratic societies, people define citizenship very differently. In elementary school, the good citizenship award typically goes to a pupil who sets a good example, respects others, plays by the rules, and hands in assignments on time. Adults practice good citizenship by taking civic obligations seriously, obeying the laws, paying taxes, and voting regularly, among other things. In a democracy, the definition of good citizenship is found in the laws, but the legislators who write the laws are freely elected by the people—in other words, a true republic at its best erases (or at the very least eases) the tension between citizenship and moral conscience.

12   Many individuals, including civil libertarians, emphasize that the essence of citizenship lies in individual rights or personal liberties. The formal requirements of citizenship in the United States are minimal (see Box 10.1), even though people the world over envy its rewards (hence the steady flow of immigrants into the United States, compared with the trickle of U.S. citizens emigrating to other countries). According to the Fourteenth Amendment, "All persons born or naturalized in the United States, and subject to the jurisdiction thereof, are citizens of the United States and of the State wherein they reside." Note that citizens of the United States are distinguished from aliens not on the basis of how they act or what they have done but simply on the basis of birthplace—to be born in the United States is to be a U.S. citizen. Moreover, the presumption is once a citizen, always a citizen, barring some extraordinary misdeed (such as treason) or a voluntary renunciation of citizenship.

BOX 10.1 FOCUS ON   Citizenship and War: Democracy and Duty

In the United States, apart from paying taxes, the demands of citizenship are quite limited. They became especially limited once the United States switched to an all-volunteer army in 1972, largely as a response to the backlash against the **Selective Service** System (often called "the draft") many considered unfair during the Vietnam War. Since then the law has been changed—citizenship no longer entails the duty of all males over the age of 18 to register for the draft or, in the event of war, to defend the country.

Defenders of an all-volunteer army argue that it is more professional and proficient, that willing recruits are likely to make better soldiers than are conscripts, and that the military provides excellent opportunities for young men and women from minority and low-income groups to acquire the self-confidence, discipline, and technical skills that can lead to high-paying jobs in the civilian economy.

Many veterans of past U.S. wars, among others, decry the ending of the draft. Others advocate making at least one year of national service mandatory for young adults who do not enlist in the armed forces.

Some who argue for bringing back the draft do so on the surprising grounds that it would make war less likely. Why? Because voters are often apathetic when an issue does not affect them directly and too easily swayed when patriotism is invoked—as it always is in war. This issue resurfaced in 2003 when President George W. Bush, in effect, declared a "presidential war"—defined as the use of force outside the United States without a formal declaration of war by congress as required under the Constitution—on Iraq.

Was President Bush justified in ordering U.S. troops to invade a country that did not (and could not) attack the United States? Is it right to send the sons and daughters of minorities and the poor to fight our wars, while the children of the rich who run the country's corporations and have close ties to the power elite never have to serve if they don't chose to? What kind of society starts wars, kills countless people in a foreign country, and calls upon the vast majority of its own people to make no sacrifices? Why not reinstitute the draft, or at least a universal national service of some sort? Questions of this nature help explain why the United States has been so deeply divided over politics in the post-9/11 era and why the war in Iraq figured so prominently in the 2008 presidential election.

After the unpopular Vietnam War, the United States abolished the draft in favor of an all-volunteer armed forces.

Continued on next page.

A Classical View

13   The minimalist view of citizenship described in Box 10.1 may provide a convenient way of distinguishing citizens from aliens (foreigners), but it does not do justice to a time-honored concept in Western civilization. To the ancient Greeks, the concept of citizenship was only partly related to accidents of birth and political geography; rather, responsible and selfless participation in the public affairs of the community formed the vital core of citizenship. Aristotle held that a citizen "hares in the administration of justice and in the holding of office." The Athens of Aristotle's time was a small political society, or city-state, that at any given time accorded a proportionately large number of citizens significant decision-making power (women and slaves were excluded). Citizenship was the exalted vehicle through which public-spirited and properly educated free men could rule over, and in turn be ruled by, other free men and thereby advance civic virtue, public order, and the common good.

14   In eighteenth-century Europe, the Greek ideal reemerged in a modified form. Citizen became a term applicable to those who claimed the right to petition or sue the government. Citizens were distinguished from slaves, who had no claims or rights and were regarded as chattel (property). Citizens also differed from subjects, whose first and foremost legal obligation was to show loyalty to and obey the **sovereign**. According to the German philosopher Immanuel Kant (1724–1804), citizens, as opposed to slaves or subjects, possessed constitutional freedom; that is, the right to obey only laws to which they consented. Kant also contended that citizens possessed a civil equality, which relieved them of being bound by law or custom to recognize any superior among themselves, and political independence, meaning a person's political, status stemmed from fundamental rights rather than from the will of another. No longer were citizens to be ruled arbitrarily by the state. Republican government came the closest to this ideal of citizenship. In the final analysis, as Kant and other eighteenth-century thinkers recognized, the freedom and dignity of the individual **inherent** in the concept of citizenship could flourish only under a republican government, and such a government could function only if its rank-and-file members understood and discharged the responsibilities of citizenship.

15   One distinguishing feature of the modern era is the extension of citizenship. In the United States, for instance, it took many years for racial minorities, women, and individuals without property to gain the right to vote and the right to protection under the law in the exercise of their civil rights. Yet, as the number of citizens (and of people in general) has risen, effective political participation for individuals has often become more difficult. It is one thing for society to embrace ideas such as citizenship for all and equal rights in theory; it is quite another to provide the civic education and social development necessary to make the ideal of a society of equals a practical reality.

sovereign ruler

inherent naturally belonging to

The chapter doesn't end here, but this passage does. Continue on to read the chapter summary:

Summary

Different governments treat the concept of citizenship in different ways. All states demand adherence to the rules (laws), of course, and most treat birth in, or naturalization into, the political order as a requirement of citizenship. In democratic states, the concept of citizenship is also tied to the ideas of equality and liberty, as well as to meaningful participation in politics, such as voting in periodic elections. This ideal of democratic citizenship dates back to the ancient Greek city-states, which were small enough to permit direct democracy (self-representation of enfranchised adults through public assemblies and plebiscites).

Political socialization is the process whereby citizens develop the values, attitudes, beliefs, and opinions that enable them to relate to and function within the political system. Specific influences on the developing citizen include the family, religion, public education, the mass media, the law, peer groups, and key political values. Political social-ization is of paramount importance; if a nation fails to socialize its citizenry on a large-scale basis, its political stability can be endangered.

paramount
supreme, foremost

Now read the end-of-chapter questions:

Chapter Questions

1. Why was the concept of citizenship of central importance to Aristotle and other political thinkers?
2. In what contrasting ways can we define citizenship? Which definition best describes your understanding of citizenship? Explain your choice.
3. It is sometimes argued that true citizenship can be found only in a democracy. What does this statement mean? Do you agree with it? Why or why not?
4. What factors influence the political socialization of citizens? Which ones do you think have been most influential on you? On your peers? Your parents?

Source: From MAGSTADT. *Understanding Politics: Ideas, Institutions, and Issues* 9e (pp.300–304; 323–324). Copyright © 2011 Cengage Learning.

1. **Highlight or underline the parts of the passage you would read to skim it.**

2. **What questions can you develop from the parts of the passage you skimmed?**

_____

_____

Continued on next page.

3. What do you predict the whole passage will be about?

_____

_____

4. Recall your own knowledge on the topic of the passage.

_____

_____

Stage Two: Study-Read

Now that you have set up a framework of what you are about to read, you are ready to study-read. Study-reading is a careful reading of an assignment during which you ask and answer questions as you read. Begin with the questions you created in the previewing stage, and refine them as you delve deeper into the details of the reading. Remember that, just like the lost traveler after receiving directions, you have a plan and now can actively get to your destination.

As you read, fill in your framework or draw a mind map with the answers to your questions. To determine whether you have truly understood the reading material, try to restate what you have learned to a classmate. If he or she cannot follow your thinking or believes you misunderstood what you read, meet with your instructor for clarification. This stage of reading focuses on understanding, so take your time and seek out help if you need it.

There are four steps to the study-reading stage:

► Study-Read Step 1: Ask and answer questions.
► Study-Read Step 2: Monitor your reading.
► Study-Read Step 3: Determine main ideas.
► Study-Read Step 4: Cross-reference prior knowledge.

Tip FROM THE Brain Doctor

Remember what you learned about the limits of working memory in Chapter 2? You can only hold a few bits of information at a time—and not for very long. Then you have to take steps to move the information into long-term memory. Apply what you learned about the methods of moving information into long-term memory as you work through this step of study-reading. If you pause to think about and process small parts of what you read, you will reduce your cognitive load and move material out of working memory and into long term memory.

Study-Read Step 1: Ask and Answer Questions

Start reading at the first heading or subheading and ask the questions you developed during the preview stage. For example, when you previewed "Political Socialization: The Making of a Citizen" on page 364, you could have asked the following preview questions:

How is citizenship defined?
What makes a good citizen?

If you were to study-read the whole chapter, you would be looking for the answers to these questions and others.

Read one complete section of a chapter at a time. Read either from heading to heading or, for more challenging material, from paragraph to paragraph. Then pause to ask and answer your previewing questions. Do not read chapters from beginning to end without pausing for questions and answers.

Study-Read Step 2: Monitor Your Reading

Textbook chapters contain too much information to remember everything all at one time. Monitor your understanding of what you have read in one section before moving on to the next, using the following thinking prompts:

1. What do I understand about what I have read so far?
2. Where in the text did I lose concentration or become confused?
3. Of everything I have read, what makes the least sense?

These questions help you separate what you do understand from what is still unclear. Interrupting your reading with thinking prompts may seem like a nuisance at first, but comprehension is more important than speed. You should pause and reflect to make sure you understand so you can quickly isolate what you do not understand and figure out the problem.

Take notes on what you read to prepare for the review stage, so you will not have to reread the entire chapter but only what is essential. Do not forget to highlight main ideas in green and major supporting details in yellow. Sometimes just writing down what

Tip FROM THE
Brain Doctor

By reading, highlighting, and then writing or note taking, you have accomplished three repetitions of the material. Add in your preview stage, and you have acquired four repetitions *before* studying for the exam. Remember how important repetition and using different pathways are for moving information to long-term memory (Chapter 2)? Look at what you accomplish by using these simple steps.

you have difficulty with helps you clarify it. If you realize that some points still confuse you, use the second prompt to identify where in the text you lost concentration or started having difficulty following the author's train of thought. This will help you pinpoint where you should reread. If after rereading, you still find the information unclear, seek help from your instructor or a classmate.

Maybe you did not lose concentration or become confused while reading. If so, chances are, you are right on track. The third thinking prompt—Of everything I have read, what makes the least sense?—encourages you to push your understanding even further. Is there an unfamiliar term or concept? Is there anything in the reading that you could learn more about? Seek a full understanding of what you read. Do not just do the minimum. Do some outside research to fill in your prior knowledge.

ACTIVITY 8E
Monitor Your Reading

Read the political science passage that you previewed on page 364.

1. Ask yourself the preview questions you created as you read. What are the answers to your questions?

2. What do you understand about what you have read so far?

3. Where in the passage did you lose concentration or become confused?

4. Of everything you have read of this passage, what makes the least sense?

Study-Read Step 3: Determine Main Ideas

As you study-read, read one section at a time and then pause to determine what the main idea of each section is. A section is usually defined as the amount of reading from one heading to the next. If a reading is very long or unfamiliar to you, you might make your sections from one subheading to the next or even paragraph to paragraph. As you determine the main idea for each section, recall the stated main idea and implied main idea strategies you learned in Chapters 4 and 6.

ACTIVITY 8F
Determine the Main Idea

Refer to the political science passage on page 364. This passage is one section (one heading and two subheadings) of an entire chapter.

1. What is the main idea for this section? Highlight it in green.

2. What is the overall pattern of organization of this section? Explain why.

_____

_____

_____

Study-Read Step 4: Cross-Reference Prior Knowledge

Suppose the teacher in your meteorology class at a college in New York City says, "It rarely rains in Seattle." Do you, as a student who grew up in Seattle, just lift up your pen and, without bothering to think about what he said, simply write it down in your notebook? Or do you say, either out loud or to yourself, "Hey, wait a minute! That isn't true!" But what if you grew up in New York and have never been to Seattle and do not know anything about it? You would probably nod your head and just write the information down in your notebook as a true statement.

Why could someone who knows Seattle tell whether the teacher's statement was true or false? That person makes a connection with prior knowledge stored in the brain about the topic of Seattle. In other words, he or she determines the statement's validity based on his or her own experience. When you connect new information with something in your memory that you already know, your neural network fires. When you check what you are reading with what you already know, you are trying to see whether you can learn something new.

On the other hand, if you have no prior knowledge about the new information, your brain will create a new memory of it. A new connection will be created and wired. However, if the new information is incorrect and is, nevertheless, wired into your brain as a new memory, you will have a problem. An incorrect memory will cause you to make mistakes in the future about what you remember and, therefore, think is true. You might be talking one day with a friend who just returned to New York after graduating from a school in Seattle and say, "You sure were lucky going to a college in a city where it rarely rains." Your friend will wonder what you are talking about and might say, "That's a good joke! Ha ha ha!" You will not understand why your friend thinks you made a joke. The two of you might even end up in an argument if you insist on firing your incorrect memory.

But if you trust him or her, you can ask your friend—who is an expert on the subject—whether it is true that it rarely rains in Seattle. Or if you do not know any people who are trustworthy, knowledgeable sources, you can go to the library or search online. When you finally have the correct information, you must consciously make a stronger memory to override the old, incorrect one that still lurks in your brain. We cannot remove information, but we can create a stronger competing network. On the other hand, if you can find no absolute proof that something you are reading is true or not, keep investigating, keep looking, keep asking, and keep reflecting. Do not let your brain work against you by keeping a specific memory of something that might not be true. Your reflection about that memory, instead, should be, "I'm not sure about this. Let me keep reading, asking, and trying to understand." Being open-minded, trying to discover what is true, and trying to see and understand will help you learn.

cross-referencing
checking what you are reading with your prior knowledge to accept new knowledge, to change prior knowledge, or to judge new information

This kind of checking is called cross-referencing. It helps readers think more critically, understand more, and learn more than just taking for granted that what they are reading is true—when it may not be.

Here is another example of how cross-referencing can help you understand and learn. Suppose in an English history course, you learn that, in 1588, England, under Queen Elizabeth, defeated the powerful Spanish navy and became the master of the seas and the greatest world power. Then, in a following term, you take a literature course on William Shakespeare (1564–1616) where you learn that Shakespeare lived in what was called a "golden age" of English culture and that Shakespeare wrote with admiration and love for Queen Elizabeth.

By cross-referencing, you come across information you stored in your memory earlier about England's history in the time of Queen Elizabeth. You can put that information together with what you are now learning about England's golden age and Shakespeare's admiration of Queen Elizabeth. "Ah ha!" you say. "Sure! England had just become the greatest world power. No wonder there was a golden age. No wonder Shakespeare admired the queen so much. This makes a lot of sense!" Now you are better able to reflect on the relevance of Shakespeare's themes about the power of royalty. You can understand and appreciate that he was living in a time when his country was the greatest world power and his queen was the most powerful sovereign in the world. Cross-referencing adds richness and depth to your studying and understanding.

You cross-reference new information by determining what is similar (comparison) or different (contrast) between new information and your prior knowledge. At first, if you are not used to cross-referencing it might take some effort and concentration. However, as you gain experience and practice, you will not only find it easier and quicker, but you will also begin to enjoy pulling together pieces of information stored away in your memory to give a fuller, richer dimension of understanding to the topic under study or discussion. The benefits of cross-referencing are:

1. If the new and prior knowledge are the same, you reinforce what you already have stored in your memory.

2. If the new and prior knowledge are different, you know that you need to continue to question, reflect, and investigate until you figure out what is correct.

3. You understand the new knowledge better.

4. You respond with more depth and completeness to your own questions, a test question, or a discussion.

Have you ever had the experience of reading something and saying to yourself, "That reminds me of something I read earlier. I have a vague recollection of it"? What do you do when this happens? Do you flip backward through the pages until you find the previous mention of the idea? Or do you just shrug your shoulders and go on reading, forgetting about that vague recollection? If you forget about it, you are, unfortunately, missing an opportunity to increase your understanding.

Page-flipping is a type of cross-referencing where you check one part of your reading with another part. Page-flipping can also be cross-referencing your reading with notes taken during a lecture or in-class discussion or with something you heard or read outside class. Whenever you are reading and have a feeling that your memory is trying to give you a recollection, stop and think. If you cannot bring up the memory, you can page-flip until you find it.

But what if your memory does not give you a recollection of ideas you read or heard earlier? How can you make sure that your memory will give

page-flipping type of cross-referencing where you check one part of your reading with something else in a reading or in your notes

you important recollections so you will pay attention to them? Simple: Cross-reference the information. This will help ensure that a firm memory will be stored in your brain.

Figure 8.1 models what an expert reader would do and think during the study-read stage of PSR.

> Use what? What would I lose? This sounds familiar.

> Movement affects health?

> Should he know or does he just think that because he is an athlete? No, he is also a doctor.

> This seems to be a main idea of this paragraph.

> It seems I have to put the main idea of this paragraph into my own words as it is not directly stated. The point the author makes is that I won't be *more* tired if I move more, but *less* tired. Moving more creates more energy.

> I have heard something like that—a saying—"energy burned is energy earned." That can be a catch phrase that can help me remember this information.

Use It or Lose It

Movement is sleep's opposite partner, the high side of a wave that fuels our health but whose value we underappreciate. Too little movement, like too little sleep, weakens and diminishes us in all dimensions of our lives. Intense movement, balanced by deep recovery, dramatically increases our capacity, not just physically but also mentally and emotionally.

"How much you move," explains Eric Heiden, an orthopedic surgeon and five-time Olympic speed-skating champion, "affects your strength, your power, your balance, how you look, how you think, how well you withstand the high winds and rain showers of life and how long you will stand. Everyone needs concentrated doses of several kinds of movement to remain fully functional."

Because our behaviors are so interdependent, the failure to exercise tends to prompt a vicious cycle. The more sedentary we become, the more we begin to avoid exercise. When we move less, we burn fewer calories, gain weight, lose strength, endurance and flexibility, and find it increasingly difficult and uncomfortable to move.

When we first met Steve Wanner, a young partner at Ernst & Young, he was working twelve- to fourteen-hour days, felt perpetually exhausted, slept poorly, and made no time to exercise. Although there is no evidence that being more fit reduces the need for sleep—elite performers typically get more sleep than average—there is considerable evidence that regular exercise makes it easier to get to sleep and leads to a higher quality of rest.

Source: From Schwartz, T., *The Way We're Working Isn't Working*, Free Press, New York, 2010, p. 79.

> This seems to be a main idea of this paragraph.

> This seems to be a main idea of this paragraph.

> I need to break this word down: I see dependent and *inter* means "between" so I am guessing that it means "between things"—dependent on each other.

Figure 8.1 Model of Study-Read Stage

Stage Three: Review

In the review stage of reading, you organize and recall what you have read. By the time you reach the review stage of reading, you should completely understand what you have read. If you do not, reviewing becomes very difficult. For example, if a traveler in an unfamiliar town arrives at her destination but cannot tell you how she got there, she will find her return trip home very difficult.

There are two steps to the reviewing stage:

► Review Step 1: Return to main idea statements.
► Review Step 2: Organize material for retrieval.

Review Step 1: Return to Main Idea Statements

Review at the end of your entire reading assignment. Begin by confirming the main idea(s). Does the main idea answer the questions you asked during the preview stage? Does the main idea seem general enough to include all the other ideas presented? Remember to highlight main ideas (in green or any consistent color you choose). This helps when you review and flip through a chapter; you can immediately recognize all the main ideas because they are highlighted.

If the main idea is not stated, infer the main idea from what you have read and write it down at the beginning or end of your reading. Some students use this symbol ∴, which means *therefore* in logic courses and *conclusion* in math courses, to label any main ideas they write down.

Review Step 2: Organize Material for Retrieval

After you have read something, organize the new information in a meaningful way, relating it to information you already know. As you learned in Chapter 2, in order to learn and retrieve information, you need to organize it in a way that makes sense to you. The more you organize and work with the information, the easier it will be to retrieve. You may want to create mnemonics to help trigger your memory or mind maps to help you visualize the relationships between pieces of information. You may prefer to outline the chapter.

Sometimes it helps to consider using the author's pattern of organization to create visuals. For example, if you know that the author uses a comparison/

Tip FROM THE
Brain Doctor

Recall what you learned about "firing" and "wiring." The preview and questioning stages are "firing" stages. Then when you review, by going back over the material and gathering details, you begin to "wire" the information into your long-term memory. This last step is just as important as the others.

contrast pattern, create a chart that shows how things are similar and different. If you know that the author uses listing or process, create a visual that shows a list or the steps to that process. Although you can create your own visuals in any manner you wish, using the author's pattern of organization helps you decide how to organize the information. You will learn more about note taking and creating visuals in Chapters 9 and 10.

ACTIVITY 8G
Organize with a Mind Map

Create a mind map for the political science passage on page 364. Put the main idea in the middle and three supporting ideas branching out, one of which should include three sub-branches with information you already know on the subject.

ACTIVITY 8A
Continuation from page 358

1. What color is the tractor?

_____

2. How many whistles are there?

_____

3. What green animal is next to the school bus?

_____

4. What is directly above the letter U?

_____

5. What colors is the butterfly?

_____

Return to page 358 to continue the activity.

PRACTICE WITH A READING PASSAGE

Prepare to Read

1. Based on the title, what do you expect the following passage to be about?

_____

2. Preview the reading. Create two questions from the title or topic of the passage.

_____

3. What do you already know about the topic of the passage?

_____

4. Study-read the passage. List the steps you will use to effectively complete this stage of reading.

_____

_____

_____

_____

Practice Forms of Mental Hygiene
By Richard Restak

1   In the nineteenth century, many psychiatrists and psychologists (William James among them) emphasized the importance of healthy mental attitudes and practices. They coined the term "mental hygiene" to describe the measures a person can take to make the brain function more efficiently. Just as the body benefits from exercise, good diet, and a temperate lifestyle, the brain works better if a person follows certain mental guidelines. The most important guideline involves not paying too much attention to our feelings. "There is no better known or more generally useful precept in one's personal self-discipline, than that which bids us pay primary attention to what we do and express, and not to care too much for what we feel. Action seems to follow feeling, but really action and feeling go together; and by regulating the action, which is under the more direct control of the will, we can indirectly regulate the feeling, which is not," according to James.

injunctions orders to do something

primal original

2   Over the years, James's point of view fell out of favor. Remember the injunctions a few years ago to "let it all hang out"? And if we needed help, there was always primal scream and other therapies that emphasized getting in touch with our feelings and, most importantly, expressing them in some way, whatever the consequences for other people's sensibilities. Additional knowledge about the brain has revealed the perils of placing too much emphasis on the unrestrained expression of our emotions. Nor can we give in to negative emotional states.

3   For instance, people suffering from depression exhibit abnormal PET scans and other measures of brain activity. Moreover, this abnormal brain activity accompanying depression can cast a pall over events of the past. When depressed we tend to dwell on the losses and hurts we've encountered in our lives. Even good things appear paltry and inconsequential when viewed through the distorting lens created by low moods. "The self-same person, according to the line of thought he may be in, or to his emotional mood, will perceive the same impression quite differently on different occasions," wrote James.

pall darkness or gloom

paltry ridiculously small, worthless

4   Research shows that brain changes indicative of depression can occur in non-depressed volunteers if they allow themselves to think sad or depressing thoughts. This result suggests that, at least in the initial stages, it is the negative thoughts and attitudes that unfavorably alter brain function, rather than the other way around. In time, as the depression deepens, this sequence may be reversed; the dysfunctional brain becomes the culprit and produces increasingly depressive thoughts, ultimately culminating in illness and even suicide. But at least, in the earliest stages, this sequence can be favorably influenced by mental attitude.

5   One important attitude change involves keeping ourselves physically and mentally occupied. Internal distress often results from having too much empty time on our hands. Physical and mental inactivity leads to boredom, anxiety, and depression. In turn, these uncomfortable states exert powerfully negative effects on our functioning. We start to dwell on the negative, perhaps a holdover from the time when our ancestors had to contend with so many physical threats to their survival, health, and well-being.

6   Today most of our perceived threats don't involve death or severe physical impairment. Indeed, most of them are the creations of our own imagination. If we could learn to take our situations and ourselves less seriously, we would be better able to cope. To be sure some of life's more serious threats, such as the loss of a job or the breakup of a marriage, are not trivial matters. But neither do they involve life or death.

7   Whatever the threat, worry and other forms of negativity make things worse because they always exert a powerfully destructive effect on the brain's functioning. When worried or experiencing other negative thoughts, we find ourselves drawn toward imagined disaster. For instance, even though we may be in excellent health, we're inclined to focus on whatever minor ills may exist at the moment. At such times, our attention is exclusively focused on the threatening and the negative—whether involving other people or just us.

8   Since the brain can keep only one thought at a time in the foreground of consciousness, it's important to emphasize uplifting rather than depressing and negative preoccupations. While this tendency toward the morbid can be overcome by encouraging positive thinking, we can't depend entirely on pure willpower. That's why it's important to keep your brain active, challenged, and curious.

morbid unhealthily gloomy, gruesome

Check Your Understanding

5. Use context clues and word part analysis to define the following words from this passage.

   - precept (paragraph 1): _____
   - dysfunctional (paragraph 4): _____
   - exert (paragraph 5): _____

6. In paragraph 1, the author uses an analogy. What is he comparing? What does he want you to infer from the comparison?

   _____

   _____

7. What is the most important guideline in paragraph 1?

   _____

   _____

8. What is James's point at the end of paragraph 1?

   _____

   _____

9. The author quotes James. Write what James means in your own words.

   _____

   _____

10. According to this passage, what happens when people think of depressing thoughts?

    _____

    _____

11. What can negatively affect brain function as discussed in paragraph 4?

    _____

    _____

12. What is mentioned as important in the last paragraph?

    _____

    _____

13. Answer the question(s) you asked yourself before you read the passage.

_____

_____

14. What is the topic of this passage?

_____

_____

15. What is the main idea of this reading?

_____

_____

16. What are four major supporting details from the passage?

_____

_____

_____

_____

_____

17. What pattern(s) of organization does the author use in this passage?

_____

_____

18. What was the author's purpose for writing this passage?

_____

_____

19. Do you detect any bias in the author's writing?

_____

_____

20. What is significant about the number of thoughts we keep in the foreground of our consciousness?

_____

_____

_____

CHAPTER SUMMARY

The PSR (preview, study-read, review) technique helps you read your college material more thoroughly because it encourages you to actively work with your memory as you encounter new material. You wire, or make connections, in your brain when you read information that is completely new to you and about which you have no prior knowledge. When you connect new information with information you already know, your neural network about that topic will fire.

The first stage of PSR is previewing, which prepares you for what you will read by giving you an overview of the content. When previewing, you skim the reading assignment and begin to develop questions about the topic and predict what the content will be about. You also recall any prior knowledge about the topic. Then as you study-read (the second stage of PSR), you ask the questions you developed in the preview stage and attempt to answer them. You also monitor your reading to make sure you are concentrating well and comprehending as you go. You must do both to thoroughly digest the new reading material. You will then determine the main ideas from the reading and cross-reference what you have read with your prior knowledge. Another way to cross-reference is page-flipping which helps reinforce what you learn. In the review stage of PSR, determine the accuracy of the main ideas from the study-reading stage. Main idea statements are most accurate after you have read the entire reading assignment. As you recall the main ideas, decide how you will organize the information. It is always best to purposefully store new information with information you already know on the subject.

Brain Connections: Self-Assessment

Draw the amount of dendrites you imagine that you have now about previewing, study-reading, and reviewing. Compare your drawing of dendrites now with what you drew at the beginning of this chapter. If the amounts are different, explain why.

✔ COMPREHENSION CHECK

▶ With what stage of PSR are you most familiar?
▶ Create a mnemonic to help you remember the stages and steps of PSR.
▶ With which stage of PSR do you need the most practice?
▶ What will you do to fine-tune your own PSR system?

POST TEST

Part 1: Objective Questions

Match the key terms from the chapter in Column A to their definitions in Column B.

Column A	Column B
_____ 1. preview	a. reading only some of the words on a page
_____ 2. skimming	b. critically reading by asking and answering questions, monitoring your reading, and determining the main idea(s)
_____ 3. study-read	c. preparing to read by skimming, asking questions, predicting answers, and recalling prior knowledge about the topic
_____ 4. review	d. a type of cross-referencing where you check one part of your reading with something else in a reading or in your notes
_____ 5. page-flipping	e. last stage of reading by returning to main idea statements and reorganizing information for retrieval
_____ 6. cross-referencing	f. checking what you are reading with your prior knowledge to accept new knowledge, to change prior knowledge, or to judge new information

Circle the best answer to the following multiple-choice questions.

7. One of the most important times to question yourself is right before you begin to read.

   True   False

8. The review stage is more important than the preview.

   True   False

9. Previewing and skimming are identical activities.

   True   False

10. Study-reading means:

   a. reading at a convenient time, when you have time to read the chapter straight through, and then making time to question yourself.

   b. asking and answering the questions you developed in the preview stage as you read.

   c. stopping to take a break after reading every 15 paragraphs.

   d. a bad habit of stopping to think about what you have read before you finish reading the entire chapter.

Continued on next page.

11. If you do not understand what you have just read, you should:

    a. focus on what you do know.

    b. seek assistance immediately for clarification from a tutor, instructor, or classmate.

    c. write what you do not understand in your journal and return to it in one week.

    d. do nothing; it is just one of many reading selections.

12. An example of active reading is:

    a. reading and walking simultaneously.

    b. completing your reading during regularly scheduled time throughout the week.

    c. creating questions so that you are reading with a purpose.

    d. playing music while you read to activate your right brain.

Short-Answer Questions

13. List the three steps of the preview stage of reading.

_____

_____

_____

14. How do you develop your questions during the study-read stage of reading?

_____

_____

15. Based on your understanding of the PSR method for textbook reading, what is the main difference between reading textbooks and reading for personal entertainment?

_____

_____

Part 2. Reading Passage   ACADEMIC READING

Prepare to Read

1. The following passage is from a sociology textbook. What does the title mean to you?

_____

2. What do you already know about the topic of this passage?

_____

3. Preview the passage, and create five preview questions.

Material and Nonmaterial Culture
By Joan Ferrante

Material Culture

1   Whatever item you named, it is part of what sociologists call material culture. Material culture consists of all the physical objects that people have invented or borrowed from other cultures. Examples of material culture are endless and include iPods, cars, clothing, tattoos, and much more. From a sociological point of view, physical objects are windows into a culture because they offer clues about how its people relate to one another and about what is important. In order to grasp the social significance of material culture, sociologists strive to understand the context during which material culture is created, the purposes for which it is used, the reasons it is modified or abandoned, and the meanings assigned to it.

Nonmaterial Culture

2   When sociologists study material culture, they are also interested in learning how it affects relationships among people. Consider the microwave. In the United States and elsewhere the microwave oven played a significant role in changing the relationships among family members—specifically, it changed norms about what and when family members should eat; it helped change beliefs about children's ability to prepare meals. To put it another way, the microwave changed aspects of what sociologists call nonmaterial culture, the intangible human creations that include beliefs, values, norms, and symbols.

Beliefs

3   Beliefs are conceptions that people accept as true concerning how the world operates and the place of the individual in relationship to others. Beliefs can be rooted in faith, experience, tradition, or the scientific method. Whatever their accuracy or origins, beliefs can exert powerful influences on actions because they can be used to justify behavior ranging from the most generous to the most violent, and they have a profound effect on behavior.

Values

4   Nonmaterial culture also consists of values, general, shared conceptions of what is good, right, desirable, or important. One classic study identified 36 values that people everywhere share to differing degrees, including the values of individual freedom, happiness, true friendship, broadmindedness, cleanliness, obedience, and national security. The study suggested that cultures are distinguished from one another not according to which values are present in one and absent in another, but rather

Continued on next page.

according to which values are the most cherished and dominant (Rokeach 1973). For example, consider the following list of potential values:

- ▶ Obedience   ▶ Modesty
- ▶ Freedom   ▶ Honesty
- ▶ Health and fitness   ▶ Self-esteem

Which value is most important to the personal principles guiding your life? Which one is least important? If you selected freedom, self-esteem, or honesty, then your values are in line with values that many Americans declare as being among the most important. If you selected obedience, health and fitness, or modesty, then your values are more in line with those Saudis define as most important (Miller and Feinberg 2002).

Norms

5   A third type of nonmaterial culture is norms, written and unwritten rules that specify behaviors appropriate and inappropriate to a particular social situation. Examples of written norms are rules that appear in college student handbooks (e. g., to be in good academic standing, maintain a 2.0 GPA); on signs in restaurants (No Smoking Section); and on garage doors of automobile repair centers (Honk Horn to Open). Unwritten norms exist for virtually every kind of situation: wash your hands before preparing food; raise your hand to indicate that you have something to say; do not hold hands with a friend of the same sex in public. Sometimes norms are formalized into laws.

6   Depending on the importance of a norm, punishment can range from a frown to death. In this regard, we can distinguish between folkways and mores. Folkways are norms that apply to the mundane aspects or details of daily life: when and what to eat, how to greet someone, how long the workday should be, how often caregivers should change babies' diapers. As sociologist William Graham Sumner (1907) noted, "Folkways give us discipline and support of routine and habit"; if we were forced constantly to make decisions about these details, "the burden would be unbearable" (p. 92). Generally, we go about everyday life without asking why until something reminds us or forces us to see that other ways are possible. Whereas folkways apply to day-to-day details, mores are norms that people define as essential to the well-being of a group. People who violate mores are usually punished severely: they may be ostracized, institutionalized, or condemned to die. Mores are regarded as the only way. Most Americans, for example, have strong mores against marrying cousins, especially first cousins. Marrying a cousin is simply inconceivable. In Iraq, however, 50 percent of marriages are between first and second cousins. In such situations the spouse is not viewed as an outsider coming into the family but a member of a kin group (Bobroff-Hajal 2006). The practice helps us to understand why family bonds are much stronger in Iraq than the United States.

Symbols

7   Another type of nonmaterial culture are symbols, which are anything—a word, an object, a sound, a feeling, an odor, a gesture, an idea—to which people assign a name and a meaning. In the United States, when someone touches the tip of the index finger to the tip of the thumb and holds the other three fingers open, it is the symbol that

mundane common, ordinary

everything is okay or a job well done. However, that meaning is not self-evident, because the interpretation of this symbol can vary. When sociologists say that the meaning of a symbol is not self-evident, they mean that positioning the hand does not universally elicit an interpretation of "okay." In Latin American countries, a hand held in this way conveys a derogatory meaning, and in France it conveys the value of "zero" or that something is worthless. In the broadest sense of the word, language is a symbol system that assigns meaning to particular sounds, gestures, pictures, or specific combinations of letters. The level and complexity of human language sets people apart from animals. In addition, language is among the most important symbol systems humans have created. When we learn the words of a language, we acquire a tool that enables us to establish and maintain relationships, convey information, and interpret experiences. Learning a language includes an expectation that we will communicate and organize our thoughts in a particular way (Whorf 1956, pp. 212– 214). For example, some languages such as Korean are structured so that speakers have no choice but to address people using special age-based hierarchical titles. For Koreans age is an exceedingly important measure of status: the older the people, the more status they can assume. As another example, in the United States the word *my* is used to express ownership of persons or things over which the speaker does not have exclusive rights: *my* mother, *my* school, *my* school bus, *my* country. The use of *my* reflects an emphasis on the individual and not the group. In contrast, the Korean language expresses possession as shared: *our* mother, *our* school, *our* school bus, *our* country. Linguists Edward Sapir and Benjamin Whorf (1956) advanced the linguistic relativity hypothesis, also known as the Sapir-Whorf hypothesis, which states that "No two languages are ever sufficiently similar to be considered as representing the same social reality. The worlds in which different societies live are distinct worlds, not merely the same world with different labels attached" (Sapir 1949, p. 162). For example, it is certainly possible to translate Korean words into English—a translator can emphasize our teacher, not my teacher—but lost in translation will be a Korean worldview that actually thinks in terms of our teacher. It is difficult for an English-speaking American who has no first-hand experience with Korean or another culture that makes the group the central point of reference (rather than the individual) to grasp thinking in terms of "our."

elicit to bring out

derogatory belittling

Source: From FERRANTE. *Seeing Sociology: An Introduction* 1e (pp. 54–58). Copyright © 2011 Cengage Learning

Check Your Understanding

4. Use context clues and word part analysis to define the following words from this passage.

- intangible (paragraph 2): _____

- formalize (paragraph 5): _____

- hypothesis (paragraph 7): _____

Continued on next page.

Circle the best answer to the following multiple-choice questions.

5. How does the author define material culture?

   a. all electronic devices that positively influence our society including iPods and cell phones

   b. only physical objects that are man-made

   c. all the physical objects that people of a particular generation use

   d. all the physical objects that people have invented or borrowed from other cultures

6. What is the author's purpose?

   a. to entertain

   b. to inform

   c. to persuade

   d. to explain

7. What overall pattern of organization does the author use?

   a. sequence

   b. definition/example

   c. listing

   d. comparison/contrast

Short-Answer Questions

8. What is the main idea of this passage?

   _____

   _____

9. What examples of nonmaterial culture can you think of? Give one example for each type.

   _____

   _____

10. Can you think of another type of nonmaterial culture not given in the passage? Are the authors correct in saying there are only four types? Explain.

   _____

   _____

BRAIN STRENGTH OPTIONS

Your project for this chapter is to apply what you have learned in a real-life application. Using a textbook from another class, apply PSR to a chapter and write a 400- to 600-word reflection to submit to your instructor. A reflection is an informal piece of writing in which you reflect on what you did and what you thought about something. A reflection is personal and there are no right or wrong answers, but it can be either complete or incomplete (see guidelines below). In this case, you will describe what you did and reflect on how the PSR process worked for you. Be sure to include every step in the process. At the end, compare PSR to how you previously read and studied and draw a conclusion. Each reflection must include the following:

1. Name of the textbook

2. Name of the chapter

3. A description of your process

4. A description of how each step in this process worked for you. What did it accomplish? How did you feel about it? What did you notice? What was going on in your mind/brain?

5. A conclusion that briefly compares your previous reading process to PSR.

Your instructor will advise whether the reflection should be submitted in writing or via e-mail. If you are using a current textbook, pick a chapter you have not yet covered so this activity will help you in your other course. If you do not have an appropriate textbook to use, borrow one or check out a library book on an academic subject that interests you. This project will take several hours. Of course, getting better at something is always helpful, and that is the purpose of this real-life project.

Taking Control of Your Textbook: Marking and Note Taking

"In a world that is constantly changing, there is no one subject or set of subjects that will serve you for the foreseeable future, let alone for the rest of your life. The most important skill to acquire now is learning how to learn."

—JOHN NAISBITT

Courtesy of Joselyn Evans

I PREVIEW THE CHAPTER, mostly to see how long it is. Then, I read straight through, taking notes as I go. I use the headings to create an outline as I read. For example, when I get to the first heading, I write down a "I" and then the heading after it. Then I read and take notes on everything important under that heading. When I come to the second heading, I write a "II" and the heading and then take notes on everything important under that heading. I keep going with the Roman numerals, the headings from the book, and the important notes until I'm done.

Writing as I read helps me monitor my understanding of the material. Sometimes when I get bored, I review what I have written in my notes and sometimes realize I have no idea what I am reading. I reread when that happens.

I also look for any bold words. Those are important. When I see a word in bold, I read the word, and then I go back and read what came before it and what came after it so I really get what it means. Just reading the definition given in the margin isn't enough. I make sure I get the whole meaning of the word before I start reading other stuff.

When I don't get something that I'm reading, I pull stuff apart and look at the individual parts. If I understand one part, I go on to the next. When I start to understand the pieces, I try to put them back together and see if I can understand the whole thing. This is how I got through calculus.

Getting the Right Mindset for
Marking and Note Taking

Understanding Textbook Parts

Textbook Marking Gets
You Right to the Point

Taking Control of Your Textbook: Marking and Note Taking

Deciding What
Else to Mark

Four Steps to
Textbook Marking

Take Control of Your
Textbook by Using
Focused Notes

Step One: Preview

Step Two: Study-Read

Step Three: Highlight

Step Four: Write Margin Notes

© Cengage Learning

Brain Connections: Self-Assessment

Draw on the brain cell how many dendrites you imagine you have for how much you know about marking and note taking.

Getting the Right Mindset for Marking and Note Taking

THE BRAIN IS WIRED TO MAKE IT EASIER TO LEARN information that affects our ability to survive. This survival instinct is a powerful learning mechanism in the brain. For example, in early human history, if someone found a location where berries were plentiful, it would be easier for that person to recall the specific location than if he were just taking a nature hike unrelated to his survival instincts. The food source was meaningful to early humans. It affected their ability to survive and was pleasurable and rewarding. How does this relate to reading and learning? If something is meaningful or pleasurable and has a significant effect on your life, it might tap into that powerful survival pathway that makes it easier to remember. While this powerful learning mechanism happens in your life without your conscious awareness, you can also tap into it deliberately to make information easier to remember. Here are two powerful strategies to keep in mind before you begin to mark, take notes, and study from your textbooks. These will set the stage for better reading and learning.

> ▶ **Make It Meaningful.** Activities that are meaningful have a more powerful impact on emotions and the brain than meaningless activities that we perform in a rote manner. Did you ever start out for a destination on your day off and suddenly realize that you were actually on the route to work? You were going through the motions without much attention and automatically went the way you frequently go. Did you ever start reading an assignment and after several pages realize that you had no idea what you just read? Your eyes were going through the motions, but your mind was a million miles away! That happens in the classroom, too, when you are supposed to be learning how to do a math equation, for example. You were looking and listening, but your frontal lobes—the thinking part of your brain—were not engaged. You did not direct your attention to the material. However, if something that you are reading or learning is meaningful to you, you learn it much more quickly because the brain focuses attention on it and gives it importance. For example, you probably learned to text using your cell phone quickly because you wanted to use that information. If you were just required to learn the steps of texting for a test but it was not something you intended to actually *do* (like maybe how you feel when you learn algebra formulas that you think do not apply to real life), you probably would not it learn as quickly.

To take advantage of this strategy, try to relate the material you read to something meaningful in your life. Obviously, becoming a faster reader with better comprehension pays off almost every day of your life, so learning to become a better reader is a meaningful activity. However, if you perceive the activities that you do in this textbook as just "school work," then you lose the meaning and may go through them in that rote, uninvolved way. The more you do with information, the more you will remember it.

The same principle applies to your other textbooks. Maybe you do not see a purpose for this information in your life. However, life is big! Statistics say that people will have seven or more different careers throughout their life. And the world is changing rapidly. We cannot really know what might be useful to us later. Knowledge is never wasted. Sooner or later what you learned will come in handy, or come up in conversation, or provide a foundation for something you need or want to learn. With this understanding, perhaps you can approach your textbooks with more purpose and attention. The best way to do this is to actually see a purpose or feel an interest in the information. If you cannot—and often we cannot—we have to summon up a way to relate it to something meaningful or take responsibility to find a way to engage with the material.

▶ **Keep It Rewarding.** As it turns out, feeling involved and engaged does more than help you recall information. When you figure something out or put forth effort to learn something and then you actually *do* learn it, you get a burst of good chemicals in your brain. You feel good. This is because the survival pathway in the brain is also called the pleasure pathway. If something is necessary for humans to survive, such as eating, then the brain makes that activity pleasurable so that we will make the effort to get food even under difficult circumstances. Learning (not just studying or sitting in school, but actually *learning*) activates the survival/pleasure pathway in the brain.

Some people are actually addicted to learning. This means that they choose to engage in this activity as often as possible because it makes them feel good. They take more courses and keep going to school. They love reading material that enables them to learn new information. They devour books. They have learned that learning is a very pleasurable activity. These are lifelong learners. Because our world is changing so rapidly, these are people that can learn, change, adapt, and continue to have a great quality of life no matter what life throws at them. Sounds good, doesn't it?

How can you take advantage of this? First, in order to get that feelgood feeling, you have to actually *learn*, and that means you have to be emotionally engaged and involved with the material. Approach a textbook with the attitude that you are actually going to *learn*, not just go through the motions.

Think about when you choose to work a puzzle or play a computer game. You can get that pleasurable feeling when you solve it, find where a piece goes, or figure out how to win the game. Now apply that to your textbook marking. When you have a reason for your reading, you will want to engage more with the material—you will want to figure it out. Sometimes when you are given the opportunity to figure something out, you may be motivated to rise to the challenge for these reasons:

1. When given this invitation, you know there is something to figure out.

2. You know that you are considered capable of figuring it out.

3. Your brain was born to figure things out.

4. Your brain enjoys figuring things out because, when the brain learns, it produces endorphins and dopamine, the feel-good chemicals.

You can, and should, take advantage of your amazing brain and its natural learning ability.

This chapter provides strategies for how to keep your attention engaged using textbook marking when reading so that you get the most out of your reading and study time.

Understanding Textbook Parts

BEFORE YOU CAN DIVE INTO MEANINGFUL MARKING and note taking, it is important to understand that textbooks include many parts, each serving a purpose to help you understand the information. Figure 9.1 shows many of the different parts that make up a textbook. Some of these parts offer important background information, definitions that you might need to reference, first-hand sources that you could access for research, or an outline of the whole book showing you how each chapter is related to the next.

Some textbook parts may be more helpful at times than others, but you should know why each is there and how to get the most from each one. Not all textbooks will include all of these parts, but try to make use of the parts that are included.

▶ **Title Page:** This page at the very front of the book gives you basic information—title, author(s), and publishing house. Do you recognize

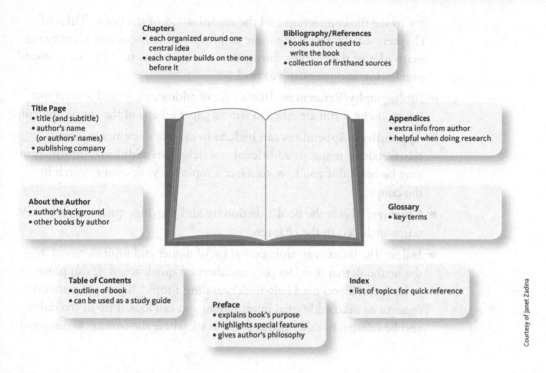

Chapters
- each organized around one central idea
- each chapter builds on the one before it

Bibliography/References
- books author used to write the book
- collection of firsthand sources

Title Page
- title (and subtitle)
- author's name (or authors' names)
- publishing company

Appendices
- extra info from author
- helpful when doing research

About the Author
- author's background
- other books by author

Glossary
- key terms

Table of Contents
- outline of book
- can be used as a study guide

Index
- list of topics for quick reference

Preface
- explains book's purpose
- highlights special features
- gives author's philosophy

Courtesy of Janet Zadina

Figure 9.1 Textbook Parts

the author's or publisher's name? What are they known for? Answers to these questions can help you decide if the information in the book comes from credible sources.

▶ **About the Author:** This information gives you background about the author and provides additional writings the author may have published. Again, this helps you determine credibility.

▶ **Table of Contents:** The table of contents gives you an outline of the whole book. Reading it lets you see how ideas are related and serves as an excellent study guide. Turn all of the headings and subheadings into questions, and try to answer these questions before an exam to see how well you understand and remember the concepts of each chapter.

▶ **Preface:** The preface usually explains the purpose of the textbook. It also may present the author's philosophy and answer some commonly asked questions about the content of the textbook.

▶ **Chapters:** The book's content is organized into chapters. Chapters build upon each other and are usually organized in a specific way to help the reader make sense of the discipline. As you preview them, try to see the connection and the organization of the book. Titles of chapters usually reveal the topic and help you to focus and identify the main idea of the chapter. Turn titles into questions to take a step toward previewing and preparing to read.

▶ **Bibliography/References:** This is a list of additional, related sources that can be useful if you are asked to write a paper on any of the course content.

▶ **Appendices:** Appendices can include items like documents, text, charts, tables, maps, or additional research. This additional information may be helpful if you have to select a topic for your own research in the course.

▶ **Glossary:** This is the book's dictionary and provides quick access to key terms included in the chapters.

▶ **Index:** The index is an alphabetical list of names and topics covered in the textbook that provides page numbers for quick access. It can prove to be useful if you need help understanding a topic. If you get stuck on a concept or need additional information, you can look it up in the index and be referred to other places in the book where the concept is discussed.

ACTIVITY 9A
Use Textbook Parts

Select a textbook that you are using this semester, and open it to your most recent reading assignment. Then pick a part of your textbook from the list of textbook parts just described, read or preview that part, and explain how that part adds knowledge to your reading assignment. Be specific.

_____

_____

_____

Textbook Marking Gets You Right to the Point

HAVE YOU EVER LISTENED TO SOMEONE BEGIN telling a story and then wondered when he would get to the point? He might have opened the story with something like, "My friend just had the best thing happen! Last Tuesday . . . no, maybe it was Monday … was Monday the 11th or the 12th?" You wait patiently for the storyteller to land on a day and move on to the good part only to have him continue with, "Her sister was there when it happened. I think her cousin was there, too. Well, he's not really her cousin. They grew up together. Their moms were best friends, I think …." Okay, okay! What's the point?

You know from experience that when a person tells a story, not all of the points are equal. Some points are more important than others. There is a recognizable structure to a story, and when a storyteller deviates from the format, the listener gets impatient. Experienced readers have similar expectations when they read textbooks. They know that not all ideas are equally important, and they expect authors to write in logical, recognizable patterns. Authors use these patterns and other clues to help readers follow their points and distinguish main ideas from minor ones. Frequently, readers mark their textbooks to flag these important points for later study. Refer to Chapters 4 and 5 to review main ideas and major and minor supporting details.

You have already engaged in a basic form of textbook marking when, in earlier chapters in this textbook, you marked the text by highlighting main ideas and supporting details in readings. Now you are going to apply this technique and add margin notes. Textbook marking is a systematic way of highlighting and labeling ideas to show how they are related to each other. Marking involves highlighting, underlining, or otherwise flagging important words, phrases, and sentences and writing margin notes, sometimes called annotations, that explain why you have marked something.

You may have noticed that lots of people, not just students, highlight and use margin notes as they read. Why? They are not studying for a test. They do this because marking important ideas as they read helps them focus and think. Marking in a book is your part of a conversation with the author. Remember from Chapter 1 that reading is defined as a two-way conversation between you and the author. You bring what you know to what you read. Your background knowledge, thoughtful questions, and careful analysis of an author's ideas are your specific tasks as a participant in this conversation. Anything less is passive reading and not enough for college-level

Tip FROM THE Brain Doctor

Remember that you can "tell" your brain what is important. There are several ways. Can you recall them? One is by paying attention with your body and your mind—sitting up straight, making sure you are in an alert state, and focusing. Another way is by doing something—some examples are taking notes, reading aloud, and drawing the information. These tasks tell the brain that you are giving this information special attention. Making marks and annotations in your textbooks is an excellent way to do this.

textbook marking a systematic way of highlighting and labeling ideas in a textbook to show how they are related

margin notes words, phrases, abbreviations, or symbols that you write in the margin to remind or explain to yourself why something is important

Tip FROM THE Brain Doctor

Research has uncovered the most powerful tool of all for preparing for a test! In this research, students were given new vocabulary words and a brief study period. Then they were given a test. Students who used typical study methods scored 30% on the test of new words, but students who used this amazing technique scored 80%! What is this amazing strategy? It is called "retrieval practice." All that means is that the students repeatedly tested themselves on the material during the study time. It turns out that although students rarely use this tool, it is very powerful for long-term retention of material. Give yourself an advantage— keep self-testing while you are studying. You will save time and effort in the long run.

assignments. The purpose of textbook marking is to help you prioritize ideas while you read and see which ideas are most important when you study. Marking also allows you to self-test before exams by using your margin notes to develop questions and your marked text to check whether your responses are correct.

Four Steps to Textbook Marking

AS YOU BEGIN TO MARK YOUR textbooks, use the reading strategies you learned in other chapters— identifying important vocabulary, main ideas, supporting details, and patterns of organization. The following four steps are used to successfully mark your textbooks:

- ▶ Step One: Preview
- ▶ Step Two: Study-Read
- ▶ Step Three: Highlight
- ▶ Step Four: Write Margin Notes

The first two steps of textbook marking should look familiar. In Chapter 8, you learned about PSR, which includes previewing and study-reading. Now you will add textbook marking as part of the preview and study-read steps. It is one more detail in the process of expert reading.

Step One: Preview

PREVIEW THE CHAPTER, just as you learned in Chapter 8. Skim over the reading, looking at the title, headings, subheadings, visuals, summary, and end-of-chapter questions. Remember, if a book does not include these resources, skim the first sentence in every paragraph to get an overview of the content.

Preview (not study-read yet) the following passage from a Western Civilization textbook, and then read the explanation that follows. This may seem like a challenging reading—because it is. By using all the reading strategies you have been taught, you can read this. Just start slowly and apply the skills you have learned. As you work through the four textbook marking steps in this chapter with this passage, you will see how you can systematically take control of any reading.

Plato and Aristotle

1   Because (Socrates) never wrote anything down, we are dependent on others for our knowledge of him. Fortunately for us, he inspired students who committed his words and ideas to paper. Socrates' most distinguished student, and our most important source of his thought, was Plato (427–348 B.C.), who in turn was the teacher of Aristotle (384–322 B.C.). Together, these men laid the foundation of the Western philosophical tradition. They were thinkers for the ages, but each was also a man of his times.

Plato's teacher

2   Socrates grew up in confident Periclean days. **Plato** (PLAY-toe) came of age during the Peloponnesian War, a period culminating in the execution of Socrates. Shocked and disillusioned, Plato turned his back on public life, although he was an Athenian citizen. Instead of discussing philosophy in public, Plato founded a private school in an Athenian suburb, the Academy. Plato held a low opinion of democracy, and when he did intervene in politics, it was not in Athens but in far-off Syracuse (in Sicily). Syracuse was governed by a tyranny, and Plato hoped to educate the tyrant's heir in philosophy—a vain hope, as it turned out.

culminating to come to completion

tyranny absolute ruler

3   In an attempt to recapture the stimulating give-and-take of a conversation with Socrates, Plato did not write straightforward philosophical treatises, but instead dialogues or speeches. All of Plato's dialogues have more than one speaker, and in most, the main speaker is named "Socrates." Sometimes this figure is the historical Socrates, sometimes merely a mouthpiece for ideas Plato wished to explore.

treatises long written paper

voluminous great volume of written work

4   A voluminous writer, Plato is not easily summarized. The word that best characterizes his legacy, though, is idealism, of which Plato is one of Western philosophy's greatest exponents. Like (Parmenides,) Plato distrusted the senses. Truth exists, but come only by training the mind to overcome commonsense evidence. The model for Plato's philosophical method is geometry. Just as geometry deals not with this or that triangle or rectangle but with ideal forms—with a pure triangle, a pure rectangle—so the philosopher could learn to recognize purity. A philosopher would not, say, compare aretê in Athens, Sparta, and Persia; a philosopher would understand the

idealism pursuit of one's ideals

??? Who is this?

aretê an ideal form, perfect idea of something

meaning of pure, ideal aretê. No relativist, Plato believed in absolute good and evil.

Plato's best-known work

5   Philosophy is not for everyone, according to Plato. Only a few people have the necessary intelligence and discipline. In the *Republic,* perhaps his best-known work, Plato displays his idealism and its political consequences. He envisioned a society whose elite would study philosophy and attain enlightenment. They would understand the vanity of political ambition but would accept the responsibility of governing the masses. Plato never makes clear precisely why they should assume this burden. Perhaps he was enough of a traditionalist, in spite of himself, to consider a citizen's responsibility to the polis [city, community] to be obvious. In any case, Plato's ideal state was one in which philosophers would rule as kings, benevolently and unselfishly.

6   The ideal state would be like a small polis: self-sufficient and closed to outside corruption like Sparta, but committed to the pursuit of things intellectual like Athens. Society would be divided into three classes—philosophers, soldiers, and farmers—with admission to each class based on merit rather than heredity. Poetry and drama would be censored. Plato advocated public education and toyed with more radical notions: not only gender equality, but also the abolition of the family and private property, which he felt led to disunity and dissension.

Plato's student

7   Plato's ideas have always been controversial, but rarely ignored. The writings of his great student Aristotle better suited contemporary tastes. Originally from Macedonia, **Aristotle** spent most of his life in Athens, first as a student at the Academy, then as founder of his own school, the Lyceum (lie-SEE-um). Like Plato, Aristotle wrote dialogues, but none survive. His main surviving works are treatises, largely compilations by students of his lecture notes. One of the most wide-ranging intellectuals, Aristotle thirsted for knowledge. His writings embrace politics, ethics, poetry, botany, physics, metaphysics, astronomy, rhetoric, zoology, logic and psychology.

examples of writings

8   Though influenced by Plato's idealism, Aristotle was a far more practical, down-to-earth thinker. His father had been a doctor, which may account for Aristotle's interest in applied science and in biology and the biological method. Unlike Plato, Aristotle placed great emphasis on observation and fieldwork and on classification and systemization.

9   Aristotle agreed with Plato about the existence of absolute standards of good and evil, but he emphasized the relevance of such standards to everyday life. Unlike Plato, Aristotle considered the senses important guides. Change, he believed, was not an illusion, but rather an

important phenomenon. Aristotle's view of change was teleological—that is, he emphasized the goal (*telos* in Greek) of change. According to Aristotle, every organism changes and grows toward a particular end and is an integral and harmonious part of a larger whole. The entire cosmos is teleological, and each and every one of its parts has a purpose. Behind the cosmos was a principle that Aristotle called "the unmoved mover," the supreme cause of existence.

teleological belief that causes and change occur in nature

10   Aristotle defined an object's aretê as the fulfillment of its inherent function in the cosmos. The (aretê of a horse) for example, was to be strong, fast, and obedient; the aretê of a rose was to look beautiful and smell sweet. As for the aretê of a human being, Aristotle agreed with Plato: Only the philosopher achieved true aretê. As a pragmatist, however, Aristotle did not imagine philosophers becoming kings. Even so, he did not advocate democracy, which he considered mob rule. Instead, he advocated a government of wealthy gentlemen who had been trained by philosophers—not the best regime imaginable but, in Aristotle's opinion, the best one possible.

examples of aretê

Source: From NOBEL/STRAUSS/OSHEIM/NEUSCHEL. *Western Civilization Beyond Boundaries* 6e (pp. 77–8). Copyright © 2011 Cengage Learning.

At first glance of this passage, you will notice that there are no subheadings and very few key terms marked in bold font. You may notice that some words are in italics and therefore worth noting. (You would be right about that.) You also might come to some quick conclusions like, it looks dry, it is about the olden days, and it has lots of unfamiliar words such as "Periclean" and "teleological." Fair enough. It is dry when you just skim the surface, but you will soon see that it is much more. Notice that the heading tells you the passage is about Plato and Aristotle. Some preview questions you could ask are:

> *What about Plato and Aristotle?*
> *What point does the author make about Plato and Aristotle?*
> *What do I already know about Plato and Aristotle?*

Step Two: Study-Read

STUDY-READING SHOULD be performed one section at a time. It is always a better idea to break up a chapter or long reading assignment into sections instead of trying to read it straight through, like you might read a novel. Handling your reading assignment in sections makes understanding the whole reading assignment more manageable. If you fully understand one part or section of your

section a manageable chunk of reading, typically beginning at one major heading and ending right before the next major heading

reading, move on to the next. If you do not understand what you are reading, you should not continue with the rest of the assignment. Instead:

- ▶ look up unfamiliar words,
- ▶ integrate the definitions of the unfamiliar words into what you are reading,
- ▶ reread what you do not understand,
- ▶ restate what you are reading into your own words,
- ▶ connect what you already know about the topic to the new information,
- ▶ review the material with another student, tutor, or instructor.

Breaking a large reading assignment into sections and monitoring your understanding as you read ensure comprehension. These steps prevent you from reading a whole assignment and realizing that it doesn't make sense to you. However, if you are still struggling, mark the difficult parts so you can ask your instructor questions.

As you focus on reading a section, try to determine the author's purpose. Mentally answer any questions you created while previewing. As you read, try to connect what you are learning to what you already know about the subject. Note that this task may take a little outside work if your background knowledge on the topic of the reading is weak. To make connections you could:

- ▶ use your campus resources to help you make sense of new information. For example, check with your reference librarians to see if faculty have special materials in your library's reserves, such as additional readings or videos on the topic;
- ▶ find a YouTube video that gives some quick background;
- ▶ meet with a tutor or someone else from your class who has a handle on the information. Talking through sections with someone else will make a big difference in your ability to understand.

Go back and begin study-reading the passage on page 401, keeping these questions in mind:

> *What about Plato and Aristotle?*
> *What point does the author make about Plato and Aristotle?*
> *What do I already know about Plato and Aristotle?*

As you read, try to connect what you are learning to what you already know—your prior knowledge. Remember to use the cross-referencing strategy in Chapter 8. What do you know about Plato and Aristotle? If you do not know anything about Plato or Aristotle, what can you do to build some prior knowledge about them before you start reading?

Are you familiar with the following words from the passage: *tyranny, treatises, aretê,* and *pragmatists?* Do not just pass over unfamiliar words. Investigate them. If there are unfamiliar words in your reading, look them up and make sure you understand them. Do not forget to use the card review system from Chapter 3 to help you to learn new words. When taking notes from your textbooks, write down vocabulary words and their definitions to make remembering them easier.

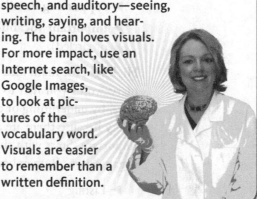

Tip FROM THE
Brain Doctor

Do not forget to use multiple pathways when you study vocabulary: visual speech, and auditory—seeing, writing, saying, and hearing. The brain loves visuals. For more impact, use an Internet search, like Google Images, to look at pictures of the vocabulary word. Visuals are easier to remember than a written definition.

Step Three: Highlight

ONCE YOU HAVE read and understood a section of your reading, you are ready to highlight in your textbook. Begin by highlighting the main idea in green as you have done in other chapters. When the main idea is implied, write the main idea after a section, using the *therefore* or *conclusion* symbol (∴) you learned about in Chapter 8 so that you know at a glance what you have written. Then highlight major supporting details in yellow. Important vocabulary words may already be in bold and may also be defined in the margins of your book, so you might not need to highlight them. If vocabulary is not in boldfaced type, highlight it in a third color, underline it, or circle it—just be consistent with your strategy so when you review your markings, you will instantly recognize what has been marked. Important vocabulary should pop out to you as you study from your textbook.

Here are some common errors many students make when highlighting textbooks:

► highlighting too much
► highlighting only interesting or familiar ideas
► highlighting something without knowing why
► not highlighting enough

The key to effective textbook marking is discrimination. Not everything you read "weighs" the same. You know that when you listen to a story. Use that same understanding as you read your textbooks. No matter what class you are taking, the following three components are always important and should be highlighted:

- ▶ **main ideas** (in green)
- ▶ **supporting details** (in yellow)
- ▶ **important vocabulary** (in another highlighter color, underlined, or circled).

Highlight the main idea of the passage on page 401 in green. Mark any vocabulary words you had to look up, such as *Periclean, idealism, teleological,* and *aretê,* by underlining or circling them. Now mark supporting details. This gets tricky because there are a lot of details and it might be difficult to tell what is important. Start with the main idea and then identify the author's pattern of organization. Remember the patterns of organization from Chapter 7:

- ▶ Listing
- ▶ Analysis
- ▶ Cause/effect
- ▶ Comparison/contrast
- ▶ Definition/example
- ▶ Sequence

Use a process of elimination. Both Aristotle and Plato are listed in the passage, but there is a stronger relationship between them than there is with just items on a list, so listing is not the overall pattern, nor is sequence because there is no series of events in chronological order. There are no organizational word clues of analysis, either. Go back to the main idea, which is:

Together, these men laid the foundations of the Western philosophical tradition.

What do you think is being discussed? Whatever you select as the pattern of organization, question it and justify it. How did they lay the foundation of Western philosophical tradition? The author does not really tell you how it happened, so it is not cause/effect. What the author does is compare and contrast the two philosophers. Note the sentence that immediately follows the main idea in the passage.

They were thinkers for the ages, but each was also a man of his times.

What is the clue word used? In this comparison/contrast, the author lets you draw your own conclusions about what elements of their thinking are still around. Clearly the author thinks these two philosophers have laid the foundation. Do you?

Now use the main idea and the author's overall organization to ask yourself questions that can lead you to the major supporting details. Some questions you might ask are:

What is the foundation of the Western philosophical tradition?
What ideas have both philosophers offered that are still around today?

Notice how these questions come right from the main idea and the overall organization of comparison/contrast. To answer these questions, go back to the passage and look at the ideas Plato and Aristotle had. Paragraph 1 introduces Plato and Aristotle. Paragraph 2 reveals that Plato had a low opinion of democracy. The rest of paragraph 2 gives background on Plato. Paragraph 3 describes the kind of writing Plato engaged in. Paragraph 4 begins to offer more ideas that Plato held. The first sentence of paragraph 4 states that "… Plato is not easily summarized." The rest of paragraph 4 (and the two paragraphs that follow) gives a summary of Plato, who believed in idealism, distrusted the senses, believed in absolute truth, and believed that things had an ideal form (aretê). Paragraphs 5 and 6 continue with Plato's ideas. In these paragraphs, you find that Plato believed philosophy was only for the most intelligent and that philosophers should rule as kings. There should be small states, social classes, public education, gender equality, and abolition of private property. All of these ideas of Plato's are details but not necessarily major supporting details. Paragraphs 7–10 offer information about Aristotle.

ACTIVITY 9B
Search for Supporting Details

1. In paragraph 7, the author uses the word *compilations*. The context clue is that this word has something to do with students and Aristotle's lecture notes. *Com-* is a prefix meaning "with or together." The root word *pile* means "a collection of things." The suffix *-ation* means "that which is," so a compilation is a collection of things grouped together. Using your knowledge of context clues and word part analysis, define the word *pragmatist* from paragraph 7.

   _____

   _____

2. Read paragraphs 7–10 of the Plato and Aristotle passage, and list Aristotle's ideas.

   _____

   _____

   _____

   _____

Continued on next page.

You now have a list of Plato's ideas, explained for you earlier, and Aristotle's ideas, which you listed. Examine both of these lists, and mark only those items that answer the questions you asked about the passage: *What is the foundation of the Western philosophical tradition? What did Plato believe that is still around today? What did Aristotle believe that is still around today?* The answers to these questions are the major supporting ideas. Everything else is minor supporting details.

ACTIVITY 9C
Use a Visual to Show You Know It

Complete the following chart. Write down ideas that each philosopher had: Aristotle's ideas to the right of the figure labeled Aristotle and Plato's ideas to the left of the figure labeled Plato. Then write down the ideas both philosophers had in common between the two figures. At the top, write down five ideas of Plato's and Aristotle's that you think are still held today.

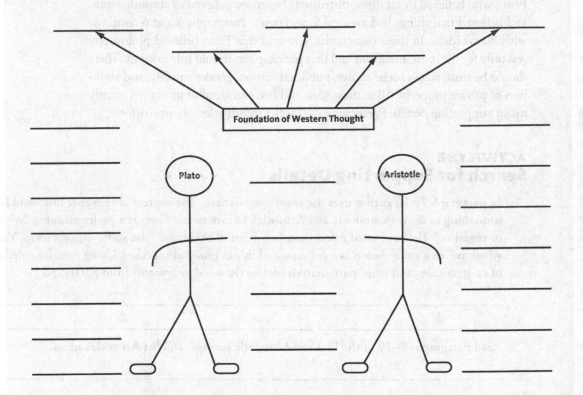

The ideas Plato and Aristotle had in common, which you decided still exist today, are the major supporting details. Go back to the passage and highlight those supporting details in yellow.

Seeing ideas that you have read in a chart such as this one helps you picture in your mind how ideas are related. Creating visuals improves understanding. You may not have time to create a visual each time you read a section of your assignment, but you will find them useful to create after reading an entire reading assignment or textbook chapter. More will be explained about creating visuals in Chapter 10.

✓ COMPREHENSION CHECK

▶ Up to this point in the chapter, what is unclear?

▶ How can you get into the right mindset to mark textbooks?

Step Four: Write Margin Notes

IN ADDITION TO highlighting, you should write a margin note if you do not understand something, disagree with the author, want to identify something new, or remember an example. Sometimes you will also need to underline additional information. When you underline something, you should note in the margin why you felt it was important. A margin note can be a symbol reminding why you marked or highlighted something, such as a *?* in the margin where something is unclear. The letters *ex* can signal an important example. *MI* can show where your underlined main idea is if you do not use a highlighter color to indicate it.

You should be able to glance at a textbook page and see where the important information is. The margin notes you make show how you understand the reading material. Table 9.1 is a list of common margin notes or annotations.

Margin notes can also be short words or phrases that bring your attention to something in the text that helps you remember and easily identify key points. For example, if you read about cell structure in your biology textbook, you learn that eukaryotic cells have nuclei and are

Table 9.1 Common Margin Notes

Textbook Information	Symbol
Important Vocabulary and Definition	def
Main Idea	MI
Major Supporting Detail	major
Minor Supporting Detail	minor
Example	ex
Don't Understand	?
Important Information	*
Identify Steps in a Sequence	1, 2, 3
Conclusion	con or ∴
Author's Opinion	opin
Biased Information	bias

Tip FROM THE Brain Doctor

Remember that the brain is designed to execute action! Taking action can help you think better. When you read a textbook, do something active. Take notes, underline, highlight, or write in the margins.

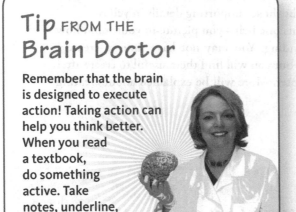

more complicated than prokaryotic cells and that an ostrich cell is eukaryotic and that bacteria are prokaryotic. You might want to write the word *ostrich* in the margin next to *eukaryotic* and *bacteria* next to *prokaryotic* so that you can remember the difference between the two types of cells.

You can and should create your own symbols. Developing a personal system of textbook marking means adopting and consistently using specific abbreviations and/or symbols to label your marked text. It is important to remember what the symbols and abbreviations you use stand for, however, as they can be easy to forget when you go back to your textbook. To help you remember your own symbols, develop a key that shows the symbols you create along with their meanings.

ACTIVITY 9D
Create Personal Margin Notes

In the left column, put the margin notes and symbols you use regularly in your textbooks, and in the right column, write down the meaning of the note or symbol. The first one is modeled for you.

Margin Note/Symbol	Meaning of Margin Note/Symbol
huh? or ???	Should make sense, but I don't really get it.

Deciding What Else to Mark

BEFORE YOU MARK SOMETHING IN YOUR TEXTBOOK, ask yourself why you want to mark it. By doing this, you are being more reflective. As a result, you will mark based on reason and not feeling. If you mark too much, everything will look important when you go back to review, completely defeating the purpose of marking. You would have to reread the whole chapter when you study if everything is marked. The goal of marking is to mark only what is the most important information so when you go back to study, the key information jumps off the page for you.

Is it possible for two people to mark differently and still both be correct? Yes and no. If an author has done a good job, all readers should get the same idea from a reading and should have the same main ideas and major supporting details highlighted. But some examples might be more helpful to one reader than another. The reader who finds them helpful might mark them in some way, but the reader who does not may not mark them at all. Others who may have less background knowledge on a topic may write more margin notes in order to gain understanding.

Knowing what else to mark, besides the main ideas, major supporting details, and important vocabulary—if more marking is even needed—depends on these three factors:

▶ **What You Learn in Lecture.** Your instructors will usually lecture on at least some of the content covered in your textbooks. When they do, pay close attention, as it is important to relate what they say to what you have read. You can judge the importance of specific information by their use of word clues such as *most important, in conclusion,* and *in summary.* You can also judge the relative importance of information from more subtle clues such as how much time an instructor spends on a topic or if the instructor repeats it—he or she is making sure you get it down for the test! Once you decide a topic covered in a lecture is an important restatement of textbook material, you should go back and mark it in your textbook.

▶ **What You Learn in a Lab.** If your class has a lab component, you have another opportunity to identify what information is most important in your textbook. Lab assignments are usually practical applications of lessons being taught in your lectures and textbook. If you are learning about the digestive system, for example, you may well have a biology lab experiment that requires you to dissect an animal to examine its digestive system. By doing this, you gain first-hand experience of what you have been learning about and a clearer sense of what is important in the digestive process. If it becomes obvious to you from participating in a lab class that certain textbook information is important, you should label or mark it using an asterisk (*) or other appropriate margin notes.

▶ **Unclear Information You Still Don't Understand.** Anything that is unclear should be marked in your textbook. You may write a *?* in

iStockphoto.com/Fai Wong

the margin beside the unclear information or another symbol that reminds you to follow up. Some students find it helpful to use sticky notes to flag unclear information. Sticky notes that stick out of a closed book, alert you to the very place in the text that was unclear. Once you have reread the information or talked to other students and your instructor to clarify the unclear points, you can remove the sticky notes and add margin notes that help you understand the text.

Go back to the passage on page 401, and write margin notes where appropriate. Do not pepper the margins with everything you can think of. Just write what you think will help you to remember the information. Some margin notes have been provided for you as a model. Remember that margin notes are like having a conversation with the author. For example, you may want to write the words *perfect form* in the margin next to the word *aretê* because *aretê* isn't a common word and having its meaning handy as you read and review will help you remember it. Another margin note might be *senses don't always = truth* written next to "… Plato distrusted the senses" in paragraph 4. That short note clarifies what "distrusted the senses" means. As you write this margin note, try to connect Plato's point with something you already know. When have you been fooled by your senses? Have you ever smelled pumpkin pie while walking through the door only to realize the scent came from a scented candle? You do not have to write these ideas down, but it is important for understanding and memory that you connect new information with information you already know.

ACTIVITY 9E
Draw Conclusions from Your Reading

Draw conclusions from the Plato and Aristotle passage on page 401 to answer the following questions.

1. What is a platonic relationship?

_____

_____

_____

2. If you looked at society today as Plato described an "ideal state," what would be the same? What would be different? (See paragraph 6.)

_____

_____

_____

3. If our cosmos is teleological and everything has a purposeful part to play in the larger goal of life, why do we have mosquitoes?

_____

_____

_____

4. Aristotle and Plato agreed that there exists absolute truth. Give some examples of ideas or norms that are absolutely timeless and eternal.

_____

_____

_____

5. What is the aretê of "student"?

_____

_____

_____

6. General James T. Conway, 34th Commandant of the U.S. Marine Corps, in an effort to entice people to join the Marines, is quoted as saying, "The battlefield will change—our values are timeless." How is he using Plato's ideas in this quote?

AP Photo/M. Spencer Green

_____

_____

_____

_____

_____

ACTIVITY 9F
Practice the Four Steps of Textbook Marking

Apply the four steps of textbook marking to the following passages. Remember to preview first, and then study-read. You do not have to break up the passages into smaller sections as they are not that long. Highlight main ideas in green and major supporting ideas in yellow, and write margin notes. Circle unfamiliar vocabulary. When you complete the four steps, answer the questions that follow each passage.

Passage 1

What Is Technology

1   Technology is the creation of new products and processes that are supposed to improve our chances for survival, our comfort level, and our quality of life. In many cases, technology develops from known scientific laws and theories. Scientists invented the laser, for example, by applying knowledge about the internal structure of atoms. Applied scientific knowledge about chemistry has given us nylon, pesticides, and countless other products.

2   Some technologies arose long before anyone understood the underlying scientific principles. Aspirin, originally extracted from the bark of a willow tree, relieved pain and fever long before anyone found out how it did so. Similarly, photography was invented by people who had no inkling of its chemistry. Farmers crossbred new strains of livestock and crops long before biologists understood the principles of genetics.

3   Science and technology differ in the ways the information and ideas they produce are shared. Many of the results of scientific research are published and passed around freely to be tested, challenged, verified, or modified; a process that strengthens the validity of scientific knowledge and helps expose cheaters. In contrast, technological discoveries are often kept secret until the new process or product is patented.

Source: From MILLER. *Environmental Science: Working with the Earth* 5e (p. 42). Copyright © 1995 Cengage Learning.

1. In paragraph 3, the author uses the word *verified*. The context clue is that this word has something to do with scientific research. Use word part analysis to define *verified*.

   _____

2. Highlight the main idea if you have not already.

3. Highlight the three major supporting details if you have not already.

4. Many examples of different technologies are given, but they are not considered to be major supporting details. Why not?

   _____

Deciding What Else to Mark

Passage 2

Why Is Sociological Research Important in Our Everyday Lives?

1   How do we know what we know? Much of our knowledge is based on tradition, a handing down of statements, beliefs, and customs from generation to generation ("The groom's parents should pay for the wedding rehearsal dinner" or "Flying the American flag at home shows one's patriotism."). Another common source of knowledge is authority, a socially accepted source of information that includes experts, parents, government officials, police, judges, and religious leaders ("My mom says that…" or "According to the American Heart Association…"). Knowledge based on tradition and authority simplifies our lives because it provides us with basic rules about socially and legally acceptable behavior. Often, however, the information is misleading or downright incorrect. Suppose a 2-year-old throws a temper tantrum at a family barbecue. One adult comments, "What that kid needs is a smack on the behind." Another person immediately disagrees: "All kids go through this stage. Just ignore it." Who's right? Much research shows that neither ignoring a problem nor inflicting physical punishment (such as spanking) stops a toddler's bad behavior. Instead, according to many researchers, most young children's misbehavior can be curbed by techniques such as making simple rules, being consistent in disciplining misbehavior, praising good behavior, and setting a good example for how to act.

2   In contrast with knowledge based on tradition and authority, sociological research is important in our everyday lives for several reasons:

1. **It creates new knowledge that helps us understand social life.** Regarding the economy, for example, sociological research has shown that the law fails to remedy much workplace inequality because it disregards unintentional and unconscious discrimination, and that workplace diversity leads to better products and greater company profits (Berrey 2009). *[diversity differences]*

2. **It exposes myths.** U. S. newspapers and television shows perpetuate the myth that suicides rates are highest during the end of the Christmas holidays. In fact, suicide rates are lowest in December and highest in the spring and fall (but the reasons for these peaks are unclear). Another myth is that more women are victims of domestic violence on Super Bowl Sunday than on any other day of the year, presumably because men are intoxicated and become abusive. In fact, intimate partner violence is common throughout the year and doesn't spike on Super Bowl Sunday (Mikkelson and Mikkelson 2005; Annenberg Public Policy Center 2008). *[perpetuate to prolong, to cause to continue indefinitely]*

3. **It affects social policies.** In many states, fatal child abuse or neglect is often undercounted because agencies vary in their interpretations of what constitutes abuse and neglect. For example, a child who is killed in an auto crash because the intoxicated parent had not placed the child in a car seat may be counted as an accident rather than parental neglect (Christensen and Therolf 2009). Sociological research can uncover such systemic flaws, and provide attorneys and social workers with the data they need to change laws that prevent children's deaths because of parental abuse or neglect.

Continued on next page.

4. **It sharpens our critical thinking skills.** Many Americans, especially women, rely on talk shows such as *Oprah* for information on a number of topics. During 2009 alone, Oprah Winfrey featured and applauded guests who maintained, among other things, that children contract autism from the measles, mumps, and rubella (MMR) vaccinations that they receive as babies, that fortune cards can help people diagnose their illnesses, and that people can wish away cancer (Kosova and Wingert 2009)—all of which are false.

Source: From BENOKRAITIS. *SOC* 2e (p. 22). Copyright © 2012 Cengage Learning.

5. **What strategies did you use to figure out the main idea?**

_____

_____

6. **What clues did you use to help identify the supporting details?**

_____

_____

Passage 3

Why the World Does Not Go Up in Flames

1   The molecules of life release energy when they combine with oxygen. For example, think of how a spark ignites tinder-dry wood in a campfire. Wood is mostly cellulose, which is a carbohydrate that consists of long chains of repeating glucose units. A spark initiates a reaction that converts cellulose and oxygen to water and carbon dioxide. The reaction is exergonic, and it releases enough energy to initiate the same reaction with other cellulose and oxygen molecules. That is why a campfire keeps burning once it has been lit.

2   Earth is rich in oxygen—and in potential exergonic reactions. Why doesn't it burst into flames? Luckily, it takes energy to break the chemical bonds of reactants, even in an exergonic reaction. **Activation energy** is the minimum amount of energy that will get a chemical reaction started. It is independent of any energy difference between reactants and products what is produced from the reaction.

3   Both endergonic and exergonic reactions have activation energy, but the amount varies with the reaction. For example, guncotton, or nitrocellulose, is a highly explosive derivative of cellulose. Christian Schönbein accidentally discovered a way to manufacture it when he used a cotton apron to wipe up a nitric acid spill on his kitchen table, then hung it up to dry next to his oven. The apron exploded. Being a chemist in the 1800s, Schönbein had immediate hopes that he could market guncotton as a firearm explosive, but it proved to be too unstable. So little activation energy is needed to make guncotton react with oxygen that it explodes

spontaneously. The substitute? Gunpowder, which has a higher activation energy for a reaction with oxygen.

Source: From STARR. *Biology: The Unity and Diversity of Life* 12e (p. 96–7). Copyright © 2009 Cengage Learning.

7. If this passage was difficult for you, what made it difficult?

_____

_____

8. Restate the main idea using your own words.

_____

_____

9. What is the overall pattern of organization of the passage? Why?

_____

_____

_____

10. How did you determine the major supporting details?

_____

_____

_____

Take Control of Your Textbook by Using Focused Notes

TEXTBOOK MARKING SHOULD NOT REPLACE TAKING notes from your textbook, but it will make the job of note taking more efficient and will save you time when studying. If you mark your textbooks effectively, your textbook becomes a kind of study guide. The ideas will be prioritized and highlighted in your text so they will stand out later as you take notes from your textbook in preparation for studying. Taking notes from your textbook and adding information and examples you already know will be a faster process because your markings have transformed the author's message into an organized framework. Ideas you add from your own experiences or class lectures can fit right into that framework.

focused notes specific pieces of information, such as vocabulary words, processes, and events, pulled from your classroom and textbook notes and placed in one chart for focused review

Focused notes is a study strategy that may save you hours of time when preparing for exams. They are referred to as focused notes because you have already identified the key points and new vocabulary. When you review your textbook markings and classroom notes, you pull out key information (vocabulary, processes, or events) and place the information in a chart. All of the information is in one spot, so you have focused your notes for review. You will need to decide what needs your focus: what is clear or unclear, what was repeated in a lecture or a lab, and what examples were provided in class.

Use a page from a notebook, and fold it lengthwise in thirds, making three columns. As you review your textbook material, section by section, go back to your highlights and margin notes and use them to create your focused notes. Create a heading for each column. The first column will be whatever you are trying to focus on. If you focus on all of the new vocabulary words in a chapter, they would be listed in Column 1. Define the words in Column 2. Column 3 is a little more flexible. Include drawings or pictures of each new word, or create a question for each so that you know you understand it. See Figure 9.2 for an example of focused notes created from passage 3 of Activity 9F. Keep in mind, however, that this passage is only one section of the larger chapter the passage came from. Focused notes would be completed after you have read the complete assignment as a review.

Figure 9.2 Example of Focused Notes

Column 1	Column 2	Column 3
Vocabulary Word	Definition	Question
exergonic	gives off energy	Why does a campfire keep burning?
activation energy	minimum amount of energy that will get a chemical reaction started	What starts a chemical reaction?
endergonic	absorbs energy	Are chemical reactions prevented?

ACTIVITY 9G
Practice Using Focused Notes

Read the following passage on how the brain works, and follow the instructions to create focused notes for the passage.

Learn as Much as Possible about How Your Brain Works

1   This is the most important factor in getting smart and staying smart. In order to do this, you don't have to become a neurologist or subscribe to scholarly journals on **neuroscience** (the study of the brain at every operating level ranging from everyday observable behavior to brain processes taking place at the level of chemicals and molecules). Here is a useful summary of the facts you should know.

2   The adult human brain weighs about three pounds and consists of about 100 billion nerve cells or neurons along with an even greater number of non-neuronal cells called **glia**

(in Greek, glia means "glue") interspersed among the **neurons**. The neurons are responsible for the communication of information throughout the brain. Especially important is the brain's outer wrinkled mantle, the **cerebral cortex**, which gives the brain the appearance of a gnarled walnut. The cerebral cortex contains about 30 billion neurons linked to one another by means of a million billion neuronal connections called **synapses**....

3   Any of the brain's 100 or so billion neurons can potentially communicate with any other via one or more linkages [synapses]...Linkages, once formed, are strengthened by repetition. At the behavioral level, this takes the form of habit. Each time you practice a piano piece or a golf swing (presuming you are doing it correctly), your performance improves. This corresponds at the neuronal level to the establishment and facilitation of neuronal circuits.

Source: From MOZART'S BRAIN AND THE FIGHTER PILOT by Richard M. Restak, M.D., copyright © 2001 by Richard M. Restak, M.D. Used by permission of Harmony Books, a division of Random House, Inc.

Complete focused notes for this passage based on vocabulary. In Column 1, write all the bolded words and any others you don't understand. In Column 2, write a definition or explanation of each vocabulary word. Use Column 3 to draw or paste a picture, create a word map, or ask a question. The first word is modeled for you here.

Column 1	Column 2	Column 3
Vocabulary Word	**Definition**	**Picture, Word Map, or Question**
neuroscience	the study of the brain at every operating level ranging from everyday observable behavior to brain processes taking place at the level of chemicals and molecules	What is the study of the brain called?

Try to recall the vocabulary written in Column 1 by covering up Columns 2 and 3 and quizzing yourself. Now cover Column 1; looking at Columns 2 and 3, can you recall the words? Were you able to define the words and recognize the pictures? This is a great study technique to help you commit key terms to memory.

PRACTICE WITH A READING PASSAGE

Prepare to Read

1. Based on the title, what do you expect the following passage to be about?

_____

2. What do you know about the topic already?

_____

3. Preview the passage, and list three questions that you developed about the passage.

_____

4. After you preview, during the study-read step, apply the textbook marking strategies you learned.
   ▶ Highlight the main idea in green.
   ▶ Highlight major supporting details in yellow.
   ▶ Mark any new vocabulary words.
   ▶ Write margin notes.

5. How familiar are you with the peace symbol? Have you ever worn one? Why or why not?

A History of the Campaign for Nuclear Disarmament: The CND Logo

1   One of the most widely known symbols in the world, in Britain it is recognized as standing for nuclear disarmament—and in particular as the logo of the Campaign for Nuclear Disarmament (CND). In the United States and much of the rest of the world it is known more broadly as the peace symbol. The peace symbol has a global history which may surprise many Americans.

2   It was designed in 1958 by Gerald Holtom, a professional designer and artist and a graduate of the Royal College of Arts. He showed his preliminary sketches to a small group of people in the _Peace News_ office in North London and to the Direct Action Committee Against Nuclear War, one of several smaller organizations that came together to set up CND.

Marilyn Volan/Shutterstock.com

First Public Appearance

3   The Direct Action Committee had already planned what was to be the first major anti-nuclear march, from London to Aldermaston, where British nuclear weapons were and still are manufactured. It was on that march over the 1958 Easter weekend that the symbol first appeared in public. Five hundred cardboard lollipops on sticks were produced. Half were black on white and half white on green. Just as the church's liturgical colors change over Easter, so the colors were to change, *"from Winter to Spring, from Death to Life."* Black and white would be displayed on Good Friday and Saturday, green and white on Easter Sunday and Monday.

4   The first badges were made by Eric Austin of Kensington CND using white clay with the symbol painted black. Again there was a conscious symbolism. They were distributed with a note explaining that in the event of a nuclear war, these fired pottery badges would be among the few human artifacts to survive the nuclear inferno. (These early ceramic badges can still be found and one, lent by CND, was included in the Imperial War Museum's 1999/2000 exhibition "From the Bomb to the Beatles.")

What Does It Mean?

5   Gerald Holtom, a conscientious objector who had worked on a farm in Norfolk during the Second World War, explained that the symbol incorporated the semaphore letters **N**(uclear) and **D**(isarmament). He later wrote to Hugh Brock, editor of *Peace News,* explaining the genesis of his idea in greater, more personal depth, ironically:

> *I was in despair. Deep despair. I drew myself: the representative of an individual in despair, with hands palm outstretched outwards and downwards in the manner of Goya's peasant before the firing squad. I formalized the drawing into a line and put a circle round it.*

6   Eric Austin added his own interpretation of the design: *the gesture of despair had long been associated with the death of Man and the circle with the unborn child.*

7   Gerald Holtom had originally considered using the Christian cross symbol within a circle as the motif for the march, but various priests he had approached with the suggestion were not happy at the idea of using the cross on a protest march. Later, ironically, Christian CND to use the symbol with the central stroke extended upwards to form the upright of a cross.

8   This adaptation of the design was only one of many subsequently invented by various groups within CND and for specific occasions—with a cross below as a women's symbol, with a daffodil or a thistle incorporated by CND, with little legs for a sponsored walk, etc. Whether Gerald Holtom would have approved of some of the more light-hearted versions is open to doubt.

Continued on next page.

---

liturgical having to do with the liturgy, the organization and content of public worship

artifacts any object made by humans

semaphore a system of signaling where flags are held in certain ways to form letters

genesis beginning

9   The symbol almost at once crossed the Atlantic. Bayard Rustin, a close associate of Dr. Martin Luther King, had come over from the U.S. in order to take part in that first Aldermaston March. He took the symbol back to the United States where it was used on civil rights marches. Later it appeared on anti-Vietnam War demonstrations and was even seen daubed in protest on their helmets by American GIs. Simpler to draw than the Picasso peace dove, it became known, first in the U.S. and then round the world, as the peace symbol. It appeared on the walls of Prague when the Soviet tanks invaded in 1968, on the Berlin Wall, in Sarajevo and Belgrade, on the graves of the victims of military dictators from the Greek Colonels to the Argentinian government led by military leaders, and most recently in East Timor.

Misrepresentation and Misuse

10   There have been claims that the symbol has older, occult or anti-Christian associations. In South Africa, under the apartheid regime, there was an official attempt to ban it. Various far-right and fundamentalist American groups have also spread the idea of Satanic associations or condemned it as a Communist sign. However the origins and the ideas behind the symbol have been clearly described, both in letters and in interviews, by Gerald Holtom. His original, first sketches are now on display as part of the Commonweal Collection in Bradford.

11   Although specifically designed for the anti-nuclear movement, it has quite deliberately never been copyrighted. No one has to pay or to seek permission before they use it. A symbol of freedom, it is free for all. This of course sometimes leads to its use, or misuse, in circumstances that CND and the peace movement find distasteful. It is also often exploited for commercial, advertising or generally fashion purposes. We can't stop this happening and have no intention of copyrighting it. All we can do is to ask commercial users if they would like to make a donation. Any money received is used for CND's peace education and information work.

Source: Copyright © Campaign for Nuclear Disarmament. Reprinted with permission.

Check Your Understanding

6. Use context clues and word part analysis to define the following words used in the passage.

- disarmament (paragraph 1): _____

- ironically (paragraph 5): _____

- semaphore (paragraph 5) (Note: The margin definition tells you what the systems of flags is, but what is the meaning of the word *semaphore* using word part analysis?): _____

_____

7. According to the passage, which of the following is *not* considered true?

   a. The peace symbol was cherished by the South Africa government.

   b. It has been banned by some as it was connected to Communism.

   c. It is considered one of the best-known symbols around the world.

   d. One of the first buttons using the Peace Symbol was made of pottery and would be among the few human artifacts that could survive a nuclear inferno.

8. To your knowledge, is there any other symbol that can be compared to the peace symbol? Explain your response.

   _____

   _____

   _____

   _____

9. Why do you think the peace symbol was at one time associated with the occult?

   _____

   _____

   _____

10. Why do you suppose the peace symbol became part of the anti-Vietnam protests?

   _____

   _____

   _____

   _____

CHAPTER SUMMARY

Textbook marking helps you distinguish important ideas from less important ones. Before marking anything in your textbooks, develop the right mindset toward learning. If what you read has meaning to you, you are more likely to remember it better. Try to connect what you read with something meaningful in your life. Also, keep the task of reading rewarding. Your brain is naturally satisfied when you figure things out or accomplish something. Use this natural tendency to keep yourself engaged in your reading.

As you begin to take control of your reading material, look at all the parts of the textbook, like the table of contents, chapters, bibliographies, appendices, glossaries, and indices. These features can be useful learning tools as they help you make sense of what you read.

Textbook marking is one way that you can keep yourself engaged as you read. There are four steps to textbook marking: 1) preview, 2) study-read, 3) highlight, and 4) write margin notes. These steps help you prioritize the information you read. At a minimum, you should aim to highlight the main ideas and major supporting details and underline new vocabulary in your reading. When you mark anything beyond the main ideas, major supporting details, or vocabulary, you should also include a margin note so that you know why you marked what you did. It is helpful is keep track of your personal margin notes so that you know what each note means when you return to the reading to review. Good textbook marking shows the relationships between ideas and can help you create efficient notes from your reading material. Focused notes is a chart strategy that you can use to categorize the important information you marked from a reading to help you study and remember the information.

Brain Connections: Self-Assessment

Draw the amount of dendrites you imagine that you have now about marking and note taking. Compare your drawing of dendrites now with what you drew at the beginning of this chapter. If the amounts are different, explain why.

✔ COMPREHENSION CHECK

▶ List and explain each step of the textbook marking process.
▶ Why is textbook marking an important part of the reading process?
▶ Where in the chapter did you lose concentration or become confused?
▶ If you could ask the authors a question about this chapter, what would you ask?

POST TEST

Part 1. Objective Questions

Match the key terms from the chapter in Column A to their definitions in Column B.

Column A

Column B

_____ 1. textbook marking

a. words, phrases, abbreviations, or symbols that you write in the margin to remind or explain to yourself why something is important

_____ 2. margin notes

b. specific pieces of information, such as vocabulary words, processes, and events, pulled from your classroom and textbook notes and placed in one chart for focused review

_____ 3. section

c. a manageable chunk of reading, typically beginning at one major heading and ending right before the next major heading

_____ 4. focused notes

d. a systematic way of highlighting and labeling ideas in a textbook to show how they are related

Circle the best answer to the following multiple-choice questions.

5. Everyone's textbook markings should be the same.

   True   False

6. Whenever I mark in a textbook, I should always write a margin note (other than main ideas highlighted in green and major details highlighted in yellow).

   True   False

7. Everyone should always get the same idea from a reading.

   True   False

8. If done well, a marked chapter can serve as a study guide.

   True   False

Short-Answer Questions

9. What are the four steps of textbook marking?

   a. _____

   b. _____

   c. _____

   d. _____

Continued on next page.

10. What is the danger of marking too much?

_____

_____

_____

Part 2. Reading Passage   POPULAR READING

Prepare to Read

1. Based on the title, what do you expect the following passage to be about?

_____

2. Do you enjoy the topic of this passage? Explain your response.

_____

_____

3. Have you taken a communications class at this point in your college career?

_____

4. Have you ever thought about the hand gestures people make as they are talking? Do you follow hand gestures to help you make meaning of a speaker's words? Do you nod in agreement or disagreement? Explain your response.

_____

5. Apply the four steps of textbook marking to this passage.

What Happens When Two People Talk?
By Malcolm Gladwell

1   What happens when two people talk? That is really the basic question here, because that's the basic context in which all persuasion takes place. We know that people talk back and forth. They listen. They interrupt. They move their hands. In the case of my meeting with Tom Gau, we were sitting in a modest-size-office. I was in a chair pulled up in front of his desk. I had my legs crossed and a pad and pen on my lap. I was wearing a blue shirt and black pants and a black jacket. He was sitting behind the desk in a high-backed chair. He was wearing a pair of blue suit pants and a crisply pressed white shirt and a red tie. Some of the time he leaned forward and planted his elbows in front of him. Other times he sat back in his chair and waved his hands in the air. Between us, on the blank surface of the desk, I placed my tape recorder. That's what you would have seen, if I showed you a videotape of our meeting. But if you had taken that videotape and slowed it down, until you were looking at our interaction in slices

of a fraction of a second, you would have seen something quite different. You would have seen the two of us engaging in what can only be described as an elaborate and precise dance.

2   The pioneer of this kind of analysis—of what is called the study of cultural microrhythms—is a man named William Condon. In one of his most famous research projects in the 1960s he attempted to decode a four-and-a-half-second segment of film, in which a woman says to a man and a child over dinner, "You all should come around every night. We never have had a dinnertime like this in months." Condon broke the film into individual frames, each representing about $\frac{1}{45}$th of a second. Then he watched—and watched. As he describes it:

> To carefully study the organization and sequence of this, the approach must be naturalistic or **ethological**. You just sit and look and look and look for thousands of hours until the order in the material begins to emerge. It's like sculpturing.... Continued study reveals further order. When I was looking at this film over and over again, I had an erroneous view of the universe that communication takes place between people. Somehow this was the model. You send the message, somebody sends the message back. The messages go here and there and everywhere. But something was funny about this.

ethological using the studies of animal behavior

Condon spent a year and a half on that short segment of film, until, finally, in his peripheral vision, he saw what he had always sensed was there: "the wife turning her head exactly as the husband's hands came up." From there he picked up other micromovements, other patterns that occurred over and over again, until he realized that in addition to talking and listening, the three people around the table were also engaging in what he termed "interactional **synchrony**." Their conversation had a rhythmic physical dimension. Each person would, within the space of one or two or three $\frac{1}{45}$th-of-a-second frames, move a shoulder or cheek or an eyebrow or a hand, sustain that movement, stop it, change directions, and start again. And what's more, those movements were perfectly in time to each person's own words—emphasizing and underlining and elaborating on the process of **articulation**—so that the speaker was, in effect, dancing to his or her own speech. At the same time the other people around the table were dancing along as well, moving their faces and shoulders and hands and bodies to the same rhythm. It's not that everyone was moving the same way, any more than people dancing to a song all dance the same way. It's that the timing of stops and starts of each person's micromovements—the jump and shifts of body and face—were perfectly in harmony.

synchrony moving together at the same time

articulation the state of being jointed, interrelated

3   Subsequent research has revealed that it isn't just gesture that is harmonized, but also conversational rhythm. When two people talk, their volume and pitch fall into balance. What linguists call speech rate—the number of speech sounds per second—equalizes. So does what is known as latency, the period of time that lapses between the moment one speaker stops talking and the moment the other speaker begins. Two people may arrive at a conversation with very different conversational patterns. But almost instantly they reach a common ground. We all do it, all the time. Babies as

Continued on next page.

young as one or two days old synchronize their head, elbow, shoulder, hip, and foot movements with the speech patterns of adults. Synchrony has even been found in the interactions of humans and apes. It's part of the way we are hardwired.

4   When Tom Gau and I sat across from each other in his office, then, we almost immediately fell into physical and conversational harmony. We were dancing. Even before he attempted to persuade me with his words, he had forged a bond with me with his movements and his speech. So what made my encounter with him different, so much more compelling than the conversational encounters I have every day? It isn't that Gau was deliberately trying to harmonize himself with me. Some books on salesmanship recommend that persuaders try to mirror the posture or talking styles of their clients in order to establish rapport. But that's been shown not to work. It makes people more uncomfortable, not less. It's too obviously phony.

5   What we are talking about is a kind of super-reflex, a fundamental physiological ability of which we are barely aware. And like all specialized human traits, some people have much more mastery over this reflex than others. Part of what it means to have a powerful or persuasive personality, then, is that you can draw others into your own rhythms and dictate the terms of the interactions. In some studies, students who have a high degree of synchrony with their teachers are happier, more enthused, interested, and easygoing. What I felt with Gau was that I was being seduced, not in the sexual sense, of course, but in a global way, that our conversation was being conducted on his terms, not mine. I felt I was becoming synchronized with him. "Skilled musicians know this, and good speakers," says Joseph Cappella, who teaches at the Annenberg School of Communication at the University of Pennsylvania. "They know when the crowds are with them, literally in synchrony with them, in movements and nods and stillness in moments of attention." It is a strange thing to admit, because I didn't want to be drawn in. I was on guard against it. But the essence of Salesmen, that is, on some level, they cannot be resisted. "Tom can build a level of trust and rapport in five to ten minutes that most people will take half an hour to do," Moine says of Gau.

6   When two people talk, they don't just fall into physical and aural harmony. They also engage in what is called motor mimicry If you show people pictures of a smiling face or a frowning face, they'll smile or frown back, although perhaps only in muscular changes so fleeting that they can only be captured with electronic sensors. If I hit my thumb with a hammer, most people watching will grimace: they'll mimic my emotional state. This is what is meant, in the technical sense, by empathy. We imitate each other's emotions as a way of expressing support and caring and, even more basically, as a way of communicating with each other.

7   In their brilliant 1994 book *Emotional Contagion*, the psychologists Elaine Hatfield and John Cacioppo and the historian Richard Rapson go one step further. Mimicry, they argue, is also one of the means by which we infect each other with our emotions. In other words, if I smile and you see me and smile in response—even a microsmile that takes no more than several milliseconds—it's not just you imitating or empathizing with me. It may also be a way that I can pass on my happiness to you. Emotion is contagious. In a way, this is perfectly intuitive. All of us have had our spirits picked up by being around somebody in

rapport
relationship

aural related to the sense of hearing/ listening

motor mimicry body motions moving with what is being said and/or heard

a good mood. If you think about this closely, though, it's quite a radical notion. We normally think of the expressions on our face as the reflection of an inner state. I feel happy, so I smile. I feel sad, so I frown. Emotion goes inside-out. Emotional contagion, though, suggests that the opposite is also true. If I can make you smile, I can make you happy. If I can make you frown, I can make you sad. Emotion, in this sense, goes outside-in.

8   If we think about emotion this way—as outside-in, not inside-out—it is possible to understand how some people can have an enormous amount of influence over others. Some of us, after all, are very good at expressing emotions and feelings, which means that we are far more emotionally contagious than the rest of us. Psychologists call these people "senders." Senders have special personalities. They are also physiologically different. Scientists who have studied faces, for example, report that there are huge differences among people in the location of facial muscles, in their form, and also—surprisingly— even in their prevalence. "It is a situation not unlike the medicine," says Cacioppo. "There are carriers, people who are very expressive, and there are people who are especially susceptible. It's not that emotional contagion is a disease. But the mechanism is the same."

prevalence
occurrences, times
something happens

9   Howard Friedman, a psychologist at the University of California at Riverside, has developed what he calls the Affective-Communication Test to measure this ability to send emotion, to be contagious. The test is a self-administered survey, with thirteen questions relating to things like whether you can keep still when you hear good dance music, how loud your laugh is, whether you touch friends when you talk to them, how good you are at sending seductive glances, whether you like to be the center of attention. The highest possible score on the test is 117 points, with the average score, according to Friedman, somewhere around 71.

10   What does it mean to be a high-scorer? To answer that, Friedman conducted a fascinating experiment. He picked a few dozen people who scored very high on his test—above 90—and a few dozen who scored very low—below 6—and asked them all to fill out a questionnaire measuring how they felt "at this instant." He then put all of the high-scorers in separate rooms, and paired each of them with two low-scorers. They were told to sit in the room together for two minutes. They could look at each other, but not talk. Then, once the session was over, they were asked again to fill out a detailed questionnaire on how they were feeling. Friedman found that in just two minutes, without a word being spoken, the low-scorers ended up picking up the moods of the high-scorers. If the charismatic person started out depressed, and the inexpressive person started out happy, by the end of the two minutes the inexpressive person was depressed as well. But it didn't work the other way. Only the charismatic person could infect the other people in the room with his or her emotions.

11   Is this what Tom Gau did to me? The thing that strikes me most about my encounter with him was his voice. He had the range of an opera singer. At times, he would sound stern. (His favorite expression in that state: "Excuse me?") At times, he would drawl, lazily and easily. At other times, he would chuckle as he spoke, making his words sing with laughter. In each of those modes his face would light up accordingly, moving, easily and deftly, from one state to another. There was no ambiguity in his presentation. Everything was written on his face. I could not see my own face, of course, but my guess

Continued on next page.

is that it was a close mirror of his. It is interesting, in this context, to think back on the experiment with the nodding and the headphones. There was an example of someone persuaded from the outside-in, of an external gesture affecting an internal decision. Was I nodding when Tom Gau nodded? And shaking my head when Gau shook his head? Later, I called Gau up and asked him to take Howard Friedman's charisma test. As we went through the list, question by question, he started chuckling. By question 11—"I am terrible at pantomime, as in games like charades"—he was laughing out loud. "I'm great at that! I always win at charades!" Out of a possible 117 points, he scored 116.

Check Your Understanding

6. Use context clues and word part analysis to define the following words from this passage.

   • erroneous (paragraph 2): _____

   • synchronized (paragraph 5): _____

   • pantomime (paragraph 11): _____

7. The author presents three major supporting details regarding how two (or more) people talk. Complete the graphic to show the three key points.

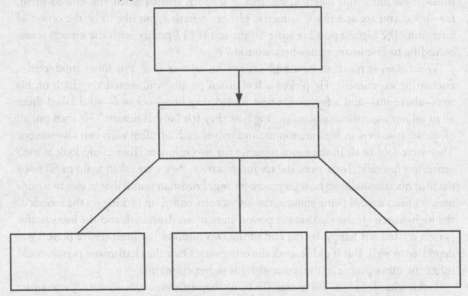

8. Based on your understanding, explain what the author means by physical and aural harmony.

   _____

   _____

9. The author never clearly explains what type of person scores high or low on Howard Friedman's Affective Communication Test. Based on what he says about the people who took it, what do you infer a high score means?

_____

_____

10. Based on your understanding of the Affective Communication Test, what do you believe your score would be if you were to take the test? Explain why it would be high or low.

_____

_____

BRAIN STRENGTH OPTIONS

Working individually or in groups of no more than three people, complete one of the following options.

1. Create a PowerPoint presentation illustrating textbook marking and annotations. Select a brief reading of about the length used in the Practice with a Reading (p. 422). Make a copy of the reading, and using what you learned in the chapter, mark it up. For example, highlight main ideas and major supporting details and write margin notes. You might define vocabulary terms or even add a picture that illustrates the meaning of new vocabulary. Be sure to include all the steps to effective textbook marking. You will have to make the sections small enough so that your audience can see a section at a time on a PowerPoint slide. You can retype or use a camera or scanner to capture the reading in sections. The more people involved in the project, the more creative your use of PowerPoint should be. You will present your PowerPoint to the class (or the instructor may have you post it online for other students to use to review the chapter).

2. Working alone, create a poster. Apply the same guidelines as in Option 1 above.

3. Working alone, take three articles from a magazine or the Internet. Highlight the main idea and major supporting details. Because you are highlighting what is actually printed, you will have to select material that has stated, not implied main ideas and details. Mark the articles by writing margin notes, using at least five symbols or notes per article.

4. Using PowerPoint or the app of your choice, create flash cards that review the material in this chapter in the form of question and response. For example, on the prompt card, you may have a blank to be filled in or a question to be answered. Create at least 30 prompts and responses. You will present the flash cards to the class as a review.

Using Visuals to Increase Your Understanding of Textbooks

MATT CORNETT

A math major at Schoolcraft College

"There is nothing in the mind which was not first in the senses."

—ARISTOTLE

Courtesy of Matt Cornett

BEFORE I CAME HERE (TO COLLEGE), visuals never played a part. One of my teachers in my earlier math courses told me that if you are ever stuck, draw a picture; it will jog your memory. And during the early math courses I was stuck a lot, especially on the story problems. You just see a wall of words; you just get so confused and befuddled. I learned that after I would stop and draw what I was reading, I was able to interpret the picture more easily than the text. But after a while of drawing pictures, I was able to look at the text and see the visuals in my head without actually having to draw them out. It was like a gateway to understanding the problems better.

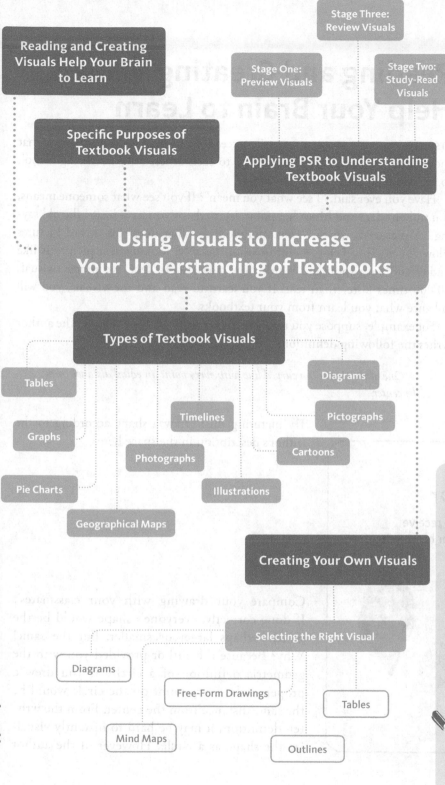

Reading and Creating Visuals Help Your Brain to Learn

Specific Purposes of Textbook Visuals

Stage Three: Review Visuals

Stage One: Preview Visuals

Stage Two: Study-Read Visuals

Applying PSR to Understanding Textbook Visuals

Using Visuals to Increase Your Understanding of Textbooks

Types of Textbook Visuals

Tables

Graphs

Pie Charts

Geographical Maps

Timelines

Photographs

Illustrations

Diagrams

Pictographs

Cartoons

Creating Your Own Visuals

Selecting the Right Visual

Diagrams

Free-Form Drawings

Mind Maps

Tables

Outlines

© Cengage Learning

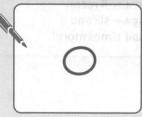

Reading and Creating Visuals Help Your Brain to Learn

VISUALS PROVIDE A QUICK, easily accessible format for information that shows you how ideas connect or relate to each other. They can bring a book to life and help explain difficult ideas.

Have you ever said, "I see what you mean"? If you see what someone means, you truly understand his or her point. Or perhaps you have heard the old saying, "A picture is worth a thousand words." What does this mean? Pictures allow you to absorb lots of information quickly; looking at a picture is like understanding a thousand words in a moment. In fact, we process visuals 60,000 times faster than text! If you learn to read and use visuals, you will enhance what you learn from your textbooks.

For example, suppose you read a textbook section about shapes. The author writes the following definition:

One of the shapes is a curved line with every point an equal distance from the center.

Try picturing this: Draw a shape according to the author's description in the space here.

Tip FROM THE Brain Doctor

Did you know that if you receive information by reading or hearing it, after 72 hours you will recall only 10% of it (if there is no additional repetition of the material)? That won't help you for the test. But if you add a visual to the information, you will recall 65%—six and a half times more!

Compare your drawing with your classmates'. If done correctly, everyone's shape would be the same! Perhaps larger or smaller, but the same! Why? Because the author provided you with the geometric definition of a circle. If you drew a proper circle, every point on the circle would be the same distance from the center. From the written definition, it may be hard to instantly visualize the shape as a circle. However, if the author provided a visual of a circle, you would instantly understand the description. It can be much easier for the brain to understand something with a visual rather than a written definition or detailed description. Imagine having both!

This chapter introduces you to two specific strategies for learning from visuals—decoding visuals and encoding visuals. When you decode visuals that are in your textbook, you interpret them. This requires that you create meaning from an author's visuals in a way that makes sense with the author's written words. When you encode visuals, you translate what you have read into some graphic form. This requires that you understand what you have read.

decode to interpret into a language that makes sense to a reader

encode to convert text into a code (in this case a visual)

Not only are visuals enjoyable, they help you to make connections with information and remember. As you learned in Chapter 2, sensory input is the first step in the memory process. People begin to learn by first taking information through their senses. Knowing this, most textbooks provide many different types of visuals to help students speed up comprehension and add to the meaning of the written content. Visuals increase your comprehension, recollection, and retention of information and bring life to the text. Think about the benefits of visuals the next time you think about skipping over them in a textbook.

Specific Purposes of Textbook Visuals

IT IS IMPORTANT TO KNOW THAT AUTHORS use a variety of visuals for specific purposes. Each visual an author selects is intended to emphasize a specific point in the text. What words say in sentences, visuals can shout in one image or table. Authors carefully select their visuals to support and reinforce ideas.

Read the following psychology passage, and then look at the photographs the author selected to support his content. The author provides you with more than a definition.

Tip FROM THE Brain Doctor

Did you know that visuals are so important to the brain that there is a scientific name for the importance? Scientists call it PSE: Pictorial Superiority Effect. What does the name tell you about the relationship between your study skills and pictures? A picture is superior to words—people remember pictures better than words.

Cohort Effects

Suppose you had been born in the 1940s. Your childhood and adolescence would have been very different from today: no Internet, computers, iPods, cell phones, air conditioners, automatic dishwashers, or appliances for washing and drying clothes. You would have listened to radio instead of watching television. Long-distance telephone calls were

Children of the 1940s and 1990s differed in their behavior because they grew up in different historical eras, with different education, nutrition, and health care. Differences based on such influences are called *cohort effects*.

a luxury. Few women or minorities went to college, and those few had limited job opportunities afterward. If you had lived then, how would you have been different?

Source: From KALAT. *Introduction to Psychology* (pp. 160–61). Copyright © 2011 Cengage Learning.

How is the author using the photographs? Do you believe that the two photographs help readers answer the author's question, "If you had lived then, how would you have been different?" The photographs provide the reader with two clearly different scenarios. If you were having trouble trying to imagine the differences, the photographs would provide you with connections to then and now. The photographs stimulate ideas and create interest.

For another example, examine the cover of the following physics textbook. Although you have not read anything from this text at this point, you can learn a little bit about the content just from the photograph on the cover. The photograph intends to create a connection with the reader. What is happening in the photograph? Is it interesting? Is it current? What message does the photograph send in relation to the title of the textbook? Think it through.

The skier is moving, which signals motion. She is moving quickly at a specific angle, which signals speed and energy. The movement looks powerful, which signals force. She is using equipment designed specifically to maximize speed and movement and most likely to account for the wind and snow. Physics is the science that deals with matter, energy, motion, and force. Do you believe that the cover is a good introduction to the textbook's content?

INQUIRY INTO
PHYSICS
SEVENTH EDITION
Wern J. Ostdiek
Donald J. Bord

© Chase Jarvis/Corbis

Applying PSR to Understand Textbook Visuals

VISUALS CLEARLY ENHANCE LEARNING, so as you read any text, be sure to carefully read any visuals that accompany the text. You will use the same stages of PSR you used in Chapter 8—preview, study-read, and review.

Stage One: Preview Visuals

DO YOU ALREADY preview textbook visuals? Previewing visuals, just like previewing text, gives you a better idea of what you will be learning. During the preview stage of your reading:

1. Read the title and caption or whatever text accompanies the visual so that you will know what idea in the text the visual illustrates.

2. Predict what the author's purpose for the visual is.

Preview this sociology passage and visual as an example.

Culture Shock

1   People who travel to other countries often experience culture shock—a sense of confusion, uncertainty, disorientation, or anxiety that accompanies exposure to an unfamiliar way of life or environment. Familiar cues about how to behave are missing or have a different meaning. Culture shock affects people differently, but the most stressful changes involve

About 75 percent of the world's people consume insects, which are high in protein, vitamins, and fiber and usually low in fat. More than two out of every three American adults are overweight or obese, the highest percentage on the planet (Flegal et al. 2010). Would we be healthier if we ate insects instead of gulping down hamburgers and French fries?

the type of food eaten, the type of clothes worn, punctuality, ideas about what offends people, the language spoken, differences in personal hygiene, the general pace of life, a lack of privacy, and concern about finances (Spradley and Phillips 1972; Pedersen 1995).

2   To some degree, everyone is culture bound because they've internalized cultural norms and values. For example, an American journalist who works in Mexico City says that perpetual lateness is common: A child's birthday party may start 2 or 3 hours late, a wedding may begin an hour after the announced time, and interviews with top Mexico City officials may be up to 2 hours late or the official never arrives. These norms are changing because of the growth of Mexico's global economy, but the more relaxed attitude of time in Mexico City (and elsewhere) can be a culture shock to someone from the United States who has grown up in a "clock-obsessed" culture (Ellingwood 2009).

3   American students who have studied abroad often experience culture shock when they return, such as in readjusting to traffic jams, the pace of daily life, and the emphasis on work above personal life. For example, a student who studied in Ecuador said that she missed the sense of community she had felt: "Back in the United States, I noticed how separate and selfish people can be at times" (Goodkin 2005).

4   A major component of culture is popular culture. Popular culture has an enormous impact on many contemporary societies.

Source: From BENOKRAITIS. *SOC* 2e (pp. 52–3). Copyright © 2012 Cengage Learning.

The title of the passage gives you a good idea about the content of the reading—culture shock. What do you already know about culture shock? Have you experienced it yourself? When? What question did you develop from the title?

Now focus on the visual. You have read the caption so you can predict the content of the visual. What do you think the author's purpose for this visual is? Unless you eat insects, you are probably shocked by the visual. The author's purpose is to convince you, the reader, that culture shock exists.

Stage Two: Study-Read Visuals

AS YOU STUDY-READ text, stop at the visuals and study-read them, too. When you study-read visuals, use the following steps:

1. Decide if your prediction from the previewing step is correct by analyzing the content of the visual.

2. Mark the visual with a symbol or note in the margin so you remember why the visual is important when you are studying.

Go back to the culture shock passage on page 437 and study-read it and the visual. In the previewing step, you may have read the title of the passage and asked, "What is culture shock?" Read the passage carefully, and look for the answer to that question. You should treat the whole passage as one section. Highlight the main idea in green and supporting details in yellow. You may want to underline important vocabulary that is not in boldfaced type or examples that help you remember main points. Write margin notes. Remember that if you mark something in the text, you should add a margin note that tells you why, unless specific highlighter colors already indicate why. Also, analyze the visual. Confirm what the author's purpose was for including it, and write a margin note next to it.

What margin note did you write? What symbol or word best captures the main point of the visual? You want to pick a word that tells you, at a glance, why the visual is important. What about the work *yuck*? It shows shock at eating insects and demonstrates the first supporting idea from the passage: *To some degree, everyone is culture bound because they've internalized cultural norms and values.*

Stage Three: Review Visuals

IN THE REVIEW stage of PSR, you go back to the main idea statement to begin reviewing and then organize your material for recall. Later in this chapter, you will learn how outlines and other visuals you create can help you organize textbook material for recall. Use these steps to review textbook visuals:

1. Recall the main idea of the reading.

2. Mentally associate the visuals that you find particularly meaningful to textbook ideas you want to remember.

If you go back to the culture shock passage on page 437, you recall that the main idea is *People who travel to other countries often experience culture shock.*

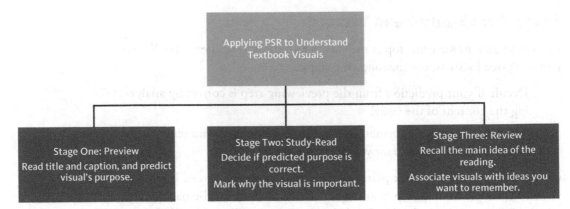

Figure 10.1 Applying PSR to Understand Textbook Visuals

What part of the visual from this passage best shows shock? Most people would say the insects on a plate.

Most of your textbook reading assignments will be longer than the culture shock passage, but the process for understanding visuals is the same—preview, study-read, and review. (See Figure 10.1.) With practice, this process can be automatic and quick.

ACTIVITY 10A
Apply PSR to Understand Visuals

1. Preview the following passage and visual from a psychology textbook. Predict what the passage and visual will be about.

_____

2. Now study-read by highlighting the main idea in green and the supporting details in yellow. Underline unfamiliar vocabulary that is not already in boldfaced type and other ideas you think may help you remember new information. Write margin notes.

Scientific Method

1   The methods of psychology rely primarily on observation, on information gathered by the senses. Because psychologists depend on observation, they typically use the scientific method

as the main tool for investigating behavior and mind. To understand the effect of subliminal messages, then, we must first employ the scientific method. Reduced to its barest essentials, the scientific method contains four important steps:

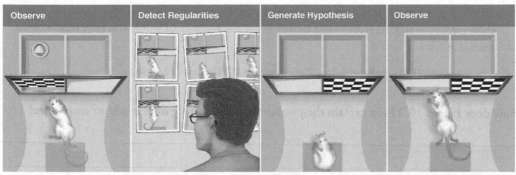

Observe	Detect Regularities	Generate Hypothesis	Observe
The rat receives food for jumping through the checkerboard panel on the left.	Over trials, the rat consistently chooses to jump toward the checkerboard panel on the left.	The rat has learned to associate the checkerboard with food, so if the checkerboard is moved to the right, the rat will jump to the right.	The rat jumps to the left, suggesting it has learned that jumping left produces food.

Figure 10.2 **The Scientific Method: Four Major Steps**

1. Observe. The rat jumps toward the checkerboard panel on the left. 2. Detect regularities in behavior. The researcher notes that the rat, over repeated trials, consistently jumps to the checkerboard on the left. 3. Generate a hypothesis: If I move the checkerboard to the right, the rat will jump to the right. 4. Observe to test the hypothesis. Here the hypothesis turns out to be wrong. The rat jumps left again instead of following the checkerboard.

1. Observe. The scientific method always begins, appropriately, with observation. In psychology, we choose the behavior of interest and begin recording its characteristics as well as the conditions under which the behavior occurs.

2. Detect regularities. Next the researcher looks for regularities in the observations. Are there certain consistent features or conditions under which the behaviors commonly appear?

3. Generate a hypothesis. In step three, the researcher forms a hypothesis, which is essentially a prediction about the characteristics of the behavior under study. Hypotheses are normally expressed in the form of testable if-then statements: If some set of conditions is present and observed, then a certain kind of behavior will occur.

4. Observe. Finally, the predictions of the hypothesis are checked for accuracy once again through observation. If new data are consistent with the prediction of the hypothesis, the hypothesis is supported.

> **scientific method** A multistep technique that generates empirical knowledge—that is, knowledge derived from systematic observations of the world.

Continued on next page.

2   Notice that the scientific method is anchored on both ends by observation: Observation always begins and ends the scientific process. This means that psychological terms must be defined in a way that allows for observation. To make certain that terms and concepts meet this criterion, psychologists often use **operational definitions**, which define concepts specifically in terms of how those concepts can be measured (Levine & Parkinson, 1994; Stevens, 1939). For example, intelligence might be defined operationally as performance on a psychological test, and memory might be defined as the number of words correctly recalled on a retention test.

Source: From NAIRNE. *Psychology* 5e (pp. 27–8). Copyright © 2009 Cengage Learning.

3. How does Figure 10.2 help explain the passage? What meaning does it add or emphasize?

_____

_____

4. What is the author's purpose for Figure 10.2?

_____

_____

5. What part or parts of Figure 10.2 could you picture in your mind to help you remember what you read?

_____

_____

✔ COMPREHENSION CHECK

▶ List the key points made in this chapter so far.
▶ Up to this point in the chapter, what is unclear?

Types of Textbook Visuals

THE TYPE OF VISUAL AN AUTHOR USES IS DETERMINED by the author's purpose for writing the text and by the content of the text. The most common types of visuals found in textbooks include:

▶ tables

▶ pictographs

▶ diagrams

▶ photographs

▶ illustrations   ▶ time lines

▶ graphs   ▶ geographical maps

▶ pie charts   ▶ cartoons

Tables

TABLES, ALSO KNOWN as charts or matrices, are visuals where large amounts of information are condensed into a format, usually using categories, that make it easy to see how different items of information relate to each other. Tables work especially well for information from history, economics, and psychology textbooks because many chapters in these books are organized by using comparison and contrast format. Tables are also used in biology, pharmacy, and nursing textbooks to show hierarchy.

table visual where large amounts of text are condensed into a format, usually using categories, that make it easy to see how different items of information relate to each other

hierarchy a ranking order of persons or things, one above the other

ACTIVITY 10B
Read a Table

1. Preview the following passage and visual from a world history textbook. Predict what the passage and visual are going to be about.

_____

2. Study-read the passage and visual. Highlight the main idea in green and the supporting details in yellow. Underline unfamiliar vocabulary that is not already in boldfaced type and other ideas you think may help you remember new information. Write margin notes.

The Phoenicians

1   A Semitic-speaking people, the Phoenicians lived in the area of Palestine along the Mediterranean coast on a narrow band of land 120 miles long. Their newfound political independence after the demise of Hittite and Egyptian power helped the Phoenicians expand the trade that was already the foundation of their prosperity. The chief cities of Phoenicia (Byblos, Tyre, and Sidon) were ports on the eastern Mediterranean, but they also served as distribution centers for the lands to the east in Mesopotamia. The Phoenicians themselves produced a number of goods for foreign markets, including purple dye, glass, wine, and lumber from the famous cedars of Lebanon. In addition, the Phoenicians improved their ships and became great international sea traders. They charted new routes, not only in the Mediterranean but also in the Atlantic Ocean, where they reached Britain and sailed south along the west coast of Africa. The Phoenicians established a number of colonies in the western Mediterranean, including settlements in southern Spain, Sicily, and Sardinia. Carthage, the Phoenicians most famous colony, was located on the north coast of Africa.

Continued on next page.

TABLE 10.1 The Phoenician, Greek, and Roman Alphabets

PHOENICIAN			GREEK			ROMAN	
Phoenician	Phoenician Name	Modern Symbol	Early Greek	Classical Greek	Greek Name	Early Latin	Classical Latin
ⴲ	'aleph	'	Λ	A	alpha	A	A
ⴰ	beth	b	B	B	beta		B
ⴷ	gimel	g	𐌂	Γ	gamma		C
ⴸ	daleth	d	Δ	Δ	delta	D	D
ⴹ	he	h	𐌄	E	epsilon	F	E
Y	waw	w	F		digamma	F	F

Source: Andrew Robinson, *The Story of Writing* (London, 1995), p. 170

2   Culturally, the Phoenicians are best known as transmitters. Instead of using pictographs or signs to represent whole words and syllables as the Mesopotamians and Egyptians did, the Phoenicians simplified their writing by using twenty-two different signs to represent the sounds of their speech. These twenty-two characters or letters could be used to spell out all the words in the Phoenician language. Although the Phoenicians were not the only people to invent an alphabet, theirs would have special significance because it was eventually passed on to the Greeks. From the Greek alphabet was derived the Roman alphabet that we still use today (Table 10.1 shows the derivation of the letters A to F). The Phoenicians achieved much while independent, but they ultimately fell subject to the Assyrians and Persians.

Source: From DUIKER/SPIELVOGEL. *World History* 5e (pp. 24–5). Copyright © 2007 Cengage Learning.

3. How does Table 10.1 help explain the passage? What meaning does it add or emphasize?

_____

_____

4. What is the author's purpose for Table 10.1?

_____

_____

5. What part of Table 10.1 could you picture in your mind to help you remember what you have read?

_____

_____

Diagrams

A DIAGRAM SHOWS the connections between related pieces of information using drawings and labels. The sections or parts of something (for example, a body, machine, plant, or building) can be emphasized clearly through the use of a diagram because the parts are labeled. Many science books use detailed, labeled diagrams of the topics they discuss.

diagram drawing with markings to show how something is put together or works

ACTIVITY 10C
Read a Diagram

1. Preview the following passage and visual from a biology textbook. Predict what the passage and visual are going to be about.

_____

2. Study-read the passage and visual. Highlight the main idea in green and the supporting details in yellow. Underline unfamiliar vocabulary that is not already in boldfaced type and any other ideas you think may help you remember new information. Write margin notes.

Energy Flows Through Ecosystems

1   Like individual organisms, ecosystems depend on a continuous input of energy. A self-sufficient ecosystem contains three types of organisms—producers, consumers, and decomposers—and has a physical environment appropriate for their survival. These organisms depend on each other and on the environment for nutrients, energy, oxygen, and carbon dioxide. However, there is a one-way flow of energy through ecosystems. Organisms can neither create energy nor use it with complete efficiency. During every energy transaction, some energy disperses into the environment as heat and is no longer available to the organism (Figure 10.3).

2   **Producers**, or **autotrophs**, are plants, algae, and certain bacteria that produce their own food from simple raw materials. Most of these organisms use sunlight as an energy source and carry out **photosynthesis**, the process in which producers synthesize complex molecules from carbon dioxide and water. The light energy is transformed into chemical energy, which is stored within the chemical bonds of the food molecules produced. Oxygen, which is required not only by plant cells but also by the cells of most other organisms, is produced as a by-product of photosynthesis:

Carbon dioxide + water + light energy → sugars (food) + oxygen

Continued on next page.

Figure 10.3 Energy Flow

Continuous energy input from the sun operates the biosphere. During photosynthesis, producers use the energy from sunlight to make complex molecules from carbon dioxide and water. Consumers, such as the caterpillar and robin shown here, obtain energy, carbon, and other needed materials when they eat producers or consumers that have eaten producers. Wastes and dead organic material supply decomposers with energy and carbon. During every energy transaction, some energy is lost to biological systems, dispersing into the environment as heat.

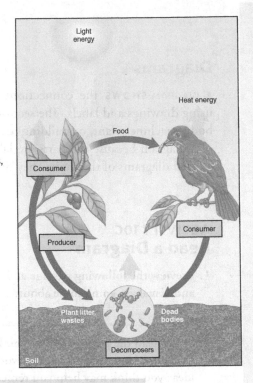

Animals are **consumers**, or **heterotrophs**— that is, organisms that depend on producers for food, energy, and oxygen. Consumers obtain energy by breaking down sugars and other food molecules originally produced during photosynthesis. When chemical bonds are broken during this process of cellular respiration, their stored energy is made available for life processes:

Sugars (and other food molecules) + oxygen → carbon dioxide + water + energy

Consumers contribute to the balance of the ecosystem. For example, consumers produce carbon dioxide needed by producers. (Note that producers also carry on cellular respiration.) The metabolism of consumers and producers helps maintain the life-sustaining mixture of gases in the atmosphere.

3   Bacteria and fungi are **decomposers**, heterotrophs that obtain nutrients by breaking down nonliving organic material such as wastes, dead leaves and branches, and the bodies of dead organisms. In their process of obtaining energy, decomposers make the components of these materials available for reuse. If decomposers did not exist, nutrients would remain locked up in dead bodies, and the supply of elements required by living systems would soon be exhausted.

Source: From SOLOMON/BERG/MARTIN. *Biology* 7e (pp. 13–14). Copyright © 2005 Cengage Learning.

3. How does Figure 10.3 help explain the passage? What meaning does it add or emphasize?

_____

_____

4. What is the author's purpose for Figure 10.3?

_____

_____

5. What part of Figure 10.3 could you picture in your mind to help you remember what you have read?

_____

_____

Illustrations

AN ILLUSTRATION IS a drawing that allows an author to show you what he or she is writing about. For example, if an author were writing about a rose, an illustration of a rose would bring additional meaning to the text. It would show the bush it comes from, a stem, thorns, leaves, and petals. It might even show some decay on a leaf or a bee flying around the flower. All of these details help readers see the idea of a rose more clearly.

illustration a drawing

ACTIVITY 10D
Read an Illustration

1. Preview the following passage and visual from a world history textbook. Predict what the passage and visual are going to be about.

_____

2. Study-read the passage and visual. Highlight the main idea in green and the supporting details in yellow. Underline unfamiliar vocabulary that is not already in boldfaced type and any other ideas you think may help you remember new information. Write margin notes.

1   A single instance underscores how differently people of diverse cultures view the world and how various ways of seeing can cause sharp differences in how artists depict the world. Illustrated here are two contemporaneous portraits of a 19th-century Maori chieftain (Figure 10.4)—one by an Englishman, John Sylvester (active early 19th century), and the other by the New Zealand chieftain himself, Te Pehi Kupe (d. 1829). Both reproduce the chieftain's facial tattooing. The European artist (Figure 10.4, left) included the head and shoulders and underplayed the tattooing. The tattoo pattern is one aspect of the likeness

Continued on next page.

John Sylvester/The Bridgeman Art Library/Getty Image

Te Pehi Kupe Self-portrait, 1826. Source: Horatio Gordon Robley's Moko; or Maori Tattooing, 1896

Figure 10.4 *Left:* John Henry Sylvester, *Portrait of Te Pehi Kupe*, 1826, Watercolor, 8¼" × 6¼". National Library of Australia, Canberra (Rex Nan Kivell Collection). *Right:* Te Pehi Kupe, *Self-Portrait*, 1826. From Leo Frobenius, *The Childhood of Man* (New York: J. B. Lippincott, 1909).

These strikingly different portraits of the same Maori chief reveal how differently Western and non-Western artists "see" a subject. Understanding the cultural context of artworks is vital to art history.

among many, no more or less important than the chieftain's European attire. Sylvester also recorded his subject's momentary glance toward the right and the play of light on his hair, fleeting aspects that have nothing to do with the figure's identity.

2   In contrast, Te Pehi Kupe's self-portrait (Figure 10.4, right)—made during a trip to Liverpool, England, to obtain European arms to take back to New Zealand—is not a picture of a man situated in space and bathed in light. Rather, it is the chieftain's statement of the supreme importance of the tattoo design that symbolizes his rank among his people. Remarkably, Te Pehi Kupe created the tattoo patterns from memory, without the aid of a mirror. The splendidly composed insignia, presented as a flat design separated from the body and even from the head, is Te Pehi Kupe's image of himself. Only by understanding the cultural context of each portrait can viewers hope to understand why either representation appears as it does.

Source: From KLEINER. *Gardner's Art through the Ages: A Global History, Volume I*, 13e (p. 13). Copyright © 2009 Cengage Learning.

3. How does Figure 10.4 help explain the passage? What meaning does it add or emphasize?

_____

_____

4. What is the author's purpose for Figure 10.4?

_____

_____

5. What part of Figure 10.4 could you picture in your mind to help you remember what you have read?

_____

_____

Graphs

GRAPHS ARE USED TO make large amounts of information easily accessible so that you can see at a glance the similarities or differences between the items being discussed or recognize trends over time, such as consumer preferences for different brands of food or clothing. It is important to read the labels on the horizontal and vertical axes so that you can correctly interpret the information provided. There are several types of graphs, each of which is used for different purposes, including bar graphs and line graphs.

graph visual that shows changes in quantities, usually with a horizontal and vertical axis

bar graph graph that illustrates information by using parallel rectangular bars of varying length to contrast information

line graph graph that displays information as a series of data points connected by straight line segments

Figure 10.5 is a graph that shows how working memory capacity changes over a person's lifetime. You may recall from Chapter 2 that working memory is the system by which you can hold a certain amount of information in your brain for a fairly brief period of time so that you can work with it, such as remembering a phone number long enough to dial it. According to Figure 10.5, a person's working memory capacity (shown by the vertical axis) changes over his or her lifetime (shown by the horizontal axis). At first it gets better and then begins a decline. You see a line that gradually goes up, peaks, and then starts going down. Generally speaking, through life your memory gradually gets better and then begins to decline. On average a person can remember from four to seven bits of information at a time. However, the number of items remembered can be affected by age. Where do you stand in this graph?

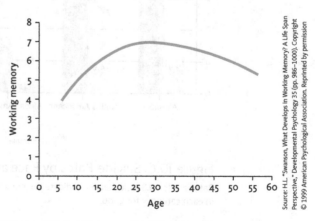

Figure 10.5 Changes in Working Memory During a Person's Life (from Swanson, 1999).

ACTIVITY 10E
Read a Graph

1. Preview the following passage and visual from a sociology textbook. Predict what the passage and visual are going to be about.

_____

2. Study-read the passage and visual. Highlight the main idea in green and the supporting details in yellow. Underline unfamiliar vocabulary that is not already in boldfaced type and any other ideas you think may help you remember new information. Write margin notes.

Race

Racial subordination may be a factor in some suicides. Figure 10.6 displays U.S. suicides in terms of race and sex.) This fact is most glaringly reflected in the extremely high rate of suicide among Native Americans, who constitute about 1 percent of the U.S. population. The rate of suicide among young Native American males on government-owned reservations is especially high, and almost 60 percent of Native American suicides involve firearms (National Center for Injury Prevention and Control, 2009). Most research has focused on individualistic reasons why young Native Americans commit suicide; however, analysts using a race-and-ethnic framework focus on the effect of social inequalities and racial discrimination on suicidal behavior.

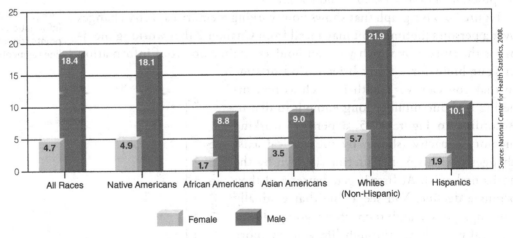

Figure 10.6 Suicide Rates by Race and Sex

Rates are for U.S. suicides and indicate the number of deaths by suicide for every 100,000 people in each category for 2006.

Source: From KENDALL. *Sociology in Our Times: The Essentials* (p. 20). Copyright © 2012 Cengage Learning.

3. How does Figure 10.6 help explain the passage? What meaning does it add or emphasize?

_____

_____

4. What is the author's purpose for Figure 10.6?

_____

_____

5. What part of Figure 10.6 could you picture in your mind to help you remember what you have read?

_____

_____

Pie Charts

PIE CHARTS ARE a specific type of chart that is presented in a circle format. Pie charts show how pieces of data relate to the whole and usually look like sliced pies. They represent data by using a circle to show the whole and slices or wedges to show how the whole is divided up. The wedges are usually in different colors and represent each component being measured.

pie chart circular visual that is divided into sections like a pie illustrating proportion

ACTIVITY 10F
Read a Pie Chart

1. Preview the following passage and visual from a sociology textbook. Predict what the passage and visual are going to be about.

_____

2. Study-read the passage and visual. Highlight the main idea in green and the supporting details in yellow. Underline unfamiliar vocabulary that is not already in boldfaced type and any other ideas you think may help you remember new information. Write margin notes.

Parenting Roles

1   Like workplace roles, parenting does not come naturally. Most first-time parents muddle through by trial and error. Family sociologists often point out that we get more training for driving a car than for marriage and parenting. For example, most couples don't realize that

Continued on next page.

raising children is expensive. Middle-income couples, with an average income of $ 77,000 a year, spend about 16 percent of their earnings on a child during the first 2 years (see Figure 10.7). Child-rearing costs are much higher for single parents and especially for low-income families if a child is disabled, chronically ill, or needs specialized care that welfare benefits don't cover (Lukemeyer et al. 2000; Lino and Carlson 2009).

2   Arguments over finances and child-rearing strategies are two of the major reasons for divorce. All in all, adjusting to marital and parental roles during adulthood requires considerable patience, effort, and work.

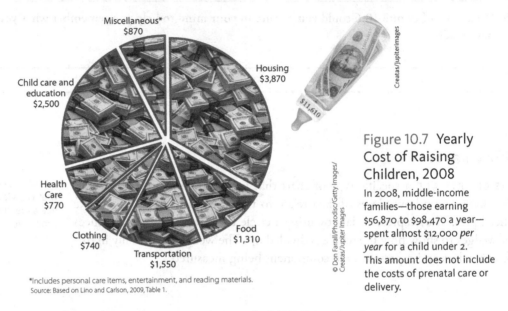

Miscellaneous*
$870

Housing
$3,870

Child care and
education
$2,500

Health
Care
$770

Clothing
$740

Transportation
$1,550

Food
$1,310

$11,610

Creatas/Jupiterimages

© Don Farrall/Photodisc/Getty Images/ Creatas/Jupiter Images

*Includes personal care items, entertainment, and reading materials.
Source: Based on Lino and Carlson, 2009, Table 1.

Figure 10.7 Yearly Cost of Raising Children, 2008

In 2008, middle-income families—those earning $56,870 to $98,470 a year—spent almost $12,000 *per year* for a child under 2. This amount does not include the costs of prenatal care or delivery.

Source: From BENOKRAITIS. *SOC* 2e (p. 78). Copyright © 2012 Cengage Learning.

3. How does Figure 10.7 help explain the passage? What meaning does it add or emphasize?

_____

_____

4. What is the author's purpose for Figure 10.7?

_____

_____

5. What part of Figure 10.7 could you picture in your mind to help you remember what you have read?

_____

_____

Pictographs

PICTOGRAPHS **REPRESENT DATA** through the use of pictures. They rely on information in the text to explain the pictures presented in the visual.

pictograph visual representing data through the use of pictures

ACTIVITY 10G
Read a Pictograph

1. Preview the following passage and visual from a sociology textbook. Predict what the passage and visual are going to be about.

_____

2. Study-read the passage and visual. Highlight the main idea in green and the supporting details in yellow. Underline unfamiliar vocabulary that is not already in boldfaced type and any other ideas you think may help you remember new information. Write margin notes.

Diffusion

1   A culture may change because of *diffusion*, the process through which components of culture spread from one society to another. Such borrowing may have occurred so long ago that the members of a society consider their culture to be entirely their own creation. However, anthropologist Ralph Linton (1964) has estimated that 90 percent of the elements of any culture are a result of diffusion (see Figure 10.8).

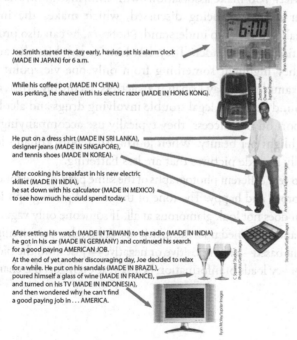

Joe Smith started the day early, having set his alarm clock (MADE IN JAPAN) for 6 a.m.

While his coffee pot (MADE IN CHINA) was perking, he shaved with his electric razor (MADE IN HONG KONG).

He put on a dress shirt (MADE IN SRI LANKA), designer jeans (MADE IN SINGAPORE), and tennis shoes (MADE IN KOREA).

After cooking his breakfast in his new electric skillet (MADE IN INDIA), he sat down with his calculator (MADE IN MEXICO) to see how much he could spend today.

After setting his watch (MADE IN TAIWAN) to the radio (MADE IN INDIA) he got in his car (MADE IN GERMANY) and continued his search for a good paying AMERICAN JOB.

At the end of yet another discouraging day, Joe decided to relax for a while. He put on his sandals (MADE IN BRAZIL), poured himself a glass of wine (MADE IN FRANCE), and turned on his TV (MADE IN INDONESIA), and then wondered why he can't find a good paying job in . . . AMERICA.

Figure 10.8 The 100-Percent American

Continued on next page.

2   Diffusion can be direct and conscious, occurring through trade, tourism, immigration, inter-
marriage, or the invasion of one country by another. Diffusion can also be indirect and largely
unconscious, as in the Internet transmissions that zip around the world.

Source: From BENOKRAITIS. *SOC* 2e (p. 56). Copyright © 2012 Cengage Learning.

3. How does Figure 10.8 help explain the passage? What meaning does it add or emphasize?

_____

_____

4. What is the author's purpose for Figure 10.8?

_____

_____

5. What part of Figure 10.8 could you picture in your mind to help you remember what you
have read?

_____

_____

Photographs

photograph a picture
made from light passing
through a camera onto film
or in digital form

PHOTOGRAPHS HELP YOU make associations with information in the text. They
help the reader see what's being discussed, which makes the information
clearer, more real, and easier to understand. Photographs can also provide more
subtle information to the reader. They can hint at any bias the author may
have because they highlight something from only one viewpoint. Consider
the following example: Lindsay Lohan is an actress, recording artist, and model
who has also found herself in legal trouble involving drugs and alcohol. When
newspapers report on her success, they typically use accompanying photos of
Lohan that highlight her beauty. When journalists report Lohan's legal struggles, they usually include pictures that are less flattering.

These are two very different photographs of the same person. The tone of the first
picture is glamorous and happy. The tone of the second photograph is markedly
different. Lohan does not look glamorous at all. If someone only vaguely knew of
Lindsay Lohan and happened upon an article about her, that person might quickly
make a judgment based—either positive or negative— just from the picture alone.
Photographs convey loads of information before text even gets the chance.

FeatureflasH/Shutterstock.com

Pool/Getty Images

A photograph has a lot to say, and an author's choice of photographs tells something about the author. Look for the tone as well as the subject matter when examining a photograph. All photographs show a point of view. What a photographer chooses to leave out of a photograph can be just as important as what he or she chooses to put in. Authors choose their photographs for a reason. Does the photograph color the way you read the text?

ACTIVITY 10H
Read a Photograph

1. Preview the following passage and visual from a culinary arts textbook. Predict what the passage and visual are going to be about.

_____

2. Study-read the passage and visual. Highlight the main idea in green and the supporting details in yellow. Underline unfamiliar vocabulary that is not already in boldfaced type and any other ideas you think may help you remember new information. Write margin notes.

Knife Grip and Positioning

1   There are different acceptable methods for gripping a knife, but there is a common method used by culinary professionals that provides control and stability. To begin, the knife is held by the handle while resting the side of the index finger against one side of the blade and placing the thumb on the other side of the blade. The hand not holding the knife is referred to as the guiding hand. The guiding hand is responsible for guiding the item to

Continued on next page.

be cut into the knife. To correctly position the fingers of the guiding hand, imitate the shape of a spider on the table. The fingertips should all be slightly tucked, yet touch the surface of the table. This guiding hand position is used to safely hold the food next to the blade of the knife.

2   Using the proper knife grip, the tip of the knife is placed on the cutting board. The guiding hand is placed next to the knife blade in the proper position, with fingertips slightly tucked under near the back half of the blade. The side of the blade should rest against the knuckle of the middle finger of the guiding hand. This position reduces the chances of cutting fingers. See Figure 10.9.

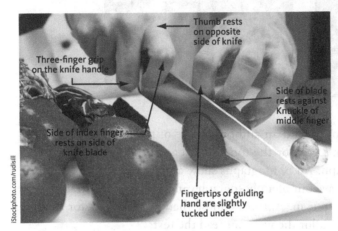

Figure 10.9 Knife Grip and Positioning

Using the proper knife grip with the knife hand, and with fingertips slightly tucked under with the guiding hand, the side of the blade should rest against the knuckle of the middle finger of the guiding hand.

Source: Mcgreal, *Culinary Arts Principals and Applications,* American Technical Publishers, Inc., 2012, p. 74.

3. How does Figure 10.9 help explain the passage? What meaning does it add or emphasize?

_____

_____

4. What is the author's purpose for Figure 10.9?

_____

_____

5. What part of Figure 10.9 could you picture in your mind to help you remember what you have read?

_____

_____

Time Lines

TIME LINES ARE visuals that are labeled marks on a line to show the time sequence or chronology of a series of events. Time lines are often used in history books to provide summaries of events that occurred over a period of time.

time line visual way of displaying events in chronological order

ACTIVITY 101
Read a Time Line

1. Preview the following passage and visual from a western civilization textbook. Predict what the passage and visual are going to be about.

_____

2. Study-read the passage and visual. Highlight the main idea in green and the supporting details in yellow. Underline unfamiliar vocabulary that is not already in boldfaced type and any other ideas you think may help you remember new information. Write margin notes.

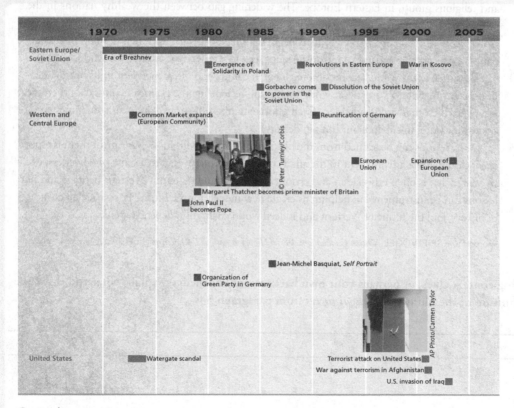

Continued on next page.

1   As the heirs of Western civilization have become aware that the problems humans face are global, not just national, they have responded to this challenge in different ways. One approach has been to develop grassroots social movements, including those devoted to the environment, women's and men's liberation, human potential, appropriate technologies, and nonviolence. "Think globally, act locally" is one slogan these groups use. Related to the emergence of these social movements is the growth of nongovernmental organizations (NGOs). According to one analyst, NGOs are an important instrument in the cultivation of global perspectives: "Since NGOs by definition are identified with interests that transcend national boundaries, we expect all NGOs to define problems in global terms, to take account of human interests and needs as they are found in all parts of the planet." NGOs are often represented at the United Nations and include professional, business, and cooperative organizations; foundations; religious, peace, and disarmament groups; youth and women's organizations; environmental and human rights groups; and research institutes. The number of international NGOs increased from 176 in 1910 to 29,000 in 1995.

2   Yet hopes for global approaches to global problems have also been hindered by political, ethnic, and religious disputes. Pollution of the Rhine River by factories along its banks provokes angry disputes among European nations, and the United States and Canada have argued about the effects of acid rain on Canadian forests. The collapse of the Soviet Union and its satellite system between 1989 and 1991 seemed to provide an enormous boost to the potential for international cooperation on global issues, but it has had almost the opposite effect. The bloody conflict in the former Yugoslavia indicates the dangers in the rise of nationalist sentiment among various ethnic and religious groups in Eastern Europe. The widening gap between the wealthy nations in the Northern Hemisphere and the poor, developing nations in the Southern Hemisphere threatens global economic stability. Many conflicts begin with regional issues and then develop into international concerns. International terrorist groups seek to wreak havoc around the world.

3   Thus even as the world becomes more global in culture and interdependent in its mutual relations, centrifugal forces are still at work attempting to redefine the political, cultural, and ethnic ways in which the world is divided. Such efforts are often disruptive and can sometimes work against measures to enhance our human destiny

4   Many lessons can be learned from the history of Western civilization, but one of them is especially clear. Lack of involvement in the affairs of one's society can lead to a sense of powerlessness. In an age that is often crisis-laden and chaotic, an understanding of our Western heritage and its lessons can be instrumental in helping us create new models for the future. For we are all creators of history, and the future of Western and indeed world civilization depends on us.

Source: From SPIELVOGEL. *Western Civilization: A Brief History* 4e (pp. 582–2). Copyright © 2008 Cengage Learning.

3. **Using context clues, or perhaps your own background knowledge, explain what you think the definition of the phrase *centrifugal forces* from paragraph 3 is.**

_____

_____

4. How does the time line help explain the passage? What meaning does it add or emphasize?

_____

_____

5. What is the author's purpose for the time line?

_____

_____

6. What part of the time line could you picture in your mind to help you remember what you have read?

_____

_____

Geographical Maps

GEOGRAPHICAL MAPS ARE visual representations of geographical areas. Authors use geographical maps to give perspective on an area they discuss. For example, an author may describe global trade and include a world map as a visual so that readers see which countries are participating against the background of the entire world. Maps are frequently used in history, political science, and anthropology textbooks.

geographical map visual representation of a geographical area

ACTIVITY 10J
Read a Geographical Map

1. Preview the following passage and visual from a world history textbook. Predict what the passage and visual are going to be about.

_____

2. Study-read the passage and visual. Highlight the main idea in green and the supporting details in yellow. Underline unfamiliar vocabulary that is not already in boldfaced type and any other ideas you think may help you remember new information. Write margin notes.

Continued on next page.

The Scramble for Africa

1   At the beginning of the 1880s, most of Africa was still independent. European rule was still limited to the fringes of the continent, and a few areas, such as Egypt, lower Nigeria, Senegal, and Mozambique, were under various forms of loose protectorate. But the trends were ominous, as the pace of European penetration was accelerating and the constraints that had limited European rapaciousness were fast disappearing.

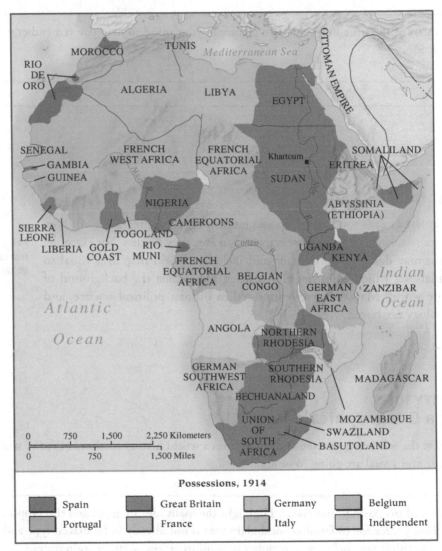

Figure 10.10 Africa in 1914.

By the beginning of 1900, virtually all of Africa was under some form of European rule. The territorial divisions established by colonial powers on the continent of Africa on the eve of World War I are shown here.

2   The scramble began in the mid-1880s, when several European states engaged in what today would be called a feeding frenzy. All sought to seize a piece of African territory before the carcass had been picked clean. By 1900, virtually the entire continent had been placed under one form or another of European rule (see Figure 10.10). The British had consolidated their authority over the Nile valley and seized additional territories in East Africa. The French retaliated by advancing eastward from Senegal into the central Sahara, where they eventually came eyeball to eyeball with the British in the Nile valley. They also occupied the island of Madagascar and other coastal territories in West and Central Africa. In between, the Germans claimed the hinterland opposite Zanzibar, as well as coastal strips in West and Southwest Africa north of the Cape, and King Leopold II of Belgium claimed the Congo.

The Motives

3   What had happened to spark the sudden imperialist hysteria that brought an end to African independence? Economic interests in the narrow sense were not at stake as they had been in South and Southeast Asia: the level of trade between Europe and Africa was simply not sufficient to justify the risks and the expense of conquest. Clearly, one factor was the growing rivalry among imperialist powers. European leaders might be provoked into an imperialist takeover not by economic considerations but by the fear that another state might do so, leaving them at a disadvantage.

Source: From DUIKER. Contemporary World History (40–42). Copyright © 2010 Cengage Learning.

3. This passage has some difficult vocabulary. Use contexts clues and word part analysis to define the following words from the passage.

   • protectorate (paragraph 1): _____
   • ominous (paragraph 1): _____
   • rapaciousness (paragraph 1): _____
   • imperialist (paragraph 3): _____

4. How does Figure 10.10 help explain the passage? What meaning does it add or emphasize?
_____
_____

5. What is the author's purpose for Figure 10.10?
_____
_____

6. What part of Figure 10.10 could you picture in your mind to help you remember what you have read?
_____
_____

Cartoons

cartoon illustration that is meant to entertain

CARTOONS ARE ILLUSTRATIONS that are meant to entertain. Cartoons usually exaggerate or poke fun at one aspect of a complicated issue. The exaggeration of one aspect or oversimplification of the entire issue is usually where the humor is. Authors include cartoons as visuals to make points in funny ways. More and more textbooks are using cartoons to lighten the mood while still making a point.

ACTIVITY 10K
Read a Cartoon

1. Preview the following passage and visual from a world history textbook. Predict what the passage and visual are going to be about.

_____

2. Study-read the passage and visual. Highlight the main idea in green and the supporting details in yellow. Underline unfamiliar vocabulary that is not already in boldfaced type and any other ideas you think may help you remember new information. Write margin notes.

Grade Inflation

1   In 1973, only 20 percent of high-school students earned an A average, compared with 47 percent in 2003. However, standardized tests show that, between 1992 and 2007, the percentage of twelfth-graders who performed at or above a basic level in reading decreased from 80 to 73 percent, whereas the percentage performing at or above a proficient level declined from 40 to 35 percent (Ewers 2004; Lee et al. 2007; Planty et al. 2008). Such data suggest that grades are rising, but learning is lagging.

2   A professor who tracks GPAs says that grade inflation "has gone wild: When students walk into a classroom knowing that they can go through the motions and get a B+ or better, that's what they tend to do, give minimal effort. Our college classrooms are filled with students who do not prepare for class" (Rojstaczer 2009: 9).

3   According to one critic, "The demanding professor is close to being extinct" because "professors are under pressure to accommodate students" (Murray 2008: 32). Grade inflation, especially in college, is due to a number of factors, both institutional and individual. Many faculty members give high grades because it decreases student complaints, involves less time and thought in grading exams and papers, and reduces the chances of students' challenging a grade. Some faculty also believe that they can get favorable course

evaluations from students by handing out high grades, and others accept students' view of high grades as a reward for simply showing up in class. Moreover, administrators want to keep enrollment up. If students are unhappy with their grades, admission application rates may decrease. Thus, inflating grades satisfies administrators and makes them look good, especially where state legislators base funding on graduation rates (Carroll 2002; Kamber and Biggs 2002; Halfond 2004; Bartlett and Wasley 2008).

4   Among other problems, grade inflation gives students an exaggerated and unrealistic sense of their ability and accomplishments. Sometimes, for example, students don't understand why their job searches are unsuccessful because "I'm an A student." In fact, many students' incorrect usage of grammar on job application forms and résumés, as well as during interviews, turns off prospective employers (Halfond 2004).

"I got an A for not smoking."

Source: From BENOKRAITIS. *SOC* 2e (pp. 270–71). Copyright © 2012 Cengage Learning.

3. How does the cartoon help explain the passage? What meaning does it add or emphasize?

_____

_____

4. What is the author's purpose for the cartoon?

_____

_____

5. What part of the cartoon could you picture in your mind to help you remember what you have read?

_____

_____

Creating Your Own Visuals

IN ADDITION TO LEARNING HOW TO UNDERSTAND VISUALS in your textbooks, you can also create your own visuals. If you are able to create visuals of what you read, then you really understand the material, which leads to better memory retention. Creating a visual can be as useful as several intense study sessions because it requires that you organize the information in a way that is meaningful to you. Your primary goal is to illustrate the relationships between the ideas in your textbook. When creating visuals, do not be concerned about how artistic you are. Just create something based on the information you are studying. Here are some general guidelines for creating visuals:

▶ Always label your visual. Do not assume that you will remember what the visual means two or three weeks later.

▶ Avoid too much detail. Focus on one task, like comparing ideas, showing cause/effect, describing a process, or labeling parts.

▶ Use color if you can to add interest and meaning. Just like the highlighter colors you have been using throughout this book, colors can also be used to indicate important vocabulary, minor details, and helpful examples or to trigger personal recall. For example, if you were to color a visual about blood circulating in the human body, you might pick red for the arteries that leave the heart (which have lots of oxygen) and blue for the veins returning to the heart (which have less oxygen). These colors illustrate the function the arteries and veins serve. What colors might you use to draw photosynthesis? Green for the leaf? Yellow for the sun? What about drawing a time line? What colors would you use to represent 1776? Why?

Before you begin to learn more about creating your own visuals, keep in mind what you learned in Chapter 2 regarding your memory—you cannot remember what you do not understand. The same idea is true for visuals. You cannot create a visual if you do not understand the text.

ACTIVITY 10L
Draw a Visual from Reading

Read the following passage, and use the space to create your own visual or interpretation of it. Do not worry about being a great artist; stick figures are fine as long as the visual makes sense to you.

If the balloons popped, the sound wouldn't be able to carry since everything would be too far away from the concrete floor. A closed window would also not work. Since the whole operation depends on the steady flow of electricity, a break in the middle of the wire would also cause problems. Of course, the fellow could shout, but the human voice is not loud enough to carry that far. An additional problem is that a string could break on the instrument. Then there would be no accompaniment to the message. It is clear that the best situation would involve less distance. Then there would be fewer potential problems. With face-to-face contact, the least number of things could go wrong.

Source: J. D. Bransford and M. K. Johnson, "Contextual Prerequisites for Understanding Some Investigations of Comprehension and Recall." *Journal of Verbal Learning and Verbal Behavior*, 11, 1972, P. 718.

Was drawing a visual easy or difficult? Why? Most people find this very difficult. You cannot remember what you do not understand, and you will not be able to create a visual if you do not understand the information. Most likely, you will not have readings that are intentionally difficult and confusing like this one was. It was created to show you:

1. Using visuals with text assists the reader's understanding of the text.
2. You cannot draw what you do not understand.

Your instructor will share the drawing for this reading with you that may help you understand the text more clearly.

COMPREHENSION CHECK

▶ What are two things Activity 10L taught you about visuals?
▶ If you are able to share your drawing with other students, discuss each others' interpretations.

Selecting the Right Visual

THE MOST COMMONLY used visuals students create include diagrams, free-form drawings, mind maps, outlines, and tables. The type of visual you choose to create will depend on the material you are trying to learn and remember.

It may also depend on the author's pattern of organization. Recall from Chapter 7 that some visuals effectively represent textbook information based on authors' specific patterns of organization. Some of the more common types of visuals for comparison/contrast, cause/effect, and sequence are shown in Figure 10.11. Remember that organizational word clues can help you to decide which type of visual to use. If a history chapter author uses words like *then* and *now*, it would be useful to organize the information using a comparison/contrast table.

When creating visuals from your textbook, it is important to include what you already know about a topic whenever possible. Attaching new information to what you know allows you to add what you have just learned to your prior knowledge where it will make it easier for you to recall. For example, if you draw a diagram to help you to remember the details of the digestive system, it will help to include parts of the body you are already familiar with, such as the head and neck, as well as showing the esophagus, stomach, and large intestine.

All of the visuals introduced here can be used for any subject, but some are better suited to specific disciplines. If you are not sure what visual might be best, refer to Table 10.3 on page 477.

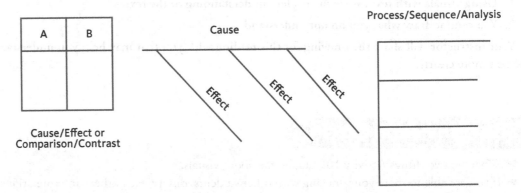

Figure 10.11 Common Visual Organizations Based on Patterns

Tables

If you recall, a table is made up of large amounts of text information, condensed into a format that makes it easy to see how different items of information relate to each other. Table 10.2 shows a way that one student decided to remember Chinese numbers. He put the English numbers in column 1, Chinese characters in column 2, and Chinese Pinyin in column 3 as a way to help him organize and remember the information. He frequently got the characters and their pronunciation and meaning confused before he organized them this way. The table allowed him to see the connections. He continues to use tables to help him learn and remember the Chinese language. This type of table could be used with any course content. For example, if you had a table about diseases, you could list the diseases in column 1, ways the different diseases are spread in column 2, and cures for the diseases in column 3.

Tip FROM THE
Brain Doctor

Images that you imagine can be just as important to the brain as images that you see with your eyes because we actually see with our brain! The eyes transport the information to the brain, but we see what the brain tells us we see. Sometimes we do not see what is actually there, as in optical illusions. Therefore, sometimes instead of actually drawing something or seeing a picture of it, you can try to clearly and vividly imagine what it looks like as you read the description. This image will help you recall the information just as if you saw a real picture. Images are powerful to the brain, whether they come from the imagination or through the eyes.

Table 10.2 **Student-Created Table**

NUMBER	CHINESE CHARCTER	CHINESE PINYIN (SPELLING)
ONE	一	yī
TWO	二	ér
THREE	三	sān
FOUR	四	sì
FIVE	五	wǔ
SIX	六	llù
SEVEN	七	qī
EIGHT	八	bā
NINE	九	jiú
TEN	十	shí

Source: Courtesy of Joseph Wafer.

ACTIVITY 10M
Create Your Own Table

1. Preview the following passage from a biology textbook. Predict what the passage is going to be about.

_____

2. Study-read the passage. Highlight the main idea text in green and the supporting details in yellow. Underline unfamiliar vocabulary that is not already in boldfaced type and any other ideas you think may help you remember new information. Write margin notes.

Science Requires Systematic Thought Processes

1   Two types of systematic thought processes scientists use are deduction and induction. With **deductive reasoning**, we begin with supplied information, called premises, and draw conclusions on the basis of that information. Deduction proceeds from general principles to specific conclusions. For example, if you accept the premise that all birds have wings and the second premise that sparrows are birds, you can conclude deductively that sparrows have wings. Deduction helps us discover relationships among known facts.

2   **Inductive reasoning** is the opposite of deduction. We begin with specific observations and draw a conclusion or discover a general principle. For example, if you know sparrows have wings and are birds, and you know robins, eagles, pigeons, and hawks have wings and are birds, you might induce that all birds have wings. In this way, you can use the inductive method to organize raw data into manageable categories by answering the question, What do all these facts have in common?

Source: From SOLOMON/BERG/MARTIN. _Biology_ 7e (p. 15). Copyright © 2005 Cengage Learning.

3. Review the information that you highlighted and your margin notes. Using that information, create a table based on this passage.

Diagrams

If you recall, a diagram is a drawing with markings to show how something is put together or works. Look closely at the student-created diagram in Figure 10.12, which was created by a nursing student trying to learn the muscles of the upper body. What details do you notice about the content of the diagram? The muscles are symmetrical (same set of muscles on each side of the body), the muscles seem to complement one another in function, muscles overlap, muscles seem bigger in the middle of the body, and there are a lot of muscles in the arms. Based on how this student drew this diagram, it is obvious she was trying to learn and remember the muscle names and their locations.

While reviewing, some students find it useful to use onion skin—a type of thin, translucent paper—to trace diagrams from their textbooks. After you trace the diagram, close the book and label the parts of the diagram on the onion skin. Then open the textbook to check your work. Tracing works well for most science courses where you are required to learn a lot of parts or processes and is an excellent way to test yourself.

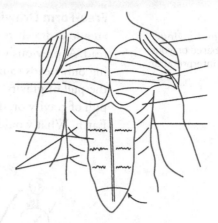

Source: Courtesy of Elise Guido.

Figure 10.12   Student-Created Diagram

ACTIVITY 10N
Create Your Own Diagram

1. Preview the following passage from a medical terminology textbook. Predict what the passage is going to be about.

_____

2. Study-read the passage. Highlight the main idea text in green and the supporting details in yellow. Underline unfamiliar vocabulary that is not already in boldfaced type and any other ideas you think may help you remember new information. Write margin notes.

Cells

    Human cells vary in size, shape, and function. The study of cells is called **cytology** (sigh-TALL-oh-jee). The **cell membrane** is the cell's outer covering. The membrane allows material to pass in and out of the cell so that the cell can receive oxygen and nutrients and release waste products. The cell's structures are housed in a gel-like substance called **cytoplasm** (SIGH-toh-plazm). The **nucleus** (NOO-klee-us) controls cellular functions and is made up of threadlike strands called **chromosomes** (KROH-moh-sohms). Chromosomes contain **deoxyribonucleic** (dee-ocks-ee-righ-boh-noo-KLAY-ik) **acid (DNA)**, which transmits genetic information. The chromosomes also have thousands of segments called **genes**, which are responsible for hereditary characteristics.

Source: From MOISIO. *Medical Terminology for Insurance and Coding* (p. 19). Copyright © 2010 Cengage Learning.

3. Review the information that you highlighted and your margin notes. Using that information, create a diagram based on this passage.

free-form drawing
drawing based on your
personal interpretation

Free-Form Drawings

Free-form drawings are drawings based on your interpretation of what you have read. As previously stated, you do not need to be a professional artist; the drawing only needs to make sense to you. Figure 10.13 represents a comparison of the pull of gravity of a 6-pound iron ball on Earth to that on the moon. The pull of gravity on the moon is only one-sixth of what it is on the surface of the Earth. What would weigh 6 pounds on Earth weighs 1 pound on the moon.

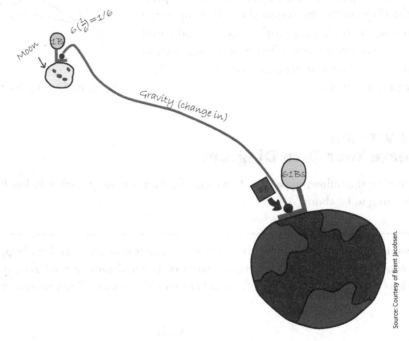

Figure 10.13 Student-Created Free-Form Drawing

ACTIVITY 100
Create Your Own Free-Form Drawing

1. Preview the following passage from a biology textbook. Predict what the passage is going to be about.

_____

2. Study-read the passage. Highlight the main idea text in green and the supporting details in yellow. Underline unfamiliar vocabulary that is not already in boldfaced type and any other ideas you think may help you remember new information. Write margin notes.

Organisms Respond to Stimuli

1   All forms of life respond to **stimuli**, physical or chemical changes in their internal or external environment. Stimuli that evoke a response in most organisms are changes in the color, intensity, or direction of light; changes in temperature, pressure, or sound; and changes in the chemical composition of the surrounding soil, air, or water. Responding to stimuli involves movement, though not always locomotion (moving from one place to another).

2   In simple organisms, the entire individual may be sensitive to stimuli. Certain unicellular organisms, for example, respond to bright light by retreating. In some organisms, locomotion is achieved by the slow oozing of the cell, the process of amoeboid movement. Other organisms move by beating tiny, hairlike extensions of the cell called cilia or longer structures known as flagella. Some bacteria move by means of rotating flagella.

3   Most animals move very obviously. They wiggle, crawl, swim, run, or fly by contracting muscles. Sponges, corals, and oysters have free-swimming larval stages but do not move from place to place as adults. Even though these adults are sessile, meaning they remain firmly attached to a surface, they may have cilia or flagella. These structures beat rhythmically, moving the surrounding water, which contains needed food and oxygen. In complex animals such as polar bears and humans, certain highly specialized cells of the body respond to specific types of stimuli. For example, cells in the retina of the eye respond to light.

Source: From SOLOMON/BERG/MARTIN. *Biology* 7e (pp. 3–4). Copyright © 2005 Cengage Learning.

3. **Review the information that you highlighted and your margin notes. Using that information, create a free-form drawing based on this passage.**

Mind Maps

Mind maps, also known as concept maps, are visuals that use shapes and lines to show the relative importance of ideas and relationships between ideas. You first read about mind maps in Chapter 4, and every chapter in this book begins with a mind map of the chapter's contents. Because they are free form in style, you decide how to organize the information. The process of determining where to place items lets you know if you understand the information you are mapping.

mind map visual that uses shapes and lines to show the relative importance of ideas and relationships between ideas

In order to start a map, you need to know the main idea and supporting details of what you are reading. You usually place the topic in the center, which becomes the core of your map with main ideas and supporting details then branching out. Figure 10.14 represents an introduction to Plato's Cave analogy. The circles directly connected to the center—Plato's Cave—are major supporting details. Those connected to the major supporting details are minor supporting details the student wants to remember.

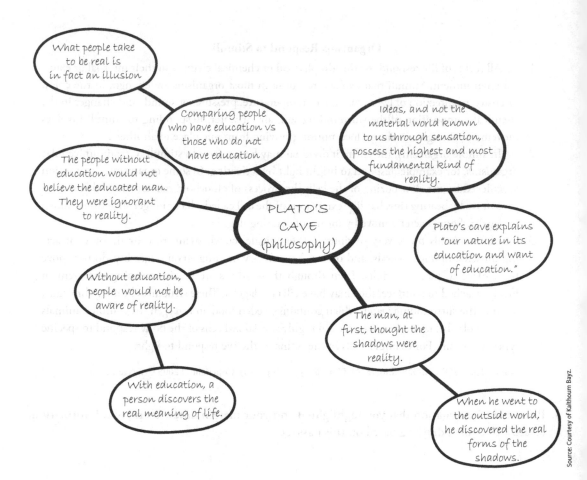

Figure 10.14 Student-Created Mind Map

Source: Courtesy of Kalthoum Bayz.

ACTIVITY 10P
Create Your Own Mind Map

1. Preview the following passage from a sociology textbook. Predict what the passage is going to be about.

_____

2. Study-read the passage. Highlight the main idea text in green and the supporting details in yellow. Underline unfamiliar vocabulary that is not already in boldfaced type and any other ideas you think may help you remember new information. Write margin notes.

Primary Groups and Secondary Groups

1   Suppose your car's battery died this morning, your sociology professor gave a pop quiz for which you hadn't studied, your computer's hard drive crashed, and your microwave stopped working. Whom might you call to vent? Your answer reflects the difference between primary and secondary groups.

Primary Groups

2   A **primary group** is a relatively small group of people who engage in intimate face-to-face interaction over an extended period. For sociologist Charles Horton Cooley (1909/1983: 24), the most significant primary groups were "the family, the play-group of children, and the neighborhood or community of elders" because they are first and central in shaping a person's social and moral development.

3   Primary groups are our emotional glue. We call members of our primary group to share good news or to gripe. Primary group members are typically understanding, supportive, and tolerant even when we're in a bad mood or selfish. They have a powerful influence on our social identity because we interact with them on a regular and intimate basis over many years, usually throughout our lives. Because primary group members genuinely care about each other, they contribute to one another's personal development, security, and well-being. Our family and close friends, for example, stick with us through good and bad, and we feel comfortable in being ourselves in their presence.

Secondary Groups

4   A **secondary group** is a large, usually formal, impersonal, and temporary collection of people who pursue a specific goal or activity. Your sociology class is a good example of a secondary group. You might have a few friends in class, but students typically interact infrequently and formally. When the semester (or quarter) is over and you've accomplished your goal of passing the course, you may not see each other again (especially if you're attending a large college or university). And you certainly wouldn't call your professor if you needed a sympathetic ear at the end of a bad day. Other examples of secondary groups include political parties, labor unions, and employees of a company.

Unlike primary groups, secondary groups are usually highly structured: There are many rules and regulations, people know (or care) little about each other personally, relationships are formal, and members are expected to fulfill particular functions. Whereas primary groups meet our expressive (emotional) needs, secondary groups fulfill instrumental (task-oriented) needs. Once a task or activity is completed—whether it's earning a grade, turning in a committee report, or building a bridge—secondary groups usually split up and go on to become a member of other secondary groups.

Source: From BENOKRAITIS. *SOC* 2e (p. 100). Copyright © 2012 Cengage Learning.

3. Review the information that you highlighted and your margin notes. Using that information, create a mind map based on this passage.

✔ COMPREHENSION CHECK

▶ Explain the differences between mind maps and free-form drawings. Explain why and when you would use one over the other.

Outlines

outline general plan of material that shows the order of various topics and their relationship with each other

Outlines are one of the most popular visuals students create. Outlines provide you with an overview or summary of information. For example, the table of contents found at the beginning of textbooks is a type of outline. It provides you with an overview of the book. Through chapter titles, headings, and subheadings, the outline serves as a guide to the framework of a text. Here is a general outline format:

I.   Topic (Roman Numeral)
   A. Main idea (capital letter)
      1. Major supporting detail (number)
         a. More specific detail (letter)
         b. More specific detail
      2. Major supporting detail
   B. Main Idea
II. Topic
   A. Main Idea
   B. Main Idea
      1. Major supporting detail
      2. Major supporting detail
         a. More specific detail

You will discover that outlines are very similar to mind maps. Mind maps use shapes and can be placed around the page, and their content is usually in no special order, except that the topic is usually in the center. What makes an outline different is that information is presented in a linear way, exact order, top to bottom. Read the following passage, and see the example of an outline that was created from it.

Enzymes

In this guide to health conditions, I describe specific problems along with the enzymes and other supplements used to treat them. Conditions are illustrated by patient success stories from my many years of clinical practice as an enzyme therapist. All patient histories are documented and, of course, patient names have been changed to protect privacy.

Source: The Enzyme Cure: How Plant Enzymes Can Help You Relieve 36 Health Problems, Lita Lee, InnoVision Health Media, Inc., 1998, p. 60.

I. <u>Topic</u> (Roman Numeral): guide to health conditions and how to treat them

   A. <u>Main idea</u> (capital letter): Enzyme therapy and other supplements can treat certain conditions.

      1. <u>Major supporting detail</u> (number): Patient success stories illustrate the success of this therapy.

         a. <u>More specific detail</u> (letter): All patient histories are documented.

         b. <u>More specific detail</u> (letter): I've had many years of clinical practice.

         c. <u>More specific detail</u> (letter): Patient names have been changed for privacy.

ACTIVITY 10Q
Create Your Own Outline

1. Preview the following passage from a public speaking textbook. Predict what the passage is going to be about.

_____

2. Study-read the passage. Highlight the main idea text in green and the supporting details in yellow. Underline unfamiliar vocabulary that is not already in boldfaced type and any other ideas you think may help you remember new information. Write margin notes.

An Effective Speech Is Well Structured

1   The structure of a speech is the framework that organizes the content. Clear structure helps your listeners follow your ideas so they can understand the points you are making. Clear structure includes both macrostructure and microstructure.

2   **Macrostructure** is the overall framework you use to organize your speech content. It has four elements: the introduction, body, conclusion, and transitions. The introduction is the beginning segment of the speech and should be structured so that you build audience interest in your topic and preview what you are going to say (you tell them what you are going to tell them). The speech body contains the main ideas and supporting material you have decided to present; it is organized into a pattern that makes the ideas easy for the audience to understand and remember (you tell them). The conclusion ends the speech, reminds the audience of your main ideas, and motivates them to remember or act upon what you have said (you tell them what you told them). The macro-structure of your speech also includes transitions, which are the phrases you use to move from one main point to the next.

3   You have studied macrostructure throughout your education as you learned to write. Now, however, you will be learning how to adapt it to oral messages. You'll see that careful attention to macrostructure is more important when you craft a speech than when you write an essay. A reader

Continued on next page.

can easily reread a poorly written essay to try to understand your intent, but an audience does not usually have the opportunity to rehear your speech. So, as you prepare each of your speeches, you will need to develop an organizational framework that enables your audience to quickly understand and easily remember the ideas you present.

4   Whereas macrostructure is the overall framework you design for your speech, **microstructure** is the specific language and style choices you use as you frame your ideas and verbalize them to your audience. Pay careful attention to microstructure while practicing and delivering your speech so that you can present your ideas with words that are instantly intelligible and guide your audience to thoughts that are consistent with your own. Practicing and using words that are appropriate, accurate, clear and vivid will help you accomplish your speaking goal.

Source: From VERDERBER/SELLNOW/VERDERBER. *The Challenge of Effective Speaking*, 15e (p. 12). Copyright © 2012 Cengage Learning.

3. **Review the information that you highlighted and your margin notes. Using that information, create an outline based on this passage.**

I. _____

  A. _____

    1. _____

      a. _____

      b. _____

      c. _____

      d. _____

    2. _____

Table 10.3 Guide for Selecting a Visual

Type of Visual	Information Visual Best Captures	Example
table	▶ depicts many kinds of information, can be made using any list of facts ▶ organizes large amounts of information, stating different characteristic of a person, place, or thing, so that a number of items and their characteristics can be viewed simultaneously ▶ compares and contrasts items easily ▶ demonstrates cause/effect ▶ useful in history, psychology, biology, nursing, pharmacy, English, literature, and economics	how something looks, where it is located, its function mammals versus amphibians the effect of gravity on objects See pages 444 and 467.
diagram	▶ represents things, places, parts, where everything is labeled ▶ illustrates sequences and processes ▶ useful in all sciences, automotive, and culinary arts	photosynthesis or the steps in creating a commercial product See page 469.
free-form drawing	▶ makes concepts concrete by creating a visual representation of text information—and for interpretation, problem solving, and reading between the lines of written material ▶ visually represents a thinking process—some people make connections using meaningful doodles connected to note taking ▶ provides personal representation and understanding of written material ▶ useful in geology, biology, literature, technology, and sciences	See page 470.
mind map	▶ shows organization of information in a nonlinear way ▶ demonstrates relationships between topic, main ideas, and supporting details in written material ▶ useful in most all disciplines	See pages 433 and 472.
outline	▶ shows linear organization of information ▶ demonstrates order or hierarchy of information ▶ useful in most all disciplines	progression of historical events feudal relationship between monarch and subjects See page 474.

PRACTICE WITH A READING PASSAGE

Prepare to Read

1. Preview the reading passage and visual. What do you predict is the purpose of the visual?

_____

2. What do you know about hypnosis? Have you ever been hypnotized?

_____

Is Hypnosis an Altered State of Consciousness?
By James Kalat

1   If a hypnotist tells you, "Your hand is rising, you can do nothing to stop it," your hand might indeed rise. If you were later asked why, you might reply that you lost control of your own behavior. Still, you were not a puppet. Was the act voluntary, involuntary, or something in between? To put the question differently, is hypnosis really different from normal wakefulness?

2   At some extreme, some psychologists regard hypnosis as a special state of consciousness characterized by increased suggestibility. At the other extreme, some psychologists emphasize the similarities between hypnosis and normal wakeful consciousness, including the fact that people who respond well to hypnosis also respond strongly to suggestions without hypnosis. Most psychologists take intermediate positions, noting that hypnotized people are neither "pretending to be hypnotized" nor under a hypnotist's control. That is, hypnosis is a special state in some ways but not others (Kirch and Lynn, 1998).

3   One way to determine whether hypnosis is a special state of consciousness is to find out whether nonhypnotized people can do everything that hypnotized people can do. How convincingly could you act like a hypnotized person?

How Well Can Someone Pretend to Be Hypnotized?

4   In several experiments, some college students were hypnotized. An experienced hypnotist then examined them and tried to determine which ones were really hypnotized.

5   Fooling the hypnotist turned out to be easier than expected. The pretenders tolerated sharp pain without flinching and pretended to recall old memories. They made their bodies as stiff as a board and lay rigid between two chairs. When standing people were told to sit down, they did not did so immediately (as hypnotized people do) without first checking to make sure they had a chair behind them (Orne, 1959, 1979). When told to experience anger or another emotion, they exhibited physiological changes such as increased heart rate and sweating, just as hypnotized people do (Damaser, Shor and Orne, 1963). Even experienced hypnotists could not identify the pretenders.

6   Only a few differences between the hypnotized people and pretenders emerged (Orne, 1979). The pretenders failed to match some of the behaviors of hypnotized people, simply because they did not know how a hypnotized subject would act. For instance, when the hypnotist suggested, "You see Professor Schmaltz sitting in that chair," people in both groups reported seeing the professor. Some of the hypnotized subjects, however, asked with puzzlement, "How is it that I see the professor there, but I also see the chair?" Pretenders never reported seeing this double reality. At that point in the experiment, Professor Schmaltz walked into the room. "Who is that entering the room?" asked the hypnotist. The pretenders would either say they say no one, or they would identify Schmaltz as someone else. The hypnotized subjects would say, "That's Professor Schmaltz." Some then said that they were confused about seeing the same person in two places. For some of them, the hallucinated professor faded at that moment. Others continued to accept the double image.

7   One study reported a way to distinguish hypnotized people from pretenders more than 90% of the time. But it might not be the way you would expect. Simply ask people how deeply hypnotized they thought they were, how relaxed they were, and whether they were aware of their surroundings while hypnotized. People who rate themselves as "extremely" hypnotized, "extremely" relaxed, and "totally unaware" of their surroundings are almost always pretenders. Those who were really hypnotized rate themselves as only mildly influenced (Martin and Lynn, 1996).

8   So, what is our conclusion? Apparently, people pretending to be hypnotized can mimic almost any effect of hypnosis that they know about. However, hypnosis is ordinarily not just role-playing. The effects that role players learn to imitate happen spontaneously for the hypnotized people.

Source: From KALAT. *Introduction to Psychology* (p. 369). Copyright © 2011 Cengage Learning.

Will hypnotized people do anything that they would otherwise refuse to do? The problem is that nonhypnotized people will sometimes perform some strange and dangerous acts, either because an experimenter asked them to or on their own.

Continued on next page.

Check Your Understanding

3. Use context clues and word part analysis to define the following words used in the passage.

   • suggestibility (paragraph 2): _____

   • distinguish (paragraph 7): _____

   • spontaneously (paragraph 8): _____

4. After reading the passage and photograph, what was the purpose of the photograph?

   _____

   _____

5. Did the photograph add to the passage? Why or why not?

   _____

   _____

6. What is the main idea of the photograph?

   _____

   _____

7. What is the main idea of the passage?

   _____

   _____

8. List the major supporting details.

   _____

   _____

   _____

   _____

9. Did you enjoy the reading? Why or why not?

   _____

   _____

10. Create a visual (your choice—refer to Table 10.3 if you are unsure which type of visual would be effective) based on this passage that helps you to learn and remember the information.

CHAPTER SUMMARY

When you examine visuals in your textbooks and create ones of your own, you increase your comprehension. Visuals help you literally see what an author means, add even more to your understanding, and can be an excellent study tool.

Approach each textbook visual in a systematic way so you can get the most from it: preview, study-read, review. Some common types of textbook visuals are: tables, diagrams, illustrations, graphs, pie charts, pictographs, photographs, time lines, geographical maps, and cartoons.

As you attempt to create your own visuals, determine the main idea of what you have read. If you cannot understand what you have read, you cannot create a useful visual. Selecting the right visual depends on what you are reading and sometimes on how the textbook chapter is organized. Common visuals that students create are: tables, diagrams, free-form drawing, mind maps, and outlines. Remember that you do not have to be an expert artist to benefit from creating your own visuals. You just have to show that you can see what your textbook authors mean.

Brain Connections: Self-Assessment

Draw the amount of dendrites you imagine that you have now about using visuals to understand your textbooks. Compare your drawing of dendrites now with what you drew at the beginning of this chapter. If the amounts are different, explain why.

✔ COMPREHENSION CHECK

▶ How does creating a visual help you learn and remember new information?

▶ If you could ask the authors a question about this chapter, what would you ask?

POST TEST

Part 1. Objective Questions

Match the key terms from the chapter in Column A to their definitions in Column B.

Column A	Column B
_____ 1. decode	a. general plan of material that shows the order of various topics and their relationship with each other
_____ 2. encode	b. visual way of displaying events in chronological order
_____ 3. table	c. circular visual that is divided into sections like a pie, illustrating proportion
_____ 4. hierarchy	d. to convert text into a code (in this case a visual)
_____ 5. diagram	e. a ranking order of persons or things, one above the other
_____ 6. illustration	f. to interpret into a language that makes sense to a reader
_____ 7. graph	g. drawing based on your personal interpretation
_____ 8. bar graph	h. visual representing data through the use of pictures
_____ 9. line graph	i. graph that illustrates information by using parallel rectangular bars of varying length to contrast information
_____ 10. pie chart	j. drawing with markings to show how something is put together or works
_____ 11. pictograph	k. visual where large amounts of text are condensed into a format, usually using categories, that make it easy to see how different items of information relate to each other
_____ 12. photograph	l. a drawing
_____ 13. time line	m. a picture made from light passing through a camera onto film or in digital form
_____ 14. geographical map	n. graph that displays information as a series of data points connected by straight line segments
_____ 15. cartoon	o. visual that shows changes in quantities, usually with a horizontal and vertical axis
_____ 16. free-form drawing	p. visual representation of a geographical area
_____ 17. mind map	q. illustration meant to entertain
_____ 18. outline	r. visual that uses shapes and lines to show the relative importance of ideas and relationships between ideas

Circle the best answer to the following multiple-choice questions.

19. Outlining can be used to:

   a. show the relationship between ideas.

   b. effectively show topics but not the details.

   c. demonstrate the main idea by representing information in a linear (top-down) way.

   d. All of the given answers.

20. Which of the following statements accurately describes charts?

   a. They can be used to organize large amounts of information.

   b. They are useful for comparing and contrasting information.

   c. Completing them lets you know how well you have learned new information.

   d. All of the given answers.

21. In order to design a successful visual, you have to:

   a. become an accomplished artist.

   b. fully understand the information you have read.

   c. use different colors.

   d. memorize all of the information in an assignment before you can create one.

Short-Answer Questions

22. Why are visuals such an important piece of the reading process?

   _____

   _____

23. If you want to represent chronology of events that occurred over a specific period, what visual should you use?

   _____

24. If you want to compare data on a specific topic over time (city population growth over the past 10 years), what visual should you use?

   _____

25. What type of information would you expect a pie chart to represent?

   _____

Continued on next page.

Part 2. Reading Passage   ACADEMIC READING

Prepare to Read

1. Based on the title and headings, what do you expect the following passage to be about?

_____

2. Create questions to ask yourself using the title and headings. Look for the answers to your questions as you read.

_____

3. What do you already know about the topic?

_____

Chapter 1 Light and Life
By Peter Russell et al.

Why It Matters

1   Claude Monet (1840–1926), a French painter, is considered by many to be the master of the impressionist form that rose to prominence in the late nineteenth century. Other well-known impressionists include Edgar Degas and Paul Cézanne. Impressionism as an art movement was characterized by the use of small visible brush strokes that emphasized light and color, rather than lines, to define an object. The artists used pure, unmixed color, not smoothly blended, as was the custom at the time. For example, instead of physically mixing yellow and blue paint, they placed unmixed yellow paint on the canvas next to unmixed blue paint so that the colors would mingle in the eye of the viewer to create the "impression" of green. The Impressionists found that they could capture the momentary and transient effects

© The Art Gallery Collection/Alamy

The Japanese Bridge at Giverny, 1918-24 (oil on canvas), Monet, Claude (1840-1926)/Musee Marmottan Monet, Paris, France/ Giraudon/The Bridgeman Art Library

Paintings by Claude Monet (1840-1926). Compared to his early works including The water-lily pond (a) his laser paintings including the japanese footbridge (b) bordered on the abstract with almost complete loss of light-blue. Monet suffered from vision degenerative disease cataracts which was diagnosed in 1912.

of sunlight and changing color of a scene by painting *en plein* air, in the open air, outside of the studio, where they could more accurately paint the reflected light of an immediate scene.

2   Interestingly, compared with his early works, which included the "Water Lily Pond" (1899), Monet's later paintings verge on the abstract, with colors bleeding into each other and a lack of rational shape and perspective. For example, "The Japanese Footbridge" is an explosion of orange, yellow, and red hues, with heavy, broad brush strokes, leaving the viewer barely able to discern the vague shape of the arched bridge. In many of Monet's later works, the colors in his paintings became more muted, far less vibrant and bright, with a pronounced color shift from blue-green to red-yellow and an almost total absence of light blues. The sense of atmosphere and light that he was famous for in his earlier works disappeared.

3   Although the change in Monet's paintings could easily be explained by an intentional change in style or perhaps an age-related change in manual dexterity, Monet himself realized that it was not his style or dexterity that had changed but, rather, it was his ability to see. Monet suffered from cataracts, the vision-deteriorating disease that was diagnosed in both eyes by a Parisian ophthalmologist in 1912 when Monet was 72. A cataract is a change in the lens of the eye, making it more opaque. The underlying cause is a progressive denaturation of one of the proteins that make up the lens. The increased opaqueness of the lens absorbs certain wavelengths of light, decreasing the transmittance of blue light. Thus, to a cataract sufferer such as Monet, the world appears more yellow.

opaque not transparent, not letting light get through

denaturation a changing of the nature of something

1.1 The Physical Nature of Light

4   Light serves two important functions for life on Earth: First, it is a source of energy that sustains all life. Second, light provides organisms with information about the physical world. An excellent example of an organism that uses light for both energy and information is the green alga *Chlamydomonas reinhardtii* (Figure 10.15). *C. reinhardtii* is a single-celled photosynthetic eukaryote that is commonly found in ponds

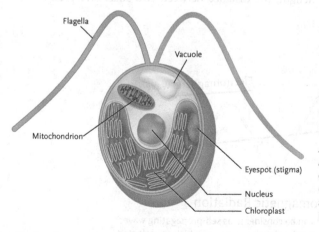

Figure 10.15
Chlamydomonas Reinhardtii

A drawing of *Chlamydomonas reinhardtii*, a green alga. Each cell contains a single chloroplast used for photosynthesis as well as an eyespot for sensing light in the environment.

Continued on next page.

and lakes. Each cell contains a single large chloroplast that harvests light energy and uses it to make energy-rich molecules through the process of photosynthesis. In addition, each cell contains a light sensor called an *eyespot* that allows it to sense both light direction and light intensity.

5   Regardless of whether the light is used as a source of energy or information about the environment, both rely on the same fundamental properties of light and require the light energy to be captured by the organism.

1.1a What Is Light?

6   The reason there is life on Earth and, as far as we know, nowhere else in our solar system has to do with distance—specifically, the distance

SOHO/EIT Consortium/ESA/NASA

Figure 10.16 The Sun

The sun is a star with a surface temperature of approximately 5000°C It generates electromagnetic radiation by the nuclear fusion of hydrogen nuclei into helium. Note the superimposed image of the Earth used to illustrate the relative size.

of 150,000,000 km separating Earth from the Sun (Figure 10.16). By converting hydrogen into helium at the staggering rate of some 3.41038 hydrogen nuclei per second, the Sun converts over 4 million tonnes of matter into energy every second. This energy is given off as electromagnetic radiation, which travels at the speed of light (1,079,252,848 km/h) and reaches the Earth in just over 8 minutes. Electromagnetic radiation moves in the form of two waves, one electrical and one magnetic, which are oriented at 90° to each other (Figure 10.17). Scientists often distinguish electromagnetic radiation by its wavelength, the distance between two successive peaks.

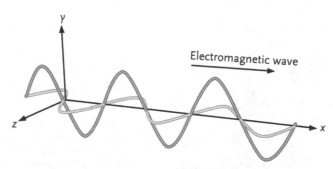

Figure 10.17 Electromagnetic Radiation

Electromagnetic radiation can be considered as self-propagating waves which consist of both electrical and magnetic waves which are oriented at 90° to each other. A wave consists of discrete packets of energy called photons.

The wavelength of electromagnetic radiation ranges from less than one picometre (1012 m) for cosmic rays to more than a kilometre (106 m) for radio waves.

7   Okay, but what is light? Light can be defined as the portion of the electromagnetic spectrum (Figure 10.18) that humans can detect with their eyes. Light or visible radiation, is a narrow band of the electromagnetic spectrum spanning the wavelengths in nanometres (1 nm 109 m) from 400 nm (blue light) to about 700 nm (red light). To avoid confusion, wavelengths just outside this range should not be referred to as light but rather as ultraviolet and infrared radiation.

8   One reason that light is a bit of an **enigma** and hard to characterize is that, although it can be described as a wave, it also behaves as a stream of energy particles. These discrete particles or packets of energy are referred to as photons. Unlike atoms, photons have no mass, but each contains a precise amount of energy. The amount of energy in a photon is **inversely related** to its wavelength. Looking just at visible light (see Figure 10.18), this means that blue light, with a shorter wavelength, consists of photons that have higher energy than longer wavelength red light. It is important to realize that although one photon contains a very small amount of energy (red light: 3.01 10 19 joules/photon; blue light: 4.56 10 19 joules/photon), on a clear summer's day, approximately 1021 photons hit each square metre of Earth each second.

enigma something that is puzzling, hard to explain

inversely related a relationship between two things where as one thing increases, the other decreases

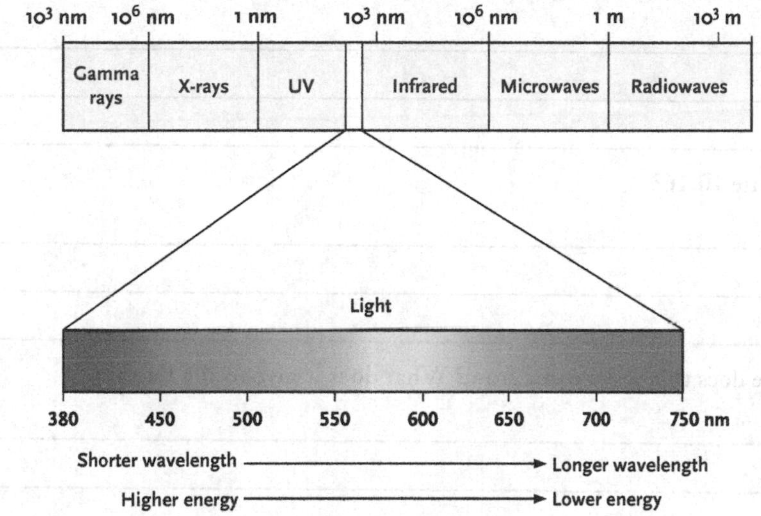

Figure 10.18 The Electromagnetic Spectrum

The grouping of all types of electromagnetic radiation according to wavelength. It ranges from very short wavelengths characteristic of gamma rays to the long wavelengths associated with radio waves. The shorter the wavelength of the electromagnetic radiation the higher the energy of each photon it contains. Light represents only a small portion of the total electromagnetic spectrum.

Source: From RUSSELL. *Biology, Exploring the Diversity of Life, Volume 1,* 1e (pp. 1–3). Copyright © 2010 Cengage Learning.

Continued on next page.

Check Your Understanding

4. List any technical vocabulary that you would need to know if this passage were an actual textbook you were studying. What strategy would you use to learn this technical vocabulary?

_____

_____

_____

5. This passage is a from a biology textbook. Why did the author begin this passage with a story about Claude Monet?

_____

_____

_____

6. Look at Figure 10.15. What part of the green alga makes energy? Which part gathers information?

_____

_____

_____

7. What can you learn from Figure 10.16?

_____

_____

_____

8. Describe Figure 10.17. Where does this wave come from? What does it give to the Earth?

_____

_____

_____

9. What was the most difficult part of this passage? If this were your textbook, what would you do to understand this difficult part better?

_____

_____

_____

10. Draw a visual that captures the main idea of the passage.

BRAIN STRENGTH OPTIONS

Below is an article with information that can be presented in a multitude of ways. The author has chosen to present it in paragraph form. Working in groups of no more than four, select five different visuals to present this information using what you learned in this chapter. You may present your project in a poster, PowerPoint, or Web page as determined by your group and your instructor. You will be graded on these guidelines:

▶ **Effectiveness of the visuals selected**: Do your visuals get the information across clearly and accurately?

▶ **Clarity of information as presented**: Are your visuals easy to read and clear to understand?

Hint: A quick read-through makes something jump out as an easy way to present this information. Do you see it? Clue: Notice that all but one item contain dates.

1   Revolutions in technology continue to cause rapid, almost unpredictable changes in career demand. Changes in technology can obsolete your job causing you to be laid off, downsized, right sized, and just plain inconvenienced.

2   Here are a few examples of jobs which were once "Hot Jobs" with high demand but are now declining or totally extinct, at least in North America and Europe:

▶ Typesetting—Has been replaced by the first Apple computers and the advent of desktop publishing. Typesetting began in the 1400's with the first printing presses. The trend away from typesetting to desktop publishing started in the early 1980s and was completed by the mid-1990s. Thousands of people had their careers upset by this trend.

▶ Secretarial Dictation—Has been replaced by individuals doing their own word processing, starting in the late 1980s as the cost of personal computers came down.

▶ IBM Punch Card Operator—Was obsolete along with IBM punch cards by ~1985. Prior to that, punch card data entry employed tens of thousands.

▶ Telex (TWX) Operator—Was obsolete by the advent of the fax machine, ~1980

▶ Fax Machine Operator—When the cost of fax machines came down, most people handled their own faxes rather than having an assistant do it. Finally, most but not all faxes gave way to email. 1980 to 1995.

▶ Telephone Operators—Once a premier job, demand was reduced significantly by touch tone systems and then later by voice recognition technology.

▶ Drafting Technician—Manual drafting using pencil and ruler was replaced by Computer Aided Drafting (CAD) in the 1980s.

Source: Robinson, Michael T., CareerPlanner.com http://www.careerplanner.com/career-articles/hot_jobs.cfm

CHAPTER
11

Understanding and Creating Arguments

"The moment we want to believe something, we suddenly see all the arguments for it, and become blind to the arguments against it."

—GEORGE BERNARD SHAW

EVERYTHING THAT I READ OR HEARD before college, I took "as is" and nothing more. Today, during lecture or while reading for a class, when I stumble upon something that interests me or strikes me as being untrue or arguable, I look into it further. The Internet, videos, and other outside resources have helped me tremendously to learn and understand more. During my second year of college, I have learned more and understand more about thinking. Most importantly, I have learned that everyone has different viewpoints and that there isn't just one way to think about something. An important lesson I have learned (and I will take with me) is to keep an open mind and do what works for me.

Making Connections

1. What is the meaning of the quotation at the beginning of this chapter? Give an example of when that situation has happened to you.
2. What is the purpose of an argument? What is the desired outcome?
3. What makes a "good" argument?
4. How can a piece of writing be an "argument" if there is only one person writing it?

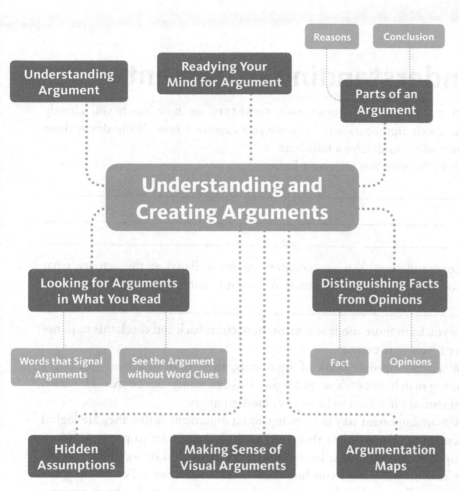

Reasons   Conclusion

Understanding Argument

Readying Your Mind for Argument

Parts of an Argument

Understanding and Creating Arguments

Looking for Arguments in What You Read

Distinguishing Facts from Opinions

Words that Signal Arguments

See the Argument without Word Clues

Fact   Opinions

Hidden Assumptions

Making Sense of Visual Arguments

Argumentation Maps

© Cengage Learning

Brain Connections: Self-Assessment

Draw on the brain cell how many dendrites you imagine you have for how much you know about arguments.

Understanding Argument

BEFORE YOU BEGIN READING THIS CHAPTER, see how much you already know about argumentation. Let's say you deserve a raise. Write down three reasons why you deserve a raise here:

Three Reasons You Deserve a Raise

1. _____

2. _____

3. _____

Congratulations! You just wrote an argument. Based on this activity, what do you think defines an argument? Write your definition here.

_____

After you learn more about argumentation, come back and check this response to see if you were correct.

When most people think of arguments, they think of a loud and angry shouting match that ends up in a fight. This can sometimes be true. However, arguments do not need to be heated, loud, or angry.

A more important way of thinking about arguments is that they are logical structures people use when they write and speak in order to persuade others to support their ideas. The logical structure of this kind of argument consists of statements including a conclusion and at least one reason. For example, if a classmate tells you that *Avatar* was the best movie ever made, she is stating a

Photofest/Twentieth Century-Fox Film Corporation

conclusion. If she continues by saying that *Avatar* had great 3-D technology and creative characters and other beasts, she is providing reasons for her conclusion. You do not have to agree with her argument. Suppose you say, "I hated *Avatar*!" That statement alone is an opinion but not really an argument. Perhaps then you add, "The story line was predictable, and the movie was way too long!" Now you have an argument. Your conclusion is *Avatar* was not the best movie, which you implied when you said you hated it. Your reasons are (1) that it was predictable and (2) that it was too long. So an argument can be defined as a conclusion backed up with one or more reasons.

argument two or more statements that include one conclusion and at least one reason that support it

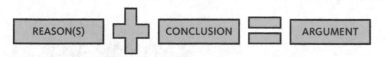

This chapter introduces you to the concept of argumentation. By no means is this, or the next chapter, intended to cover *all* aspects of argument. Whole courses are designed around the concept of argumentation. Instead, this chapter will help you realize what arguments are and will show you where to look to find them in textbooks. Once you locate the arguments, you can begin to evaluate them and then decide if you accept them as true and worthwhile. Critical readers approach all reading with a healthy skepticism. They do not just accept everything in print as necessarily true. Good readers judge based on the strength of an argument.

Knowing the basic structure of an argument, its reasons and conclusion, and being able to see these argument parts in what you read encourages you to develop your own arguments, your own reasons and conclusion, about the subject matter. When you develop your own arguments, you are thinking critically and not just accepting another person's thoughts and opinions.

Readying Your Mind for Argument

A GREAT ASIAN SAYING CAPTURES GOOD ADVICE TO STUDENTS: "Learn how to empty your cup each time that you come to learn." This simply means to come to every class as though you are learning something for the first time. Approach everything with an open mind.

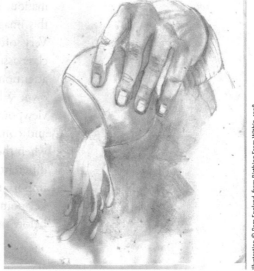

Illustration © Pam England, from Birthing From Within, 1998

One of the major dispositions—habit, state of mind, or state of readiness—of critical thinking and good argumentation is keeping an open mind. No matter how much you think you know about a subject, someone else can always bring something new to your understanding of a concept, perhaps through a different viewpoint, additional facts, or personal experiences. If you have your mind made up that you already know enough about a topic—or you believe that there is nothing more or different you want to learn about a topic—you may miss a wonderful learning opportunity. You limit yourself by getting or keeping only pieces of the picture. This is not to say that everyone is always equally right, and that there is no truth. Everyone has some truth but no one has it all. Careful consideration of other people's ideas can lead you to a greater overall understanding.

ACTIVITY 11A
Describe What You See

What do you see in this picture? It is more interesting if you are able to share this picture with another person. Did you both see the same thing? You may be surprised by what the other person sees.

Created by "R.H.," The Strand Magazine, December 1899

The picture in Activity 11A is a metaphor for seeing more than one view, and not assuming that you have all of the information. The point of looking at this image is to make a point. Very often students come to class assuming that they know what will be discussed, so they do not pay attention to new information or to reasons for a conclusion different from their own. When arguments are presented, these students focus only on their own viewpoints, reasons, and conclusions. They ignore or dismiss others' reasons and conclusions, tending to see things only one way—their own way. Then when they are tested on what they should have learned (for example, that two different pictures can be seen in one picture), they find that they are missing important pieces of information. They are not prepared because they missed key points. Critical thinking requires that you examine *all* parts of an argument before making your final conclusion. It is necessary to keep an open mind.

Parts of an Argument

AN ARGUMENT HAS TWO PARTS: a conclusion and reasons. A simple way to imagine the structure of an argument is to picture a stick house. A conclusion is like the roof and the reasons are the walls that hold it up. A solid argument is like a house with strong walls and a roof that fits properly. A weak argument has thin walls or an ill-fitting roof—or sometimes both. In this chapter, you will learn how to find an author's arguments in your textbooks. (In Chapter 12, you will begin to evaluate arguments.)

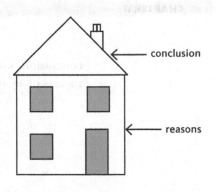

conclusion

reasons

For now, let's look at basic arguments. An argument consists of two or more statements that include one conclusion and at least one reason that supports the conclusion.

conclusion judgment or decision based on at least one reason

reason statement that explains, justifies, or otherwise supports the conclusion

Conclusion: Sociology is important.

Reason 1: It offers explanations for how people act in groups.

Conclusion: Democratic governments have the happiest citizens.

Reason 1: Citizens can choose their leaders.

Reason 2: Citizens can pick careers that best suit their talents and interests.

Conclusion

A CONCLUSION IS the judgment, decision, or opinion that someone reaches after thinking about or investigating an issue. For example, one might conclude that the San Francisco Giants are the best baseball team. Another person might conclude that eating eggs from vegetarian-fed chickens is healthier than eating other eggs. Both of these are conclusions. To qualify as full arguments, though, each conclusion requires at least one reason.

Reasons

A REASON IS a statement that explains, justifies, or otherwise supports the conclusion. Reasons can be facts, opinions, beliefs, or examples that support the

Tip FROM THE
Brain Doctor

After puberty, there is a tendency for the brain to want to make what is external conform to what is internal. This means that you want to make what you see and hear conform to the way you already view the world. Instead of the environment shaping the brain as it does before puberty, the brain wants to shape the environment. That is not to say we become closed-minded; it just means that sometimes we hear and see what we want to hear and see. This is a slight tendency, but becoming aware of this can help you keep an open mind.

conclusion. Good reasons support a conclusion well and contribute to the success of an argument.

Conclusion

↑ ↑

Reason 1

Reason 2

One could offer as a reason *The Giants won the World Series in 2012* for the conclusion *The San Francisco Giants are the best baseball team.* Or one could use the reason that *Vegetarian-fed chicken eggs do not contain the hormones found in other types of eggs* to support the conclusion *Vegetarian-fed chickens provide healthier eggs.*

Consider the following arguments:

Conclusion: Mark Zuckerberg is an effective businessman.

> **Reason**:   Mark Zuckerberg started Facebook. (This supports the conclusion that he is an effective businessman. Facebook is well-known and very popular.)

> **Reason**:   He has earned an estimated $6.9 billion. (If he has earned this much, he must be doing something right in his business, which must be successful, so he is effective.)

Conclusion: There are several reasons why consistent study is more effective than cramming.

> **Reason**:   If you study regularly every day, you will find it easier to remember what you learned.

> **Reason**:   By studying regularly, you will see the connections within course material.

> **Reason**:   The brain takes time to process information. The more you study, the more deeply you will learn new information, which means better test results.

Do the three reasons support the conclusion that consistent study is more effective than cramming? Yes, they are all relevant. Say, however, that one of the reasons states that *Joe's diner provides excellent food.* This is not a reason that supports the conclusion. It may be true, or someone's worthy opinion, but it is not a reason that directly supports the conclusion. It has nothing to do with the argument *Consistent study is more effective than cramming.* The reason(s) must support the conclusion in order for the statements to be considered an argument.

ACTIVITY 11B
Identify Conclusions and Reasons

Read the following sentences, and determine which sentence in each group is a conclusion and which sentences in each group are reasons. One is modeled for you here.

Example:

  conclusion   a. It follows that I will graduate on time.

  reason   b. I need 15 credits a semester to graduate on time.

  reason   c. I have earned 15 credits every semester for 3 ½ years.

1. _____ a. Therefore, legislation needs to address the flu issue.

   _____ b. It is estimated that 1 to 2 million Americans are infected with the virus that causes the flu.

   _____ c. In 2014, more children and women will continue to get the flu.

2. _____ a. The truth is, I am not happy.

   _____ b. I cry a lot.

   _____ c. Also, I want to be left alone.

   _____ d. For example, I sleep all day.

3. _____ a. Exercise allows you a better, more restful sleep.

   _____ b. Third, exercise lowers the risk of heart attack.

   _____ c. Second, moderate exercise improves the immune system.

   _____ d. In conclusion, there are several benefits of exercising.

4. _____ a. Additionally, critical thinking should be taught to students throughout their educational experiences (from kindergarten through college), using course content.

   _____ b. For one thing, critical thinking is not a natural ability.

   _____ c. It should be clear that critical thinking requires deliberate, continuing instruction, guidance, and practice in order to develop to its full potential.

   _____ d. Also, critical thinking is a composite of skills, standards, and dispositions.

Continued on next page.

5. _____   a. The acting was horrible.

_____   b. In my opinion, *Intruders* was the worst movie I have ever seen.

_____   c. The special effects were low budget.

_____   d. The plot did not have enough believable stuff in it to keep the audience interested.

ACTIVITY 11C
Supply Missing Parts of the Argument

Read the following statements, some of which are reasons and some of which are conclusions. Supply the missing parts of the argument. One is modeled for you here.

Example:

Conclusion: *Brian took property that was not his.*

Reason 1: An eyewitness saw Brian leave the building with the property when the alarm went off.

Reason 2: Brian had the stolen property in his possession when he was stopped by the police.

1. Conclusion: *Rap music is actually a form of poetry.*

    Reason 1: It involves creative word combinations.

    Reason 2: _____

2. Conclusion: *We, the human race, need to share the food the world produces.*

    Reason 1: _____

    Reason 2: Some countries throw away extra food and are very well-fed and healthy.

3. Conclusion: _____

    Reason 1: Reality television has lots of viewers.

    Reason 2: Reality television earns good ratings.

4. Conclusion: *Therefore, the government should outlaw the sale of guns.*

    Reason 1: _____

    Reason 2: _____

5. Conclusion: _____

    Reason 1: There are no snow-related accidents.

    Reason 2: You can swim year-round.

Looking for Arguments in What You Read

AUTHORS PRESENT ARGUMENTS IN WHAT THEY WRITE, and you have already had ample practice identifying these arguments, even if you did not know it. When you identified an author's main idea and major supporting details in a reading, you identified the main argument. An author's main idea is a conclusion, and the major supporting details are the reasons. Sometimes the conclusion (main idea) is right up front in the reading. Sometimes it is at the end. Other times, it is implied and you have to infer the meaning. Many times authors have one main argument with other smaller arguments within it. For the purposes of this chapter, we will focus on the main argument.

Main idea		Conclusion	
↑ ↑	=	↑ ↑	
Major Supporting Detail		Reason 1	
Major Supporting Detail		Reason 2	

ACTIVITY 11D
Identify the Argument

Read the following commencement speech given by Miles Levin, a valedictorian from a suburban Detroit high school. His speech is unique because of his perspective. He comes from what might be called, in the language of the Occupy Wall Street movement, the 1%. His family is privileged; his high school is prestigious. As you read, ask yourself: What are his arguments?

Preview and study-read the speech. While previewing the speech, you will notice that there are no headings, so skim the speech and access your background knowledge. What do you know about commencement speeches? What is their purpose? As you study-read, highlight the main idea/conclusion in green and the major supporting details/reasons in yellow. Make marginal notes as needed. When you are done previewing and study-reading, answer the questions following the speech.

Graduation Speech, Cranbrook Upper School, Bloomfield Hills, Michigan
By Miles Levin

1   We are here on this earth having been thrust into a random situation we did nothing to deserve, surrounded by circumstances we cannot control. Sometimes chance is kind to us; sometimes we get the short end of the stick. I think the hardest pill we'll

Continued on next page.

existential resignation giving in to the philosophical idea that people should find themselves and the meaning of life through free will, choice, and personal responsibility without the help or knowledge of absolute truth

fulminate energetically protest

vociferate shout, complain

ever have to swallow is getting less than we deserve. It stems from accepting that life isn't fair. We want it to be fair. We want so badly for it to be fair. It should be. It deserves to be. On a very deep level, we need it to be. But it's not. And whenever we fume over some injustice that has befallen us and then a wise friend reminds us, "life isn't fair," we have to admit with a certain existential resignation that they have a point; but somehow that doesn't really help at all.

2   How can I support the very existence of the universe I live in? I can't. I can only shake my head, and rather without clout. I can fulminate; I can vociferate; I can raise my banner in protest of everything that isn't as it should be in the world, but the universe is as the universe does. A pregnant woman will die in a car accident today, and I cannot change that.

3   What feels so deeply wrong about an unfair world such as ours is that it is unfair in a way that, almost by definition, doesn't make any sense. At least not to me. Some people own private jets, others don't have access to fresh water. I don't get it. So what I ask you is this: If you are born rich with blessings beyond your control, if good luck should catch you a taxi while an old man stands in the rain, if you are given the seldom talked about long end of the stick, do you have an inherent obligation to use your gifts, resources, and abilities, in a sharing and philanthropic manner? Does having good fortune come with the uninvited responsibility that we give some of it back to the less fortunate? The comfortable answer is: Yes. Feed the hungry children, absolutely. Support music and the fine arts in our school systems, absolutely. But really, no one can be blamed for what they have. You didn't choose your lot any more than a hungry person chose theirs; how can you be held accountable for chance? And I'm not just talking about money. If you are intelligent and have access to an education, can you be a janitor? If you are brilliantly intelligent, and could, if you applied yourself, cure a disease and save thousands or even millions of lives, can you be the CEO of Marlboro? Your initial reaction to my question about giving back was probably yes, we should. Our consciences are pretty clear in identifying the more generous path, but the top position at Marlboro reveals the complexity of the issue. It involves the question, "to what extent is your life your life, and to what extent must it be lived for others?"

4   On the one hand, our parents here in the audience are a perfect example of the duty to sacrifice. For the past eighteen years they have sacrificed for us, and I'm gladdened to see the pleasure they take in witnessing the fruit of that sacrifice today. On the other hand, who's to say you can't be a janitor if that's what you want to do with your life. It's not hurting anybody. In fact, it's helping people, and I mean no disrespect to janitors, but it might not be helping others as much as you could be, and is that hurting them indirectly? Put your good where it will do the most, goes the old adage. It's not, "do what you enjoy the most," and with that comes a certain submission to the greater good. Being an operative for the greater good is rarely fun or easy, but always gratifying.

5   So do you have a right to live your life as you wish? If it's not hurting others, I say absolutely. Is this being selfish? Potentially it is. Where we draw the line is both personal and circumstantial, but I beg you… give your line some reflection.

6   We cannot be blamed for the things we cannot control, but that does not excuse us from taking charge of the things we can. And while we cannot be blamed for the blessings we cannot control, that does not excuse us from at the very least appreciating them. Often, people who have been in peril but escaped unscathed while others weren't so lucky, look around and experience something called "survivor guilt." "Why do they still get to live when others must die?" they wonder. I've never liked the term. I much prefer "survivor responsibility."

7   Survivor responsibility carries no guilt, although you are enlisted to a certain moral duty by the default blessedness of your life. I suppose you could argue this is an onus forced upon you without your asking, without consideration that you might not want it, and you'd be right, but Paris Hilton could say pretty much the same thing about getting stuck with a few billion dollars. You'll have to look inward to see exactly what this responsibility means to you. I can't tell you the answer, and even if I could, I hope I'd be wise enough not to. I will say that all of us here could have been born into poverty or orphanage or oppression… yet we weren't. And I haven't the faintest clue why. As far as I can tell, it was not merit's hand that rolled the dice. I don't think of myself as a better person than he who goes hungry, and I don't think of you as better people than she who gets sick. But for some reason, we have been plopped into a world of comfort and opportunity while others starve and die. In the end, how much responsibility this puts on you to make something of yourself and level the playing field is a matter of opinion. I can tell you no absolute truth; only ask with all my heart that you consider a) what an advantage we have all been given as recipients of a Cranbrook education, and all the other blessings you couldn't even begin to count, and then b) what duties, if any, come with privilege as you head off to your colleges and onward into your futures. Would you be doing a dishonor to those without opportunity if you do not take full advantage of yours? I'm sure you're all a little nervous about college, so I apologize for the extra pressure, but please do think about it. Thank you.

onus
responsibility

Source: Reprinted by permission of Nancy Levin.

1. What point does the author make about life in paragraph 1?

   _____

   _____

2. What two examples does the author give in paragraph 2 that support the point made about life in paragraph 1?

   _____

   _____

Continued on next page.

3. Who is the author talking about in paragraph 3 when he says those who are "given the seldom talked about long end of the stick …"? What responsibility do these people have?

_____

_____

4. What important question does the author ask at the end of paragraph 3? Why is it important?

_____

_____

5. How is paragraph 4 organized (pattern of organization)? How does paragraph 4 answer the important question posed at the end of paragraph 3?

_____

_____

6. The main idea of this speech is implied, but paragraph 5 offers a big clue. What sentence in paragraph 5 helps you to infer the main idea of the speech? What is the implied main idea?

_____

_____

7. Give the reasons that the author provides to support his conclusion.

_____

_____

_____

_____

8. At the end of the speech, the author talks about survivor guilt and survivor responsibility. He says he prefers the term "survivor responsibility." What does "survivor responsibility" mean? Create your own argument to support or refute the author's idea. (You may have more than one reason.)

_____

_____

_____

_____

9. What you may not know is that Miles Levin, the author, was diagnosed with a rare form of cancer. His goal was to be well enough to walk across the stage at graduation. He made his goal, but he died shortly after, on August 19, 2007. Does this additional knowledge change your understanding regarding the arguments he presents? Explain your answer.

_____

_____

_____

_____

10. Did you enjoy the speech? Why or why not? Did the additional information regarding Miles have an impact on how you reacted to the speech emotionally?

_____

_____

Words that Signal Arguments

IN ADDITION TO questioning yourself to uncover argument parts, you can also look for words clues. Remember that a word clue is a word or phrase that signals something to a reader. In Chapter 5, you learned that word clues signal major supporting details. Since major supporting details are reasons in an argument, words that signal major supporting details also signal reasons. Table 11.1 shows some words and phrases that authors might use to signal to their readers that reasons are being listed or explained. For example, to support the conclusion that smoking should be banned on college campuses, an author might say, "*First of all*, second-hand smoke can cause cancer." The next reason could begin: "*Secondly*, cigarettes are a fire hazard in dormitories."

Table 11.1 Reason Word Clues

for example	if	may be deduced from	as shown by
since	with it	because	may be inferred from
in the first place	finally	it is reasonable that	in view of the fact
for the reason that	first of all	first, second, third	as indicated by

Table 11.2 Conclusion Word Clues

therefore	thereby showing	it follows that
the only answer can be	then	leads me to believe that
in conclusion	consequently	as a result
the truth is	implies that	so
the point I am making is	in my opinion	thus
demonstrates that	proves that	it should be clear that
hence	points to	in short
as shown by the fact	from this it follows	I conclude that
is based on	for these reasons	justifies that
the data/research suggest(s)	can be argued	the truth is
can lead to	in fact	additionally

In Chapter 4, you learned that some word clues help readers identify and follow an author's main idea. Because main ideas are conclusions in an argument, words that signal main ideas also signal conclusions. Table 11.2 shows some words and phrases that authors might use to signal to their readers that a conclusion is coming. For example, to signal a conclusion about smoking, an author may say, "*Therefore*, smoking should be banned on college campuses" or "*The point I am making is* that smoking should be banned on college campuses."

Consider the following passage from a communications textbook. Circle any words that give you a clue that an idea is a reason or a conclusion.

Causes of Public Speaking Apprehension

1   Public speaking apprehension is most commonly caused by negative self-talk. Self-talk is defined as intrapersonal communication regarding perceived success or failure in a particular situation. Negative self-talk about giving a speech increases anxiety. Negative self-talk generally focuses on a fear of being stared at, a fear of the unknown, a fear of failure, or a fear of becoming fearful. Where do these negative thoughts come from? Research suggests three common roots: biologically based temperament, previous experience, and level of skills.

Biologically Based Temperament

2   First, some public speaking apprehension may be inborn. This "communibiological" explanation proposes that for a few of us public speaking

apprehension stems from our biologically based temperament. According to this theory, people who are extroverted tend to experience lower levels of public speaking apprehension than people who are introverted. Similarly, people who naturally experience elevated levels of general anxiety and shyness tend to experience higher levels of public speaking anxiety than people who do not. Does this mean that, if you are temperamentally predisposed toward high public speaking apprehension, you are doomed to be ineffective in your speaking efforts? Of course not. Many successful celebrities are introverted and generally anxious and shy, yet all of them enjoy a great deal of public speaking success.

Previous Experience

3   Second, our level of apprehension may also result from our experiences with public speaking while growing up. In other words, some of us actually learned to fear public speaking! Research tells us that most public speaking apprehension stems from such socialization. We are socialized in two main ways: through modeling and reinforcement. Modeling is learning by observing and then imitating those you admire or are close to. Reinforcement is learning from personal experiences so that past responses to our behavior shape our expectations about how our future behavior will be received.

4   Consider your past. How did modeling affect your current communication behavior? What was oral communication like in your home when you were a child? What was it like in your community? Did your parents talk freely with each other in your presence? Did family or community members talk with each other a great deal, or were they quiet and reserved? What was it like around the dinner table or at community events? Did any of your family members do much public speaking? What were their experiences? Did they avoid public speaking if they could? If your family tended to be quiet and reserved and avoided speaking in public or showed fear about it, your own preferences and fears may stem from modeling. Modeling an aversion to speaking freely in public influenced noted Boston Globe columnist Diana White, who remarked, "In my family, looking for attention was one of the worst sins a child could commit. 'Don't make a spectacle of yourself' was a familiar phrase around our house."

5   How you have been reinforced by others in your speaking efforts also influences how well you believe you performed in the past and affects how apprehensive you feel about future speaking occasions. We have all had many "public speaking" experiences, from reading aloud during second grade, to giving an oral report in science class, to accepting a sports award at a banquet. If the responses to your speaking in the past

were generally positive, you probably learned to feel confident of your ability. If, on the other hand, the responses were negative, you probably learned to feel fearful of public speaking. So, if your second-grade teacher humiliated you when you read aloud, if you flubbed that science report, or if friends laughed at your acceptance speech, you will probably be more apprehensive about speaking in public than if you had been praised for your efforts. The public speaking apprehension you feel because of negative past experiences, though uncomfortable, does not have to influence your future performances. There are strategies you can use as you prepare to speak that will help you reduce your apprehension and be more effective.

Level of Skills

6   An important source of public speaking apprehension comes from having underdeveloped speaking skills. This "skill deficit" theory was the earliest explanation for apprehension and continues to receive the attention of researchers. It suggests that most of us become apprehensive because we don't know how to (or choose not to) plan or prepare effectively for a public presentation.

7   Effective speech planning is an orderly process based on a set of skills. If you do not know or apply these skills, you are likely to have higher anticipation reaction levels. On the other hand, as you become skilled at using the six-step speech-planning process, your preparation will give you confidence and your anticipation reaction will be lower than if you were ill prepared. The goal of this course is to help you become skilled and, in so doing, help you become a more confident public speaker.

Source: From VERDERBER/SELLNOW/VERDERBER. *The Challenge of Effective Speaking,* 15e (pp. 22–4). Copyright © 2012 Cengage Learning.

Did you circle *first* and *second* as word clues? Those words signal two of the reasons to support the conclusion. What is the conclusion of this argument? It follows the signal words *research suggests*:

> *Research suggests three common roots: biologically based temperament, previous experience, and level of skills.*

The author does not signal the third reason, but you can tell by the conclusion what the third reason is: level of skills. When authors use word clues, take note and use them to reconstruct the author's argument.

ACTIVITY 11E
Identify Word Clues

Read the following passage from a sociology textbook. Use the heading to develop a question to ask yourself before you read the passage. Use what you have learned so far in this book about main idea, details, inference, and argument to analyze the passage. Circle any word clues. Highlight and annotate the passage. Can you figure out the conclusion? What are the reasons? To determine the conclusion, look at the big picture. What is the overall point the author argues?

Multiculturalism

1   At the political level, cultural diversity has become a source of conflict. The conflict is most evident in the debates that have surfaced in recent years concerning curricula in the American educational system.

2   Until recent decades, the American educational system stressed the common elements of American culture, history, and society. Students learned the story of how European settlers overcame great odds, prospered, and forged a united nation from diverse ethnic and racial elements. School curricula typically neglected the contributions of nonwhites and non-Europeans to America's historical, literary, artistic, and scientific development. Moreover, students learned little about the less savory aspects of American history, many of which involved the use of force to create a racial hierarchy that persists to this day, albeit in modified form.

3   History books did not deny that African Americans were enslaved and that force was used to wrest territory from Native Americans and Mexicans. They did, however, make it seem as if these unfortunate events were part of the American past, with few implications for the present. The history of the United States was presented as a history of progress involving the elimination of racial privilege.

4   In contrast, for the past several decades, advocates of multiculturalism have argued that school and college curricula should present a more balanced picture of American history, culture, and society—one that better reflects the country's ethnic and racial diversity in the past and its growing ethnic and racial diversity today (Nash, Crabtree, and Dunn, 1997). A multicultural approach to education highlights the achievements of nonwhites and non-Europeans in American society. It gives more recognition to the way European settlers came to dominate nonwhite and non-European communities. It stresses how racial domination resulted in persistent social inequalities, and it encourages Spanish-language, elementary-level instruction in the states of California, Texas, New Mexico, Arizona, and Florida, where a substantial minority of people speak Spanish at home. (About one in seven Americans older than age 5 speaks a language other than English at home. Of these people, more than half speak Spanish. Most Spanish speakers live in the states just listed.)

Continued on next page.

5　　Most critics of multiculturalism do not argue against teaching cultural diversity. What they fear is that multiculturalism is being taken too far (Glazer, 1997; Schlesinger, 1991). They believe that multiculturalism has three negative consequences:

1. Multiculturalism distracts students from essential subjects. Critics believe that multi-cultural education hurts minority students by forcing them to spend too much time on noncore subjects. To get ahead in the world, they say, one needs to be skilled in English and math. By taking time away from these subjects, multicultural education impedes the success of minority-group members in the work world. (Multiculturalists counter that minority students develop pride and self-esteem from a curriculum that stresses cultural diversity. They argue that pride and self-esteem help minority students get ahead in the work world.)

2. Multiculturalism encourages conflict. Critics also believe that multicultural education causes political disunity and results in more interethnic and interracial conflict. Therefore, they want schools and colleges to stress the common elements of the national experience and highlight Europe's contribution to American culture. (Multiculturalists reply that political unity and interethnic and interracial harmony maintain inequality in American society. Conflict, they say, although unfortunate, is often necessary to achieve equality between majority and minority groups.)

3. Multiculturalism encourages cultural relativism. Cultural relativism is the opposite of ethnocentrism. It is the belief that all cultures and all cultural practices have equal value. The trouble with this view is that some cultures oppose the most deeply held values of most Americans. Other cultures promote practices that most Americans consider inhumane. Should we respect racist and antidemocratic cultures, such as the apartheid regime that existed in South Africa from 1948 until 1992? How about the Australian aboriginal practice of driving spears through the limbs of criminals (Garkawe, 1995)? Or female circumcision, which is still widely practiced in Somalia, Sudan, and Egypt? Critics argue that by promoting cultural relativism, multiculturalism encourages respect for practices that are abhorrent to most Americans. (Multiculturalists reply that cultural relativism need not be taken to an extreme. Moderate cultural relativism encourages tolerance and should be promoted.)

Source: From BRYM/LIE. *Sociology: Your Compass to a New World Brief Edition* 2e (p. 83). Copyright © 2010 Cengage Learning.

The author's topic is multiculturalism. You may have heard the word, but do you really understand what it means? Multi = many/more than one. Culture = behaviors and beliefs characteristic of a particular group, but its original meaning was "tilling the land." The meaning expanded over time, metaphorically, to mean tilling the intellectual mind. It now also means behaviors and beliefs characteristic of a particular group, but because of the origin of the word, it is implied that these behaviors and characteristics are deeply rooted, "tilled minds." So the behaviors are probably protected and justified by the group that holds them. It also is implied that these behaviors are not easily changed. What is the author saying about many or diverse cultures?

1. What is the conclusion in the first paragraph?

   _____

   _____

   _____

2. In paragraphs 2, 3, and 4, what kind of clue words stand out?

   _____

   _____

   _____

3. Paragraphs 5 shows a numbered list. What is the author listing?

   _____

   _____

   _____

4. What is the overall pattern of organization? Hint: It is not a list. How do you know?

   _____

   _____

   _____

✔ COMPREHENSION CHECK

   ▶ Up to this point in the chapter, what is unclear?
   ▶ Using your own words, define argument.

ACTIVITY 11F
Identify Arguments and Word Clues

Read the following passage, and answer the questions that follow. The first passage is modeled for you.

Example:

> (In fact) the discovery of America sparked a revolution of food and cuisine that has not yet shown any signs of abating. For example, tomatoes, chilies, and green peppers formed the first wave of American flavorings to circle the globe. Additionally, the Indian garden still grows a host of plants that
>
> *Continued on next page.*

the world may yet learn to use and enjoy. These plants may have practical uses such as providing food in otherwise unusable land or producing more food in underused land. They <u>also</u> vary the daily diets of people throughout the world and (thereby) increase nutrition.

Source: Adapted from Weatherford, J. *Indian Givers: How the Indians of the America Transformed the World.* Fawcett Columbine: New York. p. 115.

▶ Circle any conclusion word clues.

▶ Underline any reason word clues.

▶ What is the conclusion?

The discovery of America sparked a revolution in food and cuisine that is still going strong.

▶ List the reasons that support the conclusion.

Tomatoes, chilies, and green peppers formed the first wave for American flavorings; America still grows a host of plants the world may yet learn to use and enjoy; they vary the diets of people.

▶ Create a visual showing the passage's structure. Select one of the visuals you learned about in Chapter 7 (authors' patterns of organization) or in Chapter 10 (visuals in general). This example uses a cause and effect visual.

Cause and Effect Map

Discovery of America sparked a revolution of food and cusine

- Tomatoes, chillies, and green pepper first wave of flavorings
- Still grows host of plants world has yet to learn about
- Varies daily diets of people
- Increases nutrition of people throughout world

1.   One such example is when a lion approaches an ostrich that is incubating eggs or guarding nestlings; the adult bird will run some distance from the nest and flop down as if injured. It then staggers around with one wing hanging down in what is described as a "broken wing display." The lion, intrigued by the behavior and anticipating an easy meal, gives chase. Imagine its surprise when the ostrich leaps up and makes off across the savannah at high speed, propelled by its enormously powerful legs. Consider a second example. A nervous male vervet spotted an unknown vervet watching his troop from a short distance away. The resident's troop was feeding below a stand of acacia trees and the intruder had to cross a piece of open grassland between one stand of trees and another to reach them. The resident male was nervous that the new arrival might pick a fight and displace him as the troop's dominate male. So, as the stranger set out across the open ground, he gave the leopard alarm call and the intruding male raced back to the nearest tree and climbed to the topmost branches. How do animals know? The only answer can be that some animals deceive to stay alive.

Source: Readers Digest. (1994). *The Earth, Its Wonders, Its Secrets: Intelligence in Animals.* Reader's Digest: Pleasantville, New York. P. 91.

▶ Circle any conclusion word clues.

▶ Underline any reason word clues.

▶ What is the conclusion?

_____

_____

▶ List the reasons that support the conclusion.

_____

_____

▶ On a separate sheet of paper, create a visual showing the passage's structure. Select one of the visuals you learned about in Chapter 7 (authors' patterns of organization) or in Chapter 10 (visuals in general).

2.   You must rely on your reason rather than your senses, your untested opinions, or your feeling, since reason will not deceive you. With it, you will be able to distinguish what is real from what is not. In the Republic, Plato has Socrates describe a situation in which a person might desire something on the level of the senses but refuse it, using truer knowledge provided by reason. The truth is that there is only one way to know reality, and that is through reason.

Source: From MITCHELL. *Roots of Wisdom* (p. 35). Copyright © 2008 Cengage Learning.

Continued on next page.

▶ Circle any conclusion word clues.

▶ Underline any reason word clues.

▶ What is the conclusion?

_____

_____

▶ List the reasons that support the conclusion.

_____

_____

▶ On a separate sheet of paper, create a visual showing the passage's structure. Select one of the visuals you learned about in Chapter 7 (authors' patterns of organization) or in Chapter 10 (visuals in general).

3.   Hence, alertness and arousal represent the most basic levels of attention; without them a person is unable to extract information from the environment or to select a particular response. For example, alertness and arousal are low when you are tired or sleepy, which is why at these times you may miss important information or have trouble choosing the correct action. In some extreme cases, such as coma, alertness and arousal are so disrupted that the person is almost totally unresponsive to the outside world and has no control over his or her responses.

Adapted: From BANICH/COMPTON. *Cognitive Neuroscience* (p. 303). Copyright © 2011 Cengage Learning.

▶ Circle any conclusion word clues.

▶ Underline any reason word clues.

▶ What is the conclusion?

_____

_____

▶ List the reasons that support the conclusion.

_____

_____

▶ On a separate sheet of paper, create a visual showing the passage's structure. Select one of the visuals you learned about in Chapter 7 (authors' patterns of organization) or in Chapter 10 (visuals in general).

See the Argument without Word Clues

WHEN READINGS DO not offer word clues to help you identify the main argument, use other reading strategies to figure out the main argument. Just like when a main idea is not directly stated or no word clues are provided, you will use other strategies to help you find the main argument. Some of the strategies you have learned include asking questions, looking in the usual spots, and categorizing the author's points (general vs. specific). Revisit Chapter 4 to review these strategies, if necessary.

ACTIVITY 11G
Identify an Argument without Word Clues

Read the following passage from a radio and television textbook, and use the strategies you have learned to identify the main argument. Begin by reading the title and turning it into a question. Skim the passage, and then read the passage carefully, looking for the answer to your question.

Technique

1 Endowing a story with human interest is a key to good feature or documentary writing. Even if you want to present only facts, and even if the facts seem stilted and dry, you can make them dramatic. Develop them by embodying traits of the people they represent. Even if the subject is inanimate, such as a new mousetrap, toxic waste, a current fad, or a nuclear warhead, endow it with live attributes. Haven't we all run across machines that seem more alive than some people we have known?

2 Develop the script according to the same basic principles you use for writing the play and the commercial. Get attention. What is the problem or situation that requires the program to be made? For the documentary, especially, the conflict is important. Explore the people or characters involved with the subject. Develop the theme by revealing more information; in the documentary, build the conflict through the complications until it reaches a crisis point. Although major happenings create dramatic action, the little things, the human elements, are important in establishing empathy and holding the audience's interest.

3 A narrator almost always is used. But too much narration distracts. Don't let the program look or sound like a series of educational interviews or lectures. A narrator frequently can summarize information that is not obtainable through actualities. Make the points clear and concise, and even if you are propounding one point of view, be certain to include all sides of the issue as the evidence presumably builds to support your position.

Source: From HILLIARD. *Writing for Television, Radio and New Media* (p. 213). Copyright © 2011 Cengage Learning.

Continued on next page.

1. What question did you create from the title?

_____

_____

2. What main point is made in paragraph 1?

_____

3. What main point is made in paragraph 2?

_____

_____

4. What main point is made in paragraph 3?

_____

_____

5. The main idea of the passage is implied. To identify it, answer the question you asked yourself about the title. Infer the idea that the three main points from each paragraph support.

_____

_____

Distinguishing Facts from Opinions

AS YOU EXAMINE AN ARGUMENT, it is necessary for you to be able to tell the difference between facts and opinions. If the reasons of an argument are verifiable facts, then the arguments they are a part of are usually stronger. If the reasons are opinions that are questionable, then the arguments are usually weaker.

In 2010, writer Kitty Kelley wrote a biography of Oprah Winfrey. The biography was unauthorized, meaning that it was written without the cooperation or permission of Oprah Winfrey. In the forward of the book, Kelley reveals Oprah's uneasiness with the biography with the following quote from Oprah: "I live in a world where people write things that are not true all the time. Somebody's working on a biography of me now, unauthorized. So I know it's going to be lots of things in there that are not true" (pp. xii-xiii).

Biographers are supposed to report accurate information about their subjects or they risk being sued. Kelley's book does contain accurate facts, but what else does it contain? Why would Oprah be concerned?

Read the following passage from Kelley's *Oprah: A Biography*, which does contain facts, but also opinions. Notic how the opinions create a picture of Oprah for the reader. The opinions are in bold in this text (not the original) for easy detection.

1   Winfrey **blew into Chicago** from Baltimore in December 1983 when a dangerous cold wave plunged the Windy City temperatures to twenty-three degrees below zero.

2   She had arrived to host a local daytime talk show and, on January 2, 1984, introduced all 233 pounds of herself to the city by **marching in her very own parade**, arranged by WLS-TV. She wore one of her five fur coats, a Jheri curl, and what she called her "big mama earrings." Waving to people along State Street, she yelled, "Hi, I'm Oprah Winfrey. I'm the new host of A.M. Chicago .... Miss Negro on the air."

3   **She was a big one-woman carnival full of yeow, whoopee, and hallelujah.**

Source: Kelley, Kitty. *Oprah: A Biography.* Crown Publishers, 2010, p. 1.

What do you infer about Oprah after reading this passage? Is she humble? Brash? Grateful? Shy? Polite? Loud? One might infer from the passage that Oprah is proud, perhaps arrogant. These inferences come mostly from the opinions Kelley has included, not the facts. Facts are statements that can be proven and verified. The day Oprah arrived, her weight, what she was wearing, and what she called her earrings are all facts that can be researched and proven. Opinions are personal views and beliefs that cannot be proven as truth. Opinions vary from person to person and are frequently based on emotions and personal perception or bias. Did Oprah literally *blow into Chicago*? *March in her own parade?* Is she actually *a big one-woman carnival full of yeow, whoopee, and hallelujah?* These opinions reflect Kelley's perception of Oprah.

facts statements that can be proven and verified

opinions personal views and beliefs that cannot be proven as truth

Readers need to be able to separate facts and opinions as they read. When distinguishing facts from opinions, ask yourself the following questions:

▶ Can the information be verified as true? (fact)

▶ Is the information reliable? (likely a fact)

▶ Is the information an expression of someone's feelings and not able to be proven? (opinion)

▶ Is the information presented using emotive or persuasive language? (likely an opinion)

Facts

YOU SHOULD BE able to research a fact in other books or sources to confirm it. A fact does not reflect personal feelings or attitudes; it is a truth. If you want to find out when the first shuttle went into space, you can confirm the date: April 12, 1981. Or if you want to know who the first President of our country was, you would find two possible answers. Both are facts: John Hanson was considered our President before the Constitution, and George Washington was the first President after.

The following are examples of some facts. They are not opinions, feelings, or beliefs. Even though they are interesting, they are verifiable truths intended to inform you:

> Roosters cannot crow if they cannot fully extend their necks.
>
> The underside of a horse's hoof is called the frog. The frog peels off several times a year with new growth.
>
> A group of geese on the ground is called a gaggle. A group of geese in the air is called a skein.

These facts are based on either scientific research or examination of historical documents.

In the following passage from a biology textbook, the author uses facts to support his conclusion. The conclusion is highlighted in green and the reasons are highlighted in yellow:

1   We—like all plants, animals, and other organisms—are collections of atoms and molecules linked together by chemical bonds. The chemical nature of life makes it impossible to understand biology without knowledge of basic chemistry and chemical interactions.

2   For example, the element selenium is a natural ingredient of rocks and soils. In minute amounts it is necessary for the normal growth and survival of humans and many other animals, but in high concentrations selenium is toxic. In 1983, thousands of dead or deformed waterfowl were discovered at the Kesterson National Wildlife Refuge in the San Joaquin Valley of California. The deaths and deformities were traced to high concentrations of selenium in the environment, which had built up over decades as irrigation runoff washed selenium-containing chemicals from the soil into the water of the refuge. Since the problem was identified, engineers have diverted agricultural drainage water from the area, and the Kesterson refuge is now being restored.

Source: From RUSSELL/HERTZ/MCMILLAM. *Biology* (p. 22). Copyright © 2011 Cengage Learning.

The conclusion is supported by facts of biology and chemistry. Facts such as *In minute amounts it is necessary for the normal growth and survival of humans and many other animals, but in high concentrations selenium is toxic* are not based on perception or bias. Facts are proven to be true and make an argument stronger.

Opinions

OPINIONS CAN BE argued and, with proper explanation, can serve as good reasons in an argument. Authors use opinions to persuade. When you identify an opinion, try to find out what the author bases his or her opinions on. Here are some examples of opinions:

The driving age should be raised to 18.

Gas is too expensive.

21 Jump Street is the funniest movie ever.

In the following passage from a history textbook, the conclusion is based on opinions. The conclusion is highlighted in green and the reasons are highlighted in yellow.

The *New-England Courant* was the first American newspaper worthy of the name—and for good reason. It was in the hands of James Franklin, an excellent printer. In James' sixteen-year-old apprentice, his brother Ben, the press had acquired its first real writer. Some of his friends had tried to talk James out of starting the paper, Ben recalled later, deeming it "not likely to succeed." James persisted, however, and his brother, "after having worked in composing the types and printing off the sheets," was "employed to carry the papers through the streets to the customers."

Source: From FELLOW. *American Media History* 2e (p. 22). Copyright © 2010 Cengage Learning.

The *New-England Courant* may have proven over time to be the first American newspaper of quality, but the reasons presented in the passage—*It was in the hands of James Franklin, an excellent printer* and *the press had its first real writer*—are not as strong as facts. This does not mean the argument is necessarily bad. It just means that the argument is not as strong as one built on facts. If you were reading this textbook for one of your classes, you might purposefully hunt for facts to see what the author's opinions are based on. Examples of facts that could be included in this argument that would make the argument stronger are: statistics on sales of the paper, quotes of customer reviews of the paper, and evidence that the paper was used as a model for other papers. If in the end of your reading you found no facts or logical explanation to back up the opinions the author gives, you might judge the author's argument as weak.

ACTIVITY 11H
Recognize Facts and Opinions

Read the following statements. Identify each as a fact (F) or an opinion (O). Remember that a fact is something that can be proven or verified—to be either true or false. You do not personally have to know whether it is true. An opinion is a personal belief that cannot necessarily be proven right or wrong.

1. The pupil of an octopus's eye is rectangular.   **F**   O
2. A horse cannot vomit; neither can a rabbit.   **F**   O
3. Anyone, even a monkey, can paint like Jackson Pollock.   F   O
4. No wars are worth the casualties.   F   O
5. Camel's milk does not curdle.   F   O
6. The most fascinating birth of any animal is that of the kangaroo.   **F**   O
7. It is a misdemeanor to kill or threaten a butterfly—so says City Ordinance No. 352 in Pacific Grove, California.   **F**   O
8. Sugar is better tasting than salt or garlic.   **F**   O

ACTIVITY 11I
Identify Reasons of Facts and Opinions

Read the following passages, and decide whether they are based on facts or opinions. Provide explanations for your decision.

1.   The amount of light a telescope can collect increases with the square of the aperture. A telescope with a mirror that is 4 meters in diameter can collect 16 times as much light as a telescope that is 1 meter in diameter.

Source: From FRAKNOI/MORRISON/WOLFF. *Voyages to the Stars and Galaxies* 3e (p. 111). Copyright © 2006 Cengage Learning.

▶ Based on fact or opinion?

_____

▶ Reason 1:

_____

▶ Reason 2:

_____

2.   Dinosaur bones have been firing our imagination for hundreds of years. People in the Middle Ages found huge bones that were probably fossils of dinosaurs and large aquatic reptiles, which may have inspired the legends of dragons and giants.

       Source: Dodson, P. *The Age Dinosaurs,* Lincolnwood, IL: Publications International, 1993.

▶ Based on fact or opinion?

_____

▶ Reason 1:

_____

▶ Reason 2:

_____

3.   Trace elements are vital for normal biological functions. For example, iodine makes up only about 0.0004% of a human's weight. However, a lack of iodine in the human diet severely impairs the function of the thyroid gland, which produces hormones that regulate metabolism and growth. Symptoms of iodine deficiency include lethargy, apathy, and sensitivity to cold temperatures. Prolonged iodine deficiency causes a goiter, a condition in which the thyroid gland enlarges so much that the front of the neck swells significantly. Once a common condition, goiter has almost been eliminated by adding iodine to table salt, especially in regions where soils are iodine-deficient.

       Source: From RUSSELL/HERTZ/MCMILLAM. *Biology* (pp. 23–4). Copyright © 2011 Cengage Learning.

▶ Based on fact or opinion?

_____

▶ Reason 1:

_____

▶ Reason 2:

_____

4.   Temporal regions of the brain are associated with four main functions: memory, visual item recognition, auditory processing, and emotion. The hippocampus in the temporal lobes was clearly linked to memory by the famous case of H.M. In early adulthood, he underwent bilateral removal

Continued on next page.

of anterior portions of the temporal lobe for the relief of intractable epilepsy. Although the surgery was successful in reducing his seizures, he became unable to learn almost all types of new information even though most of his memories from the years before the operation were intact.

Source: From BANICH/COMPTON. *Cognitive Neuroscience* (p. 28). Copyright © 2011 Cengage Learning.

▶ **Based on fact or opinion?**

_____

▶ **Reason 1:**

_____

▶ **Reason 2:**

_____

5.   This week, Snyder did the right thing. He signed a bill allowing the sale of louder, more powerful fireworks within Michigan borders. Detractors, killjoys and nanny-staters have taken to the airwaves, using the mainstream Michigan media to whine about the dangers these devices pose. If they're to be believed, next summer our state is going to look like a snapshot of WWI trench warfare—only louder and more colorful.

Source: Friday, Robert Laurie. *The Detroit News*, 2011, December 16, p. 22A.

▶ **Based on fact or opinion?**

_____

▶ **Reason 1:**

_____

▶ **Reason 2:**

_____

ACTIVITY 11J
Identify Argument and Facts

The following passage discusses mental training. Richard Davidson is a neuroscientist who studies the brains of Buddhist monks who are experts at meditating to see how they are different from the brains of people who do not meditate. Determine the argument made in this passage and what facts support it.

Transforming the Emotional Mind

1   Davidson has been on a quest that much of modern neuroscience suggested was, to put it politely, quixotic: to discover whether states such as happiness, compassion, enthusiasm, joy, and other positive emotions are trainable. That is, do there exist techniques of mental training that can alter the brain in a way that raises the intensity of these emotions, makes them last longer, or makes them easier to trigger?

2   Take two data points. In the research that sealed his reputation for rigorous neuroscience, Davidson and colleagues discovered, in the 1970s, striking differences in the patterns of brain activity that characterize people at opposite ends of the "eudaemonic scale"—that is, along the spectrum of baseline happiness. That's fact one: there are specific brain states that correlate with happiness, as I'll discuss in greater detail below.

3   Second, brain-activation patterns can change as a result of therapy—specifically, as a result of cognitive-behavior therapy and mindfulness meditation, in which people learn to think differently about their thoughts. Jeffrey Schwartz showed that to be the case with patients beset by obsessive compulsive disorder; Zindel Segal and Helen Mayberg showed it with patients suffering from depression. Thus, fact two: mental training practice, and effort can bring about changes in the function of the brain.

4   From those facts, Davidson built his hypothesis: that meditation or other forms of mental training can, by exploiting the brain's neuroplasticity, produce changes—most likely in patterns of neuronal activation but perhaps even in the structure of neural circuitry in the sense of what connected to what and how strong those connections are—that underlie enduring happiness and other positive emotions. If that is so, then by exploiting the brain's potential to change its wiring, therapists or even individuals might restore the brain and hence the mind to emotional health.

5   Just to be clear, the goal is not merely the absence of mental illness which seems to be all that psychiatric and psychological therapies strive for these days, but the enduring presence of robust mental and emotion health.

6   "That's the hypothesis: that we can think of emotions, moods, and states such as compassion as trainable mental skills," Davidson told the Dalai Lama.

Source: From Begley, S. *Train Your Mind, Change Your Brain*. Ballantine Books, New York, 2007, pp. 220–221.

quixotic foolishly impractical

hypothesis argument

neuroplasticity brain's ability to change

1. What is Davidson's conclusion?

   _____

   _____

2. What are two facts that he presents as reasons?

   ▶ Reason 1: _____

   ▶ Reason 2: _____

Hidden Assumptions

inferred arrived at a
conclusion based on
evidence (see Chapter 7)

IN EVERY ARGUMENT, THERE ARE MISSING PIECES that can be inferred from the context of the argument. You should make these inferences so you can examine the complete argument. People know when they create an argument that they cannot list *every* reason why, for example, the Cardinals are a good baseball team or vegetarian chickens produce better eggs. Many times, reasons are left out of arguments because authors assume some basic ideas are true for most people, so stating them explicitly is unnecessary. The World Series as a competition is considered a fair contest for most people. The games, most believe, are not fixed. Therefore, one arguing that the Cardinals are the best because they won the World Series assumes that everyone believes that the World Series is fair, individual players are not taking steroids, and legitimate teams in both leagues are not omitted from the competition. If these missing or hidden assumptions are true, then winning the World Series is a fact that would lead one to believe that the Cardinals are the best team. If these hidden assumptions are not true, however, then the conclusion is faulty.

hidden assumptions ideas
or beliefs that are not stated
explicitly

Make sure you see whole arguments as you read your textbooks. Hidden assumptions need to be seen clearly, using inference skills, and judged as closely as stated reasons. (Refer to Chapter 7 for more information on inference.) Look at the following passage from a sociology textbook. Pay attention to the underlined text, which uncover the hidden assumptions the author has implied. Are these assumptions generally accepted as true?

Quantity and Quality of Schooling

1   When Gallup pollsters ask Americans about their dissatisfactions, public education is typically on the list of top problems every year. Is such concern warranted? Yes. Fifteen-year-olds in 22 countries out perform their U.S. counterparts in science and those in 35 countries have much higher scores in math, surpassing even the students in the highest achieving states in the Northeast.

2   Why are many U.S. students doing so poorly? Some believe that the typical curriculum in the United States covers "too many topics too superficially" unlike the curricula in many other countries. One reason for the superficiality of coverage may be short school hours. For example, Asian students have longer and more school days than their American counterparts. From grades one through twelve, this equated to 610 extra hours in school per year or 7.4 more years of schooling in Asia than in the United States.

3   Not all Americans endorse the idea of longer school days, even if the extra hours offer social studies, art, music or creative projects like building

model houses (to teach fractions). Instead, many parents feel that kids need some time to relax and play, and administrators worry about the additional costs of materials and teachers' salaries. Many Americans complain that the United States is falling behind other nations in academic achievement, but 44 percent feel that colleges and universities should not require students to take more math and science courses.

4   Unlike the United States, many countries identify young children with high innate ability in mathematical problem solving and then provide them with the resources (such as highly qualified teachers and specialized programs) to excel. A number of policy analysts maintain that many U.S. students are performing poorly, in mathematics and other areas, mainly because of school funding.

Source: From BENOKRAITIS. *SOC* 1e (p. 267). Copyright © 2010 Cengage Learning.

See if you can figure out the following about this passage.

Conclusion: Reason/Hidden Assumption:

_____

Reason:

_____

Hidden Assumption:

_____

Reason:

_____

Reason:

_____

Hidden Assumption:

_____

Reason:

_____

Hidden Assumption:

_____

Reason:

_____

Hidden Assumption:

_____

Now check your answers here to see how well you figured it out.

What is the conclusion? American students are academically falling behind other countries.

Reason: 22 countries outperform U.S. students.

Hidden Assumption: The process and measures comparing student achievement are the same.

Reason: Students are doing poorly.

Reason: One of the reasons may be short school hours.

Hidden Assumption: Increasing hours on school work will increase test scores.

Reason: Parents and administrators do not endorse longer hours.

Hidden Assumption: Again, increasing hours will fix the school systems.

Reason: Students are performing poorly because of inadequate school funding.

Hidden Assumption: Money will fix the problems in our school systems.

The hidden assumptions are not universally agreed upon; however, the author assumes you accept the hidden assumptions as true. Do you? This is not to say that just because assumptions are hidden that they are automatically wrong. They might not be. It is just that these particular hidden assumptions are conclusions themselves without explanations or facts to back them up. If you ignore these important hidden assumptions, you run the risk of accepting an author's argument without completely understanding it. Aim to reserve judgment until you completely understand what an author proposes. Unpack arguments in their entirety. If you do, you will see exactly what kind of reasons an author's conclusions are based on.

ACTIVITY 11K
Identify the Hidden Assumption

Read the following statements. Identify one hidden assumption for each stated conclusion.

1. Conclusion: We should enforce the death penalty. We need to stop crime.

   Hidden Assumption: _____

2. Conclusion: Of course Loki is a great dog. Loki is a black Labrador.

   Hidden Assumption: _____

3. Conclusion: Buying cheaper ingredients for our lemon drop cookies is the plan. We will save the company lots of money.

   Hidden Assumption: _____

4. Conclusion: There is nothing wrong with staying out all night. I am just having fun. My other friends do it all the time.

   Hidden Assumption: _____

5. Conclusion: This bread is not good for you. It is full of carbohydrates.

   Hidden Assumption: _____

Read the following passage, and identify the hidden assumption.

> The problem is more complex than keeping fuel in your car's gas tank. When the fuel gauge shows that the tank is running low, you fill it with gas. By contrast, your stomach and intestines are not the only places where you store fuel. Fuel is present throughout your body, especially in the fat cells and liver cells, and more circulates in your blood. Furthermore, each meal has a different density of nutrients from any other. Fortunately, you don't have to know how much to eat.
>
> Source: From KALAT. *Introduction to Psychology* 9e (p. 381). Copyright © 2011 Cengage Learning.

6. Hidden Assumption:

   _____

Making Sense of Visual Arguments

VISUAL ARGUMENTS MAY BE PRESENTED THROUGH many different types of media such as cartoons, photographs, drawings, posters, or graphics. Through visuals, the author's goal is to share his or her point of view. The author intends to convey meaning and influence the reader by persuading, inspiring, or evoking emotions and reactions. A reader needs to uncover and discover the author's implied main idea, or argument. In order to determine what the author's purpose and argument are, you will do what you do for textual arguments and determine the argument, conclusion, and reasons that support the conclusion.

ACTIVITY 11L
Determine the Visual Argument

Read the following, and answer the questions that follow each.

1.

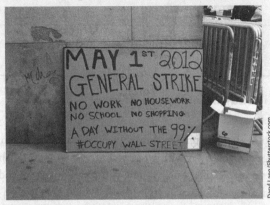

Daryl Lang/Shutterstock.com

▶ Predict what you think this visual is about.

_____

▶ What is the purpose of the visual?

_____

_____

▶ What is the conclusion that you inferred from the visual?

_____

_____

▶ What reasons can you infer from the visual?

_____

_____

2.

© Kim Kulish/Corbi

▶ Predict what you think this visual is about.

_____

▶ What is the purpose of the visual?

_____

_____

▶ What is the conclusion that you inferred from the visual?

_____

_____

▶ What reasons can you infer from the visual?

_____

_____

3. Read the following passage and the photograph that accompanies it.

M. Baumann/Blickwinkel/age fotostock

> I have very strong opinions regarding tattoos. I think that the body is a glorious canvas. Tattoos represent our inner thoughts and energy. They are beautiful. And after asking over a hundred people with tattoos if they were still happy that they got them, I was pleased to find that most people were. Not only did they love them, but said that they would be getting more soon. The truth is, most people find tattoos very attractive.

▶ Predict what you think this visual is about.

_____

▶ Read the passage and then determine what the purpose of the visual is.

_____

_____

▶ What is the conclusion of the reading passage?

_____

_____

Continued on next page.

▶ What reasons are provided for the conclusion?

_____

_____

4.

▶ Predict what you think this visual is about.

_____

▶ What is the purpose of the visual?

_____

_____

▶ What is the conclusion that you inferred from the visual?

_____

_____

▶ What reasons can you infer from the visual?

_____

_____

5.

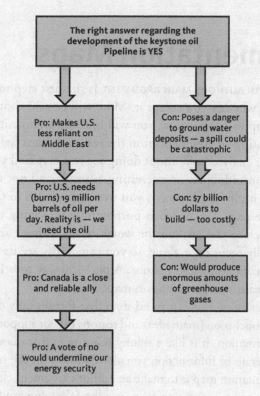

The right answer regarding the development of the keystone oil Pipeline is YES

Pro: Makes U.S. less reliant on Middle East

Con: Poses a danger to ground water deposits — a spill could be catastrophic

Pro: U.S. needs (burns) 19 million barrels of oil per day. Reality is — we need the oil

Con: $7 billion dollars to build — too costly

Pro: Canada is a close and reliable ally

Con: Would produce enormous amounts of greenhouse gases

Pro: A vote of no would undermine our energy security

▶ Predict what you think this visual is about.

_____

▶ What is the purpose of the visual?

_____

_____

▶ What is the conclusion that you inferred from the visual?

_____

_____

▶ What reasons can you infer from the visual?

_____

_____

_____

Argumentation Maps

UNCOVERING AN AUTHOR'S MAIN ARGUMENT is the first step toward evaluating it and deciding whether you accept it. More will be said about evaluating arguments in Chapter 12. For now, you will find the argument and prepare it for analysis. Isolating an argument from the rest of the text helps you not get distracted as you analyze it. Without doing so, you may find yourself getting lost in a creative introduction or interesting example and not truly analyzing the argument by itself. In Chapter 1, you were introduced to the idea of selective attention (see page 21), which is purposefully managing your concentration and focus. Before you analyze the worth of an author's argument, you need to purposefully focus on it alone, so you can clearly see its parts and the logic between the conclusion and reasons. A practical way to bring an argument to focus is to create an argumentation map.

argumentation map a mind map that focuses only on the argument

An argumentation map is a mind map that focuses only on the argument. It includes the conclusion (main idea) and reasons (major supporting details) only—no extra information. It is like a skinny mind map that does not include minor supporting details or information you already know on the subject. The purpose of an argumentation map is to make an author's argument clear and obvious.

To create an argumentation map, use the following guidelines:

1. Use separate boxes for the conclusion and reasons, and connect them with lines like as in Figure 11.1. Keep in mind that authors sometimes present the reasons first and the conclusion last.

2. Use complete sentences, not words or phrases, for the conclusion and reasons (major supporting details). If you use only single words in an argumentation map, you risk not seeing the entire argument. See Figure 11.2 for a complete argumentation map.

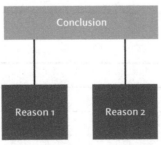

Figure 11.1 Argumentation Map Structure

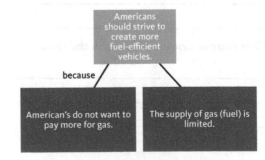

Figure 11.2 Example of a Completed Argumentation Map

Read the following passage from a humanities textbook, and see how Figure 11.3 portrays the argument the passage makes.

The Importance of Rome

1   If the origins of our intellectual heritage go back to the Greeks and, less directly, to the peoples of Egypt and the Near East, the contribution of Rome to the wider spreading of Western civilization was tremendous. In fields such as language, law, politics, religion, and art, Roman culture continues to affect our lives. The road network of modern Europe is based on one planned and built by the Romans some two thousand years ago; the alphabet we use is the Roman alphabet; and the division of the year into twelve months of unequal length is a modified form of the calendar introduced by Julius Caesar in 45 BCE. Even after the fall of the Roman Empire, the city of Rome stood for centuries as the symbol of civilization; later empires deliberately shaped themselves on the Roman model.

2   The enormous impact of Rome on our culture is partly the result of the industrious and determined character of the Romans, who early in their history saw themselves as the divinely appointed rulers of the world. In the course of fulfilling their mission, they spread Roman culture from the north of England to Africa, from Spain to India. This Romanization of the entire known world permitted the Romans to disseminate ideas drawn from other peoples. Greek art and literature were handed down and incorporated into the Western tradition through the Romans, not from the Greeks. The rapid spread of Christianity in the fourth century CE was a result of the decision by the Roman emperors to adopt it as the official religion of the Roman Empire. In these and in other respects, the legacy that Rome was to pass on to Western civilization had been inherited from its predecessors.

3   The Romans were in fact surprisingly modest about their own cultural achievements, believing that their strengths lay in good government and military prowess rather than in artistic and intellectual attainments. It was their view that Rome should get on with the job of ruling the world and leave luxuries like sculpture and astronomy to others.

Source: From CUNNINGHAM/REICH. *Culture and Values, Volume I: A Survey of the Humanities with Readings* (pp. 83–4). Copyright © 2010 Cengage Learning.

Tip FROM THE
Brain Doctor

Remember that the brain likes visuals. Mapping out an argument causes you to visualize it, and this visual, both in your head and on paper, helps you understand the information and recall it.

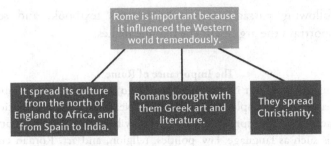

Figure 11.3 Argumentation Map Built from *The Importance of Rome* Passage

ACTIVITY 11M
Map an Argument

Create your own argumentation map using the following passage. Remember to write the conclusion and reasons in complete sentences.

Scientific Argument

Why is Earth a planet and not a dwarf planet?

This question calls for an argument based on a scientific classification. If it is to be useful, a classification must be based on real characteristics, so you need to think about the definition of the dwarf planets. According to the International Astronomical Union, a dwarf planet must orbit the sun, not be a satellite of a planet, and be spherical. A dwarf planet must not have cleared out most of the smaller objects near its orbit. As Earth grew in the solar nebula, it absorbed the small bodies that orbited the sun in similar orbits. That is, Earth cleared its traffic lane around the sun. Pluto never became massive enough to clear its lane, so Pluto is a dwarf planet. Because Earth grew large enough to sweep its traffic lane clear, it is a planet.

The dwarf planets are interesting for what they can reveal about the origin of the solar system. **How do the orbital resonances between the plutinos and Neptune confirm a theory for the formation of the Jovian planets?**

Source: From SEEDS/BACKMAN. *Foundations of Astronomy,* 11e (p. 548). Copyright © 2001 Cengage Learning.

ACTIVITY 11N
Create Your Own Argument

Using one of the prompts provided here, create an argument in support of or against it. You do not need to write a paper; just write the argument and conclusion and provide at least two reasons.

▶ Is the death penalty effective?

▶ Is torture ever acceptable?

▶ Should men get paternity leave from work?

▶ Should animals be used for research?

▶ Are we too dependent on computers?

You must use at least one conclusion word clue. Include at least two reasons using one reason word clue for each. Create an argumentation map to help you build an argument.

ACTIVITY 11O
Create Your Own Argument from a Visual

Read Figure 11.4. (Remember that you learned about bar graphs in Chapter 10.) Look at the types of data that are being shared. Using your interpretation of the data, create your own argument and argumentation map.

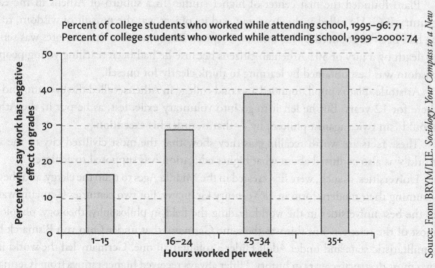

Percent of college students who worked while attending school, 1995–96: 71
Percent of college students who worked while attending school, 1999–2000: 74

Source: From BRYM/LIE. *Sociology: Your Compass to a New World Brief Edition 2e* (p. 83). Copyright © 2010 Cengage Learning.

Figure 11.4 Negative Effect of Employment on Grades among Full-Time College Students Who Work, United States

PRACTICE WITH A READING PASSAGE   POPULAR READING

Prepare to Read

1. Based on the title, what do you predict the following passage will be about?

_____

2. What do you know about the topic already?

_____

3. Before you read the passage, develop a question from its title. As you read, try to answer that question.

_____

Are Universities Worth It?
By Paul Johnson

1   A new academic year is about to start. At this time every year I find myself asking these questions: What ought universities to be doing? And are they doing it? After all, to take four years out of a young adult's life is a major investment, and we ought to be clear whether or not it's bringing in a worthwhile return. However, our societies seldom produce clear replies to these fundamental questions. The universal assumption is that higher education is valuable, and all governments are pledged to ensure that more and more people receive it.

2   Plato founded the first center of higher studies in a suburb of Athens in the early 4th century B.C. He called it the Academy, and its object was the pursuit of wisdom, to which he had been introduced by his mentor, Socrates. But remember that Socrates was sentenced to death by a jury of 501 Athenian citizens because he had been teaching young people that wisdom was best obtained by learning to think clearly for oneself.

3   Aristotle, Plato's pupil, founded a second college in Athens, called the Lyceum, and taught there for 12 years. But he left it to go into voluntary exile, lest, as he put it, the Athenians should "sin twice against philosophy"—that is, order his execution.

4   These facts are worth recalling, as they show that the most civilized city of the ancient world was also confused about what higher education was supposed to achieve.

5   Universities, as such, were first created in the Middle Ages to train the clergy, and they began assuming their modern form in 18th-century Germany. For two centuries Germany was home to the best universities in the world, leading the field in philosophy, theology, philology and most of the sciences. But this was the same Germany that under Otto von Bismarck became a militaristic state and under Adolf Hitler a totalitarian one. Germany led the world into the two most destructive wars in history. Hitler always received higher ratings from [German] students than from any other group in society, his views being strongly supported by a majority of German academics, with the world-famous philosopher Martin Heidegger setting the pattern.

6   So universities, and the education they provide, do not necessarily impart wisdom. What they do convey, in general terms, is not so easily defined. Prime Minister Vladimir Putin of Russia received a routine dose of higher education in the twilight of the Soviet Union as a prelude to entering the U.S.S.R.'s secret police community, an intellectual culture in which he still remains.

7   President Barack Obama found Harvard Law School to be invaluable in providing patrons and a fast-track entry into politics. There he absorbed the left-liberal culture that is Harvard's hallmark, which he is now applying to governing the U.S. and leading the Western World.

8   Prime Minister David Cameron had three years at England's oldest and most prestigious university, Oxford. Cameron's sojourn there was notable for his belonging (along with other members of his cabinet) to the Bullingdon, a club with a vague connection to horses and a more specific activity of consuming large quantities of champagne.

9   Such frivolities are not unknown in the U.S. The greatest disappointment in the life of Franklin Delano Roosevelt was his failure to get elected to the Porcellian, the club occupying the same position at Harvard as the Bullingdon at Oxford. FDR went on to win four terms in the White House to general but by no means universal applause.

More Than One Path to Success

10   The quality of higher education received seems to bear no relation to the success or failure of most Presidents. The two greatest, George Washington and Abraham Lincoln, had to learn the hard way. On the other hand, another distinguished President, Woodrow Wilson, first attracted notice as president of Princeton.

11   It is striking how much or how little great inventors and scientists learned at university. Thomas Edison never attended one, discovering his genius instead while working as a teenage telegraph operator. Charles Darwin went to Cambridge to study for the church but derived the greatest benefit to his career during long rambles with J.S. Henslow, a professor of botany. Darwin was known in his student days as "the man who walks with Henslow." What Cambridge did give Darwin was the opportunity to reinforce his capacity to work hard and systematically and to expand the range of his enquiring mind.

12   Indeed, the study of universities and the great men and women who have attended them leads me to think that the best of these schools are characterized not so much by what they teach and how they teach it but by the extent they provide opportunities and encouragement for students to teach themselves. The best also help to instill certain intellectual virtues in young minds, including respect for the indispensable foundation of democracy, the rule of law; the need to back up opinions with clear arguments, empirical evidence and hard work; the varying importance of resolute conviction and friendly compromise, when appropriate; open-mindedness at all times; and the perpetual need for courage in the pursuit of truth.

13   These are essentially moral qualities, which must form the basis of any university education. College presidents and trustees must satisfy themselves that this is precisely what their institutions are providing, as must corporate and individual benefactors. In the long run this is the only way we can ensure that universities justify the resources and time they consume.

Continued on next page.

Check Your Understanding

4. What is the conclusion of this reading? (Hint: It should answer the question you created before you started reading.)

_____

_____

5. Reread paragraph 7 about President Barack Obama. Is it fact or opinion? Positive or negative? Why? Share words in the reading that help you understand what the author is saying about President Obama.

_____

_____

6. What does the author imply about Germany, Hitler, and universities? What hidden assumption does the author make?

_____

_____

7. Write your own argument in response to the following question: What makes a college education worthwhile?

Conclusion: _____

Reason: _____

Reason: _____

Reason: _____

8. Why, as the author argues, should university students learn the intellectual virtue of "courage in the pursuit of truth"?

_____

_____

9. Read the following sentence from the passage, and use context clues and word part analysis to define the bolded words.

> "The best also help to instill certain intellectual **virtues** in young minds, including respect for the **indispensable** foundation of democracy, the rule of law; the need to back up opinions with clear arguments, **empirical** evidence and hard work; the varying importance of **resolute** conviction and friendly compromise, when appropriate; open-mindedness at all times; and the **perpetual** need for courage in the pursuit of truth."

a. virtues   _____

b. indispensable   _____

c. empirical   _____

d. resolute   _____

e. perpetual   _____

10. In your opinion, why would a university that encourages students to teach themselves be worth it?

_____

_____

CHAPTER SUMMARY

Arguments are logical structures that people create when they speak or write. When reading an argument, first ready your mind and "empty your cup." Entertain the fact that the argument *could* be true. Carefully read it. Then seek out the argument parts—conclusions and reasons. An author's conclusion is his or her main idea. The reasons are the major supporting details. One strategy for locating arguments is to look for word clues that signal conclusions and reasons. When there are no word clues, rely on the other main idea strategies you know—asking questions, looking in the usual spots, and categorizing an author's points.

You need to decide whether you accept arguments when you are presented with them. Determine if the reasons in the argument are facts or opinions. Identify if the author makes any hidden assumptions by using your inference skills to uncover the complete argument. When you have discovered all the argument parts, you can make an argumentation map, which is a visual depicting exactly what the argument contains. It helps you see the argument for what it really is before you begin to evaluate it.

Brain Connections: Self-Assessment

Draw the amount of dendrites you imagine that you have now about arguments. Compare your drawing of dendrites now with what you drew at the beginning of this chapter. If the amounts are different, explain why.

✔ COMPREHENSION CHECK

▶ What is one question you have about arguments?

▶ Explain why learning about arguments is considered a skill that expert readers need.

POST TEST

Part 1: Objective Questions

Match the key terms from the chapter in Column A to their definitions in Column B.

	Column A	Column B
_____	1. argument	a. judgment or decision based on at least one reason
_____	2. reason	b. statement that explains, justifies, or otherwise supports the conclusion
_____	3. conclusion	c. two or more statements that include one conclusion and at least one reason that support it
_____	4. facts	d. personal views and beliefs that cannot be proven as truth
_____	5. opinions	e. statements that can be proven and verified
_____	6. hidden assumptions	f. a mind map that focuses only on the argument
_____	7. inferred	g. ideas or beliefs that are not stated explicitly
_____	8. argumentation map	h. arrived at a conclusion based on evidence

Identify each of the following statements as fact or opinion by circling F or O.

9. Spiders are ugly.   F   O

10. The king of hearts is the only king without a moustache on a standard
    playing card.   F   O

11. Intelligent people have more zinc and copper in their hair.   F   O

12. A child's hyperactivity is all in the mind of the parent.   F   O

13. Antarctica is the only continent without reptiles or snakes.   F   O

Using what you have learned regarding argument word clues, identify the following statements by circling either R for a Reason or C for a Conclusion and by underlining the clue words.

14. For example, the medicine must be taken three times per day.   R   C

15. Hence, people need to be sensitive to the needs of the elderly.   R   C

16. I conclude that education is the key to success.   R   C

17. First of all, most students prefer staying up late anyway.   R   C

18. As a result, the purple plants are the most beneficial.   R   C

Part 2. Reading Passage

Prepare to Read

1. Based on the title, what do you predict the following passage will be about?

_____

2. What do you already know about the subject?

_____

3. Develop a question from the title. As you read the passage, try to answer that question.

_____

Language
By A. C. Krizan, Patricia Merrier, Joyce P. Logan, and Karen Schneiter Williams

1   Language can be a barrier to communication. Interactions between persons who have different native languages present communication challenges. Languages other than English can be heard in public places almost everywhere in the United States, as well as in other countries. In addition, most product directions are printed in more than one language, and universal symbols are commonly used as road and other directional signs. Although English has become the international language of business, a person's knowledge of a second language is somewhat limited because of word, tone, and non-verbal nuances that develop over time among native language speakers. Increased global contacts, along with a high percentage of U.S. residents whose native language is not English, multiply opportunities for misunderstandings among employees, clients, customers, suppliers, and other contacts.

2   Some words have different meanings and connotations in different countries and cultures. The Advertising Research Resource Center 6 at the University of Texas gives a number of examples of humorous or lost marketing opportunities because of mixed meanings in different languages. For example, the American Dairy Association's decision to extend the "Got Milk?" advertisements to the Mexico market failed because the Spanish translation was "Are you lactating?" When KFC entered the Chinese market, its slogan "finger lickin' good" came out in translation as "eat your fingers off." Chinese translation proved difficult for Coca-Cola; it took two attempts to get it right. The first translation was "Ke-kou-ke-la" because it sounded roughly like "Coca-Cola." After printing thousands of signs, company representatives discovered the phrase meant "bit the wax tadpole" or "female horse stuffed with wax," depending on the dialect. After researching 40,000 Chinese characters, Coca-Cola came up with "ko-kou-ko-le," which translates roughly to a more appropriate "happiness in the mouth."

Continued on next page.

3   Some words and phrases are difficult to translate from one language to another because of mental associations that only native language speakers have for them. For example, sports-related expressions such as "out in left field" would create translation problems in a country without baseball teams. Likewise, time-related references such as "time flies" and "time is money" have no logical meaning in literal translation.

4   The first wave of globalization made English the universal language, but current marketing strategies recognize the importance of accommodating geographic or cultural target markets. Corporations are shaping their products for local conditions and producing websites in two or more languages. American media giants such as CNN now broadcast in other languages as well as English to compete with regional, national, and international media. The number of non-English websites is growing, along with newly active Internet newsgroups that use the national language.

5   English is the common "linguistic denominator" for business. However, globalization is changing the nature of the language. With native speakers a shrinking minority of those who speak English, current thought resists the idea that students of English in other countries should emulate British or North American English. There is an acceptance that they may embrace their own local versions. Researchers are studying non-native speakers' "mistakes"—such as "She look very sad"—as structured grammar.

6   Even the use of parts of speech varies in different languages. In Japanese, the verb is at the end of a sentence. This enables Japanese speakers to begin to express a thought and watch the receiver's reaction. Depending on how the receiver reacts to a message, the verb may be changed, thereby changing the meaning of the sentence. For example, a Japanese language speaker might start to convey a message meaning, "Please go away from me now" but end up with the meaning, "Please stay with me now" by changing the verb, which is said last. Because of the importance of misunderstandings that can occur in language translations, a person with knowledge of language and language subtleties is an organizational asset.

7   Variations of English words exist even in English-speaking countries. For example, the American word for bathroom becomes loo or WC (water closet) in British English. In England, the American jello becomes jelly and jelly becomes jam. The British word for a sausage is a banger, and a car trunk is a boot. In both Australia and England, an elevator is a lift. Regional language differences exist within the United States as well. When you need a drink of water, do you look for a water fountain, a drinking fountain, or a bubbler? Do you carry your lunch in a bag or a sack? Do you refer to a carbonated beverage as a pop or soda?

8   Nonverbal language influences the receiver's understanding and acceptance of a spoken message. If message receivers perceive a difference between the sender's verbal and nonverbal messages, they are more likely to believe what they see rather than what is said. In multicultural business communication, nonverbal signals vary as much as spoken languages. Nonverbal greetings vary from a bow to a handshake, or from a hug to an upward flick of the eyebrows.

9   Not understanding cultural differences in nonverbal messages causes communication problems. For example, the Japanese consider crossing one's legs by placing one foot or ankle on the knee of the other leg to be impolite or vulgar. The preferred way of sitting is with both feet on the floor with knees together. Thumbs up in America means approval, but in Iran and Ghana it is a vulgar gesture. In addition, the social distance or individual space that persons need for comfort in communication varies in different cultures. If people stand too close when conversing, Germans, Canadians, and Americans may feel uncomfortable; in Middle Eastern cultures, however, conversations may be almost nose to nose.

Source: From KRIZAN. *Business Communication* (pp. 33–5). Copyright © 2011 Cengage Learning.

Check Your Understanding

4. Use context clues and word part analysis to define the following words from the passage.

   • connotations (paragraph 2): _____

   • denominator (paragraph 5): _____

   • emulate (paragraph 5): _____

5. What is the conclusion of the passage?

   _____

   _____

   _____

6. What are the reasons that support the conclusion?

   _____

   _____

   _____

7. One of the examples from the passage is: *When KFC entered the Chinese market, its slogan "finger lickin' good" came out in translation as "eat your fingers off!"* Is this a fact or an opinion?

   _____

Continued on next page.

8. This is a statement from the passage: *Regional language differences exist within the United States as well.* Using this statement as a conclusion in an argument you create, come up with two reasons to support the conclusion.

_____

_____

_____

9. What is one hidden assumption that the author makes?

_____

_____

_____

10. Create an argumentation map using the main conclusion from the passage and three reasons from the passage that support it. Make one of your reasons the hidden assumption you wrote in your answer to #9.

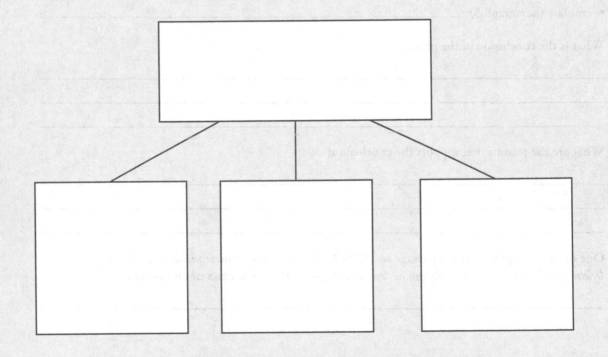

BRAIN STRENGTH OPTIONS

1. Working in a group of no more than three or individually, create a poster. The poster will contain two annotated pages. You may choose from the following options:

   a. Select a topic of interest to you (such as a medical condition, a favorite athlete, or information about a travel destination). Find information about the topic, including one page of information that you believe is based on fact and another that you feel is based on opinion. Print out both pages, and put them on the poster. Annotate the arguments, underlining conclusions and reasons. Label one "fact" and one "opinion." On the opinion, write a brief section explaining why it is opinion and not fact.

   b. Find the lyrics to two songs. One set of lyrics should contain opinions, and the other should contain only facts. Remember that you do not have to personally know if the facts are true, but you should know that they could be investigated and proven. Print out both sets of lyrics, and put them on the poster. Annotate the arguments, underlining conclusions and reasons. Label one "fact" and one "opinion." On the opinion, write a brief section explaining why it is opinion and not fact.

2. Working with one other classmate, prepare a debate in which one person speaks only in facts and the other speaks only in opinions. Each person will have a "side" or an argument. During the debate, each person will support his or her position with either all facts or all opinions. The debate will consist of three major points per person. Present the debate to the class.

3. Working individually, select a topic and present an argument on that topic.

   ▶ You must have at least three reasons and a conclusion.
   ▶ Your point must be clearly stated.
   ▶ Your argument must consist of all facts and no opinions.

   You may present this argument in one of the following ways (as approved by your instructor):

   a. PowerPoint presentation
   b. Poster
   c. Essay
   d. Oral report
   e. Illustration (The argument must be stated as captions with a picture for every statement.)

4. Find one editorial from a newspaper. Identify the argument's reasons and conclusion. You may choose one of the following formats:

   a. Poster (including the editorial)
   b. PowerPoint presentation (scanning in the editorial)
   c. Written report (the editorial as an attachment)

Reading Arguments Critically

ALEX MANION

A senior at Michigan State University majoring in earth science with a concentration in meteorology

> *"The unexamined life is not worth living."*
>
> —SOCRATES

Courtesy of Alex Manion

MANY OF THE PRINCIPLES taught in basic science classes have definite evidence to back them up and have been proven again and again. Knowing this, I accept whatever I am learning as fact. I have also witnessed the truth of these principles firsthand while working at the National Weather Service. It is generally accepted that low-pressure systems bring rain and high-pressure systems bring clear skies. I was able to look at surface weather maps that displayed high and low pressure systems and associate them with the weather outside. If a high-pressure system is sitting over Michigan, I was taught to expect clear skies. Sure enough, when I looked out the window, the skies were clear. I was able to take what I learned and apply it in the real world, solidifying that what I was learning was indeed true.

One popular argument I hear frequently about is global warming. When debates are shown on TV, the viewer sees one person arguing for a topic and one against. This setup makes it look like there is a 50/50 split on the point of view for a particular subject when, in reality, the majority of scientists believe one scenario. This makes it look like half of the general population believes in human-induced climate change where the other half believes global warming is naturally caused. These debates on TV are not always a bad thing, though. The scientific community needs opposition. When one criticizes a hypothesis, it causes the scientist to go back and make sure there is definitive proof to back what was said and that there are no loopholes in the explanation. It is important to always think critically about arguments. By doing this, you can understand any process and come up with a conclusion for yourself.

Making Connections

1. What does it mean when you deduce something?
2. Where have you heard the word *deduce* before?
3. Has anyone ever convinced you to change your opinion about something? If so, what did they do to change your mind? If no one has ever caused you to change your mind, why is that?
4. What do you think a generalization is? Look for a clue in the word itself.
5. What do you think circular reasoning would be? Look for a clue in the term.

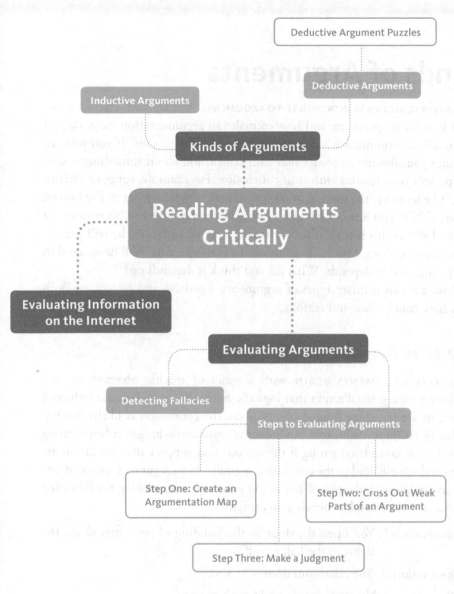

Deductive Argument Puzzles

Deductive Arguments

Inductive Arguments

Kinds of Arguments

Reading Arguments Critically

Evaluating Information on the Internet

Evaluating Arguments

Detecting Fallacies

Steps to Evaluating Arguments

Step One: Create an Argumentation Map

Step Two: Cross Out Weak Parts of an Argument

Step Three: Make a Judgment

© Cengage Learning

Brain Connections: Self-Assessment

Draw on the brain cell how many dendrites you imagine you have for how much you know about reading arguments critically.

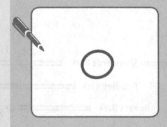

Kinds of Arguments

IN CHAPTER 11, YOU WERE INTRODUCED TO ARGUMENTS. You learned what an argument is, what its parts are, and how to make an argumentation map. As you may recall, an argument is a conclusion supported by reasons. If you want to convince your listener or reader that your conclusion about something is correct, present your reasons with your conclusion. For example, suppose a friend said, "I believe that the human brain is the most complex thing in the known universe." Will you just believe him or does he have to give you his reasons for why he believes this is true? If he wants you to agree with him, he will present all the reasons, along with his conclusion, to convince you. Will he succeed in convincing you? It depends. What do you think it depends on?

There are two primary types of arguments: inductive and deductive. Both types have conclusions and reasons.

inductive a type of argument where the conclusion is based on a series of observations and generalized to all

deductive a type of argument that makes a conclusion about a specific thing based on facts and verifiable truths or absolutes

Inductive Arguments

INDUCTIVE ARGUMENTS BEGIN with a series of specific observations and conclude with a generalization that logically follows from it. Because inductive arguments are based on limited observations, the conclusion is likely, but not absolutely, 100% verifiably true. An inductive argument is judged as being strong or weak. It is considered strong if the reasons that support the conclusion are strong and actually lead to the conclusion logically. Most arguments encountered in everyday life are inductive. What would you think after making the following observations one Monday morning on campus?

Observation 1: You open the door to the building of your first class. The lights in the hall are off.

Observation 2: The classroom door is locked.

Observation 3: No other people are in the building.

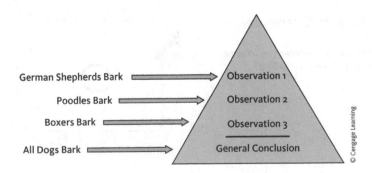

You might conclude that there is no school scheduled. You made specific observations and then came to a conclusion. You may be wrong, but your observations led you to this logical conclusion.

Here's another example of an inductive argument. After a recent study, it was concluded that students love pizza!

Papa Jozella's Pizza went to Glendale Community College, Heartland Community College, and Valencia Community College and asked students if they loved pizza. Most of the students confirmed they did.

Observation 1: Most of the students at Glendale Community College love pizza.

Observation 2: Most of the students at Heartland Community College love pizza.

Observation 3: Most of the students at Valencia Community College love pizza.

Conclusion: College students love pizza.

ACTIVITY 12A
Identify Inductive Arguments

Read the arguments provided here and explain why they are considered examples of inductive arguments.

1. The men and women of North Dakota were polled regarding an upcoming election. Eighty-five percent of those polled said that they would vote for Bette Grande. Bette Grande has won every debate. Bette Grande has the support of most business owners in the area. So, Bette Grande will most likely win the next election.

   Why is this argument inductive?

   _____

   _____

2. The Hawks won the last 11 games against the Doves. I am betting that the Hawks win tonight's game against the Doves.

   Why is this argument inductive?

   _____

   _____

3. I played poker last Tuesday and won. I played on Thursday and Saturday and won then, too. Tonight I will play and win poker.

   Why is this argument inductive?

   _____

   _____

Continued on next page.

4. I made charts to study for my last three biology exams and got As on all of the exams. I will make a chart this time, too, so I can earn an A.

Why is this argument inductive?

_____

_____

5. The detective comes into a room and sees a man lying on the floor with a sword stuck through his heart. He has seen this many times during his 30-year career. He states that the man is dead or dying.

Why is this argument inductive?

_____

_____

ACTIVITY 12B
Identify the Argument

Identify the argument in the following passage by previewing and study-reading it. Then answer the questions that follow.

> For billions of years, the man in the moon has looked down on Earth. Ancient civilizations saw the same cycle of phases that you see, and even the dinosaurs may have noticed the changing phases of the moon. Occasionally, however, the moon displays more complicated moods when it turns copper-red in a lunar eclipse. In cultures all around the world, the sky is a symbol of order and power, and the moon is the regular counter of the passing days. So it is not surprising that people are startled and sometimes worried when they see the moon grow dark and angry-red.
>
> Source: From SEEDS/BACKMAN. *Foundations of Astronomy*, 11e (pp. 32–3). Copyright © 2001 Cengage Learning.

1. What is the conclusion (main idea) of this passage?

_____

_____

2. What is one reason (major supporting detail) that supports the conclusion?

_____

_____

3. Write or find your own example in a newspaper, magazine, or textbook of an inductive argument.

_____

_____

Deductive Arguments

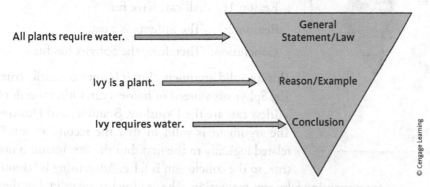

All plants require water. ➡ General Statement/Law

Ivy is a plant. ➡ Reason/Example

Ivy requires water. ➡ Conclusion

© Cengage Learning

THERE IS A difference between a statement about all things and a statement about some things. A deductive argument begins with a general statement or a general law and leads to or concludes with a statement about something specific. It is your job as a reader and critical thinker to determine if a deductive argument is valid. What does this mean? The argument has reasons that lead to only one possible conclusion, which follows logically from already accepted generalizations or truths. The first reason in a deductive argument is usually a general idea, truth, accepted theory, or other widely accepted principle. The second reason is typically a specific item that is linked logically to the first reason.

valid when a deductive argument has a conclusion that logically follows from the reasons, including the general statement/law

Reason 1: All flowers need water and sunlight. (scientific fact, not an observation)

Reason 2: A rose is a flower.

Conclusion: Therefore, roses need water and sunlight.

Reason 1: All humans breathe air. (fact)

Reason 2: Andy is human.

Conclusion: Therefore, Andy must breathe air.

While reading, you determine if an argument is valid by seeing if the reasons follow logically from the conclusion. If they do, the argument is valid.

Tip FROM THE Brain Doctor

Figuring out arguments is like figuring out a puzzle, which is rewarding to the brain and makes you feel good when you succeed. Think of it as pretending you are a detective, perhaps like Sherlock Holmes, and you are going to deduce, or uncover, the deductive argument.

Reason 1:   All humans need sleep.

Reason 2:   Jack is human.

Conclusion: Therefore, Jack needs sleep.

Once you have determined that the deductive argument is valid, you need to determine whether it is true. Just because it is valid does not mean it is true.

Reason 1:   All cats have fur.

Reason 2:   The Sphynx is a cat.

Conclusion: Therefore, the Sphynx has fur.

This is a valid argument, but it is not necessarily true. The Sphynx is a breed of hairless cat. Other breeds of hairless cats are the Donskoy, Bramble, and Dossow. The argument is valid in that the second reason is related logically to the first, but the first reason is not true, so the conclusion is false. Advertising is famous for presenting false argumentation. The arguments are valid, but they are sometimes false.

Many of the arguments you will read in your textbooks, especially in the sciences, will be deductive because these arguments are based on facts and verifiable truths that lead the reader to only one possible conclusion. Here is an example of a deductive argument from biology.

Reason 1:   All organisms are cellular.

Reason 2:   Plants are organisms.

Conclusion: Therefore, plants are cellular.

ACTIVITY 12C
Think Deductively

Read the following passages, and answer the questions that follow each.

1.   Burial of radioactive waste is the best disposal method. Yucca Mountain, however, is not the best site because it is hydrologically and geologically active. Burial at this site poses the risk of radioactive materials leaking out and contaminating surrounding soil and ground water. If a leak did occur,

ground water contamination would be a major problem. Many of the surrounding cities, including parts of Las Vegas, receive some of their water from the aquifers in the area.

Source: *ACT Victory Partial Passages*. Cambridge Educational Services: Des Plaines, Illinois. E-20, 2003.

Identify the conclusion of the deductive argument using the reasons to guide you.

Reason 1:   Hydrologically and geologically active areas are not good burial spots of radioactive waste (general statement/law).

Reason 2:   Yucca Mountain is hydrologically and geologically active.

Conclusion: _____

2.   Superficially, today's problems with the abuse of illegal drugs such as heroin and cocaine resemble the problems of alcohol abuse during the 1920s, when many people kept drinking in spite of Prohibition. There is, however, a significant difference. The use of drugs such as heroin and cocaine has never been a wide-spread, socially accepted practice among most middle-class, otherwise law-abiding Americans.

Source: *ACT Victory Partial Passages*. Cambridge Educational Services: Des Plaines, Illinois, 2003.

Of the following answers, circle the hidden assumption about this passage.

a. During Prohibition, drinking alcohol was commonly accepted among most Americans.

b. As long as drugs are available, they will be used despite laws to the contrary.

c. Most Americans consider heroin and cocaine to be in the same category as alcohol.

d. In a democracy, laws must be based on the fundamental beliefs and values of the majority of citizens.

e. American popular opinion has always been molded by the values of the middle class.

3.   Taoist philosophy, which was developed in Asia a century after the introduction of Confucianism, proposed that all forces of nature are connected and that it is necessary for individuals to become "one" with those forces. If a person is in a state of harmony or "oneness" with nature, then conflict will cease to exist. Together, Confucian and Taoist thought have permeated Chinese society, with the goal of getting citizens to be in consonance with those around them, to be in harmony with others and the rules of society. It was believed that the best way to accomplish this was through social persuasion and informal social control. Informal social control mechanisms include family members, neighbors, and fellow workers, as well as local town, city, or countywide boards that point out deviant behavior and provide sanctions.

Source: From DAMMER/ALBANESE. *Comparative Criminal Justice Systems* (p. 76). Copyright © 2011 Cengage Learning.

Continued on next page.

Identify the first reason of this passage. Remember the first reason in a deductive argument is a general principle or theory.

Reason 1: _____

Reason 2: It was believed that the best way to accomplish this was through social persuasion and informal social control.

Conclusion: Informal social control mechanisms include family members, neighbors, and fellow workers, as well as local town, city, or countywide boards that point out deviant behavior and provide sanctions.

4.   There is a basic rule involved in maintaining economic growth: The more things people must pay for, the more the economy grows. For example, if you do your friend a favor by driving her to the store, you may have advanced your friendship, but you've done little for the economy (other than using gasoline). If, on the other hand, you charge her (and report the charge on your taxes), you have added to the nation's GDP. In a similar sense, the greater the number of goods and services that can be obtained only by purchase, the better it is for economic growth. This means that some things that we would not consider desirable—a divorce, an oil spill, an illness or natural disaster— are economically positive events because they result in more money being spent. Other things that we might think are desirable, such as sharing your lawnmower, are negative because, by using something without paying for it, you hinder economic growth.

Source: From ROBBINS. *Anthro* (p. 62). Copyright © 2012 Cengage Learning.

Thinking deductively and using this passage as Reason 1 (general principle, accepted theory), what is an example of one positive event that could affect the economy and one negative event?

_____

_____

_____

_____

5.   Food irradiation has significant value in destroying the bacteria that infect the food. Irradiated food has a much longer shelf life than traditionally treated food. Irradiation destroys nutrients, but no more than normally destroyed by cooking food. Food irradiated with 10,000 rads or less of gamma rays show little or no nutrient loss. Therefore, irradiation of food should be supported.

Source: *ACT Victory Partial Passages*. Cambridge Educational Services: Des Plaines, Illinois. E-19, 2003.

What can you deduce specifically about meat, wheat flour, poultry, or other specific food items after reading this passage?

_____

_____

ACTIVITY 12D
Decide between Inductive and Deductive Arguments

Read the following statements, and determine whether they are inductive (I) or deductive (D). Ask yourself whether the conclusion *probably* follows from the statements (inductive) or does follow *necessarily* (deductive).

1. All actors are extroverts. Julia is an actress. Therefore, Julia is an extrovert.   I   D

2. A professor provides a definition of ethnocentrism and then makes the definition clearer by providing examples.   I   D

3. After reading an article that rates the quality and energy efficiency of dishwashers, you can now decide which one to purchase.   I   D

4. The detective determines that the man's brother-in-law is the murderer because his fingerprints are on the open window sill and on the murder weapon.   I   D

5. The coaches feel that the new football recruit will be of exceptional value to the team because he exhibits all of the recognized qualities of an outstanding athlete.   I   D

6. The vast majority of salespeople are extroverts. Tom is a salesperson. Therefore, Tom is an extrovert.   I   D

7. The Tigers have won all of their home games for the past two years, so they will win their next home game.   I   D

8. If the key players for the Tigers are healthy and able to play, then the Tigers will win their next home game. The key players are healthy and able to play; therefore, the Tigers will win their next home game.   I   D

9. The longer a pendulum is, the longer it takes to swing. Therefore, when the pendulum of a clock is lengthened, the clock will slow down.   I   D

10. Either the lines on people's hands are indicators of personality and life characteristics or hand-reading is a fraud. The lines on people's hands are not indicators of personality or life characteristics. Therefore, hand-reading is a fraud.   I   D

ACTIVITY 12E
Identify Deductive and Inductive Arguments

Read the following textbook passages, and highlight the conclusion (main idea) in green. Determine whether the argument is deductive or inductive, and explain why you think so.

1.   The study of brain damage is one of the oldest methods for determining brain function. A patient arrives with an injury such as a blow to the right side of the head and complains of a particular problem, such as trouble moving the left side of the body. In this way, a link is established between a brain area and its function. As early as the 19th century, it was known that damage to the left side of the brain can create very specific speech difficulties. Destruction of Wernicke's area results in a patient who cannot easily understand spoken language (Wernicke, 1874); damage to Broca's area produces a patient who can understand but not easily produce spoken language (Broca, 1861). Cases such as these suggest that different psychological functions are controlled by specific areas of the brain.

Source: From NAIRE. *Psychology* 5e (p. 69). Copyright © 2009 Cengage Learning.

Is the passage deductive or inductive? _____

Why? _____

2.   Judging from television, magazines, and books, no topic is more important to Americans than weight control. Dieting has become a national obsession, as people of all ages strive to be thinner and thus more "attractive."

Source: *Exploring Health: Expanding the Boundaries of Wellness.* Prentice Hall: Englewood Cliffs, New Jersey p.192.

Is the passage inductive or deductive? _____

Why? _____

3.   Humans give birth only to human babies, not to giraffes or rose bushes. In organisms that reproduce sexually, each offspring is a combination of the traits of its parents. In 1953, James Watson and Francis Crick worked out the structure of DNA, the large molecule that makes up the genes, the units of hereditary material. Watson and Crick's work led to the understanding of the genetic code that transmits genetic information from generation to generation. This code works somewhat like an alphabet; it can "spell" an amazing variety of instructions for making organisms as diverse as bacteria, frogs, and redwood trees. The genetic code is a dramatic example of the unity of life because it is used to specify instructions for making every living organism.

Source: From SOLOMON/BERG/MARTIN. *Biology* 7e (p. 7). Copyright © 2005 Cengage Learning.

Is the passage deductive or inductive? _____

Why? _____

_____

4.   People everywhere wonder about ultimate reality. In Asia, the question might be, Have you reached enlightenment?, Do you understand the interconnectedness of all things?, Or, are you living your life in harmony with the Tao? So in much of the world, the question of ultimate reality has nothing to do with God. Even in the parts of Africa where people have accepted Christianity or Islam, one might have asked, "Have you honored the ancestors?" In the West, the questions of ultimate reality could center around the existence or non-existence and nature of God.

Source: From MITCHELL. *Roots of Wisdom* 5e (p. 166). Copyright © 2008 Cengage Learning.

Is the passage deductive or inductive? _____

Why? _____

5.   From the same site another well preserved skull from the same time period possesses a cranial capacity of less than 600 cubic centimeters but has the derived characteristics of a smaller, less projecting face and teeth. Generally, specimens attributed to this period have cranial capacities greater than 600 cubic centimeters. However, cranial capacity of any individual is also in proportion to its body size. Therefore, many paleoanthropologists interpret the skulls as a female and male.

Source: From HAVILAND. *Anthropology: The Human Challenge* (p. 402). Copyright © 2008 Cengage Learning.

Is the passage inductive or deductive? _____

Why? _____

ACTIVITY 12F
Write a Deductive Argument

Try writing your own example of a deductive argument. Here is an example written by Nathan Wagner, a college student.

It's hard to write a good example of a deductive argument. I'm sure I read and hear them all the time….I just haven't recognized them before. Maybe this is one…. If I plagiarize my research paper for English 102, I will receive a zero in the class. That's a fact. It says so in my syllabus. That's one. If I eat canned tomato soup, I'll get cancer. No. There are people who eat canned tomato

Continued on next page.

soup and they live a long life. If I smoke, I might get cancer. No...doesn't work. This statement is true, but it's not a deductive argument. In a deductive argument, the reason is true and logically leads to the conclusion (cancer) must be true. Forget that one. I think this works: If I get my hair cut, it will be shorter. (Cutting hair makes it shorter. I am getting my hair cut. Therefore, my hair will be shorter.) Ha. That's two. I'll use one from Newton's gravity thing...Law of Gravity...If I throw my book up in the air, it will come down. There. I wrote a couple of deductive arguments.

COMPREHENSION CHECK

▶ What are the differences between deductive and inductive arguments?
▶ An interpretation of a poem is a good example of what kind of argument?

Deductive Argument Puzzles

Good problem solvers do not give up. They try experiments with several different ideas and possible solutions. Remember—sometimes the obvious answer is wrong. Read the following example:

> Ms. Lowmer works in a dress factory. Her job is to operate a cutting machine. Each time she presses the button, the machine cuts a piece of cloth two meters long. If she starts with a piece of cloth twenty meters long, how many times should she press the button in order to cut the cloth into two-meter lengths?

Source: Adapted from: Harnadek, A. *Critical Thinking Book One*. Midwest Publications, Pacific Grove, CA.

© David Crausby/Alamy

Provide a response before reading the answer.

The usual answer is ten. But the correct answer to the question is nine. Here is the reasoning: When she presses the button eight times, she will have eight two-meter lengths of cloth cut off, or a total of sixteen meters of cloth cut off. This leaves her with a piece of cloth four meters long. So, when she presses the button the ninth time, the machine cuts a two-meter length of cloth, leaving a two-meter length of cloth. So there is no reason for her to press the button a tenth time.

Before you begin solving the deductive problems, keep the following tips in mind. Good problem solvers:

▶ Never give up! Persistence pays off.

▶ Think through several options.

▶ Keep an open mind.

ACTIVITY 12G
Solve Deductive Puzzles

Try to solve the following deductive arguments. Based on the statements provided, there is only one possible correct answer. Have fun. Don't give up. *Think* it through. Draw pictures! Chart it out! Get creative! The first puzzle is modeled for you. See if you can come up with the answer on your own.

Example:
    If the wind is strong, kites are flown.
    If the sky is not clear, kites are not flown.
    If the temperature is high, kites are flown.

Assuming the statements above are true, if kites are flown, which of the following statements must be true:

    a. The wind is strong.
    b. The sky is clear.
    c. The temperature is high.
    d. a and c
    e. b and c

Try to determine the only response that is absolutely true. The puzzle does not say that all three criteria are required to fly a kite; so, the only one we know absolutely is that the sky is clear because the kites are being flown. It could be cold, but the winds are strong or the temperature could be high and the winds are not so strong. But kites are not flown if the sky is not clear. Rewrite the statements so that a, b, and c are all correct.

a. _____

b. _____

c. _____

1. You have two coins totaling 30 cents, and one of them is not a quarter. What are the two coins?

_____

Continued on next page.

2. There are no lower airline fares from Denver to Chicago than those of Anter Airlines. Which of the following is logically inconsistent with the above advertising claim?

   a. Zadina Bus Company has a Denver-to-Chicago fare that is only half that charged by Anter.

   b. Smilkstein Airlines charges the same fare for a trip from Denver to Chicago.

   c. Daiek Airlines has a lower fare from Denver to Detroit than does Anter.

   d. a and b

   e. None of the premises is inconsistent.

3. In Madeup-ville, *dob crack* means "yellow bananas." *Crack shoe hij* means "big yellow foot." And *hij pab* means "big house." What is the word for foot?

   a. dob

   b. crack

   c. shoe

   d. hij

4.

At the Races

The problem:

Five men, each with a different occupation—a banker, accountant, lawyer, engineer, and a doctor—bet on a horse race by contributing $100.00 each to the pot. The pot was divided into three cash prizes, according to how the horse placed in the race (1st, 2nd, or 3rd). In addition to cash prizes, a local merchant contributed a flat screen television, iPhone 5, and a microwave oven—to be split up as 1st, 2nd, and 3rd places. List each person's occupation, eye color, return on investment, placing of his horse, cash price, and the donated gifts won.

Directions: Compile the information from these clues into a final classification table that will give all of the required information.

The Clues:

1. The banker lost $100 on his bet.

2. The person who won the microwave oven gained $50 on his total cash investment.

3. The lawyer has brown eyes.

4. The person with gray eyes did not place.

5. The person with green eyes took first place.

6. The engineer won the T.V.

7. The person who took third place lost $50 on his cash investment.

8. The banker has blue eyes.

9. The accountant has black eyes.

10. The lawyer, even though he received a prize, lost money on his total investment.

Complete the following chart based on the 10 clues.

Occupation	Eye Color	Return on Investment	Place of Horse	Cash Prize	Donated Gift

Source: From KOLLARITCH. *Reading and Study Organization Methods for Higher Learning.* Copyright © 1990 Cengage Learning.

5. On this day, I am able to go to the tutoring center, buy paper from the bookstore, visit the student center theater, and then meet with my professor. The tutoring center is closed on Wednesday; the bookstore is closed on the weekends; the student center theater is open only on Monday, Wednesday, and Friday; and my professor has office hours Tuesday, Friday, and Saturday.

Conclusion: There is only one day of the week that I can do all of these things and that day is:

_____

ACTIVITY 12H
Challenge Yourself with This Deductive Argument

Now try something a little more challenging! Read the following story, and decide whether the statements that follow are true, false, or questionable. Provide a reason for each of your answers. For the purposes of this activity, accept each sentence as fact. Think about what information each sentence conveys before making judgments about the statements that follow. Become the detective! Ask good questions.

Karl's Day at Work

Karl had a busy day at the university. As he was driving home late that night, he stopped at a neighborhood convenience store to pick up a pack of cigarettes. After completing his errand, Karl stayed on for a few minutes to chat with the pretty store clerk. A heavy-set woman entered the

Continued on next page.

store and, brusquely pushing Karl aside, walked up to the counter. She handed the clerk a large canvas bag and insisted that the contents of the cash register be placed into it. The clerk reluctantly obeyed her order. The woman then sped away with the filled bag under her arm, leaving the clerk in tears, the empty cash register drawer still open, and Karl looking on helplessly.

Don't jump to conclusions! Sometimes the obvious is not always correct. Mark each statement with T for true, F for false, or ? for questionable. Explain why you chose the answer that you did.

1. Karl worked hard at the university that day. _____

   Reason:
   _____
   _____

2. On his way home from the university, Karl stopped at a convenience store. _____

   Reason:
   _____
   _____

3. Karl stopped at the store around noon. _____

   Reason:
   _____
   _____

4. Karl is a smoker. _____

   Reason:
   _____
   _____

5. Karl purchased a pack of cigarettes. _____

   Reason:
   _____
   _____

6. Karl made a date with the store clerk. _____

   Reason:
   _____
   _____

7. The store clerk was male. _____

   Reason:

   _____

   _____

8. A heavy-set woman entered the store. _____

   Reason:

   _____

   _____

9. The heavy-set woman brought a large canvas bag into the store. _____

   Reason:

   _____

   _____

10. The heavy-set woman brusquely pushed Karl aside. _____

    Reason:

    _____

    _____

11. The clerk put all of the money into the bag. _____

    Reason:

    _____

    _____

12. The heavy-set woman left the store with the bag under her arm. _____

    Reason:

    _____

    _____

13. The moon was shining brightly. _____

    Reason:

    _____

    _____

Continued on next page.

14. A crime was committed at the convenience store. _____

Reason:

_____

_____

15. The police were called. _____

_____

_____

Source: Adapted from: Ormrod, J. (1989). *Using Your Head: An Owner's Manual.* Educational Technology Publishing: Englewood Cliffs, N.J.

✓ COMPREHENSION CHECK

▶ Why is validity important in a deductive argument?
▶ What doesn't make sense to you up to this point in the chapter?

Tip FROM THE Brain Doctor

Being able to detect fallacies requires using your frontal lobes, the center for "executive" or higher-order functions in the brain. Good frontal lobes improve critical thinking, including the art of detecting fallacies in arguments. The good news is that practicing looking for fallacies and thinking more deeply about things help you develop your frontal lobes.

Evaluating Arguments

WHEN YOU ENCOUNTER ARGUMENTS IN YOUR TEXTBOOKS, it is best to read them with a healthy skepticism. Ready your mind to accept that the argument may be true, but do not just accept whatever is written without some analysis and evaluation of the argument. Arguments are tools authors use to persuade you to support their opinions, ideas, or beliefs. As a critical reader, you need to decide whether an argument is fair and good. It is important for you to keep asking yourself as you read authors' arguments, "Is the information presented true? Are the reasons facts or opinions? Does the conclusion logically follow from the reasons?"

Detecting Fallacies

FALLACIES **ARE ERRORS** in reasoning. Some authors have fallacies in their arguments by accident or due to their own bias. At other times, authors purposefully use fallacies when arguing to tempt you toward their way of thinking. Either way, fallacies make arguments weak and should be avoided. As a reader, you should be knowledgeable about fallacies and learn how to detect them in your textbooks or in anything you read. Once you understand what fallacies are and how to detect them, you will be able to determine if an argument is strong or weak. There are various types of fallacies. This chapter addresses the more common ones.

fallacies errors in reasoning

▶ **Ad Hominem (Personal Attack).** When authors commit an ad hominem error of reasoning, they avoid the true issue of an argument by attacking the person they disagree with.

ad hominem personal attack

Example	**Reason 1:**	I studied for the multiple-choice exam and should be ready.
	Reason 2:	I read most of the assigned chapters.
	Conclusion:	But I failed anyway because my professor is a woman who doesn't like me and is too emotional to grade objectively.

The fact that this student's professor is an emotional woman has nothing to do with the fact that the student failed the exam. The student failed because he or she could not answer all of the questions on the exam.

▶ **Red Herring.** Authors introduce red herrings, or irrelevant material, into an argument when they want to distract readers' attention away from important information that does not support their conclusion. An argument with this error leaves the original issue and moves to another one.

red herrings irrelevant material presented into an argument

Example:	**Reason 1:**	Voting yes to reduce our taxes may be a good idea.
	Reason 2:	But there are now 10 other issues on the ballot.
	Conclusion:	It is getting out of control.

The issue is to vote yes to reduce taxes. However, the argument dodges this issue by throwing in irrelevant material. The 10 other issues have nothing to do with whether someone should or should not vote yes to reduce taxes. The argument never addresses reasons to support, or not support, a vote of yes.

▶ **Circular Reasoning.** When authors use circular reasoning, instead of presenting an argument with a reason and a conclusion, they make two

circular reasoning argument in which the conclusion and reason are the same

statements that say the same thing. The conclusion is logically the same as the reason(s).

Example   **Reason 1:**   The Tigers won their game today.

                Conclusion: Because they scored more runs, the Tigers won.

Both the reason and the conclusion are the same.

▶ **Either/or Thinking.** The error in either/or thinking is that it allows for only two answers to a problem, when in fact there may be more.

Example   **Reason 1:**   I can quit eating and lose weight.

               Reason 2:   Or, I can eat and never lose weight.

               Conclusion: I am always going to be fat.

Obviously, there are other possible alternatives. Perhaps selecting healthy foods would be an option, or perhaps adding exercise would cause someone to lose weight.

▶ **Slippery Slope.** The error in slippery slope reasoning is that the author assumes that one event will most assuredly lead to another event, which will lead to another event, and so on. The author provides a chain of improperly linked conclusions as reasons to support an unjustified main conclusion. Conclusions found in this fallacy are often greatly exaggerated.

Example   **Reason 1:**   Voting for a Democrat for office will raise taxes.

               Reason 2:   As a result of the increased taxes, people will riot.

               Reason 3:   Once people begin to riot, the whole country will collapse.

               Conclusion: Voting for a Democrat will be the end of civilization as we know it.

Although voting for a Democrat *could* increase taxes, it is highly unlikely that doing so would cause the end of civilization. Voting for a Republican could raise taxes as well. One event does not necessarily cause the other chain of events.

▶ **Hasty Generalization.** Hasty generalizations are fallacies where the author makes the error of using too few or too weak of reasons to support a broad, sweeping conclusion.

Example   **Reason 1:**   My neighbor Dani is a nurse and always eats too many cookies.

---

either/or thinking argument that allows for only two solutions to a problem when there are may be more

slippery slope argument where the author assumes one event will lead to another, and to another, and to yet another

hasty generalization argument that makes a sweeping generalization without strong reasons to support it

> **Reason 2:** Judy is a nurse, and whenever we eat out, she always eats chocolate cake.
>
> **Conclusion:** All nurses eat too many sweets.

Obviously, this is a sweeping generalization. The two reasons provided may be true; however, it is very difficult to apply this evidence to all nurses. Be very aware of absolutes such as *every, never, always, all,* or *none* when they are used in arguments. Situations are usually not black and white and either/or. Remember this for tests. Unless you know an answer for certain, avoid guessing at answers using absolutes such as *every, never, always, all,* or *none*.

▶ **False Cause.** In a false cause argument, authors state a conclusion and give reasons for it, but fail to explain how the conclusion and reasons are connected to each other or provide unclear and/or faulty connections between them.

false cause argument where the author states a conclusion and gives reasons, but fails to explain how the reasons and conclusions are connected to each other

> **Example**   **Reason 1:** Dr. Jay's window is broken.
>
> **Reason 2:** My window is broken.
>
> **Conclusion:** I am positive Jake broke the windows. I saw him playing outside yesterday.

Although two windows are broken and Jake was playing outside the previous day, there is no evidence presented in this argument to prove that Jake had anything to do with breaking them. There is no proof of cause and effect.

▶ **False Authority.** False authority occurs when a celebrity promotes a product and tells you to purchase it, even though he or she is not an expert or leading authority regarding the product. Marketing departments often use celebrities to sell their products.

false authority a celebrity promotes a product but is not an expert or authority on it

> **Example**   **Reason 1:** Dwyane Wade says to buy this car.
>
> **Reason 2:** All the stars drive this type of car.
>
> **Conclusion:** The car must be good if Dwyane Wade and other stars drive it.

The error in reasoning is that unless the stars are car mechanics or experts, they may not be reliable sources of information regarding cars.

▶ **Begging the Question.** Begging the question is a fallacy where authors present a reason that is itself a questionable conclusion. The author assumes that you agree that the reason is true without providing evidence of its truth and then builds the argument on it.

begging the question providing a reason for something that is itself a questionable or debatable conclusion

Example   **Reason:**   Women are better at decorating than men are.

Conclusion: The woman in the couple should pick out the paint color for the home.

The reason, *Women are better at decorating than men are*, is debatable. It has to be proven before it can be used as a good reason for a conclusion. An author should not assume that you agree with that statement.

bandwagon fallacy where authors try to persuade you to agree to their point of view because many others already have accepted it

▶ **Bandwagon.** Bandwagon is a fallacy where authors try to persuade you to agree with their point of view because many others already have accepted it. It is the "everybody's doing it" appeal. Though the point of view might be good, the fact the "everyone agrees" is not a reason why you as a reader should accept it.

Example   **Reason:**   Everyone is majoring in engineering.

Conclusion: You should major in engineering, too.

ACTIVITY 12I
Detect Fallacies

Read the following arguments, and determine whether they contain a fallacy. The first one is modeled for you.

1. A good athlete must exercise regularly and be careful about what he or she eats. Therefore, attention to diet and a routine of exercise are necessary to a good athlete.

   Error in Reasoning?

   yes, circular reasoning

2. If you do not get good grades, you will never get into college. If you do not get into college, you will never get a job. Therefore, you will end up a homeless person in some major city.

   Error in Reasoning?

3. Trees are so beautiful in the springtime. The air seems cleaner and the grass seems greener. In my opinion, there is something so wonderful regarding the onset of summer.

   Error in Reasoning?

4. The doctor said I could either stick with his diet plan or accept being overweight.

   Error in Reasoning?

5. Hesa Geeke, mayoral candidate, suggests changing several local laws. He believes that the laws need to be more reflective of the times. He's just a Millennial. What does he know?

   Error in Reasoning?

6. Every student who earns a 3.0 grade point average or higher is eligible for the Lah D. Dah Scholarship. I have a 3.2 GPA. I will try to get the scholarship.

   Error in Reasoning?

7. If I go to the casino with Niran, I know that I will lose money. The first time I went to the casino with Niran, I lost $10. The second time I went, I lost $50.

   Error in Reasoning?

8. Johnny Depp, a well-known movie star, eats Cap'n Crunch cereal. It must be good if he eats it. You should eat Cap'n Crunch cereal.

   Error in Reasoning?

9. Judy gave an outstanding presentation in class today, and I admit that she seems like a good candidate for student council. But I am leery of someone whose parents support euthanasia.

   Error in Reasoning?

10. Men make better police officers than women. Therefore, only men should be allowed in the police academy.

    Error in Reasoning?

ACTIVITY 12J
Detect the Fallacy in a Cartoon

Write down the main idea of this cartoon and what fallacy it depicts. Be sure to explain your answer.

1. Main Idea:

_____

_____

2. Fallacy:

_____

_____

ACTIVITY 12K
Identify Fallacies in a Reading

The following passage is from a book on the environment and our efforts toward preserving it. See how many fallacies you can find. Highlight the fallacies in the paragraph and label them in the margins.

1   Yes, either we are going to rise to the level of leadership, innovation, and collaboration that is required, or everybody is going to lose—big. Just coasting along and doing the same old things is not an option any longer. We need a whole new approach. As they say in Texas: "If all you ever do is all you've ever done, then all you'll ever get is all you ever got."

2   The simple name for the project I am proposing is "Code Green." What "red" was to America in the 1950s and 1960s—a symbol of the overarching Communist threat, the symbol that was used to mobilize our country to build up its military, it industrial base, it highways, its railroads, ports, and airports, its educational institutions, and its scientific capabilities to lead the world in defense of freedom—we need to be "green" to be for today's America.

3   Unfortunately, after 9/11, instead of replacing red with green, President George W. Bush replaced red with "Code Red" and all the other crazy colors of the Department of Homeland Security's warning system. It's time to scrap them all and move to Code Green.

Source: Friedman. *Hot, Flat, and Crowded: Why We Need a Green Revolution—and How It Can Renew America.* Farrar, Straus and Giroux, 2008, p. 6.

Steps to Evaluating Arguments

YOU LEARNED IN Chapter 11 that the first step in identifying an argument is to make an argumentation map. By combining an argumentation map with other steps, you can begin to effectively evaluate arguments made in readings.

Step 1: Create an argumentation map.
Step 2: Cross out weak parts of an argument.
Step 3: Make a judgment.

Step One: Create an Argumentation Map

An argumentation map is a picture of an argument. It includes only the conclusion and the reasons. Each conclusion and reason is written in a separate box in complete sentences. The purpose of an argumentation map is to completely reveal the argument so that you can see what you are evaluating. Read the following passage from a sociology textbook, and then look at the argumentation map that follows. You will note that hidden assumptions have been added to this argumentation map, which help ensure that you understand the whole argument and encourage you to think about the reasons a little more deeply—where are they coming from? However, most important is knowing what the argument is, its conclusion, and the reason(s) that support it.

Who Decides What's Deviant?

Because deviance is culturally relative and the standards change over time, who decides what's right or wrong? Those who have authority or power. During our early years, parents and teachers define acceptable and unacceptable behavior in our everyday interactions and behavior. As we get older, we learn that legal institutions also define what is deviant, for example, not allowing us to drive until age 16 or to purchase or consume liquor until age 21.

Source: From BENOKRAITIS. *SOC* 2e (p. 119). Copyright © 2012 Cengage Learning.

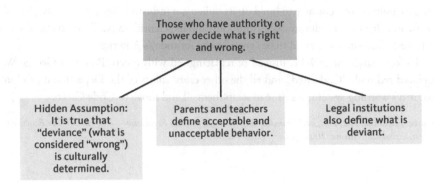

Figure 12.1 Argumentation Map for *Who Decides What's Deviant?*
Passage

The conclusion (main idea) of the passage is highlighted in green and the reasons (major supporting details) are highlighted in yellow. Those reasons and conclusions are transferred to the argumentation map in Figure 12.1. The hidden assumption included is: It is true that deviance is culturally determined. The author assumes that you agree with this statement and builds her argument on that idea. Do you agree that deviance is culturally relative? Is slavery, for example, ever good for some people in some cultures or is it always wrong? Is murder okay among some cultures? Are there no *absolute truths*?

Step Two: Cross Out Weak Parts of an Argument
In this step, you analyze the argument looking for fallacies or opinions and cross them out on your argumentation map. These weak elements of the argument (if there are any) should be discarded so that only the logical and true parts of the argument remain. See Figure 12.2 for an example.

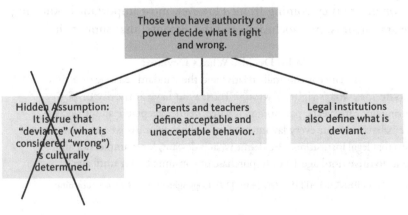

Figure 12.2 Crossing Out Weak Parts of an Argument

The hidden assumption is crossed out on the map because it is a fallacy. Which fallacy is it? It is the fallacy of begging the question. The author uses as a reason something that is debatable, not universally accepted.

Step Three: Make a Judgment

Now you are ready to judge the argument. You see it clearly. You have crossed out weak parts. What is left? Do people with power and authority decide what is right and wrong? Not always. Sometimes people with power and authority do the wrong things. A dictator of a government may say citizens who protest are deviant, but are they? Martin Luther King, Jr., broke laws and was labeled deviant, but was he? The issue is complicated. It seems the author oversimplifies the issue and makes assumptions that might not be true. This argument is weak.

Some arguments can have weak parts that you cross out and still be good arguments. The problem with the argument on deviance is that the author uses "right and wrong" without defining them (legally right and wrong? morally right and wrong?) and assumes deviant behavior is culturally determined and not influenced by others factors such as natural law or moral truth. That is a big assumption, a conclusion in itself, and should be argued, not just assumed.

Earlier in the chapter, you learned the difference between inductive and deductive arguments. As you evaluate the arguments you find in your college reading, you will discover that this knowledge comes in handy. Most of the arguments you will find in your textbooks will be inductive. As you decide whether they are weak or strong, ask yourself the following questions:

- ▶ Are the reasons based on fact?
- ▶ If some of the reasons are opinions, are the opinions wild or reasonable based on my background knowledge?
- ▶ Do the reasons logically support the conclusion?
- ▶ Are the hidden assumptions fair?
- ▶ Are there enough observations to make the conclusion reasonable?
- ▶ Can I think of an argument that goes against this argument (a counter-argument)?

If the argument is deductive, you can ask if the reasons are true and if they logically follow to the conclusion. Evaluating arguments takes practice and is not a perfect science. The goal of evaluating arguments is to truly think about what you read and examine it before you just accept it. The best way to reach this goal is to ask good questions. See Tables 12.1 and 12.2 for a checklist of useful questions to ask while evaluating inductive and deductive arguments.

Table 12.1 Evaluating Inductive Arguments

Questions to Ask Yourself	Check (√) if Answer Is Yes
1. Are observations (reasons) verifiable (able to be seen by others)?	
2. Are reasons provided in strong support of the conclusion?	
3. Does the argument appeal to reason more than feelings or unsupported opinion?	
4. Is there an absence of errors or fallacies in reasoning?	
5. Does the argument omit no significant information?	

The more checks you have, the stronger the inductive argument. You ideally should have checkmarks for at least #1, #2, and #5.

Table 12.2 Evaluating Deductive Arguments

Questions to Ask Yourself	Check (√) if Answer Is Yes
1. Does the argument start with a general principle or law?	
2. Is the conclusion specific?	
3. Are the reasons all true?	
4. Does the conclusion follow logically from the reasons?	
5. Does the argument omit no significant information?	

You should have checkmarks for #1, #2, #4, and #5 for the argument to be considered valid. You should have checkmarks for all numbers for the argument to be considered valid and true (sound).

ACTIVITY 12L
Evaluate Arguments

Read the following passages, highlighting the conclusion in green and the reasons in yellow, and create argumentation maps. Decide if there are any weak parts to each argument, and cross them out on the map. Finally, judge whether the argument presented is weak or strong.

Social Class

1   Social class has a significant impact on voting behavior. At each successive level of educational attainment, the voting rate increases. For example, the voting rate of those with a college degree (77 percent) is almost twice as high as for people who have not completed high school, and those with advanced degrees are the most likely to vote (see Table 12.3). People with the highest educational levels are usually more informed about and interested in the political process and feel that their vote counts ("Who Votes…" 2006).

2   Voting rates also increase with income levels. The voting rate of people with annual family incomes of $100,000 or more was 92 percent compared with 56 percent of those with annual incomes under $30,000 (see Table 12.3). People with higher incomes are more likely to be

employed, to have assets (such as houses and stock), and, therefore, are more likely to be aware of the costs of not voting to protect or increase their resources. In contrast, people who are unemployed usually have few assets and may be too disillusioned with the political system to vote ("Who Votes…" 2006).

TABLE 12.3

Selected Characteristics of Voters in the November 2008 Election

(a) Age

18–24	49%
25–34	57%
35–44	63%
45–54	67%
55–64	72%
65–74	73%
≥75	68%

(b) Marital Status

Married	70%
Widowed	62%
Divorced	59%
Never married	54%

(c) Educational Attainment

Less than high-school graduate	39%
High-school graduate or GED	55%
Some college or associate's degree	68%
Bachelor's degree	77%
Advanced degree	83%

(d) Annual Family Income

Less than $20,000	52%
$15,000–$29,999	56%
$30,000–$39,999	62%
$40,000–$49,999	65%
$50,000–$74,999	71%
$75,000–$99,999	76%
$100,000 and over	92%

(e) Race and Ethnicity

White	66%
Black	65%
Latino	50%
Asian	48%

Source: Based on File and Crissey 2010, Tables 1 and 2.

© Cengage Learning

Source: From BENOKRAITIS. *SOC* 2e (p. 208). Copyright © 2012 Cengage Learning.

1. **Create an argumentation map for this passage.**

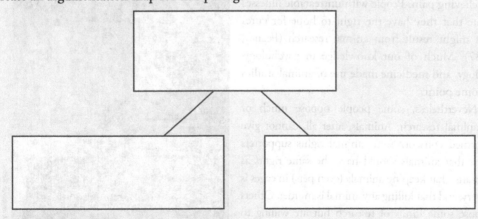

Continued on next page.

2. Fill out the following table to help you determine if the argument is strong.

Questions to Ask Yourself	Check (√) if Answer Is Yes
1. Are observations (reasons) verifiable (able to be seen by others)?	
2. Are reasons provided in strong support of the conclusion?	
3. Does the argument appeal to reason more than feelings or unsupported opinion?	
4. Is there an absence of errors or fallacies in reasoning?	
5. Does the argument omit no significant information?	

3. Is the argument strong or weak? Explain why.

_____

_____

Ethical Concerns with Nonhumans

1   Some psychological deals with nonhuman animals, especially research on basic processes such as sensation, hunger, and learning. Researchers use nonhumans if they want to control aspects of life that people will not let them control (e.g., who mates with whom), if they want to study behavior continuously over months or years (longer than people are willing to participate), or if the research poses health risks. Animal research has long been essential for preliminary testing of most new drugs, surgical procedures, and methods of relieving pain. People with untreatable illnesses argue that they have the right to hope for cures that might result from animal research (Feeney, 1987). Much of our knowledge in psychology, biology, and medicine made use of animal studies at some point.

2   Nevertheless, some people oppose much or all animal research. Animals, after all, cannot give informed consent. Some animal rights supporters insist that animals should have the same rights as humans, that keeping animals (even pets) in cages is slavery, and that killing any animal is murder. Others oppose some kinds of research but are willing to compromise about others.

Brykczynski/Anzenberger/Redux

3   Psychologists vary their attitudes. Most support some kinds of animal research but draw a line somewhere separating acceptable from unacceptable research (Plous, 1996). Naturally, different psychologists draw that line at different places.

4   In this debate, as in so many other political controversies, one common tactic is for each side to criticize the most extreme actions of its opponents. For example, animal rights advocates point to studies that exposed monkeys or puppies to painful procedures that seem difficult to justify. Researchers point to protesters who have vandalized laboratories, planted bombs, banged on a researcher's children's windows at night, and inserted a garden hose through a window to flood a house (G. Miller, 2007). Some protesters have stated that they oppose using any drug, even a medication for AIDS, if its discovery came from research with animals. Unfortunately, when both sides concentrate on criticizing their most extreme opponents, they make points of agreement harder to find.

5   One careful study by a relatively unbiased outsider concluded that the truth is messy: some research is painful to the animals and nevertheless valuable for scientific and medical progress (Blum, 1994). We must, most people would conclude, seek a compromise.

Source: From KALAT. *Introduction to Psychology* 9e (pp. 50–51). Copyright © 2011 Cengage Learning.

4. **Create an argumentation map for this passage.**

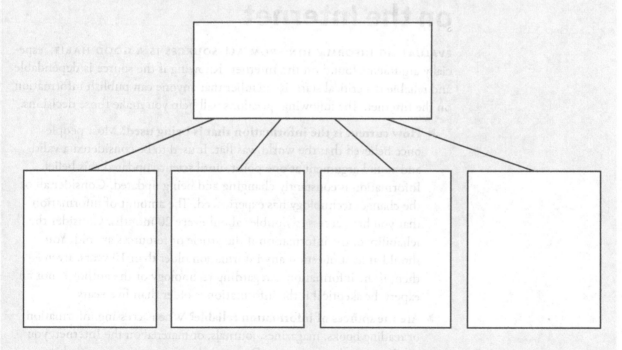

Continued on next page.

5. Fill out the following table to help you determine if the argument is strong.

Questions to Ask Yourself	Check (√) if Answer Is Yes
1. Are observations (reasons) verifiable (able to be seen by others)?	
2. Are reasons provided in strong support of the conclusion? (Is it right to use nonhuman animals for research to help mankind?)	
3. Does the argument appeal to reason more than feelings or unsupported opinion?	
4. Is there an absence of errors or fallacies in reasoning?	
5. Does the argument omit no significant information?	

6. **Is the argument strong or weak? Explain why.**

_____

_____

Evaluating Information on the Internet

EVALUATING INFORMATION FROM ALL SOURCES IS A GOOD HABIT, especially arguments found on the Internet. Knowing if the source is dependable and reliable is a critical start. Remember that anyone can publish information on the Internet. The following questions will help you make those decisions.

▶ **How current is the information that is being used?** Most people once believed that the world was flat. It used to be considered a valid and sound argument at one point, until science updated this belief. Information is constantly changing and being updated. Consider all of the changes technology has experienced. The amount of information that you have access to doubles about every 20 months. Consider the reliability of the information if the article or resources are old. You should at least question any information older than 10 years. Even then, if the information is regarding technology or the author is not an expert, be skeptical if the information is older than five years.

▶ **Are the sources of information reliable?** When accessing information or reading books, magazines, journals, or material on the Internet, you need to consider the source. Do you believe everything you read in *People* magazine? Why or why not? Knowing that a publisher is reputable is critical as you are trying to make decisions regarding the information.

If you were researching an argument about organ transplants, which would you trust more? An article in the *American Journal of Medicine* or an article in the *Ladies Home Journal*? You need to ask yourself:

▶ Who published the information?

▶ Is the source reliable? Quality publishers invest time and money authenticating information.

▶ When reading material on the Internet, consider the Web site's information for relevancy, reliability, credibility, and accuracy.

  ▶ What's the focus of the Web site?

  ▶ Is it a professional Web site?

  ▶ Is the text easy to read?

  ▶ Is the information biased?

  ▶ Is the information current?

  ▶ Is the information emotionally charged?

  ▶ Are spelling and grammar used correctly?

▶ **Who wrote the information?** Consider who has written the information you are reading.

  ▶ What are the author's qualifications?

  ▶ Is the author considered an authority or expert in the field?

  ▶ What are his or her credentials and/or degrees?

  ▶ Does the author seem to be basing arguments more on reasons or facts?

  ▶ Is the information first-hand? Or is the author interpreting someone else's work?

  ▶ Does the author have a good reputation?

Learn to become an information detective. Author information is usually located in the beginning of books and at the beginning or end of articles. Your instructor or librarian can also help you locate information regarding authorship and the reliability of specific publishing houses.

ACTIVITY 12M
Determine the Reliability of Web Sites

Access two Web sites, providing the URLs. One should be an example of a reliable source of information, and the other should be an example of an unreliable source. Explain why each was or was not reliable.

PRACTICE WITH A READING PASSAGE

Prepare to Read

Based on the title, what do you expect the following passage to be about?

1. What do you know about the topic already?

_____

2. Develop a question, using the title of this passage, to ask yourself before you read.

_____

3. Study-read the passage, highlight the conclusion in green, and write any margin notes that would be helpful to you.

_____

Handshake or Hug? Why We Touch
By Paul J. Zak

1   In the last several months, I've moved several colleagues from the handshake greeting to the hug. For my colleague Mark, it happened after the series of long intensive days working on a new project several weeks ago. Somehow all that time together made shaking hands seem too trivial. Still, it can be a bit uncomfortable to initiate a hug. Or maybe it's just a guy thing to worry about hugging another guy.

2   Come to think of it, why do we even have this ritual where with nearly everyone we meet we must touch our palms together? True, in some Latin cultures, the handshake is replaced with a kiss or two. But isn't that really intimate for people who are just friends? Why all this touching?

3   I thought I would investigate this a couple years ago. My real interest was to find out if touching would somehow make people "nicer," especially towards strangers. But I couldn't crack the lawsuit problem: if I asked participants in an experiment to touch each other, surely someone would be touched inappropriately and I would get sued. And for most of us, being forced to touch someone is weird and uncomfortable. Touch needs to be freely given and accepted to have a positive effect.

4   So, what to do? Many of the experiments I run involve blood draws, and I noticed that when one has a white lab coat on it is easy and acceptable to comfort a nervous person with a touch on the shoulder. Then it hit me: clinicians can touch us in a caring way and it doesn't bother us.

5   This is the reason I spent $6,000 on massages for strangers (and I never even got a massage myself!). Participants in this experiment came in, got a blood draw, and then

were randomized to get massaged for 15 minutes by a licensed massage therapist or to rest quietly for 15 minutes. Most people then made a single decision involving money and another person, and then received a second blood draw (a control group just did blood draw-massage-blood draw to isolate the effect of massage alone). Not surprisingly, we had no trouble recruiting 150 participants for this experiment!

6   I wanted to test a "pay it forward" idea: would massage by a therapist make you more likely to sacrifice money to help another person? And if so, why? If you have been reading *The Moral Molecule*, you'll have guessed that the target brain mechanism that would connect touch to sacrifice was oxytocin. Our idea was not without precedence: stroking the belly of rats had been shown to release oxytocin. But no one knew if touch would do the same thing in humans.

7   In September, 2008, my colleagues and I reported our results in the journal *Evolution and Human Behavior* (see www.neuroeconomicstudies.org for the details). Here's what we found. Massage alone did not raise oxytocin, but primed the brain to release this neurochemical after one received a signal of trust. This neuroeconomics experiment used computer-mediated monetary transfers between strangers to measure trust. The gist of this method is that one can take money out of one's account and entrust it to a stranger because this will cause the amount entrusted to grow threefold. The stranger can then return some money to the person who trusted him or her, or keep it all. And everyone knows that they only do this once so there is no chance to build up a reputation for reciprocity and make money by doing this task repeatedly. A full description of this approach can be found in my June, 2008 article in *Scientific American* (www.sciam.com) called "The Neurobiology of Trust."

8   We knew from research that we published in 2004 and 2005 that monetary transfers denoting trust caused the brain to release oxytocin. And we showed that there was a positive relationship between the amount of oxytocin released and the amount people choose to return to the person who trusted them—even though they were under no obligation to do so. Adding massage was like putting the human oxytocin system on steroids. Those who were massaged and trusted sacrificed 243% more money to the person who trusted them compared to those who were trusted but not massaged. And the change in blood levels of oxytocin strongly predicted this behavior.

9   Interestingly, women were more susceptible to the effect of touch: they had larger changes in oxytocin and sacrificed more money to those who trusted them. This may be why at least anecdotally, women touch others more than men. Oxytocin not only is a potent anti-anxiety agent, it activates reward pathways in the brain. Yes, our brains are designed to make it feel good to be good—even to strangers.

10   So, hugs or handshakes? Either one, along with a display of trust, is likely to cause oxytocin release and increase the chances that this person will treat you like family even if you've just met him or her. We touch to initiate and sustain cooperation. That's a pretty neat trick for a little nine amino acid molecule!

Source: Copyright © Paul J. Zak. Reprinted with permission. Paul J. Zak is the author of The Moral Molecule: The Source of Love and Prosperity.

Continued on next page.

Margin glossary:

randomized to select, design, or arrange in random way without pattern

oxytocin powerful hormone that plays a significant role in our bonding ability

precedence an earlier occurrence

primed prepared

gist central idea

reciprocity a mutual and cooperative interchange

anecdotally based on casual observation

Check Your Understanding

5. Use context clues and word part analysis to define the following words from the passage.

   - initiate (paragraph 1): _____

   - denoting (paragraph 8): _____

   - potent (paragraph 9): _____

6. Is the passage a deductive or inductive argument? Explain your answer.

   _____

   _____

7. What is the conclusion of this passage?

   _____

   _____

8. What are three reasons that support the conclusion?

   _____

   _____

9. Create an argumentation map from the main argument presented in the passage. Include one hidden assumption that you think the author makes.

10. Judge the argument from the passage as weak or strong. Provide an explanation for your judgment.

Questions to Ask Yourself	Check (√) If Answer Is Yes
1. Are observations (reasons) verifiable (able to be seen by others)?	
2. Are reasons provided in strong support of the conclusion?	
3. Does the argument appeal to reason more than feelings or unsupported opinion?	
4. Is there an absence of errors or fallacies in reasoning?	
5. Does the argument omit no significant information?	

CHAPTER SUMMARY

Learning to evaluate arguments allows you to determine if an author has made a compelling point. Being a critical reader of arguments requires that you approach your textbooks with a healthy skepticism. Be open to new ideas and arguments, but do not accept everything just because it is in print. Evaluate the strength of what is written.

To begin to examine arguments critically, you need to understand the two basic types of arguments: inductive and deductive. Inductive arguments start with specific observations and have conclusions that say something general. Deductive arguments start with a general idea or principle and conclude with a specific statement about a specific thing. Inductive arguments can be weak or strong based on the logic that holds them together. Deductive arguments are judged as valid and sound. When examining arguments, look for common logic errors or fallacies. Arguments with fallacies are weak. Nine common fallacies are ad hominem, red herring, circular reasoning, either/or thinking, slippery slope, hasty generalization, false cause, false authority, and begging the question. Make an argumentation map so you can examine an argument fully. Cross out any weak parts of the argument in the map. Then make a judgment of the argument by asking yourself the following questions: "Are the reasons based on fact? If some of the reasons are opinions, are the opinions wild or reasonable based on my background knowledge? Do the reasons logically support the conclusion? Are the hidden assumptions fair? Can I think of an argument that goes against this argument (a counter-argument)?"

As you read material on the Internet, decide whether the sources are dependable. Is the reading recent? Are the authors qualified to speak on the subject matter? Just like information that is in print, do not just accept Internet information because you read it. Critically examine it.

Brain Connections: Self-Assessment

Draw the amount of dendrites you imagine that you have now about reading arguments critically. Compare your drawing of dendrites now with what you drew at the beginning of this chapter. If the amounts are different, explain why.

✔ COMPREHENSION CHECK

▶ Where in the chapter did you lose concentration or become confused?
▶ If you could ask the authors a question about this chapter, what would you ask?

POST TEST

Part 1. Objective Questions

Match the key terms from the chapter in Column A to their definitions in Column B.

	Column A		Column B
_____	1. Deductive	a.	argument where the author states a conclusion and gives reasons, but fails to explain how the reasons and conclusions are connected to each other
_____	2. Begging the question	b.	when a deductive argument has a conclusion that logically follows from the reasons
_____	3. Inductive	c.	a type of argument that makes a conclusion about a specific thing based on facts and verifiable truths or absolutes
_____	4. Ad hominem	d.	providing a reason for something that is itself a questionable or debatable conclusion
_____	5. Either/or thinking	e.	personal attack
_____	6. False cause	f.	argument that allows for only two solutions to a problem when there are may be more
_____	7. Circular reasoning	h.	a type of argument where the conclusion is based on a series of observations and generalized to all
_____	8. Valid	i.	errors in reasoning
_____	9. Fallacies	j.	argument in which the conclusion and reason are the same
_____	10. Red herring	k.	fallacy where authors try to persuade you to agree to their point of view because many others already have accepted it
_____	11. Slippery slope	l.	irrelevant material presented into an argument
_____	12. Hasty generalization	m.	a celebrity promotes a product but is not an expert or authority on it
_____	13. False authority	n.	argument that makes a sweeping generalization without strong reasons to support it
_____	14. Bandwagon	o.	argument where the author assumes one event will lead to another, and to another, and to yet another

Continued on next page.

Identify the following passages as inductive or deductive, and explain why. Highlight the conclusion in green.

15.

> By the time of Bach's death in 1750, the Baroque style had faded in popularity. In fact, Bach's own sons thought of their father as something of an outdated old man, a not unknown attitude of sons towards their fathers. But the world was changing. Passing was the intensity of religious feeling. Gone was the love of the dramatic and grandiose. A new age had arrived, one that would see significant changes in the style of art and music.
>
> Source: From HOFFER. *The Understanding of Music* 5e (p. 200). Copyright © 1985 Cengage Learning.

Is the passage deductive or inductive?

_____

Why?

_____

_____

16.

> Elements in the same vertical column (belonging to the same group) of the periodic table have similar chemical properties because their valence shells have similar tendencies to lose, gain, or share electrons. For example, chlorine and bromine, included in a group commonly known as the halogens, are highly reactive. Because their valence shells have 7 electrons, they tend to gain an electron in chemical reactions.
>
> Source: From SOLOMON/BERG/MARTIN. *Biology* 8e (p. 29). Copyright © 2008 Cengage Learning.

Is the passage deductive or inductive?

_____

Why?

_____

_____

17.

> Fish are the major source of animal protein for more than one-half of the world's people, especially in Asia and Africa. Fish supply about 55% of the animal protein in Southeast Asia, 35% in Asia as a whole, 19% in Africa, about 25% worldwide—twice as much as eggs and three times as much as poultry—and 6% of all human protein consumption. Two-thirds of the annual fish catch is consumed by humans and one-third is processed into fish meal to be fed to livestock.
>
> Source: From MILLER. *Environmental Science: Working with the Earth* 5e (p. 153). Copyright © 1995 Cengage Learning.

Is the passage deductive or inductive?

_____

Why?

_____

_____

18. Briefly explain why you think it is important to know whether an argument you read is inductive, deductive, or includes fallacies.

_____

_____

Based on what you now know about arguments, identify whether each of the following statements is an argument. If it is, identify it as inductive or deductive.

19. I certainly hope that Tom Hanks has a major part in this film. He is my favorite actor.

_____

20. The Detroit Lions have beaten the New York Giants nine straight times. So, I'm betting on the Lions to win this game against the Giants.

_____

21. Zippy always wins when he races on a muddy track. So, Zippy will win today's race because the track is muddy.

_____

22. We interviewed 1,200 U.S. college students, and 900 of them favored 18 as the legal age for purchasing beer. Therefore, a substantial majority of all U.S. college students favor 18 as the legal age for purchasing beer.

_____

Continued on next page.

23. If you have a credit card, you will spend money you do not have. Dana has a Visa. She will spend money she does not have.

_____

24. George should not run for Student Council. He is a real jerk! Every time I see him at an event, he starts a fight.

_____

25. Class starts at 10. If I go, I will be late. So, I won't go.

_____

Read the following cartoon, and answer the questions that follow.

"If the treatment hasn't helped, Mrs. Jensen, I think the best thing you can possibly do is sue me. Litigation is often very therapeutic."

26. What is the conclusion of this cartoon?

_____

_____

27. Identify the argument being made in this cartoon.

_____

_____

28. Explain the fallacy being used in this cartoon.

_____

_____

29. What information could be added to make this a true argument?

_____

_____

30. Change the language in the cartoon so that it becomes a slippery slope fallacy.

_____

_____

Part 2. Reading Passage   POPULAR READING

Prepare to Read

1. Based on the titles of the following two passages, what do you expect the passages to be about?

_____

2. What do you believe you already know about the topic?

_____

3. Develop one question you expect these passages to answer.

_____

Passage #1

Ending Michigan's Mandatory Helmet Law Would Cost Everyone
Who Pays Insurance Rates
By Alan Reiner

1   The helmet debate has now boiled down to two divergent positions. There are the
"freedom" folks, who believe we are free to ride without the government deciding for
us what apparel to don. They say the vicious insurance industry-led campaign against

Continued on next page.

our freedom is tainted. They argue: Everyone knows that if you fall off a motorcycle at 60 miles an hour, you're going to die. Everyone knows that when you hit a car, deer, school bus, dog, gravel, oil slick or damp pavement and fall, you're going to die. Helmets won't save you.

2   And then there's the insurance industry, which believes that when any of the above-mentioned situations occur, somebody has to pay. And Michigan's no-fault insurance plan places that burden on the driver of the car, truck, bus, tractor or other insured vehicle (or really, the insurance company). And fault is not an issue. They argue: Pull out on your motorcycle in front of a bus, the bus pays. Hit a parked car, the car pays. Hit a dog, the homeowner pays. If everyone wore helmets, we'd pay less. If we distance ourselves, just for a moment, from these irreconcilable positions, we might get a better view of the brouhaha and lean toward common sense. Let's look at motorcycle racing. Granted, it differs greatly from motorcycling on public streets, but there are motorcycles, and people do fall off, run into things (more often than not at frighteningly high rates of speed) and run into each other.

3   However, everyone is headed in the same direction. Everyone's skill level is similar (classes are created to keep that in check). Everyone's motorcycle is safety checked before the race. And everyone understands the rules. No one is forced to deal with traffic signals. No one need worry about school buses or trucks or errant auto drivers. No one need worry about blind corners, joggers or four-way stops.

4   In addition, everyone signs a waiver of liability at the beginning of each race. Everyone depends on turn marshals to indicate what is happening ahead. No one is ever worried about bridge abutments, unmarked railroad crossings or drunken drivers.

5   Every racer wears an approved helmet. They also wear boots, leather, body armor, eye protection. Why? Racers pay for their own injuries. These folks want to go home at the end of the day. And race promoters want people to continue to participate in the sport. Comparing racing to the dangers on streets and highways, don't you think racers, above everyone else, should be helmetless? Of course you don't.

6   Would you ride in an automobile and leave your seat belt unfastened? Of course you wouldn't. Would you disconnect your airbags, just because you could? No. Would you run a grinding wheel without safety glasses just because? No. Stand in front of Tigers pitcher Justin Verlander without a helmet? Please!

7   And finally, to argue that motorcyclists from other states avoid Michigan and deprive our tourist industry of their money because they don't want to wear a helmet is just plain poppycock. Would a tourist flee to a new state because it didn't require seat belts?

Passage #2

By Giving Motorcyclists Choice on Helmets, Michigan Would Gain Millions
By Jim Rhoades

1   Every year, millions of dollars are leaving our state on two wheels. Michigan's outdated mandatory helmet law is sending motorcyclists racing across our borders and discouraging motorcyclists in neighboring states from visiting our state.

2   When motorcyclists leave Michigan, they take their dollars with them. That's millions of dollars that could be spent on gas, food, hotels, gifts and other items that could boost local economies. Michigan is losing out on this source of tourism money because of its outdated mandatory helmet law—the only one of its kind in the Great Lakes region.

3   Every one of our neighbors has modernized its mandatory helmet laws. The reason: Helmet laws do nothing to improve safety, and they have no impact on health care or insurance costs. Moreover, they act as a barrier to tourism.

4   Representatives from the Insurance Institute of Michigan were asked directly if insurance rates would increase if Michigan modified the helmet law. Their answer: "But with respect to passage of this legislation, is this going to have an impact on premiums across the board? No." This was in a Senate hearing in 2005. But now, they are spreading information that contradicts their own testimony, saying that the legislation *may* result in an increase to insurance costs.

testimony a statement sworn to in court as true

5   In fact, no state has ever increased insurance rates with the modification of a helmet law for adult choice—period! Saying that this "may" happen doesn't make it happen. This is a bad law based on bad science, myths and distorted data.

6   Neither do helmets make a difference in saving the lives of motorcyclists. Head injuries kill around 29% of motorcyclists involved in accidents regardless of whether they wore helmets or not, according to a Wisconsin Department of Transportation study. Wisconsin has no mandatory helmet law. Fatality rates among motorcyclists have actually gone down by 60% nationwide since 1985, and that's counting the 30 states that have no mandatory helmet law, according to the National Highway Transportation Safety Administration. Moreover, fatality rates are lower in states that allow riders to choose on helmet use.

7   More importantly, because of our law, motorcyclists in surrounding states have said repeatedly they will not visit Michigan, depriving our state of a valuable source of revenue. If Michigan's helmet law were to be modified, Michigan could stand to gain $1.5 billion in sales, tourism and other revenue, according to an economic study by Michigan Consultants.

8   By lopsided majorities in the last two sessions, the Michigan Legislature passed a plan that would let motorcyclists ride without a helmet only to have then-Gov. Jennifer Granholm veto the legislation. New legislation has strict requirements for rider education and/or cycle endorsements. In an age when everyone else is modernizing, it's about time Michigan dumped its outdated helmet law and got in the fast lane to the 21st Century.

Continued on next page.

Check Your Understanding

4. Use context clues and word part analysis to define the following words from the passages.

   - mandatory (Passage # 1, paragraph 1): _____
   - impact (Passage # 2, paragraph 3): _____
   - contradicts (Passage # 2, paragraph 4): _____

5. What is the conclusion of Passage #1?

   _____

   _____

6. What fallacies are committed in Passage #1? Explain your answer.

   _____

   _____

   _____

7. What are three of the reasons the author gives to support the conclusion in Passage #1?

   _____

   _____

   _____

8. What is the weakest reason the author gives in Passage #1? Why is it weak?

   _____

   _____

   _____

9. What is the conclusion of Passage #2?

   _____

   _____

10. What fallacies are committed in Passage #2? Explain your answer.

    _____

    _____

    _____

    _____

    _____

11. What are three of the reasons the author gives to support the conclusion in Passage #2?

_____

_____

12. Present your own point of view regarding helmet laws based on both passages. Which side do you support? Create your own argument. Then create an argumentation map of your argument.

_____

_____

BRAIN STRENGTH OPTIONS

1. Working individually or in a group of no more than three, create a poster. You may choose from the following two options:

   a. On the Internet or using another source, find an example of an inductive argument and a deductive argument.

      ▶ Each argument should be half a page to a page long.

      ▶ Print out both arguments, and put them on a poster.

      ▶ Indicate which one is deductive and which one is inductive.

      ▶ Annotate the arguments, indicating the conclusion being made and the reasons.

   b. Create a poster to teach about fallacies in arguments. Find examples of each type of fallacy covered in the chapter, and place them on the poster. Label each example, indicating and explaining the type of fallacy.

2. Working with one other classmate, prepare a debate consisting entirely of fallacious statements. One person will make his or her statement of an argument followed by a fallacious supporting statement. The second person will counter by naming the fallacy, as in "You are using a red herring" and then make a countering argument followed by a fallacious statement. The first person will respond by naming the fallacy and countering with another fallacious statement. Continue until you have presented arguments using every type of fallacious statement. Present the debate to the class or in a video, as determined by you and your instructor.

3. Write a letter to the editor on a topic currently under discussion in your school or local newspaper editorial page or of concern in your community. The letter should contain at least three supporting points, all of which must be factual. Turn in this argument in a format suitable for submitting to the newspaper. Once the instructor has approved it, send the final version to the newspaper.

4. Create a project of your choice based on the material in this chapter. Submit a written proposal of what you will do, the length of the project, and how it will be evaluated. Get the instructor's approval before you proceed.

Reading Beyond
the Words

MEE SOOK CHOO

A nursing student at the University of Michigan

"Information is not knowledge."

—*ALBERT EINSTEIN*

Courtesy of Mee Sook Choo

ONE OF THE MOST valuable academic tools that I learned while attending school to become a nurse is to think critically. While it was true that there were subjects that required me to memorize information so I could recall it, I also learned that I needed to be able to demonstrate an ability to apply, analyze, and question in order to really feel that I had the knowledge that I needed. For example, if I needed to learn the names of a certain class of drugs for my pharmacology class, I might make a list and memorize them. However, once I learned the names of the drugs, I needed to know their applications. For example, one drug may have two or more different applications. Knowing these differences requires an ability to think critically. Another example would be learning a particular skill, like patient assessment. Memorizing the steps in writing a patient assessment is only the first level. However, to really understand patient assessment, you have to know what questions to ask, be able to make accurate judgments based on the information you received, and identify contradicting statements made by the patient. Critical thinking is the key to being able to make these types of decisions and judgments. For me, critical thinking gave me the tools to excel in both my classes and my job.

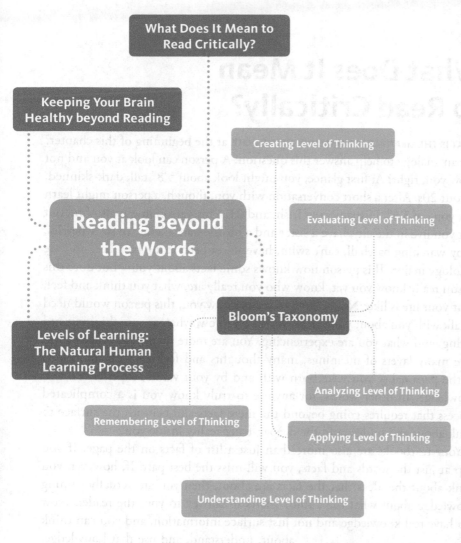

What Does It Mean to
Read Critically?

Keeping Your Brain
Healthy beyond Reading

Creating Level of Thinking

**Reading Beyond
the Words**

Evaluating Level of Thinking

Bloom's Taxonomy

Levels of Learning:
The Natural Human
Learning Process

Analyzing Level of Thinking

Remembering Level of Thinking

Applying Level of Thinking

Understanding Level of Thinking

Brain Connections: Self-Assessment

Draw on the brain cell how many dendrites you imagine you have for how much you know about reading beyond the words.

What Does It Mean to Read Critically?

WHAT IS THE MEANING BEHIND EINSTEIN'S QUOTE at the beginning of this chapter? Use an analogy to help answer this question. A person can look at you and not know you, right? At first glance, you might look about 5'8" tall, dark-skinned, in your 20s. After a short conversation with you, though, a person might learn that you are 5'6", Hispanic *and* Irish, and 21. This person might also find out that you live in the city, have a sister and a brother, are allergic to strawberries, enjoy watching baseball, can't swim, have never been stung by a bee, and are a biology major. This person now knows some facts about you—but does this person really know you yet, know who you really are, what you think and feel, what your life is like? No, because to really know you, this person would need to talk with you about your ideas, what you know, what you are thinking and feeling, and what you are experiencing. You are more than a list of facts. You have many layers of meanings, many thoughts and feelings that are shaped by the personality you were born with and by your values, experiences, and knowledge. In other words, for anyone to truly know you is a complicated process that requires going beyond the mere facts and beneath the surface to think about and understand the deeper, truer reality inside you.

Your textbooks are also more than just a list of facts on the page. If you stop at just the words and facts, you will miss the best part! If, however, you think about the ideas that the facts are about, then you are actually gaining knowledge about what the author wants to convey to you, the reader. Now you have real knowledge and not just surface information, and you can think

about, understand, and use that knowledge. You can apply it in your assignments. You can discuss it by comparing it with other information you know. You can evaluate it and then, ultimately, you can design, create, and construct from new knowledge.

You need to study-read, question, and dig deeply, and then when you *understand* and can *do* something with the information, it becomes knowledge. This is what can be inferred from Einstein's quote. But *how* do you get beyond the words on the page to the deeper layers of meaning?

Bloom's Taxonomy

BENJAMIN BLOOM, A PSYCHOLOGIST AND INFLUENTIAL PERSON in the field of education during the 1950s, categorized critical thinking into six levels. Instructors use this taxonomy as a blueprint for planning lessons and developing exam questions. For many years, only teachers knew about this taxonomy. However, it finally became obvious that if instruction and exams were being designed around Bloom's Taxonomy, students should also have an understanding of these levels to help them learn information using all six levels. Have you ever studied for an exam and believed that you had memorized all of the necessary information? Then when you took the exam, the questions were harder? The questions asked you to do something with the knowledge you memorized, but you had not studied it that way and you were not prepared.

In the 1990s Bloom's Taxonomy was revised to make it more relevant to the the 21st century, not only for teachers, but for students, too. The six levels in Bloom's Taxonomy are:

Bloom's Taxonomy a classification of levels of thinking

- ▶ **Remembering**
- ▶ **Understanding**
- ▶ **Applying**
- ▶ **Analyzing**
- ▶ **Evaluating**
- ▶ **Creating**

Because there is an order to the levels of thinking within Bloom's Taxonomy, it is often presented as a triangle. The lower, more general levels of thinking serve as the foundational levels—the triangle's base. Each level builds on the previous one, and it is necessary to understand each level before moving onto the next, higher level of thinking. Creating is the top, as it is considered the highest level and no longer foundational. However, this does not mean that the levels cannot work in unison. You may address more than one level at the same time. Mastery of the levels allows you to demonstrate

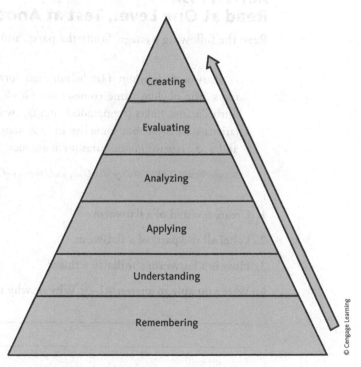

Figure 13.1 Bloom's Taxonomy

© Cengage Learning

true application and understanding of a topic. Most employers will want you to demonstrate all levels of thinking because having mastery over all levels is both desirable and necessary in order to create and produce new products and services. This is one of the reasons why the Brain Strength Options are included at the end of every chapter. These projects allow you to demonstrate your understanding and application of the skills at the highest level of thinking.

Most students are very good at learning information at the first two levels (remembering and understanding), meaning that they memorize dates, names, places, vocabulary, specific facts, and principles as well as paraphrase, make predictions, and draw conclusions. These are considered lower levels of thinking. Even though thinking through the first two levels is necessary in order to move on, you should not stop there. The next four levels (applying, analyzing, evaluating, and creating) are considered the higher levels of thinking because they require more thinking and doing. The higher levels demand that you work with the information, show your instructors (and future employers) that you have mastered it, and demonstrate your thinking. Critical reading is the ability to read, think, and understand using all six levels—and expert readers read critically.

ACTIVITY 13A
Read at One Level, Test at Another

Read the following passage. Study the parts, and answer the questions that follow.

Flatworms (phylum Platyhelminthes) form a three-layered embryo and have organ systems. The phylum name comes from Greek; platy- means flat, and helminth means worm. Turbellarians, flukes (trematodes), and tapeworms (cestodes) are the main classes. Most turbellarians are marine, but some live in fresh water, and a few live in damp places on land. Flukes and a few tapeworms are parasites of animals.

Source: From STARR. *Biology: The Unity and Diversity of Life* (p. 412). Copyright © 2009 Cengage Learning.

1. Create a visual of a flatworm.

2. Label all the parts of a flatworm.

3. How is a flatworm similar to a fluke?

4. Were you able to answer #1–3? Why or why not?

_____

_____

5. Based on what you just read, you were limited by the information provided to you. However, if you knew that you would be asked to create a visual of a flatworm, list the parts, and compare the flatworm to a fluke, what could you have done differently?

_____

_____

6. Have you found that some college exams seem to test for information that you did not read about in the most current chapter?

_____

_____

7. How do you think you can use Bloom's Taxonomy to learn more effectively?

_____

_____

This chapter will teach you how to begin thinking about textbooks beyond the literal *who, what, where*, and *when*. This type of information is a great starting point, but it is not enough to get you through most courses. College courses build off each other. By the time you reach upper-level courses, it is assumed that you have mastered the foundational course information.

Remembering Level of Thinking

BLOOM'S remembering level of thinking is the most literal level and considered the first level. It is the level you use when you recall facts or recognize the correct answer from a list in a multiple-choice test question. Remember the hypothetical person described earlier in the chapter? The one who is 5'6", Hispanic and Irish, and 21? Understanding these facts about someone is an example of understanding at the remembering level of thinking.

This is considered lower-level thinking because you do not even have to understand the material to answer questions based on this kind of rote memory. You can just look at a reading and write answers and not even comprehend the text.

Instructors question their students at the remembering level when they want to be sure they know common terms, specific facts, basic concepts, principles, methods, and procedures used in their discipline. Examples of words used in exam questions that require this level of thinking include *define, describe, label, list, match, reproduce, select*, and *state*.

remembering level of thinking literal level of thinking

ACTIVITY 13B
Provide Just the Facts, Please

List 30 facts about yourself. Keep these facts for Activity 13D later in this chapter.

_____	_____	_____
_____	_____	_____
_____	_____	_____
_____	_____	_____
_____	_____	_____
_____	_____	_____
_____	_____	_____
_____	_____	_____
_____	_____	_____
_____	_____	_____

ACTIVITY 13C
Think at the Remembering Level

Read the following passage taken from a sociology textbook.

Status

status ranking or social position in society

1   For most people, the word *status* signifies prestige: An executive, for example, has more status than a secretary, and a physician has a higher status than a nurse. For sociologists, status refers to a social position that an individual occupies in a society (Linton 1936). Thus, executive, secretary, physician, and nurse are all social statuses. Other statuses that are familiar to you include student, professor, musician, voter, sister, parent, police officer, and friend.

2   A status refers to any societal position within a culture. Statuses can be (and are) ranked, but sociologists don't assume that one position is more prestigious than another. A mother, for example, is not more important than a father, and an adult is not more important than a child. Instead, all statuses are significant because they determine social identity, or who we are.

status set a collection of social statuses that a person occupies at a given time

Status Set

3   Every person has many statuses at the same time (see Figure 13.2), and together they form her or his status set, a collection of social statuses that a person occupies at a given time (Merton 1968). Dionne, one of my students, is female, African American, 42 years

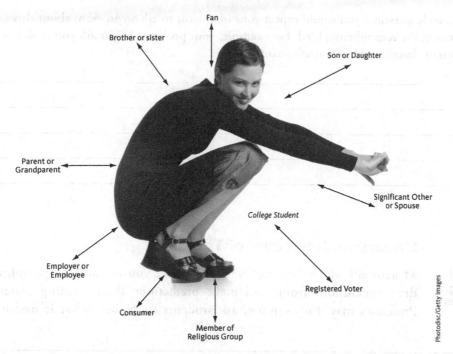

Fan

Brother or sister

Son or Daughter

Parent or Grandparent

Significant Other or Spouse

College Student

Employer or Employee

Registered Voter

Consumer

Member of Religious Group

Photodisc/Getty Images

Figure 13.2 Is This Your Status Set?

The status of college student is only one of your current statuses. What other statuses comprise your status set?

old, divorced, mother of two, daughter, cousin, aunt, Baptist, Maryland voter, supervisor at a bank, volunteer at a soup kitchen, president of her homeowners associations, country music fan, and stockholder. All of these socially defined positions (and perhaps others as well) make up Dionne's status set.

4   Status sets change throughout the life course. Dionne's statuses of child, single, and high school student changed to married, parent, and bank employee. Her status of married changed to divorced, and she added the status of college student. Because she will graduate next year and is considering remarrying and starting an after-school program, Dionne will add at least three more statuses to her status set and will also lose the statuses of divorced and college student. As Dionne ages, she will continue to gain new statuses (grandmother, retiree) and lose others (supervisor at a bank, or wife, if she is widowed).

5   Statuses are relational, or complementary, because they are connected to other statuses: A *husband* has a *wife*, a *real estate agent* has *customers*, and a *teacher* has *students*. No matter how many statuses you occupy, nearly every status is linked to that of one or more other people. These connections between statuses influence our behavior and relationships.

Source: From BENOKRAITIS. *SOC* 1e (pp. 82–3). Copyright © 2010 Cengage Learning

Continued on next page.

Write five example questions you would expect your instructor to ask on an exam about this passage written at the remembering level. For example, your professor might ask you to define the term *status* or describe what Dionne's status set is.

1. _____

2. _____

3. _____

4. _____

5. _____

Understanding Level of Thinking

understanding level of thinking level of making predictions and inferences and paraphrasing

AT BLOOM'S understanding level of thinking, you are able to paraphrase, draw conclusions from, and make predictions about reading material. Professors may, for example, ask students to explain what is meant by

Tip FROM THE Brain Doctor

As you get to higher levels of thinking, the frontal lobes get more involved. The frontal lobes have been called the "executive brain" because they specialize in the kind of things that an executive does: organize, plan, analyze, synthesize, delay rewards, assign priorities, keep emotions in check, use good judgment, and focus attention. If the brain were an orchestra, the frontal lobes would be the conductor.

The brain develops in response to input and experience. For example, some scientists took a newborn kitten and covered one eye with a patch. They did not harm the eye. A few months later, they took off the patch, and the cat was permanently, functionally blind in that eye. Why? Because the connections from the eye to the brain were not being used, the brain pruned them away. There was no sensory input coming into the brain from the eye.

By the same token, to develop your frontal lobes so that you are a high-functioning adult, you must engage in the kinds of activities that develop the frontal lobes. These higher-order-thinking tasks contribute to that. Think of these activities as growing a better brain!

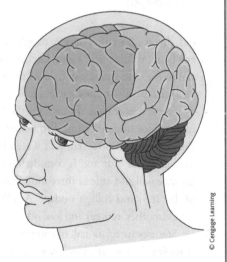

© Cengage Learning

a specific statement, paragraph, or concept. Professors question students at this level to check whether they understand what facts and principles mean, can interpret charts and graphs, can estimate the future consequences implied by data, and are able to translate verbal language into mathematical formulas and vice versa.

Examples of words used in questions at the understanding level include *explain*, *infer*, *summarize*, *rewrite*, *convert*, *defend*, *distinguish*, and *predict*. When you are preparing for an exam, you can use these same words to devise questions to test yourself on your comprehension of textbook material.

ACTIVITY 13D
Summarize the Facts

In Activity 13B you were asked to develop a list of facts about yourself. Give your list to a classmate. Each of you should write two paragraphs based on the other person's list. In the first paragraph, summarize the other person's list, combining details and omitting less important details as necessary. In the second paragraph, make two plausible inferences from the facts in the first paragraph.

ACTIVITY 13E
Think at the Understanding Level

The following passage is taken from a book titled *Actual Innocence: Five Days to Execution and Other Dispatches from the Wrongly Convicted* by Jim Dwyer and his coauthors. The questions that follow are written at the understanding level of thinking. The answers to these questions cannot be found word for word in the text but are instead conclusions you should draw from the passage.

1 On the evening of December 19, 1974, a short documentary film was shown on the local NBC newscast in New York. In it, a young woman walks in a hallway. A man lurks in a doorway, wearing a hat, leather jacket, and sneakers. The man bursts from the doorway, grabs the woman's handbag, and runs straight toward the camera, full-faced. The entire incident lasts twelve seconds.

2 After the film was shown, the show presented a lineup of suspects. The viewers were provided with a phone number and asked to choose the culprit from among the six, or to say that he wasn't in the lineup. "We were swamped with calls," Robert Buckhout, a professor

Continued on next page.

at Brooklyn College who organized the experiment, would write later. They unplugged the phone after receiving 2,145 calls.

3   The "thief" was seated in lineup position Number 2. He received a grand total of 302 votes from the callers, or 14.1 percent of the 2,145. "The results were the same as if the witnesses were merely guessing, since on the basis of chance (1 out of 7, including the "not in the lineup" choice), we would expect only 14.3 percent identification of any lineup participants, including Number 2," Buckhout wrote in an article with the charming headline NEARLY 2,000 WITNESSES CAN BE WRONG.

Source: Dwyer, Jim, Neufeld, Peter, Scheck, Barry. *Actual Innocence: Five Days to Execution and Other Dispatches from the Wrongly Convicted.* New York: Doubleday, 2000, pp. 43–44.

1. Using the title of the book, what do you infer is the main point of this passage?

_____

_____

2. Predict what the callers would say if they were told that their responses were incorrect. What reason do you think they would give for wrongly identifying the thief in the lineup?

_____

_____

_____

3. Create two of your own understanding-level questions about this passage.

_____

_____

Applying Level of Thinking

applying level of thinking level of applying what you have learned

BLOOM'S applying level of thinking requires you to solve problems by selecting and utilizing the appropriate concepts, principles, or theories you already know. For example, if you learn about the process through which a bill becomes a law in your political science class, you could work out the status of a piece of legislation before Congress and what steps still need to occur for it to become a law.

Professors ask questions at this level to see if students are able to solve mathematical problems, demonstrate correct usage of procedures or methods, create charts and graphs, use familiar concepts to understand new information, or apply theories to real-life situations.

Examples of words used in questions at the applying level include *change, compute, demonstrate, discover, manipulate, modify, prepare, show, solve, apply,* and *use.*

ACTIVITY 13F
Think at the Applying Level

Read the following passage, and answer the applying-level questions that follow.

> Detailed knowledge of the brain processes that underline language has emerged in recent years. For example, there appear to be separate brain areas that specialize in subtasks such as hearing words (spoken language of others), seeing words (reading), speaking words (speech), and generating words (thinking with language). Whether these patterns of brain organization for oral, written, and listening skills require separate activities to promote the component skills of language and literacy remains to be determined. If these closely related skills have somewhat independent brain representation, then coordinated practice of skills may be a better way to encourage learners to move seamlessly among speaking, writing, and listening.
>
> Source: Bransford, Brown, Cocking, eds., *How People Learn: Brain, Mind, Experience, and School.* Washington, D.C.: National Academy Press, 1999, p. 110.

1. If you were a teacher, how would you use the information in this passage to help your students learn?

   _____

   _____

   _____

2. A friend is having trouble learning. How would you help this person figure out how to solve his or her problem?

   _____

   _____

   _____

3. Create your own applying-level question about this passage.

   _____

   _____

Analyzing Level of Thinking

AT BLOOM'S analyzing level of thinking, you take a difficult or complex concept, such as democracy, mitosis, or phonics, and break it apart into the smaller ideas or parts it is made up of. Once you break a concept down into its essential parts, you will have a much clearer understanding of what it means and how the different elements interact with each other. Mentally reassembling them back into the larger concept using your own words and examples further adds to your knowledge.

Consider this example: A 19-year-old student on a university swim team comes in second in an important race. The concept he wants to analyze is *Why didn't I win?* The parts that make up this concept are the variables that contributed to his performance: what he ate that day, how much he practiced, his ability to concentrate, his level of nervousness, his sleeping habits, his mental attitude, and the strength of his competitors. After some thought, he realizes that the problem is not his competitors, but his own behavior. Specifically, he has been staying up late and not practicing good concentration techniques during practice. He decides his lack of sleep and lack of focus are more likely the reasons for his lackluster performance.

Professors question students at the analyzing level to see if they are able to recognize fallacies in an author's reasoning, distinguish between facts and opinions, or take apart the organizational structure of a work and recognize how the different parts interact to form the whole.

Examples of words used in questions at the analyzing level include *break down, differentiate, discriminate, infer, outline, classify,* and *trace the growth of.*

ACTIVITY 13G
Analyze How the Brain Is Like an Orchestra

List all the ways the brain is like an orchestra. Hint: Think of everything you know about an orchestra (activate your existing neural network), and then think about how that information relates to what you have learned about the brain throughout this textbook.

Orchestra

1. _____   6. _____

2. _____   7. _____

3. _____   8. _____

4. _____   9. _____

5. _____   10. _____

Ferenc Szelepcsenyi/Shutterstock.com

Brain

1. _____   6. _____

2. _____   7. _____

3. _____   8. _____

4. _____   9. _____

5. _____   10. _____

Source: Copyright Janet N. Zadina, Ph.D. 2009. May not be reprinted without permission.

ACTIVITY 13H
Think at the Analyzing Level

Read the following passage, and answer the analyzing-level questions that follow.

1   Thanks to technology and to the Internet, all children now are children of the globe,
not just children of the neighborhood where they live. Today's tech-savvy kids already
have the tools for global learning at their fingertips. Gone is the day when education was
synonymous with a building housing a teacher and a blackboard. Today, the opportunities for learning beyond the school walls and beyond the school day abound, enabling

Continued on next page.

students to connect the local to the global and back again. Globally oriented schools can do the following:

2   Harness technology to tap global information sources, create international collaborations, and offer international courses and languages online, especially to underserved communities. Information and communication technology is our greatest asset in internationalizing education. It allows students to access information from every corner of the world, to overcome geographic barriers, to communicate and collaborate with their peers in other countries, to publish findings, and to share words, images, and videos with a worldwide audience—even to talk to one another in real time.

3   Lack of timely educational resources about other parts of the world was once a major constraint on teaching about the world. Today's students can tap into free, relevant information and networks from around the world; but at the same time they need to learn critical-thinking skills to assess the wealth of global information that can be found online. Online courses can allow students access to languages or other internationally focused courses that are not available in their local school district. And Internet-based, classroom-to-classroom projects, which allow students to learn *with*, not just *about*, their peers in other countries, are a forerunner of what one day will become truly global classrooms. These learning opportunities made possible through technology are powerful for all students but are especially valuable in rural areas, where global connections or local diversity may be limited.

Source: Jacobs, Heidi Hayes, ed. *Curriculum 21: Essential Education for a Changing World* Alexandria, VA: ASCD, 2010, pp. 107–108.

1. **Differentiate between non-global and global education in either a paragraph or a visual.**

_____

_____

_____

_____

_____

_____

_____

_____

Non-Global Learning	Global Learning

2. **Create your own analyzing-level question about this passage.**

_____

✔ **COMPREHENSION CHECK**

▶ What in the chapter up to this point is unclear?
▶ Explain the purpose for understanding and using Bloom's Taxonomy.

Evaluating Level of Thinking

BLOOM'S evaluating level of thinking, involves making a value judgment based on specific criteria rather than on one's own opinions. The process of asking questions, evaluating answers, and developing or acknowledging criteria to use in evaluating information involves thinking at a very high level. Consider a juror's task at a trial. Individual jurors cannot judge the defendant based on their own personal experiences or biases. They have to follow specific criteria outlined in the law and interpret that law based on the judge's directions.

Similarly, different academic disciplines have rules or guidelines for evaluating whether information is valid and therefore acceptable. Here are some

evaluating level of thinking level of making a judgment

general questions you can ask yourself as you begin to evaluate the quality of information and arguments in your textbooks:

▶ Are the author's arguments based on research?

▶ Does the author argue inductively or deductively? What reasons does the author use to support what he or she says?

▶ Does the author appear to be biased? Does he or she use emotive language?

▶ Do I agree with what the author is saying? Why or why not? On what do I base my evaluation?

Students sometimes fail to prepare for an exam at the evaluating level of thinking because the questions can be difficult to formulate and the answers are not always objective. But it is important to ask evaluation questions because they challenge you to think critically about what you read and not passively accept what you are being told. They also require you to analyze an author's arguments using the specific criteria relevant to his or her discipline and to develop your own arguments using those same criteria.

Professors question students at the evaluating level to see if they can assess the validity of a conclusion; judge the artistic merit of a play, poem, or sculpture using widely accepted standards; or evaluate the logic of written or spoken material. Examples of words used in questions at the evaluating level include *justify, support, defend, appraise, judge,* and *conclude.*

ACTIVITY 13I
Think at the Evaluating Level

Read the following passage. Provide definitions in the margin for all of the bolded words. Then answer the evaluating-level questions that follow.

Space Junk

1   On February 6, 1971, astronaut Alan Shepard famously hit some golf balls during his walk on the moon. Although he claimed that one went "for miles and miles," it actually still rests on the moon's surface today and did not achieve escape **velocity**. Even though there are no golf balls in lunar orbit, there is plenty of orbital debris or space junk circling the earth. Spent rockets and dead satellites, Ed White's glove, flecks of paint, crystallized urine, and other **detritus** make up 94 percent of the stuff that floats around the earth along with operational satellites. (The glove stayed in orbit for only about a month.)

velocity
speed

detritus
fragments
resulting from
disintegration

2   There are also remnants of Project Needles (official name: Project West Ford), a 1960s plan to orbit tiny strips of metal to be used as antennae in a worldwide communication system. (These are the "lost Air Force needs" referred to by Glenn.)

3   In early 2009, the International Space Station had a close call with a piece of micro-meteoroid orbital debris. According to NASA, approximately nineteen thousand objects larger than ten centimeters in diameter are known to exist; there are also an estimated five hundred thousand particles between one and ten centimeters and tens of millions of particles smaller than one centimeter.

4   The space agency points out that although "collisions with even a small piece of debris will involve considerable energy," NASA has a surveillance network to monitor debris during space shuttle missions, and the shuttle can be maneuvered away from an object if the chance of collision exceeds one in ten thousand, which occurs about once every year or two. The International Space Station is well shielded and can withstand the impact of debris as large as a centimeter in diameter.

Source: Malesky, K. *All Facts Considered: The Essential Library of Inessential Knowledge.* John Wiley and Sons, Inc.: Hoboken, NJ, p. 138–139.

remnants small parts or traces remaining

1. Judge the space practice that takes place in the passage. Should there be regulations? If so, who would enforce them? What would be the punishment for not adhering to the regulations?

_____

_____

_____

2. Do you agree with the concept of Project Needles? What do you base your opinion on?

_____

_____

3. Create your own evaluating-level question about this passage.

_____

Creating Level of Thinking

BLOOM'S creating level of thinking is considered the highest level of thinking. It requires you to arrive at an understanding of the larger picture or meaning by combining the individual elements that contribute to it and being able to create from

creating level of thinking level of being able to create a bigger picture after combining parts

it. For example, suppose you want to create a quilt for your bed that somehow reflects your life. You decide to use pieces of fabric that have special significance to you. You choose pieces of an old receiving blanket your mother used when you were a baby, a dress you wore for an elementary school picture, parts of a suede glove that belonged to an old boyfriend, a sheet that covered the armchair in your dorm room, and a faded cotton shirt worn by your father who died last year. You arrange all these pieces to form one big rectangle and border it with pieces of blue fabric, your favorite color. Although your quilt is made up of a combination of different fabrics, it is itself one bigger item. By undertaking this project, you have created a number of important memories into one picture of your life.

Being able to synthesize information is important in college because professors will ask you to think about discrete items of information in order to arrive at a deeper, more comprehensive understanding of the larger topics they relate to. Unlike analyzing level of questions, which ask you to break ideas down into smaller units, the creating level of questions ask you to bring ideas together to create a larger picture. For example, you may be asked in a political science class to explain how Hitler gained power in pre-World War II Germany. By synthesizing information about the political situation, the economic state of the country, and the culture of the German people at the time, you can answer the larger question of how the combination of these factors set the stage for Hitler's rise to power.

Professors question students at the creating level of thinking to see if they are able to use different concepts and principles to arrive at a new understanding of complex issues; write about a well-organized theme; present a persuasive speech; write a creative story or poem; create a scheme for classifying objects, events, or ideas; or propose a plan for research. Examples of words used in questions at the creating level include *categorize, write, relate, reconstruct, design, create, compose,* and *tell.*

ACTIVITY 13J
Think at the Creating Level

Read the following passage from *Dave Barry Hits below the Beltway*. Even though the passage is intended to be humorous, it demonstrates the skill necessary to synthesize different items of information in order to create an explanation of a larger topic. In this passage, the larger idea of government is pieced together using people and ants to explain what government is and how it works.

Why Do We Have Governments

1   Why do we have governments?
2   This is a hard question, and, like so many hard questions, the best way to answer it is to consider ants. When you see an ant on your kitchen floor, it appears to be an insignificant insect scurrying around randomly, so you stomp it into a little smear without a second thought.

3   But if, instead of stomping the ant, you were to get down on your hands and knees and follow it, something fascinating would happen: Your head would bonk into the wall, because the ant has scurried into a hole. So I'll just tell you where the ant goes: It goes to a nest containing an ant colony that is every bit as complex and organized as a human society. In fact, it is more organized, because there are no teenagers.

4   Yes, even ants—tiny creatures with a primitive brain no larger than that of a psychic-hotline caller—have a government. The ant government operates on what political scientists call the "Smell System," whereby your role in society is based on what chemicals you secrete. At the top of the hierarchy is the queen, who is elected unanimously by the other ants after a very brief political campaign that consists of hatching.

5   "Hey!" the other ants say. "This smells like the queen!"

6   Most of the other ants smell like workers, so they spend their lives scurrying around looking for food and exchanging important chemical information with the other ants they bump into ("I'm an ant!" "Hey, me too!") Also, there are a few winged ants, whose job is to scare you by flying around your house pretending to be termites. (This is the only form of entertainment that ants have.)

7   Ants are not the only animals that have government. Similar organizational structures can be found throughout nature: Monkeys form troops, birds form flocks, fish form schools, worms form bunches of worms, intestinal parasites form law firms, etc. In other words: Governments are natural. All animals form them, including humans. In a way, we are like the ants scurrying across our kitchen floor: We give our Cheez-It fragments (tax money) to the colony (government), and in return we enjoy the many benefits provided by the colony (the Federal Avocado Safety Administration).

8   Of course human beings are far more advanced than animals; we do not elect the president of the United States based on how he smells. As cerebral beings, we are much more interested in other qualities in our president, such as height. As a result, we here in the United States have developed a sophisticated, highly complex government structure involving three major branches. (Among other animal species, only woodpeckers have more.)

Source: "Why Do We Have Governments" from Dave Barry Hits below the Beltway by Dave Barry (pp. 5–6). Copyright © 2001 by Dave Barry. Used by permission of Ballantine Books, a division of Random House.

1. Examine the word *hierarchy* in the following sentence from the passage: *At the top of the hierarchy is the queen, who is elected unanimously by the other ants after a very brief political campaign that consists of hatching.* Use context clues and word part analysis to define the word.

_____

2. Create your own creating-level question about this passage.

_____

3. Design a fictitious government structure for an animal group not mentioned in the passage. Using the information provided in the passage as a guide, include the details on your criteria for selecting a leader, the role of followers, the types of taxes you would impose, and the various branches of government.

Use Table 13.1 to help you prepare for exams by asking yourself questions from the different levels when studying. To use this chart effectively, select a level of thinking. Then use the verbs provided in the middle column to develop your practice test questions at that level. The third column gives you ideas for projects that demonstrate that level of thinking. By learning about the different levels of thinking, you are able to explore all possible question types.

Table 13.1 Verbs and Types of Activities Associated with the Levels of Bloom's Taxonomy

Level of Thinking	Verbs Associated with Level		Types of Activities Associated with Level	
Remembering new information: Remembering	define label locate draw identify select state name	describe match recall order recognize relate list show	definitions use a dictionary use text reading list information match words with definitions	
Understanding new information: Understanding	explain express paraphrase summarize predict compare	extend restate rewrite recognize translate	summary outline analogy collage	poster reflection paper examples
Using/applying new knowledge: Applying	apply change solve modify sketch produce	demonstrate illustrate interpret use write predict	photograph list mind map puzzle	essay written from an outline diagram
Breaking down information into component parts: Analyzing	analyze outline infer break down separate investigate classify trace the growth of differentiate	discriminate compare contrast experiment question test solve manipulate	model graph conclusion	questionnaire report

Level of Thinking	Verbs Associated with Level		Types of Activities Associated with Level	
Judging the value of knowledge: Evaluating	apprise compare recommend assess conclude criticize solve	critique judge justify support defend argue	group discussions recommendations	court trial editorial survey
Putting the pieces together to design/construct: Creating	combine construct formulate what if reconstruct produce categorize write relate	design assemble compose plan propose distinguish hypothesize	article play song game Brain Strength Options	book cartoon experiment poem

ACTIVITY 13K
Apply the Levels of Thinking

Using Table 13.1, identify the activities you would recommend based on the levels of thinking required.

1. Critique a newspaper article regarding the current elections

   What level of thinking is required?

   _____

   What activity would you recommend and why?

   _____

   _____

2. Outline a chapter in your psychology text

   What level of thinking is required?

   _____

   What activity would you recommend in addition to the outline and why?

   _____

   _____

Continued on next page.

3. Explain how photosynthesis works

   What level of thinking is required?

   _____

   What activity would you recommend and why?

   _____

   _____

4. Label the parts of the foot

   What level of thinking is required?

   _____

   What activity would you recommend and why?

   _____

   _____

5. Design a lesson plan for your internship

   What level of thinking is required?

   _____

   What activity would you recommend and why?

   _____

   _____

ACTIVITY 13L
Apply Bloom's Taxonomy to a Textbook Reading

Preview and study-read the following passage from a sociology textbook. Highlight the main idea in green and the major supporting details in yellow. Write margin notes as you see fit, and then answer the questions that follow.

Some Benefits and Costs of Technology

1   The ever-accelerating pace of change means that most U.S. children born after 2000 are now using technologies that didn't exist just a decade ago. Indeed, much of this "iGeneration" views even those in their 20s as outdated in their tech skills (Rosen 2010).

2   Technology may be creating greater generation gaps than in the past, but many Americans view the major technological and communications advances in a positive light. There is a greater division of opinion, however, over whether social networking sites or Internet blogs have been changes for the better (see Table 13.2). According to another recent national survey, 68 percent of Americans see technology companies as having a positive impact on the country,

Table 13.2 Opinions of Technological Changes

Technological Changes	Percentage Saying that the change has been "for the better"
Cell phones	69
E-mail	68
Internet	65
Increased surveillance/security	58
BlackBerrys/iPhones	56
Online shopping	54
Social networking sites	35
Internet blogs	29

Sources: Based on Kohut et al. 2009, p. 2.

compared with large corporations and the federal government (25 percent each), Congress (24 percent), and banks and financial institutions (22 percent) (Allen 2010).

3 Should the average American be less upbeat about technology changing for the better? Let's first look at some of its benefits.

Some Benefits

4 Technological advances have for some time offered benefits such as performing surgery, tracking people's medications, and monitoring children and older family members from afar using webcams. In other cases, robotic devices have performed repetitive, dirty, or dangerous tasks, including digging deep wells, testing military equipment, and locating bombs.

5 DNA testing has provided millions of people with information about their genetic predispositions for diseases such as emphysema, cancer, and Huntington's disease (an incurable neurological disorder). Having such information has helped doctors and patients make more informed healthcare decisions (Harmon 2008).

6 More than one-third of Americans age 65 or older falls each year. The economic cost of falls, including hip fractures and replacements, is about $75 billion a year. Low-cost wireless sensors in carpets, clothing, and rooms allow doctors to monitor an older person's walking and activity. As a result, physicians are reducing falls by devising exercise programs for specific muscles or changing medications to eliminate dizziness (Lohr 2009).

7 Some scientists also maintain that use of the Internet has enhanced human intelligence: As people have more access to information, they become smarter and make better decisions. In effect, as the digital systems that people rely on become faster and more sophisticated, so will our capabilities in working on solutions for problems such as the growing population density, the spread of pandemics, and global pollution (Cascio 2009).

Continued on next page.

predispositions
to make more
likely to suffer
from

density
degree of
concentration

pandemics
diseases spreading
throughout an
entire region

Some Costs

8   Cell phones, the Internet, and other forms of telecommunication bring people together and provide quick access to a wealth of information. Some argue, however, that the Internet, especially, has made us more sedentary and lazy, and that the ease of online searching and browsing has limited our ability to concentrate, to read without distractions, and to think (Carr 2008). Others worry that the iGeneration expects an instant response from everyone they communicate with, and has little patience for anything else (Rosen 2010). A more common concern is that virtually every technological advance in telecommunications reduces privacy.

9   Many companies routinely collect information about people as they click from site to site on the Internet. Much of this Web tracking is done anonymously, but a new crop of "snooper" sites is making it easier than ever before for anyone with Internet access to assemble and sell the information, including your name, Social Security number, address, and which sites you've visited on almost any topic, product, or service. The data come from a variety of sources, including public records on campaign contributions, property sales, and court cases; networking sites where people provide information about themselves, their jobs, relatives, and friends; and even Netflix, where marketers can track the movies that customers have watched and rated (Sarno 2009; Singer 2009, 2010).

10   Many Americans are vulnerable because they're not very knowledgeable about privacy laws. For example, only 22 percent know that if a Web site has a privacy policy, the site can share information about you with other companies without your permission (Turow et al. 2009). Another increasingly common intrusion on privacy is by health and life insurance companies that pay only about $15 per search to other companies that prepare health "credit reports." They have accessed at least 200 million Americans' 5-year history of purchases of prescription drugs, the dosages and refills, and possible medical conditions. With such reports,

insurance companies can charge some customers higher premiums or exclude some medical conditions from policies. Even worse, according to some health experts, some insurance companies have misinterpreted the information and denied coverage (Nakashima 2008; Terhune 2008).

Source: From BENOKRAITIS. *SOC* 2e (pp. 328–330). Copyright © 2012 Cengage Learning.

1. (remembering) List three benefits of technology.

   _____

   _____

2. (understanding) Using your own words, summarize the main points of this reading in five sentences or less.

   _____

   _____

   _____

   _____

   _____

3. (applying) Interpret the meaning of the cartoon that accompanies the passage.

   _____

   _____

   _____

   _____

4. (analyzing) Outline the passage to differentiate the major and minor details presented.

   _____

   _____

   _____

   _____

   _____

   _____

   _____

Continued on next page.

_____

_____

_____

_____

_____

_____

_____

_____

_____

_____

_____

_____

_____

5. (evaluating) Use this passage to evaluate whether technology enhances human intelligence. Support your response with information from the passage along with information you know.

_____

_____

_____

_____

6. (creating) In what way(s) does Table 13.2 relate to the main idea of this passage?

_____

_____

_____

_____

_____

Levels of Learning: The Natural Human Learning Process

WHILE BLOOM DEVELOPED HIS SIX STAGES OF THINKING using experience and critical thinking, Rita Smilkstein identified the six stages of the natural human learning process (NHLP) by research with more than 10,000 people, from students through elementary, middle, high school, college, and graduate school to university educators, about their process of learning. When asked how they learned something outside school, every group identified similar stages, leading to the research-based conclusion that there are specific, sequential, natural stages of learning (see some of the NHLP research results in Chapter 1).

Compare the NHLP's stages with Bloom's stages. You will see that its six stages are also almost identical, suggesting that learners progress through Bloom's stages of thinking because they are experiencing the NHLP's stages of learning.

It is important to note that both the NHLP and Bloom's Taxonomy expect that to learn something new, you must connect it with something you already know about the topic. This is the first stage of the NHLP (motivation) and Bloom's Taxonomy (remembering). For example, if you are going to read about psychology, think about what you already know about psychology. If you do not already know anything on the topic, then you will need to investigate or research more on psychology to begin to know something and connect the new topic to. Otherwise, you will not be able to fully understand the topic. You will feel lost. Has this ever happened to you?

At the second stage (beginning practice, understanding), you practice relating what you are reading to what you know. Does the reading make sense to you? Can you see or comprehend how it relates to your own knowledge or experience? If not, is *it* wrong or are *you* wrong? If you cannot relate it to what you already know, you will need to become familiar with the new ideas and information in the reading. You will have to practice relating the new material to what you already know until you have

Tip FROM THE Brain Doctor

The brains of participants in a research study were scanned while they studied. Those who used multiple mental strategies had better memory performance. You have learned many strategies in this book. Apply as many as you can each time you study, and you will make the most of your study time, learn more effectively, and remember the material better!

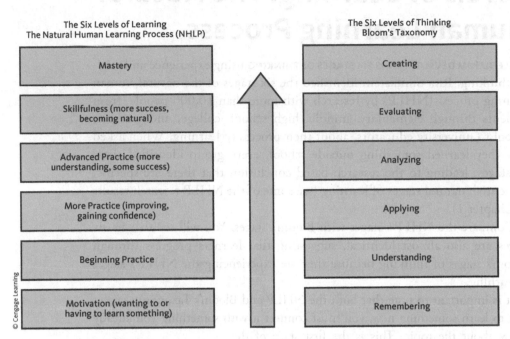

Figure 13.3 Comparing the Natural Human Learning Process (NHLP) and Bloom's Taxonomy

gone beyond to learn something new and can begin to comprehend the new material.

At the third stage (more practice, applying), you continue reading the text and see how it applies, not only to your own experiences but also to what else the reading tells you. Sometimes you might need to page-flip or cross-reference to relate the new ideas to previous ones. Then you continue practicing to see how the previous material and the new material relate. When you are learning new material, applying what you already know to the new topic will help you understand the new topic more completely and easily.

In the fourth stage (advanced practice, analyzing), you understand and analyze (know the parts and how they relate to each other) the text. To support your understanding of a text, you are able, with advanced practice, to identify or present an analysis of the ideas or information in the text.

In the fifth stage (skillfulness, evaluating), you now have your own ideas and understanding about the topic, possess a certain amount of skill with the new information, and you are able to evaluate and make decisions about the text. You understand other ideas about the topic and are able to determine whether you agree or disagree. This ability to perform an evaluation of ideas or parts from one or more texts gives you an even deeper understanding so that you can skillfully, with evidence, write or talk about your understanding.

Finally, in the sixth stage (mastery, creating), you are able to fully integrate the new information you have mastered from your text with other information you already know to create new knowledge. Your ability to master text material, integrate it with your prior knowledge, and create something new from it, is based on all the learning and thinking you have done in the previous stages.

Knowing that there are different levels of thinking, you can approach your textbooks with a greater expectation of learning. Aim for a deeper, more critical reading of your textbooks by questioning yourself at the six levels of Bloom's Taxonomy and actively experiencing the six stages of the NHLP.

ACTIVITY 13M
Identify the Steps of the NHLP

Using your own words, describe each of the six steps regarding the natural human learning process. How are they similar to Bloom's Taxonomy?

1. _____
   _____

2. _____
   _____

3. _____
   _____

4. _____
   _____

5. _____
   _____

6. _____
   _____

Keeping Your Brain Healthy Beyond Reading

APPLYING WHAT YOU LEARNED IN THIS CHAPTER about how to read at higher levels can also make you a better thinker. Not taking everything you hear at face value is an important mental trait. Applying what you learn in one situation to another situation in your life makes you more intelligent and effective. Being intelligent is about more than a score on an IQ test. It is operating at higher levels in your everyday thinking and interactions. Applying, analyzing, and creating are desirable and marketable job skills that will contribute to your success when you graduate and apply for a job of choice.

You have learned so much about your brain, reading, and learning in this textbook that will benefit you throughout your life. But, there is more to being a good learner, a good student, a good employee, a good parent, or a good citizen than just being an expert reader. You need to maintain a healthy brain at all stages of life for everything that you do.

As you have learned through this book, your brain changes as a result of what you do—it demonstrates plasticity. So remember that the activities that you engage in, the habits you have, and your persistent thoughts and attitudes all serve to form your brain as it will be later in life. If you persist in negative habits, behaviors, or thoughts, you will become more negative. So keep a positive attitude!

Some research has shown that exercise grows new neurons in the hippocampus, which is involved in memory. Much research has shown the importance of exercise for a healthy brain. Keep in mind that oxygen carries fuel to the brain, so getting oxygen to the brain through exercise is beneficial. Get up and move around when you are studying or working at a desk. Make walking a daily habit. Instead of complaining about how far the parking lot is on campus, enjoy that walk. Get some aerobic exercise weekly. Strength training has also been shown to be beneficial.

Diet affects brain health. Avoid trans fats as indicated by the words "partially hydrogenated" on food product nutrition labels. Avoid excess sugar. Get plenty of antioxidants with fruits and vegetables. Keep in mind that you grow your body and brain every day with the choices that you make.

Statistics show that the average person today will have seven careers in a lifetime. This means that you will be a lifelong learner. This textbook has prepared you to read and learn effectively so that you can continue to adapt to changing society and your changing interests.

ACTIVITY 13N
Follow Up with a Reading Survey

Now that you have completed this textbook, check your current knowledge of your reading skills and strategies by taking the following survey for a second time. Read each statement, and respond based on your current reading habits. Be honest with yourself. This is a way to help you discover how well you are applying the strategies you have learned. Write *Y* if the statement correctly describes you or what you currently do or *N* if it does not.

_____ 1. I make every attempt to learn the words I do not understand while reading. (See Chapter 3.)

_____ 2. I create questions to ask myself before I begin to read a textbook chapter. (See Chapters 4 and 8.)

_____ 3. When I decide to read a chapter, I start at the beginning and read straight through, often forgetting most of what I read. (See Chapters 1, 4, and 8.)

_____ 4. I highlight main ideas consistently so that I can review the key points of a chapter easily. (See Chapters 8 and 9.)

_____ 5. Thinking at different levels has nothing to do with reading at different levels. (See Chapter 13.)

_____ 6. I do not make connections between what I know and new reading material. (See Chapter 1.)

_____ 7. When I detect an argument in my reading assignment, I locate and evaluate the reasons supporting it. (See Chapter 11.)

_____ 8. Detecting fallacies helps me to understand authors' conclusions more effectively. (See Chapter 12.)

_____ 9. I am always able to identify the main ideas of textbooks. (See Chapters 4, 5, and 6.)

_____ 10. Sticking to a schedule seems too rigid for me. I'm too spontaneous to stick to a regular reading plan. (See Chapter 1.)

_____ 11. When I read, I try to locate organizational word clues. (See Chapter 7.)

_____ 12. Having a good attitude is related to how well I read. (See Chapters 1 and 2.)

_____ 13. It is important to actually say to myself that I intend to remember specific information in my textbook chapters. (See Chapter 2.)

_____ 14. Using authors' patterns of organization is not an important reading skill. It is more of a writing skill. (See Chapter 7.)

_____ 15. I create visuals for my most challenging textbook information. I use different visuals based on the type of information presented. (See Chapter 10.)

Continued on next page.

_____ 16. Tracking my concentration will not improve my ability to read. (See Chapter 1.)

_____ 17. I always look for clue words to help me gain deeper insight into the author's meaning. (See Chapters 7, 8, 9, and 13.)

_____ 18. I often try to create a metaphor to help me remember. Making comparisons makes recall easier. (See Chapters 2 and 6.)

_____ 19. I give up on trying to figure things out. It is a waste of my time. (See Chapters 6 and 7.)

_____ 20. I use specific colors to identify main ideas and supporting details when marking my textbooks. (See Chapter 9.)

To calculate your score, your instructor will provide you with the answers of an expert reader. For every answer you have that matches that of an expert reader, give yourself 5 points.

Your Score: _____

100–95 Outstanding	Outstanding application of critical reading and thinking strategies.
90–85 Above Average	Above average application of critical reading strategies.
80–75 Average	Additional knowledge of skills and strategies will strengthen your ability to read and think more effectively.
70–65 Marginally Adequate	You may have difficulty getting the most out of your college textbooks. Additional knowledge of skills and strategies will strengthen your ability to read and think more effectively.
60 and below Needs Work	You will benefit from learning and applying the strategies learned in this course. Not only will the strategies help you academically, but they will also benefit you in the world of work.

Compare your score on this survey with the score you earned the first time you took this survey, (in Chapter 1). How is your current score different? What changes did you note in your reading strategies?

You know that knowledge is power. The more you read, the more you know, and the ability to use information in a meaningful way will always give you an advantage. How will you use what you learned from this book? How will you read your textbooks now as an expert reader?

PRACTICE WITH A READING PASSAGE

Prepare to Read

The following sociology passage includes the results of a study of the American ritual of the marriage proposal. Twenty engaged couples were interviewed and studied and parts of the conclusions of the study are provided in this passage.

1. What is a *ritual*?

_____

2. What do you already know about marriage proposals?

_____

3. Develop a question, using the title of this passage, to ask yourself before you read.

_____

4. Preview the passage by reading the title and headings. Then, study-read the passage, highlighting the main idea in green and the major supporting details in yellow. Write margin notes as necessary.

5. Circle all new vocabulary, and provide the definitions as margin notes.

The Proposal Script
By David Schweingruber, Sine Anahita, and Nancy Berns

1   The majority of the proposals in this study contained five elements. Three were found in every proposal: (1) the man asking the woman to marry him, (2) the man presenting the woman a ring, and (3) the man orchestrating the proposal as a "surprise." Another element, the man getting down on one knee, was found in 17 of the 20 proposals. The final element, the man asking permission of the woman's father, was found in 12 of the 20 proposals.

Man as Proposer

2   A universal element in the proposals of heterosexual couples we interviewed was that the proposer was the male member of the couple and the audience was the female member. Breaking this rule, as only the female member can do, did not result in an official engagement. In fact, switching the roles may turn the proposal into a parody that produces amusement, instead of the usual romantic feelings. As one woman explained:

> I actually, as a joke, the week before, on our one year anniversary, I put in the card, I'm like, "I love you so much. Will you marry me?" And he just looked at me and he's, like [with intonation of amused scolding], "Oh, Julie."

parody joke, mimicry

Continued on next page.

Another woman twice asked her boyfriend to marry her and even gave him a ring. He wore the ring but did not take her proposals seriously. The couple did not consider themselves engaged until he asked her to marry him....

The Importance of the Ring

3   Although the man's verbal request that the woman marry him was important, words without an engagement ring did not make a complete proposal. The presentation of a ring made it clear that what was going on was an engagement proposal. This was a strong necessity not only for the first audience, the woman, but also for the secondary audience. Without a ring, the proposal was not yet appropriate as a public story and did not provide the official marking of their future as an engaged couple. The following two examples illustrate the change in the woman's emotions from hope to disappointment when she realized that her boyfriend was not presenting a ring and thus the proposal was not a "real" one:

> I actually kind of faked her out that night [shortly before the actual proposal]. [laugh] I acted like I was getting something on the couch, and I was on one knee, and I had my hands closed, and she was getting all excited then. And so like I go, "Molly, will you marry me?" And I open my hands up and there's nothing there. And ... [she] told me how mean that was and that the next time I do that it'd better be real. [laughs] (male)

> He said, "... will you marry me?" And I said, "Yes." And then he pulled out this ring box, and in it was a ring made out of pine needles, and I started to cry because I was expecting my real ring. And so I started to cry and he's like, "I promise I'll give you the real ring as soon as I can" and all this stuff. And so I was trying to be really nice about it, but in my head I was going, "Oh my gosh. I want my diamond."... So after doing that for about two minutes, then he pulled a box out of the other pocket, and it had my ring in it.... I still have the pine ring, but I like this one better. (female)

In the first case the proposal was transformed into a humorous rehearsal. In the second, the joke (until it was resolved) ruined the performance and created the impression that the proposer did not understand the script and, consequently, might not be serious about becoming engaged. Not all women shared the opinion that a proposal without a ring would be illegitimate. However, if there was no ring, some sort of explanation, such as financial **exigency**, was required....

exigency something that is urgent, demanded, necessary

prima facie at first view or glance

4   The ring was just as important, or even more important, during the secondary performances. The presence of a diamond ring on the woman's ring finger acted as *prima facie* evidence to the couple's friends and family that they were indeed engaged. The secondary audience may in fact demand that the ring be produced. For instance:

> I think the first thing my mom said is, "Let's see your finger," because she knew he was going to ask so we just kind of broke [the news], you know, told everyone what happened and that we were engaged and let everyone know. (female)

Surprise

5   The proposal was supposed to be a "surprise" but only in a limited sense because an agreement to marry had already been reached by all of these subjects. The woman expected that a proposal would be made. What was supposed to surprise her was when and where the proposal would take place. Whether surprise was achieved varied within our sample. At one extreme, the woman knew that the proposal was imminent. She knew the ring had been purchased, and she suspected that she would be proposed to that day. The surprise was in the details. Her fiancé said, "We both knew it was coming, and we both knew it was going to happen that night, but she didn't know exactly how it was going to happen."

imminent due soon, coming

6   At the other extreme, the woman knew that the man would someday propose to her, but the time and place of the proposal caught her off guard. "He surprised me. That was his big thing 'cause we both knew that we'd be getting married. He was afraid that I was going to say I thought this was coming, and I didn't." Note that although this woman "had no idea" the proposal was coming, the couple had discussed the ring. She had also previously given her boyfriend instructions about what she expected from the proposal.

7   One of the purposes of the surprise was to allow the woman to respond spontaneously to the proposal. As one woman reported:

> It kind of swept me off my feet ... If I know something's coming up, I can kind of plan for it and kind of prepare myself for it. But this, I just had none of that so maybe it was just like complete raw emotion when you just don't expect anything, you can't have any feeling preplanned or anything. You just kind of react and it seemed ... more genuine that way. If you don't plan out what you're going to say before or after ... if it just happens, maybe it's more true.

This outpouring of emotion was an expected part of the proposal and not just by the women. Respondents reported the outpouring of emotion that accompanied the proposal occurred in various ways. First, respondents reported weeping and not understanding what was going on. Second, they reported that they could not remember parts of the proposal because they were overwhelmed by emotion. Finally, men reported that performances were disrupted by emotion and some of their plans were abandoned....

Down on One Knee

8   Seventeen of the 20 men got down on one knee during the proposal. Another was down on both knees. The two exceptions were explained by the circumstances. One couple got engaged while looking at the stars as they sat in a car (it was too cold to go outside). The other proposal involved the man turning around to show his girlfriend the ring balanced on the end of a hockey stick. In many cases the woman had earlier requested that her boyfriend get down on one knee. This element of the proposal exemplified much of the entire ritual in that it clearly indicated that a proposal was taking place, but its origin or original meaning was unknown to the people who

Continued on next page.

were participating. Specifically, the man getting down on one knee signaled that the proposal was beginning and the presentation of the ring and the verbal request to marry were imminent. When respondents were asked about the meaning of this element, they were able to come up with possible meanings but indicated that they did not know the "real" meaning or had not even given it much thought. For instance:

> I don't know. Maybe it's like going back to tradition, man trying to be submissive to his wife. Who knows really, but it just seems like the **chivalrous** thing to do, I guess, you know, because you're asking and when you get lower than the other person, you're supposed to be submissive. I don't know what it means really, but I like it. (male)

9   The lack of a tradition of men's submission to their wives suggests that this man's **hypothesis** was incorrect. The elements of the engagement proposal are important because they convey that a proposal is going on, not because of other symbolic meanings. Getting down on one knee is uniquely useful in communicating a proposal is taking place because it is rare during typical interactions.

Asking Permission

10   Twelve of the 20 men asked permission from their girlfriend's father before proposing. As with the proposal itself, asking the father was a performance with dual audiences. By asking his girlfriend's father's permission, the man acted out his respect for his future father-in-law, his hope to have his father-in-law's blessing, and his desire to join the family. His secondary audience was his girlfriend, who viewed asking permission as a romantic gesture and often specifically requested it. In fact, she might have been a more important audience than her father.

> I told them [my girlfriend's parents] that after careful consideration I would really like to marry Shari and wanted to know if that was all right with them, kind of knowing that it was, but they said that that was really all right with them and that was about it. Really it was kind of more of a formality for her than directly involved with us. (male)

11   As with other sex-specific requirements of the script, most couples did not make the connection between the script and its seemingly sexist symbolism, i.e., its suggestion that the woman is owned by her father, who is empowered to turn her over to her future husband. Couples liked it not only because it was "traditional" but also because women liked to involve their fathers in the event. As one woman explained:

> I thought it was kind of nice.... I just think it would make [my dad] feel special to be involved in that way and stuff, and I think that it really did make my dad feel good that he called and asked him. I mean my dad obviously ... loves Dan, and we both knew that he wouldn't say "no" or anything, but it's just kind of nice to have him involved that way.

One woman who thought the process "takes out the independence of the woman" still encouraged her fiancé to "notify" her father because he was "old-fashioned" and

---

chivalrous marked by honor and courtesy usually describing a man's behavior toward a woman

hypothesis assumption

"I knew he'd get really excited about it and feel like he was part of the process.... It gives my dad a story to tell." Only one woman indicated a strong objection to her boyfriend asking her father, saying, "I'm my own person, and my dad has nothing to do with it." Another woman, though, said she thought that asking her father was more significant than asking her, because "then I knew that he was really serious." Only four of the 12 men who asked permission from their girlfriend's father also asked permission from her mother.

From David Schweingruber, Sine Anahita, and Nancy Berns, "The Engagement Proposal as Performance," *Sociological Focus* 37(2), 2004. Reprinted by permission of the North Central Sociological Association.

6. Why is the marriage proposal called a "script" in the passage's title? How is the marriage proposal a ritual?

_____

_____

7. What reasons does the author give to support the main idea? What are the parts or elements of the ritual?

_____

_____

8. What pattern of organization does the author use? How do you know? What organizational word clues helped you determine the pattern?

_____

_____

9. Examine the "Asking Permission" section of the proposal script. How can it be seen as sexist? How can it be look at as endearing?

_____

_____

10. Do you agree with the author's main idea (conclusion)? Why or why not?

_____

_____

_____

11. Design a scenario for the the perfect marriage proposal. Use three of the five elements described in the passage.

12. What level of questioning are questions #9, 10, and 11?

_____

CHAPTER SUMMARY

Bloom's Taxonomy began as a teaching tool for instructors to use to help their students achieve more complex levels of thinking. The six levels of Bloom's Taxonomy are remembering, understanding, applying, analyzing, evaluating, and creating.

The natural human learning process (NHLP) is a specific, sequential, natural process that people go through as they learn. Working through Bloom's six levels of thinking actually prompts you to go through the six steps of the natural learning process. The end result is higher-level thinking.

In the first stage, you must learn something new and recall what you already know on the subject you are reading. Doing this helps you establish a place in your brain where the new information will go. In the second stage, you practice relating what you are reading to what you already know. This establishes a place for your knowledge to grow. In the third stage, you take what you understand from the reading and apply it to other parts of the reading and the information you already know on the subject. In the fourth stage, you analyze the parts of what you are reading to see how each part stands against what you already know and the rest of the new reading material. In the fifth stage, you evaluate what you have learned, allowing you to make decisions about the information. In the last stage, the highest level of learning, you create a big mental picture of the new information, which also includes what you already know. Then you can create from what you have learned.

Knowledge of Bloom's Taxonomy and the NHLP not only helps you explore many levels of thinking. It also provides a blueprint for upcoming exams and future learning experiences. Remember that instructors will test you with questions at the various levels of thinking to ensure that you are learning. If you know these levels and test yourself beforehand, you will perform better on exams. More importantly, you will become an expert reader and a better thinker.

Brain Connections: Self-Assessment

Draw the amount of dendrites you imagine that you have now about reading beyond the words. Compare your drawing of dendrites now with what you drew at the beginning of this chapter. If the amounts are different, explain why.

✔ COMPREHENSION CHECK

▶ Where in the chapter did you lose concentration or become confused?
▶ If you could ask the authors a question about this chapter, what would you ask?

POST TEST

Part 1: Objective Questions

Match the key terms from the chapter in Column A to their definitions in Column B.

	Column A		Column B
_____	1. Bloom's Taxonomy	a.	level of breaking information down into parts
_____	2. evaluating level of thinking	b.	level of making a judgment
_____	3. remembering level of thinking	c.	literal level of thinking
_____	4. understanding level of thinking	d.	a classification of levels of thinking
_____	5. applying level of thinking	e.	level of being able to create a bigger picture after combining parts
_____	6. analyzing level of thinking	f.	level of applying what you have learned
_____	7. creating level of thinking	g.	level of making predictions and inferences and paraphrasing

Circle the best answer to the following multiple-choice question.

8. Which of the following is an example of critical reading and thinking?

   a. developing mnemonics to recall important dates from a book on World War II

   b. understanding the main ideas of a large biology chapter

   c. understanding the concept of area in geometry, working out the problems at the end of the chapter, and figuring out the areas of shapes outside the Student Union

   d. disregarding a new article in a magazine because it disagrees with what the textbook says

Read the following scenarios, and determine what level(s) of thinking is (are) involved. Explain your answers.

9. Toni was assigned a psychology chapter to read. She was asked to:

   ▶ critique section one of her chapter, using her own words.

   _____

   ▶ write a poem regarding the chapter's main idea.

   _____

   ▶ define the words in the section regarding the Bell Curve Theory.

   _____

Continued on next page.

10. How can an understanding of Bloom's Taxonomy and the natural human learning process help someone in future college and work assignments?

_____

_____

_____

Part 2. Reading Passage   POPULAR READING

Prepare to Read

1. Based on the title, what do you expect the following passage to be about?

_____

2. What do you already know about the subject?

_____

3. Develop a question from the title. As you read the passage, try to answer that question.

_____

4. Study-read the passage and highlight the main idea in green and the major supporting ideas in yellow.

Empress Wu
By T. Walter Wallbank and Alastair M. Taylor

1   One of the most remarkable women in world history, famed for her vices as well as for her strong and able rule, governed China from about 660 to 705. The Empress Wu began her career as a concubine in the harem of the third T'ang emperor. When the emperor died, Wu and all the other concubines, according to custom, had their heads shaved and entered a Buddhist convent. Here they were expected to pass the remainder of their lives. Wu, however, was too intelligent and beautiful—as well as too **unscrupulous** to accept such a fate. Within a year she had won the new emperor's heart and had become honorable, his concubine. According to a hostile tradition, she first met the new emperor in a lavatory when he was paying a ceremonial visit to the convent.

2   Wu rose steadily in the new emperor's favor until, after accusing the empress of engaging in sorcery, murdering her baby daughter, and plotting to poison her husband, she was herself installed as empress. According to the official history of the age, "The whole **sovereign** power passed into her hands. Life and death, reward and punishment, were determined by her word. The Son of Heaven merely sat upon his throne with hands folded."

unscrupulous does not follow what is right

sovereign state with defined territory

3   After the death of the emperor twenty years later, Wu installed two of her sons as successive puppets. She ruthlessly employed secret police and informers to suppress conspiracies against her. Finally, in 690 at the age of sixty-two, she usurped the imperial title and became the only woman ever to rule China in name as well as in fact.

4   To legitimize her usurpation, the empress was aided by a group of unscrupulous Buddhist monks, one of whom is reputed to have been her lover. They discovered in Buddhist scriptures a prophecy that a pious woman was destined to be reborn as the ruler of an empire that would inaugurate a better age and to which all countries would be subject. Not only did the monks identify Wu as the woman in the prophecy, but they acclaimed her as a divine incarnation of the Buddha. The T'ang capital was renamed the Divine Capital, and Wu assumed a special title—"Holy Mother Divine Imperial One."

usurpation a wrongfully takeover

5   Despite her ruthlessness—understandable in the totally unprecedented situation of a woman seeking successfully to rule a great empire—the Empress Wu was an able ruler who consolidated the T'ang Dynasty. She not only avenged earlier Sui and T'ang defeats at the hands of the northern Koreans who had been subject to the Han, but she made all of Korea a loyal vassal state of China. Yet because she was a woman and a usurper, she found little favor with Chinese Confucian historians. They played up her vices, particularly her many favorites and lovers whom she rewarded with unprecedented honors.

unprecedented nothing like it before

vassal under her protection

usurper one who seizes and holds power wrongfully

6   Among those who gained great influence over the aging empress was a peddler of cosmetics, famous for his virility, who was first made abbot of a Buddhist monastery, then palace architect, and finally commander-in-chief of the armies on the northern frontier. At the age of seventy-two, her favorites—and reputed lovers—were two young brothers of a type known as "white faces" (men who were physically attractive but otherwise of no account), whose powdered and rouged faces were a common sight around the palace. When the empress appointed a younger brother of her two favorites to an important governorship, her leading ministers successfully conspired to put her son back on the throne. The two brothers were decapitated in the palace and the Empress Wu, the founder and only member of the Wu Dynasty, was forced to abdicate.

virility wide range of masculine characteristics viewed positively

conspired plotted something together

abdicate give up the throne

Source: From WALLBANK, CIVILIZATION PAST & PRESENT, 5th Edition, © 1985. Reprinted by permission of Pearson Education, Inc., Upper Saddle River, NJ.

5. Use context clues and word part analysis to define the following words from the passage.

• successive (paragraph 3): _____

• incarnation (paragraph 4): _____

• consolidated (paragraph 5): _____

Continued on next page.

Now complete three of the essay questions provided here. Every student's essay answer will be different based on the key word in the individual assignment. Be sure that your answer corresponds with the specific question. Every essay answer must have a minimum of five sentences. Be sure to cite specific examples from the passage to support your main idea. Your main idea sentence will be determined by your question.

6. Compare and contrast yourself with Empress Wu.

7. Criticize or critique the essay. (Example: *The author did not present a fair picture of Empress Wu.*)

8. Define Empress Wu as a tyrant. (Example: *Empress Wu is a tyrant because....*)

9. Describe Empress Wu.

10. Discuss Empress Wu as a leader of a country. (Example: *Empress Wu had both good and bad qualities as a leader.*)

11. Evaluate Empress Wu as a leader. (Example: *As a leader, Empress Wu...*)

12. Explain why Empress Wu was forced off the throne.

13. Illustrate why Empress Wu would be disliked.

14. Interpret Empress Wu's behavior.

15. Justify the decision to remove Empress Wu from the throne.

16. List how Empress Wu got to the throne.

17. Outline the rise and fall of Empress Wu.

18. Prove that Empress Wu was a good leader.

19. Relate the behavior of Empress Wu in office to a leader that you know of.

20. Review the rise and fall of Empress Wu.

21. Summarize the history of Empress Wu.

22. Trace the rise and fall of Empress Wu.

Source: Copyright Janet N. Zadina, 2002

BRAIN STRENGTH OPTIONS

1. Working individually or in groups of no more than three, create a poster portraying each level of Bloom's Taxonomy. The purpose is not just to list the levels. Instead, give an example of each level by listing an activity that would represent it. Use your creativity, but be consistent throughout the poster and make sure all levels are labeled.

2. Working individually or in groups of no more than three, choose one of the following prompts based on the story of Empress Wu on page 632.

   a. Draw a series of pictures (like a comic book) that illustrates Empress Wu's story.

   b. Write a song that illustrates Empress Wu's personality or tells her story.

   c. With your group, act out Empress Wu's story.

   d. Make a PowerPoint presentation or poster that compares Empress Wu with a current person. Include at least four points of comparison or contrast.

   e. Find a movie that you think is a modern-day version of Empress Wu's story. Present to the class at least four points of comparison. The movie does not have to have a political theme; it can relate in terms of personality or cause and effect or in other ways.

   f. Turn Empress Wu's story into a movie that you design in the form of a movie poster. Use pictures to illustrate your casting, scenery, and relevant symbols. Include at least four sentences that describe the movie and motivate viewers to attend.

   g. Your idea (obtain approval from your instructor).

Appendix
Test-Taking Strategies

Test-Taking Self-Assessment

TAKE THE FOLLOWING QUIZ TO DETERMINE THE STRENGTH of your test-taking strategies. Answer *Yes* if the statement is characteristic of you and *No* if it is not. Preferred answers with explanations are provided following the quiz.

1.	I never seem to have enough time to finish an exam.	Yes	No
2.	I answer all exam questions. I leave nothing blank.	Yes	No
3.	I read the directions twice before answering the exam questions.	Yes	No
4.	While taking multiple-choice tests, I select the first answer if it seems correct.	Yes	No
5.	I always double-check my answers.	Yes	No
6.	When I answer essay questions, I organize my thoughts as I am writing.	Yes	No
7.	I always match the grammar used in the question with the grammar used in the correct answer.	Yes	No
8.	If I am unsure of the answer, I avoid those that use absolute words.	Yes	No
9.	I often change my answers when taking objective tests.	Yes	No
10.	I answer questions I know well first.	Yes	No
11.	If I get nervous, I take a few seconds to take a deep breath and know that it is normal to experience momentary blocks during an exam.	Yes	No
12.	When writing an essay exam, I understand the difference between the terms *evaluate, summarize, contrast, prove,* and *justify.*	Yes	No

Now compare your answers to those provided here. If you find that any of your answers are different, take some time to review the information in this appendix.

1. **No:** Plan on using time management when taking tests. If you have 50 minutes to answer 50 questions, make sure you spend no more than a minute per question. Skip over questions you do not know the answer to right away, mark them in some way, and plan to come back to them later. Do not waste time on questions that you are not confident about as all questions are usually equal in point value.

2. **Yes:** Good habit. Try to never leave any questions blank—there is a chance your guess might be right and you will get the point value for it.

3. **Yes:** Good habit. Students sometimes get questions wrong because they do not read the directions correctly. If you are asked to select the best answer, then you do not want to select the first answer that seems correct as it may not be the best answer.

4. **No:** Cover up the multiple-choice options provided and try to answer the question yourself. Then see if your answer is one of the options. If so, it most likely is correct.

5. **Yes:** It is a good habit to double check your answers. It can be easy to make careless mistakes, but do not change your answer unless you are very certain your initial response was wrong.

6. **No:** It is more effective to spend a third of your time before writing your essay exam answer brainstorming to organize your thoughts. Outline your answer and then write it completely. If you write it before fully thinking out your answer, it becomes difficult to add or change paragraphs as more ideas come to you.

7. **Yes:** If the question is in present tense, the answer most likely will be also.

8. **Yes:** Unless you know for certain that the answer is correct, absolutes, which include words like *all*, *always*, and *never*, are usually wrong.

9. **No:** Unless you are certain an answer you selected is incorrect, it is best not to change your initial answer.

10. **Yes:** When you answer questions that you are positive you know the answers to first, it saves you time to focus on the more challenging questions and relaxes you by building your confidence. Using this strategy is rewarding.

11. **Yes:** Breathing deeply is good for you and your brain. It sends good chemicals throughout your brain, making you feel calmer, and it also provides a needed boost of oxygen to the brain, which often provides clarity and calm.

12. **Yes:** It is good to know test-taking vocabulary. Often, students know the answer to a test question, but they do not understand what is being asked and then answer incorrectly. If a test question asks a student to contrast an apple and an orange, but the student writes an answer that shows similarities between the two fruits, the answer would be wrong, even if what the student wrote was factually correct.

Preparing for a Test

THERE ARE SEVERAL STRATEGIES YOU CAN USE TO HELP you prepare to take a test. Most importantly, you need to understand and learn the information you are being tested on. However, there are other strategies that can help you feel prepared. These strategies will give you confidence. Think of them like a floating device as you "jump in" and take an exam. Even if you are a good swimmer, the extra assistance keeps you afloat should the waves of questions suddenly feel rough. If you have studied and know the material, your knowledge and confidence will guide you through.

▶ **Prepare early.** You can begin preparing for tests on the very first day of class. Review your syllabus and your textbook(s). A syllabus is your contract with your instructor. Put test dates in your planner, calendar, or schedule so you always know when they are. Schedule dates to study for tests so that you know how to plan for the test. Also, take the time to go through your textbook's table of contents to get an idea of what you will be learning. When you are aware of when and what you will be studying and when exams are coming, you will feel less anxious.

▶ **Avoid cramming.** Cramming is the enemy of concentration. If you try to cram several weeks' worth of information into one day of studying, you will not be able to concentrate on the information long enough to thoroughly understand it. During a test, your confidence will be shaken as you scramble to answer the questions correctly. Study every day for each subject that you had that day. Remember that the more you fire a network in your brain, the stronger it is. Repetition is key! If you spend a few minutes every day reviewing, think how many repetitions you will have before the test!

▶ **Review often.** Plan reviews as part of your regularly weekly study schedule. Reviews are much more than reading and rereading assignments. Make sure that you also read and review lecture notes and ask yourself questions on the material you do not know well. Review for several short periods rather than one long period. You will find that you retain information better and get less fatigued. Your brain needs time to process information. Review Chapter 9 for strategies to help you take more effective notes.

▶ **Make study time intentional.** When you study, it is sometimes useful to use special items, like wearing a specific sweatshirt or hat. This gets you in the mindset to study and can also signal to family members or roommates that you are studying. When they see your item, they know to give you the time and quiet you need.

▶ **Test yourself.** Create flashcards using your textbook markings to test yourself on concepts or vocabulary words that may be giving you trouble. Develop questions from the green-highlighted main ideas and yellow-highlighted major supporting details. Use the card review system (CRS) for new vocabulary (see Chapter 3). Review the cards in random order. Test yourself over and over (see Chapter 2 for more on retrieval). From your flashcards, create a pile you can answer easily and a pile for questions that stump you. It will help you know where to focus your time.

▶ **Think big**. Focus on the big picture. Often, you will be able to plug in the minor details if you understand the bigger picture. Study your margin notes—the items that you identified as being the "main points" of your reading. If you understand the bigger picture, it makes it easier to remember some of the details that support it. If you focus on a million details, sometimes the main idea and larger picture get lost and become difficult to remember.

▶ **Ask questions beforehand.** Make sure you fully understand what you will be tested on. Ask your instructor what course content the exam will cover and what kinds of test questions you should prepare for. Find out if the exam is open-book or open-notes. If it is, remember to bring the allowed items with you. Review Chapter 9 for strategies to help you take more effective notes.

▶ **Bring all the necessary supplies.** Come prepared for the exam. Bring more than one pencil or pen. Bring a calculator, if appropriate, and scrap paper to brainstorm or draw to aid your memory retrieval.

▶ **Get a good night's sleep.** A rested brain concentrates better. Research shows that sleep helps to consolidate learning—it helps you remember what you learned!

▶ **Eat beforehand**. Start with a good breakfast. What you really need on the morning of a test is a combination of complex carbohydrates and protein: peanut butter on whole-wheat toast with a glass of orange juice is a good choice. Avoid large quantities of caffeine, sugar, and fat, and do not eat too much or you will feel sleepy. Do try to stay hydrated by drinking water.

Coping with Test Anxiety

TAKE THE FOLLOWING SELF-ASSESSMENT, and honestly answer how each statement relates to you and tests by marking it as True or False.

Test Anxiety Scale
Developed by Lois McGinley

_____   1. While taking an important exam, I find myself thinking how much brighter the other students are than I am.

_____   2. If I knew I was going to take an intelligence test, I would not feel confident and relaxed.

_____   3. While taking an important exam, I perspire a great deal.

_____   4. During class examinations, I find myself thinking of things unrelated to the actual course materials.

_____   5. I feel very panicky when I have to take a surprise exam.

_____ 6. During a test, I find myself thinking of the consequences of failing.

_____ 7. After important tests, I am frequently so tense my stomach gets upset.

_____ 8. I freeze up on tests and final exams.

_____ 9. Getting good grades on one test does not seem to increase my confidence on the second.

_____ 10. I sometimes feel my heart beating very fast during important exams.

_____ 11. After taking a test, I always feel I could have done better than I actually did.

_____ 12. I usually get depressed after taking a test.

_____ 13. When taking a test, my emotional feelings interfere with my performance.

_____ 14. During a course examination, I frequently get so nervous that I forget facts I really know.

_____ 15. I seem to defeat myself while working on important tests.

_____ 16. The harder I work at taking a test or studying for one, the more confused I get.

_____ 17. As soon as an exam is over, I try to stop worrying about it, but I just can't.

_____ 18. During exams, I sometimes wonder if I'll ever get through school.

_____ 19. I would rather write a paper than take an examination for my grade in a course.

_____ 20. I wish examinations did not bother me so much.

_____ 21. I think I could do much better on tests if I could take them alone and not feel pressured by time limits.

_____ 22. Thinking about the grade I may get in a course interferes with my studying and performance on tests.

_____ 23. If examinations could be done away with, I think I would actually learn more.

_____ 24. On exams I take the attitude, "If I know it now, there's no point in worrying about it." But I still worry.

_____ 25. I don't understand why I get so upset about tests.

_____ 26. I do not study any harder for final exams than for the rest of my coursework.

_____ 27. Even when I am well prepared for a test, I feel very anxious about it.

_____ 28. I do not enjoy eating before an important test.

_____ 29. Before am important examination, I find my hands or arms trembling.

_____ 30. I seldom feel the need for "cramming" before an exam.

_____ 31. The college should recognize that some students are more nervous than others about tests and that this affects their performance.

_____ 32. It seems to me that examination periods should not be made such intense situations.

_____ 33. I dread courses where the instructor has the habit of giving "pop" quizzes.

Source: © Lois McGinley. Reprinted with permission.

SCORING: Total the number of "true" answers you have. This is your test anxiety score.

▶ A score of 12 or below ranks in the low test anxiety range. However, you may not realize that a little anxiety is good. It can keep you on your toes and help you concentrate. If you are too relaxed, you may miss key words. Stay relaxed, but maintain focus.

▶ A score of 13 to 20 ranks in the medium test anxiety range. Although you probably handle stress well, you may benefit from learning some test-taking strategies to help you feel more confident.

▶ Scoring 21 or greater is a good indication that you experience considerable anxiety when taking tests. Meet with your instructor to learn more about the resources that are available on your campus to help address your issues and focus on all the strategies presented in this appendix. Many students experience test anxiety, but there are many ways for you to overcome the anxiety.

Sometimes students perform poorly on a test not because they did not study but because their anxiety over the test impairs their thinking. This is quite common in math classes, for example, and is known as "math anxiety."

The brain is designed to respond to threat with a survival mechanism. However, this mechanism has a negative effect when it comes to learning and test taking. When you feel "threatened" by a test, you put your survival mechanism into motion. Your best plan is to keep these threat alarms from going off in the first place. Thinking of a test as a challenge rather than a threat will keep the negative reactions of stress from going into action and making it harder to think well. It is only one test, not your identity. Mentally reframe your approach.

If the threat (fight-or-flight) alarm has gone off, you need to kick it back out. The brain has a feed-forward and a feed-backward system. When you think about a test, you may get anxious. This sends signals to the body, such as tightened muscles and faster breathing. This system helps you in a dangerous situation, like running from a tiger, but this kind of response hurts you when you are taking a test. However, you can send a different message _back_ to the brain. Slow breathing sends messages to the brain that all is calm and all is well. Forcing yourself to take a few calm breaths sends a message to the brain to turn off the anxiety. Taking a few slow breaths before every test can help you to combat the threat that your brain perceives.

▶ **Practice deep breathing exercises.** The following exercise is helpful when you are feeling stressed. Do this exercise the night before and the morning of an exam, if possible. Deep breaths will oxygenate the brain, giving it energy and allow it to function optimally. Stand up and stretch by reaching high with both hands. Try to reach for the ceiling. Slowly bend over and touch your toes. Let your arms loosely dangle by your feet. Repeat. Now position yourself so that you are comfortable and close your eyes. The preferred way to complete the remainder of this exercise is to lie down on a couch, floor, or bed. If you prefer to sit, make sure that your posture is good, keeping your back straight. Do not cross your arms or legs. Take a deep slow breath and slowly count to four. Exhale slowly, again to the count of four. As you exhale, notice how your body relaxes and becomes calm. Breathe deeply again to the count of four. Exhale to the count of four. While continuing to take deep breaths, relax all of your muscles one group at a time. Tell each muscle group to relax: face muscles, eyes, mouth, and forehead. Drop your tongue from the roof of your mouth. (When we are tense, our tongues stick to the roofs of our mouths.) Relax your neck, shoulders, chest, and upper arms. Continue to breathe deeply. Notice how your body relaxes and becomes calm. Relax your hands and each finger. Relax your stomach. Relax your upper back. Now relax your lower back. Relax your upper legs. Relax your knees; again, notice how your body relaxes and becomes calm. Relax your lower legs. Relax your feet. Relax each toe. Keep breathing deeply. Let the anxiety go. Take notice of how good you feel. You feel relaxed and calm. Enjoy how good you feel. Appreciate how you have created this calm and peaceful atmosphere within yourself. Keep your attention on your body. Wait a few moments before opening your eyes. When you open your eyes, you will feel refreshed and peaceful.

▶ **Stay calm**. If you have prepared well for an exam, you can be confident that you will do well. Taking a few deep breaths right before the test starts helps you relax and focus your concentration. Close your eyes and think about your deep breathing exercise and the calm feeling that you had.

▶ **Think positively**. Decide that you will get the most out of each class session and from your instructors. Thinking positively increases your ability to concentrate in the classroom and do well on exams. Sometimes the answers will come if you keep a clear head and don't panic.

▶ **Do not take things too seriously**. Keep the test in perspective. A test is an opportunity to show your instructor what you have learned. If you have studied your best, know that you have given it your best. If you fail a test, it does not mean that you are a failure. It just means that you may need to try different approaches to how you study. Meet with your instructor and find out what you missed and what you can do better next time.

Practicing Time Management during Tests

▶ **Arrive early on test days.** Research indicates that sitting in your regular seat may help to improve your memory and concentration. If you intend on sitting in your seat, make sure to arrive early enough to secure it. Arriving early will also give you the opportunity to breathe deeply and organize your materials and thoughts.

▶ **Avoid distracters.** Avoid the same distracters during test time that you would during study time. Do not sit next to your friends or by windows or doors if at all possible. Try to sit as close to the front as you can in case your instructor writes important directions on the board. This will also decrease the distraction of other students' test behavior.

▶ **Do not be concerned if other students finish before you do**. Set a pace that is comfortable for you.

▶ **Answer the easy questions first**. If you have 50 minutes to answer 50 questions, pace yourself. If each item is worth the same amount of points, do not spend five minutes on one question when you could be correctly answering four others. Skip over the questions you are not sure about, mark them with a question mark, and return to them later, if you have time. Oftentimes, reading other easier questions will trigger your memory, which will help you find answers to the questions you struggled with. Then, when you tackle more difficult questions, do not panic if the answers do not immediately come to mind. Relax. Breathe. And silently talk yourself through the question and its solution.

Answering Test Questions

▶ **Skim the test.** Before you start answering questions, skim the whole exam to get an overview of what to expect.

▶ **Read all of the directions**. It is important to know exactly what you are being asked to do. Also, listen to any verbal test instructions carefully, and be sure that you understand any last-minute changes the instructor may announce.

▶ **Read each question carefully and identify its purpose.** Ask yourself, "What information is this question asking me to provide?" Circle clue words to help you focus on the question's purpose.

▶ **Read the questions as they are, not as you would like them to be.** Do not add more to the question so that it fits the response you want to make rather than the one being asked for.

▶ **Do not become flustered by unfamiliar words and phrases.** Try to determine the meaning of unfamiliar words using context clues that you learned in Chapter 3. Then translate the question into your own words. If you are unable to determine the meaning, mark the question so that it is easy to locate later, and come back to it. Very often, a question presented later on in the exam may use the word or concept and define it. Come back to it later.

▶ **Do not change your answers.** Your first instinct is usually right, but do change your response if you are absolutely sure it is wrong or you made an accidental error. If you are unsure, leave your responses alone. Do not let your doubt cloud your concentration.

▶ **Use your memory strategies for retrieval.** You will do better on exams when you consistently use memory strategies while studying because they help you store and efficiently recall what you have learned. See Chapter 2 to review memory strategies.

Strategies Specific to Objective Tests

OBJECTIVE TESTS ARE exams where the questions have only one right answer. Question types include multiple-choice, true-and-false, matching, and fill-in-the-blank. There is usually no disputing a correct answer.

Multiple-Choice

▶ **Answer multiple-choice questions yourself.** Attempt to answer multiple-choice questions without looking at the answer choices first. This practice will make you more likely to choose a correct answer when you look at the options and see one that matches your answer. It will boost your memory and increase your confidence when your answer matches one of the options.

▶ **Do not make assumptions.** No matter what kind of answer pattern you think has been established in a test, do not assume anything. It is possible to have four correct "c" answers in a row. Stick with what you absolutely know or think is correct.

▶ **Write on your exam.** Unless you have been directed to not write on the exam, mark up your exam. Cross off the answer options you have eliminated. Underline key terms in the question. Draw pictures to help you remember what you have learned.

▶ **Make sure your answer is the best answer.** If you are asked to select the best answer, do not select the first correct answer. Make sure it is actually the best answer. If you are unsure, skip it, and return to it later. Just because an option is true does not mean that it answers the question correctly. If you are asked to pick the best answer, read *all* of the options and then decide which one answers exactly what is being asked.

▶ **Avoid absolutes and universals**. Avoid answer options that use absolutes, such as *all*, *every*, and *always*. These tend to be wrong. Rather, select options that say *often*, *most always*, and *in many instances*, as these tend to be correct.

▶ **Avoid double negatives**. <u>Not</u> <u>un</u>important = important. If something is unimportant then it is not important (remember the prefix *un-* means "not"). However, if it is <u>not</u> unimportant, then it is important. Two negatives equal a positive.

▶ **Note the grammar used in multiple-choice questions and answers.** If you choose an answer that does not fit grammatically with the question stem, you have probably chosen the wrong answer. Make certain the verb tense matches in the question and in the answer options. For example, if you are asked, "Who wrote the novel *The Caper*?" the verb tense should match.

   a. Jim and Raul will have written the novel *The Caper*.

   b. Professor Anter wrote the novel *The Caper*. (correct)

   c. Sandy JJ writes the novel *The Caper*.

▶ **Remember that most multiple-choice tests include a main idea question or questions.** Make sure you understand the main idea of everything you read.

True-and-False

▶ **Underline key terms.** This will help you focus on exactly what you are being asked to determine the correctness of.

▶ **Watch for any inaccuracies.** If any part of the statement is incorrect, the whole statement is false.

▶ **When in doubt, guess true.** There are usually more true statements on exams than false because it is easier for an instructor to write factual statements.

▶ **Remember absolutes and universals.** As discussed above in strategies for multiple-choice questions, questions that use absolutes (words such as *always*, *never*, *every*, and *all*) are usually false.

Matching and Fill-in-the-Blank

▶ **Study often.** Because these types of tests require you to memorize facts, study regularly and vary your study methods so you create more pathways for learning the information. Repetition and rehearsal are keys to success for these types of tests. Matching questions require you to know specific information, but you can see possible answers. Fill-in-the-blank questions can be one of the most challenging types, especially if you have not studied, because there are no options from which to guess.

▶ **Learn the discipline-specific vocabulary.** These types of questions usually focus on key terms from the textbook and discipline, so make sure you are familiar with them. Learn the names of key people, places, things, and events introduced in the material on which you are being tested. Learn key processes introduced.

Strategies Specific to Essay Exams

SUBJECTIVE TESTS ARE exams where your thoughts are required, like responding to an essay prompt. You provide the complete response based on a question presented to you. Although your instructor will most likely have key features you need to address for points toward your grade on a subjective test, you can show how much you know using your own thoughts.

▶ **Write on your exam.** Underline key terms in essay questions so you know exactly how to answer and what needs to be included.

▶ **Brainstorm.** It is usually a good idea to spend one third of your time brainstorming. List all the information you know about the topic; then organize it. Very often, students jump into writing and end up forgetting key information.

▶ **Understand exam terminology.** The way questions are written can give you clues about how to answer them. If you do not understand exam terminology, you can perform poorly on tests even though you know the material. Study the following terms, which frequently appear in test questions and essay exams.

  ▶ **Analyze**: Look at individual parts and examine each critically.

  ▶ **Compare**: Bring out the points of similarity.

  ▶ **Contrast**: Bring out the points of difference.

  ▶ **Criticize**: State your opinion and support your opinion by using examples.

  ▶ **Define**: State the meaning of a word or concept; place it in the class to which it belongs.

  ▶ **Describe**: Tell about, give an account of or characteristics of something.

  ▶ **Discuss**: Present a detailed argument or consideration of a topic.

  ▶ **Enumerate**: List and explain each point in concise form.

  ▶ **Evaluate**: Make a judgment based on specific criteria.

  ▶ **Explain**: Make clear, tell how to do by giving an example. Tell as is.

  ▶ **Illustrate**: Use a chart, word picture, diagram, or concrete example of what you are being asked to "illustrate."

- ▶ **Identify**: Establish the essential characteristics.
- ▶ **Infer:** Draw a conclusion based on given facts that allow you to make a prediction.
- ▶ **Interpret**: Present the subject at hand in understandable terms.
- ▶ **Justify**: Show good reasons for, give evidence to support your position.
- ▶ **Outline**: Summarize by using a series of headings and subheadings.
- ▶ **Prove**: Establish the truth by providing factual evidence or logical reasons.
- ▶ **Sequence:** Arrange events or a process in a meaningful order, from beginning to end.
- ▶ **Summarize**: Provide a brief overview of the main idea and major details.
- ▶ **Synthesize**: Put the pieces together, combine the parts into a coherent whole.
- ▶ **Trace**: Review in detail, step by step.

What to Do After the Test

JUST BECAUSE YOU HAVE FINISHED THE TEST does not mean your learning is over. These are some strategies you can use immediately after you have taken a test or after you have received your grade.

- ▶ **Write in your journal.** Predict how well you believe that you did. Comment on your study techniques and if you think there is any room for improvement. Were there certain test questions that you were not prepared for? Why were you not prepared?
- ▶ **Reward yourself.** If you honestly prepared for the exam, take a mini-break. You have earned it. Perhaps go out for a meal or a movie or be with family and friends.
- ▶ **Analyze what you got wrong.** Once you receive your test back, use it as an opportunity to learn what you may have missed. Find out why you answered incorrectly. Get clarification from the instructor if the correct answer does not make sense to you. Write down the questions missed and explanations in your journal. Also, return to the page in your journal where you wrote your prediction. Write down your score next to your prediction as a confirmation or as a signal that you need to do something differently. If you did not get the score you thought, meet with your instructor or a tutor.
- ▶ **Use the test as a study guide for final exams.** Past tests make great study guides to help you prepare for the final exam, which is usually cumulative.

Index

Note: f represents figures and t represents tables

conclusion, 570. *See also* inferences
    defined, 497
    drawing of, 413–414
    identifying, 499–500
    using text to support, 281
    word clues signaling, 506, 506t
connections. *See also* associations; synapses
    encoding and making, 72–77
    establishing, 74–75
    strategies for making, 72–73, 76–77
    suggestions on making, 73–74
conscious encoding, 51
consciousness, 186
context. *See* environment
context clues, 101–114, 174, 174t
    defined, 100
    identifying, 104–105
    opinions and, 104
    in passages, 107–111
    paying attention to, 100
    practicing with, 106
    specialized vocabulary, for defining, 129–130
    in textbooks, 112–113
    types of, 102–104
    using, 102
corpus callosum, 200
creating level of thinking, 616–618
critical reading. *See also* Bloom's Taxonomy
    arguments and, 544–591
    brain health and, 622–624
    defining, 8, 594
    learning levels and, 619–621
    strategies for, 8
critical thinking, 100
cross-referencing
    benefits of, 375
    defined, 374
    during study-reading, 373–377

D
daily reading plan, 30–32
deadlines, 65
declarative memory. *See* semantic memory
deductive arguments, 549–562

challenging, 559–562
deductive thinking and, 550–553
evaluating, 571, 572t
inductive and, 553–555
puzzles of, 556–562
    solving, 557–559
writing, 555–556
deductive thinking, 550–553
definition/example patterns, 327–329
    defined, 328
    identifying, 329
    visual for, 328, 329f
    word clues for, 328, 328t
definitions as context clues, 103–104
dendrites, 12–16, 14f
    growing, 15
    natural learner and, 12–16
    neural networks and creating, 21
details, defined, 157
diagrams, 445–447, 468–469, 469f
    creating, 469
    defined, 445
    reading, 445–447
dictionary, 100
diet and brain, effect on, 622
diminishing returns, 64
discrimination, 406–407
distracters, 25–26. *See also* distractions
distractions
    checkmark monitoring system and, 28–29
    concentration and, 25–32
    daily reading plan and, 30–32
    fighting, 25–32
    journal writing and, 26–28
    learning environment and, 29–30
doodling, 25

E
either/or thinking error, 564
emoticons, 266–268
emotions
    detecting, 265
    learning, effects on, 33–34

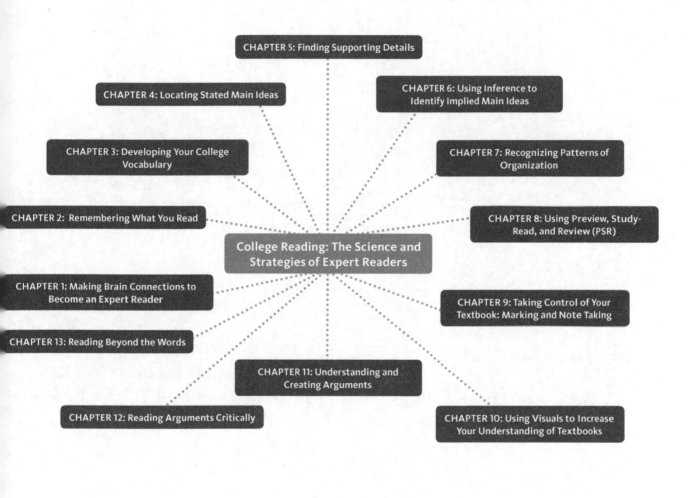

CHAPTER 5: Finding Supporting Details

CHAPTER 4: Locating Stated Main Ideas

CHAPTER 6: Using Inference to Identify Implied Main Ideas

CHAPTER 3: Developing Your College Vocabulary

CHAPTER 7: Recognizing Patterns of Organization

CHAPTER 2: Remembering What You Read

CHAPTER 8: Using Preview, Study-Read, and Review (PSR)

College Reading: The Science and Strategies of Expert Readers

CHAPTER 1: Making Brain Connections to Become an Expert Reader

CHAPTER 9: Taking Control of Your Textbook: Marking and Note Taking

CHAPTER 13: Reading Beyond the Words

CHAPTER 11: Understanding and Creating Arguments

CHAPTER 12: Reading Arguments Critically

CHAPTER 10: Using Visuals to Increase Your Understanding of Textbooks